AVALONIAN ÆON

From Glastonbury Festival to 2012
A Personal Occult Odyssey

PAUL WESTON

AVALONIAN ÆON
PUBLICATIONS

"Avalonian Aeon - From Glastonbury Festival to 2012.
A Personal Occult Odyssey."

This first edition published 2010 by
Avalonian Aeon Publications, Glastonbury, England.

ISBN: 978-0-9557696-2-7

A CIP catalogue record for this book is
available from the British Library.

Design, diagrams and text styling by
Bernard Chandler, Glastonbury. www.graffik.co.uk
Cover painting and inner illustrations by Yuri Leitch.

Text set in Monotype Plantin 10/12pt.

Printed and Bound in Great Britain by
CPI Antony Rowe, Chippenham and Eastbourne.

DEDICATION

To
Andrew Collins.

And in memory of
Bernard G
who died during the final stages of the
completion of this work.

ABOUT THE AUTHOR

Paul is a Psychic Questing, Reiki,
Crowley, Fellowship of Isis, Scientology, Adi Da,
Kriya Yoga, Mother Meera, Druid, Osho, Gurdjieff,
Anthony Robbins firewalking, UFOlogical,
Avalon of the Heart, 2012 kind of guy.
He lives in Glastonbury.

www.avalonianaeon.com
www.aleistercrowley666.co.uk
www.mysteriumartorius.co.uk
www.avalonianaeon.blogspot.com

Previously published by the same Author:

Mysterium Artorius -
Arthurian Grail Glastonbury Studies

Aleister Crowley and the Aeon of Horus -
History • Magick • Psychedelia • UFOlogy

ACKNOWLEDGEMENTS

Mother Meera. Her incalculably astounding blessings have accompanied and infused the entire process of the writing of this book over a ten year period. Om Namo Bhagavate Mata Meera.

Rachel and Michael. Home is where the Avalon of the Heart is.

Andrew Collins was magnificently generous in granting me complete access to three years worth of his diaries and nearly a hundred tape recordings for material on the Glastonbury Zodiac, Crystal Chambers, and 1989-91 psychic questing. I have barely skimmed the surface of that astounding archive, unique in the annals of magic and psychic research. He also checked in detail the *Holy Light* and *Glastonbury Zodiac Vision Quest* sections.
www.andrewcollins.com

Deborah Cartwright (née Benstead) recalled the Seventh Sword and Glastonbury Zodiac quests in an invaluable series of taped interviews and brainstorming sessions. Her contribution to the *Pact with the Devil* section in particular was considerable.

Yuri Leitch created a magnificent rendering of my vision for the book cover. He has also contributed significant artwork throughout the text
www.yurileitch.co.uk

Bernard G. His legend is at the core of psychic questing. It's a privilege to present some of his stupendous material for the first time in print.

Caroline Wise gave much-valued encouragement and shared priceless details of the 1988 Giza Crowley manifestation.

Chandira Hensey helped with many of my early Glastonbury lectures and was closely involved in my mid-nineties adventures.

Storm Constantine set the wheels in motion that provided the computer this book was begun on.

Yvan Cartwright did the necessary tinkering to get it functional.

Bernard Chandler. His type-setting and graphics work, nearness, availability, and flexibility, has been further proof to me of fourth-dimensional processes at work in this book.

Elahn Keshava, Jay Angali, Vivienne Goodwin, and the whole Sangha crew helped create the sacred space of the legendary miraculous group pilgrimage journeys from Glastonbury to Mother Meera in Germany. Some of the Sai Baba section was written during one of them.

Kathy Jones, Mike Jones, and all at the *Isle of Avalon Foundation,* encouraged my Glastonbury lectures and early appearances of some of the material in this book as articles in the *Avalon* magazine.

Celia Thomas focuses the Fellowship of Isis *Isis of Avalon* Iseum that provided the title for a crucial chapter in the book.

Also significant thanks to
Claire Chroston, Robert Coon, Kerry Dar (formerly Horrigan), Kay Dayton, Oliver and Tish Gillespie, Dave Hobbs, John Horrigan, Alex Langstone, Dana Lee, Fee McBride, Joshua, Lisa Mundy, Jane Satchwell, Denise Stobie, Phil Stretch, Richard Ward.

Further acknowledgements for important encounters during the decade-long writing process are due to *Anthony Robbins, Mother Amma, Andrew Cohen, Leonard Orr,* and *Swami Shuddhananda* (from whom the gift of grace bestowed on all who receive initiation into the Kriya Yoga of Babaji).

CONTENTS

LIST OF ILLUSTRATIONS

INTRODUCTION

"Better any number of quests, even if some are illusory, than the arid pretence that there is no quest at all."

Geoffrey Ashe. *Avalonian Quest.*

"Jerusalem... Rome... Mecca... Lhassa - and of these Glastonbury has the largest residue of unused power."

John Cowper Powys. *A Glastonbury Romance.*

"We are here and now among you."

The Shamen. *Phorever People.*

IMAGINE WHAT IT WOULD BE LIKE IF, over a period of years, whilst attending and dreaming of Glastonbury festival, listening to rock music, and taking drugs, some of the books you read seemed to become interactive? Imagine if you heard a true story so extraordinary it was like something out of Harry Potter or *Lord of the Rings*? What if you stepped into that Glastonbury saga, and discovered it was part of the greatest paranormal drama played out in Britain in the 20th century, became part of it, and wrote a book about it filled with more detail than had ever been made public before? How do you think that might feel? Welcome to my life.

I believe that the sheer immensity of the potential total Glastonbury experience has yet to be adequately expounded and celebrated. The music festival alone represents a vast cultural event, the scale of which may perhaps be only vaguely intuited by the consensus media. How many people of different generations have now attended this extraordinary gathering that has become almost as much a part of the British social calendar as Wimbledon, the FA Cup final, and the last night of the proms? A significant proportion have been amazed and exhilarated by what they've experienced. Many have been inspired in numerous ways to in some way change their lives. They've been touched by some kind of magic. These people are out there somewhere. The case studies have not been collected. A definitive arrangement would never be possible.

I attended eight Glastonbury festivals between 1979 and 1987. From the very first time, the event became the focus of my yearly calendar. My journeys to the West Country increasingly coincided with moments of transition in my greater life. The mythology of Glastonbury itself exerted an ever-greater pull on me. Eventually I realised that something mysterious was in motion. I was taken beyond the festival into the magic and mystery. It became clear that was always what was really happening. I'd been set up somewhere, somehow. How I followed that process of discovery, cultivating it all the way, is what this book is all about. I believe that many people have a similar process at work within their own lives. In sharing how I have learned to discover and interact with the mystery, I hope to encourage others to find their own results.

In these pages is the first published account of the entire quest partially depicted in Andrew Collins' *The Seventh Sword* that concluded before the artefact had been discovered. The chapters *The Path of the Dragon, Initiation of the Oracle, From Hell, Babylon Rising,* and *Pact with the Devil* contain material not seen in print before. *Holy Light* and *Aegypt* in turn feature previously unpublished material from legendary visionary Bernard G, best known for his role in Andy's cult classic *The Black Alchemist*. This covers a pivotal period in Collins' work that began in the Glastonbury landscape and led to the remarkable Egyptian odyssey detailed in *Gods of Eden* and *Beneath the Pyramids*, a journey that would lead to tangible discoveries concerning the Giza underworld.

There is certainly much here that could be considered controversial. The realm of the paranormal is pretty much taken for granted. There are some outlandish manifestations. It is inevitable that some will never believe in their authenticity. What can be confidently stated is that these events are depicted in their true context. Locations, dates, and conversations have been taken from tapes and diaries and are reliable. If, after all that, the reader feels that psychic questers must have been tricked or deluded at, for example, a waterfall in Wales, we were nonetheless definitely there and our reasons for being there are as explained in the text. There are some decidedly dark episodes as well. I believe they help indicate an inescapable aspect of the total 'personality' of Glastonbury and magical work in general. I'm not aiming for white-light sainthood here.

The terrestrial zodiac is the centre of the narrative. I'm entirely aware that its very existence is in doubt by all consensus standards. There is no archaeology or historical documents to confirm it. Nonetheless it has served as an immense consciousness expander for a number of people. The story of the linking to Giza by Bernard G is a definitive example. I would hope my treatment of it will at least serve to grant it credibility as a potent psychogeographical influence.

A lot of the story is permeated with casual drug use but the reader will note that gradually alcohol and acid diminishes to nothing and the frequency of cannabis intake falls away as part of the unfolding of what comes to be revealed as the inner dynamic of my life. I haven't done drugs for 17 years now and am teetotal. I have a total acceptance of the role those practices played in my life but would stress that perhaps my mental preparation was unusual and would not recommend adopting similar behaviour.

The work also features an extensive overview of the global work of the remarkable American visionary Robert Coon. His involvement in Crowley, Glastonbury and the 1987 Aztec calendar dates later popularised by José Argüelles would converge with Andy's work and my own Glastonbury adventures in a striking manner that forms the climax of this book.

It's worth noting how a lot of the material here was written and the problems that presented. The 1989-91 psychic questing adventures were recorded on tapes, primarily by Andrew Collins. The crucial 1990 Glastonbury Zodiac adventure produced excruciating difficulties. Andy made a set of tapes primarily oriented to recording the experiences of the group's main psychic, Deborah Cartwright (née Benstead). He didn't bother recording his own context-setting comments and visualisation procedures. Alex Langstone also had a set of tapes that did record Andy but Debbie was so faint as to be inaudible. I had to listen to six C90 tapes, transcribe almost the entire contents, then join them together, edit out what I deemed irrelevant, and render the remainder readable.

This is a big book. I make no apologies for that. One of my prime intentions was to convey the gradual build-up of input overload and relentless intensity because that is exactly what I experienced. The narrative pay-offs that sometimes fulfil events many years before them need to be seen in their total arc to appreciate the real dynamic of the story. *Avalonian Aeon* has nonetheless been significantly trimmed. Almost the entire contents of my first two books, *Mysterium Artorius* and *Aleister Crowley and the Aeon of Horus*, were originally contained within it. Readers of those works will note that some material still features in *Aeon* but in a significantly different and expanded context that does not detract from its reappearance. The original intention was to feature the magical work done with the seven swords once the set was complete. This story, with its millennial Giza background, haunted by the Nephilim, and full of expansive global material pointing still further to 2012, must await the follow-up, *Aquarian Phoenix*.

Paul Weston.
Glastonbury.
May 11th 2010.

PART ONE

FESTIVAL DREAMING

"Pure folly is the key to Initiation."

Aleister Crowley.

"Excess in youth is necessary for life."

William Blake.

"The secret of life consists in sharing the madness of God."

John Cowper Powys.

FLOATING ANARCHY

"It was ragged and naïve, it was heaven."
David Bowie. *Memory of a Free Festival.*

JUNE 21ST 1979. STONEHENGE. DAWN.

A new epoch was beginning. Margaret Thatcher and the Ayatollah Khomeini had recently come to power. Both developments had been greeted with a mixture of strange enthusiasm and intimations of horror. It was impossible to foretell what lay ahead but I had intuitively felt a need to look elsewhere for my salvation. I left a steady job and consensus reality behind. The legendary Stonehenge free festival had been sending out a clarion call to me for years. I'd been aware of the event from the time of its inception in 1974, when, as a fifteen year old living in South East Essex, I'd heard mention of it on Radio Caroline. I was a fledgling hippie, filling my head with psychedelic era Beatles music and early Pink Floyd. On the longest day, sitting in a classroom at school, I indulged in a fantasy of the spirit of the 1967 Summer of Love descending, like tongues of fire, on the mysterious ancient temple.

A lot of media publicity attended the event, and the whole issue of free festivals, during that summer of 1974. It had all ended in tears at Windsor, when the police forcibly dispersed a group of hippies. A school friend of mine had been present there and recounted a terrifying tale. He said that he had seen a policeman drag a pregnant woman out of a tent and kick her in the stomach. History was quite a passion of mine. I knew all about Hitler and Stalin and the nightmare atrocities that had blighted the century. This was different. We were supposed to be the good guys. Now I was no longer sure who 'we' were. If you tried to act out the ideal of the Summer of Love it could end up like that.

During the following years, rock music was my religion. I would listen to Radio Caroline for hours whilst reading the *New Musical Express*. It was a golden age of rock journalism and that served me well. An article by Mick Farren on the Doors set me on the road to an obsessive interest in the band. If I knew that Jim Morrison was known to have read a book, I would make a point of finding it and reading it as well. This led me to Nietzsche, Frazer's *Golden Bough*, and most importantly of all at the time, Aldous Huxley's *Doors of Perception*. The erudite mystical British author had been a major influence on the birth of the psychedelic era with his account of experiences on mescaline. The Doors had taken their name from it. I read it repeatedly. Just like it seemed perfectly normal to listen to a favourite album a huge number of times, I would read articles and books again and again. Another Farren article on the burgeoning weird cult scene clued me in to the existence of the notorious Aleister Crowley. As a Led Zeppelin fan I was most interested to learn that guitarist Jimmy Page had a serious interest in the man known as the Great Beast and later discovered that he actually lived in a former home of his on the shores of Loch Ness. To use Huxley's terminology, rock was a door in the wall for me. It potentially led to so many things.

In my studies, it seemed perfectly clear that heroin was garbage and I never remotely contemplated taking it at any stage, from that day to this. LSD and cannabis seemed entirely different propositions. I came across accounts of the use of acid in psychotherapy. I was enthralled by stories of mystical mythic visions. I noted the name of Timothy Leary, hearing of his use of the *Tibetan Book of the Dead* as a manual for hallucinogenic journeys into inner space. He had created a version of it entitled *The Psychedelic Experience*. When I discovered that my favourite Beatles track, *Tomorrow Never Knows*, was influenced by Leary's Tibetan-flavoured text, I was determined to find out as much as possible about the subject. It seemed that all of my favourite music had been clearly inspired by acid, so I was led to what seemed a logical conclusion: I had to take some. Fortunately those were the innocent days before drugs were easily available in schools and I didn't know anyone who could get hold of it. Nonetheless, along with a fellow voyager named John, I made it number one priority. I was seventeen before the inevitable happened and the music of the Doors helped me to break on through to the other side.

As the years went by I had continued to be aware of the Stonehenge festival. I was always busy with exams, at school and then sixth form college, but I was determined that I would get there one day. In 1978 I got a job in the Civil Service. Looking at the people I was working with, I became horrified at the prospect of creeping normality setting in and developed a prodigious appetite for reading as widely as possible in all mind-expanding subjects. I eventually resolved that I would resign from my job in time to attend the Stonehenge event and then move on to a larger legal festival at Glastonbury that was scheduled for June 1979.

By the time of the solstice dawn the Civil Service was a distant memory of some other life. I tried to review what I'd just been through. What a glorious chaos it had been, the transition from employment to this mythic reality. I had wandered, staggered about, for three days and nights, past tepees, amongst fire eaters and jugglers, through a large group of naked people having a tug of war in a pit of mud, and so on. The culture shock was unending, amplified unto infinity by a constant diet of drugs. During the few hours of darkness a clear primordial sky of multitudinous stars had heaved and breathed over me. One night a few of us had come across a small clearing amongst the tents, presided over by a group of tepees. Two large guitar amplifier speakers therein blasted out Jimi Hendrix's *1983: A Merman I Should Turn to Be* and never had any music sounded more awesome. I distinctly felt myself levitate six inches above the ground. What could you expect if you took acid in the middle of all this? Ten years on, I really felt as if I'd made a connection to the energy of the sixties.

On the night of the 20th I dropped more acid and watched a superb performance by Here and Now. This legendary hippie/punk fusion band had made their reputation by playing all of their gigs as freebies. Their anarchistic lyrics over a soundscape of searing glissando guitar and spacey keyboards, usually accompanied by an intense lightshow, gave them a cult following. They were perfect for what was happening at Stonehenge.

> *"Here and Now is Floating Anarchy.*
> *Don't you know it's the only way to be? –*
> *Violence is caused by governments, armies, police force."*

I knew by then something of the story behind the early days of the festival. Many years later, in C. J. Stone's *Fierce Dancing*, I discovered more. It was a bittersweet tale of visionary beauty, joy, death, and a boot stamping on a human face forever. One man is clearly identified as the prime force behind it, a man whose life story has passed into the realm of mythology. Phil Russell, better known as Wally Hope, was born into a wealthy family, growing to become a trickster prankster acid head and sun worshipper. On holiday in Ibiza, a trip-born vision seized him. He wanted to take the great solar temple of Stonehenge back from the dour control of the state and return it to the people. The ceremonies of the modern Druid Orders there didn't seem to do it justice. A total

NEW JERUSALEM

THE PILTON FESTIVAL has gradually attained the status of some kind of cultural institution. It makes the front pages of most national newspapers and gets covered by TV and radio. The scale of the event has become immense. Many local causes benefit from the profits and organiser Michael Eavis has become something of a hero. Much opposition and hostility had to be overcome over the years before this level of success. In fact the story of the festival is inextricably intertwined with that of the place it is always associated with. Glastonbury.

It had all begun in summer 1970 when Methodist dairy farmer Eavis attended the Bath festival and liked the music and colourful hippie types in evidence. He contemplated the idea of a similar sort of gathering at his own Worthy Farm, which his family had worked since 1894. Later that year, in September, a small-scale event took place. A mere 1,500 people saw Marc Bolan's T. Rex headline. It was enough of a success to be noticed but Eavis lost money nonetheless.

At this point, visionary initiative was added to the dynamic. Andrew Kerr had been personal assistant to Randolph Churchill, Sir Winston's son. When Randolph had died, Kerr sought a fresh outlet for his energies. He read John Michell's *The View Over Atlantis* and was inspired by the idea of reviving the celebration of the summer solstice. He had the funds to set his dream in motion. Initially he had considered Stonehenge to be the ideal venue. The mysterious weavers of destiny were keeping back something special for the stones though, something that required a particular cast of characters. Glastonbury was to press the 'on' button. After the success of the small Pilton gathering, Kerr realised the possibilities of the site and approached Michael Eavis who readily agreed to his plans. A charming tale tells how Kerr was atop Glastonbury Tor when he saw a rainbow that seemed to descend onto the Worthy Farm area. This confirmed for him that it was the necessary location.

John Michell's book, published in 1969, had become an instant Earth Mysteries cult classic, presenting a comprehensive survey of a widely varied field. Its ideas permeated the whole of hippiedom. Various notions that had previously been held only by obscure eccentrics now reached thousands of impressionable minds.

The modern idea of 'Earth Mysteries' can be said to begin with the work of one man. Alfred Watkins was a Herefordshire merchant who travelled the country as part of his work. He developed antiquarian interests and was always fascinated to hear local landscape legends told by members of families who had lived in the same, virtually unchanging locations, for countless generations. This helped prepare his sensibilities for a moment of revelation. In 1921, at Blackwardine, Herefordshire, he was admiring the view when a strange intuition came over him. It was a way of perceiving the landscape differently and it seemed to represent a glimpse of an archaic forgotten worldview. He sensed a web of lines linking holy places and ancient sites: mounds, old stones, crosses, ancient crossroads, churches on pre-Christian sites, legendary trees and holy wells. They all seemed to stand in straight alignments that ran over beacon hills to cairns and mountain tops. When he came to investigate his vision on maps it appeared to be confirmed. Such features fell on straight lines with a frequency he felt to be above chance. Particular names seemed to regularly appear along such alignments: Red, White, Black, Cold, Cole, Dod, Merry and Ley. The last gave the phenomenon a name that's stuck and since travelled the world. *Ley lines*.

Watkins' discoveries were published in the 1925 work, *The Old Straight Track*. It attracted a small group of enthusiasts who formed a Straight Track Postal Portfolio Club and went on picnic-type outings to further his studies. It was all seen as a kind of charmingly eccentric manifestation of the inter-war years. The archaeological establishment barely deemed it necessary to refute the book. Watkins was not alone in looking at prehistoric sites in an unconventional way. At that time the idea of astronomical alignments at places like Stonehenge was already being discussed. It was Watkins who managed to stimulate a wider interest though, and he will always be remembered as the pioneer.

This whole way of looking at the landscape proved to be a potent beginning to a recovery of an ancient way of relating to the land. Other cultures were looked at with fresh eyes. John Michell provided a supremely eloquent, poetic vision of what these studies seemed to suggest.

Australian aboriginal spirituality provided fertile ground for comparison and stimulation. Their mythology told of a primordial period of creation known as the dreamtime, when the landscape was brought into its current form by the activities of divine beings whose deeds formed the eternal exemplary models for human behaviour. Paths across the land called songlines connected sacred sites. At certain times in the calendar it was necessary to walk these lines to revitalise them and ensure their proper alignment to the forces of creation by singing the very songs by which the world had been brought into being.

Ancient China yielded fine fruit in the form of the art of Feng Shui. The Chinese had a complex culture concerning the land as a living entity that needed to be related to in a state of harmony. To this end, buildings were sited in accordance with precise laws. The energy of the life-force, symbolised as a dragon, moved in channels through the land and ebbed and flowed depending on the nature of the terrain, whether mountain and valley and so on. Subtle procedures could aid and enhance its beneficial effects in an individual home and in the larger design of towns and cities. A wrongly placed building could bring misfortune and ill health to occupants. The art is still in use in the present day and can therefore be investigated in great detail.

All over the world, traditional societies had a way of interacting with their locale that had many points in common. In the light of these cross-cultural studies, it seemed valid to look at British legendary traditions and prehistory in a similar way, searching for indications of the same kind of patterns. An exciting picture was revealed. The megalithic stone circle at Avebury had been considered by the 18th century antiquarian William Stukely to be a serpent temple of the Druids. We now know it considerably predates them but the serpent idea seems to gel with the Chinese concepts. The serpent perhaps symbolised the life energy in the ground. Alfred Watkins had originally felt that the leys were practical means of navigation. In later life he began to acknowledge the possibility that they had more esoteric purposes. John Michell affirmed that they marked paths of earth energy. It seemed the megalithic builders had a way of understanding this force and perhaps the ley system served a similar function to the Chinese Feng Shui arts. Dowsers are a modern example of people who appear to be sensitive to invisible forces beneath the ground, whether water, magnetic currents, or something more unclassifiable. Such types have always existed and it seems likely the megalithic people could have made use of them.

British folklore concerning dragons was looked at with fresh eyes. The English patron saint, George, is of course the most famous of dragon killers, closely followed by the Archangel St. Michael. It is interesting to see how many churches dedicated to Michael are situated on hilltops. Glastonbury Tor is the obvious example. One of John Michell's most important and enduring visionary insights was to notice an apparent alignment of Michael churches across the south of England. This has become the world's most famous ley line. It stretches from St. Michael's Mount in Cornwall, through his churches at Brentor, Burrow Mump in Somerset and the Tor, proceeding on through Avebury stone circle and into Norfolk and the abbey at Bury St. Edmunds. It travels across the longest continuous stretch of land in southern England. Many more churches dedicated to St. Michael fall upon it. The suggestion is that the dragon force in the landscape was recognised by early Christians and certain esoterically-inclined church builders of the Middle Ages. It became equated in the popular mind with the Devil. Michael was considered to be the ideal figure to keep these forces in check, due to his role in the *Book of Revelation* 'War in Heaven'. The real nature of Michael's relationship to the dragon force and what he himself may truly represent is an ongoing study. The original formulation of the line has set countless pilgrims off along it. It is now officially marked on a National Trust direction-finding plinth on the summit of Glastonbury Tor as the 'dragon path'.

The second part of Michell's book claimed to reveal a cosmology of sacred geometry and mathematical mysticism that the builders of sites, from Stonehenge to Glastonbury Abbey, and even Egypt's Great Pyramid, had in common. The suggestion is that they all may have been heirs to knowledge that was a relic of some unknown previous culture, generally thought of as 'Atlantis'. This canon of thought has formed a major part of the wisdom tradition of humanity, supposedly being passed down through the ages by the likes of Pythagoras and Plato, the Masons, the builders of the Gothic cathedrals and so on. Music has been an integral part of it, as its laws are believed to show how the harmony of creation functions. Even if one is not mathematically minded it can be an intoxicating experience to try and follow Michell's elucidation of these ideas.

The most evocative example in the book is the suggestion that the geometrical plan that Glastonbury Abbey was constructed upon was deliberately intended to duplicate the pattern of the city of the New Jerusalem in the *Book of Revelation*. A similar geometry may, perhaps, be found in the layout of Stonehenge. Glastonbury Abbey was considered to be its successor in a new epoch. That this is so is not only suggested by the geometrical grid-plan but also by the existence of an apparent ley alignment that travels right up the centre of the abbey and the aptly-named Dod Lane just outside it, to Stonehenge. The complex unfolding of the geometry and the Stonehenge, Glastonbury, Egypt connection was further elaborated in Michell's next book, *City Of Revelation* (later revised as *The Dimensions of Paradise*).

The contents of *The View Over Atlantis* hung in the air, like an esoteric energy transmission, around the inception of the 1971 Pilton festival. Powerful forces were at work. The story of the famous pyramid stage is a good example. In 1970 Bill Harkin was camping with a friend on the south coast of England. One night, gazing at the stars over the sea, he experienced an intense feeling of light. He decided to allow himself to be guided by it and they set off in his car, navigating solely through the vibe, with no sense whatever of any destination. Eventually they saw a road-sign for Glastonbury and arrived at the Tor. The synchronisation beam got them there in time to meet a group of extravagantly dressed hippie characters descending from the summit. One of them was Andrew Kerr. He and his friends were on their way to meet Michael Eavis to discuss the possibilities of a solstice festival the following year. Harkin fed them with tea, honey and oatcakes. They exchanged phone numbers. The next Wednesday, Harkin was out driving when he saw a vision of Andrew Kerr's face on an upcoming phone-box. He immediately stopped and rang him. The news was that the festival had been given the go-ahead and that Kerr and his associates were moving in to Worthy Farm to begin the preparations. Harkin offered to help them that weekend. On the Thursday night he dreamt of a stage with two beams of light forming a pyramid. He was impressed enough to take the morning off work and make a small cardboard model of his vision. Within a few days he arrived on the festival site. Kerr showed him a location he had dowsed as being auspicious for the stage to be constructed upon. Harkin recognised his dream landscape. Before long, his model was on a table at the farm and a phone call was being made to John Michell for advice on the sacred dimensions for the pyramid stage.

When the whole thing finally came to fruition months later, Kerr introduced the bands with this inspiring invocation: *"Glastonbury is a place far too beautiful for yet another rock festival. If the festival has a specific intention it is to create an increase of awareness in the power of the Universe, a heightening of consciousness and a recognition of our place in the function of this, our tired and molested planet. We have spent too long telling the Universe to shut up; we must search for the humility to listen. The Earth is groaning for contact with our ears and eyes. Universal awareness touches gently at our shoulders. We are creators being created and we must prove our worth."*

What followed became a mythic event. After the massive downer of Altamont in 1969, Pilton showed there was still plenty of life in the hippie dream and its ideals had not been permanently sullied. Fortunately for posterity, the festival was filmed by David Puttnam and Nicholas Roeg and later released as *Glastonbury Fayre*. The event worked on many levels. Most obviously, it was a rock festival and a truly impressive line-up was assembled. Traffic, Arthur Brown, Daevid Allen's Gong, Fairport Convention, David Bowie, Hawkwind and Quintessence, provided a time capsule of the musical vibe of the era.

Many of the musicians were serious in their esoteric interests. The story of Daevid Allen, for example, represents a good case study. He was a personal friend of Robert Graves, the poet and novelist. Graves magnum opus *The White Goddess* dealt with what he believed to be the primordial religion of humanity; veneration of the divine feminine principle. He also supplied a very interesting introduction to Idries Shah's seminal work *The Sufis,* published in 1964. This book suggested that most of the esoteric ideas circulating in Europe during the Middle Ages had been inspired by, and sometimes directly monitored by, mystical schools operating from within Islam. It was a contentious but fertile hypothesis. Perhaps the most fascinating example concerned the wandering troubadour minstrels who had played a large role in the dissemination of Arthurian literature. A case could be made for their connection to Saracen groups in Spain. It seemed the Celtic mythos was deemed suitable to be the carrier of other ideas. The troubadours sang the praises of 'the Lady' and extolled the virtues of a cult of 'Courtly Love'. They fitted Graves' criteria of true poets. This remarkable movement had helped to mellow out the brutal aristocratic warriors of the time with a sense of the chivalric ideal.

Graves was a long-term resident of Deya on Majorca. The village was located at the foot of a small mountain capped by a church, on a site supposedly once sacred to the moon goddess Diana. In the spring of 1966, Daevid Allen was also living there and feeling himself being pulled towards some imminent initiatory event. All of the omens seemed to point towards Easter Sunday, which was also a full moon. An American visitor brought with him some of the legendary Owlsley acid. On Good Friday, Daevid chanced upon Robert Graves who took him for an exhilarating ascent of a steep hillside path. Graves gave forth a freeform discourse on themes from *The White Goddess.* It seemed to Allen that he experienced some kind of *"bio-energetic power transfer by osmosis"*. He felt that he was being empowered to *"take a burden of fame and responsibility"*, to become a modern troubadour. On the full-moon Sunday he ingested the psychedelic sacrament

Allen experienced his partner Gilli Smyth as the Goddess in her many aspects. The climax of their acid sex session annihilated his normal sense of identity, leaving him as *"zero in infinity"*. Somewhere in all this he began to sense the presence of beings, entities of some kind, *"spiritual gardeners, like experimenting doctors from another dimension"*, who were moving part of him into another realm and mode of functioning. He was aware that others were being similarly manoeuvred, *"all being prepared for a common purpose in the hope that at least one of us will succeed in manifesting this mysterious purpose in the difficult field of dense physical reality"*. The feeling took form in a vision of being on a stage. A large rock festival audience were giving him rapturous applause. There was a vibe of love and soul connection. *"Looking up I see with psychic vision an enormous luminous cone of etheric light which is simultaneously drawing astral shadows up from deep below us and dissolving them in the downpouring radiance focused at its peak. As I look out into the audience I see that same light sparkling sweetly in their eyes."*

It was this experience that moved Daevid Allen to enter the field of rock music. He was a founder member of Soft Machine (named after the William Burroughs novel), noticeable on the London scene during the golden daze of the UFO club, in 1967, amidst the early careers of Pink Floyd and Jimi Hendrix. It was the later Gong project that finally made him feel that he was moving towards the fulfilment of his vision. Allen consciously considered Gong to be a magical endeavour, *"a Self Initiation to the Path of the Heart through the medium of Rock Music"*. Their first British appearance was at Pilton. The sound of Gilli Smyth's 'space whisper' vocals actually begin *Glastonbury Fayre,* to the visual accompaniment of atmospheric shots of the pyramid stage.

Gong became a great musical family who nurtured many fine talents. Steve Hillage emerged from their ranks. Their classic line-up recorded a trilogy of albums notable for a mixture of superb and innovative musicianship, whimsical humour, and transcendental magic and mysticism. A full-blown Gnostic invocation featured on

You. World traveller Daevid Allen made his British base in the Glastonbury environs and published the autobiographical *gong dreaming 1* from there in 1994.

One of the most striking performances in *Glastonbury Fayre* was given by Arthur Brown. This was the man who had appeared on *Top of the Pops* in 1968, wearing a flaming head-dress, proclaiming in an unsettlingly powerful voice, *"I am the God of Hellfire"*. Arthur was a kind of daemonic vaudeville trickster artiste. He dug into the shamanic roots of showbiz and rock to invoke an archaic gnosis disruptive of the grey comforts of consensus reality. He didn't disappoint at Pilton. In front of the stage were three burning crosses. On either side of them stood a robed figure holding a flaming torch. To some of the clearly tripped-out audience the blazing triangle of light of the pyramid stage must have seemed like a doorway into another dimension. On the threshold of that realm, the hierophant Arthur invoked the appropriate energies through into manifestation. With his face painted black and white, dancing like a jerky marionette possessed by some voodoo deity, he intoned:

> *"Let, from the Father and the Mother, Come forth the son.*
> *Out of Chaos, bring forth the forms."*

That was one aspect of the dynamic energies that were inspiring the alternative realities of the hippie dream. Directly after Arthur Brown's appearance in the movie, a major complementary force in that process can also be seen. Once again a sea of people dance before the stage, but this time they are themselves singing. In joyful ecstasy they are chanting *Hare Krishna.* They part to let a car slowly drive through, showering it with flowers. It contained the thirteen-year-old Guru Maharaj Ji, leader of the Divine Light Mission. In the aftermath of The Beatles interest in Maharishi Mahesh Yogi's Transcendental Meditation and George Harrison's promotion of the Hare Krishna movement, many began to look eastwards for inspiration. Like a number of the influences that erupted into mass consciousness at that time, Hinduism and Buddhism had been powerfully present with a small, cultured and creative minority for most of the century, but this level of exposure was something else altogether.

Guru Maharaj Ji was, in 1971 in Britain, the most well-known and successful Indian export. His father Sri Hans Ji Maharaj was a spiritual master with thousands of followers. He had founded the

Divine Light Mission, teaching a form of initiation called *The Knowledge*. This was supposedly an esoteric wisdom that had been in existence since ancient times and been transmitted from generation to generation. At any one time only one 'Perfect Master' was alive who was able to pass it on. When his father died in 1966, the eight-year-old Guru Maharaj Ji inherited the mantle. It may seem a bit odd that a child could be expected to effectively represent such wisdom but *The Knowledge* was not just a series of meditation exercises but an energy transmission. The young man had received something beyond information and ideas from his father. Entering into connection with him rendered others susceptible to the mysterious process.

The combination of his youth and the high level of wealth that seemed to surround him made the teenage guru a media magnet. His highly publicised first visit to Britain in 1971 coincided with the Pilton festival. At the peak of his success, a small, slightly plump, Indian-featured figure, dressed in white, sitting on a specially prepared chair, he addressed the audience from the pyramid stage. *"Every materialistic thing is perishable. You should know such a thing as is un-perishable, the Holy Knowledge of God and that is within you."*

Arthur Brown's performance was suggestive of the way of self-mastery, of magic, the way of the western magus. A lonely path.

> *"Nobody's here to show you how.*
> *Nobody's here to help you now.*
> *You have to face yourself alone."*

> *"In my image, by my Will,*
> *do I hereby create all forms and distinctions."*

By its side is the apparent opposite, a way of austerity, surrender, devotion, and mysticism. The guru.

> *"I can help mankind and everybody of you by giving*
> *that Knowledge."*

Perhaps the real stars of the movie were the audience. At the slightest excuse a huge drumming session would develop, ecstatic dancing begin, and clothes be discarded. An attempt at a Christian Service went that way. Many normals were somewhat perturbed by the spectacle of naked people crawling around in mud, licking the ground. Spliffs were mightily in evidence. Tripped-out weirdos stared into space and beyond for the cameras.

By all accounts a splendid time was had by all. All except the local residents, who had felt like they were on the receiving end of some sort of alien invasion. A number of the festival-goers and others who had connected to it inevitably became interested in Glastonbury itself. The place loomed large in *The View Over Atlantis* and John Michell's earlier classic of psychedelic UFOlogy, *The Flying Saucer Vision.* Strange hippies had been visiting the town in small numbers since the mid-sixties. Now they became increasingly visible, getting banned from local pubs and not exactly welcomed with open arms.

By the mid-seventies a few idealistic types had settled there. The opening of the now-famous *Gothic Image* shop began the transformation of the High Street into the New Age Mecca it has now become. They were strange and testing times for the town. Flourishing industries had gone into terminal decline. Many locals became unemployed. Complex economic factors were to blame. The arrival of a load of weirdos and the changes in the High Street were all but simultaneous and came to be inextricably linked in many minds. A mythos developed whereby the decline of Glastonbury's industries and the closing of many old shops had actually been caused by the hippies. Unfortunately the most extreme forms of this belief attribute to the recent arrivals qualities not unlike those that the Nazis saw in the Jews. The bottom of the High Street has been referred to as the 'hippie ghetto'. Get rid of these people and everything will be okay. The 1971 event had set all this in motion, so it wasn't surprising that there was little local enthusiasm for a repeat. It would be eight years before another opportunity arose for a major gathering.

In 1979, after the dreamtime solstice journey, I awoke to the first full day in my new surroundings. Glastonbury festival proved to be another shock to the system but a subtly different one from Stonehenge. The site was far larger. There were more people. And it was legal. We were allowed to be there and that made a big difference to the general atmosphere. Music was ostensibly the centre of gravity. There were stalls. Food, books, and counterculture paraphernalia were for sale. Various organisations representing causes political and spiritual had tents amidst what was a kind of hippie village. An interesting selection of music played from the sound system of the stage (which unfortunately wasn't a pyramid this time) between acts. Different eras were brought together, at least in my head, by hearing Tubeway Army's then current hit, *Are Friends Electric?* and It's a Beautiful Day's 1967 *White Bird*.

Something else was also happening. At one of the stalls I bought an A4 size booklet called *The Glastonbury Giants* by Mary Caine, on the alleged terrestrial zodiac. It was she who had presented the idea on *Nationwide* in 1976. As I sat around in my open altered state, I glanced at it, throughout the festival. She believed that the great earthwork edifice had been constructed by Sumero-Babylonians. I wasn't aware of any confirmatory archaeology. The way it was written made it difficult for me to assess. I felt it was important somehow though. I knew I had to persist with it. There were things that would reveal themselves to me. I would understand the cryptic, allusive, poetic text one day.

Another group of friends arrived from Essex with fresh energy, ready for mayhem. Gary set about intoxicating himself in a manner remarkable for its single-minded intensity. He began by consuming an unhealthy amount of Abbot Ale. I avoided this respected brew following a sad episode, at the age of seventeen, when I had attempted to climb out of the emergency exit of a bus that was, unfortunately, in motion. No such qualms inhibited Gary. Having attained to a rarefied state of raving delirium, he now invited the rest of us to partake of his speciality party-piece, a Rasta cone. This was a monster spliff involving an intricate arrangement of Rizla papers, an entire packet of twenty cigarettes, and a quarter of an ounce of dope. Even in his generally incoherent state he was able to construct this engineering marvel. As the time came to light it, the whole scenario seemed to take on a mythic quality. Maybe a kind of salute and dedication was required? We were positioned such that a fine view of the distant mystic Tor commanded our attention. Some deep instinct inspired Gary to rise, unsteadily, to his feet and raise the monstrous artefact, like Excalibur, towards the sky. Facing the Tor he gave forth a strangulated sound that was both the proud affirmation of a warrior and the last gasp of a man who was about to write-off the rest of the day. The cone was lit, and after taking some mighty tokes, he passed it on whilst spiralling into a slumped heap in the remains of one of the previous night's bonfires. As he dribbled and gurgled most of the group of chums were focused on his antics. I remained transfixed by the Tor. Something was being communicated to me. Of this I was certain.

To celebrate the peak of the festival, I took yet more acid. It was a very different experience to Stonehenge, subtle but ultimately deeper. The mystic input was making itself felt. With eyes closed, I entered into an Arthurian Glastonbury reverie. Something of the ambience of Mary Caine's booklet was permeating my mind. I seemed to imagine a Merlin-type figure viewing the whole landscape from above and also taking the festival into his comprehension. This was not a vivid visual episode but an apprehension on some other level.

The climax of the stage entertainment was provided by former Gong keyboard player Tim Blake's performance of his synthesiser epic, *New Jerusalem.* The lyrics showed he had been reading John Michell's books. Blake was ahead of Jean Michel Jarre in pioneering the combination of electronic music and lasers. The presentation was spectacular. Turns were being taken looking after Gary, who had sacrificed basic motor skills and mouth-brain co-ordination to bring us the sacrament of the cone. This became quite surreal to me. As I helped a man to walk who barely even knew who he was, let alone where he was, synths and lasers tingled my acid consciousness as these words emanated from the stage:

> *"Pyramids and Stonehenge are ley lines to this place,*
> *City of Revelation, that governs inner space.*
> *So now, tune in your auras, let solstice music sound*
> *and build New Age vibrations and feed them to the ground.*
> *For here, inside these valleys, that are so full of energy,*
> *we'll build a New Jerusalem, with love, from you to me."*

A mist had arisen in those very valleys whilst the set was being played and, for some, it was a combination that proved unforgettable. The depth of the experience expanded with time. A mighty mythos had been downloaded into my brain that was to change my life forever.

DARK SATANIC MILL

BACK IN ESSEX I realised that the solstice events had blown my brain to pieces. It was enough to try and assimilate it all. Some of my friends tried to keep the festival spirit alive by constructing a tepee in a hidden place on Hadleigh Downs, not that far from the ruined castle. A lot of time was spent there in the summer of '79.

For now, Floating Anarchy somehow had to be paid for. The spectre of money loomed ever larger. I was unemployed. Something had to change. By autumn, I was working in a factory. I had to wear ear-plugs or risk deafness from the relentless machinery. In the dark satanic mill I was trapped in a surreally monotonous routine. I stood in front of a machine that dealt with planks of wood. One edge of them was sprayed with black paint. The other had a strip of plastic glued to it. The planks went along a kind of conveyor belt. As they came out I checked each edge for correct application of paint and plastic and then piled up the planks on a pallet. When 150 planks had been thus stacked, I wheeled the pallet to one side and began again. That's what I did all day long, five days a week. My Stonehenge and Glastonbury memory reveries helped keep me sane. I couldn't exactly spend eight hours a day thinking about nothing but that though. A whole load of tedious trash wafted across my sky of mind. As days and weeks and months rolled by, even if books and profound acid experiences presented seemingly new opportunities for contemplation, I experienced annoyance at my physical inertia and its accompanying mental misalignment.

Things began to change. I made a point of not going out and indulging in drink and drugs during the week. On the way home from work each day I walked along an unmade track that sloped gently downhill for about a mile. Something inspired me to push against the fatigue and see if I could stir up my latent energy. I began to jog. A year before, still smoking cigarettes as well as dope pipes, I'd suffered a long-term cough that had needed half a bottle of Benylin a day to deal with. I'd started each day by staggering into the bathroom to retch up green muck. I permanently gave up cigarettes and eased off on the chillums. To be able to run a mile and to feel exhilarated at the end felt like a major triumph. It was the start of a lifelong love of running. I had resisted the apparent inertia of my circumstances and found an increasingly healthy dynamism in their midst.

I decided that I wanted to go to university. It would have to wait for the October 1980 intake. As one decade moved into another I entered into an inner directed purification process. I gave up smoking dope and drinking. I had no desire to consume any alcohol at all. In fact, I never drank in quite the same way ever again. The initial abstinence lasted ten months, until I went to university. I didn't smoke any dope for the same amount of time, although I did consume hash cakes and coffee. After only a few weeks of such healthiness, with no weekend intoxications, my energy was building to the extent that I simply had to resign from my job. I had no deliberate intention to not work again for the rest of the year but that is eventually how things worked out. This enabled a superb period of intensive book reading to further prepare me for my coming adventure.

THE ENIGMA OF ALEISTER CROWLEY

ONE NIGHT IN MARCH I dreamt that I was in the company of an imposing bald-headed man in a darkened room. My immediate thoughts on waking were that it was Colonel Kurtz, as portrayed by Marlon Brando in the movie *Apocalypse Now,* which I had recently seen twice and been profoundly affected by. Later that day, whilst browsing in a bookshop, my attention was suddenly transfixed as I discovered a copy of *The Great Beast,* John Symonds' biography of Aleister Crowley. I would have grabbed it and immediately devoured it anyway but the thought that, perhaps, it was Crowley who I had dreamt of the night before, added to the sense of excitement. Symond's work is entirely unsympathetic, expressing scorn, mockery and contempt for his subject wherever possible. Nonetheless it did nothing to diminish my fascination.

The *"wickedest man in the world"* was what the *Sunday Express* called Crowley in the nineteen-twenties. *"A man we'd like to hang."* Here was the King of Depravity. A bisexual drug addict who practised the worst forms of black magic. A man who, according to a coffee table book on the occult I once saw, *"regularly practiced human sacrifice"*.

One particular quote seems to represent the hardcore of the legend of infamy. It's in Crowley's book *Magick,* from a chapter entitled *On the Bloody Sacrifice. "For the highest spiritual working one must accordingly choose that victim which contains the greatest and purest force. A male child of perfect innocence and high intelligence is the most satisfactory and suitable victim."* In a footnote Crowley then says *"he made this particular sacrifice on an average about 150 times a year between 1912 and 1928"*. The quote is thrown up again and again in exposes by Christian authors and even allegedly serious occult writers. The very last sentence of Crowley's *'bloody sacrifice'* chapter says *"you are likely to get into trouble over this chapter unless you truly comprehend its meaning"*.

So let's think about this one. We're being asked to take this passage as evidence that Crowley murdered 150 children a year from 1912 to 1928. This would make him unique in the annals of crime. It's strange how he got away with it really. Rather odd that we have no record of any of the victims. No witnesses. No evidence. Although expelled from certain countries and refused entry to others, he was never arrested for any offence, let alone served a jail sentence. Some of his books were banned, even burned as pornographic. He lost a libel action in Court. The little matter of those child murders seems to have been ignored.

Perhaps there's another explanation. Crowley was a great jester and loved to write in code. He put cryptic meanings into his books that only those with a certain commitment to the subject would be able to understand. Although he didn't mind being upfront and shocking in some of his poems, *Magick* was a serious work which he hoped to see remain in print and reach a wide audience. The late twenties were a time when he'd seen himself condemned and works like James Joyce's *Ulysses* and D. H. Lawrence's *Lady Chatterley's Lover* made unavailable through their use of material related to sex. The *"male child of perfect innocence and high intelligence"* concerned a magickal practice involving sperm. It's as simple as that.

Yes he did, here and there in rituals during his career, kill an animal, and I personally don't approve of that but broadly speaking, the legend of infamy is a smokescreen of nonsense. What lies behind it?

Crowley was a poet hailed in numerous literary journals as a genius. His work was included in the *Oxford Book of Mystical Verse* but he was also responsible for what has been considered to be some of the vilest pornography in the English language. At one time he had been a world-record mountaineer, having climbed higher in the Himalayas than anyone else. He played chess to the standard of a Grand Master, demonstrating the ability to play two games at once blindfolded, thus displaying extraordinary abilities of visualisation and concentration. He was one of the first westerners to immerse themselves in the study of eastern religion, having travelled extensively in Arab countries, India and China. In the first decade of the 20th century, he practiced physical and mental yoga with great dedication. Many works later to become famous in the West were familiar to him such as the *I Ching, Tao Te Ching, Bhagavad Gita, Dhammapada* and Patanjali's *Yoga Sutras.* He was the first person of any note in the West to systematically experiment with the full range of consciousness expanding drugs ie, hashish, mescaline, ether, cocaine and heroin. For better or for worse, the psychedelic revolution of the sixties was inspired more by him than anyone else. Crowley has also been considered to be either a pioneer or a monstrous sexual degenerate for the endless lovers, both male and female, that he had throughout his life.

First and foremost though, Crowley comes down to us as the magician, the occultist. A member of the most famous occult group of the 19th century, the Golden Dawn, he went from there to believe he had received a communication from a non-human entity, an angel for want of better terminology, who gave him a new Bible for a new age or *Aeon*. This work was *The Book of the Law* and it contains the phrase which is most strongly associated with him, *"Do what thou wilt shall be the whole of the Law."*

This was one man. And this is the enigma of Aleister Crowley. Picture the effeminate homosexual side of Crowley and Crowley the pornographer. Can we then see this man 22,000 feet up the Himalayas without oxygen? Can we see the junkie likewise? Could we picture Quentin Crisp or Sid Vicious in that context? As Thelemic writer Gerald Suster clearly stated, *"debauched degenerates don't set world mountaineering records"*. Contrariwise, how about Chris Bonington? Can we see him returning from an Everest trip to write a book of mystical or pornographic verse and proclaiming himself to be Logos of the Aeon of Horus? What about some of our recent esteemed poets such as John Betjamin or Philip Larkin? Can we see them performing ancient ceremonies in the Great Pyramid or rites of sex magick with prostitutes or taking psychedelic drugs? As for yoga, can we imagine some of the sweetness and light types who get attracted to it composing poems such as *On the Delights of Passive Pederasty,* and *Of Dog and Dame,* or going big-game hunting?

This indeed is the enigma of Aleister Crowley. We all have different facets to ourselves but in Crowley they are written large. Very large. Any one of his different aspects would serve most people for a life's work. I wondered how to get to the essence of the man?

The study of his procedures was an obvious starting point. Crowley had a sort of recipe for preparation. As well as his studies magickal and mystical, he had great knowledge and insight on the latest developments in science, philosophy, mathematics, art, literature, and psychology. One of his most significant achievements was to synthesise his worldview in terms that seemed to fit the New Physics. *"The Method of Science. The Aim of Religion."* He recommended that, before tackling the Great Work of Magick, the aspirant should get their minds and bodies in order. Get fit, become competent in some athletic skill, some physical path. Study philosophy, comparative religion, and science. Understand the world around you in its own terms without necessarily losing yourself in it. If, neglecting this kind of balanced groundwork, you start trying to play games with reality you'll simply wreck yourself and have no fruitful understanding of the results. This was probably the best advice I could receive in readiness for my coming time at university.

TRIPATHON

PRIOR TO MY DEPARTURE there was one great focus leading me on: the summer solstice. I was disappointed that no repeat of the Glastonbury festival was planned. That still left Stonehenge. I psyched myself up for it. On arrival, I immediately took acid and raced to put my tent up before the effects came on. Because I wasn't smoking or drinking I attempted to stay tripping the whole time. This is a foolhardy enterprise. If you take acid two days running you have to double the dose to get an effect. Not only that, it's unlikely to match the first day's high, as so much energy will have been expended and no proper time for regeneration allowed. In fact it can get a bit wonky. It would be a few years before I would really get to understand this when I read Robert S. de Ropp's *The Master Game*. These drug binges use up enormous amounts of energy. We know that certain physical activities burn up so many calories an hour etc. An acid trip undoubtedly does that, but it also burns up stuff that western science maybe hasn't got names for yet. Ideally these episodes require good preparation and time for recuperation. I learnt this the hard way that year by staying awake for three days and nights. By the end I felt like some ghost, haunting the site, rather than having any tangible connection with it.

One considerable change from '79 was that we were allowed amongst the stones on the solstice. A big circle of police turned their backs whilst some wild merrymaking went down. Big chillums were smoked as *Om Namaha Shivaya* was chanted. Naked people danced around. The obligatory Hopi Indian elder said his piece. In the midst of all this were some Druids as well.

As I walked around the site, during my three-day tripathon, I'd been disturbed to feel what I took to be the deeper vibe of the festival and I didn't think it was just paranoia induced by my fragile, hallucinatory state. Compared to the previous year there were a significantly larger number of people and their numbers increased, it seemed, with each of my circumambulations of the site. I was aware of a lot of hardcore biker types, who had not been noticeable in 1979. Punks as well. It soon became clear that the two contingents didn't get on. I heard tales of unpleasant violence. It seemed that some of the bikers felt it was 'their festival.' I was a student of the sixties and worried that I was seeing Woodstock mutate into Altamont. The whole thing simply didn't carry the same amazing vibe of '79. Nonetheless when I returned home it was perfectly obvious that a further mutation of my consciousness had occurred.

I began to read up on the history and mythos of the ancient civilisations and particularly the British landscape more systematically than ever before. The works of John Michell shone like a beacon in this field for me. A long chapter in Colin Wilson's *Mysteries* entitled *The Path of the Dragon* was repeatedly gone over. And the attitude of Crowley began to permeate my being. As the time drew near for my departure for university I sought to mark the rite of passage. To this end, in late August, I had my head shaved in Buddhist/Hare-Krishna monk manner.

DEMONIC POSSESSION

MY FIRST FEW DAYS AT UNIVERSITY made me wonder if I'd made a huge mistake. The place was crawling with normals. When initially applying for a place I had very clearly stated that I was not prepared to share a room with anyone. The photo of myself I'd supplied had been taken just after Stonehenge and showed me psychotically intense. I had written on my application form that I had a "highly evolved lifestyle". This undoubtedly anti-social ploy was immediately validated when I saw the kind of people living in my hall of residence. In the room directly opposite mine was a vicar's son. He was a campanologist. For the uninitiated, that's nothing to do with his sexual orientation. It indicates a passion for bell-ringing. Many students soon engage in the time-honoured ritual of the pub-crawl. This lad and his mates went off on church-crawls. They would drive around to see how many different sets of church bells they could ring in one evening. He once invited me into his room to listen to an album he had of various well-known pop classics played on hand-bells. I sat, stunned, listening to

Yellow Submarine. Quite clearly, sharing with such a person was not an option. He was a nice guy but –. In a room directly next to me was another Christian. He used to regularly listen to a Sunday morning church service on his radio, loud enough for it to be clearly audible through the walls.

By isolating myself in the midst of such horrors, I was able to magickally attract the necessary people and experiences to me. I soon began to hear tales of a woman first year student, living in the same hall as me, who had rapidly gained the reputation of being a nymphomaniac. It seemed logical to research the truth of this rumour. Before long I had verified its accuracy. Having got to know her, what interested me even more, was to hear of what had happened to her just before coming to university. She had undergone a full-blown classic demonic possession episode. This had involved her getting dangerously loud and larey as a parade of celebrities such as Sid Vicious, Nero, and Hitler put her through her paces. This little problem had only been resolved when a Catholic priest did a complete bell, book, and candle number on her. I was curious to know what having sex with someone who had been possessed by Hitler would be like. Ah, the follies of youth! Did I really believe that she had played host to the genuine spirits of the Fuhrer and his maties? Not necessarily. What I was sure of was that this gorgeous young woman had a passionate intensity that brought forth immensely powerful energies from within her that her normal life was not able to accommodate. This elemental rawness was something I wanted to connect with.

A brief, most pleasant, sexual association unfolded. We actually formed an abiding friendship beyond the initial jollies. One particular memory sums up the flavour of our involvement at that time. After a party, one Saturday night, we had retired to my room. I awoke the next morning with her sleeping by my side. The sun was shining through the curtains and highlighting a poster on the wall, an image by H. R. Giger, famous for his work on the *Alien* movie. It featured his version of Eliphas Levi's Baphomet, the goat headed androgynous being that formed the famous image that most tarot depictions of the Devil derive from. As I stared at it, and contemplated the strange history of the woman sleeping beside me, the sounds of a radio church service filtered through the wall from my neighbour. It was one of those moments that throws you back on yourself. One of those mysterious episodes that begs one to enquire, "Who the fuck am I and what is my life all about?" It seemed fairly obvious that strange days lay ahead.

Despite this promising start it was still hard work to find many interesting people. Once I had, I realised that my no drinking/no dope smoking policy was going to leave me in a class of one. Maybe it was a bit early in my life to take such a final step. I made a policy decision that it would be acceptable to venture back into the realm of dope smoking and drinking.

AEON OF HORUS

THE YEAR'S END was dominated, for me, by the horrific murder of John Lennon. It made me take stock of how important the music and career of the Beatles had been in shaping my own development. This naturally took me into a retrospective review of the sixties. Many people compared the event of Lennon's death to the Kennedy assassination. That moment in 1963 seemed to have acted as a kind of 'on' button that began an astonishing period of acceleration and intensity. The Beatles were very much a part of the whole process. Lennon's death seemed to indicate some kind of closure and to invite attempts at summarising.

The journey of John Lennon had been a remarkable example of how far things could move in a short period of time. In 1964 he had been singing, *"I want to hold your hand"*. A mere two years later he was encouraging his listeners to,

> *"Lay down all thought, surrender to the Void, it is shining,*
> *it is shining.*
> *That you may see the meaning of within, it is knowing,*
> *it is knowing,*
> *that Love is all and Love is everyone, it is Being,*
> *it is Being."*

Within another year it had come to,

> *"Limitless undying Love, which shines around me like a*
> *million suns,*
> *it calls me on and on, across the universe."*

I found it intriguing that he had arranged for Aleister Crowley to be among the group featured on the *Sgt. Pepper* album cover.

The famous shaven-headed image can be seen along the top row on the left. There's little to indicate that Lennon really knew much about Crowley at all, beyond his reputation as drug pioneer and general wild man. Nonetheless, out of that matrix of influences, I began to intuit a bigger picture.

I was born in 1959. My parents were of the generation involved in the Second World War. I came to consciousness in the sixties with a growing awareness of an amazing contrast between two decades only twenty years apart. I have very early memories of Beatlemania. In 1967 as the Summer of Love unfolded I can remember *San Francisco* on *Top of the Pops* and some vague sense of Flower Power. During the same period I developed a passion for history, looking at picture books about the world wars.

The Nazis perplexed me. Film footage of the gigantic Nuremberg rallies brought me out in goose pimples. Hitler was totally strange. There simply wasn't anybody else remotely like him. The British culture of the time, which I somehow took to be represented by the George Formby and Will Hay movies that were still regularly shown on TV, and the old songs that my father and uncles remembered with nostalgia, *The Lambeth Walk* and so on, was completely different.

The theme of the ongoing mystery of the two diverse decades continued to intensify for me. It began to dawn on me that history felt like a mighty weird affair. I read top historians and took on board arguments for economic, sociological, and technological determinants but for all the growing mass of data and ideas that filled my head something that felt like it ought to be cohering wasn't.

If you look at what was happening in Germany following their defeat in the First World War, their treatment by the Allies with the Treaty of Versailles and the economic troubles of the twenties, a resurgence of an aggressive nationalism seemed inevitable. That doesn't account for the strangeness and severity of form it took. With the sixties, it is possible to point to a number of economic and technological factors that made the emergence of some sort of youth culture highly likely. That doesn't really explain why it turned out to be such an outrageous party. The drugs certainly made a difference but they simply can't bestow talent on mediocrities. How remarkable that as Hitler, Himmler, and their associates reached the climax of their endeavours at Stalingrad and Auschwitz, so the grouping that included John Lennon, Bob Dylan, Jim Morrison, Jimi Hendrix and Mick Jagger, were coming into incarnation.

It seemed to me that the main players of the Nazi nightmare and the swinging sixties were rather specialised groups. They were uniquely over-qualified for the situations that they were born into. The group of characters who were available to take the whole thing to the limit and beyond seem to have been assembled by a brilliant casting agency. The usual ways of looking at history didn't satisfactorily explain to me why it all turned out to be quite so hideous, quite so ridiculously brilliant. I felt there was a deeper mystery trying to reveal itself.

The most important event of Aleister Crowley's life had occurred in Cairo in April 1904. The episode began when his wife Rose started to experience uncharacteristic trance states, firstly conveying a message to Crowley that *'they'* were waiting for him. The Egyptian god Horus was considered to be of central importance.

Crowley took Rose to the Cairo Museum on March 21st to see if she could identify an image of the mysterious deity. She passed by a number, which greatly pleased Crowley, as he was irritated to see his wife seeming to have a melodramatic episode like the kind of fake mediums he despised. Amidst the 'Boulak collection', a group of items brought from another museum that had closed in 1890, she then exclaimed "*There he is,*" pointing down the end of a corridor to an exhibit that was not yet clearly in view. It turned out to be a wooden funerary stele of one Ankh-af-na-Khonsu, a Priest of Mentu, a God of War, dating from about 725 BC. On it was an image of Ra Hoor Khuit, who is a kind of amalgam of Horus and Ra. This was interesting enough but what clinched the matter for Crowley was seeing that the exhibit number was 666. This famous number, attributed to the Great Beast of the *Book of Revelation,* and the happy hunting ground of numerologists and nutters down through the ages, was one that Crowley had already personally adopted as his own. His parents had been members of a fanatical Christian sect and his mother had used the name of the Beast to castigate her young son. He had happily accepted this as a token of rebellion. Educated pagans consider that it represents the energy of the sun. John Michell expounds on it in such a manner. From that point onwards, Crowley realised that something of magical importance was happening and allowed himself to go along with the strange adventure.

The climax came when Rose's psychic material instructed the couple to keep a noon appointment over three days in a specially prepared room with writing material in readiness to receive something important from a messenger of Horus who had identified himself as Aiwass. The old world was ending and a newly dawning epoch, the Aeon of Horus, was just beginning. Crowley was to be its prophet.

At exactly noon on April 8th, the first day, the Beast heard the voice of Aiwass, seeming to originate from a point over his left shoulder, behind him in the furthest corner of the room. During the course of the three sessions, *The Book of the Law* was dictated. Aiwass introduced himself as *"minister of Hoor-paar-Kraat"*. Elsewhere known as Hor-pa-Kred, and in Greek as Harpocrates, this is the infant Horus, usually pictured with a finger to his lips, making a gesture of silence. In a magickal sense, this represents the sealing of a formula that has been put out into the world. Each chapter contains the words of particular forces pictured on what Crowley came to call the 'Stele of Revealing'.

Arched over the whole scene was Nuit, goddess of the night sky. The first chapter is hers. It is ironic to realise, considering Crowley's reputation as misogynist and abuser of women, that the words of Nuit represent one of the first clear indications of the return of the Goddess in the magical literature of the time.

(All following quotes from the *Book of the Law* are representative selections from the respective chapters condensed together with verse numbers referenced.)

3. *Every man and every woman is a star.*
12. *Come forth, o children, under the stars, & take your fill of love!*
13. *I am above you and in you. My ecstasy is in yours. My joy is to see your joy.*
15. *They shall gather my children into their fold: they shall bring the glory of the stars into the hearts of men.*
29. *I am divided for love's sake for the chance of union.*
32. *– the joys of my love will redeem ye from all pain.*
41. *The word of Sin is Restriction.*
    There is no bond that can unite the divided but love.
51. *Also take your fill and will of love as ye will, when where and with whom you will! But always unto me.*
53. *This shall regenerate the world, the little world my sister, my heart and my tongue unto whom I send this kiss.*
    – ecstasy be thine and joy of earth.
57. *Invoke me under my stars! Love is the law, love under will.*
61. *I love you, I yearn to you.*

I who am all pleasure and purple and drunkenness of the innermost sense desire you.
Put on the wings and arouse the coiled splendour within you: come unto me!

A winged disc is pictured on the stele. In Egyptological terms, it depicts an aspect of an early predynastic form of Horus, from a cult centre at a place called Behdet. This name was later given to the famous Horus temple at Edfu and other places of his worship. As defender of Ra he would travel the sky as a winged disc hunting Ra's enemy Set. Chapter Two is his words, but his energy is named as Hadit, which is understood as a mathematical metaphysical principle.

6. *I am the flame that burns in every heart of man, and in the core of every star. I am Life, and the giver of Life, yet therefore is the knowledge of me the knowledge of death.*
9. *Remember all ye that existence is pure joy; that all the sorrows are but as shadows; they pass & are done; but there is that which remains.*
20. *Beauty and strength, leaping laughter and delicious languor, force and fire, are of us.*
22. *I am the Snake that giveth Knowledge & Delight and bright glory, and stir the hearts of men with drunkenness. To worship me take wine and strange drugs whereof I will tell my prophet, & be drunk thereof! They shall not harm ye at all. It is a lie, this folly against self. The exposure of innocence is a lie. Be strong, o man! lust, enjoy all things of sense and rapture: fear not that any God shall deny thee for this.*

Powerful and inspiring words but amongst them were some with a more disturbing flavour.

21. *We have nothing with the outcast and the unfit: let them die in their misery. For they feel not. Compassion is the vice of kings: stamp down the wretched & the weak: this is our law and the joy of the world.*

The third chapter gives full expression to such sentiments. It is the voice of Ra-Hoor-Khuit.

3. *I am a god of War and of Vengeance.*
11. *Thou shalt have danger & trouble. –*
    Worship me with fire and blood.
18. *Mercy let be of: damn them who pity! Kill and torture, spare not, be upon them!*
51. *With my Hawk's head I peck at the eyes of Jesus as he hangs upon the cross.*
54. *I spit on your crapulous creeds.*
55. *Let Mary inviolate be torn upon wheels: for her sake let all chaste women be utterly despised among you!*

For some years Crowley rejected the work because of passages like these. He considered Chapter Three to be *"gratuitously atrocious"*.

There have been previous Aeons, also symbolically presided over by Egyptian deities. Isis ruled the matriarchal epoch of the great mother goddess. Osiris was a dying and resurrected god, typical of the mystery cults of the Mediterranean world. Jesus and Christianity demonstrate the triumph of that form. Horus inevitably partakes of qualities of both his parents but is an individual beyond them. This individuality is perhaps the most characteristic form of what is now unfolding, for better or worse. *"Do what thou wilt."*

I felt that, if nothing else, *The Book of the Law* can be seen as prescient prophecy, all but unique at the time. In 1904, Britannia ruled the waves with the greatest empire in history. Although there had been wars in the 19th century, there had not been one involving all of the major powers together since the time of Napoleon, a century earlier. The unification of Germany had been a powerful and disruptive event, but the royal families of Europe were related and a system of alliances had been forged that seemed to guarantee peace and security. Progress in science and industrialisation had been extraordinary. There was a confidence that all problems could and would be solved. Despite Darwin, Christianity appeared to remain as the centre of gravity of European civilisation. Any voice suggesting that this whole world was to go up in flames would not have been heeded. Nonetheless, within a decade that process most certainly began. The First World War ravaged Europe's morale, leaving it wide open for the Nazi denouement.

I also began to feel that the concept of the Aeon of Horus offered, at the very least, a superb poetic metaphor to help understand the enigma of the 20th century. The apparent diversity of the Nazi era and the psychedelic sixties masked a greater unity. They were both part of the same underlying process involving the breaking down of old forms. It could be argued that the Nazis destroyed western civilisation. They manifested so many of its governing ideals in hideous forms that, for many people, patriotism, patriarchy, strict self-discipline, respect for authority and love of one's country with its history and traditions, could never be the same again. The Nazis seemed to embody and amplify things that were present in the whole of European culture. They revealed something horrendously rotting at the heart of civilisation. The baby boomer generation that powered the sixties instinctively sensed that rot and had no desire to recreate the pre-1939 world. In the middle of all this, it seemed to me that there had been an explosive unleashing of knowledge and energy, symbolised by Hadit, *"the flame that burns in every heart of man, and in the core of every star"*. Nuit's admonition to *"arouse the coiled splendour within you"* may have seemed obscure in 1904 to all but scholars of arcane Hindu texts, but by the sixties they seemed to sing with prophecy. LSD and the atom bomb, DNA and the space programme, were all examples of our mental horizons being expanded as never before, as the light within matter itself was unleashed.

The process was entirely neutral but its effects on the life of the world varied, from Nuit calling us to return to her as she arched over the Summer of Love, to the ferocity of Ra Hoor Khuit as he presided over Auschwitz and Hiroshima. These mind-shattering opposites were part of a law of nature, the general flavour of a dawning epoch, which was inescapable.

This was the nature of the epoch I had incarnated in. It was against this bigger picture that I began to assess my passions. The new age of Horus could be studied from the matrix of the world wars, a kind of European Aeon. The upheavals in Biblical lands might be seen as a Middle-Eastern Aeon sub-division. The Glastonbury festival and the whole *View Over Atlantis* package could not be separated from that wider context. The extraordinary seemingly spontaneous social and spiritual experiment unfolding in Somerset might be considered to be manifestations of the Avalonian Aeon. I wondered how my future experiences might configure to deepen my understanding? Would my dimly stirring intuitions be affirmed or not?

* * *

DIVINE-DIABOLIC SOLSTICE GNOSIS

"This is the function of the creative imagination that it can find a marriage of Heaven and Hell in the most grotesque, humiliating, sordid, and apparently trivial event."
John Cowper Powys. *Autobiography.*

AFTER ANOTHER NEW YEAR cut-off from drugs and booze, 1981 began with me feeling very strongly motivated. There was an immediate sense of being in training for something. I did some yoga and went for a short run first thing most mornings and joined a karate class. My intuition was sound. I needed all the preparation and stamina I could muster for what became a colossal year. By Easter I had completed my hibernation. The karate eased off and some dope smoking began. I was happy to learn that there was to be a festival at Glastonbury again. It seemed that the best possible recipe for celebration after the stress of exams would be to go to the Stonehenge gathering and then on to Glastonbury, as I had in 1979. I had my golden memories to inspire me.

At this point, I bought a colossal novel that had been increasingly attracting my attention in the university bookshop. *A Glastonbury Romance* by John Cowper Powys has been described by Colin Wilson as, *"Possibly the greatest novel of the twentieth century, and one of the great mystical masterpieces of all time."* I'd first become aware of Powys in Wilson's *The Occult.* As I found out more about him, it became obvious that he was an astonishing blend of Grade A weirdo and mystical creative genius. This kind of combination, so clearly present in Crowley, was always fascinating to me.

Powys described himself as, *"a fatally dangerous sort of monster, a satyr-monk, a wicked mystic"*. He believed that he *"was, or at least would eventually be, a magician; and what is a magician if not one who converts God's 'reality' into his own 'reality,' God's world into his own world, and God's nature into his own nature?"*. Many accounts testify that he was possessed of unique charisma. His friend, the writer Louis Wilkinson, spoke of *"a beauty of a transfixing power for those who saw and heard him. – full of life, full of beliefs, full of the power to communicate his abundance"*, *"every gesture – was extravagantly highly coloured, fantastical, theatrical, maniacal even, but it all made a tremendous mark"*. There was a, *"vital force of John's whole identity, and his power of, his genius for breaking all bounds and bonds with it"*.

"I could and can very well understand anyone thinking of or indeed worshipping him as 'god-like'."

He was born in 1872 into a huge and astoundingly talented family. Two of his brothers, Theodore and Llewelyn, were highly regarded authors as well. His father became vicar at Montacute, within visual range of Glastonbury Tor, thus introducing the young John to the Somerset landscape. He was a bit of a slow starter in his literary career. An early long philosophical poem originally entitled *The Death of God*, later renamed *Lucifer*, from 1905, seems an interesting statement of heretical intent.

For nearly thirty years, Powys was a public lecturer in the United States. Rather than addressing academic audiences he sought out an interested general public to sound forth on great literature. By all accounts, they were amazing daemonic theatrical performances. He described them as *"a sort of focussing, through one single twisting, leaping, shuffling, skipping, bowing, and scraping human figure, of some special comic-tragic vein in the planetary consciousness"*. Powys felt that, *"the old Druidic spirit, the spirit of Taliessin of the many incarnations, took possession of me!"*. The subsequent, *"Druidic hypnotism of speech"* might produce a, *"magic message, from the gods of the old world to the market place of the new – something it was, from those far-off 'sacred hills', from Glastonbury Tor, from Cadbury Camp"*. His later long-term partner Phyllis Playter first saw him at one of these legendary events. He spoke with such intensity on Dostoevsky that two of the audience fainted!

This overflowing life force was a sign of astonishing inner depths. Central to his peculiar psychology, especially in his early years, was a prodigious polymorphous perversity sufficient to provide work for a whole convention of psychoanalysts. He made no attempt to hide this, recording its many forms in an immense *Autobiography*. *"I gave complete rein to so many manias and aberrations that those who knew me best must often have wondered how far in the direction of a really unbalanced mind I was destined to go."*

Powys was a man who happily accepted immense paradoxes in his nature, exploring them for the sake of his art, developing an intense sense of the simultaneity of good and evil in the divine. Sadistic thoughts overwhelmed him but he felt vivisection was the very embodiment of evil, becoming a vegetarian. Beautiful images rapidly distorted into hideous forms. The repulsive was also somehow humorous. His malaise continued until terrifying hallucinations developed. Throughout his life he was plagued by recurring stomach ulcers and bouts of bad health but lived to ninety-one years of age, still writing in his eighties.

He went through a phase of compulsive hand washing, avoiding touching door handles in fear of the pestilence they carried. His whole sense of touch became dangerously warped-out. Contact with anything made of cotton was inordinately distressing. Linen sheets were repulsive. He later made an all-encompassing sensuality his major mode of being, cultivating it as a magical mystical technique, a *"power of rousing a peculiar exultation in yourself as you confront the Inanimate, an exultation which is really a cosmic eroticism"*. This usually began with the contemplation of some natural object. Powys felt that, *"From every plant and from every stone there emanates a presence"*. His apparently separate identity dissolved in stillness so that his awareness seemed to blend with whatever he saw. *"I could become inanimate objects. I could feel myself into the lonely identity of a pier-post, of a tree-stump, of a monolith in a stone-circle; and when I did this I looked like this post, this stump, this stone."*

Initially, all things feminine freaked him out. Trees and flowers with female organs were disgusting. Birdsong was irredeemably tainted by the possibility of some of the choir being female. A terror of growing breasts developed. In the grip of this mania around sex and femininity, he actually got married. Whenever his thought turned to the fact that children are the result of sexual union he became almost physically ill. Such was his fear of sex with a virgin that his poor wife was forced to endure surgical deflowering to facilitate their physical union. Any feminists who feel she should have told him to fuck right off probably have a point. On the basis of some unconvincing reasoning he never mentioned his wife or mother or any other women in his *Autobiography*. He was indubitably, a sick puppy. A man in this kind of condition would be unlikely to get invited to give a workshop at the Glastonbury Goddess Conference.

And yet this strange crank, *"had what was undoubtedly a strong erotic desire to embrace the magical loveliness of the world, just as if that vast mysterious Presence was a feminine being"*. He was searching for, *"the finding of the 'eternal feminine' in Matter itself"*. Later in his life, he would pray every day to the ancient goddesses Demeter and Cybele for the sake of the health and well being of his brothers and also for the destitute of London and New York. The legendary dancer Isadora Duncan sent Powys multitudinous red roses and put on a performance for him alone in his flat of which he later said, *"It was as though Demeter herself, the mater dolorosa of the ancient earth, rose and danced."* The climax of *A Glastonbury Romance* would portray a man returning to the embrace of the Great Mother, characterised as the very source of all nourishment and creativity.

The extreme end of the spectrum of his boundary-less power-charged psyche seemed to exist in a semi-magical paranormal zone. On one occasion Powys apparently bilocated. He predicted to a friend that he would somehow appear to him later in the night, after he had physically departed. Hours later he did indeed manifest, clearly recognisable but glowing strangely white. He later refused to discuss how he had accomplished the feat. Colin Wilson speculated that it was because he actually didn't know. People who angered Powys suffered misfortune so regularly that he adopted a discipline of praying for his enemies in an attempt to restrain this function, which was beyond his conscious control.

He began to withdraw from the lecture circuit to settle down to a period of stunning literary achievement. The tumultuous intensity of his passionately paradoxical inner life provided the dynamism to create a huge corpus of work. His first major novel, *Wolf Solent*, appeared in 1929. The 1932 *A Glastonbury Romance* has been generally considered to be Powys' masterpiece. Its virtues are present in a large number of his later novels, including *Weymouth Sands, Maiden Castle, Owen Glendower, Porius,* and *The Brazen Head* (an outrageously strange haunting work for a man in his eighties). His *Autobiography* has been rated as one of the greatest in the English language. Colin Wilson said that, *"The most remarkable thing about these novels is their 'nature mysticism' and their incredible vitality; it is clear that he has tapped some subconscious spring and the result is a creative outpouring that has something of the majesty of Niagara Falls."*

Glastonbury was a place that Powys considered to be a, *"reservoir of world magic"*. The overall intention in writing his great novel was to portray, *"the effect of a particular legend, a special myth, a unique tradition, from the remotest past in human history, upon a particular spot on the surface of this planet together with its crowd of inhabitants of every age and of every type of character"*. The *"special myth"* is the book's heroine, the Grail, *"much older than Christianity itself"*, for, *"ages before any saint or Saviour of our present Faith appeared in Glastonbury – the earth-goddess had her cauldron of the food of life safely guarded in our Island of the West"*. *"Its hero is the Life poured into the Grail. Its message is that no one Receptacle of Life and no one Fountain of Life poured into that Receptacle can contain or explain what the world offers us".*

So Powys had decided to make the landscape, history, and mythology of Glastonbury a character in his novel. The different elements cannot be separated. They constitute an elusive something that can interact with a person as strongly as a human character, stirring passion, idealism, madness, asceticism, horror, mysticism and eroticism in all possible combinations. Iain Sinclair has referred to Powys as the grandfather of Psychogeography. This term, originating with the French surrealist anarchists, the Situationists, refers to how geography and environment influences psychology. The mindset of an individual may make a considerable difference to how that person experiences a location. A mystic and a moron may find the Taj Mahal to be far from identical in their perceptions. In *Glastonbury Romance* Powys enters all of these realms with dazzling genius.

The simplest level of the narrative concerns the interplay of two contending forces. Phillip Crow, a powerful industrialist who despises the Glastonbury mythology, tries to effectively take over the town and turn it into a dark satanic mill. At the same time a religious revival is underway, focused by John Geard, a mystical preacher obsessed by the redemptive power of the blood of Christ but with a dark earthy side that hints at the pagan Merlin. He sets up a kind of Grail cult at the Chalice Well. The climax comes when a huge flood washes the works of both men away.

The novel weaves a huge multi-dimensional organismic tapestry, seen from what Colin Wilson calls the, *"Gods-eye point of view"*. As Powys stated, *"There are no less than six major love affairs, one murder, three births, two deaths, and one raising from the dead"* amongst the forty different characters who fill its thousand pages. An all-pervading Wordsworthian pantheistic nature mysticism depicts the landscape, weather, trees, animals, insects, ghosts, dreams and thoughts, the events of the past, as equally significant to the actions of its human characters, who play out a drama that is more erotic, albeit less explicit, than D. H. Lawrence, and as rustic and fatalistic as Thomas Hardy, a drama conforming to a deep subtle script of Grail mythology that most of its protagonists are unaware of.

The literary critic and great champion of Powys, G. Wilson Knight, wrote in his study of him, *The Saturnian Quest*, that, *"We are on a border-line between spirit and matter: we are reminded that sex-lust is really less physical than psychic; and yet psychic imponderables here have body. Thoughts are felt hovering; souls go astral travelling in sleep;*

past experience lives in present locality; spirits of the dead are active." Mysterious indeterminate external intelligences wryly characterised as the *"invisible watchers of the Glastonbury aquarium"* observe the whole drama. *"The manipulation of this vast concourse of themes and persons, treated simultaneously in width and in depth, is staggering, and the realism attained remarkable." "The psychological and spiritual insights show a daring and a penetration in comparison with which many great classics fall to the level of escapist fiction. A Glastonbury Romance is less a book than a Bible."*

The whole vast edifice is built on a gnostic heretical conception of the divine, obviously wrought from the paradoxical tensions in Powys' own psyche. He states that,

> *"there is no consciousness, whether of demiurge, demon, angel, elf, elemental, planetary spirit, demi-god, wraith, phantasm, sun, moon, earth, or star, which is not composed of both good and evil."*
> *"Both the two great forces pouring forth from the double-natured First Cause possess the energy of sex. One is creative, the other destructive; one is good, the other evil; one loves, the other hates, but through both of them pours forth the magnetic energy that moves and disturbs the lethargy of Matter. Both of them have abysmal levels in their being that transcend all that we at present know of the duality of life and death."*

I was astounded by the brilliance of the novel. It immediately leapt into second place behind James Joyce's *Ulysses* in my personal ratings. One of the things that the two novels had in common was their vibrant attitude of life affirmation, even amidst tragedy. Powys gives compassion and dignity to nearly all of his characters. Only a truly ghastly murderer seems entirely evil. With the obvious sense of Powys' titanic genius, I also wondered why the author wasn't better known? He may well be the most neglected figure in English literature.

The story soon attracted my attention beyond its style and conception. Early on in the narrative, one of the principal characters, John Crow, comes to Glastonbury via Stonehenge. Encountering the megalithic circle at night he is overwhelmed by its primal timeless power. I had already experienced one powerful Stonehenge to Glastonbury journey and I was eagerly anticipating another. The fact that John Crow had a fateful meeting at Stonehenge that prefigured a coming dark destiny didn't fully register. I simply felt that Powys' prose was potentially priming me for appreciation of some subtle nuances that might be present on the upcoming pilgrimage. It was encouraging my burgeoning sensitivity to the intense flavour of June.

There was no doubt that it had become my favourite month of the year. The combination of the peak of the hours of daylight and the unfolding of the great sprouting that emerged from the glorious blossoms of May created a potential dreamtime for those not trapped by a normal routine. The vibe seemed to call out for a certain quality of weirdness. All of these feelings, which I had been becoming more aware of for years, became very clear and strong in me then. I entered into June with a distinct consciousness of its magic. My whole mythos of the solstice pilgrimage to the West Country had become an integral part of it.

The sacred month had barely begun when it took on a darkly dangerous flavour. I'd got very friendly, through a shared interest in drugs and derangement, with a few fairly wild people. On the whole I demonstrated a demeanour of restraint in comparison to them. One of my friends suggested that it might be a jolly jape to wander up a nearby road, to where some animals were kept, and bludgeon a pig to death with sledgehammers. The potential perpetrator had a perverse porcine preoccupation. He felt that any situation could be greatly improved by the introduction of a large number of squealing piglets greased in butter. Squealing piggies, yes. Sledgehammers and death, no. I declined the invitation. I also heard tales of a party in the town, attended by only a few students, where a donkey, kept in the large garden, was sodomised by a group of local skinheads who were out of their brains on booze and drugs. "You should have been there," my friends enthused, but I did not pine away with any sense of loss.

On a day between exams I felt that, rather than revising further, I would be better served by slowly ingesting successive acid blotters. The afternoon was an amenable, sunny one. By evening, with more people about, I started getting some beers in. An odd mix of characters fell into each other's company. Some were tripping like myself, others just drinking. Our collective state of mind became increasingly bizarre. After the bar shut we retired to someone's room.

It's difficult to chart the ensuing conversation. Sufficient to say that an hour or so later we could be found marching defiantly down the middle of a road, some in balaclavas, clutching petrol bombs. A small electricity sub-station proved to be boringly fire proof.

We maniacally searched for a satisfyingly flammable low-risk target. One building that was narrowly rejected was later discovered to have people living in it. Finally, a wooden hut in a field was torched. It's nicely burnable contents rapidly produced spectacular flames that roared up above the surrounding trees to a height of about fifty feet. The season had inspired its unconscious possessed priests to perform some kind of fiery solstice ceremonial but what aspects of the sun it was acknowledging and invoking were unclear for the moment. Who knows what weirdness that locale might have witnessed in bygone eras? Unbeknownst to us, the genius loci may have been demanding the resumption of archaic rites. A clairvoyant eye might have seen dudes dressed in animal skins and antlers emerging out of rippling smoke to dance around us, waving flaming torches. We broke Olympic sprint records to get away before the fire brigade turned up. The next morning at breakfast, having not yet slept, I did wonder what the fuck I'd been playing at and did not get a good feeling about it. There was no time to ponder. In a few hours I faced the second of my psychology exams.

A week later I had an annoying gap of four days before my last exam freed me up to go to Stonehenge and Glastonbury. I couldn't just sit around and revise. A manic thirst for action compelled me further onwards. I decided to fit in a swift visit to Essex to check out my friends' plans for the solstice. By lunchtime on Saturday, I was sitting outside a pub, enjoying supreme June sunshine and smoking a spliff. Talk of Stonehenge was in the air. The great gathering had already begun. Everyone agreed it would be magnificent to be there at that very moment. A mate named Paul went with the mood and offered to take a car-full down there immediately. It was a tempting idea but I had to be able to get a train back to university the next day in order to attend Monday's exam. He assured me we would be back by the next morning, so I jumped in.

The resulting escapade was magnificent. The weather maintained its definitive solstice-time flavour. We got on to the site and all dropped some Yin and Yang acid blotters, including Paul, who was supposed to be driving us back to Essex just over twelve hours later. The acid was beautifully pure. The stage sound system blasted out Steve Hillage's *Green* album. The music seemed to come up out of the earth like the dragon current of John Michell's books. In a moment of total perfection, Here and Now performed. It was still daylight so no lightshow this time. The sound was not so overtly spacey but their hearts were still coming from the *Floating Anarchy* zone. This was back to the vibe of '79 for me. The whole day was better than anything I'd experienced in 1980. On one of the nearby tumuli we later took in the whole panoramic scene of the motley crew spread out before the majestic megalithic edifice. Again an amazing vibe seemed to be coming up through the earth into our bodies. The sun set. The body of Nuit emerged to pulsate over and through us. Time dissolved. Daylight began to return. Still totally tripped-out, we left. The fact that our driver, who was taking us along motorways and so on, was on LSD, never perturbed me in the slightest. The vibe was good. I got back to my parent's home by about seven. After a rest but no sleep, I got up and set off on yet another immense journey. That night, dissolving into comatose kip back in my hall of residence, I looked back on an incredibly long day. I'd woken up in Essex on Saturday and had no sleep since. In between I'd gone all the way to Stonehenge and back and fitted in an outstanding psychedelic experience. It was a superb testimony to the value of being willing to act spontaneously. I couldn't wait to return and then go on to Glastonbury. The next day saw my last exam. Following that, after one day's rest, it was time to get back into the dreamtime again.

On Wednesday June 17th I undertook another journey to Stonehenge. I had arranged to meet two university friends who were heading down from London. The guys had finished their exams before me and had gone to the capital for chemical jollies. Having met them and sampled the Stonehenge scene, I intended to go on to Glastonbury by Friday. On the long coach trip I read *The View Over Atlantis* in its entirety. The weather was superb and it was mighty fine to look up from the visionary text and gaze across the kinds of landscape so eloquently extolled within it. Rolling fields, distant hills, hazy steeples, high blue sky. Eternal June. The sun began to set as I entered the mystic west and felt my skin tingling with the sense of impending magic. It was a Powys-type moment. Something, "*a wave, a motion, a vibration, too tenuous to be called magnetic, too subliminal to be called spiritual,*" was passing between me and, "*the divine-diabolic soul of the First Cause of all life*".

Once I arrived at the festival site I soon found some people I knew from Essex. Yet again it was a case of score some acid, take it, and then hope I could get my tent up before its effects made all further progress impossible. I made a point of grabbing a fair few tabs to stock up for Pilton and also distribute back at university on my return. The Essex crew were not particularly close friends. Most of the 1979 contingent were going straight to Pilton. I wanted to make sure that I managed to meet my university mates. I wasn't particularly settled when I took the acid so when it started to come on I went wandering. This started me off on what became an all-night walkabout. I took in the vibe of the place as I had done in 1980. This time I was conscious of being on my own. I had no contact with anyone. As hours went by I began to feel that the people I was expecting to meet weren't going to show. In my altered state I tried to work out what difference that would make to my plans. I didn't feel like I wanted to hang around at Stonehenge. I would have much preferred to get to Glastonbury as soon as possible.

At dawn I was still staggering around the site, increasingly *"drunken with the magnetism of these prehistoric monoliths"*, in the manner of Powys' John Crow. I noticed a guy sitting in front of his tent with some cigarettes and Rizla papers. I had some dope so I offered to share a spliff with him for the use of his smoking material. We began to chat. He was living in a city on the south coast. I casually mentioned that I only knew one person who lived there. He knew that person. The conversation expanded. It had begun as an amusing case of 'small world' but it soon turned increasingly strange. He had lived in Essex, near to me. He knew many friends of mine and spent time in our local pubs. The cherry on the cake was discovering that he had actually sat outside my parent's house in a car whilst a mate of his came in to score some dope during a sort of party there the previous year. He was going on to Pilton later the same morning. It seemed obvious we should travel together.

I remembered how tiring the 1979 trek from Stonehenge to Glastonbury had been after being awake all night. I hadn't slept since waking up in my hall of residence. I'd already had a long journey and had then walked around for about eight solid hours. The prospect of what lay ahead was daunting. I decided to leave myself an additional option. I bought some speed. It was no longer a drug of choice. I'd taken it about once a week for the whole of 1977. For a while it had been brilliant. After that the come-downs had become increasingly arduous, along with a feeling that it was eating my bones from the inside out. On this occasion I considered it could be an emergency measure. Of course I would be totally wasted by the time I finally did sleep but I was arriving a day before the festival began and therefore had time to recuperate.

My companion and I hitched into Amesbury and then took a bus to Salisbury. This was where we needed to make the connections to get us to Somerset. At the bus station I sat down on a bench and started to have another look at *The View Over Atlantis* whilst my new friend got something to eat in the canteen. Out of the corner of my eye I noticed a police car drive past. I realised that it might be a long time before I had another opportunity to eat and decided to grab a quick bite in the canteen before the bus came. I went in and stood in the queue, contemplating whether a Cornish pasty would taste hideous after a night on acid. Suddenly I felt a hand upon my shoulder. I turned around to find a policeman standing behind me. He asked me if I would mind accompanying him outside. I was walked over to a parked panda-car where his driver colleague was waiting. It was the same car I had noticed moments before. They had seen an obvious hippie Stonehenge festival type get up and walk away the moment he'd seen them. This seemed sufficiently suspicious to warrant further investigation.

For a few moments I entertained the fantasy that their search of my rucksack would not reveal my barely concealed stash of drugs. I was soon disillusioned. There probably wasn't much point in telling them that I didn't usually take speed. What was more important was the worry that the amount of acid I had was large enough to make me seem to be a dealer. I assured them that I tended to take enormous doses of it. I had rapidly entered another reality. I was placed in the back of the police car and grilled by the boys in blue as I was driven away into the unknown. Once we stopped, I was marched, wearing mirrored sunglasses and a wide velvet hat with a big artificial flower in the side of it, in full view of curious members of the public, across a forecourt to some police building with my arm bent round behind my back. It was like being in a movie. I couldn't help laughing. I asked the coppers if they seriously thought I would try and make a break for it when they had my student travel card with my name, photo, and address on it? They replied that a few had done so in their experience and they were taking no chances.

Once actually inside, I soon stopped laughing. A grim station sergeant requested that I remove my shades. I was a little worried that my still-dilated pupils would not help the situation but it was bad enough to be going on with anyway. I was fingerprinted. Next it was into a cell and the instruction to strip. I had known enough people who had been knocked about a bit by the police for me to feel increasingly worried. When Timothy Leary used to talk about the importance of "set and setting" for an ideal psychedelic session

I'm sure he had something more harmonious in mind than stripping for a policeman and being told to bend over. Fortunately that was as far as the nightmare developed. My apprehenders were decent enough and also realistic. One of them told me that he didn't think my arrest would make the slightest bit of difference to me and that I'd probably do some acid the moment I got to Glastonbury. I confirmed that this was an entirely accurate assessment.

I was let back out onto the street with an appointment to appear in court in Salisbury in August. I got back to the bus station feeling somewhat different to when I had initially arrived. Obviously my travelling companion had long since departed as he had gear on him as well and needed to swiftly get away. I was going to Glastonbury for certain but it wasn't going to be like 1979. Of course it was a colossal bummer to get busted. It was even possible that I might go to prison for a few months. I'd read of cases where people with less drugs on them than I'd been nabbed for had gone down. Most powerful of all were the uncanny feelings aroused through pondering on the incredible synchronicities that had apparently set the whole thing up. I had to acknowledge that it seemed very much that it was supposed to happen. The list of random factors leading up to it was impressive. Firstly, the friends I'd arranged to meet hadn't showed. If they had I would have spent an extra day at Stonehenge. My meeting with my travelling companion was a fairly outlandish thing in itself. It had led to me thinking that it was obvious I should go to Pilton with him that morning. Why had I decided to buy some speed at the last moment? We hitched into Amesbury. If we'd had to wait just a little bit longer we'd have got a different bus into Salisbury and arrived at a later time. As for when we did get there, why didn't I go straight into the canteen? And, of course, what factors led to the police car driving past at that crucial moment as my brain thought of food? Where had the coppers been that morning that set them up to be there then? It was simply too much and a mind-bendingly brutal contrast to my spontaneous swift tripping visit to Stonehenge a mere five days before.

I reflected on the recent events of my life. I couldn't escape the conclusion that all of this was connected to the deranged petrol-bombing episode. It wasn't like I believed there was an Old Testament-type God sitting on a cloud somewhere who had seen me being naughty and was now punishing me. It wasn't as simple as that. Powerful forces had been stirred up. That ritual fire (and it certainly seemed now to have been revealed to be such a thing) had served as a beacon marker for a crossroads. Those accompanying spirit shamans had perhaps been conducting some initiation on my behalf. In my state of emotional vastation, it was easy to formulate such fancies. I believed that a truth had been revealed to me. If I went further down the road represented by the night of flaming madness my life would go right off the rails. It wasn't what I was supposed to be doing. Period. Never mind anyone else and their karma, or any issues of moral codes and so forth. It was a practical demonstration of how the dynamic of my life worked. I had to understand it and act accordingly. Nonetheless, I had to be grateful to that dark fire of the night. It was all supposed to happen that way. I scanned my memory for any other events that had been so clearly synchronistically engineered. There weren't any. Once again I arrived in Somerset as part of a life-changing event.

It was late evening when I disembarked from the bus in Glastonbury, this time alone, and began the gigantic walk to Pilton. In later years special festival buses were laid on from the town. That luxury was a fantasy then. A hard slog lay ahead. I had dozed a bit during the long journey but had still not really slept. I empathised with John Crow's epic walk at the start of *Glastonbury Romance* when he came to the limit of his physical endurance. The contrast to the radiance of my 1979 solstice epic was immense. In the two years since then I had thought about it so much. I had dreamed of returning and reconnecting to that tangible magic. That dream had motivated me through my time in the factory and my first year at university. Not once had I ever contemplated the possibility that my return would be in such circumstances. Awakening in my tent the next morning, my strongest feeling was a quest for chemical oblivion. When I met up with my Essex friends it turned out that many of them had also been busted in a series of separate episodes on their way down. A few mates clubbed together to give me a bit of money and some drugs. I began to perk up a bit. The weather was fine and I was in sight of the Tor once again. I resolved to make the most of it.

After a two-year gap, the festival had clearly changed. This time it was specifically focused on the CND cause. There were more people. Something about the music on offer seemed to symbolise the differences between the departing seventies and emerging eighties. Tim Blake had been billed to appear but didn't. This was a drag as I'd really been looking forward to seeing him again, having made something mythological in my mind of his 1979 performance. One night the bill was topped by an early performance by New Order. They were a long way from the electro-dance phenomenon they later became. Less than a year after the death of Ian Curtis, they carried a glacial coldness from their origins as Joy Division. It fitted my general condition. In the course of the weekend I did some acid. It was a neutral average kind of affair. In the end I was grateful that it hadn't turned into a screaming bummer. I wasn't exactly set up right to do some. I even took some speed. That was also fairly uninteresting. Such was my emotional state that even this definitive upper could barely affect it. I didn't know it at the time but it was to be the last occasion I would ever take any. I've never had the slightest twinge of an impulse to do so since.

The solstice itself did seem to be a very long day. I began to notice something about the greater environs of the Glastonbury landscape. Staring into the sky, I felt a quality that Powys had commented on concerning the misty rim of the horizon, *"that peculiar Somersetshire blueness which is neither air nor vapour, water nor cloud, but a phenomenon, an entity, unique to itself."* A *"mystical blueness"*. He had also noted that Glastonbury is, *"a place that's famous for its twilights"*. In June, on a clear sunny day, it seems to take about a hundred years to get dark. After the solstice sun had set, an exquisite afterglow lingered in the form of a fading rosy light across the hills. Not even the greatest of the Pre-Raphaelites could have done it justice. No wonder that the ancients had been drawn to the place and that it still aroused the poetic, mystical faculties. I was touched by an unbearable sense of something hanging in the air, just out of reach, shrouded with poignant nostalgia, beckoning, calling to the heart like a prayer.

On Sunday August 16th I set off for Salisbury to appear in court. I told my parents that I was going to an all-night party and then on to spend the day in Southend, so they wouldn't see me again until the following evening. I was only too aware of the very real possibility that I might end up phoning them the next day to give them the surprise news that I was about to start three months in prison. This would unquestionably devastate them and I hoped, as much for their sake as mine, for a better outcome. I had to appear in court at 10.30 on Monday morning. There was no way that any public transport could get me there in time if I left from Essex on the same day. I had to travel down the night before. My financial situation was such that overnight accommodation was not an option. A grand fantasy emerged to compensate for my terror. I would try and spend the night in Salisbury Cathedral. I imagined that it might be possible to get in there and then hide so as to spend an unforgettable time in the company of ghostly monks, perhaps obtaining some kind of sanctuary and blessing before my ordeal.

My senses were heightened to an almost hallucinatory level as I disembarked, just after ten o'clock, in an unfamiliar town with such a profound unknown ahead. For starters, I had never before not known where I was going to sleep. I soon located the cathedral and my mind was transported beyond its troubles. The magnificent building with its 404ft spire, the highest in England, was floodlit. Somewhere inside it an organ was being played. The night before had been a full moon and as I arrived at the already majestic scene, it was ascending from the horizon, as if directly next to the cathedral from my vantage point. *"From the dim shores of ancient anarchy," "The patroness of all defiers of man's laws,"* as Powys had characterised it. The numinous combination of floodlit cathedral, music, and moon, would have been sufficient to give me cold tingles whatever the state of my life but in the circumstances of that time it was unbearably beautiful. I settled down on a bench to take in as much soul food as was available whilst the opportunity lasted.

The music stopped just before eleven. I was now faced with the daunting challenge of finding a safe space to doss undisturbed. I wasn't that surprised to find the cathedral locked. I wandered off in search of an acceptable bed and soon suffered a definite setback. I didn't realise that I was in an area known as Cathedral Close. The immediate environs were surrounded by a wall that looked like it could maybe date from the Middle Ages. Within its locale were a number of buildings including a fair few modern ones. There were big gates within the wall and it turned out that they were locked at eleven. I had to stay within the cathedral zone all night. A delirious time unfolded. I never slept at all. I heard every chime of the cathedral clock, each quarter of an hour. I spent time in a number of entirely unsuitable uncomfortable places and found they were always too exposed, leaving me feeling too vulnerable to go to sleep. Eventually I found some school buildings and curled up in a shivering ball behind a stack of wooden pallets. By six o'clock I could hear the sounds of the world beginning to stir, traffic and footsteps, so I moved on again.

It is certainly not advisable to turn up for an appearance before a magistrate, where the need to impress is paramount, looking like you've just spent the night sleeping rough. There was no way round this. I sat outside the court room waiting my turn, and studying the specimens of humanity around me. The big moment came and went in a blur. I was not sent to prison. My punishment was a fine of a few hundred pounds and arrangements would be made for me to pay in instalments. Ripples of relief and gratitude flowed through me. I went out into the sunshine to begin the rest of my life.

HOLYEST ERTHE

COUNTING UP MY MONEY I decided I could afford to have a little celebration. I went into a bookshop to see what was on offer. I came away with a history of Glastonbury that primarily covered the story of its abbey, *King Arthur's Avalon* by Geoffrey Ashe, and Gurdjieff's autobiography, *Meetings with Remarkable Men.* I started reading Ashe on the train journey home, feeling it was material I was well primed for after the experience at the cathedral.

A Glastonbury Romance, for all its vast length, doesn't really give much historical detail about the place. The abbey ruins are featured. They make an atmospheric backdrop for various lovers meetings. One character is plagued by vague ghosties that are being stirred up there. A vast spiritual presence of Christ crucified spreads out to permeate the ethers of the town over an Easter weekend. The rest of the time, its thousand years of devotions linger like a waft of incense sometimes detected in the air. There's mention of an ancient Lake Village that's stated as being a centre of goddess worship. The principle character, Geard, actually drowns in its vicinity during the climactic flood, seemingly returning to the embrace of the Great Mother. Powys had given me a considerable ambiance. Geoffrey Ashe was about to provide a real history lesson but he emphasised something Powys would have understood.

Firstly, one has to wonder what it was that attracted people to Glastonbury in the past? The most fundamental thing seems to be a mysterious quality of the landscape itself. For example, the Tor can be seen from a considerable distance away. It totally dominates the visual field. As one approaches it and circles around it, a continual shapeshifting is occurring. It presents a different aspect from every vantage point. And yet, there are places in the town where the Tor cannot be seen. The view from its summit is extensive but does not include the abbey, which is hidden by Chalice Hill, apart from the late addition of the abbot's kitchen. The Tor tower, which is clearly visible from miles away, doesn't really seem that tall when you're inside it. The early inhabitants of Britain led lives far more intimately connected to the land than most people do today. The distinctive qualities of the Glastonbury environs would suggest it was a place of the Otherworld. In those far-off times much of the area was underwater as well. The Tor and its adjoining hills would have been virtually islands. Despite subsequent draining much of the spell remains intact. The whole locale seems to participate in an endlessly shifting perspective.

Ashe begins his Glastonbury history around the 3rd century BC when Celtic settlers created a lake village, built on platforms on stilts in water, in the vicinity of present-day Godney. The settlement flourished and had trading links as far away as the Baltic. The most obvious local landmark was the Tor. In Celtic mythology there are traditions of islands of the dead and hills that were entrances to the underworld. It seems reasonable to suggest that the Tor, as a hill and island, could have been sacred to the locals at least. They may well have buried their dead nearby. If that had been the case, it would imply a Druid presence. They presided over all aspects of Celtic religious life. Christian material from the Dark Age period contains some tantalising hints about the place's sanctity and the sort of beliefs surrounding it. St. Collen was summoned to pay his respects to Gwyn ap Nudd, who is Lord of the Tor, King of the Faeries and ruler of the underworld known as Annwn that Powys had so strongly affirmed as part of Glastonbury's identity. Atop the Tor, Collen somehow enters Gwyn's otherwordly castle where a feast is in progress and music and beauty are all around. Not being much of a party person, Collen splashes holy water everywhere and the whole scene disappears like a mirage. An early charter from the abbey period mentions a Celtic name that the place may have been known by, Ynys Witrin, often taken to mean 'Isle of Glass'. It is difficult to say much about the Glastonbury area during Roman times. There have been finds indicating their definite presence but suggestive of a few large houses rather than a whole town.

It is at the beginning of the Roman era that one of Glastonbury's greatest mythological events is supposed to have occurred. Joseph of Arimathea, who the New Testament tells us provided the tomb for Jesus, journeyed from Palestine to make his home in Somerset, either in 37 or 63 AD. No written forms of this story exist prior to the Norman conquest. This mythos has become perhaps the most enduring of all Glastonbury tales, resolutely refusing to dissolve before the sceptics, attracting and repelling people with equal force. Ashe makes the interesting point that academics often react just as irrationally as mystical space-cases to this material. The derisive tone of many detractors can be every bit as emotive as the devotional mystic. The Joseph story has left us with perhaps the last functioning medieval-type saintly relic. Supposedly he arrived at Wearyall Hill and planted his staff into the ground. It sprouted and became the famous Holy Thorn. The current form of the story doesn't appear during the days of the abbey but the thorn is of a type originating in the Middle East. Perhaps a Crusader brought it. Ashe delights in affirming how the enigma of Glastonbury often manages to supply such typically annoying little details to irritate the sceptic.

The Arimathean mythos has impacted significantly on the greater life of the nation. An extreme form of the tale has Joseph as the uncle of Jesus. He came to Britain with the young Christ as part of an involvement in the Cornish tin trade. It appears to be this idea that inspired William Blake to write the words that, now known as *Jerusalem*, have since been set to music and become our 'second national anthem'.

> *"And did those feet in ancient time*
> *Walk upon England's mountains green?"*

I'm not quite sure if the sceptical academics and general haters of Glastonbury would like to remove all such manifestations from our culture. I would refer them to the works of Jung, Joseph Campbell, and Mircea Eliade concerning myth as a vital natural human function, necessary to the health and sanity of the individual and body-politic, and a measure of the well-being of the society it arises from. I would affirm that there exist certain special numinous places, somehow able to inspire the tribal tales that any culture needs to understand its identity and needs, its potential destiny. As Geoffrey Ashe connected me ever more strongly to its history, I became increasingly convinced that Glastonbury seems to be such a place, a place where history and mythology, two hemispheres of one greater brain, are almost impossible to separate.

The stories tell that Joseph and his associates were given land by a local ruler of some kind. On it was built the first church in Britain, a small circular wooden affair. Twelve huts surrounded it. Such was the legendary foundation of Glastonbury Abbey. Unfortunately none of this material exists in documentary form before the Normans. Sceptics can refute it all as typical examples of an institution seeking to validate itself through the creation of an illustrious legendary pedigree.

What can be confidently stated is that when the Saxons appeared they found a piously venerated small church, redolent of a mysterious antiquity. Rather than act as conquerors, they accepted what was in place and tried to create a functional unity with the resident Britons. Geoffrey Ashe recognised in those events signs of Glastonbury's real importance. *"It is a national shrine, standing for the creative reconciliation of races and provinces. – Here was the original haven of the faith which made the country a single realm after the interval of Saxon division. Here the Britons and Saxons first learned to live at peace, and the vision of the United Kingdom was born."*

With the onset of the Norman era the figure of Arthur began his astonishing ascendancy. Somewhere around 1135 Geoffrey of Monmouth's *History of the Kings of Britain* appeared. This supposedly non-fiction work, which told of the deeds of Arthur to a large audience for the first time, achieved immediate major success. This was the preset to the most generally famous events to occur at the abbey. In 1184 the old church was destroyed by fire. This was seen as a national disaster. Henry II agreed to rebuild in a manner worthy of Glastonbury's status. A tale is told that during a visit to Wales he was informed that Arthur was buried in the grounds of the abbey at a specific location. After the fire, amidst the reconstruction, the opportunity arose to investigate. In either 1190 or 1191, the monks began to dig. They found a hollowed oak trunk, set at an angle in the ground. It contained skeletal remains. A skull showed the marks of a fatal blow. A leg bone affirmed a man of impressive stature. Most evocative of all was the presence of a second skeleton. Long golden hair was still intact but crumbled to dust on touching. Arthur and Guenevere. Or so the story goes. The whole business is still a matter of fetid controversy over which protagonists of different theories readily foam at the mouth. Cynical critics generally consider that the find was a huge hoax, perpetrated for the purpose of fund raising in the aftermath of the fire. The bones were interred in an impressive black marble shrine, the former site of which is now denoted by a sign in the abbey ruins.

From that moment Glastonbury became identified with the Isle of Avalon. This is yet another area of rancid disagreement. The discovery of the grave seemed to suggest some sort of logic: if Arthur was laid to rest at Avalon and he'd been found at Glastonbury then it must be Avalon. The Celtic traditions of islands of the dead don't really suggest there was only one of them. The name 'Avalon' may well have originally referred to a location other than Glastonbury. What cannot be doubted is that all of the characteristics of Avalon are present in Glastonbury. If it isn't the original one it probably fits the bill even better. We can perhaps recover the details of the place the name derived from. Different theories have been propounded. A good case can be made for Anglesey. Chances are that, unless one is a powerful clairvoyant, such other locations may not feel like a living reality. The new Avalonians would affirm that Glastonbury remains a *functional* Isle of Avalon to this very day and, beyond the sneering of the debunkers, it is that which is of most importance.

So began a golden age. The Arthurian mythos with its quest for the Grail inspired the whole of Europe. Glastonbury's fame as his resting place gave it a unique status. The abbey and its lands were almost an independent state, having been granted unique privileges by successive monarchs. Abbots sought to outdo each other with ever-larger building projects. Apart from old St. Paul's it became the longest church in England. The blessings of Our Lady of Glastonbury seemed tangible. The previous night, gazing out of the train window as I'd travelled into an uncertain future, I'd known that it was no ordinary journey I was on. By late afternoon on the way home, I was in awe. The level of input had reached overload. I put the book down and surrendered to delirious fatigue.

When I got back to Essex I was soon off to the pub for a more intense celebration. Exotic cocktails disappeared down my throat. I had scarcely slept since the previous morning. The whole stress of the night out in Salisbury had left me unable to handle much intoxication. On returning home I vomited into a waste paper bin at the side of my bed. By August 1981 it really felt that that kind of thing was well past its sell-by date. Salisbury Cathedral, the grace of my escape from prison, the doorway into Glastonbury Abbey, were too incongruous a juxtaposition against pissed-up puking, even for someone such as myself, who had come to embrace paradox and the unity of opposites. That was the last time I ever got myself into such a condition. Although I didn't know it at the time, my drinking days were on the way out. Something was changing.

The next morning, despite being profoundly knackered by the recent events, I was pleased to find that I'd not lost my appetite for input. It was back into *King Arthur's Avalon* for its conclusion. I was thoroughly sobered by a glimpse of horror, of the murder of the dream, acted out on the bloodstained pages of real history in November 1539. Onetime Renaissance *wunderkind* Henry VIII perpetrated perhaps the greatest British cultural atrocity. His dissolution of the monasteries was carried out in a needlessly wanton manner. What happened at Glastonbury was the worst example of the entire process. The elderly abbot, Richard Whiting, was set up on a blatantly false charge of treason. Along with two colleagues, he was sentenced to death. The King's Einsatz Kommando hit-squad stretched and tied the old man on a hurdle. This was dragged by a horse through the town, past the abbey, and up to the summit of the Tor, where gallows had been erected. There the three men were executed. Whiting's head was removed and placed above the abbey gate. The rest of his body was cut into four pieces that were displayed in nearby towns. Ashe raises some disturbing points about the ghastly scenario. It would require considerable effort, in wet and muddy November, for a horse to drag a man tied to a hurdle up to the top of the Tor. The construction of the gallows there was no easy task either. The summit is renowned for the strong winds that often blow across it. If the sole purpose of the deed was to instil fear in the population then why not do it in front of the abbey, in the middle of the town, where everyone could potentially see it? There's an unsettling hint of impractical stranger motives amongst the executioners. The three bodies strung up on a hill suggest a blasphemous parody of the crucifixion and archaic sacrificial rites.

The abbey library was trashed. Pages of priceless manuscripts were found as litter in the streets. The bones displayed as Arthur and Guenevere's were lost. Who knows what modern forensic science could have told us if they were still available? The monks were dispersed. Before long the majestic edifice of the building was pillaged for raw material. One of its later owners used gunpowder to blow great holes in the walls to satisfy his materialistic priorities. The Grail Chalice of British Christendom disappeared, leaving a wasteland behind.

For hundreds of years Glastonbury seemed to go into a kind of suspended animation. At the beginning of the 20th century the abbey ruins were put up for auction and passed into the hands of the Church of England. In 1908 a Bristol architect named Frederick Bligh Bond was placed in charge of archaeological excavations there. I already knew from John Michell's books a little of the amazing saga that followed. Bond quickly achieved notable results. A chapel mentioned in records but physically lost was located. Further good work followed. Boosted by his success, Bond was rash enough to reveal his unorthodox methodology. Automatic writing was used to contact the spirits of the departed monks, who referred to themselves as the 'Company of Avalon'. They had, in a way, become part of the realm of Annwn. Directions for digging derived from such psychic sessions. They also helped to enhance the heresies that Bond saw in the architectural form of the abbey. It was he who had stated that numerical codes, suggestive of esoteric ideas, were embodied in the geometry of its design. Bond was removed from his post. This extraordinary episode heralded the rebirth of Glastonbury. For those willing to consider such possibilities, the dynamic appeared to come from the invisible realms, from spiritual forces linked with the mysteries of Arthur and the Grail, Joseph of Arimathea and a whole host of saints. It gave hope that eventually, the horrors perpetrated by the syphilitic king and the profoundly bad karma of his national church, born in blood, could one day be annulled and transcended. Geoffrey Ashe didn't wax quite so lyrically about it but I was stirred to such fancies.

My journey to Glastonbury in June had actually led to me making a stronger connection to the place, but in ways I could never have anticipated. I'd experienced a sense of it as an other-world apple orchard paradise in 1979. In 1981 it had shown me how it could also function as an entrance to the underworld. And the two visions were not separate. Each implied the other. There was treasure in the underworld. Amongst the departed shades of Avalon, its hideous martyrdom and ghostly monks, was something so beautiful it was almost painful. It seemed to be best symbolised as the mystery of the Grail. That mystery, as Powys had felt, stretched across the whole of Glastonbury's history, somehow embracing both the pagan and the Christian. Now that the summer had played itself out I could intuit a spooky unity in what had happened to me. Primed by the sensibilities of Powys, after my Salisbury ordeal I was in a superb state of heightened sensitivity to read *King Arthur's Avalon.* The vision of the floodlit cathedral, with the full moon beside it and the celestial organ sounds emanating from within were readily on hand to stimulate me to reverie over the glories of Glastonbury Abbey. The possibilities of imprisonment and so on were a kind of purgatory or test of the Grail Knight. I went straight from that, with no sleep, into Ashe. I'd never had such an amazing preparation for reading a book before. It was being given a perfect invitation to make a gigantic impression on me. It did.

MASTERS OF WISDOM

FIRED UP WITH THE INTENSITY OF MY LIFE, I went straight into my other Salisbury purchase, *Meetings with Remarkable Men.* Gurdjieff is perhaps the most enigmatic and haunting magus figure of the 20th century. Like Crowley, he has been reviled as a charlatan. Others have seen him as a superhuman ambassador of esoteric schools. *Meetings with Remarkable Men* can barely be validated in any of its details. Nonetheless those who were closest to Gurdjieff accepted its essential veracity. He was born sometime between the 1860s and 70s, in the multicultural melting pot of Armenia, an area of the Caucasus that had been in the middle of wars and migrations of different races for millennia. It had recently passed from the control of Turkey to Russia. His father was a kind of bard who had memorised a vast storehouse of ancient tales, none of which he wrote down. One day the young Gurdjieff read details of the translation of some cuneiform tablets recently excavated in Babylon. They told the tale of the *Epic of Gilgamesh.* He was amazed to recognise the story as one that his father told. This meant that oral tradition was capable of preserving material in undistorted form for thousands of years. It raised the question of what other survivals may be retrievable. Gurdjieff and his friends engaged in a quest for ancient knowledge. In the ruins of a Greek Orthodox monk's cell, a manuscript was discovered. It told of a group known as the Sarmoun Brotherhood. This esoteric society had originated in Babylon and gradually migrated. Here was the evocative idea that some Christians had been guardians of hidden knowledge, passed secretly down through the ages, avoiding inquisitors and iconoclasts. There were hints that Sarmoun still existed. Gurdjieff made it his life's work to find them.

All manner of lyrical adventures followed. A map of 'pre-sand Egypt' led him to the Sphinx. There was an expedition across the Gobi desert. Finally, after being led blindfolded on horseback and across a perilous ravine, Gurdjieff arrived at the Sarmoun Monastery. He was initiated into their mysteries. They had preserved a tradition of sacred dance. The movements had complex meanings. In learning to perform them the dancer would need to enter into a profound altered state. A whole cosmological system could be taught through them. Gurdjieff later achieved great success in Europe and the USA through public presentations of dances and music allegedly originating from esoteric sources.

It was always maintained that the Gurdjieff Work was essentially 'Esoteric Christianity'. He was born into a Greek Orthodox family and was buried to their funeral service. Evocative statements were made claiming that the liturgical details of early Christianity, which were better preserved in the Eastern churches, derived from the Egypt of the Pharaohs. There was also a science of number and proportion, known to architects and builders, which could create places that inevitably induced altered states in those who entered within them. The combination of the appropriate ceremonial and music in such temples and churches was a true science and had been largely lost.

The essential principles of Esoteric Christianity lie at the core of all religion. In Islam, similar wisdom has been transmitted through Sufi schools. Until recently most textbooks on the history of religion would state that the Sufis are simply the mystics of Islam. Many of the groups themselves affirm that they are the carriers of wisdom from the very dawn of humanity. The Sarmoun Brotherhood may have seeded schools in central Asia with their knowledge. Possible candidates are a mysterious order called the Khwajagan or Masters of Wisdom. They may in turn have inspired one of the most important Sufi sects, the Naqshibindi. According to Idries Shah, some of the wisdom kept by the Sufis was transmitted to Christian Europe. Following on immediately after my connection to Glastonbury Abbey, I inevitably wondered if some form of that ancient wisdom had been in operation there? A few days after returning from Salisbury I realised that I'd experienced a level and intensity of input unparalleled in my life so far.

MIND GAMES

THE NIGHT OF PETROL-BOMB INSANITY had certainly carried some weird energy with it. Strange episodes later befell two of my collaborators. One of them was booked on a helicopter flight to the

Isle of Wight but was held up and missed it. The helicopter crashed. Lives were lost. I felt that something was clearly inviting him to take a look at his life and where it was going. He disagreed and pursued a path into the realms of heroin and its attendant mentality. The other mate lived to regret his one dalliance with the demon scag. He'd never done it in his life or even contemplated it until one night, pissed-up at the university bar, he was offered some and took a small amount home in silver paper. Shortly after that his flat caught fire. All of his clothes were destroyed. Vital course project work going towards his final degree mark was also incinerated. In fact there was virtually nothing of his personal possessions left for the fire brigade to retrieve. Nothing that is apart from the silver paper containing heroin. I saw this very clearly as a similar event to my own. It was strange to me that he didn't. After his court appearance he got drunk and went out vandalising things.

The remaining part of the summer break was dramatically different. I now had a future. I could look ahead to a second year at university. The vibe was significantly helped by the arrival of a large quantity of John Lennon acid blotters. The name derived from a big sheet of blotting paper soaked in LSD. A design was printed on it of the cover of Lennon's greatest hits album, *Shaved Fish*. The story was that this large piece of art, containing thousands of doses of acid, was openly taken through Customs and shown to the officers who didn't know what it was. A mate of mine had a big portion of it and was happy to let me sell some at a profit. Whereas in the past I had helped sort out a few friends in the acid department and also shifted small amounts of dope, this emphatically put me into the dealer category.

Two weeks after my court appearance I was unloading a hundred trips at a free festival in Norfolk. Was I totally insane? After what I'd been through why was I taking such huge risks? The money was certainly good but I had a sense of an idealistic Leary-type crusade to expand people's consciousness. During that weekend I, of course, sampled the goods. It seemed appropriate to listen to *Shaved Fish*. During *Mind Games* I experienced some sort of chemical satori.

> *"Love is the answer, and you know that for sure.*
> *Love is the flower, you gotta let it grow.*
>
> *Yes is the answer, and you know that for sure*
> *Yes is surrender, you gotta let it go."*

I was listening to this as I was coming up on quite a hefty dose. An ecstatic opening of my whole system ensued. Great shudders accompanied its purifying force. I cried buckets. I knew with total certainty that what Lennon was singing about was *true.* In fact it was the only truth worth knowing. Without that foundation, everything was bullshit. It was that feeling that propelled me into even more dangerous territory.

In September I spent Friday nights at a notorious pub in Southend, the *Top Alex.* I shifted a hundred blotters each time. It was not unknown for undercover police to operate in there. People had been busted immediately outside before. To say I was easy to pick out would be an understatement. Most of the regulars were hippie or biker in appearance. Something of the zeitgeist of the time was influencing me. August had seen the notable chart successes of Soft Cell with *Tainted Love* and the Human League with *Love Action (I Believe in Love).* It was the shape of things to come. I was the only person in the *Alex* wearing a kind of white tuxedo jacket. I was also the only male with purple hair and black eyeliner. The white winklepicker boots were likewise a one-off. Any one item of my appearance was sufficient to identify me. I would walk in there with a hundred blotters and out with hundreds of pounds. I could have easily been busted or robbed. I wasn't. The events from June to September had been extraordinary. As I returned to university in October I was loaded up with acid and dope and ready for extreme weirdness.

THE BURNING SQUIRRELS OF SATAN

IT WAS SOON APPARENT that my second year was going to be very different from the first. I was in a new room and the fresh influx of students had a far higher percentage of drug users and people showing signs of interest in esoteric subjects. University life can produce culture shock for the unprepared and many chances for rich learning experiences beyond the general curriculum. I was always aware that I was not an average specimen of the student genus. I was a little older than most for starters. My general interests, consumption of drugs, and intensity of consciousness helped to set me apart. Having tasted the world of employment, I was under no illusions as to how wonderful and desirable it was. Therefore I recognised this time of my life as a unique opportunity to live and behave in a way that might never be possible for me again. Nonetheless I soon discovered that in some areas at least, I was dangerously naive.

It began on a Friday night with no obvious social prospects beyond intoxication. I had vaguely noticed that in our dining hall a Christian Union barn dance was scheduled. An event of more insipid mediocrity would have been difficult for me to imagine. The strange destiny that drives my life had other plans for me though, as two divergent universes were about to collide. Towards the end of their rocking evening, the format was changed to include the playing of music more likely to entice a wider selection of punters. Going in there and being blasted by the Human League had a better appeal than taking my partner by the hand and praising the Lord. As I walked by, I was approached by someone who asked me if I wanted to come in. My response was to affirm that I would do, on condition that the Christians reciprocated by attending a devil worship party the following week, for Halloween. It proved to be a tragic mistake for me to assume that evangelical types may possess a sense of humour or irony in such matters. The shocked response to my suggestion led me to feel that some good sport lay within, so I joined the throng for some deliberate baiting. Within a short time, I was being confronted by a distraught individual firmly holding up a crucifix to my face, proclaiming grimly, "*we* shall win".

I retired to my room, amused by his antics and fired up for some more fun. I grabbed my copy of Crowley's *Magick: In Theory And Practice* (which, to be honest, at that point, I barely understood at all) and wandered out into the communal kitchen and proclaimed, to those gathered there, that I intended to perform a ceremony. I showed everyone the images of the ritual postures of 'Apophis-Typhon' etc, and then returned to my room. When I re-emerged, the kitchen had mysteriously filled with a large number of serious-faced people, many of whom I did not recognise. Word had rapidly spread. They turned out to be Christians determined to thwart my fiendish enterprise. One followed me back down the corridor to my room and communicated to me the definite impression that a kicking was on the cards if I persisted. With mocking scorn and bravado I backed down, amazed at how the night's events had galloped away, out of control. This was only the beginning.

Some of my fellow students had led sheltered lives to say the least. One lad, living in the same block as me, had never heard any music other than church and classical before coming to university.

I was barely able to believe that was possible. Others such as he helped create a Halloween debacle. It was set in motion by the misunderstood antics of two friends of mine. Andy Lawrence had attracted my immediate attention on the first day of term when he moved into a room in the same corridor as me. His dress sense was somewhat unique. Obviously inspired by hippie rock band Gong and their trilogy of albums featuring 'Pot Head Pixies', he often wore long pointed gnome hats, tie-dyed boilersuits and suchlike. This was the kind of person I had expected to meet at university and had lamented the absence of in my first year. Even his trombone playing was somehow endearing. He was not a hardcore chemical case like myself but we became firm friends.

He soon met up with and then introduced to me another boiler-suit wearer. Pete Wilson was a bookish type with interests similar to my own. I recognised his potential to be thoroughly corrupted. I felt sure I'd soon have him dancing naked round a bonfire worshipping Pazuzu. It wasn't long before he was crawling out of my room, on his hands and knees, vomiting, after I'd filled his head full of drugs and played him a Vangelis album in the dark with only the luminous glow-stars on my ceiling to orientate him. Fifteen years later, when I initiated him as a Reiki Master, we laughed that, in certain respects, the same head-mashing process was still in motion.

Andy and Pete were noticeable eccentrics and their association with a known dodgy geezer, i.e. me, was remarked upon. A kind of guilt by association was set to work both ways. On Halloween night the two of them gathered in Pete's room. An album of Native American Indian chanting and drumming was put on. Andy had obtained some coloured smoke canisters and decided that now would be a good time to open the window and let one off. The smoke proved to be thicker than anticipated so they now adjourned outdoors. A pair of shoes owned by Andy had come to the end of their natural lifespan. It seemed an auspicious time to give them a good send-off. Just outside the residential block they set fire to them and danced in a circle as Andy chanted in Latin, with the sounds of the Native Americans still coming from Pete's window. At the climax of the proceedings another smoke canister was set off, producing a great green column from the burnt offering. Many nearby watching eyes interpreted the events according to their own peculiar mind-sets. It was later discovered that a number of girls, watching from the block opposite, had locked themselves into their rooms, believing the column of smoke to be a demonic manifestation. More remarkable still was the widely told tale that the burning shoes were, in fact, a squirrel sacrifice.

The first whispers of this rumour reached Andy a few days later. His immediate response was to buy a plastic squirrel from a garden centre. He then inserted a six-inch nail through its head, applied some blood red paint and hung the resulting artwork in his window. Other feedback didn't seem to gel very easily with reality. When Andy had first entered Pete's room that night he had been carrying a teapot. It was a particularly distinctive one as it had a Pot Head Pixie design painted on it taken from the Gong *Flying Teapot* album cover. A Christian had passed him in the corridor and given him a suspicious look. It was later reported that Andy had been seen entering the room holding a Ouija board. At least two cases of perplexing faery glamour seemed to have been at work, whereby shoes became squirrels and a Pot Head Pixie Flying Teapot became a Ouija board. The teapot hallucinator had become further unhinged as the night progressed until, convinced that teapot/Ouija board plus Native Americans and green smoke equals Black Mass, he had run off, weeping in terror into the night, to find the hall warden.

The combination of this whole episode with my own performance the week before helped a unique sociological event unfold. In many ways it was one of the most educational experiences I underwent at university. I certainly learnt more from it than much of my course work. Within a week I had been called before the hall warden and faced with allegations of being a black magician. I was happy to own up to a deep interest in the occult but laid out for him very clearly how the fear, cultural conditioning, and downright stupidity of certain people, had let their humourless imaginations gallop away with them. I confessed to having been foolish to bait them but the situation was now ridiculous. He seemed satisfied with my explanations and my pledge to tone down my act a bit. Andy and Pete were likewise called upon to give an account of their behaviour.

I expected that to be the end of the matter. In fact, as the weeks went by, it became clear that some kind of folklore was rapidly building up and spreading widely. A nearby hall of residence had a screening of Stanley Kubrick's *The Shining*. At the end, a Christian conspiratorially approached the hall warden and told him "this kind of stuff is going on over the road". I was sneaked a copy of minutes for a meeting of hall wardens and presidents where the matter of 'occult events' was raised. It was stated that this was a serious matter and should be stamped out immediately. This was a gathering of academics and they seemed to accept the reality of the rumours and allegations. I was completely stunned by this. Immediately I protested to my own warden that this was simply not acceptable.

The eighties became a decade of spectacular evangelical insanity. My own personal favourite episode involved one Jim Brown in Ohio. He led seventy-five young people in a mass burning of recordings of the theme tune to *Mr Ed*, the TV comedy about a talking horse. Brown believed that *A Horse is a Horse* played backwards revealed the message, *"Someone sung this song for Satan"*.

I synchronistically found a copy of Norman Cohn's *Europe's Inner Demons* at this time. Cohn is a real intellectual heavyweight. His most famous work, *The Pursuit of the Millennium,* detailed religious and social upheaval in the European Middle Ages inspired by the *Book of Revelation.* It's an astounding work, full of barking-mad crusading utopian visionaries and the bloodbaths surrounding their bizarre careers. He also investigated anti-Semitism from the starting point of the infamous *Protocols of the Elders of Zion.* This forged work was widely circulated at the start of the 20th century in Russia, and later in Nazi Germany. It purported to reveal an international Jewish conspiracy aimed at world domination. With *Europe's Inner Demons,* Cohn turned his attention to the witch trial mania. He noted continuity with discoveries in his earlier studies.

Throughout European history, groups of people have been vilified and demonised. They are often accused of strangely similar crimes. The earliest Christians were believed to indulge in the grossest of orgies. They were supposedly cannibals with a particular taste for babies. They had no respect for the existing social status quo and were happy to see it collapse. Some sought to actively encourage the process. Once Christianity triumphed, the Jews came to be considered guilty of the same kind of activities. The witch-burning era saw the whole syndrome in its most extreme form. Cohn argues that, because the early Christians and Jews were never guilty of any such non-existent crimes, we should look very carefully at the witch trials as well. The book ultimately suggests that there never were any real witches at all, as no genuine evidence was ever produced to substantiate the basic package of allegations. I tend to feel that is a considerable oversimplification. I was very impressed though, by his laying bare of the basic social myth of the demonic outsiders and their activities. I doubt if I'd ever experienced the reality of such historical analysis with such vividness in my life before. Whilst I was reading about it, a manifestation of the same kind of process was actually happening to me. Once a certain mythological 'on' button had been pressed, educated people simply ceased to think coherently and fell in with the collective dynamic. These clean, moral, righteous, religious types were more zombied-out than a festival full of hash-heads. I shuddered to think of the famous words of Nietzsche: *"It is not their love for men but the impotence of their love for men which hinders the Christians of today from - burning us."*

I had seen a numinous vision of Salisbury Cathedral by full moon light. I had immediately afterwards made a connection to the eternal form of Glastonbury Abbey. Through studying the Gurdjieff Work, Esoteric Christianity had been revealed to me. My most tangible connection to Christians, though, had involved me being on the receiving end of an inquisitorial witch-hunt. It was a confusing business but it was enough to show that strange forces were still at work in my life

What of the other incarnate demons that tried to open the hellmouth on that eldritch Halloween? Having been unmasked as the slaves of Satan where did their lives go from there? Andy Lawrence went on to receive commissions from showbiz luminaries in need of specialised services for their productions. On one occasion he created a giant sandwich for the use of Russ Abbott. A two-legged camel costume graced the *Little and Large Show.* Perhaps his greatest moment was his work on *Blackadder's Christmas Carol,* helping to dress the cast for a futuristic sci-fi sequence, including the character of 'Nursy' as a sort of Dalek. Pete Wilson followed his muse and achieved multiple successes in *The Library of Avalon* poetry and short story competitions. Such are the wages of sin.

As the year drew to a close it seemed to me that I had been comprehensively set up as a rebel, devil, and heretic. Of course I was responsible for the events that had set the whole sequence in motion but it certainly felt as if fate was manipulating me. I could never have anticipated the manner in which it all unfolded.

* * *

FEAR AND LOATHING OF THE BIRDIE SONG

IN EARLY DECEMBER, a remarkable opportunity arose that tested all I had learnt during that weirdest of years. A nearby hall of residence booked for their Christmas Ball an act guilty of appalling cultural atrocities: the Tweets. Earlier in the year they had scored a hit in the pop charts with their uniquely hideous *Birdie Song*. This involved a performance, dressed in bird costumes, with a characteristic dance, whereby, in the midst of repeating grotesque pantomimic synthesised birdcalls and handclapping, they flapped their wings and turned around in a circle, encouraging others to imitate them. The whole thing suggested a bad acid nightmare to me. I happened to know someone who was involved in the general arrangements for their arrival. They had stipulated that they required a large bottle of vodka between them. At this point I realised that a bad acid nightmare was indeed within my power to produce. I still had in my possession a large amount of acid in blotter form. An irresistible idea occurred to me: I could put a monster dose of it in the vodka, leave it to soak for a few days, remove it and then hand the bottle to the Tweets. I discussed this indubitably evil plan with a few friends and we wondered about the possibilities of making it happen.

In the week leading up to their performance, I indulged in delicious drug-fuelled imaginings of the potential for utter carnage that might be unleashed. I could vividly picture the scene. The end of term Christmas Hall Ball. Large numbers of happy young students, eager to enjoy themselves after their academic exertions and relax with their friends, prior to returning home to their parents for Christmas. Party time. Tinsel and balloons festoon the hall. Many are already a bit merry. Music plays as a group of girlies have a little jig around their handbags. The star turn of the evening is happily awaited. An innocent anticipation of fun and frolics pervades the place. In their dressing room the Tweets, a bunch of good decent blokes, swig from the communal vodka, looking forward to the gig ahead. They don their bird costumes.

Time passes and now they're in full swing. Up on stage they go through their Birdie dance and, with great mirth, the crowd join in. There are mighty guffaws and hearty belly laughs. The now very merry Dolly Dingbats, tinsel in their hair, are executing a veritable shamanic stomp around their handbags. Up on stage it's business as usual for the Tweets. They've been through the whole routine countless times before. Hang on a minute though. As the heinous chemicals begin to take effect, inside their heads something different *is* starting to happen. The music they're playing seems to be echoing strangely. It sounds warped and not at quite the right speed. One of them feels his fingers elongate and become uncomfortably rubbery. He loses the sense of the music he's trying to play. Another sees the end of his guitar wobble, bend, and start melting like one of Salvador Dali's clocks.

> *This bird costume feels really weird. I can't tell where my skin ends and it begins. I never noticed the others looking like that before either. The way all the flashing lights are moving across their costumes, floating, seething, green and purple. Their eyes. Are there really people in there? No. This is fucked up. Something's badly wrong here.*

To the poor lads of the Tweets, the raucous audience begin to take on the vibe of a Hieronymous Bosch painting. Leering, sweaty, warty, purulent faces seem to bark menacingly. Their gyrations suggest preparations for human sacrifice. It's all some kind of Hammer horror voodoo ceremony and the Tweets, in their cult costumes, are the leaders. All these people are here because of them. They have all been brought together for some nightmarish purpose. It has to end. Must escape.

Fast forward. Later that night. Just outside the dining hall where the gig took place. Blue lights flashing. The sound of a helicopter overhead. There's broken windows in the hall. It's empty and dimly lit in there now. Chaos is strewn across the floor. Broken bottles, shards of glass, smashed chairs, an overturned table. Look closer. Beer. Blood. And a sad, pathetic sight. A discarded handbag decorated with tinsel. Outside again, a priest, eyes downcast, slowly shakes his head as a traumatised group of youngsters, some weeping, others with dishevelled or ripped clothes, some bandaged and bleeding, are led away by police and nurses. The scene pans out. Ambulances. Police cars and wagons. Television crews. Photographers. People talking earnestly into microphones against the backdrop of lamentation. Focus back in on a figure, dressed in a bird costume, strapped to a stretcher, his glazed eyes insanely dilated, screaming gibberish, thrashing around, being loaded into the back of an ambulance. More tumult now over by one of the adjacent residential blocks. A group of police in full riot gear, helmets, body-armour and shields, have cornered a figure against a wall, where a searchlight from the hovering helicopter has projected the shadow of its bird costume. A few policemen cautiously advance, brandishing electric cattle prods, towards their cornered prey. Howling like a wild beast he prepares to take on all-comers, a Mansonesque Foghorn Leghorn.

One week later. An official visitor at a psychiatric hospital is shown the terrible legacy. He is led down a corridor of reinforced doors where screams fill the air. A door window shutter is drawn aside to reveal a figure, dressed in a ridiculous bird costume, slumped on the floor. He is mute in the catatonic despair of a hellishly intense introspection nightmare. It is explained that he refuses to take off his bird costume and responds with astonishing violence to any attempt to remove it. It is considered that, for now, it would be dangerous to administer any more medication and it is best to leave him as he is. Indeed a similar state of affairs pertains with one of his comrades but with one major difference. Further on down the corridor another opened shutter reveals a Tweet slamming himself, full speed into the walls, repeatedly. Noting his observers, he launches himself, screaming, at the door. Smashing his bird-masked head against the window he falls back, unconscious on the floor.

The nation's newspapers left no stone unturned in their crusade to uncover the truth behind the outrage. It didn't take long to reveal the culprit. Headlines screamed the appalling details.

TWEETS DRUG NIGHTMARE AND THE BLACK MAGIC FIEND

BIRDIE SONG MONSTER'S DISCIPLES BURNT SQUIRRELS

TWEETS AND THE OCCULT: THE TERRIBLE TRUTH

The day of destiny rapidly approached and reality considerations came to the fore. Of course I never went ahead with my maniacal plan. Regardless of the inevitability of my being easily caught and imprisoned and the whole of my future life being ruined as I acquired a reputation for monstrous evil that I would never be able to lose, the real issues at stake involved the total violation of every ethical code on the planet. There was no way I could believe that it was the True Will of the Tweets to undertake such an experience. To force it on them contravened all Thelemic principles. It was also clearly not in the spirit of Timothy Leary's second great Neurological Commandment: *"Thou shalt not alter the consciousness of thy neighbour without his or her consent."*

MAGNETIC CENTRE AND ETERNAL RETURN

"The point is that a different understanding of time and a different feeling of I are linked together."
Maurice Nicoll. *Living Time.*

AS 1982 BEGAN, I was coming into contact with ideas that would have an incalculably immense effect on me. Following on from my reading of *Meetings with Remarkable Men*, I had developed a big appetite for information on the life and teaching of Gurdjieff and entered into the new-year reading *The Fourth Way* by P. D. Ouspensky, a leading advocate of his work. The ideas within it seemed to enter into every realm of my life and shine a clear light upon them. Gurdjieff's critique of the general state of humanity seemed pessimistic at first. He stated that most of us can be said to be asleep in a trance of distraction. Each of us believes in a unique individuality but, on closer examination, most cannot demonstrate any real unity of functioning. We are full of small separate personalities. One part may proudly proclaim the intention to stop smoking, take up a regime of exercise, follow some idealised spiritual path etc. The 'I' that likes to smoke or overeat or take drugs, be sexually deranged and so on, will later on assert its own claims and the lofty talk will be worthless. We have many I's. They can all be *"caliph for an hour"*. Work on oneself involves the conscious cultivation of a 'magnetic centre'. It is the responsibility of this aspect of oneself to seek out those influences conducive to the maintaining and expansion of its function.

What does that mean in the real world? The feeling of it can be better grasped by looking at it alongside another of Gurdjieff's teaching ideas. Ouspensky discusses the concept of 'food'. He takes it beyond the usual definitions. As well as what we eat in the normal sense, the case is made for regarding air as food. If anyone thinks it isn't, try living without it for a while. Most stimulating of all was the classification of 'impressions' as food. What we input through our senses can nourish or poison us. To take an extreme example, a person feasting everyday on splatter movies, hardcore porn and horror, someone who regularly read the literature of hate, racism etc, would be thoroughly poisoning themselves. Contrariwise, a person who immersed themselves in great art, literature, music, and the religious classics of the world, with a view to changing themselves for the better, would be getting some kind of higher food vitamins and protein. Although just what constitutes appropriate input is hugely debatable and variable, the basic principle is a call to some sort of conscious awakening. Gurdjieff suggested that once this process was really in motion, somehow one magnetically attracted to oneself the necessary higher influences. The world was full of them, but to the average tranced-out sleep-walking person they were all but invisible. I tended to feel that I was essentially already doing this. The year before had been a freaky demonstration of *something* educating me as to what was good for me and what most definitely wasn't. I seemed to be being pulled towards something and made gradually more aware of its subtle way of working. As I became more conscious of the process in motion it accelerated, as I was now also more strongly drawing it towards me. That something was waiting to reveal itself at some future moment but was also already happening.

I could feel the mysteries of time in that paradox. This was another topic that was also being hugely stimulated in early 1982 by reading Mircea Eliade's *The Myth of the Eternal Return.* I have been strangely perturbed by time since I was a small child. I can first remember it in relation to the *Batman* movie in 1966, when I was seven. I used to watch the TV series and saw that a movie was in the offing. I thought that there was something weird about feeling that I would probably get to see the film and that would be in the future. When I was actually in the cinema it would be the present moment and then it would rapidly recede into the past. I tried to imagine looking back from months later, on this event that was still some way off, and feeling it as long gone and also remembering when I had first thought of the whole sequence. All the way through the run-in to seeing it, I kept returning to this pattern of thought. I eventually saw the film on a Thursday. From that point on, every subsequent Thursday for some time, I would stop to ponder that it was now one week since seeing *Batman*, two weeks, and so on up to about nine, before I dropped the whole thing.

There was something mysterious about time that I just couldn't get my head round. Over the years I developed a lot of neurotic obsessive behaviour around dates and anniversaries. I used to note when I'd watched some rubbish movie on TV by circling the date on my calendar and then counting off weeks and months away from it. I can still remember to this day that I watched *The Purple Mask,* starring Tony Curtis, on November 23rd 1971. The apex of this derangement occurred in 1972. Walking to school, on March 24th,

I noted some horse manure in the road. I idly wondered how long it would be before the passing of cars and the weather removed every last trace of it. I duly made a circle on my calendar and noted the gradual diminishment of the pile of poo. Miniscule amounts of it still remained there a year later. I realised I was undoubtedly the only person in the world who a) knew that there was a tiny amount of horse manure in a crack in the road, and b), had a record of the date it had been deposited. Fortunately I went into a kind of spontaneous remission after this event, perhaps unconsciously realising that to go any further in that direction was not a good idea. Nonetheless, the general thing about time persisted.

In other respects this strange mental functioning did serve me well. By the age of ten I had got all of the main dates of the history of the two world wars indelibly memorised. The whole sequence of Hitler's expansionist policies from the remilitarisation of the Rhineland through to the attack on Poland was quite clear to me and I found it totally bizarre that my father, who had fought in the Second World War, got confused over what had happened in what order. I didn't realise it at the time but all of this was providing me with invaluable intellectual foundations and a general emotional disposition in relation to information. It wasn't just dull neurosis. I was passionate about my interests. I felt a strange contempt for people who were merely lukewarm about their lives.

With the reading of Eliade a great elation overcame me. I discovered other ways of experiencing time that seemed to validate at least some of my personal rituals surrounding it. It seems entirely natural to believe that time moves in a straight line, from the past, through the present, and into the future. This is the process of history. The Bible contains such a cosmology. There was a beginning of time, with God's creation of the universe, and there will be an end of it. From *Genesis* to *Revelation*. Common sense appears to bear this out. Our bodies age in a clearly linear sequence. The path from infancy to old age and death seems obvious and apparently inescapable. The deeds of our long vanished ancestors are in the past. The days of Stonehenge and the pyramids are gone, never to return. There is, however, a significant part of the life of the world that is repetitive. On this planet we have the cycles of day and night, the returning seasons, the movements of heavenly bodies in the sky. Nature appears to teach that what disappears will return. And there are many people, even in modern technological societies, who have strong experiences suggesting that they may have lived before this life, that something of them is eternal.

Western civilisation, with its servant science, has been so successful, has demonstrated so many tangible results, that other ways of experiencing time and history have been all but forgotten. Pre-industrial traditional societies often demonstrate a profoundly different worldview. *"Neither the objects of the external world nor human acts, properly speaking, have any autonomous intrinsic value. Objects or acts acquire a value, and in so doing become real, because they participate, after one fashion or another, in a reality that transcends them."* That greater reality consists of the deeds of deities and mythic ancestors, which represent the blueprint for all subsequent actions in a culture. *"In the particulars of his conscious behaviour, the 'primitive', the archaic man, acknowledges no act which has not been previously posited and lived by someone else, some other being who was not a man. What he does has been done before. His life is the ceaseless repetition of gestures initiated by others."*

Construction rituals recreated the cosmogonic act. An archetypal model was imitated. Sacred centres in tribal lands establish divine harmony by bringing down to the earth the celestial perfection. Locations in Egypt, Sumeria, and central Asia were supposedly mapped out firstly in the sky, and then brought to earth. Settlement in new, unknown, uncultivated territory was equivalent to the divine act of creation. Chaos was transmuted into cosmos.

> *"Man constructs according to an archetype. Not only do his city or his temple have celestial models; the same is true of the entire region that he inhabits, with the rivers that water it, the fields that give him his food etc. The map of Babylon shows the city at the center of a vast circular territory bordered by a river, precisely as the Sumerians envisioned Paradise. This participation by urban cultures in an archetypal model is what gives them their reality and their validity."*

A large section of the book deals with the topic of the regeneration of time. Every culture has had a concept of the end and beginning of a temporal period and ways of acknowledging it. Many are profoundly different to what we are now used to. Traditional cultures have periodic ceremonials for the annual expulsion of demons, disease and sins, amidst rituals for the days on either side of the New Year. The expulsions are part of a process that literally abolishes the past. There is an *"attempt to restore, at least momentarily, mythical and primordial time, 'pure' time, the time of the instant of the creation"*. Every New Year is a resumption of time from the beginning, that is, a repetition of the cosmogony.

The clearest examples of all this come from Babylon. Their New Year ceremonials, known as the *Akitu*, seem to have kept a basic form that dates from the earliest Sumerian times. They therefore represent the earliest 'historical' civilisation. The *Akitu* lasted twelve days. During this time the creation story, the *Enuma Elish* was repeatedly recited in a Temple of Marduk. He had become the principal Babylonian deity. It was said that the creation of the world and the human race had come about as a result of his combat with a primordial water serpent of chaos named Tiamat, who he had slain and then dismembered, using her severed pieces to make earth and heaven. (Devotees of the Goddess may feel that Tiamat has been unfairly treated. She was originally conceived of as a womb of creation, an essentially benevolent force. The Marduk story could be taken as an example of patriarchal forms violently supplanting an older matriarchal culture.) Actors mimed the epic saga. The most important point is that they weren't just commemorating the events in the creation drama, they were repeating, actualising the cosmogonic passage from chaos to cosmos. *"The mythical event was present: 'May he continue to conquer Tiamat and shorten her days!' the celebrant exclaimed. The combat, the victory, and the Creation took place at that very moment."*

The *Akitu* also contained a festival of fates known as the *Zagmuk*. Omens for each of the twelve months of the coming year were determined. In effect this helped to *create* the year. It was "*a period of chaos when all modalities coincide*". All of the normal conventions of social behaviour were dissolved. The dead were allowed to return. There were orgies, the reversal of social roles (slaves as masters etc.), feasting, *"a reversion of all forms to indeterminate unity"*. *"a repetition of the mythical moment of the passage from chaos to cosmos"*.

The king embodied divinity on earth. He was responsible for the regularity of the rhythms of nature. In the New Year ceremonials he had the duty of regenerating time. It all concluded when he ascended a ziggurat step pyramid to a temple on its summit. Here he engaged in a rite of sexual union with a sacred hierodule priestess who embodied the Goddess. In this it could at least be seen that something of the significance of the Goddess remained. Here was a tangible acting out of the rebirth of the world and humanity.

Similar conceptions of time are present throughout the ancient world. They can be found, in varying degrees, in Vedic India, early Rome, Germanic tribes and amongst the Egyptians. I got a very strong sense that our Christmas and New Year festivities contain many survivals of the archaic mentality. In the rites of mistletoe and the office party, in the feasting and drunkenness and *auld lang syne*, were the modern forms of the *Akitu*. Quite clearly they served profound human needs. There seemed to be a cyclical sense of dissolution and regeneration in all this. The psychology of the New Year's resolution speaks clearly of it. A new year carries something of the feeling of the possibility of an abolition of the past and a genuine new beginning. Eliade's exposition of the complete mind-set behind such events expanded my understanding immensely.

I seemed to be thinking and feeling like an ancient Babylonian. I'd had a weird sense since childhood that the past cannot really be completely gone and that something of the nature of anniversaries means that the events they commemorate are somehow present. My bizarre obsessive behaviour around time was an attempt, however unconscious and distorted, to express this. I felt that Eliade validated my weird experiments with time and this encouraged me still further.

This led me to ponder upon my personal summer solstice mythos and what the pilgrimage to the West Country had come to mean for me. I realised that many of the motifs from the Babylonian *Akitu* were present in my Glastonbury experiences. Christmas and New Year are powerfully noticeable in our society because most of the culture participates in some way. The summer solstice was, for some, becoming an equally significant time. For me it always seemed to be a focus for transitional events of renewal and regeneration. Being a student was a contributory factor, as the academic year ended round about then. My festival experiences had certainly been *"a period of chaos when all modalities coincide"* and *"a reversion of all forms to indeterminate unity"*. Time had been dissolved. Solstice dawn was some kind of eternal now, a moment in the dreamtime. The normal forms of consensus reality ceased functioning. There was most certainly great intoxication. I already realised that I probably felt all of this more strongly than most. I knew I was evolving a personal mythos. Once again my understanding of Eliade encouraged me to feel that I was gradually revealing some knowledge or intuitive understanding that was already present in me and wasentirely in sympathy with the worldview of the ancients.

Looking at Glastonbury with the eyes of Eliade was very useful to me as well. The zodiac on the landscape had been allegedly created by Sumero-Babylonians. I contemplated the ideas concerning mapping out a celestial archetype of perfection on a new territory, of acting out the cosmogonic process from chaos to cosmos. It was easy to think of prehistoric Somerset as a series of hills arising out of primordial waters of creation in the manner of some ancient myth. The emergence of this land, subtly imbued with the very shapes of the laws of heaven, was an idea that was intoxicating to contemplate. The terraced Tor could evoke the image of a ziggurat. It was an obvious sacred centre. And this zodiac was perhaps the generator of our subsequent national mythos. The Arthurian Grail stories, with their call to vision quest, could easily be seen as examples of Eliade's theme of the imitation of mythic figures whose deeds form the exemplary eternal models of perfection for human behaviour. If the zodiac was pure fantasy, the mysteries of the abbey remained to suggest the bringing down of heavenly archetypes of perfection to earth. The geometry of its grid-plan represented the dimensions of the New Jerusalem. Or at least there were those who believed it did. I had most definitely decided to allow myself to follow that train of thought as far as it could possibly lead me.

Eliade enabled me to place the Glastonbury mythos in an expanded context through comparative data. It was not in any way diminished by this analysis. I became still further convinced that a living authentic mythical reality was accessible there. I was confident that the more I studied the religions of the world and allowed them to mutate my everyday life, the more I learned to think in other categories, the greater chance there would be for the mystery to reveal itself to me.

ON THE INADVISABILITY OF PUBLIC DRUG DEALING

THE EASTER HOLIDAY BREAK turned out to be an important time for me. Back in Essex, I'd scored some acid blotters and headed off to Southend and the *Top Alex* to further supplement my student grant. I got there quite early on a Friday, when there weren't many people about. I wanted to do my business quickly and get out of there. The first person I sold to shouted across the half empty room to a mate of his, "ACID!," pointing at me. I wondered why he didn't get a megaphone out and ring the local police station while he was at it. Something dissolved in me that night. These people generally knew next to nothing about Leary. If they knew anything about Crowley it could probably be written on a postage stamp and was likely to be untrue. They were only interested in getting intoxicated rather than opening their doors of perception to the perennial philosophy. A lot of their terminology around the subject indicated the real motivations. How many times had I heard someone proudly tell me how 'out of it' they were? I occasionally responded by affirming that I was "into it, incredibly into it in fact". I think that perhaps the 'it' that people were so happy to get out of had once been taken to mean the grim consensus of single vision and Newton's sleep but I didn't know anyone who seemed to understand it that way. 'It,' to all intents and purposes, appeared to mean 'reality'. I also drew a definite distinction between being 'high' and being 'wasted'.

The intensity of the regulars' quest for oblivion can be perhaps best demonstrated by a case involving a guy slightly known to me. His experimentation was so unique that it eventually featured in the BMA journal. He had put some hallucinogenic mushrooms into a liquidiser and then poured some of the resulting goo into a syringe, injecting himself with it. For about five seconds it was apparently quite an interesting hit. However, his arm soon doubled in size, turning purple, and his head swelled into a sort of hideous Elephant Man parody. This curtailed the jollies and required the attendance of an ambulance. He survived. I always knew that I would eventually need to escape from such a climate. In spring '82 my ideological crusade and career as an acid dealer ended. It just wasn't worth the risk and it didn't conform to my sense of right livelihood any more. I continued to sort out for a few mates at university for a little while longer but my evangelical public ministry was concluded.

I never set foot in that pub again. This was a prescient decision. 1982 was a ghastly year for the *Top Alex* regulars. A large number of them died. The final toll was well into double figures. Bike crashes were mostly responsible. Shortly after my last visit, heroin began to appear in increasing quantities. It had never really been present during my six years of attendance. Some of the deaths were overdoses. The climax came when the resident DJ was stabbed to death in there. I knew a number of the deceased, although not very closely. Some of them had bought acid from me. The whole scenario was sufficiently unusual to warrant a TV documentary.

The management changed and a new policy barred all the old regular hippie biker types. It was the end of an era in Southend. The reverberations lasted for a number of years. I continued to hear of more of the old crew who had passed on. I'm extremely glad that I extricated myself from that matrix when I did but I won't forget or negate the fact that it was the place where I had swallowed my first-ever tab of acid and many glorious times had been had therein.

APOCALYPSE AND THE CONSCIOUS CIRCLE OF HUMANITY

THE APPROACH OF JUNE saw me inevitably turning my mind towards the great solstice pilgrimage. The Stonehenge festival was on. Unsurprisingly I had no desire to attend. I would go to Worthy Farm and I most certainly would not travel with any drugs. My faith in a certain something to deliver what I needed was undiminished by the previous year's underworld nightmare. If anything, it was enhanced. I was the better for it all. My appetite for the Glastonbury mystery continued to increase.

The first day of the Pilton festival was the wettest in Somerset for forty-five years. This was not a positive sign. My travelling companion had bravely smuggled a large lump of dope into the site. We soon bought a little hubbly-bubbly pipe and settled down to business. I was electrified to discover that the movie of Gurdjieff's *Meetings With Remarkable Men* was to be shown in the film tent, late on the Sunday night, the eve of the solstice. I could begin that sacred day in the Gurdjieff zone. It seemed there was a subtle resonance here for me with the events of the previous year that had linked my festival experiences with my connecting to Gurdjieff's book. I resolved that no matter what else happened, I would see the film. Making sure that I did would be my centre of gravity for the whole festival.

Saturday was dry but the rain had already done enough damage to turn a lot of the site into a quagmire. Only by maintaining a suitably Gurdjieffian intensity of self-remembering awareness did I manage to avoid falling over. Sitting on some bin-liners in the main arena field, we brought out the hubbly-bubbly and relentlessly smoked it. The weekend settled into the dreamtime. An interesting assortment of musical entertainment was paraded before us. The Chieftains stood out with a superb performance of their traditional Irish dance music. Van Morrison, Jackson Browne, The Blues Band. One day just blurred into another. It was something played between acts that lingered as my most delicious musical memory: the 12 inch version of *Tainted Love/Where Did Our Love Go?* by Soft Cell.

At one point, Sir George Trevelyan appeared onstage. He has often been referred to as the Grandfather of the New Age movement in Britain. A Cambridge graduate, he went on to teach history at Gordonstoun, later becoming a pioneer in adult education. From the concept of a balanced curriculum for the whole person, arose his brainchild, The Wrekin Trust. Thoroughly permeated with Rudolf Steiner's mystical Christianity, he evolved into a visionary prophet, inspiring many with the ideals of the necessity of world transformation and the infusing of spiritual values into our corrupt culture. He had been present in 1971 and makes some brief appearances in *Glastonbury Fayre*. By June 1982 we had reached the peak of the Thatcher years. Everyone had been stunned by the Falklands War. Regardless of any considerations as to whether or not the task force should have been sent, it seemed clear that the Government exploited the emotions of the situation and the propaganda of patriotism to further an agenda that reached beyond the war situation. It all helped to widen the divisions that were already getting ever larger in Thatcher's Britain. I considered myself to be a patriot. I honoured a spirit and continuity that stretched from the megalithic circles and white horses carved on hillsides, through Boudica to Arthur, the glories of Glastonbury Abbey, Chaucer, Malory, Drake, Shakespeare, Milton, Nelson, William Blake, and on to the finest hour of 1940. I could happily stand in the ruins of Tintern Abbey in early spring, reading Wordsworth's immortal lines. The whole vibe of the Falklands was a long way away from all that. It disgusted me. I'm sure that most of the people sitting listening to Sir George felt likewise. Once again the festival was in aid of the CND cause and in the aftermath of an actual war, the issues seemed all the more vital. Trevelyan was eloquent on the problems we faced. He was a man who resonated to Britain's great poetic heritage and saw the likes of Blake as prophets and shamans of the tribe, inviting us all into the realm of spirit, which is ever present if we but learn to look at things afresh.

The climax of his short discourse came with the suggestion that if everyone got together in a mass meditation, the energy of our collective thought could create an impenetrable dome above us that would be able to withstand a nuclear explosion. This was an idea he had recently dealt with in his 1981 book *Operation Redemption.* In there he stated an extreme New Age form of the case for nuclear disarmament. He speculated as to what might happen if *"the Folk-Soul of Britain were taken over and fully impregnated with the Christ power, so that all its members were also filled with a universal compassion and love. If then, as a nation, this country refused to involve itself with killing and threw itself solely on the Divine protection of the Living Christ, the land would be surrounded and covered by a dome and shield of High Mana. – the Russian rockets fired at our unresisting land, would, when they reached the protective barrier, simply disappear!"* There was only one problem with this beautiful theory. It was complete bollocks. It seemed to me to be a bad case of what's been called 'confusing the planes'. I fully believe that prayer and meditation can cause changes in subtle realms that have a knock-on effect in consensus reality. Mind can influence Matter because they're not really separate. I'm prepared to accept the claims of the Transcendental Meditation movement that the crime rate may drop in a location where a large number of people are regularly meditating. It may well be that the actions of world leaders could be influenced for the better by an upping of the intensity of the inner plane climate. Dissolving a mass strike is something else altogether. If it comes to the crunch and an actual physical nuclear weapon has exploded, no amount of prayer and meditation will prevent everything at its epicentre being annihilated. Period.

I found all of this to be distressingly close to the fundamentalist Christian idea of 'the Rapture'. Supposedly when Armageddon comes, the righteous will be taken bodily into heaven and not suffer a scratch. The rest of the population will be left to endure bigtime smiting and smoting. The modern forms of the theory stated that, in the event of a nuclear war, the true believers would be saved in such a manner. It was profoundly disturbing to note that Ronald Reagan, a man with a potential finger on the button, accepted this idea. Trevelyan's way of thinking affirmed that spiritual practices were a physical safeguard against an Armageddon scenario. Become righteous and be saved. Yes, we *must* become saints to save the world, but if the bomb drops the saints fry with the sinners. Maybe they go and sit with God or attain auspicious rebirth. That's another realm of discourse altogether. As far as I was concerned the meditational nuclear umbrella and the Rapture were both dangerous escapist fantasies.

This all led me into a depressing consideration of the politics and issues of the time. It was an era of appalling polarisation. Everything seemed to be divided into opposite extremes. If someone supported a single Tory idea, a cacophony of voices would be ready to label them as a complete Nazi who was barely concealing genocidal tendencies. Certainly my 'patriotism' would have been thus construed. It didn't necessarily mean that I wanted to repatriate all immigrants and gas homosexuals but there were people around me at university who would have drawn those conclusions. Contrariwise, the braying jackass Young Conservatives I knew were only too happy to denounce anyone who was a tiny bit concerned about a nuclear holocaust as a pinko leftie paid agent of Moscow and subverter of church, state and heterosexuality. It seemed that it was very difficult not to get trapped in an ideological prison.

I hated Thatcher. There I was at a CND festival. Did I even fully endorse the cause? My knowledge of history suggested to me that fear of the Bomb really had kept us from a Third World War. That didn't mean that nuclear power wasn't disastrously abusive of the planet and therefore a supremely bad option as a source of energy for our technological society. It said nothing about the way in which the superpower conflict had been displaced to be played out in innumerable smaller wars that had crippled the Third World. Of course the arms race and the resources squandered on it was insanity. The integrity of many of the prime movers behind CND and the quality of their ideals and thinking was beyond reproach. The example of Bertrand Russell had inspired many. Decades later though, it became clear that the movement really had been infiltrated and exploited for political purposes by Moscow just as the braying jackasses had always said it was. Back then in the eighties, I knew enough about the workings of intelligence agencies to feel that it was more than likely to be the case. I saw Ra-Hoor-Khuit towering over Hiroshima and felt the deadly tension of the Aeon of Horus. It was bad but it could have been a lot worse. Sometimes it was a case of choosing the least deadly option when the cumulative effect of centuries of stupidity kept any good options too far out of reach. There were many ideas I contemplated then that, on their own, could have backed me into either of the extremist positions. I could also have been told that I was 'inconsistent' and had simply not thought things through. If I wasn't so full of spaced-out fantasies, I would have to come down on one side of the fence or the other.

In the midst of the hubby-bubbly smoke I was infinitely grateful to have the Gurdjieff Work to feed on. He had been my main source of nourishment for the whole of that year so far. Connecting to the movie was my festival focal point and as it drew nearer, I pondered on the problems that Trevelyan had raised for me, using the fragments of an unknown teaching that Gurdjieff had transmitted to Ouspensky. I'd read *The Fourth Way* back in January. All of the material in it is also presented in Ouspensky's *In Search of the Miraculous.* This work became my most read book of the eighties. Ouspensky had met Gurdjieff in 1914 in Russia. Colin Wilson suggested that their meeting was as significant as that of Plato and Socrates. I came to endorse that opinion. The historical situation in Russia during the period that the two worked together was a perfect backdrop for the demonstration of the power of Gurdjieff's ideas. It began with the archaic Romanoff dynasty still in place as the First World War broke out. Gradually, insane chaos emerged. Russia's badly led, ill-equipped forces were trashed by the German war-machine. Morale nosedived. The rumblings of the revolution were heard. Before long, a whole dynasty and culture was swept away and Ouspensky faced exile or death. For people with a feeling for history those events in Russia are amongst the most mind-blowing of the 20th century.

Ideas that may have seemed outlandish or pessimistic were revealed by the events of the time to be spine-tinglingly insightful. Gurdjieff had said that we are machines, slaves to certain natural laws and processes that are as mechanical as a motor car. If people were remotely awake they would never submit to going off to war and likely death. The leaders of great nations are likewise sleepwalkers through the strange workings of unknown dynamics.

Ouspensky had difficulties with these ideas until an event he witnessed brought them to life. He saw a truck loaded with artificial limbs on its way to the front. They were for legs that had not yet been blown off but it could be calculated that they would be. There was something so mechanical about this process, something so lacking in conscious awareness, that the insanity of the situation was revealed in all its ludicrous horror. If those legs hadn't been blown off yet then why on earth did they have to be? The process was surely stoppable. On one occasion, when Gurdjieff was discussing the horror of the war and the hollowness of the ideals it was being fought for, someone asked him what he thought of the pacifists? *"They're even worse,"* was his classic reply.

There was a particular function of the mass sleepwalking mind that helped perpetuate the trance that enabled the world-historical madness to continue. Gurdjieff called it 'Formatory Thinking'. It is basically that process whereby people are compelled to think and feel in terms of opposites such as black and white, wrong or right, left and right, and so on. This manifests in rigidity in one's personal life and in the greater horrors of religious conflicts and wars between rival political systems. I could see it being played out all around me. It had turned British political life into a vulgar cartoon. On the larger stage Ronnie 'Rapture' Reagan stood against the evil empire of the Godless Commies and megadeath was a possible outcome.

Gurdjieff held out the hope that there are some who stand outside the common influences, who have freed themselves from that which psychically enslaves the rest of humanity. He appeared to be a representative of esoteric schools who sent him to examine the capacity of westerners to understand their work. I'd read enough of the teachings to be entirely convinced that they really did embody something truly extraordinary.

Thus was I primed as I dropped some acid on the Sunday afternoon. I had no more interest in the musical entertainment and went off on my own for a marathon walkabout. Finally, after hours of wandering around, I honoured my prime intention and found my way to the film tent. I was not in a hallucinatory space by then. My perceptions were simply enhanced and along with that, my emotional consciousness. I felt things deeply. I'd imbibed the vibe of the festival. Now it was time for some real food. Peter Brook's film of Gurdjieff's book was never going to outgross *Star Wars*. I don't really know what anyone would make of it who wasn't already familiar with the book. Filmed in Afghanistan before the Russian invasion, the photography helps set the lyrical, timeless feel of the narrative. I'd read a lot about the Gurdjieff dances but never actually seen any. The climax of the film, set in the monastery of the Sarmoun Brotherhood, featured a performance of some of them. In my heightened state the sacred dances moved me to my deepest core. It seemed perfectly obvious that they represented proof of the reality of higher states of consciousness and of groups of people who understand and permanently function from them. This was what Gurdjieff had called "the conscious circle of humanity". What I'd seen demonstrated in the movie simply doesn't originate from the normal realm of life. I got the feeling that most of the audience hadn't exactly come there deliberately to watch that specific film. It was raining and the tent offered a haven for assorted casualties. Memories of Salisbury and the path to that tent seemed to suggest to me that the whole thing was somehow primarily for my benefit. I'd made my strongest connection yet to the most potent influence on my year so far, at the very beginning of the solstice itself, and at Glastonbury. The symmetry between June '81 and '82 was enough to give me cold shivers. After a few hours'rest, with perhaps no sleep at all, it would then be time to return to university. I would be a zombie by the end but it was worth it. I had fed on some powerful impressions.

In the last few days of the summer term, I discovered I had failed an exam and would need to resit. There was actually a possibility I would not be able to return for my third year. I also entered into a romantic involvement with a beautiful young woman named Rosanne. In my darkened room, lit only by the glowstars on the ceiling and filled with the perfume of strawberry joss-sticks, we dissolved into the dreamtime, to the constant soundtrack of Steve Hillage's pioneering ambient classic instrumental album, *Rainbow Dome Musick.*

To be suddenly removed from such bliss and placed back at my parent's home, with little money and my university life in peril of termination, was a severe shock. It may not have been as heavy-duty as the previous summer's potential jail sentence but I was weary and all such hassle was not welcome. I overcame the obstacle of the failed exams and started my final year at university. As I returned to my old room (which still smelt of strawberry joss-sticks three months later), I couldn't believe my luck. I was being given another trip on the merry-go-round. I reconnected with Rosanne in the rainbow pleasure dome. Things were moving fast though. It was not intended to last.

THATCHER, KALI AND NAKED ATHLETICS

1983 STARTED WITH ME FEELING very conscious that I was entering into my final six months at university and a bit of hard work should be on the menu. I stayed off the drugs and booze for the first few months but was more interested in reading large numbers of Colin Wilson books than attending to my set work. Eventually common sense prevailed and I focused on the dissertation I had to submit towards the final marks in my study of religion course. I chose for my subject matter the lightweight topic of Nazi occultism. The big question was what I would do on completing my degree. I had no idea at all. No sense of any potential career. I had recently entered into a new relationship with a first year student named Jane, and the whole thing was developing in a serious manner previously unknown in my life. I was happy enough to see where that led me. A lot of people still hung around the university environment after finishing their studies to take stock and continue to enjoy the fun, good company and social culture. Jane still had two years left so I opted to stay put. A group of her female friends were intending to get a shared house in the summer for the year ahead. They were amenable to us joining them. This helped take any stress out of the final terms and allowed me to enjoy them for the golden times they were.

For me, that year, Pilton was charged with emotional energy. I had just completed my final exams. A huge epoch of my life was about to end. In a few weeks time I would be officially leaving university. The vast, unknown future beckoned, full of mystery. The June weather had already been remarkable. Solar energy was switched full on. It was one of those rare times when the fantasy of what the festival should ideally be like was almost matched by the reality. It was also the first time that I'd been to Glastonbury with a girlfriend and that felt very auspicious. The combination of dope and heatwave exerted a horizontal pull. I did manage, with the help of some acid, to be up and ready for Saturday night's headlining UB40. Standing at the top of the main hill, looking down across the natural amphitheatre arena to the pyramid stage, the view presented a magical otherwordly spectacle. Innumerable sparkling faery lights, hallucinatorily spectrum haloed, flickered and danced as the music sent its waves rippling through the audience. In combination with the laser show the total effect was an unforgettable experience. UB40, with their worldly political concerns, may have seemed a long way from Tim Blake, but in their own way they were up for building a New Jerusalem as well. They sounded magnificent because the immense heart beating through their music was amplified unto infinity by the qualities of the venue they were playing and the state of mind of their audience.

It was not lost on me that Thatcher had just secured another term of office. Earlier in the month I had made the futile gesture of voting for Michael Foot's Labour in the general election. I always knew it would be a purely symbolic act. Compared to Thatcher's dynamism they were a hopeless mess, but I wanted it to be noted in the Cosmic Hall of Records that I did exercise my right to vote and I most definitely did not vote for *her*. A disturbing dope reverie had focused what I had come to feel about that extraordinary creature. It was a vision that lingered and intensified, assuming mythic potency. I could see Thatcher as the cremation-ground aspect of the fearsome Hindu goddess Kali. She stood with her foot upon the prostrate form of William Blake's Albion figure, the naked personification of our island realm. Her tongue was extended, lolling obscenely, unnaturally long. A necklace of severed shrunken heads, once belonging to trashed cabinet ministers, adorned her. Multiple arms brandished weapons of destruction. In the background were scenes of the exploding *Belgrano* and inner cities in flame. There was a feeling that the Falklands might only be the preamble to ever-greater horrors.

The come-down from the very wholesome Saturday night trip was a shade intense. Camped immediately behind us was a group of London geezers who had obviously never been in the midst of anything like Pilton before and were experiencing culture shock. When we left the tent to go and see UB40 I heard them talking about dropping some acid en-masse, and all for the first time. I made a point of noting this and intended to keep my intuitive vibe radar attuned to their potential presence and condition later on. In the early hours we had retired to the tent. My acid ingestion meant that I was unlikely to nod out for a while. I became acutely conscious of all sound outside, which the drug mutated and amplified. I heard the now delirious cockney characters return to their camping area. Listening to the complete dissolution of their normal mode of being was quite amusing at first. Then one of them began to express the desire to "get those tents in front of us and the people in them and throw them on the fire". Oh dear. Charlie Manson and Altamont vibes here in England's green and pleasant land. I did not feel that to be murdered at Glastonbury festival, with my girlfriend, whilst under the influence of acid, was the ideal conclusion to my university days. The group dynamic and energy processes that were played out in that potent matrix amongst the London nutters defy description. I was convinced, as only a person on acid can be, that my own consciousness, from within the tent, somehow involved itself in the complex negotiations whereby the fledgling murderer was dissuaded of his intentions. I don't know how long the whole thing lasted but eventually I felt that the vibe had shifted and I could finally relax into sleep.

The next morning, on emerging from the tent, I cast half a glance in the direction of the cockney crew. They had been totally Glastonburyed. I was greatly heartened when a group of chanting Hare Krishnas merrily wandered by and the previous night's potential Manson said he fancied tagging on the end and joining them. The London boys had come to the festival full of urban paranoia and streetwise geezer-type front. A night on acid and you could chuck them in a pool full of dolphins and leave them to invent a new religion. "Set and setting", as Tim Leary used to say. The possibility of re-infection with the urban disease would be a major challenge for them to face on their return. I live in hope that at least some of these cases succeed in permanent transformation.

The day that we left the festival and returned to the university hall of residence was actually the summer solstice. That evening, I began to feel a little agitated and despondent. Yes, we had been to Glastonbury and the festival had been brilliant, but I hadn't done anything specific to honour the solstice. As the long June evening reached the mellow sunset afterglow stage, Jane and I went for a wander up to the nearby running track, which was pleasantly situated near a grove of trees and a sheltered lane, where lived the piggy who two years previously I'd been invited to bludgeon with a sledgehammer. It was one of those scenarios where nostalgia is already present whilst the events are occurring. A definitive June evening. A landscape of eternal memory. The final few days of my time at university. All senses converging in the knowledge that I would remember this for the rest of my life. Nobody else was around to intrude on the dream. A sudden inspiration struck me. I would do something to celebrate the solstice after all. I removed all of my clothes and ran 400 metres around the track. This satisfied my sense of need for some kind of solar ritual and sealed the occasion securely in my memory banks forever.

NEW HORIZONS

HAVING MOVED INTO A SHARED STUDENT HOUSE with Jane and the group of ladies I shall refer to as the 'Love Cats', the next phase of my life began at the end of the year. Just before Christmas a small newspaper advert looking for 'Trainee Hypnotherapists' caught my eye. I went for an interview and was accepted, thus entering into the holiday period charged up with the sense that my life was going somewhere interesting and that after my amazing times at university I wasn't going to end up in some boring normal job. Unfortunately the organisation that trained me allocated their practitioners locations on the basis of set distances away from other members. My home city was fully subscribed. I would have to try and establish myself in a small town, a train journey away.

During the spring, I was full of the material preparations for my great hypnotherapy adventure. I didn't need to do any more studying so I could also look toward Glastonbury and the solstice. To that end, I started to read up on Arthurian and Earth Mysteries material. The way the timing worked out, it seemed that the festival would mark yet another transitional period of my life. The year before had seen the end of my time at university. Now I was about to start a new and unusual career. This was sufficient to make everything very vivid and charged with significance.

That year I travelled down on the actual solstice. I was happy enough to be making such a pilgrimage on a special day. Memories of '79 and '81 made for interesting comparisons with my new life. Jane was driving. Joining us was her sister, Rachel. At the festival site a large group of people from university had gathered. I had decided that once I actually began my hypnotherapy practice I would stop smoking. I was intending to make a living helping people to quit so it seemed a matter of integrity. It was possible that the coming spliffs would be my last ever. That was indeed a strange thought.

The weather remained good. I prepared to engage in the now traditional Saturday night acid experience. Elvis Costello was scheduled to headline. He didn't really strike me as a pyramid stage, laser light-show type of act. I would have much preferred Tim Blake. It started to rain. A dismal light drizzle. The combination of that and Costello did not induce a transcendental state. Fortunately I had brought with me a powerful tape machine that I was going to use in my new career. Tim Blake was switched on with me standing far enough from the stage for the tape to drown out miserable Elvis. I could now listen to *New Jerusalem* with an accompanying laser show. A crowd of people gathered round me, many expressing the opinion that my sounds were more appropriate for Saturday night at Pilton than what was actually on stage.

On the way home we ventured into the town of Glastonbury itself. For the first time in my life I visited the Tor, Chalice Well, and the abbey. We began by climbing the holy hill. It was a superbly sunny day that helped heighten my receptivity to its atmosphere. The extensive view from the top seemed to expand my mental horizons simultaneous to the drawing of my vision out across the landscape. It was strange to look back on how the place had pulled me in over the years. It seemed as if the festival had been the lure to draw me to it.

From the summit of the Tor can be seen a smaller dome-shaped hill that lies nearby. This is now known as Chalice Hill. The famous well and its gardens lie at the base. Chalice Well is a great example of how much mythology has become connected to Glastonbury. Supposedly Joseph of Arimathea had brought the Holy Grail there. In one version of the tales the Grail was a chalice. In another it was represented by two vials containing blood and sweat from Jesus. These had either been left in the well itself or buried in Chalice Hill. There was a link between the sacred artefacts and the red colouration of the well water. There was a chamber beneath the well that had been the place of Druid sacrificial rites. Arthur's half-sister Morgan le Fay was also somehow involved due to her association with the Isle of Avalon. Unfortunately few of these tales can be traced back very far, even to the time of the abbey. As for the underground well head, it was only underground because of a significant silting of the valley that had occurred after the Tor and Chalice Hill had been deforested in the early Middle Ages. It had originally stood above ground. It seems unlikely to date from Druid times although exactly when it was built is not entirely clear. Archaeology had unearthed a stump of yew dating from the Roman period. There are yew trees in the gardens to this day. These famously sacred trees have an established connection to places of the dead. To find them near a 'blood spring' and in the vicinity of a hill considered to be a possible entrance to the underworld seems significant. There's no way the ancients wouldn't have felt the place to be important.

Rather than rubbishing its modern mythology it might be better to try and be open to the qualities of a location that could attract such beliefs. Powys had placed the only truly miraculous elements of his novel at the well, stating that, *"No sacred pool, in Rome, or Jerusalem, or Mecca, or Thibet, has gathered such an historic continuum of psycho-chemical force about it."* *"This chalybeate fountain on this particular hillside had been the scene of such a continuous series of mystic rites, going back to the neolithic men of the Lake Village, if not to the still more mysterious race that preceded them, that there had come to hang about it a thick aura of magical vibrations."* The charismatic Merlin-like preacher John Geard cures a terminally ill cancer patient after standing naked in the well and invoking its healing energies. He later appears to resurrect a dead child at the opening ceremony of his strange Blood of Christ Grail cult centre there.

It was an ideal time of year to make a first visit and connect to the potent enchantment. The gardens were in full bloom. This truly was a healing place, removed from the profane concerns of the world, a place where one could be nourished and revitalised. It was easy for me to feel that those seemingly tired old legends were somehow alive in that clearly vibrant space.

In 1981 I'd been introduced to the history of Glastonbury Abbey in memorable circumstances. On entering its grounds for the first time I felt both melancholy and inspired. Seeing a mere fragment of the once noble edifice brought me to ponder on the events of 1539. Despite that, the atmosphere of the place was such that I had no difficulties in believing that the ghostly monks remained as witnesses to the eternal form of its true glory. This was, at the very least, supreme romance. Having visited the real Glastonbury sites for the first time it was that which lingered in the eternal June memory matrix. The festival was definitely becoming secondary to me. As my life obviously expanded with the start of my new career, so likewise the Glastonbury connection seemed to deepen.

Within a month I was ready to begin the next phase of my life. I had found an office to rent. A phone was connected. Adverts were placed in the local papers and shop windows. I was fortunate to get on a government Enterprise Allowance Scheme whereby I was paid a fortnightly sum of money during the first year of my business in order to help me make a go of it. In this at least, I had something to thank Maggie for. I settled down to await the first call. True to my ideals, I stopped smoking. I perhaps bent the rules a little by deciding to allow myself to ingest cannabis orally. Five months went by before I actually did.

Over the Christmas period, I realised that the memory of my first ascent of the Tor had somehow seemed to gather to itself the emotional charge of satisfaction that I felt from the whole year. With the rebirth of the sun at the winter solstice, the feeling expanded into an increasing appetite for all things Avalonian and even more anticipation than usual about the inevitable June return to Worthy Farm. As 1985 began though, my immediate main concern was to ensure the success of my hypnotherapy practice.

In March it seemed as if I was being given a good opportunity to get results in my attempted career. In those days there were various promotional options available for people on the Enterprise Allowance Scheme. I was entitled to a free mail-shot going out to a few hundred addresses. What I had to do was provide the promo material and the envelopes and find the ideal addresses. This was quite a task. It didn't take long to exhaust all of the potentially pertinent local clubs, societies and associations. This left me randomly working through the local phone directory for the rest. It was mind-numbing work. A seemingly hopeful sign appeared though. I was contacted by a local free newspaper wanting to do a feature on my hypnotherapy practice. It felt like a great opportunity. I was interviewed in my office and was entirely happy with the way that I'd communicated. The piece was expected to appear on a particular date so I decided to time the posting of my mail-shot to coincide with it. I was sure I'd get a result.

I posted my material off at the end of March and a long wait began. In retrospect perhaps the fact that I read *The Book of Heroic Failures* a few days later was an indication of my higher self trying to communicate to me with its usual sense of humour. The newspaper article never appeared. In fact, from the day of my interview, the newspaper itself never appeared again. Some sort of industrial action repeatedly delayed its publication until, eventually, it closed down altogether. I received two replies to my mail-shot. One consisted of a returned envelope with the legend 'Deceased!' by the side of the addressee's name. The other was a phone call from a gentleman who thought the whole thing was some kind of prank set up by his mates. At this point it became obvious that I was entering into a realm of serious difficulties. Once the government scheme payments stopped I was scuppered. I simply didn't have the resources to keep afloat whilst waiting for a change of luck. The way things had worked out I had to ask myself if I was really supposed to be doing this. The obviously available alternatives all seemed nightmarish so I simply tried to carry on.

Putting such concerns to one side, I allowed myself to give over to the vibe of the spring season with its inevitable Glastonbury focus. I resolved to dive into the whole enormous field of the Earth Mysteries and Arthurian studies as never before and keep going relentlessly until the summer solstice. I'd done something similar the previous year but this felt different. As my career seemed to collapse, all of my emotional energies went into my Glastonbury mythos. It would be easy to see it as some kind of compensatory process. The compulsion was so overwhelming and felt so right that I did not seek to question it.

THE GREEN STONE

IN 1981 MY PASSIONATE RELATIONSHIP with books had entered a new level of intensity as their contents increasingly affected my life in strikingly strange ways suggestive of a guiding intelligence. These were not dead words. This stuff was *alive* and interactive on a profoundly deep destiny level. *Glastonbury Romance* had permanently mutated my sensibilities. Its power had announced itself with the timing of its appearance in my life so that the fateful narrative of an arduous journey between Stonehenge and Glastonbury essentially synchronised with my own. The subsequent events led to my Salisbury Cathedral priming for *King Arthur's Avalon* and also *Meetings with Remarkable Men*, a book that returned on a higher level of manifestation at the next Glastonbury festival. *Europe's Inner Demons* had appeared with notable timing as well. The realisation of such a process at work was exciting and inspirational. It power-charged my quest for suitable impressions to feed Magnetic Centre. The next instalment could come at any time. Maybe it already had but a slight time delay meant some sort of stunning pay-off lay just ahead.

On April 30th, the pagan feast of Beltane, I wandered into a bookshop to browse. In the section on the paranormal and general weirdness, one book caught my eye: *The Green Stone* by Graham Phillips and Martin Keatman. The cover picture showed a ruined castle on a hill with a large green sparkling jewel in the foreground beneath it. Intrigued, I then scanned the back. *"It began with a series of bizarre psychic messages - unbelievably specific, incredibly accurate - and utterly terrifying. They suggested the existence of mystic occult powers which transcended comprehension. Soon the quest for the Green Stone led the researchers into an awesome confrontation with the powers of evil. For the Green Stone was the Meonia Stone of the ancients, mysteriously linked to the Knights Templars and the Rosicrucians- and the key which could unlock the terrible force of the place of darkness."* That was enough for me! The coming night's entertainment had been decided. I had not the faintest conscious awareness that I was encountering a portal of destiny and that one day I would step into the story I was about to hear for the first time.

I started reading after my evening meal. The amazing tale began in the realms of UFOlogical studies with an abduction case that had occurred in Essex in 1974. The pseudonymous Avis family, John, Sue, and their three children, were travelling by car, along a country road at night, when they saw a strange blue light in the sky. It dropped out of sight as they rounded a corner, suddenly driving into a bank of green mist. On returning home they realised that they had somehow lost three hours. During the next few years, inspired to radically change their lifestyles through such means as giving up smoking and drinking and becoming vegetarian, they also became increasingly plagued by disturbing dreams and assorted poltergeist phenomenon. Weirder still, they seemed to develop ESP abilities and an affinity for the ancient mysteries of the British landscape. Eventually, in 1977, they contacted a young UFO researcher named Andrew Collins. He introduced them to a hypnotist. The father of the family recalled being taken into some kind of alien craft and medically examined. It's worth remembering, in these days when alien abduction stories have become part of popular culture, that this was the first recorded British case and knowledge of the few American ones was not widespread at that time. It seemed as if the 'alien' experience had been a trigger for the family's general expansion of consciousness. They believed that they remained in some sort of communication with the alien intelligence. From this came prophecies that a group of people would soon be brought together for some important tasks, including a psychic conflict of some kind. Andy Collins made a record of the details for future reference.

What was intriguing about the case was the link between a 'contact' and the wider spectrum of the paranormal. Andy met up with Graham Phillips, who was researching similar topics. He too had encountered people who had psychically intuited a coming-together of a group in the centre of England for a quest into realms beyond their understanding. The two men founded an organisation called *Parasearch*. They were soon to be joined by UFO and paranormal investigator, Martin Keatman. He introduced them to Marion Sunderland. In the scorching summer of 1976 her daughter Gaynor, who was nine at the time, was walking in a lane near their Welsh home when her attention was drawn to something glinting in a field. She saw a silver oval-shaped object, about thirty feet across, sitting there motionless. Two humanoid entities, seemingly male and female, were nearby. Gaynor proved to be a very interesting case study for Martin. She seemed to be psychic and believed that the entities were still in contact with her. In the following years the family had experienced a wide spectrum of unusual paranormal episodes. It seemed that something wanted to clearly demonstrate that the UFO phenomenon does not exist in a vacuum but connects to bigger issues. The Aveley and Sunderland cases were extraordinary. They helped to provide a unique range of investigative experience for the young *Parasearch* team that helped to prepare them for a quantum leap. The UFOlogical side of the Sunderland family experiences was covered in *Alien Contact* by Jenny Randles and Paul Whetnall. This was only the beginning.

The meeting of the team with the Sunderlands seemed to create an atmosphere of charged intensity, a feeling of imminence. One evening in October 1979 Graham Phillips went into a strange altered state of consciousness. A voice that was seemingly not his own began to speak through him. This was not something that Graham was used to. The message claimed that all of the events that had drawn them together were part of a huge process relating to unfinished business dating from the time of the Pharaoh Akhenaten. Andy Collins, in true researcher mode, tape-recorded the whole session. Or at least he thought he did. When they tried to replay it moments later, what came out was Graham's voice, as if echoing in a large hall, repeating the name of Akhenaten over and over again.

Akhenaten is one of the most famous and compelling figures in Egyptian history. Andy and Graham knew nothing of the man when his name was first mentioned. He had reformed Egyptian religion by abolishing worship of multiple deities. In their place he set up a monotheism devoted to the Aten, represented by the sun and its rays. He had built a new capital city in its honour. The generally received interpretation of his reign suggests that he was an unworldly space-case and general weirdo, although many have sung his praises as mystic and precursor of the later monotheisms. Foreign policy was neglected. The priests of the banned cults were less than happy. Akhenaten's end remains unknown. Perhaps he was murdered. What is certain is that before long his gleaming new city had been trashed and all references to him and his religion throughout Egypt erased. Tutankhamen was born into this situation and was a victim of the fall-out. His original name had been Tutankh-aten. The Aten had to be amended to Amen to affirm the re-ascendancy of the powerful Pharaoh-making priesthood of the god of that name.

Graham decided to see if he could get back into the same state on the following evening. What came out was a sort of history lesson on Akhenaten's life and times. The real points of interest were things that could not be found in any history books. It was stated that certain initiates of the megalithic peoples of Britain were in contact with the Pharaoh's inner circle. They were the guardians of the secret knowledge behind the stone circles and landscape alignments. This knowledge had been abused and they sought to entrust its pure form to the mysterious Pharaoh.

A group of inhabitants of Akhenaten's city had left Egypt when things got dangerous and went on a major walkabout. Some of them got as far as Britain. They founded a colony in the Midlands. Later Celtic settlers became connected with it. They were the bearers of a powerful secret magical lore. In subsequent centuries it was passed down by small enclaves within a lineage of occult societies such as the Knights Templar. The task that they had been involved in was now being passed on to *Parasearch*. The Templars had been famously suppressed. The anniversary of their demise happened to be the next day, October 13th. The site of the Egyptian colony still existed. It was at a place called Berry Ring. The group must be there that very night, at midnight, as the 13th began. Two tape recorders had recorded perfectly this time. Maps were consulted. Berry Ring was located. Andy, Graham, and Martin managed to be there at midnight. No ghostly Egyptians appeared but they all felt a distinct unmistakeable *something*. They knew that an 'on' button had been pressed and that nothing was ever going to be the same again. Later checking revealed that the October 13th Templar date was completely correct, as were large amounts of the Akhenaten material. None of this knowledge was consciously in Graham's mind. The group were prepared to believe that something paranormal was truly in motion, something immense and important.

So was established a modus operandi for what came to be known as psychic questing. It involved a willingness to be open to spontaneity, whereby you could suddenly find yourself at midnight, at some ancient site, that you may have scarcely heard of when you got up that morning. There was a conscious suspension of disbelief in order to work with information from trance states, dreams, omens, synchronicities and so on. If historical research could show that some of the messages were accurate, and none of the details necessarily inaccurate, then it was considered acceptable to take a gamble with the material and work with it.

The unfolding events began to pull in a larger cast of characters who were able to contribute their own strange experiences to what rapidly expanded into a truly epic scenario. Graham's trance messages went on to talk about how the megalithic initiates had used their occult knowledge to create a talismanic jewel, a green stone. It was imbued with an energy that was capable of counter-acting some malevolent force that had somehow messed with the integrity of the British ley system and also caused a lot of grief to many others at that time. The green stone was given over to Akhenaten's associates. They had returned it to Britain. It was the major part of the secrets handed down across the ages. Some Templars had worked with it and this had brought against them the same evil forces that had worked against the Megalithic culture. It was in the possession of Mary Queen of Scots and people associated with the later Gunpowder Plot. By this time it was known as the *Meonia* stone. After the Guy Fawkes debacle it had been hidden and disappeared from view. A Victorian occult group had become involved in a quest to retrieve it. This had also activated opposition that resulted in their destruction. Destruction did actually mean, in many cases, death. *Parasearch* had to find the real physical green stone by October 31st. It was actually out there. An object of incalculable arcane power, once in possession of an Egyptian Pharaoh and Mary Queen of Scots. And the energy unleashed by this quest would inevitably attract the bad guys. Outlandish though the story was, the messages were significantly validated by the accuracy of all manner of trivial historical details. Nothing contradicted the basic narrative.

The Gunpowder Plot details were crucial as this was the time when the stone was hidden and it had not surfaced since. They were led by the messages to a place called Harvington Hall, onetime residence of Humphrey Pakington, who had been keeper of the green stone. In his home were paintings called *The Nine Worthies* that held clues to the stone's whereabouts through some kind of code. The place existed, as did the man and the paintings, although connections to the 1605 plot could not be established. A visit was inevitable. *The Nine Worthies* were a well-known artistic topic of the period. They represented famous heroes such as Arthur, David, Samson, Alexander etc. The grouping was not always the same. Six remained on show at Harvington Hall. Graham noted that the figures holding swords were all depicted with their arms held over their heads in the same stylised gesture. It was known as the St. George Parry.

The pace further accelerated when Marion Sunderland had a psychic impression of a sword lying on a stone slab at the bottom of some water. A strong unpleasant smell of rotting vegetation was present. Arthur. A hand holding a sword aloft. A sword under water. Images and themes seemed to be coalescing. Maps were studied of the Worcestershire area where the 1605 trail had gone cold. A Knight's Hill was located. A nearby lake was known locally as 'Knight Pool'. On October 22nd a psychic message was received by Alan Beard, who was part of the larger group brought together by the quest. He contacted *Parasearch.* As he knew nothing of the sword developments, his communication was very suggestive. He said that they needed to find something else first before they could find the stone. It would then lead them to it. He specifically stated that it was a sword and that it could be found near an old mill. A check of the maps showed a mill in the immediate proximity of the Knight's Pool. He also said that they had to go there as soon as possible as the opposition was already activated.

Later the same night Andy and Graham set off from their Wolverhampton home on a journey to destiny. Paranoia was in the air. The upcoming escapade would be a significant gauge of the reality behind the whole weird business. What if they actually found a real sword? That would of course be magnificent but it would mean that the rest of all the messages would probably be true as well. It was a ripping yarn and had been a great game but this sword could lead to the Meonia stone of the ancients and possible confrontations with malevolent forces. They arrived at the isolated location and began to circumnavigate the lake. The ruins of a mill were located there, but the building was too recent to connect to 1605. Hours elapsed as the two men strained their brains to look for clues and inspiration. The only other structure in sight was a bridge. First inspection also indicated its date was too late. The foundation stones looked a lot older though. The arch was newer but the rest seemed promising. Examining the foundations more thoroughly, they reasoned that if something was concealed amongst them it would be on the side that overlooked the lake and which was not as eroded by the water current. Perhaps it might be concealed behind a stone. Harvington Hall had been full of secret hiding places for priests. Andy suggested that nine stones down and across would fit the coded clues. They took a guess as to where to take the count from and then clambered down into the vegetation and water to clear a way to it. Marion Sunderland's vision had shown rank rotting vegetation and they were now very much amongst it. It took a long time but they finally gained access to the place that seemed the best bet. A further half-hour with a penknife and trowel removed the target brick. A torch was shone into the resulting hole. In the recess a shape was clearly visible. A long dagger or short sword! This was a reality-smashing event. After the initial major emotional shock, which had included Andy bursting into tears, they grabbed the thing and got the hell out of there. Back in Wolverhampton the cleaned short sword revealed an inscription, *'Meonia Fore Marye'*. It was going to be a late night for me. There was no way I was going to put this book down until I'd finished it.

The sword was supposed to lead to the stone. What now? As Andy and Graham secured their remarkable find, Gaynor Sunderland was dreaming of connected events. She saw what could well be the moment when the sword was hidden in the bridge. She had been unaware of their activities that night. Marion had a brief vision of an avenue of trees near water and was sure the stone lay nearby. They had less than a fortnight to find it. There followed a vertiginous sequence of psychic attacks and general sinister weird episodes, amidst visions and dreams of nasty magical ceremonies, as it appeared that the dark forces in opposition were out to thwart them.

On October 29th Gaynor and Marion were taken to Knight's Pool. Gaynor asked for the sword and stood with it atop the bridge. She then took the hilt in both hands and stretched out her arms, turning slowly around, using it as a kind of psychic direction finder. Pointing in a particular direction, she announced that there was an old ruin about a mile away and they should go there immediately. They were led to a tower that was all that remained of a mock 18th century castle. The stone itself would not be there but a further vital clue would be revealed. Gaynor wanted to go inside the building but it looked unsafe. Once inside they soon heard sounds from above them. There was a thudding and crashing, a moving about suggestive of some large animal. Amidst falling masonry they hastily exited. Once outside they lingered awhile to see if the creature in the tower revealed itself. More than likely it was a big bird. Nothing was forthcoming so they returned home.

Maps were scanned again in the hope of further clues of the kind that had led them to the Knight's Pool. There was a bend on the

River Avon called the Swan's Neck. Marion had read that Mary Queen of Scots was known to some by the code name of Swan. The group's research into the Rosicrucian backdrop of the 1605 events had already shown that the symbol of the swan had had widespread significance for many European groups involved in mystical political intrigues at that time. Gaynor was not present during the swan deliberations. That night though, she dreamt that she returned to the tower by moonlight. A great white swan launched itself from the top. Around its neck was a leather pouch, tied by a cord. She knew that the green stone was within it. She awoke at dawn with the certainty that a swan's neck was the resting place of the Meonia stone. In Wolverhampton Graham also stirred at dawn, filled with a sense of urgency. Something told him he could not afford to wait. He had to get up and go to the Swan's Neck straight away. The opposition was very near. He acted on the impulse. The avenue of trees that Marion had seen was soon located. In the grip of a growing panic Graham's intuition focused on a slight rise on the ground. After digging two holes with a trowel, he was excavating a third when he hit something hard. It was a metal rectangular box, covered in some sort of resin. He used a penknife to open it. Inside was a small silver box. Within that was a green stone. The incredible artefact had been retrieved just in time to meet the Halloween deadline.

What about the actual artefacts? Could conventional means of research shed any further light on them? Marion became convinced that the sword did not date back to the days of the Gunpowder Plot. She took it and the casket to a museum in Chester to see what the experts made of them. The sword was indeed likely to date from the 19th century, whilst the casket could be up to five hundred years old. This began an extensive consideration on the Victorian side of the story, an epic in its own right. It centred on a place named Biddulph Grange, near Stoke. This was an impressive, almost stately home with themed gardens containing buildings and statues modelled on different countries and historical periods. There was a kind of mock Egyptian temple there. A woman named Mary Heath had been active within it. She was the main psychic in the Victorian group and it was increasingly felt that her spirit presence was guiding them all in the present day. It was never possible to confirm her existence but the mind blowing denouement came when it was discovered that the very house in Wolverhampton where Graham and Andy lived had been the scene of a climactic occult ceremony, featuring the Victorian group, which had gone disastrously wrong and led to their dispersal. The opposition had temporarily triumphed. Obscure names and details picked up psychically had been verified through local records. It had supposedly happened in the cellar. No wonder so many strange phenomenon occurred there. Once again the group had to deal with the residue of past unpleasantness.

The Meonia stone was not just a talisman against evil. It had other purposes. On the night of Boxing Day 1980 a remarkable dream of Graham Phillips opened up a further portal into the past. He saw Akhenaten lying dead on a stone slab in a chamber covered in hieroglyphics. In his headband was the green stone. Around the slab stood nine small white pyramids. A group of people entered and each took one of the pyramids before leaving along a corridor. These people were going to take the stone and the mysterious pyramids to Britain. Graham awoke with the phrase *"the nine lights"* in his head. Further dreams, visions, and automatic writing from the Meonia group, told the story of how this small band of Egyptians had visited nine sacred sites in the south of England and somehow left aspects of the total energy of the green stone at them by some mysterious use of the little pyramids. That energy was still present and the locations needed to be found so that the stone could reconnect to its complete power and functions. None of the holders of the stone since those days had done this.

The mini-quest was to begin on New Year's Day. Each site would have a spirit guide, a physical guardian and a spirit guardian. The guide would lead them to a particular place. They would then find a person who could tell them some piece of history or folklore about it that would lead them to the spirit guardian. Summoning it with the stone would release the light. Each light had to be retrieved in sequence. Only then would the clues to the next be revealed.

I paid particular attention to the fact that, after successfully completing the process at places such as Avebury and Wayland's Smithy, the fourth light was at Glastonbury. The Zodiac theorists had talked of Sumero-Babylonians in Somerset. Now I contemplated the idea of a small group of Egyptian initiates coming there with a specific task three thousand years ago. It was implied that these people already knew something of the places they were visiting in a seemingly deliberate sequence. There was contact between the two cultures. The incredible green stone appeared to be potent proof of that. Now, in 1981, something of the Glastonbury-Egypt connection was being reawakened. Andy and Graham were led to a house near the Tor in search of clues to the spirit guardian. This led to the discovery that a phoenix was associated with the Tor. Satisfied that this was what they were looking for, the group now climbed to the summit. There they summoned the phoenix. As with the previous sites, this was done in the spirit of a deliberate suspension of disbelief. For example, at Wayland's Smithy, after learning of some local folklore, Graham had ended up kneeling on its top, bowing three times, and asking for the help of elves. This had been immediately followed by a sudden howling gale and the feeling of a huge surge of energy surrounding the stone, indicative of the return of one of the lights. So it was atop the Tor. Strong winds are not exactly unknown up there, but the one that appeared with the summoning of the phoenix was of sufficient intensity to alarm the tourists around them. Although no clear reference of this distinct detail was made in the book, the Aquarius effigy of the Glastonbury Zodiac is in the form of a phoenix. The Tor was the main part of it. Summoning the phoenix had done the trick. Perhaps the Zodiac and the wandering Egyptians were part of an even bigger picture, an ever-greater mystery.

As the night wore on my brain began to suffer input overload. The lights were retrieved. This set up a climactic confrontation with the forces of evil that was worthy of a Spielberg movie. Yet more psychic attacks. Still more historical information. Finally, a special-effects bonanza at a place called White Ladies Priory in Staffordshire. Graham had had another classic magical dream to set the group up for what they knew would be their toughest test yet. He had seen a strange three-dimensional eight-pointed star of a particular size and colour design. It was necessary to actually construct the thing. All the details were retained on waking. In conjunction with the stone, it could somehow summon a force strong enough to finally defeat the ancient evil that had festered in the landscape for so long. Gathered together in the priory at night, the terrifying screeching of some unearthly thing, moving through the air towards the group, had announced that the game was on. It seemed to circle above them. The noise became a howling. Cue the power of the green stone. A blinding light and an ear shattering crash. A few moments later another huge flare illuminated the landscape for hundreds of yards around. Another crash. Another blinding flash, this time lingering for several seconds. Two spheres of light then joined and exploded together into brightness too powerful to look upon as a final hideous cry echoed through the night.

An outlandish tale. It seemed to me at the time that it was a cross between *The Holy Blood and the Holy Grail* and Colin Wilson's *Poltergeist*. Remarkable historical research and speculation interspersed with outrageous paranormal events, and all involving a group of seemingly normal people. Something felt totally authentic about it all. I believed the events had happened as described. I wondered what it would be like to hang out with these characters. Would the weirdness rub off? Was there still more to come? It had more than justified the late night. I couldn't understand why I hadn't already heard about this incredible saga. It deserved to be famous.

ANCIENT WISDOM

FROM THE START OF THE YEAR I'd been feeling the pull of the Glastonbury festival more strongly than ever before. Reading *The Green Stone* set me up very nicely for the culmination of my great study course in preparation for it. I read thirty-four books in eight weeks. It involved more concentrated effort than I'd put into my university courses. All of the books on Glastonbury that I already knew were consumed again. A particular set of new associations made a very strong impression.

One of the most notable visual aspects of Glastonbury Tor is the terracing on its slopes. On a sunny day it can be distinctly delineated by the play of light and shadow. A generally held theory contends that it derives solely from medieval agricultural practices. In recent times others have come to feel differently. The occultist Dion Fortune, who had a home in Glastonbury between the wars, wondered if the hill might have been deliberately sculpted in remembrance of a prototype holy mountain on some other continent. She had Atlantis in mind but the general idea would prove to be fruitful in later speculations.

In 1944 Geoffrey Russell had a mystical experience in Ceylon. Struggling to understand its meaning he produced a drawing of a pattern featuring various circles. He felt that it was something to do with the human brain. Nearly twenty years later he saw a picture of a sevenfold labyrinthine maze design that had been discovered on a rock face near Tintagel and was considered to be perhaps three thousand years old. He was stunned to recognise essentially the same design that he had drawn. This inspired him to undertake a study of the topic from both a historical and psychological perspective.

Mazes are most famously associated with Crete and the tale of the Minotaur. A particular maze pattern, known as 'Cretan' and septenary in form, of which the Tintagel case is one example, can be found in many places around the world. The most striking result of Geoffrey Russell's journey of discovery was his theory that the Tor terracing is a unique three-dimensional form of the Cretan septenary maze design.

Russell linked his postulated Tor maze to a famous Welsh Dark Age tale, *The Spoils of Annwn.* It's an early story of Arthur in which he and his companions go in search of a wonder-working cauldron that seems to be a precursor of the medieval Grail. One of the featured locations is Caer Sidi. This is taken to mean the turning or spiral castle. Russell believed this motif shows a memory of maze-threading ceremonials. Somewhere in this mystery, the secret of the Grail waits to be revealed. Were Dion Fortune's idea of the Tor as a representation of a sacred mountain or temple prototype and Geoffrey Russell's maze theory mutually exclusive or could they somehow have an underlying connection?

In two inter-related books, *The Ancient Wisdom* and *Avalonian Quest,* Geoffrey Ashe entered into an extensive consideration that helped to put the mystery of the sevenfold Glastonbury maze in a remarkable context of expanded perspective. After my intense introduction to his work with *King Arthur's Avalon* I was well disposed towards sampling some more.

The starting point of *The Ancient Wisdom* journey is an investigation of the mystique of the number seven. Why is it considered so important? At first it seems that the Bible is the obvious reason for this. God made the world in seven days and therefore his chosen people structured their lives and culture around that, hence a seven-day week and so on. The presence of numerous sevens in the Old Testament shows the attempts by the Jews to align themselves with God's pattern of creation. This was picked-up on by the authors of the New Testament, in particular the *Book of Revelation,* where a septenary feast features fifty-four groupings of seven. All of this was then carried forward into the culture of the Middle Ages where it was commonplace to think of seven colours of the rainbow, notes of the musical scale, metals, archangels etc.

Jerusalem was considered by the Jews to be the centre of the world. It was literally the place where the process of creation began. At the centre of the centre was Solomon's temple. Everything about it was designed to embody divine laws. The presence in the temple of the seven-branched candlestick, the Menorah, affirmed the sacredness of seven. Even stranger was the belief that the hill where the temple stood, known as Zion, was the highest point on Earth. This is particularly odd as the nearby, plainly visible, Mount of Olives is obviously taller. The world was considered to be flat and circular with a mountain at its centre. There are perplexing anomalous references to this mount in the Old Testament. Psalm 48, verse 2 refers to *"Mount Zion in the far north"*. Why the north?

Closer investigation reveals that the Babylonians had revered the number seven before the Jews. It seems that some of their ideas were passed on during the formative process of the writing of the Old Testament, in the time of the Babylonian captivity. Some academics argue that the Babylonian numerology stems from their knowledge of the planets, which they counted as seven. This list consisted of the visible planets of pre-telescope days, Mercury, Venus, Mars, Jupiter and Saturn with the addition of the Sun and the Moon. It seems however that the list was manipulated to align with an already established sacrality of seven. The Sun and Moon were not always included in planetary counts. Other cultures numbered them differently. The Chinese, for example, had five.

In Babylonian sacred culture seven appeared as part of a complex of closely connected concepts, some of which had been introduced to me by Mircea Eliade in *Myth of the Eternal Return.* In the city of Babylon was a circular 250 feet tall, seven-tiered ziggurat, known as the Etemenanki, *"the Temple of the Foundation of Heaven and Earth"* and the *"Mount of the Mountains of all Lands"*. It was considered to be the centre of the world, the point of creation and its cyclic regeneration. On its summit was a temple where the climax of the *Akitu*, was acted out between the king and the priestess who represented the goddess. It was believed that through the ziggurat's centre ran a mystical axis, a 'bond' or binding post, connecting the realms of earth, underworld, and sky. The heavens rotated around its top. Here was one area though where there seemed to be a discrepancy between mythic and physical reality. Anyone standing on the top of the ziggurat and looking up to observe the sky could soon see that the pole star pivotal point was not directly above but off to the north. The world mountain temple seems to have been a model of an original located elsewhere.

Earlier Mesopotamian cities had similar ideas. Ziggurats had seven levels. The Sumerian capital Nippur's temple was known as the *'House of the Mountain'*. The city had a wall with seven gates. There were also significant sevens in the Sumerian Underworld, into which their 'bond' or binding post, of cosmic unity extended. They feature in one of the most famous stories of the ancient world, the descent of the Goddess Innana who became the Babylonian Ishtar. She encountered seven judges at seven gates who demanded that she remove an item of clothing at each until she reached the heart of the underworld naked. The motif of the septenary path that reaches a centre by a difficult route suggests comparisons with mazes. Whilst the Sumerians clearly influenced the Babylonians, the mystery of the displaced centre of the heavens remains. The two cultures occupied essentially the same geographical region. The pivot of the sky would still be somewhere in the north.

Seven appears in the context of the sacred centre, the creation point, the heart of the world, both above and below ground, at Jerusalem, Babylon, Nippur and the Greek Delphi, which Ashe also examined in some detail in *The Ancient Wisdom*. It is not omnipresent throughout the ancient world but further examples of the familiar package of symbols do occur in some far-flung locations.

The idea of the world mountain as centre and starting point of creation is widespread in Asia. It is best known as the Mount Meru of Hinduism that has the familiar celestial pole star axis through its centre around which the heavens revolve. Remember that in Jerusalem and Babylon, the temples were not physically aligned in such a way, hence the need to somehow identify them with a prototype in the north and thereby partake of its archetypal potency. Meru was not believed to be located in India but to the north, where the migrating Indians had originated from. Ashe wondered if the references to *'Zion the far north'* were suggestive of a diffusion of a set of ideas from a point of origin connected to the Meru mythos.

Mount Meru has been portrayed with seven tiers. It is the home of the seven Rishis. They are human but endowed with divine qualities. These Masters of Wisdom are revealers of knowledge at the start of new cycles of history. They keep an eternal watch over the affairs of humanity. Blavatsky's Himalayan sages seem very similar. Gurdjieff's career was surely not unconnected.

In ancient times the polar constellation was Draco, the dragon serpent. The sky revolved around it. Finally, through looking at the heavens, Ashe found his source for the mystique of seven. It is in the seven stars of the constellation of Ursa Major, the Great Bear, considered to be the abode of the seven Rishis. Its stars circled about the centre of the sky and could be used to locate it. It therefore will always be in immediate proximity to the axis of the world mountain. Nations which had early versions of the sacred seven cultural package lived in latitudes where the constellation was always visible. It disappears in the later forms of Hinduism, as the Indians travelled south and it vanished from their sky. Ashe delivered detailed evidence of the significance of Ursa Major in many cultures down through the ages. The Sumerian Nippur was considered to align with it. Babylonians called it the bond of heaven. As far as I was concerned, the source of the sacred seven had been identified.

Having travelled so far, Ashe has to acknowledge that Blavatsky was there before him. In *The Secret Doctrine* she had stated that the first form of the sacred seven is visible in heaven as Ursa Major. She, in turn, derived this from the work of Gerald Massey who had said precisely that in his work, *The Natural Genesis,* published in 1883. The other associations he links to it are a very intriguing mix. He talks of Ursa Major being a visible symbol of a goddess. Artemis was born in the celestial circle that its movements traced around the polar axis. He also links the constellation with the world mountain and even the spiral labyrinth, specifically the so-called 'Cretan' form, which he claims, *"represents... the seven encirclers of the Great Bear"*. Massey's suggestion of the proto-myth behind this material is of a primal mythic mountain, *"the Mount of the Seven Stars... which represented the celestial north as the birthplace of the initial motion and the beginning of time"*. On this seven-tiered Meru, the Great Goddess was enthroned. The world revolved around it and other sacred mountains were copies of it. Ashe marvels over the accuracy of Massey's insights and wonders how he may have come by them. They're all the more remarkable as Massey was a firm believer in the Egyptian origin of culture and primarily investigated its roots in Africa. Ashe is willing to concede that perhaps Massey had come into contact with some genuine occult tradition.

From looking at the associations of Ursa Major with bears, Ashe proceeds to the climax of his journey. He is led into the Siberian realms of the Altai mountain range, with its sacred Mount Belukha, and archaic shamanism. In this region can be glimpsed the oldest currently discoverable forms of the complete seven package. Mammoth ivory carved with seven circles of dots was discovered at an Altaic cave burial. Perhaps this was the first stirring of what evolved into the septenary maze design?

All of this was more than enough to light up my inner Glastonbury landscape but more was to follow. The Altai region has also been the focus of another immense quest, for a fabled realm most famously known as Shambhala. For the Tantric Buddhists of Tibet and Mongolia, who believe it to be the home of a system of secret wisdom, Shambhala represents a living and vital reality. Some of this is embodied in the teachings of the Kalachakra, which means 'Wheel of Time'. Its origins are believed to predate Buddha, who visited Shambhala himself to be initiated in its mysteries. On the one hand it has a tangible physical location but also strange qualities which can hide it from the profane, making it all but invisible to the outside world. Its pilgrims are somehow summoned by subtle inner means.

The Ancient Wisdom and *Avalonian Quest* also introduced me to the remarkable Stephen Jenkins who had worked as a teacher in Mongolia and been initiated into a type of Tantric Buddhism that included Kalachakra Shambhala teachings. High-ranking Lamas had told him that a European had visited Buddha. They believed him to be a Celt. He received Shambhalic initiation. In the midst of this mysterious episode the 'presence' of Shambhala was transplanted to Britain. Apparently the Lamas had been deliberating about the whole business for at least a century. They stated that Shambhala once had a literal physical existence in the Celtic Britain of the last centuries before Christ. I went on to find Jenkins' excellent book *The Undiscovered Country* where he put forward the possibility that it was actually Glastonbury. There's not exactly a lot of archaeology to back this one up but it was a marvellous mystical, poetic idea that set my mind off on strange, suggestive tangents.

Ashe and Jenkins raised the possibility that something of the Central Asian ancient wisdom package made its way to Britain. The Glastonbury landscape seems to speak eloquently of it once the code is broken. The Tor combines many of the familiar motifs. The alleged septenary spiral maze appears to have sculpted it like a ziggurat. It could easily accommodate world mountain concepts. There seems to be an association of both paradise and underworld around it. Ursa Major has been known as 'Arthur's wagon' and his very name is generally taken to mean 'Bear'. The Celts originated in Asia. Was it all in the past tense? Shambhala was generally believed to be still functioning. Could there possibly be any way in which a living connection could be made in the present day through Glastonbury?

One aspect of the maze mystery helped to further expand my sense of Glastonbury's uniqueness. We still have the impressive remains of Stonehenge and Avebury to ponder over. It is possible to speculate on what may have been done at such places, what they were for. Psychics can give evocative suggestions. Neo-pagan orders can perform ceremonies, such as the one I witnessed at Stonehenge in 1979. A mystery always remains. With the Tor maze there is much we don't know but one thing seems certain. People would have walked its path. It seems that, in past times, the Tor may well have been largely covered in trees. The maze perhaps wove its uniquely three-dimensional path of gradual ascent through an enchanted wood. It would take a long time to walk it. The process would surely have induced an altered state of consciousness. This may well have been reinforced by ceremonial procedures presided over by the officiating site guardians. It has been plausibly speculated that there may have been a stone circle of some kind, or perhaps a large single standing stone, at the summit. The actual centre of the maze appears to be a large rock, generally known today as the 'egg stone', placed just below the summit. The entrance at the bottom is supposedly situated where two smaller stones lie. Various stages of the path could have been marked in a similar way. Some have felt that the destruction of the Tor church by an earthquake (not a lot of British churches have met such a fate), leaving today only a large upright structure that resembles, from a distance, some kind of megalithic obelisk, to be an expression of the mysterious hill's personality, asserting its archaic and eternal predisposition. The totality of that numinous effect is lost to us. The trees and the megaliths are gone. The path remains though, and therefore can be walked again. Altered states may still be on offer. A glimpse of the mentalities of its creators could be possible. Despite the suggestion that the maze could stimulate a visionary experience, Geoffrey Russell didn't seem to have contemplated the option of actually walking it. Geoffrey Ashe did. During the summer of 1979 he spent long hours on the Tor tracing the path, eventually producing a small booklet on its navigation.

It soon became clear that the time was ripe for this initiative. The ancient wisdom package has a number of different layers. One of them very strongly indicates the powerful presence of the primordial Great Goddess and it was from this direction that an attempt was soon made to re-forge a living link to an archaic past. In *Avalonian Quest,* the story is told of how, over the May-day period in 1980, which coincided with the full moon that year, a large group, initially consisting of about forty people, walked the maze at night by flaming torchlight. They were focused by Kathy Jones, who was inspired by the idea of the Tor as an ancient site of goddess veneration. I was now primed with a whole set of numinous associations for the Tor which helped me to appreciate the potency of this event with heightened emotional consciousness. The idea of the world mountain, the throne of the goddess as the axis of the heavens, the Babylonian ziggurat and the Ursa Major connection, had all coalesced deep inside the mythic matrix of my brain. To picture modern priestesses, ascending the Tor by the light of flaming torches, gave me cold tingles all over. It was as if Innana/Ishtar was returning from the underworld to take up her rightful place again as Queen of Heaven.

The great group that began the ascent did not all complete it. Some who did reach the summit had at first felt a sense of anti-climax. Nothing obvious had been done to conclude the process. Monica Sjöö, a major figure in Goddess spirituality, gave a vivid account of what happened next. They tried to stay the night there but were forced to leave by a lightning storm. As they walked down, flashes of lightning produced eerie visual effects, whereby the whole landscape was lit up like a kind of photographic negative, with light but no colour. This would switch on and off, rendering the darkness all the more dark and disorientating. The total effect was conducive to a trance state. Sjöö felt that the original maze creators were aware of inherent qualities in the local environment and were somehow able to make use of them, through a kind of fine-tuning the design, to amplify such manifestations.

The strongest, most inspiring feelings that I took away from *The Ancient Wisdom* and *Avalonian Quest* was that Glastonbury is not just a repository of history and mythology in the past tense, some kind of museum. That which has given it its unique identity remains alive and functioning, potent with power for transformation. As the heavens revolve in their vast cycles, archaic mysteries reveal themselves again. There seemed to be a far better case to be made for the existence of the maze than the zodiac and yet there was a typical Glastonbury enigma here. It was only at this point in time that its pattern, which had been there since its creation, somehow became visible again and the possibilities of walking it returned. My grounding in Eliade's work also reminded me of what I personally felt was somehow a vital theme in the mix. The Babylonian Etemananki ziggurat, believed to be the centre of the world and starting point of creation, was supposedly involved in a cyclic process involving the abolition and regeneration of time. Might there once have been similar beliefs about the Tor and could they suggest something about its future?

FLIGHT OVER THE CITY OF REVELATION

SOME SAD NEWS IN EARLY JUNE gave me pause for thought. The Stonehenge festival had finally been trashed by the authorities. A group of travelling people, on their way there in their mobile homes, had been corralled into a field by the police. In what became known as the Battle of the Beanfield they became the victims of a sustained violent assault clearly designed to intimidate and dispirit them. Even the generally hostile media seemed to recognise that the intensity of the force applied was totally disproportionate to the 'threat' these people posed. I will remain forever grateful that I experienced a glimpse of the festival at its best in '79.

My journey to Pilton commenced on Thursday June 20th, in the late afternoon. As per usual, change was in the air. Pete Wilson had got it on with Jane's sister Rachel. The four of us were travelling to Glastonbury as a prelude to a brave and idealistic venture. We had decided to all move into a flat together. The trip started uneventfully enough. As twilight began so too did heavy rain. The nearer we got to Pilton the more traffic began to build up. We had anticipated arriving in time to get our tents up in fading daylight and retire for a decent kip. The solstice dawn and sunrise weren't considered to be options after such a long journey. To be in the sacred zone was enough.

A few miles away from the site, the traffic came to a complete halt. The rain got heavier. Time elapsed. It was almost dark and the car had not moved an inch. The duration and intensity of the rain already made it obvious that the place was going to be muddy. Putting up a tent was likely to prove problematical. Although no drugs had been consumed it became increasingly strange inside the car. I don't know what we talked about but it seemed as if we dissolved into a twilight zone as hour after hour went by and rain ceaselessly beat against the windows. The chaos was due to a police experiment in controlling the festival traffic. By dawn we had barely moved a hundred yards. At that point our sense of what sort of time lay ahead of us was not wildly optimistic.

And so began the first of the great Glastonbury mud-baths. It had rained a lot in '82 and got quite muddy but there had been long dry periods. This was a whole new ball game. For the first two days it barely seemed to stop. A sea of slush engulfed the entire site, as if to absorb it all back into primordial ooze. All thoughts of seeing any bands dissolved. We spent long periods in the tents. Eventually I sprinkled some dope into a cheese roll and settled down to read John Michell's *City of Revelation.* Before we departed I had completed the whole book.

By way of a surreal contrast, at one point, wandering around the site during a dry interlude, we came across a field from which helicopter rides were being offered. For £5.00 each, four people could fly over the site. I'd finished John Michell's other masterwork, *The View Over Atlantis* on the first day there. The prospect of a potential view over the Glastonbury Zodiac was very appealing. Of course we went for it. After the isolation tank effect of the car in the rain and traffic jam, followed by the tent, it was somewhat strange to be suddenly powerfully rising up into the air, with the panorama of the vast campsite and the wider Glastonbury landscape spreading out around beneath us. It was input overload. I registered the Tor but no ancient effigies seemed visible across the ground. It was all too swift and vertiginous. I had barely adjusted to my new condition when it was over.

Amongst the teeming multitudes I bumped into a former girlfriend from university days. Jane Satchwell had first met me during the time of the burning squirrels debacle but had not fled screaming. I'd lost touch with her after leaving university. Now here she was and in a bit of a pickle as she'd had a row with the guy she'd arrived with and was now without a rucksack for her camping gear. As we were in a car I could spare mine and lent it to her. She would be passing through my home town later in the summer and could return it to me then. This meant me re-establishing contact with her again.

On the Monday that the festival dispersed, the weather was mercifully dry. This encouraged us to go into Glastonbury. Once again I climbed the Tor. Later on we visited the Chalice Well and the abbey. I was nicely set up to get it on with the ghostly monks, having just read John Michell on the sacred geometry. In the most well known New Age shop of the time in town, *Gothic Image,* I bought a poster of a solstice sunrise at the Tor. I also grabbed a number of postcards of Glastonbury views and associated subjects such as a representation, in stained glass, from the local church of St. John the Baptist, of Joseph of Arimathea. Amongst the books I noticed a few copies of an Earth Mysteries publication called *Earthquest News*. Something about it interested me so I bought two different editions.

TRANSITION

WE RETURNED HOME to the last days of my time in the house with the Love Cats. There was packing to do and a move across town to accomplish within a week. I still managed to look at some of my new input. I was intrigued to discover that *Earthquest News* was published by Andrew Collins, who had been involved in the Green Stone saga. He was based in Essex. In fact one of the articles involved spooky goings-on at a pub I had once frequented. It was also interesting to see that Park Wood, a site at the centre of the Glastonbury Zodiac, was up for sale and lots of inner and outer plane turbulence was surrounding the event. This was reported by Anthony Roberts, whose name I knew from the anthology *Glastonbury: Ancient Avalon, New Jerusalem* which I'd bought at Pilton '82 and reread only a few weeks before, at the start of June. He was obviously a friend of Andy's. In one of the magazines, Andy mentioned that he had been led to Park Wood himself, in 1983, by psychic material from Marion Sunderland. There was so much going on and I was in such a daze that I had little time to really ponder too deeply on this information.

The move to a new home was accomplished on the last night of the sacred month of June. The flat was above a shop and significantly more plush than most student homes, although not more expensive. We were lucky and we knew it. At the end of the first week of settling-in I contemplated what form our living room decoration should take. I had lots of Glastonbury piccies. After eating a little piece of dope I started to arrange some on the wall above the electric fire. The centre-piece was the poster of the Tor solstice sunrise. Around it I placed some cards of Glastonbury views, Joseph of Arimathea and so on. In the middle, beneath it, was William Blake's *Glad Day,* the naked Albion, personification of Britain. To the far left and right were some Tibetan posters, which had also been recently bought at Pilton. All of this imagery remained in place for the year we lived there, helping to create a certain ambience.

The grim fact that my hypnotherapy practice was floundering could no longer be avoided. It had been obvious from the end of April. My intense focus on the build-up to the solstice had pushed the issue to one side. There was nothing more to distract me. I was in my new home and Glastonbury was all over the walls. It had been played out. June had passed and the solar current was in decline. It was quite clear that it was all over. This was a profound shock to the system. I was unemployed for the rest of the year. At least it afforded the opportunity to carry on reading ridiculous numbers of books.

I had to acknowledge that the huge dynamism that had taken me to university and kept me around its environs for six years had now run out of steam. One option suggested itself. I could return to Essex to avail myself of its prosperity and the group of friends I still had there. Employment prospects would surely be better. I put the idea to Jane. It would be far more of a significant move for her than me. She was up for it. On completion of her teacher training the following June, she would try and find work in Essex. This now changed the whole energy of my situation. However bleak the immediate vista was, I knew that yet another huge transition would be upon me by the time of the next Glastonbury festival. I could enter into the new-year well psyched-up for action.

On January 21st 1986 I idly turned on the TV, having noticed in the *Radio Times* that an interesting-looking programme was being screened that night. It was part of a BBC series entitled *The Strange Affair Of...* This episode concerned the Glastonbury legends. At first there were no surprises. It seemed the subject would be in for a bashing. Then avuncular presenter Bob Symes stated that, *"believers in the existence of the Zodiac have now received a fresh charge to their batteries from a very unusual story indeed. From two young researchers who seem to have been led to the zodiac and around it by an unseen guide"*. We then saw the figure of a casually dressed, short-haired young man walking on a hill top. *"Andy Collins lives in Essex and is following what he calls a 'psychic journey'."*

Symes related how a psychic message had led Andy and a friend of his named Cara to a place near Glastonbury called Kingweston. They were looking for a lion and, *"a hill called Golgotha, 'the place of the skull' in The Bible, where Christ was crucified"*. The two were seen entering the churchyard at Kingweston. Cara explained how, when kneeling within the church, she had seen *"a sequence of images related to solar energy, such as a solar disc and a king with a crown sitting on his throne"*.

Having been given a clue about a lion and then the image of a solar disc, the two were now found, in combination, a few hundred yards down the road from the church. On the front wall of an old house was a large circular plaque depicting the sun with a lion's head at its centre. *"It was as if something was pointing to the fact that Kingweston was a centre for solar energies."* Only after this did Andy discover that they were immediately adjacent to the area of the Leo figure in the Glastonbury Zodiac.

The next clue led them on to Golgotha itself. Brief details passed by me in a blur. Andy summed it up: *"it would almost appear that the Leo figure is the Guardian, the gateway into the Zodiac. Once you're within it, it's as if some subtle psychic whirlwind will take you from site to site, like some great Arthurian adventure, a quest for the Holy Grail."* Symes then concluded. *"It's a weird and intriguing story and if you think it's unlikely it's worth knowing that six years ago another psychic quest sent Andy and his friends to a lonely pool in Worcestershire. When Andy explored, as the psychic message directed, he found hidden there, a short sword."* A few photos I recognised from *The Green Stone* were shown on screen and then Symes returned holding the actual sword itself. *"Its very existence suggests that psychic quests can and do produce real results."*

This was hugely interesting to me. The Glastonbury Zodiac may not be archaeologically verifiable but something authentic could well lie at the heart of its mystery. That was enough to be going on with for the time being. In fact, the TV programme would retrospectively seem like an immaculately timed portent of what my return to Essex would bring.

My employment situation altered as I began working for an agency on temporary assignments. This covered factories and so on. It was great to have money coming in and because the tasks didn't last that long there was a sense of variety. I was also amongst a group of the most over-qualified temps imaginable, as there were a number of recent graduates in a similar transitional state to myself and they made good company. I soon ended up on a long-term job in the post-room of a building society. Conditions were comfortable, and as spring came on I began to feel increasingly good. Of course I knew that a big adventure awaited me in the summer with a move back to Essex.

I travelled to Glastonbury on Friday June 20th. Rachel was unable to come due to exams and Jane's teacher training commitments meant that we'd miss the first day's entertainment. She and I travelled down with Pete. We were praying that the great mud-bath would not be repeated and thankfully it wasn't. One of the main focuses for me was the presence of a superb full moon in the night sky. I considered its coincidence with the full-sun solstice period to be auspicious. On that Sunday night, in a heightened state I stared up at it, entranced. I began to talk to Jane and Pete about how magnificent it would be to behold it from the Tor. As in previous years, the weather was erratic. Things became briefly stormy. There was an isolated clap of thunder and my nose started to briefly bleed. The sky cleared and the moon beamed out again. The idea of a trip to the Tor took hold and we began to seriously ponder its possibilities. Could we realistically expect to leave the site, when many people would already be departing, drive to Glastonbury, and then return without getting snarled up in any traffic jams? It wasn't a commonsense plan but we went for it anyway. Amazingly enough, the whole thing went smoothly. At midnight we were standing on the Tor, feeling the pull of the awesome moon. A few others were also present. All spoke in whispers as if to hold the spell in place.

This was the first time I'd been there at night and a whole new quality of the place seemed to communicate itself to me. On a number of occasions I had looked at the last few pages of *A Glastonbury Romance* where Powys evoked the Great Mother. Something of the mood he conjured up came alive in me as never before. It was a vista of eternity, a perspective from whence the epochs of a personal life are barely the blink of an eye. *"Out of the Timeless she came down into time. Out of the Un-named she came down into our human symbols. Through all the stammerings of strange tongues and murmurings of obscure invocations she still upholds her cause; the cause of the unseen against the seen, of the weak against the strong, of that which is not, and yet is, against that which is, and yet is not."* The divine feminine, *"moves through the generations from one twilight to another; and of her long journeying from cult to cult, from shrine to shrine, from revelation to revelation, there is no end"*. She brings, *"the breath of what is beyond life and beyond death; and none, but such are covenanted as her own, discern her goings and her comings"*.

Geoffrey Ashe's account of the 1980 torchlight maze threading by the modern priestesses had immediately entered very deeply into my mythic consciousness. My feeling of the Tor as a centre of archaic ceremonies was now immeasurably amplified. It was very easy to imagine a torchlight procession ascending the maze path in some ancient epoch. Who were these people and where would they have come from? Would they have been guardians of the site who lived around its slopes? Maybe some of them came from the scattered settlements out on the marshes. Imagine a group setting off from one of the Lake Villages in oak log canoes, as the full moon rose above the distant dark shape of the Tor to cast its rippling reflection across the waters. Perhaps, as the group came nearer, they could see the maze terraces twinkling with faery fire-light as the guardians of the otherworld island stood in attendance with flaming torches. It would have been quite something to make that slow journey across the lapping watered lake, past wind rustled reeds and the sudden flapping of disturbed birds. Where were they going? To the land of what? The Great Mother and her Grail? Gwyn the Lord of the Underworld? All of that in some extraordinary combination I didn't yet understand? What would these people have been feeling? What would they have been about to experience? I could almost picture their faces. It was all so near and yet so long ago and, *"The days of the years of men's lives are like leaves on the wind and like ripples on the water."* By the Tor tower, bathed in full moon light, I felt the poignant sense of standing on the threshold of another moment of significant change in my life. Like the 1983 solstice nude 400 metres, it became part of my eternal memory matrix.

Early in July, I returned to Essex. Jane and I found a flat near Southend. I got a job in a hospital as a fill-in whilst trying to return to the Civil Service, which seemed like my best available option. In November I finally returned to my old job. I entered a grade lower than I'd left in 1979, despite the acquiring of a degree, so anxious was I to secure my place. I assumed I could easily enough ascend the ladder. My new working colleagues perplexed me. Standards seemed to have spectacularly dropped. One young woman told me she would have preferred to work for the Metropolitan Police. When I asked her why, her jaw dropping reply, "So I could beat up niggers", stunned me into silence. I began to wonder if I'd made the right move. Spliffs and a few beers began to creep back into my life.

* * *

HIGHWAY TO THE END OF THE NIGHT

"Take a journey to the bright midnight."
Jim Morrison.

I BEGAN 1987 WITH A SENSE of not knowing quite what was happening and, in the meantime, it was best to cultivate my fitness. I joined a local gym and started regularly working out. Social life was a bit limited. Work was crap. In Spring I got a sort of promotion into a data processing section that at least involved a pay rise. A number of the largely female staff came to work as if dressed for a night at the disco. It was the era of the 'Essex Girl' and I have to say the mythology was often justified. There were a few decent people there though, to keep me sane.

It didn't seem long before Pilton was upon us again. Jane was now a full-time teacher and couldn't go. I went down there with an old friend who I'd known since infant-school days. Nick had led a colourful life. He could probably be called an acid casualty. He'd find that idea amusing. 1979 had been a big year for him as well. After visiting Pilton and mixing lots of psychedelic mushrooms with repeated readings of Carlos Castaneda's books, he found himself in a mental hospital. His adventures would fill a book. An amazing dynamism propelled him. In 1982 he'd managed to find his way out to India and travel around alone, which is more than most normal 'sane' people could handle. He was doing okay until he started smoking opium with a group of naked saddhus. After that he recalls episodes such as being taken in chains by the Nepalese police to see the Frog God. Having been deported from the country, he was committed to a mental hospital the moment he returned to England. A lot of people had big problems dealing with him. I loved the guy and was quite happy to drive down to Glastonbury with him.

We smoked a stupid amount of very strong spliffs and got into some interesting spaces. Unfortunately one big feeling kept on returning. It was getting increasingly obvious that Jane and I were drifting apart. I couldn't see us lasting much longer. Where the hell did that leave me? My job was stifling. I was treading water. Where were the great ecstasies of my university days? This was what I pondered on the solstice, amongst the largest Pilton crowd yet.

On the last night I found myself alone as Nick had crashed out early in his tent, in preparation for the long drive home the next day. I wandered into the Hare Krishna marquee and a wild party.

The shaven-headed ones were chanting in a total frenzy but it communicated to me a genuine devotional bliss. A group of them huddled together in a circle and went into head-banging mode reminiscent of a Status Quo concert. To my amazement some of them started doing back flips and general acrobatics. The energy and overall vibe was the best thing I experienced at the whole festival. The next day, on the way out, I tried to talk Nick into visiting the Tor but he said he didn't want to because he'd already been there before years previously. I simply didn't think in those terms. The Tor wasn't somewhere you visited only once. We drove off with me wistfully watching it disappear into the distance.

The period following on from Pilton was not at all a happy one. Ending a five-year relationship was unknown territory that I had no maps for. By the time it got to August an unpleasant daydream was increasingly haunting my days. There was a stretch of railway line that ran across Hadleigh Downs. I contemplated going over there one night and putting my head on it. It became like a guided visualisation meditation. I evoked all of my senses to make the scene as vivid as possible. I imagined getting the bus to Hadleigh and seeing many places for the last time. I would walk down the road onto the downs, with the body of Nuit above me, seeking *"peace unutterable, rest, ecstasy"*. The climax of the sequence was the feeling of my face pressed against the metal railway line as it vibrated amidst the overwhelming roar of the sound of the approaching train.

A rapid descent into intense drinking and dope smoking began. Weighing myself, I discovered I'd lost a stone. One morning, the moment I got out of bed, I felt a dull throbbing pain in my guts. I staggered into my living room and began crying my eyes out. The thought of that railway line filled up more and more of the day. On August 31st, shortly after rising, a calm strong inner voice informed me that I could not possibly continue in this manner. It was a case of either, kill yourself now, or start the rest of your life. If you're going to put your head on that railway line do it today or drop the whole thing. I accepted this. How to decide which path though? The mind was totally useless. I opted to toss a coin. If it came down heads, I would stick my head on the line that very night. If it was tails, I would stop drinking and smoking and get down the gym, get out running on the street and just see where that got me. It came down tails. I would surrender to an acceptance of life in its totality and try and cultivate some level of being that could no longer become falsely identified with either extreme of agony and ecstasy. I would carry on. My strange life was surely leading somewhere further. Suddenly I was curious to see just what would happen if I persevered. Maybe, I hoped, this might be like the Salisbury ordeal from which came all manner of extraordinary things.

It seemed as if one part of me was having a word with another. Just who or what was the 'I' in all this? A part of me that was experiencing grief was being advised by a larger, wiser, aspect of my total-self that somehow seemed to know a greater truth. I could understand it in Jungian terms. Whatever it was, the bit of me that was living on a day-to-day basis was glad to give over to it. At that point I didn't really have the luxury of examining it. I would simply see where it led me.

PART TWO

QUEST

"Our perfected selves whisper to us from the future."

Terence McKenna.

"There are certain subjects which, if we wish
to preserve the even and relatively meaningless
tenor of life, are best left alone.
The Glastonbury Zodiac is one of them."

Mary Caine. *The Glastonbury Zodiac.*

INTIMATIONS

IN NOVEMBER 1987 I read *Communion* by Whitley Streiber. This famous work, which was later filmed, tells the story of the author's alleged encounters with Extra-Terrestrials. Everyone I knew who had read it seemed to be polarised by extremes of response. Some detested it, losing no opportunities for mockery. An episode involving an anal probe, featured in the movie, was the cause of much hilarity. Others used it to fortify their religious beliefs about the space brothers' intervention on Earth.

The book had a profound impact on me but not for any of the usual reasons. I felt it was probably the best contactee account that I'd read, but I wasn't overly concerned with determining whether or not it was 'true'. What stirred me at great depths of my being was a theme that ran through the book that I felt to be supremely evocative in the manner of some archaic myth that hints at the hidden realms of one's deeper life.

In the course of the story, Streiber had a series of experiences that stimulated memories of events that his conscious mind had no recollection of. These events were by no means trivial. As they were uncovered it became clear that they represented the most important, the most fundamental events of his whole life. Gradually he began to realise that the life he thought he was living was not his real life at all. The other, forgotten life was, in fact, more 'real'. It was the hidden dynamic of his true destiny and had, in effect, been 'living' him. This realisation, this process of catching up on himself, created a turn around in his sense of self that permanently mutated his feeling of identity.

I wondered if there was a similarly mysterious, secret coherent dynamic, functioning from some other realm outside of the range of my normal perception that was somehow 'living' me? During an obvious phase of major change in my life, I was open to such possibilities and hoped I was ready to pick up on any clues to lead me on.

I soon had worldly concerns to focus on though. For complicated reasons my landlord wanted me out of my flat. I had just a few weeks to make new arrangements. It simply wasn't possible. I was left with no option but to stay with my parents until I could find somewhere decent to live. By the end of January '88 I was back with them. To say this was a shock to the system would be an understatement. One little detail summed it up. In the mornings I had to get the same bus into work, from the same bus stop, as I had in 1979, before I'd resigned to set out on my voyage to Stonehenge, Glastonbury, university, a career as a hypnotherapist and a five-year relationship. This was taking the idea of eternal return a little bit too far. It would have been easy to get depressed. I resolved to make the best of it. Money could be saved and I could concentrate on getting ferociously fit for the next phase of my life, which I simply had to believe was soon to come.

PRIESTESS OF THE FINEST HOUR

ONE DAY, IN MID FEBRUARY, I bought *Priestess* by Alan Richardson, a magical biography of Dion Fortune, second only to Crowley as the greatest British occultist of the 20th century. The cover of the book attracted me, a dreamy mystical painting of a moonlit female figure standing by the sea. I did have some familiarity with Fortune's work. Her novels, *The Sea Priestess* and *Moon Magic,* occupy a unique place in the history of occult literature. They were both written in the thirties, when it seems that inner plane events were in motion that led to the post-war revival of witchcraft and the general return of the Goddess. Numerous models existed for the male magician magus-type. From the Renaissance to Crowley, there was a certain way of being, a particular style that the would-be adept could take on board. For women it was different. The burning times had left unfavourable archetypes associated with witches. The most notable British sorceress was Morgan le Fay, from the Arthurian cycle. Helen Mirren's portrayal of her in *Excalibur* typifies her general depiction as a scheming manipulative malevolent figure, largely responsible for the doom that befalls the King. If the figure of the Priestess was to return, somehow she needed to be rehabilitated, restored to the fullness of her functions. People had to have an idea in their heads of what such a figure would be like and how she might feel and behave in the modern world. *The Sea Priestess* portrayed the immortal character of Vivien Le Fay Morgan, who became Lilith Le Fay in *Moon Magic.* She embodied the qualities of the Arthurian sorceresses, but in a way that revitalised their mystery, expanding what they represent and opening up vistas that speak of a lineage of profound antiquity.

Fortune also demonstrated the way of the Priestess in her personal life. She wrote and lectured extensively. Equally important to her was the practical teaching of ritual magic to small dedicated groups.

On some occasions she took on the function of a Priestess of Isis, dressing in robes and brandishing a sistrum rattle.

A little book of hers called *Avalon of the Heart* that I had first read in 1985 sung the praises of Glastonbury. It was she who had drawn attention to the Tor's terraced tracks, thus helping to set Geoffrey Ashe off on a remarkable journey. Appropriately enough, his home at the foot of the hill had once been occupied by her. Great importance was placed on the Arthurian tradition. In common with Rudolf Steiner, Fortune believed that Arthur was not just a single historical individual but a title passed on through the ages. She further expanded this idea to include Merlin and Morgan, believing that the lineage began in Atlantis. Merlin's involvement in the conception of Arthur told of a deliberate magical genetic engineering, whereby the Atlantean stock of Igraine was mixed with the Celtic blood of Uther. It wasn't exactly an idea that had a lot of history to back it up but it nonetheless seemed to speak of some arcane truth. The Arthurian mythos had been greatly revived by poets and painters during the 19th century. Fortune was trying to revive it in a different way. She believed that it is possible to work with the collective mind of a race through the magical use of its mythic archetypes. Bringing forth the Priestess figure helped pave the way for the return of the witch and the Goddess. Working Arthurian magic at Glastonbury could likewise affect the inner life of the nation.

An extraordinary test of such beliefs formed the climax of Dion Fortune's life. In *Priestess* I first learned of some remarkable events that had occurred during the Second World War, events that substantially fleshed out my knowledge of the occult backdrop of that conflict. I came to feel that they represented Glastonbury's finest hour and it seemed strange to me that they were not better known. To any occultists of the time it was obvious that the Nazis were making use of magical techniques. They had helped to mobilise a nation's consciousness through the manipulation of folklore and mythology. The energy unleashed by this was immensely powerful and had easily swept all before it. Dion Fortune felt that a British response was urgently needed. We had plenty of traditions of our own that could be invoked. The mediocrity represented by years of appeasement and non-entities like Neville Chamberlain needed to be transcended. What followed was a new departure in the history of magic.

Shortly after the start of the war, letters were sent out every week to a group of associates across the country. They contained details of visualisation meditations that were to be carried out in unison every Sunday morning. The focus was to be Glastonbury Tor. Imagery gradually built up over a period of months. The participants would find it coming to life and developing of its own accord. Feedback would be exchanged and this would influence the next sequence. It was believed that messages from discarnate sources were received. To begin with, the scene consisted of a large cavern inside the Tor. A red rose on a cross of gold hung in the air. For those initiated in the Golden Dawn tradition this was seen as a more detailed glyph covered in magical symbols. Three rays of light, red, purple, and blue, emanated from a point above and behind the cross. The fully developed form of the imagery saw Christ at the apex of the converging rays. The purple light was central, reaching down behind and beneath the cross. At its base could be seen the Virgin Mary, holding a chalice. The red beam came down at an angle to the left of the cross and culminated in an image of Arthur, sitting on a white horse and holding Excalibur aloft. To the right of the cross, the blue ray projected a vision of Merlin, holding an orb of sovereignty. To me, it seemed a very powerful equilibration of Britain's pagan and Christian heritage. When it mattered, they functioned from a space of unity. From this inner plane realm, spiritual forces streamed through into the soul of the nation fortifying it against the potent will of Nazism. That's what Dion Fortune and her associates believed and my temperament inclines me to agree with them.

Immense forces were surely at work. Dion Fortune gave her all during the war. She died shortly afterwards, exhausted on all levels by the intensity of her efforts. The rebirth of Glastonbury had begun at the start of the century with Frederick Bligh Bond's work at the abbey. The Magical Battle of Britain effectively completed that process. Whatever forces were at work waited almost another thirty years before their next major manifestation.

Priestess was the first book on such subjects I had read since 1985. I devoured the book in two days, finishing it during my afternoon tea break at work, sitting by my VDU amongst the disco dollies. It was one of those February days when the sun shines quite brightly in a clear blue sky and there is a definite sense that spring is starting to stir. I stared out of the window and asked myself, "Do I still believe in the Avalonian quest?" The answer came back immediately, "of course I fucking do!"

* * *

EARTHQUEST

AT THE END OF MARCH a story in a local newspaper drew my attention to the formation of some kind of psychic group called Earthquest with an initial meeting on April 5th. That was my birthday. And I knew that 'Earthquest' name. "*Psychic Carole Young and mysteries writer and Researcher Andy Collins, both from Leigh, are the forces behind Earthquest.*" "*Andy has worked for over 10 years with talented psychics nationwide in his quest to unravel landscape mysteries, often discovering artefacts hidden in the ground. He said in 1979 in a psychic quest he found a sword bearing the Mary Queen of Scots coat of arms and a green jewel in a 17th century brass casket in Worcestershire.*" An opportunity had arisen to meet someone who had been involved in the most outrageous paranormal saga that I had ever heard of and also done work in the Glastonbury Zodiac. The birthday timing did seem to emphasise that here was something I should definitely respond to!

On the evening of my twenty-ninth birthday, I made my way to the upstairs function room of *The Ship* pub in Leigh-on-Sea. It was packed solid, with many people standing at the back and around the edges. Earthquest was actually being re-launched. The group had begun in Essex a few years earlier but drifted apart as is often the case with such undertakings. The bespectacled nattily dressed Mr Collins presented an extensive slide-show lecture covering the full range of his remarkable work over the years. I was delighted and excited to hear of Green Stone and Glastonbury Zodiac events. He was currently completing a book concerning the most recent strange episode in his life. This was the saga of the Black Alchemist. It seemed a fascinating, intense tale of hardcore occultism. Indubitably dark stuff indeed, but I was not put off in any way by the prospect of potential involvement. There was no doubt in my mind that Andy was completely honest in the presentation of his experiences and that all of this stuff was the real thing. I wanted to be on board. I knew with total certainty that I would be back for the next meeting.

From that point on I went out of my way to attend any public event that Andy put on in the area. I greedily absorbed every bit of information I could about his amazing experiences. He'd led quite an interesting life. Leaving school with no qualifications, he was in London during the beginning of the punk era. In the spirit of the time, he'd helped form a band named Disease, whose career had been short-lived due to the unfortunate inability of any of its members to play a musical instrument. Andy had been a friend of Tony Parsons and through him had met many of the prime movers on the punk scene of the time. Parsons was writing for the *New Musical Express* and was just entering into his tumultuous association with Julie Burchill. There was talk of him and Andy moving into a flat in London together. In a moment of destiny, Andy decided to stay put in Essex and concentrate on his growing interests in UFOs and the paranormal, whilst also pursuing a career in journalism.

In a short period of time, his energy and persistence had made him one of the top UFO researchers in the country. This was how he'd come to investigate the Aveley abduction that I'd read about in *The Green Stone*. The whole spectrum of what had most fascinated me about UFOlogical studies, the overlap with the paranormal and occultism, was strongly present in Andy's early work.

Talking to him about his Glastonbury experiences, I soon discovered something that I considered to be a bit spooky. His zodiac quest, which had been featured on TV, had been spread over two years. It had come to a climax in June 1985. In fact, this episode was simultaneous to my presence at the great Pilton mud-bath of that year. During the torrential rain, entirely alone, he had thrown himself into a weir in the Sagittarius figure at midnight, as part of a death-rebirth test of his intentions. He emerged intact from the heavily swollen river to set off on an incredible visionary journey across the Glastonbury landscape. It reached a mind-bendingly psychedelic conclusion when he encountered the Ship of Solomon and climbed on board, in a state where the nature of reality was difficult to determine. The end result was a kind of gnosis that involved a massive download of ideas and information.

In all that time Andy was never more than a few miles away from me. I'd actually been up in a helicopter scanning for signs of the Zodiac. If I'd had some powerful binoculars and knew where to look, I could have spotted him, driving along in his car or walking in a field, playing out a destiny that would connect us in some way nearly three years later. I couldn't help but entertain the idea of a further witness to those events. Some other consciousness of indeterminate nature, beyond normal spacetime, perhaps one of John Cowper Powys' invisible watchers of the Glastonbury aquarium, was aware of both of us and whatever the future held. When I left the site and got to Glastonbury itself, I found copies of *Earthquest News* and learnt of Andy's Essex connections. I read about the whole business of the proposed selling of Park Wood and the magical turbulence around it. Now I discovered that the auction had been on the solstice, as I'd arrived at the festival, and the outcome was acceptable. After months of reading a huge number of books (a sequence that had begun with *The Green Stone*), and feeling I was on for something big at Pilton '85, I had arrived in the matrix of the Glastonbury Zodiac simultaneous to the major geomantic issue of Park Wood being resolved and the strongest magical events in the Zodiac as a whole since its rediscovery, in the form of Andy's reality-busting experiences.

In 1985 I consciously knew nothing of any of this but, in 1988, I became convinced that some part of me *did* know. From that moment, I was always going to return to Essex and meet Andy and have this mysterious Glastonbury connection expanded. It was already signposted when I read *The Green Stone* as my hypnotherapy business floundered. The processes present through my weird interactions with *Glastonbury Romance, King Arthur's Avalon, Meetings with Remarkable Men,* and *Europe's Inner Demons* had now crossed a major threshold. This was exactly the sort of thing I had dimly intuited was possibly lurking beyond my conscious awareness after being strangely moved by Streiber's *Communion*. Was this initial revelation just the tip of an iceberg? How much more was waiting to be uncovered? It was clear that the next phase of my life had now properly begun.

There was further pleasing symmetry when Andy brought his friend, the artist Chesca Potter, to give a slide lecture for the Earthquest group. She had been responsible for the picture on the cover of *Priestess.* Looking back a few months, it seemed that my reading of that book, which had caused me to reaffirm my dedication to the Avalonian quest, was the start of the whole amazing expansive process that was now so rapidly emerging. Chesca had been involved in some of the zodiac quest herself. Seeing her art it was blindingly obvious to me that it was in a class of its own. Her perfect marriage of exemplary technique and numinous deep inspirational connections to the land and its archetypes induced an immediate rapturous reverie in me. Chesca would later go on to create two tarot masterpieces, the *Greenwood* and *Celtic Shaman* decks, amongst a huge outpouring of magnificent works.

Within six weeks of meeting Andy I had found a new home in Southend. It was an upstairs flat in a converted terraced house, very near to the centre of town and my place of employment. I was now working in the VAT Head Office. It's a good thing that so many tangibly positive things were happening in my life then because this new phase of my career appeared initially to be an abyss of meaninglessness. Having moved into my new home I wondered how I would decorate it and thereby claim the space for my own. I soon had the idea to recreate the wall of Glastonbury piccies I had put up in July '85. This affirmed for me my reconnection to the place and also the sense of increasing mystery over the pull of the destiny that I now felt had been working then.

SUPER PSYCHICS

ONE OF THE THINGS that had most impressed me about the Green Stone story was the way that accurate psychic information had been produced in abundance. I soon got to hear far more detailed versions of those events and realised that in fact the psychism was even more spectacular than at first appearance. The book suggested that Gaynor Sunderland had been the centre of gravity of the strange phenomenon. Her role was undoubtedly crucial but Graham Phillips had probably been the driving force. As things had got going he'd developed extraordinary abilities himself. The historical details he'd come out with, tracing the story from Akhenaten and megalithic Britain through to Victorian times, were full of names, dates, and places that were readily checkable. Many of the Victorian names were very obscure but eventually traced. Andy came to refer to this talent as Direct Information Psychism and those with the rare ability to manifest it as Super Psychics. After the Green Stone saga had played itself out, Andy had left the Midlands and returned to his original home of Essex. He set up an earlier version of Earthquest to see if it was possible to duplicate the kind of events that had happened around the Meonia group. He met a man named Bernard who soon demonstrated all the classic abilities of the Super Psychic.

I heard many accounts of Bernard's prodigious talent. What really appealed to me was that he didn't need any of the trappings of the Victorian medium or New Age channeler to get a result. Andy would meet up with him at a pub. They'd settle down with some beers and cigarettes and have a chat. As the conversation turned to esoteric matters, Bernard would begin to pick up information and start relaying it. A pub full of people and a juke-box didn't make any difference. He didn't even necessarily close his eyes. Andy would tape record or take written notes of each session.

To adequately convey the kind of information he produced I feel it's necessary to give an extended example. On one evening, the subject turned to the Middle Ages. Bernard came up with 37 pieces of information in quick succession. They were all on a topic that had not been discussed before.

1) There is a medieval castle at a place called Coucy in France.
2) A family of the same name owned it.
3) Coucy was in an area called Picardy.
4) It's not far from Paris.
5) The castle was constructed around the 12th century.
6) It was built upon an earlier structure.
7) The land was once owned by Clovis, the French King.
8) It is large and positioned on a very significant strategic point.
9) It had five towers, four at the corners and one large central one.
10) Over the entrance to the castle was a base relief of a knight without armour fighting a lion.
11) In front of the entrance is a statue complex of four lions.
12) One of the lions is devouring a child.
13) Nearby is a standing cross.
14) A group of monks there performed a kind of ceremony there that involved circling the cross and then pouring the contents of a cup over the lions.
15) There is a complex of tunnels and chambers beneath the castle.
16) There is a central chamber beneath the central tower.
17) Thirty-seven steps lead down to the central chamber and three corridors lead away from it.

18) More steps lead up to the tower from the ground floor.

19) There is a large banqueting hall in the castle with a raised dais at one end.

20) Behind the dais are carved reliefs of the Nine Worthies (remember them from *The Green Stone*?)

21) Six of them are: Hector, Charlemagne, Alexander, Arthur, Godfrey de Bouillon, and Judas Maccabeus.

22) This hall contained battle standards to the left and right of the stage.

23) Servants with torches stood on either side of the hall during banquets.

24) There is also a smaller hall featuring female Worthies.

25) The banqueting hall was constructed during the 14th century.

26) Someone named Ingelram de Coucy had built it.

27) He built it to honour his wife.

28) Her name was Isabella and she came from a very important family.

29) Her family connected to previous questing work.

30) Bernard drew the family coat of arms and named the colours.

31) Ingelram de Coucy was tall, dark roundish face and bearded. Seemed a very powerful character.

32) He was strongly connected to the King, possibly an Ambassador.

33) The Germans occupied the castle during the war.

34) It was badly damaged then.

35) It is now just a ruin.

36) The Germans tried to locate treasure there.

37) Ingelram was the last of his dynasty.

The important thing about this kind of material is that it's checkable. Andy's later research revealed that the castle was built in the 13th century. Nothing could be found about the wartime German treasure hunt. Other than that, thirty five of the thirty seven points proved to be accurate. That's a good batting average. Bernard was, like Frederick Bligh Bond, a suitably prepared vehicle. His strange experiences over the years had stimulated an interest in medieval history, heraldry and so on. This seemed to help an input of material that had never been present in his head in the first place. Of course, sceptics will simply never believe this. It would always be assumed that he had prior knowledge.

The castle was only *one* of the topics covered that evening. A few minutes later, Bernard was pouring out the same quality of material about something else altogether. He'd been doing it every week for *years.* Direct Information Super Psychics can function that way. Compare this with the ramblings of most New Age channelers or even the successful psychic espionage of remote viewing experiments. The level of quality was outrageous. Bernard had made a major contribution to Andy's Glastonbury Zodiac work. The saga of the Black Alchemist revealed his abilities functioning at their most intense level.

THE ANGELIC GIFT

I WASN'T THE ONLY ONE to have taken heart from the 1986 screening of the *Strange Affair* Glastonbury TV documentary. Colin and Gelly Paddon had good reason to applaud it. The contents helped to validate the most mysterious adventure of their lives. It had begun in August 1985 with an extraordinary dream of Colin's. A wood full of ferns. A large fallen log. A small clearing. In its centre, a tall shining angelic figure: white robed, long blond hair, pale face. In each hand he held a short sword. They were being offered to Colin, who stepped forward and took them. The dream repeated a few nights later. He had the sense that he recognised the location as near to their Milton Keynes home. There was a feeling that the swords really existed and needed to be found. The Paddons were not strangers to mystical matters. They and a few friends shared an interest in the Qabalah. A meditation at Milton Keynes Buddhist peace pagoda yielded a few more details. The angelic figure with the swords was there again. On the ground was an oak leaf on a stem by a forked twig and two white down feathers.

An outing to the nearby woods was arranged. After a lot of wandering around, the large fallen log was spotted. Nearby was the clearing. Colin inspected the ground. There on the floor together were the oak leaf on a stem, forked twig, and white down feathers. They were obviously in the right place. Now what? What was the likelihood of some shining being materialising and giving them the swords? They reasoned that the swords might well somehow already be there. Colin got down on his hands and knees to where the shamanic clues lay. Removing them, he began to pull at the clod of turf they lay on. Pulling up a section about one foot square revealed a stunning sight. Suddenly visible were two oval shaped silver knobs, seemingly the ends of something stuck in the ground. Initial investigation failed to budge them. Considering the strange events that had led them there, perhaps they were supposed to be grasped together. Colin gave it a go. Out of the ground emerged the two swords of his dreams.

About six months later, the Glastonbury documentary was shown. Colin was out working that night so Gelly made a point of videoing it as they were both great lovers of the place. The programme didn't really have any great surprises until Andy appeared. At the end of the section on his zodiac adventures, the Green Stone story was mentioned and the Meonia sword shown. It was clearly identical to the ones found in the wood. When Colin returned the footage was repeatedly replayed. They contacted the BBC. Less than a week after the programme was shown, Andy was sitting in the Paddons' living room inspecting their remarkable artefacts. Colin shared his feelings on the subject. He was sure there were more of the mysterious swords waiting to be discovered until a set of seven was complete. At the time of the discovery of the first sword nobody had ever suggested that there would be more. On the weekend of filming for the documentary, back in 1984, Andy had a vision of a group of knights coming together who would be recognised by the swords they bore. He felt that somehow they would come to him. At that time he hadn't linked it with Meonia. Now he could see the fruits of that weekends' filming and began to wonder.

One thing that did need to be cleared up was the use of the theme of seven swords in productions that had been seen on TV by large audiences. A story from *Robin of Sherwood* featured seven swords created by the Saxon smith god Wayland that were used in an evil ceremony to raise Lucifer. *The Omen* movies had the seven stilettos of Megiddo that helped to battle the Anti-Christ. Was Colin Paddon familiar with this material? Could it have influenced his ideas on seven swords? He had no conscious recollection of any of it. Time would tell if the quest for seven swords was a goer or not.

AVALON OF THE HEART

"Glastonbury is a gateway to the unseen."
Dion Fortune.

EARLY IN THE SPRING, I had learnt that there wouldn't be a festival at Worthy Farm that year. So much else was going on in my life that I gave it little thought. On the first day of June I took a day off work to read *Avalon of the Heart* again. It's a compendium of a series of short articles Dion Fortune had written about Glastonbury during the thirties. There's a certain amount of repetition. The Avalonian mythos of Arthur, Excalibur, the Grail, Morgan le Fay, Joseph of Arimathea and the Holy Thorn gets presented in a manner that scarcely gives a nod to any credible history. There are eloquent powerful passages however, that conveyed to me more about my inner feelings for Glastonbury then anything else I'd read. I already knew that *"Legend and history and the vision of the heart blend in the building of the Mystical Avalon"*. I believed that it was that Mystical Avalon, the Avalon of the Heart, calling me.

Dion Fortune wrote that, *"She is all beauty, our English Jerusalem. The paths that lead to her are ways of loveliness and pilgrimages of the soul"*, and wondered if we *"miss much when we abandon the ancient custom of pilgrimage?" "Every race has its holy centres, places where the veil is thin"*, that contain, *"power to quicken the spiritual life and vitalise the soul with fresh enthusiasm and inspiration." "Where strong spiritual emotions have been felt for long periods of time by successive generations of dedicated men or women - especially if they have had among them those who may be reckoned as saints because of their genius for devotion - the mental atmosphere of the place becomes imbued with spiritual forces, and sensitive souls capable of response are deeply stirred thereby when they come to it." "Glastonbury is a spiritual volcano wherein the fire that is at the heart of the British race breaks through and flames to heaven."*

A powerful idea took hold of me. I should be in Glastonbury for the solstice, regardless of whether the festival was on or not. I could spend a night on the Tor, where there was certain to be a gathering.

For, "*there are tides in the inner life, and on the crest of their flood we are very near to heaven. There are times when the power tides of the Unseen flow strongly down upon our earth, and there are also places upon her surface where the channels are open and they come through in their fullness of power. This was known to them of old time, who had much wisdom that we have forgotten, and they availed themselves of both times and places when they sought to awaken the higher consciousness*". Glastonbury Tor, at dawn on the summer solstice, was surely such a time and place.

The pilgrimage feeling became progressively stronger as the month went on. It seemed likely that I would be travelling alone. I'd never been there without having been to the festival. It would also be the first time I'd spent an entire night on the Tor. I was intending to go through the month of June with no drug input. This would be the first time I'd done such a thing since I formulated my personal mythos of the sacred month and my West Country journeys. Everything about the upcoming adventure suggested something new.

On Monday June 20th I undertook a long journey involving trains and buses that cost more than I could sensibly afford. On arrival, as I ascended the path that went by Geoffrey Ashe's house and into the Tor field, I gave a psychic nod to Dion Fortune, whose words, some perhaps written in that very house, had catalysed my journey a few weeks before, and continued to guide me. As I began to climb the Tor itself, I deliberately contemplated the powerful sequence of events that I'd experienced in the last year. Pilton '87 seemed like aeons ago, another life altogether. I may not have put my head on that railway line, but something more than just a relationship ended then. It was nine years since my first solstice pilgrimage to Glastonbury. The memories of those visits were incredible snapshots of rites of passage, magnificently accentuated and accelerated by the Avalonian dynamic. This focusing on my Glastonbury connection was a deliberate magickal act to raise my emotional consciousness and thereby render myself more receptive to whatever was about to follow. It was a kind of invocation that stated who I was, where I was at, and my willingness to engage the next stage.

As I reached the top, I joined quite a throng. There must have been a good few hundred up there. Along with this, I also noted that the vibe-reading was immensely powerful. I could easily feel surging tides of what I can only describe as earth energies. I'd had a sense of such things at Stonehenge in 1981 but I'd been on acid then. I hadn't touched any drugs for six months. It felt like I was wading through thigh deep water. I thought of Fortune's "*times when the power descends and spiritual forces are rushing in like the tide up an estuary*". I tangibly slowed down. There was a definite global tribal vibe amongst those who had "*come to open their souls to the fiery forces going up like dark flames from the Tor*". The tower was full of drummers. Rippling raucous rhythms emanated from within. Waves of chanting vocals carried sacred prayers from other epochs and dimensions skywards. Didgeridoos, clouds of dope smoke. A whole psychedelic sensorama embraced me, welcomed me, with immediate overwhelming affirmation. It was the 1979 vibe, but more besides.

I heard for the first time the Hopi Indian sun chant.

Kuwatay lano lano mahotay,
hiyano hiyano hiyano

and its accompanying English translation,

We are all one with the infinite sun,
forever and ever and ever.

The whole shamanic drum-out scene was exhilarating. It was alive and vital, anchored in the earth, resonating to its powerful heartbeat, calling us back to the body and its revitalisation. A sense of mystical connection to the land, the seasons, and the heavens, is natural to all humans. Our sick, alienated industrial culture, has taken us so far away from that it seems weird to people now. I'd recently seen the *Glastonbury Fayre* movie for the first time and really loved the way that spontaneous drum-outs had permeated the whole festival. I was now in the middle of a concentrated dose of it. There was a sense of wanting to spread the word. I felt like it would be great to somehow find a group of people to do such things back in Essex.

Out of the backdrop of definitive hippie celebration emerged a sequence of strongly focused episodes. A group of people clad in white stepped forward. They were Sufis, involved in what was known as Universal Peace Dances. I'd been keeping my eye on Sufism from the perspective of the Gurdjieff Work and Idries Shah. There were plenty of other aspects of its innumerable manifestations.

Peace Dances had been created by an American, named Samuel Lewis, during the nineteen-sixties. He was connected to the lineage of Hazrat Inayat Khan who had founded a Sufi Order in the West during the same period that Gurdjieff was in France. Lewis had studied the sacred chants of the world's religions and came up with a sequence of simple circle dances that have a kind of folk devotional quality. The combination of singing and movement, for all its apparent simplicity, was able to generate powerful emotion. The group went through their paces. The combination of Hindu, Native American, Islamic, and Christian chants with movement was inspiring. It made me feel that I'd really like to be directly involved in something similar one day. On a far off summer day, fifty years before, Dion Fortune and some of her associates had spontaneously performed a '*Dance of the Elements, whirling like dervishes'*, on the summit of the Tor. They may have been the first to do such a thing in a few thousand years. Now it had come to this.

The didgs and singing in the tower continued in the background. The multitudes increased. Amongst them was a group of Geordies. They were partaking of their own special cultural rituals: the mass imbibing of multiple cans of *Newcastle Brown* ale and the repeated intoning of the sacred anthem, *Blaydon Races*. As a Catholic might solemnly give over to a night's worth of *Hail Mary* or a Tibetan Buddhist settle into a long round of *Om Mani Padme Hum*, so did the Geordies devote themselves to their arcane hymn. The rising and falling tides of their passionate recitations formed an ebbing flowing soundscape behind the successive Tor top group performances.

La Illa Ha Illa 'Llahu Hu
Oh! lads ye should a' seen us gannin
La Illa Ha Illa 'Llahu Hu
Passin' the folks upon the road just as they were stannin
Ya Shafee, Ya Kafee
Thor wis lots o lads and lasses there aall wi smilin faces
Ya Shafee, Ya Kafee
gannin alang the Scotswood road to see the Blaydon Races.

The Peace Dancers completed their work as twilight settled in. I remembered my only previous visit to the Tor at night, during Pilton '86, when I had bathed in the beams of a majestic full moon. I'd come to celebrate a solar event but I knew that the primal night carries its own blessings. The intensity of the vibe increased.

A London based Wiccan group now made their own contribution. I'd noticed them when I first arrived, an obvious clan of some kind, with bags of food and paraphernalia. Modern pagans honour seasonal festivals such as the solstices and equinoxes. Witchcraft revivalists call them Sabbats. Ideally they should be commemorated in fine style. It soon became apparent that this crew meant business. Between the Tor tower and the National Trust direction finding plaque at the summit's edge, a brazier was positioned and a fire kindled. The group stood around in a large circle and took off their clothes. Respect. It wasn't exactly warm up there and the random multitudes were a bit larey. The sight of naked female flesh inspired a strong response of veneration of the divine feminine from the Geordie mystics. "Fucking 'ell she's gerrin her tits out like."

> The lasses lost thor crinolines an' the vails that hid their faces,
> Aa got two black eyes an' a broken nose I' ga'n te Blaydon Races.

A well-ordered ceremony began. Invocations at the four quarters.

> *"Ye Lords of the Watchtowers of the East, ye Lords of Air; I do summon, stir and call you up, to witness our rites and to guard the circle."*

I watched, transfixed, exhilarated. When I'd read accounts of the maze ascent of 1980 there'd been a sense that something climactic had been missing. After all the effort, the final completion was just out of reach. I felt that what I was witnessing supplied the necessary added ingredient.

From the presiding naked Priestess, the famous words of the 'Charge of the Goddess' seemed to speak on behalf of some aspect of the ancient history of the landscape around us, something that Dion Fortune had certainly recognised in her life's work. It was returning like a great flood tide. As Powys had noted, "*evermore she rises again, moving from the mists of dawn to the mists of twilight, passing through the noon-day like the shadow of an eclipse and through the midnight like an unblown trumpet, until she finds the land that has called her and the people whose heart she alone can fill*".

Here was a statement of magical intent for the new aeon.

* * *

> *"Ye shall be free from slavery; and as a sign that ye be really free, ye shall be naked in your rites; and ye shall dance, sing, feast, make music and love, all in my praise. For mine is the ecstasy of the spirit, and mine also is joy on earth; for my law is love unto all. I who am the beauty of the green earth and the white moon among the stars, and the mystery of the waters, call unto thy soul. Arise and come unto me. I am the soul of nature. From me all things proceed, and unto me all things must return. All acts of love and pleasure are my rituals. I have been with you from the beginning; and I am that which is attained at the end of desire."*

The group joined hands and began circling to the singing of assorted pagan chants.

> *"We are all part of the Goddess and to her we shall return,*
> *like a drop of rain, merging with the ocean."*

Eventually the circle opened to invite the rest of us to join in. Before long, I was hand in hand with naked witches, circling around a fire singing

> *"We are the old people, we are the new people,*
> *we are the same people, wiser than before."*

Magnificent! This was *exactly* the sort of thing I'd felt ought to be happening at a place like Glastonbury Tor on the eve of the summer solstice. I took note of everything. Once again I strongly felt that I'd really like to arrange something like it myself one day. Eventually the ceremony ceased. Exhausted by the intensity of their efforts, even the ululations of the Geordies subsided. The tower now became the focus. Didgs till dawn. Singing and smoking into the dreamtime. Impressions blending into each other. More pagan chants.

> *"The Earth is our mother, we must take care of her."*

By the time of the first faint signs of daylight, I wondered if I was the only person there not under the influence of any drugs. It was fine though. I was alone but not lonely. I was consciously abiding in something bigger than any stonking spliff I may have missed out on, keeping "*vigil in the high places when the cosmic tides are flowing and the Powers of the Unseen are changing guard and the rituals of the Invisible Church are being worked near the earth*".

The crowd was gradually increased by further multitudes of people of all ages and appearances. When the sun finally appeared, I looked around me. It was a strange sight to see so many in contemplative silence, responding to the various promptings of their inner lives that had brought them there to honour this moment. Many of the dawn newcomers looked entirely normal. Some were quite elderly. They wouldn't get a passing glance in the street. Where had they all come from and what were their stories? Nobody would ever know the full details. The cumulative alchemy of this cast of characters was something that was unique and beautiful. This was a poignant taste of the Avalon of the Heart. There we all were in the dreamtime. Somehow, I felt that everyone who had ever stood atop the Tor at a summer solstice dawn was in some way present, as indeed were those who in linear time were yet to come. The sunrise, although not as spectacularly perfect as Stonehenge '79, spread the rays of a golden dawn to the land and its pilgrims.

People slowly departed, leaving the all-night casualties behind. I dozed on a stone seat in the tower. Sleep is not really possible when some bearded Hare Krishna-type character in orange robes is sitting next to you, chanting and blowing a conch shell. About seven o'clock, a man dressed in nothing but a French beret set at a jaunty angle approached me. "Hi. I'm Aubrey. Would you like a banana?" Politely, I declined. It was time to make a move. I descended from the holy mountain, gazing down and across to the foot of Chalice Hill and what had once been Dion Fortune's high veranda. From reading her biography some might feel that she would have very much disapproved of the night's fun and games on the Tor, which really couldn't have been remotely anticipated during her lifetime. More words of hers nicely summed up my immediate feelings and suggested to me where her spirit might now be at. "*Avalon cannot be claimed by any sect as their private sanctuary. It belongs neither to artist nor to anglican, neither to psychic nor to pagan. All these have their part in Avalon, and none can deny the rest.*" It had been what the Sufi Peace Dancers called a Universal Service and it felt to me like it was profoundly imbued with the energies of Avalon's *'Invisible Church'*. I knew it would take a while for the whole thing to sink in and work its way through my system. That was fine. Right there and then, in the present moment, I felt magnificent and that was all the measure of the event that I needed.

I'd brought a copy of *The Green Stone* with me. It seemed good to go over it again at that moment in my life and fix it in my memory timeline. I anticipated that I could probably read the whole book on the journey home and still be able to get some sleep. There was an Earthquest meeting that night. No matter how knackered I was from my exertions, I was going to be there. I'd learnt the value of microdotting mythic solstice memories for future inspiration. I knew I was in the midst of a total classic. The decision to travel down on my own, regardless of the absence of the festival, had been gloriously vindicated. The weather was fine, the journey comfortable. I did manage to read the whole of *The Green Stone*. Of course I pondered the sequence of events since my first reading of it in '85. The story fascinated me more than ever. However much Andy's current Black Alchemist saga interested me, what I really hoped for was that somehow the Green Stone epic would kick-off again and I could be involved.

I got to the Earthquest meeting easily enough. Andy had something special set up. A few years previously he had spent some time on the island of Mount Athos, investigating the Greek Orthodox monasteries there, with their awesome icons. He'd taken lots of slide photographs and arranged them into a magnificent presentation. He was using a projector that enabled two slides to fade in and out of each other. The musical soundtrack was David Sylvian. I'd been aware of him in the band Japan back in my university days. They'd initially seemed like an arty bunch of pretty-boys and I'd not given them much attention. The classic song *Ghosts* had changed all that. I now discovered that Sylvian had gone on to a strong solo career, collaborating with the likes of Robert Fripp. Instrumental passages from the album *Gone to Earth* were used to enhance the Athos imagery. It was stunning. Cold tingles ran riot over me. So did the solstice end. It had been an embarrassment of riches.

8/8/88

I MADE A POINT of letting Andy know that if he ever wanted help on any Black Alchemist adventure, I was up for it. In early August just such an event arose. What came to be called black questing would become a major part of my life for the next three years. A lot of the details have been covered in Andy's books *The Seventh Sword* and *The Second Coming*. It would be impossible in a work less than a thousand pages long to do justice to the many full-on sagas that were running simultaneously in those days. I'm only going to mention a certain amount of it in passing here. It's necessary to give a taste of my personal and magical development against the constant climate of the time. It also helps form a backdrop against which some Glastonbury events may be better understood.

The Black Alchemist story had begun in 1985. Out on a quest in the landscape, Bernard had been psychically led to find an inscribed stone spearhead hidden in a churchyard. This had caused him to make a mental link with its creator and his unusual magical practices. It proved to be difficult to sever the connection. More artefacts were uncovered and the enigmatic character of the Black Alchemist loomed ever more largely. The psychic link worked both ways. Andy and Bernard had seemingly trespassed on his territory and work. He left calling cards in Essex. A kind of magical battle commenced.

Bernard again demonstrated his amazing abilities as he picked up detailed information on obscure figures such as the 4th century AD alchemist, Zosimos of Panopolis. There was a death threat against Andy. Although the Black Alchemist was engaged in a very individual work, he didn't operate out of a vacuum. There were associates. One of them was a woman who seemed to link in with a story of apparent black magic that had been written of by Toyne Newton in *The Demonic Connection.* A shadowy group allegedly named the Friends of Hecate were operating in the south of England. They in turn were part of a larger network of loosely affiliated groups who sometimes acted in unison for special purposes. Work was done outdoors at sites of ancient sanctity and the motives usually seemed well dodgy. These people wanted to exploit the energy matrix of Britain for their own agenda.

Some of the most memorable material in *The Black Alchemist* concerned the great hurricane of October 1987. A number of people had experienced visions and dreams that night of themes that linked with the goddess Hecate. There were wolves, fierce hags and so on. She is linked with storms. It was felt that when the hurricane got going it had unleashed primal energies that stimulated archaic bits of the brain. The Black Alchemist and the Friends of Hecate had realised that a unique magical opportunity was presenting itself and had immediately got to work. Anything done on a night like that would be rendered doubly potent.

Andy was convinced that the Black Alchemist was a real person and he wanted to meet him face to face, ideally by finding him in the middle of nowhere, up to strange business. The ending of the book had been inconclusive in some respects because he hadn't managed to do it. As far as the writing was concerned, it reached a cut-off point. The real-life story itself continued.

In early August 1988, a number of people known to Andy had a series of disturbing psychic visions. Some of the material had elements in common. They were indicative of something big brewing. Bernard was in the thick of it. What became a complex picture began with a simple, striking image. The Black Alchemist, hooded and robed, stood atop a tumuli-type mound. He was holding two daggers crossed above his head. Later sessions saw the same mound at sunset. He was now encircled by a group of robed figures. In his arms he held a young motionless child, its skin charred black by fire. There were flashes of other locations. Bonfires in woods. Somehow all linked together. A secluded clearing in a wood. A pit about three feet deep and four feet across. A female figure clad in dusky raiment silhouetted by its side. A libation of golden liquid, the hive-stored labour of bees, poured into the pit, propitiating Hecate. From her life-generating womb, a child of fire. *"I, by my power, turning air into water, and water again into blood, and solidifying it into flesh to form a new human creature - a boy - and produce a much nobler work than God."* A spearhead suspended in mid-air, pointed downwards. *"The wanderers are on the move. The wolves cry to the night. Dark forces tear at the threads."* A male voice, *"enhance birth"*. The feeling of *"white fire"*. A series of events underway, set to climax on the mystically potent 8/8/88. A symbolic birth mediated through wolves, white fire and a blackened child. Co-ordinated activity across the south of England. The culmination of the rites to Hecate. The focus: Paradise Mound near Eastbourne.

Andy told me what was going on. He intended to travel down to the mound and see if some hardcore group of occultists really did turn up to do nasties. I was invited along and unhesitatingly accepted. The way the whole thing was appearing we had to contemplate the possibility that the characters we could encounter might not be of a particularly cheerful disposition. It was difficult to tell to what degree the dead baby imagery was symbolic. Also along for the jolly journey was Earthquest regular and Southend musician Mike Oliver. He was a warm-hearted humorous character and his presence helped balance out the grimness.

The Paradise Mound was situated a long way from any roads. A half hour trek began the evening. We were set to meet up with some friends of Andy's. In the meantime we hid ourselves away and spied on the mound. After sunset, in the beginnings of twilight, some movement attracted our attention. A lone middle-aged man was briskly walking by, looking all around him as he did so. It was an incongruous sight. He gave the impression of someone in a hurry to catch the morning train but we were in the middle of nowhere. Maybe he was a scout, making sure the coast was clear. Letting him pass, we cautiously ventured out behind him as he stood at the top of a ridge behind us. Unfortunately, he then turned around and saw us. If he was reporting back to any base camp, our cover was blown.

That night we enjoyed a great luxury, something that showed that magic was moving toward the 21st century. 1988 was part of the ancient epoch prior to the complete takeover of the world by mobile phones. At that time they were mainly a yuppie and drug-dealer accessory. Andy had borrowed a brick-sized one for the night. He'd asked Bernard to regularly tune-in to the situation and let him know if anything important arose. Shortly after the odd episode of the brisk walker, the phone rang. Bernard warned of a lone man, surveying the area to make sure all was clear. Also something about a hound of some kind. Maybe the man was walking a dog. This was fairly startling. It was enough to convince me that some sort of weirdness was definitely afoot.

Whilst Andy was still on the phone, the rest of the crew arrived. Amongst them were two notable figures on the London scene, Caroline Wise and John Merron. It was also reassuring to have on board occultist Dave Rankine. He'd done a lot of work with Hecate and knew her very well. As twilight gave way to darkness the vibe shifted. It always does at dusk and dawn. They're considered to be the times when the veil between the worlds is thinnest. Less than two months before, on the Tor for the solstice, I'd got a quite tangible sense of the vibe of real *magic*. On the Paradise Mound I felt it again. There was nothing expansive and celebratory about it this time. The more sensitive amongst the group felt powerful presences nearby. Some sort of magical battle was about to kick-off. We gathered on the mound in a circle and visualised a spiralling cone of electric blue light around us. More than one person psychically saw a white wolf with red eyes approaching. Dave Rankine saw it in the form of Hecate's familiar, the three-headed hound, Cerberus. He banished it in her name and its variant forms disappeared. Others followed. They were seen to leap towards the circle, only to dissolve as they came into its light. The phone rang again. Bernard knew we were now gathered on the mound in a globe of light and that hostile forces were trying to drive us off. Hearing the full details, he focused his mind still further on the situation. Down in Eastbourne, there was frustration and anger as the plans for the night were thwarted. A room where a robed female figure intoned from a manuscript whilst half a dozen figures sat before her. There was an attempt being made to drive us away. It wasn't going to work. The strange birth of the child of fire would have to be accomplished some other way.

The worst of it was over. We moved out of our circle. There were still many hours until dawn though. Many people saw shadows in the night form into the archetypal robed hooded figure of the Black Alchemist and advance towards them. I know. I was one of them. I'm not exactly a stranger to the distortions of perception that can occur in the early hours of the morning. Being outdoors can enhance them. During the years of my heaviest drug use, I'd been inspired by the poet Rimbaud to try and teach myself to hallucinate as much as possible. I'm aware of what the mind can bring into certain situations. Our heads were full of the Black Alchemist story. Even if the psychic stuff was 'real', by 3am we were probably just mildly hallucinating. Maybe. It's the feeling that went with it. Later that week I saw, or thought I saw, the same figure in a corner of my bedroom. I intoned aloud the classic Essex banishing, "fuck off you wanker", and it dissolved.

As the year progressed I went off on an increasing number of similarly flavoured adventures. We commemorated the first anniversary of the great hurricane in clammy fog at Chanctonbury Ring. On the night of Halloween, I was standing on the Long Man of Wilmington at one am. If it sounds a bit grim that's because it was. It was also very exciting. At the same time, I was rapidly running out of money. The savings I'd made whilst living with my parents were soon eroded. My weight began to fall. I was being paid monthly. By the last week, I tended to be living on rice and potatoes enlivened with curry powder. At the end of October, I weighed two and a half stone less than I had in February. I went down with flu. I had scarcely had a day's illness in years. My job was utter shite. On one level, things seemed a bit bleak. It would be easy to think that it was all an indication that I'd taken a wrong turn. There I was, immersing myself in a climate of decidedly nightside magic, with weight falling off me and poverty and ill health beckoning. That was only part of the story. A far bigger game was afoot and by the year's end the mystery of my life had expanded even further.

HELEN AND THE BEAST

ALONG WITH HIS GLASTONBURY TALES, there was another episode from Andy's past that came to thoroughly fascinate me. It involved that ongoing study of mine, Aleister Crowley. I got to know of a story that formed a powerful prequel to the Green Stone saga, although it was not mentioned in that book. It dated from Andy's time as a UFO researcher. On New Year's Day 1979 there had been many reported sightings of strange lights in the sky across the south of England. A number of people contacted Andy and were sent UFO sighting forms for completion. Amongst the group was a lady named Helen from South London, who contacted him again in the coming months to report more sightings. These had culminated in a 'missing time' episode when she had been drawn to her front door to gaze at a motionless blue light in the sky. Returning indoors, feeling that only a few minutes had elapsed, she discovered that in fact, twenty minutes had passed. This was the kind of thing that greatly interested Andy at the time. He had worked on the first three so-called 'abduction' cases reported in Britain (Aveley being one of them), and Helen's story looked potentially interesting. He arranged to meet her on March 24th. Sure enough, under hypnotic regression from Andy, a standard-issue story of being beamed aboard an alien spaceship and medically examined duly appeared. By 1988 his attitude towards such manifestations had considerably changed but back then it seemed to be exciting new territory.

More interesting by far was what followed next. On the night after the regression she had a complex vivid dream of a past life as a witch, who had been burnt at the stake in the French Pyrenees on the seventh day of the seventh month in 1556, the very day on which she was supposed to become High Priestess of her coven. Andy had featured in all this as her lover and magical associate. Obviously, this was enough to secure a return visit from Andy and more hypnosis. Following this session Helen seemed to become strangely psychic and started picking up bits of witch lore and history. This helped to confirm a pattern that Andy had seen before, suggesting that many people who have UFO experiences may have an unusual general background. The UFO acts as a trigger for a wider spectrum of paranormalia. The Aveley case was a classic example.

Things began to rapidly accelerate and Helen picked up that, to resolve the karma of the past, she and Andy should perform a series of witchcraft-flavoured rituals, primarily on the 7/7 date. There was a lot of detail concerning the magical paraphernalia for the ceremonies. This included an image of a wand with a golden top in the shape of a head, wearing a sort of jester's hat. On being quizzed by Andy, she went on to pick up that it represented the 'triformis Janus head'. It bore the number 666 and had once belonged to 'Perdurabo'. This was a magical name of Crowley's and the wand is quite well known. Andy knew this but it was clear from Helen's bookshelves and general personality, which was of a straightforward Londoner, that she had no idea what any of her material referred to. Andy was told to make a replica of the wand for himself.

The ceremonies were performed and this resulted in a further threshold crossing. Helen now believed herself to be in psychic communication with Crowley. From Andy's point of view this was an unprecedented adventure and, regardless of whether one could say for certain if the whole thing was genuine or not, he was happy enough to go along with it, if only to see what on earth happened next.

The magical core of her visions focused on the spring of 1904 in Egypt. She saw what appeared to be an 'Equinox of the Gods' ceremony that had begun the series of events leading to the reception of *The Book of the Law*. Eventually she seemed to view the actual writing of that text. Crowley was sitting at a desk, wearing a kind of kaftan and baggy trousers. Before him was a quill pen and sheets of paper, some of which already contained writing. Also visible on the desk were books and a paperweight. On his hands were two rings, one of which was a large red ruby. She could hear nothing but could smell unpleasant pipe tobacco. She mentioned another unseen presence in the room. The most striking aspect of this vision was the fact that her vantage point was seemingly from the same place that the voice of Aiwass had been heard.

With the connection to Cairo 1904 thus made, the next level of intensity began. Crowley began to talk to and even physically appear to Helen with increasing frequency. He began to dictate to her a supposed *Inner Book of the Law.* It became apparent that he had big work for Andy and Helen to accomplish. Andy never got to see the writing in progress. The instructions were for them to go to Sicily and perform a ritual at the site of the old Abbey of Thelema that would regenerate the work begun there. Crowley would somehow enter into Andy and he would then receive Helen's channelled text. The date was set for November 1st. Helen even received an unexpected windfall that would pay for the excursion.

All these psychic shenanigans were occurring over the summer of '79, as the cast of characters who played out the Green Stone story were assembling. *Parasearch* had established connections with many psychics across the country. Along with the increasing number of prophecies suggestive of a major task at hand, that would bring together a group of people in the Midlands, there were also warnings. Andy began to tire of the amount of times his strange situation with Helen seemed to be broadcasting across the ethers, and assorted psychics who knew nothing of the facts told him to stay well clear of her.

Gradually the sheer weight of numbers began to impress him. He conceded to a worried Graham Phillips, who had also been trying to persuade him to disconnect from the Crowley scenario, that if one more psychic warning arrived he would back out. This conversation occurred just as they were about to enter a UFO Convention in London. That afternoon Martin Keatman first introduced Andy and Graham to Marion Sunderland. They all talked about her family's experiences. Later in the day Marion approached Andy again, this time in an agitated state. She told him of a powerful psychic vision she had just received concerning a woman of dubious motives near to him and how it was absolutely imperative that he have nothing more to do with her. This incident is briefly alluded to in *The Green Stone* but no mention is made of Crowley and the whole background to it. Andy immediately rang Helen to tell her he was backing out.

The situation seemed to be resolved until Helen contacted Andy again. The time for the projected trip to Sicily was getting nearer. She talked of Crowley instructing her to retrieve documents he had hidden and that these and the *Inner Book of the Law* would be up for grabs if Andy co-operated. It was tempting and he vacillated. Once again Marion came through with precise psychic information. She also told him that if he went along with it all it would not just have a deleterious effect on him but the whole group of people around him. Something that was meant to happen wouldn't be able to. This, finally, was enough to get him to say a definitive 'no'.

Marion invited Andy to visit her and her family the next day, Sunday 23rd September. That evening she spoke again of the feeling that something important was soon to happen, and that Andy needed proof of this. Shortly after midnight, with the children in bed, Andy sat chatting with Marion and husband Fred. The couple were fully in view to him, seated either side of the fireplace.

Suddenly, a tooth was seen to fall out of thin air in front of them, hit the mantelpiece and break in two before landing on the carpet in front of the fireplace. One of the children had recently lost a tooth but the manner of manifestation was completely inexplicable. Andy had a clear view of the Sunderlands throughout. Neither of them had moved at the moment the tooth appeared. It seemed to be some sort of apport, a materialisation phenomenon. It was that bizarre event that convinced Andy that he'd made the right move. The later feeling was that if he had gone out to Sicily the entire Green Stone saga would never have happened.

This was an amazing story but it had elements that were perplexing to me. Crowley was portrayed as a malevolent influence. Andy had read John Symonds' biography and taken its general ambience on board. Even though he confessed that, in some respects, he considered Crowley to be a sort of hero to him, he nonetheless felt that he was basically one of the bad guys. He'd never read some of the material I was familiar with such as Israel Regardie's *The Eye in the Triangle* which gave a positive portrayal. I had the feeling that somehow Andy had connected to a distorted frequency through a number of synergetic factors. His own knowledge of Crowley's life, filtered through the contempt and moral vilification of Symonds, affected the nature of the psychic magickal experiences. Helen picked up on and amplified this via her own temperament. It was a heady cocktail. Against the backdrop of the bigger picture of the developing Meonia story, I had to accept that it was a dangerous energy and could have wrecked something awesome that most definitely needed to happen. The whole cast of characters had been assembled by cosmic-coincidence control-centre with above average care and attention, so why had the test on the threshold taken that specific form? I had been given an enigmatic koan to solve.

One detail in the story provided a clue. During the July ceremony connected with the witch past life Helen had experienced a dark formless energy in the room that felt in some way consciously disruptive. She even collapsed on the floor as a result of its presence. A few days later she identified it with the name *Choronzon.* It was directly afterwards that Crowley first came on the scene.

The strange name is in fact famously associated with the Beast through one of the most important episodes in his life. He walked across the Algerian desert with his disciple and lover, the mystical poet Victor Neuberg in 1909, experiencing apocalyptic visions worthy of *Revelation* and performed a ritual to confront Choronzon.

John Dee wrote briefly of a *Coronzon*, describing it as *"that mighty devil"*. It appeared to occupy a role similar to the serpent in the Eden story, at least as far as the church portrayed it, a force that exploited the lower wilfulness of humanity. Crowley adopted a variant spelling which due to the fame of his association has carried through. He categorised Choronzon as *'Dweller in the Abyss'*. He has also become known as the Demon of Dispersion, associated with fear, insanity, lies, malice, and restriction. This force, says Crowley in his *Confessions, "is not really an individual"*. The Abyss is filled with false forms, egoic distortions, and *"each such chance aggregation asserts itself to be an individual and shrieks, 'I am I!'"*. This is in contradistinction to the True Will informed by Knowledge and Conversation of the Holy Guardian Angel. In purely Jungian terms it was a major encounter with the Shadow side of the psyche. Crowley believed that the process was successful. A number of critics have doubted this and wondered if he did irreparable damage to himself. Neuberg undoubtedly was traumatised for the rest of his life by what occurred.

The basic idea is that on the threshold of any great achievement in personal and magical development forces arise, virtually as a law of nature, taking on forms appropriate to the circumstance that embody whatever may be capable of preventing its full success. A distortion onto a side route or outright failure may be a result. At the centre of the process may be a figure that carries an archetypal charge of danger and fear to be confronted and understood. This seems to be what happened in 1979 and the Dweller on the Threshold theme would later return in different forms. Each scenario will require a unique response. Sometimes proceeding through fear would be correct. In this case it does seem Andy made the right move in backing down. A bigger picture would eventually reveal itself.

In October '88, Andy prepared a small booklet entitled *Helen and the Beast* and gave a lecture on the subject at the annual Thelemic Conference in Oxford. The whole story was obviously vibed up by this amount of attention. It would be a few months before we realised just how much was being set in motion.

* * *

AGGRAVATED CRYPTOMNESIA

IN DECEMBER, after putting up my Christmas decorations, I smoked a few spliffs. It had been the most drug-free year since I'd first indulged over a decade before. I started to read *The Black Arts* by Richard Cavendish, a book that featured the Qabalah. For the whole of the eighties I'd been sporadically reading books that featured this massive topic. The Qabalah was the centre of gravity of the Crowley and Golden Dawn systems of magic. Dion Fortune had written a major book about it. The most well known manifestation of the Qabalah is a diagram known as the Tree of Life. It contains three pillars with a grouping of ten spheres around them. Twenty two paths link the spheres. They are associated with the letters of the Hebrew alphabet. There's a whole filing cabinet of symbolism surrounding every aspect of the tree. For some reason, I simply hadn't been able to retain information about it. I couldn't even remember the names of all of the ten spheres. The Qabalah featured in Questing work. If I was going to progress further with it and my Crowley/Golden Dawn studies, I had to comfortably internalise the basic data.

One Saturday night, after a smoke, I noticed the reflection of a Christmas tree light shimmering on the surface of one of the Glastonbury post-cards on the wall that formed part of the arrangement I'd recreated from my home in 1985. It was a picture of the Tor covered in snow. I stared at it, strangely transfixed. The light started to take on the form of a naked young woman like Botticelli's Venus. I'm a bit short sighted and wear glasses to watch TV. I put them on and the clarity of the vision actually increased. A few feet away from the picture was another of the same size, showing the Tor in spring, with Chalice Hill in the foreground, covered in flowers. I felt that would be a more appropriate backdrop for Venus so I swopped the images over. Sitting back down, I immediately registered a change of atmosphere. There was a feeling of intensity in the air. I remembered something of what I'd recently been reading about the Qabalah. Amongst the many layers of symbolism pertinent to each sphere, there are groups of magical mythological archetypal images. Wasn't the vision of Venus amidst the greenery of spring quite appropriate to the sphere of Netzah? I checked Cavendish. Yes. It was indeed a most excellent Netzah image. Good. I was starting to retain that sort of data.

I changed my focus to take in the general arrangement of all of the 1985 pictures on the wall in front of me. Some Qabalists think of the tree of life in terms of nine spheres. The usual final tenth, Malkuth, represents the world as we experience it, the consensus, built of four elements. The next sphere up the tree, Yesod, begins the journey into other realms. It is the 'foundation'. Without any preamble, I simply noted that, if I took my actual living room as Malkuth and my fireplace as Yesod, my pictures were arranged pretty much in three columns that fitted the Tree of Life structure, including the Daath sephiroth that is sometimes omitted. The Netzah image was in exactly the right place. I idly wondered if any of the other pictures were in any way appropriate to their apparent place in the Qabalistic arrangement. At the top of the right column, in the position of the sphere named Chokmah, was an image of the head and shoulders of Joseph of Arimathea, holding his staff. It was the one that came from a window in the church of St. John the Baptist in Glastonbury High Street. Looking at the necessary references, I was startled to discover that the image of a bearded man holding a staff was actually one of the magical images associated with Chokmah. That was odd. Beneath Chokmah lies Chesed. A wise male ruler on a throne is the usual visual there. I had a Tibetan Buddhist poster there. It did feature a seated wisdom deity. Not a bad fit. The Yesod fireplace had a photo of my mother upon it. There are mother goddesses linked to Yesod but I wasn't making too much of it. Then I turned to the image at the centre, in the sphere of Tiphereth. It was William Blake's *Glad Day: the Dance of Albion,* a naked man of perfect proportions, surrounded by a blaze of golden light. This was a definitive Tiphereth image! It would probably be difficult to find a better one. I was now totally freaked-out. What the hell was going on? Some part of me automatically continued the process. The Daath image was the biggest of them all. It was a poster of the solstice sunrise behind the shadowy shape of the Tor. Looking through various sources, I noted the symbol of a watchtower on a mountain. Hmm. Above it was the only other non-Glastonbury image. It was a Druid ceremony at Stonehenge. This would be Kether, the crown. I guess the circle of stones were a bit crown like but again, I wasn't going to make too much of that. What I already had was more than enough.

* * *

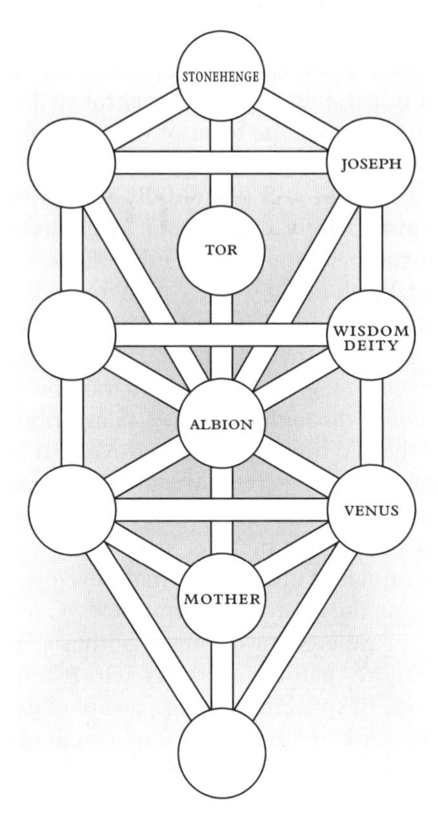

I took stock of the situation. Including Daath, there are eleven spheres of the Tree of Life. I had taken one of them to be the actual room itself and another to be represented by the fireplace/ hearth as the 'Foundation' of Yesod. That left nine images arranged in three columns. Of those nine, four were extremely appropriate to the relevant spheres and two had imagery that was at least suggestive and by no means irrelevant. I'd had to swap over two of the 1985 images to switch the whole thing on but once it was revealed it seemed very much a structure that was already there. There wasn't the remotest chance that the whole thing was entirely accidental. Back in 1985, stoned amidst a pile of piccies in my old home, some part of me was acting under guidance. My bodily vehicle was a bit wobbly but enough of the inspiration could be expressed.

There's a word that describes this kind of thing. It's 'cryptomnesia'. It refers to when something has been read and then consciously forgotten but lingers to resurface in a way not necessarily recognised. I had read bits and pieces on the Qabalah for nearly a decade but didn't think I'd internalised it at all. Quite clearly I had. It was a case of cryptomnesia but to me, a bit of an aggravated one.

I had a word to describe the form of the phenomenon but it was not an evaluative term. My experience could not be reduced to *just* cryptomnesia. It was still profoundly mysterious to me. How did it work? I immediately came to an overwhelming emotional apprehension of the personal significance of the event. Some part of me knew the Qabalah in 1985 better than my conscious personality did in 1988. That knowledge wasn't simply stored in some filing cabinet of data either. It had been used in a creative application. Not only that, it was magical material. It was the Qabalah and its expression had come through images of Glastonbury. I'd got them on the same day that I'd bought *Earthquest News.* It had all come out of that mysterious 1985 matrix. I already felt something uncanny about the events of that time. Now I discovered there was more to it. It was all part of a bigger picture.

My Streiber stimulated intimations had developed quite extraordinarily throughout the year to this moment. Catching up on the whole of 1988, I formulated a working hypothesis. There was a part of me that knew more than my everyday self. It functioned beyond normal perceptions of spacetime. It was aware of great moments of destiny in my life years in advance of 'me' catching up on them. In effect, it was the real 'I' that was living my life, or it was at least considerably closer to whatever such a mystery could be truly said to be at that stage of the game.

With the picture pattern revealed, I proceeded to enhance it by placing more appropriate images in the less successful areas. A postcard of the vesica piscis cover of the Chalice Well went up in Binah. It was another one of the postcards I'd bought in June '85. Blake's *Ancient of Days,* God measuring out the creation, went into Kether. More changes were soon made until there was a goddess statue on the fireplace and the entire tree was represented.

Andy had made a kind of personal tradition of going down to Glastonbury on New Year's Eve, to be on the Tor at midnight. He decided that he was up for it again in '88 and invited me to join him. Also on board was Chesca Potter. I felt that it was a remarkably symmetrical end to the year. Chesca's painting of Dion Fortune on the cover of *Priestess* had been the door opener to my recommencement of the Avalonian quest and my meeting with Andy. To walk with them past Dion Fortune's old home, now occupied by Geoffrey Ashe, on the way to an ascent of the Tor and the entrance to a new year, was like a waking dream, it was such a condensed symbolic representation of everything that 1988 had been for me. After all that had happened, I couldn't think of anywhere better to be. It was yet another magnificent Glastonbury transitional moment. Although it didn't compare to the solstice epic in terms of numbers, the vibe was very good. From within the tower, I gazed out of the door across the lights of Glastonbury town, seeming like sparkling candles in a far off otherworld. I felt sure the coming year would inevitably be even more extraordinary. We now knew that another Meonia sword had been discovered. It was in Tintagel, in an Arthurian hall of some kind. Details were a bit sketchy but the associations of the location made an interesting story very likely.

PERDURABO ENDURES BEYOND THE END

"Alas the Master; so he sinks in death.
But whoso knows the mystery of man
Sees life and death as curves of the same plan."
Aleister Crowley.

BARELY HAD 1989 BEGUN when an amazing story set my head on fire. It had begun the previous autumn when Earth Mysteries researchers Paul Devereux, his wife Charla, John Merron, and Sue Boyd-Lees had bought a house in Brecon to serve as a base to run courses and organise excursions. A cruise journey to Egypt was arranged to check out some of the prime locations. A number of unusual and interesting people soon booked up. Marion and Gaynor Sunderland were going. It was decided to take the Green Stone along. Caroline Wise was also involved.

Shortly before departure, the Devereuxs were presented with a strange discovery. Near to their new home was a house where the *Ley Hunter* magazine was published. During renovations, its owner had found a long discarded shoebox in the attic. He felt that the contents might be of interest to them, although he didn't really know what they were. Caroline Wise certainly knew. It contained the original material for Aleister Crowley's funeral service, known as the Last Ritual, previously believed to be lost. There were uncorrected proofs, with corrections by Lady Frieda Harris in pencil, not set in type. There was copperplate artwork by her as well. It was a remarkable discovery in any circumstances. Being on the verge of a trip to Egypt, scene of Crowley's greatest revelation, rendered it all the more unusual.

Caroline felt it would be good to acknowledge the magical strangeness of the situation. Part of the tour itinerary included a dawn meditation at the Great Pyramid. She suggested reading some of the funeral rite aloud there. The Giza plateau is a supreme necropolis. It would be on November 1st, a time in the western magical calendar very much considered to be a feast of the dead. Her plan was accepted. The journey began.

In Egypt, during the underworld hours prior to the November 1st dawn, Caroline dreamt of Anubis. In the form of a human body with a jackal head, he lay on a slab in a black chamber. He sat up, seeming as if ready to speak. Before any words could be heard, an alarm clock broke the dream. A later check revealed that her partner of the time, back in England, had exactly the same dream that night.

The group assembled under the gaze of armed guards. Special permission had been obtained to be present on the Giza plateau. It was one of those periodic times when the place is off-limits to tourists for various reasons. About thirty people sat down in a horseshoe shape directly in front of the Great Pyramid. They tried to best cultivate a meditational space by closing their eyes and relaxing.

Paul Devereux began to read from the last rite, from Crowley's *Hymn to Pan.*

> *"Thrill with lissome lust of the light,*
> *O man! My man!*
> *Come careering out of the night*
> *Of Pan! Io Pan!"*

Caroline felt the urge to open her eyes. Her attention was immediately drawn to the striking sight of a group of jackals that appeared around the lower levels of the stepped edifice. They scampered around and then one picked its way up a little further, until taking up a sitting position right in the centre of the triangular facade. This was more than a bit odd. Something then made her look upwards at the apex of the pyramid. A figure was sitting there. It was Aleister Crowley. He was wearing a turban and a red and white striped pyjama number, similar to an outfit he was famously photographed in.

He sat with arms folded out in front of him, slowly rocking from side to side. Despite the great height and distance he was clearly visible, and therefore somehow of giant proportions. Caroline later described the apparition as *"inhabiting space in a strange way"*. The vision was not just a brief flash. It seemed to last for a few minutes at least. The experience was strangely neutral. One part of Caroline's mind calmly registered that she was seeing Aleister Crowley sitting atop the Great Pyramid but there were no feelings of surprise, curiosity, amazement, fear, or exhilaration.

John Merron had seen the jackals as well. As the reading commenced, he saw two of them climbing the pyramid to also take up a central position, as if guardians of a portal. He likewise found his attention moving upwards to see Crowley in the same Arabic clothing. To John though, he was standing and strangely gesticulating, as if engaged in some mysterious ceremonial summoning. Both Caroline and John briefly looked away and then Crowley was gone. The Devereuxs had seen something of the figure as well and readily identified it as Crowley. One group member who had chosen to stand apart from the meditation saw a flash of blue white light behind one of the other pyramids at the time of the reading. The rest of those seated on the ground had not felt the urge to open their eyes and missed the astounding manifestation.

A few months previously I'd pondered the saga of Helen and the Beast. Crowley had a role in the Green Stone story. It had seemed to be a negative one. I didn't totally believe that. Almost a decade after those events he had manifested again, in the immediate proximity of the stone, and there had been nothing malevolent about him. Nobody cross-referenced dates at the time but I later found what I took to be significant correlations. The funeral material had been discovered on October 15th. Andy wasn't aware of this, but he spent the following week going over old events in detail, as he prepared his booklet prior to delivering his lecture on October 22nd. The group left for Egypt on the 24th. Crowley appeared on November 1st. This was the same date that Andy had been instructed to be at the Abbey of Thelema in 1979. I was sure that Andy's renewed interest in the Helen story was not separate from something that was building up and had also expressed itself in Cairo. Something told me I was being drawn into all this for a good reason. I trusted the process completely. It would be nine years later, in the 93rd year of the Thelemic epoch, at Glastonbury, before I finally understood.

SEVEN

AT THE START OF 1989, two more Meonia swords were discovered. It happened in the Midlands and involved people who knew Graham Phillips and his associates. In the summer of 1988 Charles Topham and Angela Reeve were on holiday near Caernarvon. In the coming days they drove around the Snowdon area and the car broke down on two separate occasions in the village of Beddgelert. The place attracted both Charles and Angela. They felt it would be a nice place to spend Christmas. When they later arrived at a holiday flat, there was a strong feeling to do some sort of psychic work there. A makeshift Ouija board seemed to facilitate contact with a Druid from the nearby hillfort of Dinas Emrys. This location was associated with the infamous Vortigern, who according to the standard mythos best told by Geoffrey of Monmouth, was a king of some kind who, in the chaotic aftermath of the Roman legions' departure, made the catastrophic mistake of inviting Saxon mercenaries into Britain. He had a reputation for treacherous duplicity and weakness. It is also associated with Merlin through the famous tale of his outwitting of the Druids who had tried to sacrifice him in order to prevent the repeated collapse of the fort's tower. He psychically saw the real cause as two dragons fighting beneath the ground. The Druid told Charles and Angela that they would find a sword beneath a rock. This was not such a wild prophecy as might at first appear. Many swords from the time of Vortigern have been found in the area. None revealed themselves though.

A few weeks later, after returning to the Midlands, Angela found a flat in an old farm building near Coventry. It sat beneath a huge outcrop of sandstone. The moment they moved in it was obvious that a vibe was building up. During the first week, Charles woke to see a tall figure in the bedroom, shining with an iridescent electric-blue glow. He was not exactly prone to such experiences. Rune readings suggested imminent important events. A few days later Charles had an overwhelming urge to visit a boot fair in a pub car park in Coventry. They were regular features there that the couple had visited before but given up on due to their persistent dismal contents. It was not a huge affair. Ten cars or so. Charles was pulled over to a table set up by a small van. On it were two Meonia swords. The stallholder said they were Victorian and came from a house clearance. He wanted six pounds for the pair. He had a deal! They recalled the words of the Druid contact. Now that they were living under a rock, a sword had certainly come to them, come to them both in fact.

When Charles Topham was still a teenager he had got involved with an esoteric group. At that time he was indiscriminately into Atlantis, flying saucers, the whole caboodle. A couple of elderly members of the group seemed to take him under their wing. It turned out they had known Dion Fortune and been involved in her work. There were photos of a car excursion, perhaps as far back as the late twenties, featuring Charles's new friends and Dion Fortune herself. It's an interesting lineage connection.

Andy responded quickly to the news. He arranged for the couple to meet with the Paddons at a convenient motorway services. The four swords would come together. My first appearance in Andy's later book, *The Seventh Sword,* was at that event. It was fairly bizarre to be handling the swords and hearing paranormal tales amongst teeming multitudes of normals. This brought the total of Meonia swords up to six. A very strong feeling hung in the air that another one would complete a set that could enable some mysterious purpose to fulfil itself. The pace was quickening. The game was afoot.

1989 developed into an above-average year of drama and strangeness on the domestic and world stage. Psychic questing adventures often seemed all the more memorable set against such a backdrop. The same day that the four swords were brought together for the first time happened to coincide with Salman Rushdie discovering that he had major problems following the publication of his *Satanic Verses.* There was always a sense that there was something a bit apocalyptic about the seven swords quest. As it hotted-up, global events seemed to justify that. We were part of a bigger picture.

It was also interesting, as we headed off on some of the black questing escapades that would later feature in *The Second Coming,* that we would encounter at M25 service stations huge groups of young people in search of that night's Rave. A youthquake every bit as potent as 1967 and 1977 was in motion and a lot of consciousness was being altered. It all made for a feeling of excitement, imminent change, and big possibilities. This was a great zeitgeist for magical activity.

As the year went on, a group of regulars began turning up for all of Andy's events and becoming part of Earthquest. Already in place was Alex Langstone, who had known Andy for a number of years and been part of the earlier Earthquest group. He was a clubbing

New Romantic Gothic mutant in the early eighties and developed interests in Wicca, Dion Fortune and Celtic Christianity. John Horrigan and his wife Kerry had appeared at the start of 1989. John was a unique individual; an arm wrestling, rock climbing, shooting and fishing, all-purpose action-man ex-paratrooper and Freemason, to name just a few of his talents. He drank in one of the hardest pubs in Southend. It wasn't long before he became an indispensable member of the group and began to show remarkable psychic abilities.

Kerry brought along her sister Lisa Mundy as well. They were both above-average psychics. Their childhood had been a bit unusual, in as much as the family home in a council flat in London could have been renamed Amityville. A catalogue of weirdness became normal. The foot of a bed levitated. A typewriter's keys worked independently of any human agency (unfortunately there was no paper in it). There had been a spooky occasion when their father had been knocked over by an invisible force. He had spoken of his own childhood experiences of a poltergeist that had moved furniture into impossible positions. My own favourite of the spooky tales concerned the girls' bedroom wallpaper. It displayed pictures of circus clowns. Sometimes it emanated unpleasant odours. Both sisters had recurring "am I dreaming or not?" experiences where a clown procession left the wallpaper to march around the room in a macabre manner. Grandmother told of seeing faeries when a child. Lisa and Kerry spoke of further joint memories that couldn't be differentiated from a dream, when nan had spoken of matters UFOlogical to them and something had been seen in the sky through a window, something they later recalled as having somehow 'landed'. Lisa's partner Karl Dawkins also later joined us. He was another hard-man with a surprising psychic sensitivity. As this unusual collection of people assembled, none of us could remotely imagine what we were letting ourselves in for.

* * *

BRITISH MUSIC

"Something eternal - universal - the very breath of freedom lives in this land. It stretches out, embracing the whole of humanity. It still speaks to us through the hills and the valleys, the rocks and caves mentioned in the Arthurian legends. The winds and the waves sing of it, the atmosphere is full of it. It is necessary to find contact with this invisible Power which, in only one of its forms, appears as the Arthur of the legend. This Power in reality is the Eternal Spirit of this country – Could we but realize this, a cultural element would be born again, English in its innermost depths. It speaks to all human beings wherever they live and to whatever nation they belong."

Walter Johannes Stein. *Is King Arthur a Historical Character?*

HAVING WRITTEN, PUBLISHED, AND PUBLICISED *The Black Alchemist*, Andrew Collins was looking towards his next project. He intended to write a full account of his Glastonbury Zodiac experiences. Preparation would include a return trip around some of the sites during the summer solstice period. It seemed likely that this would stimulate typical questing adventures. To me, this was perfection. I recognised great opportunities and the clear and obvious sense of being totally in the right place at the right time. This was exactly the kind of sign I had anticipated, following the Glastonbury Qabalah event, to indicate that a new level of the game had appeared. Andy's original zodiac quest had climaxed in June '85 at the exact same time that those Avalonian images configured together in my head. This was the next turn of the spiral.

With the example of '85 to inspire me, I reasoned that if my head were stuffed to bursting point with every level of Arthurian and Glastonbury studies, I would be better primed for whatever may follow. Initial preparation required the cultivation of an ongoing mood, an ambiance, a constant background evocation. I knew from previous experience that a relentless combination of history, art, literature, poetry, music, magic, and mysticism, could bring me levels of pleasure that were erotic in their sensual whole-body intensity. In this state of openness, Magnetic Centre became alchemically active. Synchronicities increased. Appropriate information and experience would come towards me. I was pacing myself to reach a level of maximum intensity during the summer solstice period when the possibility of a whole new level of Glastonbury adventures beckoned.

Barely had I formulated this intention when perfect means for creating that special mood became known to me. An old friend of mine turned me on to the music of Ralph Vaughan Williams. I soon came to feel that his *Lark Ascending* and *Fantasia on a Theme by Thomas Tallis* are definitive evocations of the British landscape. Williams composed these pieces just before the First World War. To me, they carry an incredible nostalgia for a vanished world and lost generation, but they also speak of some more archaic mystical quality of supreme sublime beauty that remains an ever-present force emanating from the very earth of our sacred sceptred isle.

In 1989 my acid intake had ceased. I hadn't made a conscious decision to stop taking it, but in accordance with the mysterious inner laws of some super-conscious process, my use of it had stopped although I was still occasionally smoking. Back at my flat I added a few spliffs to the Vaughan Williams experience and found that it was a mighty fine combination.

Encouraged by my unexpected pleasure in this material, I searched in Southend library for anything similar. I soon found the *English Suite* of Hubert Parry, who had been a teacher of Vaughan Williams and is mainly remembered for setting Blake's *Jerusalem* to music. I was amazed by how much I liked it. There were friends of mine who would have preferred to listen to some German morphine addicts screaming their brains out and bashing bits of metal together in some warehouse in Berlin. I taped the *English Suite* and initially played it every day for weeks. Before long, I was grooving on the great British musical revival of the late 19th and early 20th centuries and firmly believing that the sudden appearance of vast amounts of what was clearly appropriate input affirmed my purpose.

I eventually came to discover a whole crew of interesting characters whose sounds stimulated my reveries. A number of the composers were mystically inclined with interests in Celtic and Arthurian mythology, faery lore, and so on. These guys were not of the status of Beethoven and Wagner but they are unfairly neglected. Elgar, Bax, Bantock, Butterworth, Delius, Finzi, and Ireland, all helped to back up Vaughan Williams very nicely, creating a constant soundscape. And then, there was Rutland Boughton.

Long before the great gatherings at Worthy Farm, Glastonbury had once been famous for its festivals. There had been an era of music and costume pageants there. Dion Fortune had spoken nostalgically of it in *Avalon of the Heart,* with the sense of it being already departed. Onetime occupier of the Chalice Well gardens, Alice Buckton, had staged and filmed a large-scale event in 1922 that included a parade of characters in historical costumes marching down the High Street accompanied by assorted town worthies and local soldiers based in Glastonbury's Drill Hall. Powys caught something of the flavour of the period, albeit in his own distinctly daemonic way, featuring a huge Christian/Arthurian Passion Play staged by the Tor in his novel.

Rutland Boughton dreamed of establishing an English venue for musical festivals to set alongside the great Wagnerian events at Bayreuth. He was a composer of operatic dramas and an advocate of community artistic projects. Circumstances combined to bring him to Glastonbury with an Arthurian musical drama he sought to stage. Promised money and resources didn't manifest. An ambitious plan to build a huge theatre had to be abandoned. He was left to do the best he could with the Glastonbury Assembly Rooms, a comparatively small venue.

The results were remarkable. Working with a mix of cultivated local talent and professionals, Boughton created a sequence of successful festivals over a period of years between 1914 and 1926. There wasn't enough space for an orchestra in the Assembly Rooms. Most of the music accompanying a series of operas was played on piano. A string quartet was as extravagant as it got. By all accounts a skilful combination of well-managed vocals with dance, lighting, and scenery, nonetheless proved to be excellently effective.

Although the festivals heavily featured Boughton's own compositions, there were many performances of other British works including historical pieces from Tudor times. Lectures were also given. The scale of the events expanded to make use of other venues and short tours. Notable personalities such as Vaughan Williams chilled in the Assembly Rooms. George Bernard Shaw was a great supporter of Boughton. Elgar made approving noises from a distance.

Various factors were always working against the enterprise though. The initial festival opened the day after the First World War began. This immediately put limitations on the scale of its future potential. Boughton was also a committed communist whose private life offended the still prevalent Victorian Christian mentality. Firstly, he dared to live with someone he wasn't married to, and later entered a relationship with a student over twenty years his junior who he went on to marry.

Boughton was blessed with one gigantic success. He had made

an opera from a story by 'Fiona Macleod', *The Immortal Hour,* a tale of Celtic Irish faery lore. It had been performed with the usual low budget resources in Glastonbury. Dion Fortune remembered her viewing of it as, "*a unique privilege*", "*a thing never to be forgotten*". The work was given a chance on the London stage with a full orchestra. It became the most successful British opera ever. A virtual cult grew up around it as some devotees returned for repeated viewings.

Eventually Boughton's political correctness seems to have stifled his creative faculties. It is generally considered that his work gradually declined. He died in 1960, all but forgotten, as the new epoch dawned in Glastonbury. The received opinion seemed to be that his aspirations for establishing Glastonbury as a rival to Bayreuth weren't matched by his talents. He just wasn't good enough. Gradually a Boughton revival got underway. In the eighties the first full recording of *Immortal Hour* was released, along with some orchestral works. A symphony was broadcast by the BBC. Recordings were released in 1989. Critics and public alike realised the material actually sounded rather good.

I felt that Boughton was expressing something of the Avalon of the Heart, which in turn was part of a larger something that could be called 'British music', to expand a term from the supreme psycho-geographical seer and magus of modern English literature, Peter Ackroyd. I believed that I was connecting to an indigenous landscape songline. Literature, poetry, and architecture, were part of that 'music'. Its 'musicians' were not necessarily patriots in the general limited sense of the term. Nonetheless Blake, for example, and Boughton, both voices of dissent in many ways, expressed something distinctly British.

I noticed that Vaughan Williams and John Cowper Powys were both born in 1872 and lived to truly ripe old age, producing stunning work well into their seventies. As people they were considerably different. In his *Autobiography,* Powys gives little space to music. To me though, both men expressed something poignant and powerful that was quintessentially of the land and its history. I soon came to feel that I had to re-read *A Glastonbury Romance* in its thousand-page-plus entirety. If I didn't do it I would be letting myself down. Once again I was awe-struck by Powys' titanic genius. *A Glastonbury Romance* and the music of Vaughan Williams became inseparable in my consciousness. Powys had said that, "*the symbolism of the Grail represents a lapping up of one perfect drop of noon-day happiness as Nietzsche in his poignant words would say, or as Nature herself, according to the hint given us by Goethe, whispers to us in more voices than at present we are able to hear, or to understand when we do hear*". A particular Avalon of the Heart reverie of mine became my personal expression of that idea: a May morning on the Tor, the unique Somerset mystical misty blueness of the sky around the horizon's rim providing a perfect backdrop for ascending larksong. Blossom and blooming abound as the landscape rolls away like surging strings, a hymn of ancestral voices, ever young and hopeful.

My classical music mentor then introduced me to the awesome glories of Renaissance sacred choral music. One piece immediately established itself as the ultimate soundtrack for my Glastonbury Abbey dreams. It was *Spem in Alium* by Thomas Tallis (who had provided Vaughan Williams with such magnificent inspiration), a composition for forty voices. Tallis was writing during the aftermath of the dissolution of the monasteries and his work seems full of a poignant nostalgia for a lost paradise. I had cultivated the feeling that an eternal form of Glastonbury Abbey exists on some other realm of perception. There, the monks of the Company of Avalon continue their daily services. A celestial choir perpetually intones sacred prayers amidst this magnificent scene, as Grail light shines through the stained glass windows, infusing the place with supernal blessings. *Spem in Alium* completely caught the vibe of how I felt such a choir would sound. It was like the chanting of angels. I knew that the liturgical recitations of the medieval monks would not have sounded the same. It didn't matter. Tallis took me into a realm of unbearable beauty. I went through a phase of listening to an album featuring *Spem* last thing each night, whilst doing forty-five minutes of yoga breathing. I could still hear the celestial voices when I woke up the next morning.

The feeling of a primordial past somehow still living through the very land itself and the ongoing mythos it generates became ever stronger for me. The land has a consciousness of some kind. A voice that can be heard. A feeling that can be communicated. At certain places and times, on hills at dawn and sunset, by wells, streams and rivers, in moonlit woods, amongst poignant ruins and remains, it lingers on, surprisingly potent, waiting to inspire in diverse circumstances; poets, soldiers, musicians, mystics, militants, all ages and genders across the whole social spectrum.

I had fully invoked the necessary ambiance. A number of powerful ideas were coming together. I was feeling that, at least in some poetic sense, Glastonbury, the Avalon of the Heart, is a perpetual choir helping to compose and to play 'British music', an expression of some vast mystical landscape mystery. All of our great artists, from the designers of Stonehenge and Glastonbury Abbey through to Powys and Vaughan Williams are part of Albion's greater perpetual choir. Its supreme symphony, in which untold multitudes have participated in innumerable ways in every epoch from the megalithic to the present is the mythos of Arthur and the Grail.

ARTHUR AND THE GRAIL MYSTERIES

IT WAS MOVING FOR ME TO REALISE how long I'd been interested in Arthur. When I was still in infant school, my mother read me bedtime stories by Enid Blyton. This was undoubtedly a formative time of destiny. I could have been introduced to any one of a number of works by the prolific author. I was spared *Don't be Silly Mr Twiddle!*, *The Adventures of Mr Pink Whistle,* and the decidedly dodgy, *The Three Golliwogs.* My mother's choice was *Tales of Brave Adventure,* stories of King Arthur and Robin Hood. From the moment of my first hearing the opening words of the chapter *The Enchanted Sword, 'There once lived a King called Uther Pendragon'*, I was hooked. The intensity of my interest ebbed and flowed over the years but always remained. My early visits to Glastonbury festival re-stimulated the appetite.

1981 had been a crucial year in my Arthurian education. John Cowper Powys and Geoffrey Ashe both impacted powerfully upon me at an extraordinary time of my life. In that year also, the magnificent movie *Excalibur* had appeared, and repeated viewings of it had increasingly stirred my archetypal imagination. Its richly realised scenes were like living oil paintings, passionately enlivened by the rousing music of Wagner and Orff. A mythologically literate script linked the vivid tableaux together. The background to the film was an interesting one. Director John Boorman had read *Glastonbury Romance* in the fifties and was inspired by the desire to make some kind of movie based upon it. He had come to Glastonbury and sat atop the Tor as far back as 1961, full of this idea. He kept the hope alive throughout the time that he made his name in the movie business with such masterpieces as *Deliverance.* Eventually it became clear that it simply wasn't going to happen. The impetus was channelled into *Excalibur,* where the quirky depiction of Merlin was influenced by Powys' portrayal in his last great novel, *Porius.*

I'm not going to cover all of the history and theories on the Grail Romances here but there are some strands relevant to the Glastonbury adventures that follow. Rudolf Steiner stated that, "*Fundamentally speaking, the phrase the 'Holy Grail', with all that it entails, means the reappearance of the essence of the eastern mysteries.*" Mystery cults were a vital part of religious life throughout the ancient world. They included both public ceremonials and more selective initiations focused on seasonal dramas of death and resurrection featuring gods and goddesses. Deities such as Sumero-Babylonian Tammuz and the Phoenician-Greek Adonis are examples of beings intimately linked with the seasonal drama, veritable vegetation deities, infused with the spirit of life. Adonis was wounded in the thigh by a wild boar and died. He was loved by Aphrodite who arranged for him to spend only half of the year in the underworld. These cults sometimes featured feasts where special mixing-bowl cups known as kraters carried sacramental liquids now considered to have been probably psycho-active. G. R. S. Mead and Jung both mentioned the possibility of links between the classical krater and the Grail. Steiner talked about the 'Arthurian Mysteries', an initiatory current of esoteric knowledge that served as a conduit for astrological gnosis from the days of Egypt and Babylon into the Christian era with Arthur as a sun king.

J. G. Frazer's epochal epic *The Golden Bough* had collected together vast amounts of data from the world's religious history and folklore pertinent to these themes. He came to feel that much of it demonstrated a fundamental belief that the king and the land are one. The vegetation deity lives within him, so the monarch's vitality is linked to the fertility of the earth. When he is healthy the crops thrive, when he declines, the land does with him. As a result, he may have to be ritually killed by a healthy successor.

Something about all this reminded Arthurian scholar Jessie Weston of the recurring theme of the wasteland in the Grail tales. The figure of the Fisher King, who appears in many of the stories, seems to be a Frazerian monarch in decline. He has a mysterious wounding through the thighs, often taken as a euphemism for impotence. His whole kingdom suffers with him. In *From Ritual to Romance,* published in 1920, she argued that Romance literature derived from myth, and because Frazer believed that myth derived from ritual, the Grail tales could likewise have such a foundation.

Jessie Weston, using Frazer as her inspiration, whilst not ignoring the Celtic sources, also sought additional roots far more widely, coming to the inspiring hypothesis that there may have been a direct continuity linking ancient fertility rites with the Grail Romances. Something of the classical mystery cults lingered. The Christian connection could have been cultivated by Gnostic groups during the early centuries AD before they were suppressed. Jesus could be seen as the ultimate dying and resurrected mystery cult deity. There may well be greater links between early Christianity and the old cults than the later churches were willing to admit. Some kind of sect may have lingered and the Grail procession and artefacts seen by the knight Perceval in the medieval stories could be a glimpse of their workings.

Weston's theories don't have much credibility amongst Arthurian scholars today but their cultural impact has been significant. T. S. Eliot's *The Wasteland* was one of the most important poems of the 20th century. Its structure was shaped by *From Ritual to Romance*. My own favourite movie, *Apocalypse Now*, has many levels of narrative. Hints of its depths come when Colonel Kurtz's book collection is shown to contain Weston. He himself is a Fisher King figure in the midst of a wasteland, and knows it. The 'King and the land are one' theme was also used to great effect in *Excalibur*.

The mystery cult motif is also discernable in Hermeticism, the most contentious of all the possible influences on the Grail Romances. What is Hermeticism? In the early centuries AD, Alexandria surpassed Rome as a multi-cultural centre. People from all over the empire and beyond gathered there. Its gigantic library was legendary. Indian 'Gymnosophists' and Persian Magi met with Jewish Mystics, Greek philosophers, Egyptian magicians and Gnostic Christians in a climate of cross-fertilisation and tolerance. Works from the ancient cult centres of Babylon and Assyria were available for inspection. Extraordinary mixtures resulted. Much of the foundations of the whole western magical tradition were laid there. Beliefs that later resurfaced during the Renaissance and in the Golden Dawn can be traced back to the fabulous matrix of Alexander's city.

The Egyptian god Thoth and the Greek Hermes became identified with each other. They were both associated with communication between the human and divine realms, and with writing and magic. The figure of Hermes Trismegistus, the thrice-great, emerged from this. He came to be seen as someone who had lived as a human being but been divinely inspired to reveal mysteries to the human race. In some versions, he attains immortality. A number of authors wrote works in his name, which are collectively known as the

Corpus Hermeticum, on mystical, magical, and philosophical themes, often featuring Egyptian deities. They tend to emphasise the harmony and inter-relationship between all of creation. The mysterious art and science of alchemy also developed from the same mix of influences.

Between the triumph of Christianity, with its subsequent library, book, and heretic burning, and a 15th century Renaissance revival, there's a period of about a thousand years where the whole thing seems at first glance to have disappeared. The usual story tells how, after the fall of Constantinople to the Ottoman Turks in 1453, scholars from the old Byzantine Empire brought previously unavailable books to the west. Part of this process enabled Marsilio Ficino to translate Hermetic works for Cosimo de Medici. This material had a massive influence on the Renaissance. A case can be made for Hermeticism being *the* major impetus behind it. The art of Botticelli, for example, seems to be suffused with its inspiration. Is it at all feasible that any such material may have influenced the Grail literature? Moslem Spain could have been a source. Many scholars from there made connections with the Christian world.

The most famous of all the Grail Romances, Wolfram von Eschenbach's *Parzival* was probably written between 1200-1210. The story does seem to contain influences from entirely different sources than the other works of the time that lend themselves readily to esoteric interpretations. Wolfram boasted that, regardless of other versions, he had the correct story. He got it from Kyot, a Troubadour from Provence, who had found the tale written in Arabic by Flegetanis, a Jewish astrologer of some kind in Toledo who "*saw with his own eyes in the constellations things he was shy to talk about, hidden mysteries. He said there was a thing called the Grail, whose name he had read in the constellations*". "*A host left it on earth and then flew away up over the stars.*" There are two basic positions concerning Kyot. He is either a fictional device or a real historical individual functioning in the midst of heresy.

In Wolfram's version the Grail is not a chalice or platter, but a green stone fallen from heaven during the Luciferic rebellion and once guarded by the angels who had been neutral in that conflict. By the power of this *lapsit exillis*, the phoenix is burnt to ashes and then reborn from them. Health and youth can be bestowed upon humans who see it. On one day of the year, Good Friday, the dove of the holy spirit comes to rest upon it and the stone is able to provide, "*the best food and drink in the world*".

'Lapsit exillis' may be the most debated words in the whole Arthurian corpus. Perhaps it means 'stone from heaven'. Maybe it doesn't really mean anything in itself but refers to something else that looks very similar. The usual candidate is *Lapis Elixir*, the Philosopher's Stone of alchemy. Given the nature and properties of Wolfram's Grail, this seems a reasonable theory.

One of the works within the *Corpus Hermeticum* is called the *Krater*, sometimes translated as simply, *The Cup*. The text takes the form of a discourse given by Hermes to his pupil Tat who interjects with questions.

> *"Tell me then, father, why did God not impart intellect to all men? – It was his will, my son, that intellect should be placed in the midst as a prize that human souls may win. – And where did he place it? – He filled a great Krater with intellect, and sent it down to earth; and he appointed a herald, and bade him make proclamation to the hearts of men 'Dip yourself in this Krater, you who are able; you who believe that you will ascend to him who sent this Krater down.' – Now they who gave heed to the proclamation and were baptised in intellect, those men got a share of gnosis."*

By intellect is meant not simply the human faculty of rational thinking but the Greek word *Nous*, the very Mind of God. The Krater symbolises the Monad, the ultimate oneness of the divine from which flows an endless outpouring in which a conscious baptism may be possible. Michael Psellus commented on the Hermetic *Krater* text clearly equating Nous with the Holy Spirit of Christianity. The wafer bearing dove of Wolfram could easily be seen an image of Nous.

The most fruitful speculation on Wolfram may perhaps be found in *The Krater and the Grail: Hermetic Sources of the Parzival* by Henry and Renee Kahanne. For the Kahannes, "*Hermetism's krater then, is the same as Wolfram's gral: the symbol around which a select ethico-religious brotherhood gathers*". They even put forward a complex etymological argument that derives the very word Grail from the classical Krater. The obvious problem is that Wolfram's Grail is usually thought of as a stone. The theory is advanced that the *stein* of Wolfram is initially used in a context that echoes a section in the Hermetic *Krater* where, after a glimpse of God, the sight attracts the soul toward the divine like a magnetic lodestone. The *Parzival* stone is a metaphor for the Grail and says nothing of its true form. Parzival receives teachings about religion of which he had been ignorant from a magus-like character called Trevrizent. The Kahannes believe his name derives from Hermes' epithet 'thrice greatest'.

Wolfram portrays a Grail procession and feast. Twenty five ladies appear in a sequential set of groupings that the Kahannes ingeniously interpret as representative of a Hermetic cosmology that shows the journey of the soul towards the divine. The first four women are the four elements. They are followed by eight celestial spheres, twelve signs of the zodiac, and finally, the Grail bearer, the Monad, the ultimate One. Each group also carries a number of lights that "*may well represent the constituents of the soul in its various phases on the way back to God*". In the first instance, the four physical elements are balanced by spiritual elements of soul and intellect so four ladies, two lights. It works it way up through a Gnostic Qabalistic-style schemata until all is unified in the one light.

I am entirely aware that the Kahanne's work, along with Steiner and Weston, is extremely contentious and that literary and historical scholars of the Grail Romances do not endorse their theories. My assessment of the validity of ideas includes what could be considered as their usefulness. Where can I get to with them? How can they help me? The possibility of mystery cults and Hermetica influencing what could be called Grail culture would come to open up some extraordinary vistas for me when immersing myself in what came to be revealed of the bigger picture around Andy's questing work.

My 1989 Arthurian input would ultimately provide the foundations of what became my first book, *Mysterium Artorius.* A lot of history as well as mythology is portrayed there. I looked into the Dark Age Arthur and the roots of the stories that came to be associated with him. Primarily I came to be in awe of the incredible period of a century or so from around 1130 to 1230, a timescale crucial to the evolution of Glastonbury and the way it is perceived today, when, in the background of the emergence of the Plantagenet dynasty, the marriage of Henry II and Eleanor of Aquitaine and the reigns of their two sons Richard and John, can be found the crusades, the rise of the Templars, the building of the Gothic cathedrals, the developing cult of the Virgin Mary, and the full-blown appearance of the phenomenon of Arthur and the Grail as the modern mythology of Glastonbury was shaped by the alleged discovery of his grave and the first appearance of the Joseph of Arimathea mythos. All of this served to create a poetic mystical mindset conducive to appreciation of the Glastonbury Zodiac mystery. I would carry my critical faculties into the adventure but I would not let them get in the way of any expansive experience that worked on other parts of my brain.

YE FOUNDATIONS AND YE DISTANCES

ONE OF THE MOST IMPORTANT AND MYSTERIOUS figures of Glastonbury's entire history looms very large during this time. Henry I had asked a nephew of his named Henry of Blois to become abbot of the abbey, which he did in 1126 whilst still in his twenties. He came from an area in France notable for an early influence on the Gothic cathedral culture and the rise of the Templars. Henry was considered to be an academic prodigy. The learning and philosophy behind the new style of architecture would have been part of the general mindset he brought to his new appointment at Glastonbury. He was also a man with a taste for classical statues and high living.

With the special permission of the pope, Henry also uniquely took on the simultaneous role of Bishop of Winchester, then the main royal city in England. He soon got down to serious business, initiating huge building programs, both ecclesiastical, at Glastonbury and Winchester, and secular, with a host of castles around the country. Glastonbury was soon transformed from a chaotic mess into the richest abbey in England. Many new buildings, including a bell tower, were constructed. The old church remained intact at that time and would surely have been given much attention by the new arrival.

Henry was patron of William of Malmesbury. His historical work on Glastonbury Abbey, *De Antiquitate Glastonie Ecclesie,* appeared in 1129, within three years of Henry arriving, the same year he became Bishop of Winchester, within one year of the Templars becoming an official Holy Order, and before the appearance of Geoffrey of Monmouth. It's most famous passage strongly suggested the presence of some esoteric mystery within the Old Church. "*One can observe there upon the paving, in the forms of triangles and squares, stones carefully interlaced and sealed with lead. If I believe that some sacred mystery is concealed under them, I do no harm to religion.*" The powerful royally connected abbot would surely have had some kind of control over what William published, so it seems likely he was happy to let an idea circulate that's served as what Robert

Bauval would call a 'Hermetic device', still drawing people into its mystery almost a millennia later. It featured in the psychic communications from Bligh Bond's Company of Avalon monks. A variety of clairvoyants, some of whom were not even in the country and knew nothing of Glastonbury lore, received some suggestive fragments hinting that,

> *"Our Abbey was a message in ye stones. In ye foundations and ye distances be a mystery." "All ye measures were marked plaine on ye slabbes in Mary's Chapell and ye have destroyed them". "In the designing of the Floor lies the future prophecy of Glastonbury, together with the inward secrets of Christianity."*

Bernard of Clairvaux, a major mover and shaker on the continental Gothic cathedral and Templar scene, referred to Henry as rival pope, old wizard of Winchester, and even whore of Winchester. It is possible that he and others were already keeping an eye on events in Glastonbury before the Arthur's grave event brought it European fame. Bernard's pointed remarks about Henry may indicate the rivalries of different groups vying for influence.

When the old church, with its esoteric floor-plan, was destroyed by fire in 1184, the new Mary Chapel was constructed, deliberately reproducing its original geometrical dimensions, which in turn appear to have served as the matrix for all subsequent extensions. The time of its rebuilding broadly coincides with the reconstruction of Chartres Cathedral, also following a disastrous fire, from 1194 to 1220. Few would now doubt that Chartres could be considered to be a book in stone. The official guide books accept the use of gematria in the proportions of the architecture, whereby the length between two features may embody through associations between numbers and letters some Biblical passage further expressed in statuary, and so on. The New Jerusalem of *Revelation* was a consistent inspiration for the decorative imagery of numerous ecclesiastical buildings of the Middle Ages. Considering that its geometry is so much a part of the biblical narrative, is it really likely that the cathedral builders, schooled in the seven liberal arts of which geometry was such an important element, would not have considered somehow utilising the design in their work? What are the chances that not the slightest nuance of such concerns was present in the newly emerging form of Glastonbury Abbey? The heavenly city is depicted within a cube. Bligh Bond believed that just such a cube formed the basis for a major cosmological geometrical Qabalistic gnosis expressed in the abbey architecture.

The romantic might perhaps be willing to entertain the idea that the spirit of the great cathedrals revived during the 19th century in accordance with some mysterious greater timing and began to communicate to those with the temperament to understand. The French novelist Victor Hugo had expressed something of this in relation to Notre Dame. In *A New Model of the Universe* Ouspensky wrote of a visit to Paris in 1914 when he had felt that, "*the real history of humanity, the history worth speaking of, is the history of the people who built Notre Dame*". He believed that, "*The building of cathedrals was part of a colossal and cleverly devised plan which permitted the existence of entirely free philosophical and psychological schools in the rude, absurd, cruel, superstitious, bigoted, and scholastic Middle Ages. – the Church was made an instrument for the preservation and propagation of the ideas of true Christianity, that is, of true religion or true knowledge which were absolutely foreign to it'.*

This intimation was further elaborated in 1926 with the publication of *Le Mystere des Cathedrals* by an author known only as Fulcanelli, an enigmatic figure whose true identity rapidly took on the form of a legend the modern form of which portrays him as a semi-immortal alchemist who occasionally manifests in spectacular circumstances. Regardless of such mythology, the book was obviously an arcane classic of the highest order.

Fulcanelli claimed that the cathedral of Notre Dame was a vastly complex book in stone. The statuary and its placement within the architectural scheme represent a Hermetic alchemical Qabalistic philosophy, an illuminated Gnostic inner Christianity. There had been hints of such ideas before but Fulcanelli's work definitively established such an ambiance around the Gothic cathedrals. Chartres has become the main focus for such ideas in modern times. Fulcanelli's alchemical interpretation stated that the first substance, the *prima materia* from which the universe was created, "*the very essence of things*", is one and the same with *mater*. The cathedrals dedicated to the Virgin are alchemical temples demonstrating God's creation of life, "*the transformations of the original substance*" for, "*in the Ave Regina, the Virgin is properly called root (salve radix) to show that she is the principle and beginning of all things. 'Hail, root by which the Light has shone on the world.'*"

The Bligh Bond work can be seen as part of a bigger picture that Ouspensky and Fulcanelli also helped express. Thanks to a triumph of barbarism over civilisation we don't have decorative carvings and statuary at Glastonbury to lend themselves to Fulcanelliesque interpretations and that is a lamentable loss but, thanks to Bligh Bond, Glastonbury Abbey can now stand alongside Notre Dame and Chartres as an eternal beacon of Esoteric Christianity.

PERLESVAUS: PORTAL TO THE TEMPLE OF THE STARS?

WE HAVE SEEN HOW SOME THEORIES have linked the Grail with an alleged ancient wisdom tradition of which Glastonbury may once have been an outpost. The Tor maze supposedly shows a physical sign on the landscape of a millennia old link to Central Asia. There are hints that some Grail literature was the work of initiates who were expounding ideas from beyond the Christian Celtic Anglo French cultural matrix. One major mystery of Glastonbury and the Grail remains to be examined. It may be a key to the greatest Glastonbury treasure of all or simply the most deluded of all Avalonian dreams.

Chretien de Troyes and Wolfram von Eschenbach wrote the most important of the early Grail Romances. Another work from the same period is of vital significance to the Glastonbury Zodiac mystery. *Perlesvaus,* often known as the *High History of the Holy Grail,* was written in an old form of French by an unknown author. It's stated that, "*the Latin from whence this History was drawn into Romance, was taken in the Isle of Avalon, in a holy house of religion that standeth at the head of the Moors Adventurous, there where King Arthur and Queen Guenevere lie*". This is an obvious reference to Glastonbury Abbey and is usually taken to infer that it must have been written following the grave scenario. A landmark quite likely to be the Tor is described in the story, suggesting that the author had some local knowledge. Perceval is portrayed as a descendant of Joseph of Arimathea. The man and the Grail are featured in the text, but never linked specifically to Glastonbury.

Most critics generally believe that *Perlesvaus* was written in the decade 1200 - 1210. Whoever did write it, and wherever they were based, they were familiar with Welsh Celtic mythological material. *Perlesvaus* is permeated by it, perhaps more extensively than any other Grail Romance, particularly featuring that most disturbing of motifs, the severed head. Despite that, it's also more militantly crusadingly Christian than the other works of the time. Resistors of the New Law of Christ are brutally killed.

There are a number of significant elements in the story that are unique. The 'Grail' changes form. It is clearly stated that it has five aspects, each manifesting amidst the usual light and fragrance. These are: 1) A crowned king crucified. 2) A child. 3) A man wearing a crown of thorns, bleeding from the forehead, palms, feet and side. 4) The fourth form is unspecified. 5) A chalice.

The Fisher King actually dies, a detail at odds with most versions of the Grail story where his healing is of paramount importance. The tales usually feature a scene where Perceval sees the Grail in its castle but then fails to ask a simple question that would have secured the prize and healed the King. In *Perlesvaus* he puts right an earlier failure at the Grail castle but not by asking the right question. He takes it by force of arms. Arthur and Guenevere have a son named Lohot. Their union is usually portrayed as childless. Lohot is murdered, and in another unique development, Guenevere subsequently dies of grief.

Alongside Perceval, Gawain and Lancelot feature as major characters of the quest. Arthur is also involved and can be seen as making up a fourfold grouping of heroes but his adventures are proportionately less than the other three who move through a recurring landscape of castles, chapels, forests, and meadows, meeting a bewildering sequence of maidens, hermits, knights, kings, deceitful dwarves and the occasional demonic giant.

There are a number of bizarre and grotesque set-pieces. When Perceval defeats the Lord of the Fens, who had stolen his mother's land, he has eleven of the Lord's men beheaded and their blood drained into a vat which their leader is then lowered head first into and left to drown. At one point, two artificial men created by sorcery who wield giant hammers beat out the brains of nearly fifteen hundred people. In an ongoing vigorous round of combat, jousting with lances and swordplay on foot is portrayed in grim detail as armour is ripped and rendered, limbs and heads are hacked off, and horses collide and crash to the ground. Maidens, innocent and otherwise, are whipped, beaten, and killed as blood flows and piteous lamentations fill the air. The kind of person who likes to count how many times goats appear in the Bible and things like that might be gainfully employed totting up the numbers of severed heads featured. Here and there, an obliging hermit interpolates an interpretation for the benefit of the puzzled protagonists of the strange events they are experiencing. The explanations seem odd and unconvincing, usually hinging on the Old Law of the Jews and the New Law of Christ. The great Arthurian scholar Roger Sherman Loomis has stated, "*the author seems at times deranged*", demonstrating "*savage vindictiveness*" and "*a taste for the gruesome*". Norma Lorre Goodrich went even further, referring to him as "*a psychopath like the filthy Marquis de Sade*".

A modern reader might also note that, although there are some fascinating snippets about the Grail, its five changes and so on, it doesn't really seem to be that important to the story. A lot of other themes appear to be far more predominant.

One maverick critic has given considerable time and ingenuity to the enigma of *Perlesvaus.* Hank Harrison is probably best known as the father of rock and movie star Courtney Love. Father and daughter have had a bit of a tempestuous relationship to say the least. She accused him of feeding her LSD as a small child when he was manager of the Grateful Dead. He propounded the controversial theory that her famous husband Kurt Cobain died not through suicide but murder. Far more interesting to me is Harrison's decades-long interest in the Grail and all matters pertaining thereto. He studied at the Warburg Institute with the legendary Frances Yates.

Harrison has produced a number of essays which centre on *Perlesvaus,* the mystery of its authorship and the nature of its meaning. Their content is contentious and provocative, unlikely to convince academics. Although I am far from comfortable with a lot of his details, I get the feeling of that *something* that does lead into the true temple of the mysteries being conveyed.

One statement by him is worth remembering whilst entering into the material he has assembled. "*The Grail is not an object, but rather an initiation, a ceremony, which transforms the supplicant from simple soul to brilliant mind.*"

The early Romance authors used what is generally considered to be a kind of literary convention, claiming to refer to source material of some kind, a mysterious lost book of the Grail. With the story of Arthur's grave being so famous, it may be that Glastonbury was invoked in the way Wolfram talked of Spain. They could be stylistic devices to gain credibility. There might be no truth in the assertions at all. Harrison contends that such a work really existed and was in fact the *Perlesvaus.* He goes further still by claiming that it was written by Henry of Blois who in turn was making use of an even earlier text.

Harrison portrays *Perlesvaus* as a multi-levelled initiatory document, as esoterically loaded as Wolfram's *Parzival.* It contains material that reaches back through Celtic Druid times to the megalithic era. It also includes connections with the earliest years of Christianity and its links with the Qumran community, the generators of the Dead Sea Scrolls. Something of this was present in the background behind the rise of the Templars and the Gothic cathedral epoch. Harrison postulates the existence of some sort of cult of which Blois was connected that was behind the first crusade and had deliberately set out to recover obscure relics and knowledge of the early days of Christianity. There are strands of mystery cult Hermeticism as well.

The story of *Perlesvaus* really gets going with some adventures of Gawain, who Harrison sees as *"a young Templar initiate on a pilgrimage through prehistory and that he represents the hopes of more than one alternative religious faction"*. His character embodies some very archaic strata. His best-known role in the story of the encounter with the Green Knight connects back to the kind of shamanism of the hunt seen painted on cave walls. "*I see, in Gawain, Lancelot and Perceval, different faces of the old tricephalic god (Hermes Trismegistus). The trefoil spiral at Newgrange, date 3100BC represents the same idea.*" In the Grail castle, the usual procession appears and a feast begins. Gawain has three sightings of the Grail. The first occurs when two damsels appear with the cup and a lance, which is allowed to bleed into it. "*Gawain gazes at the Grail and it seems to him that there is a chalice within it, albeit there was none at the time.*" The next time he, "*seemed to behold in the midst of the Grail the form of a child*". In the final appearance, Gawain sees the crucified Christ, pierced by a spear. These transformations may echo the qualities of Celtic regenerative cauldrons. Despite having begun his quest in full knowledge of Perceval's earlier failure and being repeatedly prompted by his fellow diners, Gawain is so awe-struck by these visions that he neglects to ask the right questions. The Fisher King is absent from the hall during the feast. Angels rather than squires bear the candelabra. The Grail hovers in the air at one point. There are twelve knights present, who are all over a hundred years old, although they don't look it.

Harrison believes that the Fisher King has been deliberately portrayed in *Perlesvaus* with features suggestive of both the Templar and Cathar initiates. "*The Fisher King is Hermes guarding the Krater Hermetis, the God of light guarding the inner chamber, the priest of*

Eleusis guarding the womb of the Great Goddess." Ultimately, "*the Fisher King is the final composite of the tricephalic hero fulfilled, aged and seeking an heir*". "*Perhaps part of the Grail vision is the realisation that one must eventually take over the job of the Fisher King. This is a great responsibility, without question identical to the Masonic tradition wherein the master of the temple retires and selects a successor.*"

After Gawain's failure, the quest is taken up by Lancelot and finally, Perceval. The Grail Castle actually gets captured by the bad guys but Perceval single-handedly sorts out this little problem barely half way through the story. Before he does so, there is an enigmatic brief moment when his presence is sufficient to ensure the long prophesied opening of a tomb that turns out to contain his ancestor Joseph of Arimathea. Not a lot is made of this potentially momentous event. With the Grail castle secure, a second narrative dynamic leads up to a finale where Perceval finally takes on a major villain, the Black Hermit, who is in fact none other than Lucifer, the Lord of Hell. It has been suggested that the action deliberately models the *Book of Revelation*. The overcoming of the Black Hermit seems very brief and underplayed for the dramatic climax of the book. Perceval unhorses and wounds him. He is not actually killed. His followers seize him, uncover a huge pit and fling him in. This happens to Satan in *Revelation*.

Is it feasible that Henry of Blois could have written this text? A lot of the general ambiance suggests the time after his death when Jerusalem had been lost to Saladin. It was perceived as a calamitous event indicative of the Last Days of *Revelation* having arrived and provoked an intense crusading zeal exemplified by Richard the Lion Heart. The cultural spiritual mood of the time was considerably different from when the holy city was in the possession of the crusaders a few decades earlier. The feeling in *Perlesvaus,* with its intense violent advocacy of the New Law of Christ, seems to reflect this.

What we know of Henry suggests a man of some considerable culture and refinement. He did strongly involve himself in politics but is the repeated brutal graphic violence of *Perlesvaus* really his style? I don't feel it is. If Henry was responsible in some way for the majority of the text, another additional later level of material would need to have been interpolated. Harrison's *Perlesvaus* speculations may seem outlandish but he was not the first to find strange inspiration from it.

* * *

THE MALTWOOD ENCHANTMENT

"Knowest though not Asclepius that our land is the image of heaven, the representation on Earth of every celestial ordinance? Our land is the temple of the world."
Corpus Hermeticum. *Asclepius.*

KATHERINE EMMA SAPSWORTH was born on April 17th 1878 at Woodford Green, Essex. Her father, who seems to have been a typical staid Victorian type, had served as the local mayor. Her mother painted and was generally into literature and the arts. Sister Mary Elizabeth became a professional landscape artist. Brother Arnold became a collector of art, philanthropist and traveller, exploring the River Amazon. Katherine was fortunate to attend a school founded by one Charles Barlow Ingham. He was dedicated to women's emancipation and gave the girls the chance to develop their intellectual and creative potential. The curriculum included world history and mythology, poetry, literature, art and architecture, music, painting, and woodcarving.

In 1896 she entered the Slade School of Fine Art, studying sculpture. In 1901 she married a childhood friend, Oxford graduate John Maltwood. He became a wealthy businessman, gaining the unique distinction of inventing the *Oxo* cube. This enabled him to support his wife's interests. The earliest major influence on Katherine was the Arts and Crafts movement. This mid-19th century idea held that industrial civilisation was destroying human values. Its main prophets were William Morris and John Ruskin. Both men idealised the Middle Ages and championed a Gothic revival and the concept of the dignity of the working man. One of Ruskin's great sayings was "*industry without Art is brutality*". There was a sense of art and craftsmanship as a redemptive force in society. Beauty was considered to be as necessary to survival as food and shelter. It was ideas such as these that inspired the inception of the Pre-Raphaelites. Their espousal of Arthurian themes was part of an overall cultural preparation that primed Katherine Maltwood for a coming moment of destiny.

Her first major sculptural work, *Magna Mater,* was exhibited by the Royal Academy in 1911. Commissioned by an American Arts and Crafts guru named Elbert Hubbard, who was a supporter of feminism, liberal divorce laws, yoga, health food and mysticism, it depicts a central female Blakean figure bound and held in place as a mass of humanity struggles around her. An accompanying carved text states, "*great travail is created for every man from the day he goes out of his mother's womb till the day he returns to the Mother of all things*". The work seemed to be a statement supportive of the women's movement of the time. Hubbard's wife Alice wrote to Maltwood saying, "*I have paid the tribute of tears to your Magna Mater. She is our shrine. She is part of us.*" Between 1911-30 her sculptural works were regularly exhibited at the London Salon, Royal Academy and other London galleries.

During the period of the First World War, Katherine had begun to frequent the bookshop of John M. Watkins in London. It was a major source of eastern and Theosophical literature. Watkins had met Blavatsky and liked to speak of her. She was never an active member of the Theosophical Society, but subscribed to their journals and had articles published therein.

A period of extensive travelling began. India was visited in 1917. A Nile cruise in 1919 saw her photographed sitting on the knees of a statue of Rameses II at Luxor. Her interest in Egypt became an abiding one. She later produced an alabaster group named *Infinity*, also entitled *Isis, Horus and Osiris.* Japanese Buddhist sites were investigated in 1920. When John retired from business in 1921, they embarked on a world tour that took in Greece, Italy, Egypt, North Africa, Palestine, Arabia, India, Ceylon, Malaysia, Bali, Sumatra, Java, China, Korea, Japan and Canada. Artwork was acquired that formed the beginning of the Maltwood Collection. Further such travels filled the decade.

Katherine became increasingly involved with eastern philosophy. This was part of the immense cultural legacy of Blavatsky, who had inspired many artists to look beyond Europe. There was a Buddhist lodge within the British Theosophical Society that became independent in 1926. Its founder, Christmas Humphreys, was a friend of Maltwood. Both admired the work of D. T. Suzuki, the pioneering advocate of Zen in the west. He later stayed with Katherine on several occasions when visiting England.

The Arts and Crafts inspiration was mutating into the ideal of the sculptor as '*idol maker*', the potential revealer of spiritual truths, guide to those on the mystic path. In 1927 Katherine put on an exhibition in her London studio. She tried to set the place up as a temple and her works as shrines of some kind. Gold curtains divided different sections of the room. Music was playing, provided by an organ and a string quartet.

In the same year, Maltwood was the thinly disguised heroine of a novel entitled *The House of Fulfilment* by an old friend of hers, the pseudonymous Lily Adams Beck. Set in British Imperial India amidst a stifling social scene, some of the characters recognise the unique spiritual possibilities of their locations and follow an inner calling. Brynhild Ingmar the sculptor lives in a state of yogic Buddhist perfection, exhibiting Francis of Assisi-like affinity with animals. She initiates a male into mystical mysteries and they journey to Tibet, searching for manuscripts of the ancient wisdom. Katherine's real sculptures are featured and expounded upon. They are treated as works of the utmost significance. The pace is lyrical and sedate, a kind of Dion Fortune novel set in Tibet, until the climax where Ingmar gets captured by bandits. When she resists some of their less gentlemanly advances with judo one wonders what this reflects of the true Maltwood. It seems that a heroic North West Frontier Raj-style rescue will be necessary but mysterious yogic powers win the day. It's a measure of her stature and charisma that those closest to her felt such veneration towards her. After her death in 1961, her husband John simply said, *"she was a Goddess"*.

It is against this overall backdrop that the work for which Katherine Maltwood has become most well known must be seen. After the First World War, the Maltwoods had bought a home at Chilton Priory, near the village of Chilton Polden in Somerset, within sight of Glastonbury Tor. It served as a base for their global travels, gradually becoming increasingly significant. Built in the 19th century in the style of the prevalent Gothic Revival, with castellated walls and a tower, it looks like some kind of ecclesiastical building but it's not. The place was full of genuine medieval relics acquired by its creator, the antiquarian and collector, William Stradling. There were bits and pieces from old churches in the vicinity, including floor tiles from Glastonbury Abbey.

Madame Blavatsky believed that in immemorial antiquity initiates of the primordial wisdom tradition had gone walkabout with some kind of zodiac package. A passage in *The Secret Doctrine* referring to a centre that one of these groups had established in the Gobi desert was later quoted by Katherine Maltwood in her own *Enchantments of Britain*. *"As above so below. Sidereal phenomena, and the behaviour of the celestial bodies in the heavens were taken as a model, and the plan was carried out below on earth. In the same manner and on the plan of the Zodiac in the upper Ocean or the heavens, a certain realm on Earth, an inland sea was consecrated and called 'the Abyss of*

Learning'; twelve centres on it in the shape of twelve small islands representing the zodiacal signs - two of which remained for ages the 'mystery signs' and were the abodes of twelve Hierophants and masters of wisdom. This 'Sea of Knowledge' or learning remained for ages there."

The timescale and exact details of the important subsequent events are unclear but what we do know is that extraordinary inspirations came to Katherine in her study room in the tower. Gazing through enchanted scrying-glass windows out around the far-reaching panoramic view of the Somerset landscape, the inner vision of the mystic artist responded to subtle inspirations. Can we imagine the priory as a peaceful spring sunset silence settles across the landscape? A light shines from the windows of Katherine's tower, attracting our vision towards it. As we draw nearer, the room becomes visible. A woman sits with her back to us, reading at a desk. Coming closer we can see that the book rests over a large map spread out on the table underneath it. We can approach and look over her shoulder. Just what is it that has so thoroughly focused her attention? She's putting the book to one side and is staring intently at what is now revealed as a detailed map of the Glastonbury landscape. Taking up a pen, she begins to draw a shape formed by a river, roads, and field boundaries. A lion. She stops, sits back and stares at what she's done. Outside in the twilight, a soft breeze suddenly stirs. A few faint stars are becoming visible. The atmosphere has changed. Right out across the land beyond the priory, back in the direction of Glastonbury, something seems to ripple. Rising upwards, looking down and around, we can somehow discern shapes of light, stretched out in a vast circle. Some of them seem familiar. Are they signs of the zodiac?

In 1925 Maltwood approached the publisher Dent with a map she had produced seemingly inspired by *Perlesvaus*. Quite how the inspiration came remains unclear. It would soon develop considerably further. There was an episode where a group of damsels await a knight who could clear a pass of a lion, "*so fell and horrible that never was none seen more cruel*". It kept getting killed but still returned. The lion has heraldic associations. It was the epoch of King Richard the 'lion heart' who supposedly introduced the beast to our coat of arms. It appears in a number of Arthurian tales. There's nothing obviously unusual about its appearance at first glance.

The lion was somewhere in the back of her mind as she scanned maps of the area. Something about a particular configuration of varying features attracted her attention. It seemed as if a vast leonine form, three miles long, was emerging from the landscape. Somerton, once the Saxon royal capital of Wessex, lies between its paws. The place seems to have lingering solar associations appropriate to a lion connection. There is indeed a Red Lion pub in the town. In a wooden roof within St. Michael's church, medieval balls have been found from a time long pre-dating the formation of the Football Association. The roots of the national game are suggestive of archaic rites where the ball represented the sun. An ancient road named Somerton Lane delineates the lion's back. Copley Wood covers the top of his head, serving as the mane. The ribs and front part of its hind leg are outlined by the River Cary, the nose, mane, and tail by streams that run into it. Raised earthworks shape the jaw. A red-earthed footpath supposedly shows its tongue. Lion claws have been excavated from Romano British graves near Charlton Adam, which lies at the rear of the figure. This bizarre combination of elements was enough to convince Katherine Maltwood that the huge lion was really there and that the author of *Perlesvaus* knew of it in some way. The four main hero figures, Arthur, Gawain, Lancelot and Perceval may represent the four seasons of the sun. Their adventures could occur over a very specific landscape. Recalling the presence of other strange creatures in the narrative, she went back to it with fresh eyes. She later recalled the moment in *The Enchantments of Britain*. *"Obviously, if the lion was a nature effigy then the dragon, griffin and the giants etc., must be likewise; perhaps this was the most thrilling moment of my discovery."*

Guided by the same kind of combination of topographical features that had revealed the lion, and some advice from a Theosophical astrologer friend, Katherine Maltwood went on to find a sequence of similar landscape figures that apparently represent a complete zodiac with a circumference of about thirty miles. Included were the usual ram, fishes, and a scorpion for example. The apparent symmetry of the design seems impressive. Firstly, we have zodiacal images in correct sequence pivoting around a central point. The heads of all but one image face west. Winter signs are placed in the north, four of which are partly drawn by the River Brue, summer signs lie in the south, four drawn with the aid of the River Cary. Eight of the effigies are similar in size, approximately 6,000 yards in breadth. There are three human figures in the group, Sagittarius, Virgo, and Gemini, which are taken to represent a father mother and child trinity and form an equilateral triangle. If laying a planisphere of the same scale as the landscape zodiacal circle down upon a map, the stars of the various constellations do tend to lie within the bounds of the alleged effigies. This enables one to say that a particular star has a definite corresponding location on the ground. This is the Hermetic 'As above, so below' par excellence. Primarily the configuration has come together through some extraordinary process in nature that has been recognised and then enhanced through human agency.

Maltwood concluded that this Glastonbury zodiac was the true round table of Arthur. The king himself was part of it, as the mounted archer of Sagittarius. Here was his original titanic form, asleep in Avalon. It was the Arthur figure that helped Maltwood to determine when the mighty work was constructed and by whom. Sagittarius has been variously linked with ancient deities whose names seem similar to Arthur: ie Assyrian Assur, Persian Ahura, and Phoenician Melkarth. Glastonbury's Sagittarian archer seems to have a bearded face and pointed cap suggesting a middle-eastern look. Maltwood states that he is aiming directly at the star Aldebaran, in Taurus. The Mesopotamian rivers Tigris and Euphrates rise at the spring equinox. Today the sun enters Aries at that time. When, due to precession of the equinoxes, it had been in Taurus, Aldebaran was synchronised with the rivers as Sirius once was with the Nile inundation. It began the Babylonian New Year festivities that were regulated by Marduk. Katherine Maltwood came to believe that it was during this period, around 2,700 BC, that the landscape zodiac was constructed by wandering initiates of some Middle Eastern mystery cult. The Bull's Eye arrow alignment is perhaps a tad adrift and indicates Maltwood working to prove an idea she favoured.

One considerable difference between the Glastonbury design and conventional zodiacs served as further evidence to Maltwood of its Babylonian provenance. The Aquarian effigy is supposedly in the shape of a phoenix. This figure looms all the more prominently due to its linking with Glastonbury's most notable landmark, the Tor, which forms most of its head. The bird holds the Chalice Well in its beak! Maltwood mentions the tale of the Chaldean bird Zu who forced entry into the chamber of destiny and seized the tablets of fate. Zu was taken to represent Aquarius.

The most notable of all design differences comes with the absence of any depiction of Cancer. In its place is a ship representative of the nearby constellation of Argo Navis. This vessel is of considerable significance to the general design and the mysteries it embodies. It corresponds to the Grail Romance Ship of Solomon. Details of the vessel and its narrative importance vary in the romances. It features briefly in *Perlesvaus.* There's more detail in the *Quest Del Saint Graal* though. Sailing in the Glastonbury landscape version is the divine child of Gemini. The masts of the vessel converge at the Zodiac's central point.

Perhaps the most convincing of all the effigies is not actually part of the zodiacal twelve. There is supposedly a guardian dog of the sacred round table. Its nose is at Burrow Mump, a kind of mini-Tor that some have speculated may be artificial, also with a ruined Michael church on its summit, that forms part of John Michell's famous ley. The nearest town of any size is Langport. An old Somerset song tells how

> *"The Girt Dog of Langport has burnt his long tail*
> *And this is the night we go singing Wassail."*

'Girt' means large. An impressive number of evocative place names cluster around the area where Maltwood saw the effigy. His tail is at Wagg! There are two Head Droves near his head, Earlake Moor by his ear, *Cur*ry Rivel on a front paw. Even if a huge effigy doesn't exist, these are strong indications of some kind of dog tradition in the vicinity.

Maltwood believed that the author of *Perlesvaus* was a Templar and was convinced of their presence and influence in early medieval Glastonbury. In accordance with general occult lore, she accepted that their mysteries influenced the Rosicrucians. Both groups were considered to be part of the infinitely older mysteries of Freemasonry, of which Maltwood had a long-term interest. She believed that the Craft had ancient roots in Middle Eastern cultures and included some knowledge of the stellar gnosis she was uncovering around Glastonbury. The Gemini figure had an arm raised at an angle suggestive of a Mason's square. Their lost word was analogous to the Grail. She was initiated into a female lodge during the period of her Glastonbury research.

In *A Guide to Glastonbury's Temple of the Stars* published in 1935, and *The Enchantments of Britain,* published in 1944 after a move from Britain to Canada, Katherine Maltwood put forward her ideas on the Glastonbury Zodiac and its connection with *Perlesvaus.* A set of aerial photos were also taken for a now rare companion volume. Like Alfred Watkins *Old Straight Track*, academics scarcely registered Maltwood's works. British magicians of the time don't seem to have been particularly aware of her either.

Temple of the Stars did find prestigious support amongst the most elitist of the contemporary European occult cognoscenti. In his short essay, *The Land of the Sun*, Rene Guenon suggested that some of the divergences from the usual zodiacal designs were actually a point in favour of the archaic authenticity of the Glastonbury configuration. Libra is represented by a dove, rather than the usual scales. The bird is placed near the centre of the design at the summit of the converging masts of the Argo Navis ship and could be taken to appear as if flying from the Arthur figure's head. The actual stars of Libra do not fall on the effigy but those of Ursa Major do. Guenon noted that, *"the celestial scales were not always zodiacal, but were at first polar, the name having been applied originally to the Great Bear, or to the Great Bear and Little Bear taken together"*. The axial alignment of the Glastonbury Zodiac is polar. The stars of Ursa Major and Draco the sky serpent, home of the former pole star, are found around its centre. Guenon believed in a Hyperborean primordial polar centre literally once situated at the roof of the world that was the source of the ancient wisdom. With axial displacement and cultural drift, things shifted south and west. Here we connect with Geoffrey Ashe's quest. His Altaic Shambhalic centre is one step removed from the original source in Guenon's version. Once again Glastonbury is conceived as an outpost demonstrating certain motifs of a prior package. Ashe postulated the World Mountain, the maze and the number seven as the giveaway code. Guenon was likewise an advocate of the World Mountain but saw in the Maltwood revelation some of his own significant signs. Probably prompted by the attention of his onetime mentor Guenon, the Italian fascist magus Julius Evola also accepted the Zodiac, stating in *The Mystery of the Grail* that, '*Glastonbury was itself in prehistoric times a centre of the primordial tradition*'.

Whatever we may make of Katherine Maltwood's Glastonbury Zodiac work, one has to take into account the preparation and the vehicle of its inspiration. She was the kind of person whose life was decades ahead of its time. Travelling the world on an unending quest, she sought to work for the spiritual hierarchy she believed is trying to help humanity through crucial times of transformation. Her background education and accomplishments were impeccable. *Magna Mater* speaks volumes. As a woman, a creative artist and a mystic, she helped to demonstrate a role model for the emerging epoch as surely as Dion Fortune's novels and Priestess work. And Glastonbury was her centre of gravity as well.

MARY CAINE AND THE DRUIDIC COSMOLOGY

IN 1950 ROSS NICHOLS, later to found the Order of Bards, Ovates, and Druids, wrote an article on *The Great Zodiac of Glastonbury* for the *Occult Observer.* He noted the presence of what he considered to be Druidic motifs and teachings within the Somerset design. Much of this had already been noticed by Katherine Maltwood but Nichols gave it greater emphasis. The father mother divine child trinity was considered particularly important. Most notable of all was the multiple meanings in the Gemini design. The child in the boat with the converging three masts and dove whose body and wings seem to reiterate the arrow-head symbol at their apex appeared to represent a complex glyph full of Druidic teachings. The deity Hu Gadarn saw three pillars of light in which were contained all divine knowledge. Three converging pillars became an ideogram of God's name, in a similar manner to the Hebrew Tetragrammaton.

A problem here is that a lot of material accepted by various Druid orders has similar controversies to the Hermetica surrounding it. Age and authenticity are topics of constant contention. Nonetheless, the teachings are mystically and magically potent. Druids are a kind of archetype of the western collective unconscious with Merlin their prime embodiment. The very word, along with Witch, can set people off on extraordinarily fertile chains of association and creativity. Just as the constant evolution of the Arthurian mythos is a measure of its power and durability so likewise the aura of the Druid shines brightly. If we look solely at the Dark Age Arthur or the Druids portrayed by Caesar we may be missing the point. Combine the two with Glastonbury and you would be best prepared by accepting that the journey will be one in an exalted realm where myths are born, poems created and symphonies heard, where visions of zodiacal figures may emerge from the landscape.

In 1961 artist Mary Caine joined the London Order of Druids. It was in such company that she first heard of the Glastonbury Zodiac. Initially sceptical, she decided to write to Katherine Maltwood in Canada with detailed questions. She received a reply from John stating that his wife had died just three months before. It was at the same time that Caine had first heard of her work. There was a sense of synchronicity. Mary came to feel that in that period of time, the work was in some sense handed over to her to carry on. Accompanied and supported by her husband Osmund, who was also an artist, she became a tireless champion of the landscape enigma. The couple never lived in Glastonbury but spent extensive time in the area.

From the mid-seventies to early eighties, Mary Caine promoted her pamphlet, *The Glastonbury Giants* (which had first pulled me into the mystery at Pilton in 1979), and full-length book, *The Glastonbury Zodiac: Key to the Mysteries of Britain.* The Caines also created a charming video. Featuring Vaughan Williams' *Fantasia on a Theme by Thomas Tallis,* it plays as a quintessential piece of Earth Mysteries, an impressionistic poetic evocation of British Music. It probably didn't get much exposure on archaeology courses.

True to her roots, Caine emphasised Druidic aspects of the Zodiac, alongside the Arthurian ones. She took her exegesis into realms that would have pleased the British Israelites. This group, whose heyday had been in the 19th century, tended to believe that the Celts had been the Lost Tribes of Israel. Caine also makes much of Wearyall Hill, the fabled location for Joseph of Arimathea's visit at the start of the Piscean Age. The hill is one of the Pisces fishes and therefore the perfect place for such a mission to help key in the coordinates for the Christian epoch.

The most famous aspect of Mary Caine's work was her noticing through aerial photography a most remarkable configuration of woodland on Dundon Beacon that looked like a conventional face of Christ. The fact that it happened to lie over the exact area already identified as the head of the Gemini being rendered it all the more peculiar. It has become the most widely distributed image connected with the Glastonbury Zodiac. Mary Caine was inevitably drawn to refer to Blake's question, "*did the countenance divine shine forth upon our clouded hills*?" It was also notable that the very peak of the hill, where beacon fires had once been lit, was the area on the effigy's head where the yogic third eye was situated. The name of the Druidic bard Taliesin meant 'radiant brow' and this seemed to fit the general mythic mix of the Gemini figure very well. In recent years the trees have been cleared and the image no longer exists.

* * *

THE FLYING SAUCER VISION

"The sun-machine is coming down and we're gonna have a party."
David Bowie. *Memory of a Free Festival.*

JOHN MICHELL'S FIRST BOOK, *The Flying Saucer Vision,* was, as the author later acknowledged, *"a genuine artefact of 1967"*. Its concluding chapter was entitled, *The Dragon, the Holy Grail, and the Flying Saucer.* The work exemplified a way of thought that had been developing since the full advent of the UFO phenomenon a decade earlier. It had been observed that weird lights in the sky were often seen in the vicinity of ancient sites. Some wondered if they used ley lines to navigate by. Before long, folklore and sci fi had met and recognised they had lots in common.

In the midst of an increasingly psychedelic zeitgeist it was possible to think new thoughts. If the Glastonbury Zodiac could only be fully appreciated from the air did that mean it was deliberately constructed not just to make a microcosmic mirror of the heavens on earth but to perhaps play a part in interaction with Extra-Terrestrials? Michell pondered this in his Grail chapter. Do the classic accounts of blinding light and spectral visitations in the romances refer to a class of events that includes Fatima? Is a flying saucer cult the '*basis of all religion*'?

Britain's most prestigious (in terms of social standing) UFO enthusiast was Brinsley le Poer Trench, the Earl of Clancarty, who used his position in the House of Lords to try and initiate top-level investigation of the subject. With a background in Blavatsky, he was a big fan of Katherine Maltwood, stating in *Men Among Mankind* that, *"If the Age of Aquarius is to be the age of the Regeneration of Man, it is to Glastonbury and to the Temple of the Stars that we must look for information regarding our immediate future."* He thought of Arthur as connected to celestial mysteries of the measuring of time through the revolution of Ursa Major. Trench did cover some interesting material in his books. It is perhaps unfortunate though that, alongside the Glastonbury Zodiac, he became an advocate of extreme forms of the Hollow Earth theory. There are hostile aliens down there. Maltwood's theories don't exactly gain credibility through association with such ideas.

Trench could be considered a sober academic in comparison with Elizabeth Van Buren, whose 1981 *Lord of the Flame* was probably the most extreme Glastonbury Zodiac space brothers opus. Early on in the proceedings, the reader discovers what they are in for. "*The Secret of the Great Pyramid and why it had been placed on the desert sands of Egypt by our brothers in Space was revealed to me while writing this book.*" Her somewhat controversial main theme is that "*Lucifer is Christ's twin brother*". The mystery of divine twins was a theme that Trench also examined. A sibling relationship between Venus and Earth is postulated, bringing in Blavatsky and Velikovsky for support. Before long, the big questions are getting asked. "*Was Christ a Venusian?*" Well, look at *Revelation* 22:16 "*I am the root and the offspring of David, and the bright and Morning Star.*"

Castor and Pollux are the two brightest stars in the constellation of Gemini. "*Do they represent the Heavenly and Earthly Twin? – Is there another race of god-like men who live in the stars, our brothers of the Cosmos, our twin brothers?*" The whole mix of imagery around the Glastonbury Zodiac Gemini is brought in to the discussion. One of the twins is the giant figure with Caine's Christ head simulacra. The other is depicted by Maltwood as a griffin or hawk that also stands on the rudder of the great Glastonbury Zodiac ship. Its tail lies between the Leo lion's paws. There is a Castle of the Griffons in *Perlesvaus* where Lancelot visited. He was forced to feed a small dog to the creatures in order to escape. Its owner kept some of the beasts and a lion in an underground chamber. *Gryphon* was one of grades in the mysteries of Mithras which Maltwood speculates may have been present in the area. *Lion* was another and we have seen that lion claws dating from Roman times have been found in the vicinity of the Leo figure. Underground chambers were often the scene of the cult. There are some intriguing nuances here but they are not explored by Van Buren. To her, "*the Griffon bird represents Horus-Christ*".

A huge amount of obscure esoteric lore gets a going over, including the Sirius mystery and Geoffrey Ashe's Ancient Wisdom investigations. A Himalayan Lama is quoted telling Andrew Tomas that Lucifer was a '*godlike giant*' ET who had come to help accelerate human evolution. When the next cycle began, he refused to step aside. We are now entering the Last Days and the Lord of the Flame is set to return. Despite the seeming crankiness of much of the material, some of her other thoughts on the Glastonbury Zodiac are rather intriguing as we shall see.

* * *

FROM ATLANTIS TO AVALON AND BEYOND

ANTHONY ROBERTS WAS BORN IN MAY 1940 during the magical Battle of Britain. He came to the Avalonian mythos from a background of anarchistic activism. As an advocate of the CND cause he broke into an American airbase as far back as 1963 in an attempt to disable some of the planes. He and his wife Janet met through campaigning against the imprisonment of Nelson Mandela. He was repeatedly arrested at political protests and attained maximum street credibility by starting a fire in the foyer of the Dorchester Hotel as a statement against capitalism. Working as a librarian at the London *Evening News* and then *The Times* allowed him the freedom to become an autodidactic polymath. He developed a mystical conviction of the eternal true nature of the spiritual tradition of Britain as best exemplified by William Blake.

Reading Geoffrey Ashe's *King Arthur's Avalon* as a teenager in 1959 had introduced him to Glastonbury. He first visited the place in 1965. In 1967, John Michell's *The Flying Saucer Vision* opened him up to the UFOlogical earth mysteries connection and most importantly of all, the Glastonbury Zodiac. In tumultuous 1969, a moment of destiny arrived. One night he and Janet were driving along the A3 when both spotted a large hovering silver ball conspicuously shining in the night sky. They stopped the car to get out and focus on the startling sight. A smaller silver ball and a red light appeared to differentiate themselves from the main mass. The climax came when a line of tiny lights slowly filed into the big silver ball. Having absorbed the smaller lights, the object began to move away. The Roberts' tried to pursue it in their car. It responded by seeming to follow them, keeping visible directly over the car through the sunroof. Finally, it shot up in the sky and disappeared from view. The whole thing had lasted about twenty minutes. The couple were profoundly life-changingly moved by the mysterious episode.

Something of the mixed blessings of UFO experiences manifested only a few days later when Tony was knocked off his scooter by a car. The injuries sustained required six months off work but enabled him to undertake a marathon reading and writing stint that helped to launch his first book. *Atlantean Traditions in Ancient Britain* was published in 1971, and as the work's title suggests, was very much a product of the Earth Mysteries scene of the time. It featured an extensive treatment of the Zodiac.

Roberts became one of the most charismatic figures in the field. Mary Caine saw him as, "*a returned Atlantean, an ancient Briton, a Druid*". He expressed passionate prophetic raptures and rages, unafraid of any controversies and consequences. As a result of this personal style, he attracted and repelled people in equal proportions.

Although firmly based on Maltwood and Caine, Anthony Roberts' work on the Zodiac was given an individual flavour through his development of a concept that I feel is his most significant contribution to the field of the Earth Mysteries: *Geomythics.* He wrote of "*Myths that coalesce the physical aspect of specific place and object with the relatedly subtle forces of symbolic patterns and their functioning supernatural powers, as seen through the processes of magic*". This was a form of Powys Ackroyd Sinclair psychogeography. The Glastonbury Zodiac was "*a perfect geomythical symbol*".

Glastonbury: Ancient Avalon, New Jerusalem followed in 1976. It was a compilation of articles with Roberts as editor and an afterword by Colin Wilson. It featured twelve pieces as a deliberate resonance with the twelve hides of land given to Joseph of Arimathea and the twelve signs of the landscape zodiac. A large section by Mary Caine repeated her basic Zodiac theories in sign by sign detail. Other articles spoke of further landscape figures allegedly discovered in the Glastonbury environs, the Polden hound and Aller Dragon. The possible existence of more British terrestrial zodiacs was also discussed. The anthology was perhaps the high water mark of Glastonbury Zodiac exposition and acceptance.

Roberts praised Glastonbury as "*a planetary beacon and powerhouse of the spirit*", prophesising that, "*The revolutionary revival of Albion's true spirit will be the precursor of a New Age and that apocalyptic revival will spring from the eternally universal fountain head that is Glastonbury. The Day draws nearer.*"

REALITY CHECK

BEFORE PROCEEDING INTO the furthest-out zones of the Glastonbury Zodiac mythos it is worth pausing to take stock of some of the diverse elements present in the brew and address consensus concerns. To begin with, we have the Maltwood interpretation of *Perlesvaus.* Much ink has been expended by critics in search of an understanding of this unusual text but a zodiacal aspect had yet to be expounded by the time of *Temple of the Stars.*

If it is really there, it's buried pretty deep. It may well be that the author was working with strands of various tales that contained sub-texts the meaning of which he was unaware. There are a number of big events in the story that the Maltwood/Caine corpus conveniently ignore. The fifteen hundred people getting their brains bashed out with giant hammers and the drowning in a vat of blood and suchlike don't feature much in the zodiacal exegesis. The hostile critic can be forgiven their scepticism.

Maltwood mentions that the *Quest del San Graal* stated enigmatically that, *"The Round Table was constructed, not without great significance, upon the advice of Merlin. By its name it is meant to signify the round world and round canopy of the planets and the elements in the firmament, where are to be seen the stars and many other things."* It also mentions the table of the Grail feeding four thousand people and 150 bulls. It was "*in a meadow*". This does seem to clearly indicate that it covers a large area on the land. It might have been more useful for Maltwood's argument if *Perlesvaus* said something similar so clearly but the quote does hint at strange ideas about the Round Table existing somewhere in the background around the beginning of the 13th century.

The first mention of the Round Table comes in the *Roman de Brut* of Wace. This was a translation into French of Geoffrey of Monmouth that included considerable additional material, the Round Table being the most notable. Where Wace got the idea from is yet another area of constantly conflicting theories. Perhaps it derived from Celtic tales circulating amongst the Bretons. Maybe it was inspired poetic invention?

In the Grail Romances and historical documents of the period there are three meanings for the term Round Table. One is the most obvious, a table to eat a meal from. It also means a chivalric institution, an order of knighthood. In that context it will tend to mention large numbers of people. Wace uses both designations. Taken as a whole, the Grail Romances use the term Round Table to describe an institution more often than an eating place, although that's not how later times remember it. The third meaning is that of a tournament of some kind, a pageant, a show, an invocation of chivalry, featuring jousting and feasting. These gatherings were often inspired by the Arthurian mythos. The famous Winchester Round Table may well have been constructed as an accompaniment to such an event. This could be sufficient explanation for the seemingly odd romance references.

Scholars of Maltwood's time believed many things about British pre-Roman history that would now be called into question. Many of her apparently wild theories arose out of such a background of ideas. For example, in *Enchantments of Britain,* she quotes L. A. Waddell from his *Origin of Britons and Scots* who claimed that the Welsh originated in Sumeria. "*We discover that the 'Cymry' of Wales derive their name from 'Sumer'.*" Various traders and colonisers had come to ancient Albion by about 2700 BC. The Celtic Caer Sidi starlore was a mutated form of the Mesopotamian cultural package. This was a variant on widely stated beliefs of the time. The reputable Arthurian scholar John Rhys (who Powys used extensively for researching his great novel) considered that Somerset meant 'Land of Summer'. Druidic material of debatable authenticity spoke of the Cymry being led from the east, from a "*Summer Country over the hazy sea*". If that wasn't discouraging enough it is a tad unfortunate that one of Waddell's most used words is 'Aryan'. He is in fact so enthusiastic in his advocacy of it that his works are popular today amongst mystics whose sensibilities could be described as somewhere to the right of centre.

So what was happening in Somerset round about the period when wandering Sumerians are supposed to have disembarked circa 2700 BC? There was certainly a lot going on in the area by Neolithic times. Trees were being cleared using axes made from stone seemingly imported from distant locations. Wooden trackways crossed the Somerset Levels through the marshland. These constructions constitute what are amongst the oldest roads in the world, having been individually dated to periods between 3806 to about 2500 BC. The tracks had a limited lifespan and were primarily for use during the more flooded times of the year. Cattle were driven across them. Canoes docked at the ends of some. The culture that produced them was obviously well organised and with manpower resources. The people were not isolated. They had contact with the world beyond. Somewhere in the middle of that timescale the Sumerian genesis of civilisation with the wheel, writing, decimal counting etc., can be dated. The famous lake villages were some considerable time later, a few hundred years BC only.

The Sumerians were also pioneer seafarers but could they possibly have travelled as far as Britain? There is a total absence of any archaeological proof here. Even the idea that Egyptians could have travelled the same way a millennia later is hugely contentious. A few Egyptian artefacts have been discovered in Britain but it has been generally considered that they arrived via middlemen and it doesn't mean direct contact. The best that can be said is that the current absence of proof for Sumerian travellers cannot be equated with impossibility.

If they did travel to Somerset they would have found a landscape significantly different from today and this has a major bearing on the Zodiac theory. The issue of the Argo Navis vessel represents the best case in point. It's unique in the Glastonbury Zodiac for a number of reasons. Of all the effigies it's the only one that depicts a man made object, the rest are animals or humans. It contains straight lines, a feature obviously not found in nature. That implies that, assuming the thing is actually there in the first place, it must have been engineered by humans rather than being some mysterious artwork of Gaia. The problem is that the whole area was marshland until the period from 1790 to 1820. The moors were then drained and rhynes built across the flat area. It's those rhynes that define the ship, so it wasn't there in the medieval period and certainly not in Sumerian times.

A strange local custom gives pause for thought though. In nearby Minehead an inverted boat is dressed as a horse. This apparently commemorates a phantom ship that entered the harbour without anyone on board in the distant past. Earth Mysteries advocates will suggest that a location can influence the creativity of its inhabitants. The people who laid out the rhynes to form the ship needn't necessarily have had a clue about what they were doing. Strange forces simply prompted them to conform to a latent pattern. Perhaps, millennia ago, some impressive vessel really had sailed into the vicinity, leaving an indelible trace in site memory.

Both Maltwood and Caine made the dangerous leap of logic that all references to zodiacal lore in British mythology derive from the Glastonbury Zodiac. It simply doesn't follow that a reference to the stars in Welsh literature encodes the Glastonbury gnosis handed down through Druidic initiates.

Geoffrey Ashe has always maintained a certain scepticism about the Zodiac. First and foremost, he simply can't see the figures in the land even when they're pointed out to him. He has wondered if an experimental control group were shown various aerial photos of the British landscape that included the Temple of the Stars but were not identified as such that anyone would spontaneously pick out the image of a lion or a boat. Katherine Maltwood was a sculptress after all. She was predisposed to seeing potential shapes in things.

I consider the point to be a valid one. How many people, not already familiar with the Zodiac hypothesis, when seeing an image of the Tor, would say it looked like a phoenix? Some might compare it to Mesopotamian or Mexican step pyramids. The vast majority I'm sure, if pressed to liken it to anything, would probably opt for symbolism of the female form. Local RAF pilots refer to the Tor tower as the 'nipple'. The Pre-Roman cultures of our islands often linked rolling hills and summits with Goddess figures. It is ideas of this kind that have found far wider response in the recent times.

Geoffrey Ashe himself can take some credit for inspiration that amounts to more than a mere suggestion. In a novel of his, *The Finger and the Moon,* there is a numinous vision of a vast primordial goddess figure whose body is made from the Glastonbury landscape. She stands up, '*ten thousand feet tall'* and walks. Another form of the vision is repeated in *Avalonian Quest.* In *The Goddess in Glastonbury,* Kathy Jones details the basic Ashe configuration along with her own inspiration whereby, "*the side-view of the Isle of Avalon presents the profile of a giant Goddess lying down lengthways*". "*Stonedown is the head of the Goddess, sinking back into the landscape. The Tor rises up as Her left breast and Her ribcage. Chalice Hill is Her pregnant belly. Bere Lane marks Her hips and Wearyall Hill is Her left thigh and leg, Her foot sinking into the ground towards the nearby town of Street.*"

This vision has become an inspiration for the now well-established, always extraordinary, Glastonbury Goddess Conference, an event of increasing significance in the way the mystic background of the town is perceived worldwide. There's no archaeology for this vision either but the inferences seem more valid than the Zodiac theories. It's not at odds with history.

ELLIPTICAL NAVIGATIONS THROUGH GLOBAL CHAKRAS TOWARDS THE OMEGA POINT

AS THE SEVENTIES MOVED INTO THE EIGHTIES the next major champion of the Glastonbury Zodiac was another global visionary like Katherine Maltwood. Robert Coon has described himself as *"an immortalist philosopher who has been initiated into all major World Religions and has unified Cabalistic Invocation, ley-line and earth chakra research, and astrology into the Magickal Art of Celestial Alchemy"*. Coon is a lineal descendant of Mormon founder Joseph

Smith. The origins of this famous sect are fascinating. The story is that an angelic being named Moroni appeared to Smith and led him to uncover some strangely inscribed tablets. By some mystical process he was able to decipher the script and thereby create the *Book of Mormon*. It told the wild tale of the lost tribes of Israel going walkabout and crossing the Atlantic to settle in the Americas. Much scorn has been heaped on the idea but it seems to broadcast across the psychic airwaves in a manner suggestive of a weird truth.

This family heritage proved useful on July 1st 1967, at the peak of the Summer of Love, when Robert was living in Boulder, Colorado. Just after midnight, "*a Physically Immortal human from the Realm of Shambhalla instantly and fully materialised within my room. He was not a shimmering vision, but rather a rock solid, Clear human being as real as you or me. This man wore a white robe, held a wooden staff in one hand, had long white hair and beard. He looked incredibly ancient - yet had the radiant Flesh of Eternal Youth*". This dude was none other than the Prophet Elijah, who Coon came to identify with Merlin, Hermes Trismegistus, and Enoch.

He somehow communicated to Robert a kind of enormous cosmic download that was to be released to the world in astrologically determined stages over the coming decades. What rapidly developed was a vision of the birth of the Aquarian Age from a location in Southern England. The 'global heart chakra' would open there and an 'Omega Point' be activated that would lead to the unfolding of the Planetary New Jerusalem and the widespread attainment of physical immortality! Within a few months Robert had narrowed it down to the specific location of Glastonbury, a place that he had never visited. The big event there was scheduled for 1984, 17 years in the future. There was much to be accomplished in the interim.

Robert's first major published work on the Glastonbury Zodiac was the superbly titled *Elliptical Navigations through the Multitudinous Aethyrs of Avalon* in 1983. This was later updated to *Voyage to Avalon*. Anthony Roberts wrote an introduction in which he said that, "*The opacity, facilitated by the jewelled prose, is a necessary initiatory construct that is designed to trigger the psychic synapses... and so enable the reader to soar into the glittering realms of 'another reality'.*" This prepares the reader for a unique journey into the Zodiac, which Coon considered to be "*a Great Synchronicity Machine weaving myths and legends from past, presents, and future*".

Whatever one's opinion on Immortalism, Coon does seem to

have validly identified a number of its motifs in the Glastonbury mythos. We have Arthur himself, dead but not dead, waiting to return. There's the Aquarian phoenix, reborn from its ashes. Joseph of Arimathea is powerfully connected with resurrection and brought the alchemical cruets of that process with him. The New Jerusalem blueprint can be seen as an important precursor to the physical resurrection seemingly spoken of in *Revelation.* Mystical poems, surreal juxtapositions of apparently unconnected but magickally cohering information, and outlandish prophecies, are woven in and out of expositions of a thirteen sphere 'Enochian Cabala'. A vital part of the alchemical Coon blend is his acceptance and advocacy of the work of Aleister Crowley. There's a powerful Thelemic flavour throughout. He is also a great lover of literature with an appreciation of Powys. The mix has not been to everyone's taste but from the moment I first read *Elliptical Navigations* in 1989 I was vastly entertained and inspired.

Over the years Robert spent a tremendous amount of time visiting the Zodiac sites and researching them in local libraries and museums. Mary Caine made a few adjustments to Maltwood's images of the effigies. Coon continued this procedure. The most notable example is in Scorpio. Katherine Maltwood had confessed to considering her delineation of the figure as being the least satisfactory. Mary Caine made major changes to it that virtually amounted to a new version. Coon dumped them both in favour of an eagle. This sort of manoeuvre lends fuel to the critics who would say that if it's really there in the first place then you just can't validly do that kind of thing. Maltwood and Caine thought in terms of landscape engineering by real people. Coon tends to feel that natural forces are at work, albeit divine ones, and the emergence of the Zodiac is not a finished process. The figures are changing in the present day. People do interact with them and help them along but something more mysterious is involved.

Katharine Maltwood and Mary Caine didn't really offer up any suggestions about what one could actually *do* with the Zodiac. In a 1993 booklet, *The Glastonbury Zodiac,* Robert Coon stated that "*Things can be done in this area that on the macrocosmic scale connect and work out into greater dimensions, so I have always worked with it from the view point of what can be done working with the Zodiac can be useful for planetary healing, for spiritual evolution on the earth*". In many of his works he recommends visiting sites at times of new and full moons and when the sun enters the Zodiac signs. So, to be clear about what that means, if it was a full moon in Leo, try and be somewhere good in the Leo figure, ideally at the exact time, even if that might be in the middle of the night. At the exact moment when the sun enters a particular sign, be somewhere on it and maybe ding a Tibetan bowl and offer up prayers and invocations to assorted appropriate deities and angels and so on. Perhaps a whole year could be spent completing the circuit. It seems inevitable that interesting processes would be triggered by such actions.

Robert Coon's Global Chakra and Omega Point theories are probably the most important new developments in Glastonbury Zodiac exposition. In yogic systems, a subtle internal anatomy is believed to be present in seven primary centres, known as chakras, located along the spinal column and up into the brain. They are normally symbolised as lotus flowers, of different colours, with varying numbers of petals, and a series of associations like the spheres of the Qabalah. Cultivating a harmonious flow of life-force through them, thus ensuring their proper opening and functioning, is an essential part of the inner yogic arts. The concept of global chakras provides a context with which to understand Glastonbury's place in the larger picture of the world sacred sites and how they might relate to each other. Such locations are believed to be places of interface with the deeper levels of the mysterious planetary organism. Ley lines have been likened to the meridians of acupuncture, showing subtle channels for the circulation of the life-force around Gaia's body. The planetary chakras concept has now become a mainstay of New Age thinking although few credit Robert Coon with being one of its original advocates.

The first published reference I'm aware of that specifically refers to global chakras and their locations is in Kenneth Grant's *The Magical Revival*, published in 1972. This amuses me, as Grant is a leading exponent of Thelemic magick, and some of his later books are amongst the most hardcore works of the Left Hand Path one could ever hope to come across, enough to give most New Agers a fit of the vapours. Coon is clear that he developed his ideas independently.

Grant stated that the base chakra is "*concentrated in an occult centre in California that is only now becoming dynamic; it will prove to be a magazine of tremendous power during the evolution of both man and the planet in the present Aeon of Horus*". This is Mt. Shasta, which has indeed become a major zone of New Age manifestation. The sexual centre is located somewhere in the region of ancient

Sumeria, a cult centre of the Yezidis. The solar plexus centre is not directly named. Two centres serve as the world's heart chakra. One is in a mountain beneath the ocean off the coast of Peru, the other is at Glastonbury. The throat centre is Cairo. The third eye region is trans-Himalayan: Shambhala.

Grant's locates his thousand petalled lotus crown chakra at Arunachala, a sacred mountain in southern India. The beliefs about this holy hill are most striking and can be fruitfully compared with the Tor mythology. The famous Himalayan Mount Kailash has been referred to as the abode of Shiva. Arunachala is considered to actually *be* Shiva, who says in the *Skanda Purana* that coming within a thirty mile radius of Arunachala "*shall by itself suffice to burn off all defects and effect union with the Supreme*". Its name is taken to mean form of light, meaning unmoving fire or light. This is suggestive of Shiva's subtle form. It is believed that a column of light runs down the centre of the hill from an infinite height above. Other channels of subtle energy are also present. A scripture dedicated to the hill states that its true form is the *Sri Chakra* yantra. This is a geometric design. In esoteric Hinduism a yantra reveals the true nature of the deity it represents and the method of its invocation. The New Jerusalem geometry could be considered to be a kind of yantra.

If the archaic site has become known in the west, it's mainly due to its association with the 20th century pristine peerless saint, Ramana Maharshi, who spent most of his life at the foot of the mountain. He actually considered Arunachala to be his Guru. One could say that the mountain has revealed itself to the modern world through his vehicle. Sri Ramana is known as a supreme exemplar of the philosophy known as Advaita Vedanta that affirms no separation between the individual and universal consciousness. The suggestion is that there's nowhere to go and nowt to do because we're already there if we did but know it. The Maharshi conveyed the reality of this realisation through his overwhelming presence, quite often in silence. Indeed, he tends to be associated with silence and the realm of the formless. This is the Arunachala transmission of unmoving fire or light.

Beyond that though, some strange phenomenon accompanied his relationship with the holy hill. Speaking of its inner light beam, Kenneth Grant states in *Outer Gateways*, "*Down this column, as down a pathway cut through space by the beams of the full moon, swarm the unearthly siddhas who, while upon earth, reside within the caverns of the hill*". These are mysterious inner plane dudes of vastly ancient provenance who can manifest in whatever way they choose. Maharshi said that "*A number of siddha purushas live on this mountain. It is perhaps with a desire to see me that they come and go assuming various shapes.*" Strange lights have been seen over Arunachala and have often given the impression of being under some kind of conscious control. When Maharshi died a bright light was seen moving slowly across the sky that then appeared to enter the hill. The Indian *Tripurarahasya* has a tale of a hill containing an entire universe within it. Someone who gets inside returns to find aeons of time have passed. Think of faery lore and the shining ones of the hollow hills and the recent links with UFOlogy so excellently elucidated by Jacques Vallée and John Michell. Think of Glastonbury Tor.

Coon's chakra list is slightly different. Shasta is the base. Lake Titicaca is the sexual centre, Uluru or Ayers Rock in Gondwana/ Australia, the solar plexus, Glastonbury the heart, Great Pyramid the throat. The third eye is not fixed. He refers to a '*mobile Shambhalic focus*' which he believes to be currently active at Glastonbury. The crown chakra is Mount Kailas simply designated as Himalayan. Other New Age versions have put Shasta as the crown.

So where is this all going? Why are these revelations occurring now? Pierre Teilhard de Chardin was probably the most influential and extraordinary Catholic thinker of the 20th century. His ideas brought him into repeated conflict with the Vatican. In *The Phenomenon of Man* he postulated a further strata of the life of the planet above the biosphere. "*A glow ripples outward from the first spark of conscious reflection. The point of ignition grows larger. The fire spreads in ever widening circles till finally the whole planet is covered with incandescence.*" This is the *noosphere,* the 'thinking layer'. The collective mindstuff of expanding humanity is creating an ever more powerful field of consciousness around the planet. It seems that, "*evolution is an ascent towards consciousness – therefore it should culminate forwards in some sort of supreme consciousness*". Every consciousness can centre everything partially upon itself, can centre itself upon itself and is "*being brought more by this very super-centration into association with all the other centres surrounding it*". "*Because it contains and engenders consciousness, space-time is necessarily of a convergent nature. Accordingly its enormous layers, followed in the right direction, must somewhere ahead become involuted to a point which we might call Omega, which fuses and consumes them integrally in itself.*"

"*Far from being mutually exclusive, the Universal and Personal (that is to say, the 'centred') grow in the same direction and culminate simultaneously in each other." "The Future-Universal could not be anything else but the Hyper-Personal - at the Omega Point." "By its structure Omega, in its ultimate principle, can only be a distinct Centre radiating at the core of a system of centres; a grouping in which personalisation of the All and personalisations of the elements reach their maximum, simultaneously and without merging, under the influence of a supremely autonomous focus of union."*

If the Vatican didn't rush to embrace these expansive ideas, there were many in the New Age realm that did. They seem to express something generally present in the zeitgeist airwaves.

Robert Coon believed that the global Omega Point would be activated during a rare conjunction of Mercury with Easter Sunday sunrise in 1984 from Glastonbury Tor. In the visionary realm, a crystalline green emerald rose would open within the hollow hill. He positioned himself to be part of the human side of the process. From that moment, "*The Spirit of that Summer of Love in 1967 has now been reborn in 1984 as the Phoenix rises from the Heart of Glastonbury.*" Fundamentally, "*the Messiah is the Global Omega Point activated at sunrise of Easter 1984 on Glastonbury Tor. We each partake of union with the Messiah to the degree that we dedicate our Hearts, Wills, and Actions to the unfoldment of the Great Truth of Everlasting Life now radiating eternally from the Heart of Ancient Avalon*". A perfect expanding circle of clear sky seemed to appear directly above the Tor and continue radiating outwards for days. This phenomenon was supposedly visible from satellite photographs.

EMBRYOGENESIS OF THE WORLD SENSORIUM

OLIVER REISER was a Professor in the Philosophy department at Pittsburgh University for fifty years. He wrote a book on the Zodiac entitled *This Holyest Erthe*. I can't really imagine a British philosopher writing a book about the Glastonbury Zodiac that mentioned Atlantis and quoted Blavatsky as an authority. A lot of the so-called history in the book is a bit wonky. It's only a short work but perhaps takes the Zodiac corpus to its most extreme and extraordinary expression.

Thanks to Lovelock's Gaia hypothesis it's no longer thought to be wildly eccentric to believe that our planet can be considered to be a living organism. Ecological studies have increasingly shown the awesome level of interconnectedness of all the many systems that function in the world. Many have found the contemplation of this interconnectedness to be a doorway to a form of mysticism. Does the planet dream? Are some of the world's most famous ghosties, monsters and general strange events manifestations of the mind of Gaia? What function do human beings serve in the midst of all this? Our consciousness is the most specialised yet seen here. Are we in effect part of a bigger picture of the planet evolving, coming to consciousness of itself and its place in the Universe? Is our apparent individuality, our separation, an illusion? Are we somehow the cells of a global brain? Reiser was speculating along these lines quite a while before the New Agers took it on board. He'd been influenced by Teilhard de Chardin. He also tried to see the unfolding of the history of human cultures within the frame of that bigger picture.

Here's a condensed sample of Reiser's mind at work. It's worth reading over it a few times.

"For a complete theory of any complex social phenomenon one requires a full-blown philosophy of history and theory of man... This will be a non-linear and wholistic interpretation. In that more complete statement two facets will receive further elaboration:
(1) there will be an organismic theory of the earth as a living entity, with human society as a part of that evolving creature; and (2) there will be a theory of the origin of human consciousness in terms of its bi-polar sources in (1) the human nervous system, and (2) the radiation belt (or psi field), the two poles generating the 'world sensorium'- the guiding field which controls the psychosocial evolution of mankind.

On the side of the earth organism, we have long argued the case for the doctrine of the evolution of a giant earth-creature, the idea that the earth is indeed a living being, with the plant and animal kingdoms forming (functionally) the entoderm and ectoderm of the giant earth-egg, with the human race constituting the maturing nervous system of the embryo and individual persons serving as the 'neuroblasts' of the creature. We have urged that the eastern and western hemispheres are analagous to the right and left lobes of the human brain, together constituting the armature of an earth dynamo spinning out the lines of force ('wires') of the coming electromagnetic society.

Accordingly the planetary cortex of the electromagnetic society gives rise to its radiation-belt 'elecroencephalograms.' These are the lines of force of the psi-field that are associated in cause-effect relations (feed-back) with the two halves of the earth-armature and the subordinate ganglia of the global cogitatorium. The evolving system of life is operated by the energy of the sun (as the ancient Druids knew), which elaborates the essential substances (e.g., chlorophyll) that the earth-egg requires.

The human beings (neuroblasts) of the differentiating forebrain are not yet the perfect neurons they will later come to be. This, of course, implies that human history, the rise and fall of nations, the migrations of peoples, cultural diffusions, and the rest, are phases of the rhythmic pulsations of the planetary electroencephalograms, playing like electric signs over a bank of lights."

"We hold that consciousness is a manifestation of a feed-back polarity between the human cortex and the environing 'radiation belts' of a 'world sensorium', this latter being our substitute for the Noosphere of Teilhard de Chardin. These postulated fields - or psi-belts - have their 'magnetic moments'... synchronicities between levels or planes of action-patterns, which are the secular-historical events occurring over the surface of the earth and reflecting a kind of electromagnetic induction. The field-aspects constitute the akashic records which provide the prototypes that may constitute the morphogenetic images in the various eras of human endeavour and achievement."

Imagine developing a mindset like that and then settling into the enigma of the Glastonbury Zodiac. Reiser pondered on the Aquarian phoenix, trying to divine its possible message for the emerging age. A problem seems to appear. "*How is it possible, at one and the same time, for the Tor Hill to be Mrs. Maltwood's 'Phoenix' and Mr. Russell's 'labyrinth'?*" The resolution is contained in perhaps the most far-out single sentence ever penned on the mystery of Glastonbury. "*Is it possible that the labyrinth will turn out to be the morphogenetic field pattern for the embryogenesis of the World Sensorium?*" What? Geoffrey Ashe quotes this remarkable speculation in *Avalonian Quest* in a gently ironic way, suggesting that this kind of thinking shows how far the Glastonbury madness can affect people. Okay. What does Reiser mean?

We are now willing to believe that our planet may be alive. It might have an evolving consciousness. Humans could have the important function of serving "*the maturing nervous system*". Reiser believed that human awareness cannot be separated from the radiation belts of the World Sensorium, the global brain. This brain uses us to become conscious of itself.

The whole process unfolds through mathematical laws, geometric forms. The Tor maze may model a brain pattern. It could be a place where the World Sensorium expresses itself in a manner that brings humans into an increased accelerated relationship with itself. They may become consciously attuned to it. Any form of interaction at all helps the process along. The maze could be seen as the brain of the Aquarian phoenix. The consciousness attainable through it represents the blueprint, the morphogenetic field pattern, the shape of the coming epoch. It has lain comparatively dormant but now is the time of its activation. Remember also, that the maze pattern may well be a signature sign of an ancient wisdom that is likewise part of the total package potentially activated. The embryogenesis of the World Sensorium, the coming to birth and maturity of the planet's consciousness can be crucially affected by whether or not the Aquarian phoenix is able to fulfil its total potential function. This idea helps deepen the sense of Robert Coon's Tor Omega Point vision.

We've come a long way from *Perlesvaus*. With my mind primed by such ideas and information on the Glastonbury Zodiac, I was nicely prepared to appreciate the unique journey of Andrew Collins into the heart of its mystery. I disappeared into the most epic and extraordinary magical mystical story I had ever heard. When I reappeared I was actually inside the middle of that story myself.

* * *

THE HOLY LIGHT

"Once, the world was not as it has since become. It once worked in a different way than it does now; it had a different history and a different future. Its very flesh and bones, the physical laws that governed it, were other than the ones we know.

Whenever the world turns from what it has been into what it will be, and thus earns a different past and a different future, there is a brief moment when every possible kind of universe, all possible extensions of Being in space and time, are poised on the threshold of becoming, before all but one pass into nonexistence again; and the world is as it is and not as it was, and everyone in it forgets that it could ever be or has ever been other than the way it is now.

And just as the world is thus turning from the what-has-been into the what-is-to-be, and all possibilities are just for a moment alight and one has not yet been chosen, then all the other similar disjunctures in time (for there have been several) can become visible too."

"I discern the shadow of another story and another world, symmetrical to it, and yet as different from it as dream is from waking."

Aegypt. John Crowley.

"There are those who will say that the keys cannot be found. Heed not those of little heart. The inner chamber still radiates."

William de St. Clere.

THE FIRST STIRRINGS HAD BEEN IN JANUARY 1981. Andrew Collins and Graham Phillips had come to Glastonbury on the Lights of Knowledge quest in the Green Stone story. Graham had picked up psychically that it was next in the sequence of sites that reactivated the stone. As they drove along the road from Wells to Glastonbury, at the point where the Tor came into view for the first time, Graham started glimpsing, and hearing, a phoenix rising from the ashes of a still crackling fire. On their arrival in the town, Graham felt they should go first to Wearyall Hill, where he might receive more information on what they had to do. There, standing next to the Holy Thorn, he scanned the horizon and suddenly pointed to a large house at the base of the Tor, stating clearly that here they would find the town's physical guardian. He had no idea why he should feel that. The two followed up this single lead, and were disappointed when no one answered the front-door of the Victorian red-brick building. About to give up, Andy noticed that over the road was a line of small cottages, one of which bore the name of Phoenix. The pair knocked on the door, only to be told by the owners that the people they really needed to talk to were the previous occupiers Tony and Jan Roberts, who had moved away a year or so beforehand. It was the people next door in St. Michael's Cottage who finally gave them the Roberts' current address and phone number.

From a telephone box a little way down the road, Andy spoke for the first time to Jan Roberts (Tony being out that afternoon). She explained to him the Glastonbury Zodiac Tor Aquarian phoenix idea. There was actually a carved relief of the fire-bird on St. Michael's tower. The two questers now had their answer to the riddle of the Phoenix. As the sun slowly sank over the horizon they scrambled up the Tor and, at the exact moment of sunset, Graham received the Fourth Light, the name for which was given as 'Vision'.

As a result of this, Andy soon met up with Anthony Roberts on the premises of the *Times* in London, where he was gifted with a copy of *Glastonbury: Ancient Avalon, New Jerusalem.* In retrospect, it was a nexus point of destiny.

The Green Stone story played itself out. Andy returned to live in Essex, setting up the first version of Earthquest to see if psychic questing could be duplicated elsewhere. He didn't see much of the original group but they all stayed in contact. One day in January 1983, Graham Phillips briefly visited. He had picked up on a location in Somerset named Kingweston, feeling there was something important for Andy there and he needed to tell him. There were no further details.

Later in the month, Andy was conducting a meditation with the Earthquest group. The intention was to try and pick up information about a local site. Something else wanted to make itself known. One of the group stalwarts, Dave Hunt, saw a celestial snake encircling a night sky like, *"the rim of a huge whirlpool"*. Another Earthquest regular, Ian Dawson, could see two medieval knights holding spears in front of a doorway. Carole Young spoke of a sun king on a golden throne, feeling he was directly connected with Andy. She sensed a Glastonbury Grail connection. Andy was having a night of above-average psychism himself. Like Dave, he had seen a serpent stretched around the sky. The seven stars of Ursa Major were particularly noticeable. Then the heavens had fallen to earth like a collapsing tent covering the landscape.

An inner voice directed him to find a hill near Glastonbury

where some kind of enlightenment awaited. The visuals shifted to a tree-covered summit. The green fields all around seemed to carry the feeling of Somerset. Amongst them were a cluster of three hills on each of which stood a Calvary cross displaying an image of Christ crucified. Andy knew that his vantage point was known as 'Golgotha', meaning the 'place of the skull', the name of the site of the crucifixion. This location was near Glastonbury and was important. He had to find it.

Again the whole scene dramatically changed. Andy saw a great medieval battle in the Holy Land. It was the siege of Jerusalem by the knights of the first crusade. Atop the ramparts, the defenders fired arrows and hurled objects down on the attacking soldiers. One figure on the ground came into sharp focus. His battered shield displayed the heraldic device of a red rampant lion against a golden background. All of the other imagery around the lion faded, leaving it shining in light. There was a feeling that this family were the guardians of some extraordinary esoteric secret. It was something to do with the Grail, the Plantaganets, and the secrets of divine kingship. Another British green countryside landscape now appeared behind the lion. The animal seemed to settle into it, somehow overlaid across its features. Andy knew that this place was also in the vicinity of Glastonbury. From the little that he had heard about the alleged terrestrial zodiac, he felt that this was surely an indication of the Leo figure. The scene further changed to the sunlit interior of a small church. The name 'Kingweston' floated through Andy's mind with the feeling that a carved lion's head was nearby and somehow the place would lead to the mysterious Golgotha. As he returned to normal consciousness he remembered that Kingweston was the place Graham Phillips had mentioned just a few weeks before.

When everyone compared notes afterwards, Andy realised that something was definitely in motion. It didn't take long to establish that Kingweston was a tiny hamlet in Somerset, very near to the lion of Leo effigy in the Glastonbury Zodiac. This was more than enough to warrant further investigation. An opportunity to visit there was immediately available. Andy had just begun a relationship with a woman named Cara Trimarco who had recently moved from Southend to Glastonbury. He was already intending to see her there the following weekend. It was clear that this was interestingly timed.

On Saturday January 29th 1983, Andy and Cara visited All

Saints Church Kingweston. Its tall spire is a notable local landmark, uncharacteristic of the style of other churches in the area. This is because most of the building only dates from the 1850's. A Norman entrance archway and nearby font are all that remain of an earlier structure. There had been something standing during the historical period of the crusade vision. No obvious depiction of a lion's head revealed itself.

At this time Cara had limited enthusiasm for Andy's questing interests and had not manifested any overt psychism. Nonetheless she expressed a definite sense of feeling a powerful atmosphere in the church and encouraged Andy to try and tune in to it. Accepting this idea, he was soon inspired to kneel down with his back to the high altar, facing towards the west wall by the Norman entrance and font. With closed eyes he immediately got the strong impression of a medieval knight, dressed in chain mail and surcoat, who had knelt there likewise centuries before. The figure arose to walk down the central aisle, which had an earthen floor, disappearing through some kind of portal in the west wall into a landscape of wooded hills. Andy knew the knight was heading towards Golgotha. Whilst this was happening, with no knowledge of what he was experiencing, Cara psychically saw the kneeling Andy as a knight.

Settling into her own attunement with the place, she saw it filled with golden light. It seemed to form the focus of a solar wheel of energies. Beyond that was a serpent turning in the sky, mounted knights, crusading scenes. Jerusalem. A sun king connected with the Somerset locale. A great concealed treasure. Andy was impressed. He hadn't mentioned anything to Cara about the imagery from the night of the Earthquest group meditation that had set him off on this journey. The sudden bout of unprecedented psychism on her part confirmed very strongly for him that a major game was afoot.

Once outside, strolling down a lane near the church, the couple spotted, on the wall of a building called the Old School House, a four-foot diameter carved circular stone plaque depicting a lion's head whose mane formed sunrays. Here was a clear indicator of Leo and the solar wheel atmosphere of the church. Why choose such an embellishment for a building? It seemed like someone had given expression to the subtle ambiance of the location, even if they hadn't been fully conscious of it. This was an example of what came to be called site perpetuation in psychic questing.

Later that day, Andy and Cara sought the advice of Tony and

Janet Roberts in the *Rainbow's End* café in Glastonbury High Street. He expanded their sense of the Leo locale, telling them as Katherine Maltwood had noted, how the main town within it, Somerton, had once been the seat of the Saxon kings of Wessex. That went some way to explain the sun king imagery. Golgotha was a mystery though. The discussion was enough to inspire Andy and Cara to spend the evening in the Red Lion pub in Somerton. Discussion turned to Graham Phillips. It was he that had first mentioned Kingweston. Perhaps he might produce further inspiration. Andy tried to call him from the pub phone. He was staying with the Sunderland family in North Wales, so there was an immediate link with the Green Stone crew. The whole group there agreed to have an immediate session to see if they could help Andy. Whilst this was happening, Andy and Cara tried to further tune-in themselves in the midst of a noisy Saturday night pub scenario. Andy saw the Golgotha hill again but from a different angle. His psychic attention zoomed in on a fairly large house at the base of the tree-covered hill. Inside the building people in robes were holding swords in the air. The weird ceremonial was something to do with the Knight's Templars. A crypt or cave. More ritual activity. Was it in the basement of the house or somehow set into the hillside? The owner knew about Golgotha. Cara could see a throne, angels, Egyptian figures, and a buried gold casket. She was reaching the point of input overload.

Time to check what was happening in Wales. Marion Sunderland felt that the Golgotha hill was near a druidic grove called the 'Eye of the Dragon'. It was a place with associated Celtic flavoured legends and was frequented by witchy types in the present day. Gaynor had seen Andy's car driving along a narrow country road flanked by hedges on either side. It stopped by a wooden gate from where could be seen a lightning struck tree. Find the tree and Golgotha would be located. Graham felt a definite alignment between the Eye of the Dragon wood and the Place of the Skull.

The next morning, Andy and Cara met up with Tony and Janet Roberts again. Tony gave Andy a further gift. This time it was his own well-thumbed copy of Maltwood's *Temple of the Stars*. He clearly realised that Andy was already involved in a unique Glastonbury adventure that needed to be fulfilled. The story of the previous night was told. Tony immediately recognised the Eye of the Dragon grove as being Park Wood, the very centre of the Zodiac and a place dear to his heart. It aligned to the stars of Draco, the heavenly dragon. One of its stars, Kochab, was the exact centre of the Glastonbury Zodiac and she suggested that this enabled the whole thing to be dated as it had been the pole star around 2,700 BC. The eye or gullet of the dragon aligned to Kochab. The stars of Ursa Major also fell in the vicinity.

That night, the vibe was tangibly building. A gale-force wind had arisen. Andy and Cara felt the call of powerful forces. Something was waiting for them outside in the darkness. There were no definite plans for the evening. They would head out in Andy's car, maybe stop at some pub or another, and await inspiration. Out beyond Glastonbury, the primal night asserted itself. Park Wood was pondered for a potential visit. Cara didn't feel the time was right. Driving aimlessly around country lanes, they suddenly recognised the distinctive shape of Kingweston church, now dark against the night sky. Accepting their unintended return as the necessary omen, they struggled through the wind to huddle in the porch and try and further attune to the mysterious situation. The whole feeling of the place was spectacularly different from its daylight solar glory. It seemed darkly brooding, full of watching presences.

Cara slipped into a remarkable state of psychic receptivity. She felt that a journey into an underworld abyss was beckoning and it was necessary to conquer any fear in order to undertake it. She started to see two dark figures standing sentinel-like before a stone gateway. This was another image that followed through from the initial Earthquest meditation. Andy could see a medieval broadsword tumbling down through a stone shaft. Cara was sure that the guardians must be passed. She then saw a knight with a lance lying in a sepulchre. He was bathed in light. This chapel had to be passed through too. Cara was experiencing journeying down a tunnel and through the chapel. The scene changed. The same knight was now a giant, lying outdoors silhouetted by moonlight. She confidently stated that the knight lay in the Gemini figure of the Zodiac and they had to go there immediately. In an unprecedented deep trance she then said in a strange fluent monotone, "*I can show you the knight. His head is Dundon Beacon, the Hill of Golgotha*".

Andy was aware of the location. He'd driven past it on a few occasions but hadn't made the Golgotha connection. He unhesitatingly agreed to go there straight away. Cara sat silently in the car, seemingly still tranced-out. Suddenly she exclaimed, "*There's the knight*", pointing out across countryside lit by an almost full moon. Stopping the car, Andy gazed out across the fields in total amazement.

There, sculpted by rolling hills, was the giant figure, its skull-like head formed by Dundon Beacon. The lunar artistry even seemed to show the knight's shield.

They drove nearer to the hill to get a closer look. A stile was spotted in a gap along the hedgerow that lined the road, so Andy stopped the car. As they approached it, the outline of a dead tree could be seen in the field just beyond it. The path from the stile led up to the summit. Gaynor's brief psychic impression came to mind. They had found the tree and located Golgotha.

According to Katherine Maltwood, the Gemini figure of the Glastonbury Zodiac was mainly formed by two adjoining hills, Dundon Beacon and Lollover Hill. The stars of Gemini and Orion fell in the vicinity. The Beacon was indeed the head. The place was the site of a ditch and bank earthwork that seemed to have been occupied from Neolithic times through to the Celtic Iron Age. Maltwood suggested it had been a centre for some kind of underworld death cult, perhaps not unlike the Annwn Gwyn Tor associations. The place name supposedly meant the 'Fort of Don', whose attribute was wisdom. Andy's initial visionary sequence had told him he would receive some kind of enlightening wisdom on the Golgotha summit.

The *Perlesvaus* zodiac correspondences attribute the Gemini giant to Arthur's son Lohot, a character unique to that romance. He had the unusual habit of lying down to sleep on the bodies of giants he had just killed to replenish his strength. Sir Kay, who is not portrayed as the usual loyal attendant of Arthur, jealously beheads the sleeping Lohot and brings the trophy to Arthur, blaming it on the giant Lohot had slain. Maltwood said that Dundon Beacon was the head of Lohot with Lollover Hill as the rest of his body.

Moving beyond Katherine Maltwood, Andy investigated what others had to say about the Zodiac. He looked further into Tony Roberts' *Glastonbury; Ancient Avalon, New Jerusalem* anthology, encountering for the first time the work of Mary Caine. He now fully clocked something he'd barely noticed before: the aerial photograph of the remarkable head of Christ image formed by the trees and contours of Dundon Beacon. On Good Friday each year, a procession walks from Compton Dundon church to the top of Lollover Hill, carrying a large wooden Calvary cross that they erect on the summit. It's left there until Easter Sunday when it is returned to the church. A further link with Golgotha. Although far from unique in Britain as a whole, this is the only location in Somerset where such a practice is maintained in the present day.

With Golgotha identified, attention returned to the original medieval visionary stimulus. Who might have established the association initially? The Knights Templars were the obvious candidates for crusaders with mystical interests. They were notoriously linked to alleged veneration of a head of some kind. A striking painted wooden panel head of Christ can be found at the important Templar site of Templecombe, only fifteen miles away from Dundon. They conducted ceremonies in underground crypts that represented the Holy Sepulchre. Andy recalled the house he had psychically seen the previous night where strange ceremonies were held. He needed to check if it really existed. If it did, he would be able to find it somewhere around the base of the hill. The owner might prove to be very interesting. What if the Golgotha idea was still being worked in the present day? Tony Roberts communicated tales of a 'tradition' linking Dundon with the Templars and rumours of a cave in the hill where death-rebirth initiations occurred. It was all a bit vague.

The amazing burst of psychism that led from the Earthquest meditation to Kingweston and Dundon had all happened in less than a week. After that the trail went cold. It wasn't until the end of June that the next stage announced itself. The starting point was once again an Earthquest gathering. This time Andy led the group in trying to pick up specifically on the Zodiac. Another striking vision came to him. He saw a female figure with corn coloured hair and a white floral dress surrounded by a golden aura. An image worthy of Botticelli. Some kind of sun queen. Rapid scene changes followed. More medieval warfare, but this time much closer to home. Men with swords and staffs. Smoke rising from burning villages. A royal court. Laughter and music. A colourfully dressed jester cartwheeling across a dirt floor. Three sombre muddied chain-mailed knights on horseback moving slowly across a wasteland type landscape, wet and bleak, the sense of it being undoubtedly England. The scene panned out to reveal them following a simple wooden cart with solid wheels, pulled by a tired looking horse. It was being driven by a hooded male figure. Sitting in the back of the cart was an obviously unhappy woman wearing a black-cowled cloak. She was holding in her arms a young child wrapped in cloth. The whole group were clearly concerned about the possibility of ambush. The woman was fearful of her identity being revealed.

As he witnessed this apparent forgotten historical drama playing out before his inner eye like a movie, Andy's mind was full of questions. Who were these people and what was this all about? Answers immediately came to him. The child was actually heir to the throne. The woman was *"the daughter of Henry and the sister of Stephen"*. Andy's mind reached out for more information. Stephen was the king but what was the woman's name? Ma–Ma–Ma–. Was it Mary? He couldn't get it. The child was in danger from Stephen. He must be hidden away somewhere safe. Why was he seeing this? What, if anything, did it have to do with the Glastonbury Zodiac? *"Near to Glastonbury they rode. Kingweston is nearby. Find the baby, the divine child."* The final phrase echoed around Andy's head as he returned to normal consciousness. This time the rest of the group's imagery didn't help push the thing forward. It simply reflected what had already happened. Only Andy's material was suggestive of the next stage.

The historical period in question was soon identified. The woman, the sun queen, was the Empress Matilda, daughter of Henry I, and cousin (not sister) of Stephen of Blois, who had married Geoffrey of Anjou, founder of the Plantaganet dynasty, and given birth to the child who later became Henry II. Her Empress designation dated from a previous marriage to the Holy Roman Emperor. The scenes of warfare were a conflict over succession between Matilda and Stephen in which Henry of Blois had been involved. Andy's initial vision was an intriguing introduction to Matilda as it was in many ways appropriate to an image of the Empress in the Tarot major arcana.

Were there any links to Glastonbury? Matilda's army was based in Bristol and Somerset and held territory in the general West Country vicinity. The Empress had owned land within the Zodiac. This included the chapel and manor of Somerton in the Leo figure and land at Camel near Virgo. Somerset gentry had strongly supported her in the civil war. They had been led by her half-brother Robert of Gloucester, who was a patron of Geoffrey of Monmouth, author of the major work primarily responsible for the great interest in Arthur.

The source of the River Cary, whose course partially delineates the Virgo figure, is at Castle Cary. There are very few signs of any castle there now but in Matilda's time it was the location of one of the very largest in the country. A gigantic edifice with walls in places twenty feet thick was the scene of an epic siege where its defendants who were loyal to Matilda were forced to surrender to Stephen's troops. The family in residence originally had the suggestive name of Perceval.

Katherine Maltwood had discovered the signs initially in the same order that Andy had come to them: first Leo and then Gemini. Now Andy was being led into Virgo. The route didn't make astrological or geographical sense but he was determined to allow the classic questing process to guide him.

The timing of Andy's vision was again fortuitous. The following weekend he was to share a stall at the London Festival of Mind, Body and Spirit with Mary Caine. He was able to give her a full account of his adventure so far. Caine confirmed that Andy's Matilda material was worth pursuing. She herself had come across a story that the infant Henry II had been hidden in the Glastonbury Zodiac! It had been in a place called Babcary. An old lady in the post office there had been the initial source of the tale. It had recently resurfaced again in an article. Babcary is in the Virgo effigy that Mary Caine linked with Ceredwen and the divine child Taliesin. It's actually in the womb area of the figure so that's quite an interesting place to conceal a royal baby. Caine took the place name to mean 'Mother Carey's baby'. It should be noted that biographers of Henry consider that he did not spend his early childhood in Britain and that Mary Caine was aware of this.

Barely a mile away from Babcary was the most notable site in Virgo. Wimble Toot is a tree-capped tumulus, taken to be the breast of the Virgo goddess. So, a mere four days after Andy's Matilda visions, he was given exactly the confirmation and further stimulus he needed from the leading living advocate of the Zodiac. Another long gap intervened though, before he was able to take up the next stage of the challenge.

By the end of 1983, Andy's relationship with Cara had ended. He was now involved with Chesca Potter. It was in her company that he first visited Wimble Toot on New Year's Day 1984. Once Mary Caine had pointed him in the site's direction, he had decided to try the experiment of not reading anything further from her books about the place. It would be a test of his psychism. Shortly after arriving, to clear blue skies and biting wind, Andy saw a vision of what he took to be the site guardian, standing at the centre of the low tumulus. It was a young woman with sharp facial features and long dark hair that was drawn together to a point upon her crown. She wore a simple black dress and held a large pottery vessel that Andy felt contained a libation. Wondering who she might be, Andy saw wooden huts on a platform above water. It was clearly the Lake Village. This woman had lived there and came out to the

Toot on some mysterious archaic religious errand. Her pottery vessel contained sea-food. Here was a glimpse of what Powys had intuited as the Lake Village's adoration of the Great Mother through the cult of the cauldron of plenty, of death and rebirth.

Hungover from New Year's Eve in the *Rifleman's Arms,* Andy felt that he had got a sufficient result for the day. He was happy that Virgo was the next sign in the sequence and that the necessary psychic preliminaries had been followed. He and Chesca prepared to depart. As they walked back across the field from the Toot, Andy heard a loud female voice shouting "Don't leave me". This was his first ever clairaudient experience. It seemed to have been an ancient echo carried on the wind. He assumed it came from the priestess guardian he had just seen.

Back in his car, having gathered initial impressions and experiences of the site, Andy now referred to Mary Caine's book. '*As Black Annis the witch she shrieks in the wind on Annis Hill near her head.*' Black Annis was a Celtic dark-crone goddess, ruler of the night and rider of storms. She was not unlike Hecate. Ritual sacrifices were offered to her at the start of August to secure her blessings for the harvest. In the gathering and reaping there's always a hint of death and the underworld. The archetypal medieval figure of Death that we see in the Tarot is generally known as the Reaper. Andy couldn't help but feel he had heard the cry of Black Annis herself. The site guardian had perhaps been propitiating her. This carried forward the underworld theme.

Chesca was a friend of Robert Coon and his wife of the time. As a result of this, Andy and Robert were able to meet and compare notes. The invisible watchers of the Glastonbury aquarium, so beloved of Powys, no doubt gathered in force to observe the coming together of two such remarkable men. And something certainly held a potent enchantment in place that prevented them from cross-referencing their lives in one crucial area. That would have to wait. It was not yet the ninety-third year of the Aeon of Horus.

What Robert was immediately able to tell Andy was the identity of the current occupier of the house at the foot of Dundon Beacon that had attracted psychic attention. It was one of the most charismatic, controversial, and enigmatic figures on the Glastonbury scene at the time. Tim Henry had recently appeared in the lead role in a play by Rollo Maughfling about the life of Aleister Crowley, staged in the town's Assembly Rooms. Robert Coon acknowledged the excellence of his performance in *Voyage to Avalon.* All kinds of occult rumours circulated about Henry that he seemed to enjoy tremendously. There was a consistent theme in some of them. He apparently engaged in neo-Templar ceremonials. People from all over Europe, in particular France and Switzerland, would periodically converge on his Dundon home for unspecified swords and robes type shenanigans. Or so the stories went. This was startlingly close to Andy's psychic material. He knew that he would have to try and meet Tim Henry.

When he did, in early 1984, it was a bit of a disappointment in some ways. Henry was hardly likely to discuss his inner life with a complete stranger, especially if other people were involved who would probably prefer secrecy. He played the enigmatic card very strongly. What he did say, which was really what Andy was most looking for, was that he was aware of Dundon Beacon being known as Golgotha. No details or context were forthcoming despite Andy's clear desire to know more. On one level in the obscure unfolding drama, Tim Henry fulfilled his role as guardian of the site and its mysteries.

In March, some time after her relationship with Andy had ended, Cara returned to Dundon Beacon. Climbing to the summit she saw a brief psychic glimpse of a white robed woman with a headdress that covered most of her face like a veil. This was followed by a medieval knight who she recognised from the initial visions from Kingweston. Once upon the beacon summit a strong urge compelled her to sit down and tune in. She immediately felt herself to be dressed in the white attire of the woman she'd just seen. A radiant blue aura surrounded her. From this strange perspective, Cara saw the nearby landscape in its medieval past. The hill's base had seemingly been covered in trees. Through that forest rapidly rode the Kingweston knight. His name was – Roger. No. Robert. He was being pursued. Three other knights on horseback, clad in Templar regalia, red cross on white surcoat, were trying to overtake him. He had to find safety with Brother John. A brief flash now of a monkish figure tending a herb garden in the grounds of some large ecclesiastical building. Suddenly the single knight fell from his horse. He ran into thick undergrowth to hide. The vision faded.

Pondering on the brief but intense experience, Cara began to feel that the knight called Robert was a past life of Andy. He had physically been to Kingweston and Dundon. He had even frequently travelled between Essex and Glastonbury as Andy was now doing. Andy had stayed in touch with her and communicated the Zodiac developments, such as the move into Virgo. Cara felt that Dundon still required a bit of attention. She wrote to him giving the details of her experience knowing it would be filed in his immense archives for possible future reference.

Back in Essex, someone who Andy had not yet met but would play a crucial role in his life had been slowly strategically manoeuvred in his direction over a period of years. The final decisive push was about to occur. It would dynamise the medieval frequency of the Glastonbury Zodiac quest into ever-greater levels of intensity.

A dream on the night of January 5th 1984 was the decisive moment. A great bank of fog faintly lit by spectral moonlight. A gently whistling breeze moving through it, carrying a sense of mysterious presence. The light within the fog was somehow spiralling outwards now. It cleared a corridor in which was revealed the silhouette of a dark, robed, monk-like figure, with bowed cowled head, thrown into sharp focus by the light and swirling mist behind and around it. The classically ghostly gothic apparition looked up, revealing a serene face and eyes that communicated wisdom and compassion. "Who are you?" the dreamer asked. *"Wulfgar."* "What are you? What do you want of me?" *"I am here to guide. It is time. You must now tell him."* "Tell who?" *"The one of the dreams. He who will rekindle the heavenly fire and move the Great Wheel."*

The monk now gestured back into the swirling vortex of light and fog. Visions formed across its rippling shifting form. They were scenes familiar to the dreamer. They were in fact his own dreams. Vivid scenes repeatedly replayed since his childhood. Battles of Crusaders and Saracens. The pyramids of Egypt. Swirling mists over British green hills. Geometric patterns. Star constellations. Religious buildings. And a monk with upraised arms. This Wulfgar had been present somewhere in the back of his inner life for years. Now the whole process had clearly crossed a new threshold.

"Now is the right time. He will understand. The past is the present. Your destinies linked. Fate awaits you both in the church of Danbury. You must meet, and soon." The shadowy form of the monk dissolved in the tunnel of mist as Bernard awoke with the word "soon" echoing in his head. It was 3am. He knew that this extraordinary dream had to be recorded as fully as possible before any of it was forgotten. Leaving his wife asleep in bed, he got up and went downstairs to write it all down.

Shortly before his marriage he'd destroyed a whole box full of visionary psychic material that he'd been accumulating for years, in the hope that the phenomenon might cease and he could enjoy a normal life. The flow continued though. Dreams guided him onwards. He came to feel that there was someone who could make sense of the extraordinary inner life he'd kept secret for decades. That person was gradually drawing ever nearer. In 1981 he saw an advertisement in *Essex Landscape Mysteries* magazine for a journal called *The Supernaturalist*. A powerful intuition told him that the mysterious character he was waiting for was behind the publication. Bernard cautiously exchanged a few letters with local Earth Mysteries researcher Andrew Collins. Years passed. They never met. Bernard trusted the inner dynamic to force the pace when the time was right. The amazing dream was the sign he was waiting for. He wrote to Andy suggesting that he might like to investigate the medieval mysteries of the Essex town of Danbury.

What was it about the place that was potentially interesting? Inside the church are carved oak effigies of three recumbent knights. Two date from a period around 1272-1307. The other is a little later, circa 1320. They are all depicted in chain mail and surcoats with a sword and scabbard. Their legs are crossed and their feet rest upon lions. Within that format are individual features such as the positioning of their hands and swords. There is no real consensus on the meaning of such details. No extant records of the time record their identities. An 18th century vicar suggested that they may have been members of the St. Clere family, who held lands in Danbury during the 13th century. Records state that the family had used the north aisle of the church as a private chapel for the interment of its members.

In recent years the St. Clere family (whose name became the modern Sinclair) have become increasingly well known as linked to esoteric mysteries of various kinds. This began in the early eighties with the publication of the immensely influential *The Holy Blood and the Holy Grail*. According to its claims, a shadowy secret society named the Prieure de Sion has supposedly been involved in mystical machinations behind the scenes of European politics for at least a thousand years. Their work connects to the story of the Knights Templar and Freemasonry. The Sinclairs are named as important figures within the drama.

A search for the origin of the St. Clere family name soon finds itself in the realm of mystery. At first one is led to a 9th century hermit from Rochester in Kent, named Clare or Clair, who travelled to France and set up a hermitage on the banks of the River Epte.

His efforts earned him canonisation and his name was then given to a nearby castle. A family that lived there took on the name, although unrelated to the hermit saint. In Latin the original form of St. Clere, 'Sancto Claro', means 'Holy Light'. The mystical scholar Harold Bayley, in a famous work entitled *Archaic England,* suggested that the name Sancto Claro was linked to the St. John's Eve bonfires. He noted an example from the parish of St. Clere in Cornwall, a place with a long tradition of midsummer fires. The oldest reference to the locations name is as 'St. Cler'. Bayley believed that it referred to the fires as well as the family. Perhaps the family themselves believed that their name derived from the midsummer fires? The coat of arms of the Danbury branch showed a 'sun in its glory', to use heraldic terms. This was a golden sixteen-rayed sun on a sky blue background. In medieval times, a family coat of arms was a language unto itself, capable of communicating all kinds of subtleties to those in the know. Its details would be chosen with care.

The St. Cleres came to Britain with William the Conqueror, rapidly becoming one of the most powerful families in Britain. Three family lines emerged, English, Scottish and French, that functioned independently of each other. One of the Scottish branch of the family built a late medieval church now acknowledged as a major esoteric set-piece: Rosslyn. They owned land in most counties. There are suggestions they were involved in political subterfuge around the monarchy.

In Danbury, four William de St. Cleres succeeded each other as lords of the local manor and are often confused with each other. The fourth William put money into reconstructing Danbury chapel into the parish church of St. John the Baptist. He died in 1283 without an heir. Some of his lands were given to two members of the Northampton branch of the family, Robert de St. Clere and John FitzSimon.

The Danbury mystery was deepened by the so-called 'pickled' knight. In 1779 some workmen were digging a grave in the north aisle near one of the effigies. They discovered an inscriptionless lead coffin. Inside it was another made of elm. Beneath its lid was a thin cement shell covered in a resinous substance. The breaking of that revealed a perfectly preserved body lying half submerged in a thick aromatic liquid containing flowers and herbs. It appeared to have been treated with embalming fluid. The skin was firm although discoloured on the face. A full set of white teeth remained in place. The body was covered in a white linen shroud. He was described as a 'hearty youth' about five feet tall. The discovery was a local sensation and the body was put on display before being reburied. This strange discovery is not entirely unique. A few other examples from the same general period exist. The process had more than a hint of the orient about it, in particular, Egypt. Crusaders could conceivably have come into contact with such practices.

In March 1984, after he had begun to correspond with Andy about Danbury and the St. Cleres, Bernard had another extraordinary dream. He found himself looking at what appeared to be a scene from medieval Danbury. A chain mailed knight on horseback was leading a funeral procession. The heraldic image of a black eagle was visible on his red knee-length surcoat. Behind him came two men pulling a wooden handcart. On it was a body covered with a sheet. A further two men on horseback, knights in chain mail and blue surcoats, accompanied the cart. The two dismounted, giving the reins of their horses to men in black and brown leather clothes. They then went to stand at either side of the cart with their heads bowed. The leading knight remained mounted. The whole group moved slowly towards the church, which did not have its tower. Along the route on each side was a single line of serf types, each holding a flower. The only sounds were those of horses' hooves and cart-wheels upon the stony path. An incline near the church was too much for the men pulling the cart. After a nod of assent from the knight in red, some of the villagers assisted. When they reached the church, the knight dismounted and walked up to the open door. He took out his sword and handed it hilt first to someone standing there and then removed his headgear. His face was clearly visible as he entered the church. At that point Bernard awoke.

His immediate feeling was that he had witnessed the funeral procession of the pickled knight. There were many details in the dream that could be investigated. The type of outfits that the knights were wearing, loose knee-length coloured surcoats with heraldic devices, were worn in England between 1200 and 1325. The church was seen without a tower. It was built in the late 12th century, with the tower being added at the beginning of the fourteenth. This also fitted the 1200 to 1325 period. All the effigies seemingly matched it as well. The real clincher was the knight in red with his black eagle heraldic emblem. During the period in question one prominent figure known in the area used such a device. He was William de Valence.

The man's life represents another incredibly complex saga of interconnected families. To cut an extremely long story short, his were very close to the St. Cleres. He became Earl of Hertford and used the castle there as his base. This is less than thirty miles from Danbury. He died in 1296. Further investigation made a good case for the pickled knight and the earlier effigy being the fourth William de St. Clere. He was actually a cousin of de Valence and their known biographies show that they would inevitably have met. At the time of the funeral, de Valence was known to be in the country. The two blue surcoated knights in attendance would have been William's heirs, Robert de St. Clere and John FitzSimon. These gentlemen are the candidates for the later effigies.

It was Bernard's communication of this dream in a further letter to Andy that convinced him that a meeting was essential. This was psychism of a quality not seen since the days of the Green Stone. On one level, the Essex mystery was a self-contained topic unto itself. It led to one of Andy's earliest works, *The Knights of Danbury.*

A larger perspective was soon revealed. Andy often drove down to the Glastonbury environs during this period of time to visit Zodiac sites out of curiosity and general information gathering rather than through definite psychic clues. At the end of April 1984, he made a significant discovery. It was in the church of St. Michael and All Angels in Somerton. Within the chapel of the Holy Spirit is a glass cabinet on a wall displaying historical information. The St. Clere solar coat of arms was displayed. The information shown indicated that they owned land in the vicinity. The Sancto Claro were Lords of Stapleton in Martock. From the Chancery Rolls of 1303 a quote mentioned, '*Robert de St. Clere to collect knights fees for marriage of King's eldest daughter.*' Further research connected the Somerset branch to the Essex group. The Robert de St. Clere who owned land in Somerton was very likely to be the Danbury man. The historical period of the St. Cleres he was investigating was within a century of the publication of *Perlesvaus* and the famous Arthurian events at the abbey. The church at Somerton dates from the same early 13th century period, although plenty of the visible features are later additions. It became officially a County town in 1278. The Grail Romances had been the sensation of Europe. Was it possible that a family like the St. Cleres could be in the vicinity without any knowledge or interest in such matters?

On May 6th, Andy and Bernard finally met in Danbury church. They discussed the amazing funeral dream and the ongoing historical research. Much of it was coming from an obscure anonymous 1887 book, *The Sinclairs of England.* Three days later, Bernard was reading that weighty tome. He got the feeling that the work should continue in Somerset. A great drowsiness overcame him and he was forced to lie down, rapidly falling asleep. Vague figures filled his mind. Words drifted in and out of awareness. *'Holy light'*, *'heavenly'*, *'hidden is Leo'*. The figure of Wulfgar then appeared. He was holding a glass ball that began to brightly shine. In that sphere Bernard saw three knights on horseback, pursuing a man on foot through a wood. Bernard was sure that the location was not Essex. On waking, he intuited that the St. Cleres were involved in a magical struggle with certain Templars. They protected the knowledge of an awesome ancient mystery.

A series of visits to Danbury church by Andy and Bernard provided the details of the whole story surrounding this episode. More medieval visions featuring the church appeared. The scenes were vivid enough to feature architectural details that, like the funeral dream, helped to affirm a psychically received date of 1285. Bernard repeatedly saw a gathering of five people in the chapel. William de Valence, dressed in armour, was standing with his back to the altar. Robert de St. Clere, wearing a divided surcoat of blue and red with a kind of elongated Seal of Solomon image on it, was kneeling with his back to him, head bared, displaying shoulder length light coloured hair and a beardless face. He looked towards three sitting men. They were John FitzSimon, and two other St. Cleres from another branch of the family, Phillip and William. The three were dressed in everyday clothes. There had been discussion about whether Robert was worthy to undertake some significant and dangerous task. One of the seated men, dressed in black with black hair and beard, got up and approached the kneeling knight, whose sword was placed on the floor in front of him. He made gestures in a circular motion over his head that invoked blue and yellow rays of energy. His hands were then cupped and the coloured energies released over Robert's head, blending together as green. A pouch was then placed around his neck. It contained a ring with a six pointed star inscribed upon it.

The questing knight was then warned of the *'Fraternatis Malus'*, the Brotherhood of Evil, and told he was to find the *'Templum'*, or Sanctuary. Bernard eventually entered into psychic communion with the third William de St. Clere of Danbury and he gave further guidance. The Templars were referred to as *"those who butcher under the pretence of the cross – fools to themselves. They think they hold the truth. They do not. – They call it Avalon. They do not know. Their being is bloodshed"*. Andy and Bernard were directed to *"the place you know. The one that burned. It did not destroy the cause. We carry on"*. Quite obviously, this is not 13th century lingo. Subsequent visions of apparent historical events with an audio component have likewise been somehow filtered through the recipient's brain. Does this invalidate the content? I personally don't believe it does. I am willing to see where such material leads and, in 1984, Andy certainly was. Here were tantalising hints. Esoteric business was already occurring in Glastonbury when the Templars were formed. There may have been subtle conflicts of interest. Remember Bernard of Clairvaux's denunciation of Henry of Blois. Hank Harrison believed that the great fire of 1184 was arson. The affair of Arthur's grave may have provided an opportunity to increase the influence of certain factions.

These visions of the Danbury preparation of Robert de St. Clere for a mystical quest were not seen with the detached perspective of someone involved in a remote viewing experiment. There was someone else in the church as well and it was from his eyes that Bernard was looking. Phillip de Clara Vallis was the son of John of Brabant, brother of Marie, the wife of the King of France, Phillip III. It was suggested that the French king knew of his mission and kept its existence a secret. Phillip had died in 1285. This helped narrow down the timescale for the visions. Phillip had travelled from the vicinity of an abbey amongst swampy lands in France. Clara Vallis was the name given to a valley in the Auxe of France by none other than Bernard of Clairvaux. Phillip was fully briefed on the situation and was to act as a kind of bodyguard to Robert on his journey. He had been raised by the St. Cleres. It was beginning to look like, on one level, Andy and Bernard were involved in a past-life saga.

Bernard felt that the two had been sent to an area on the outskirts of the Leo figure. Something about a 'Queens Chamber' connected with a triangular piece of land. Andy recognised this as the tuft on the tail of the lion at Christians Cross.

Eventually, the full details of their journey were revealed. Robert de St. Clere and Phillip de Clara Vallis had travelled in disguise on a fateful journey to Somerset. It was September 20th 1285. Robert stood between two large oaks on the top of a sloping hill. He was holding his sword with both hands, point vertically down on the ground. Phillip was a few hundred yards away watching him and the general scene. Suddenly he saw five men appearing from a nearby wood bearing down on his companion who had not yet spotted them. Before he could warn Robert, Phillip was surprised from behind and run through with a sword, falling dying to the ground. Bernard looked down on the body and the two attackers who stood over it. The next day he awoke with two strange scar-like marks on his chest and back corresponding to the areas pierced by the sword in the vision. The fatal attack on Phillip de Clara Vallis alerted his companion. Robert de St. Clere fled with the group in pursuit. He ran down the hill slope into a meadow, coming to a stone gateway that led into a complex of buildings around an inn. A group of people who obviously knew him had horses prepared in a courtyard. They rode out to confront his pursuers.

A few days later Robert was ambushed again. He had been riding along a dirt track through a dense wood. A stream had been forded by two stone marker pillars. Bernard saw from above that another path crossed over some way ahead. The trees prevented Robert from seeing his pursuers until it was too late. Three mounted knights barred his path. One grabbed the reins of St. Clere's horse in an attempt to force him to dismount. *"You have something which belongs to our master. Our mission is to retrieve. It is not for your family to decide how to use the power it invokes."* Robert denied possession of any such item and warned them that he had companions nearby. Taking advantage of their brief indecision, he broke free of his pursuers.

The fleeing man reached some kind of sanctuary where friends helped him. A servant was despatched with a message. He was seen entering a dining chamber in Glastonbury Abbey and talking to the abbot, John of Taunton. There was a sense of urgency. The abbot left the table and walked down some concealed steps into an underground vault. Within it was a megalithic type stone, a bit taller than an average man. A group of nine men in black sat around a horseshoe shaped table behind the stone. The abbot touched the stone, seeming to invoke some unknown force.

It was after this that Robert's plight became more desperate as the events seen firstly by Cara and then in Bernard's initial vision in Wulfgar's glass ball unfolded. He was cornered again, unhorsed and chased through a wood, being forced to hide in a ditch to escape.

The spirit of William de St. Clere became more forthcoming about the esoteric details of the zodiac quest. Robert's ring *"was handed to our forefathers by Khunata, a man of the words. He had the keys and could walk through the circle. He is the fashioner of the ring. Our forefathers pass on the knowledge through the ages. Only the ones with the signs of the colours will succeed. They retread the steps of the ancients".* The mysterious Khunata came from a place, *"where the sun burns the head and swells the tongue".* The practice of preserving bodies, that the St. Cleres of Danbury adopted, came from his tradition. So Robert's ring was *"not a ring of the finger. It is the ring of colours and numbers decided at birth. To say Robert wears the ring is true. He does, but not on his finger. The pouch contained these colours and numbers of Robert and they were to sit on the stone at Glaston".*

A further vision showed what happened when Robert de St. Clere eventually arrived at the abbey after his pursuit. The abbot led him down into the underground chamber. Robert knelt by the stone, with one hand upon its side. Around the horseshoe table were nine members of the St. Clere family in black monk-type robes. One of the nine put a kind of upturned cup on the top of the stone. He then ritualistically raised his hands and brought them together over the stone. As he parted them, colours could be seen in a similar manner to the Danbury preparatory blessing. The whole stone then became increasingly colourful. It started at the base with a reddish orange and moved through a rainbow sequence to the top whilst the man's hands were still over it. Bernard felt there was an important solar aspect to all this and then heard the word 'Teitan'. Teitan is a Chaldean solar deity whose gematria adds to 666. Bligh Bond had suggested that this number was an important key to the numerical codes of the abbey's geometry. Church authorities tend to have their own feelings about it so that didn't help his case much. The vision progressed as the officiator then took a cup from the horseshoe table. It contained liquid. A few drops anointed the stone. This produced sounds, and the colours became translucent and moved rapidly up and down the stone until becoming pure white light. Somehow Robert's colours and numbers had been fed into the stone. The vision concluded with the black monk saying, *"the threads will part and become as one. All souls will join in the songs".*

The underground chamber has so far eluded archaeologists. Glastonbury lore is full of tunnels though and the abbey is often implicated. John of Taunton's abbacy was a time of major events and big building projects. Ten years before the alleged Robert de St. Clere episode, in 1275 an earthquake had destroyed the Norman chapel of St. Michael on the Tor. In 1278, the same year that Somerton became a county town, Edward I, the notorious Longshanks so memorably portrayed in *Braveheart,* visited the abbey with his Queen and the Archbishop of Canterbury to inspect the bones of Arthur and Guenevere prior to their internment in a lavish tomb, an occasion synchronised with the consecration of a new High Altar. Considerable attention would have been given to Glastonbury. A remarkable measure of the power of the abbey as an institution was demonstrated by the fact that the King himself was unable to hold assizes there due to prior royally established laws that made the place almost a kingdom unto itself. He had to move his entourage outside of the twelve hides to do so. The abbot was obviously a national figure able to wield worldly power and inevitably at the centre of some levels of intrigue, even if only in terms of ongoing rivalries with the Bishop of Bath and Wells. Glastonbury's influence was at its peak. The extraordinary psychic scenarios involving him need to be appreciated in that context.

Around this time, Bernard visited Canterbury Cathedral with his family and viewed what is known as the Opus Alexandrinum mosaic. He mentioned to his wife that there was a similar one on the floor in Glastonbury Abbey and it included a zodiac and lines set into the stones. Having virtually no knowledge of the abbey's history he didn't realise until he spoke to Andy that it no longer existed. He was able to see it still with his inner eye so clearly that he could draw it and discuss it in detail.

The design on the floor of the Old Church referred to by William of Malmesbury and Bligh Bond's monks was apparently reproduced in the new Mary Chapel, signifying the position of the original building. John Michell had paid particular attention to it when suggesting that the abbey's foundational geometry embodied the ancient wisdom code and represented the New Jerusalem celestial archetype during the Christian cycle.

* * *

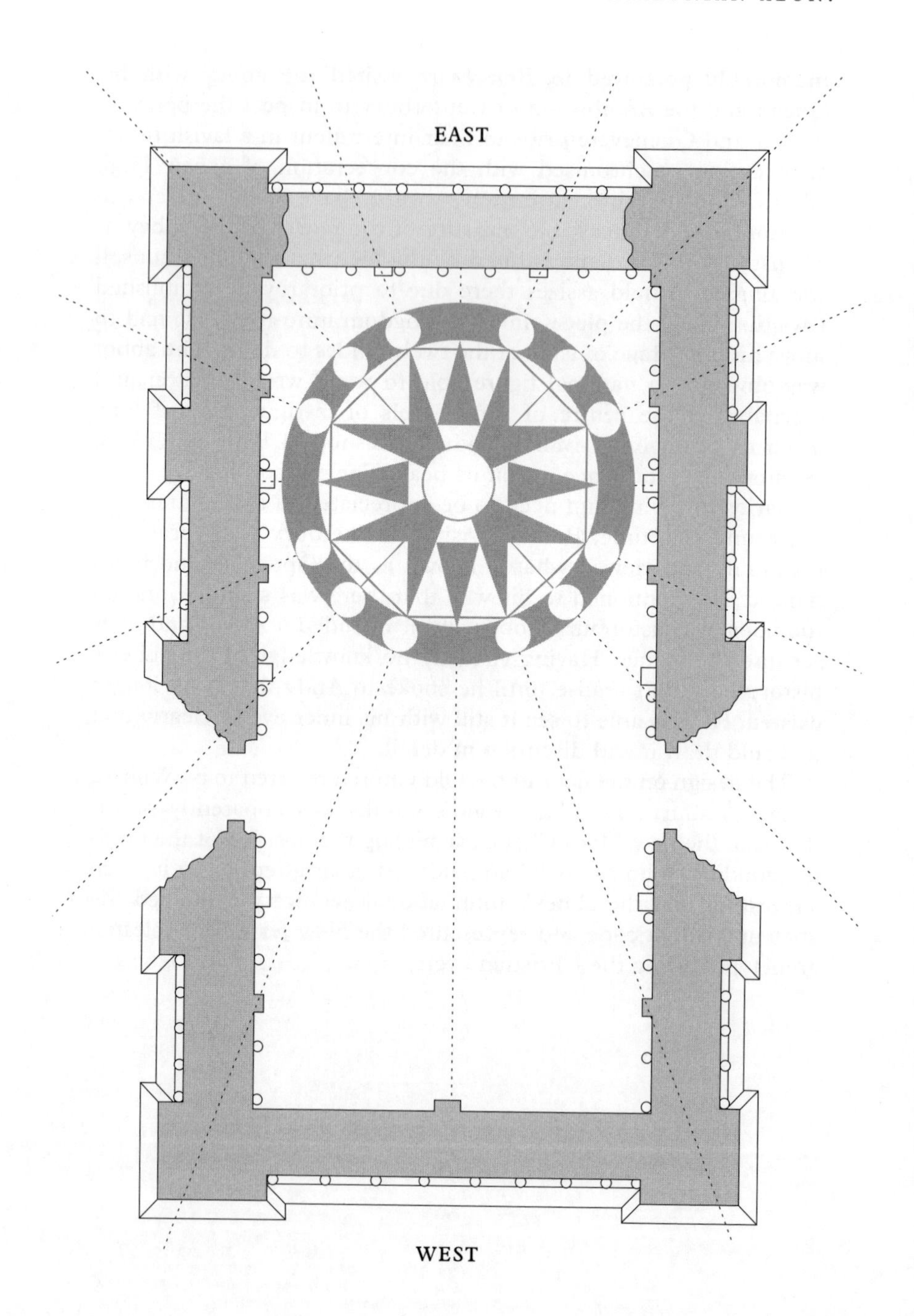
EAST
WEST

Bernard saw an outer and inner circle. Within the two were twelve spheres, in four groups of three, containing symbols for the signs of the zodiac. In the middle of the inner circle was a square. Its corners could not be seen as they were cut across by a Maltese cross whose points reached out to the edge of the inner circle. From the sides of the square that were visible, four triangles reached out to the edge of the inner circle, indicating the cardinal points. Sixteen lines ran out from the centre of the design, through the twelve spheres and four triangles beyond its outer circle to sixteen small pillars along the base of the chapel walls, each about two feet tall, on which were further symbols. The twelve lines passing through the zodiacal signs could be continued out beyond the building to the locations of the fabled twelve huts and further across the Glastonbury landscape and beyond.

The twelve zodiacal spheres and central point were coloured gold by ochre tiles. The outer circle in which the spheres were set was red terracotta as was the Maltese cross and cardinal point triangles. Beaten lead lines marked the geometry of the design. Somehow the whole thing was to be perceived as in motion. Each part of the levels of geometrical design was revolving. The Maltese cross was moving at one speed, the triangles from the square at another. A series of colours was produced by this that came to form one colour. The colours also had sound correlations.

At the end of August 1984, in Danbury church, with William's guidance, Bernard began to see an Egyptian vision, a dark windowless room lit by torches. A sarcophagus. On the dark blue ceiling was a spiral of stars. *"Khunata formed the wheels and colours from the stars. There are others of the line."* The names Sahure, Neferirkare, Niuserre, and the place name Abusir. It turned out that those gentlemen were all early fifth dynasty rulers, circa 2,500 BC, buried in pyramids at Abusir, and connected with a solar cult. Sahure's tomb does have gold stars on a dark blue ceiling. Andy was not able to discover if they were in a spiral. Again, this astounding access to real names and places was a strong encouragement to go along with the adventure. The implication was that somehow the St. Cleres had connected with ancient Egyptian wisdom. Whether this had occurred during the crusader epoch or sometime before was unclear.

Andy and Bernard prepared to physically visit Glastonbury at the time of the autumn equinox. A few weeks in advance Bernard began having more of his typical trademark psychic visions. He saw himself entering a church with Andy. The usual meticulous detail was there. A font with four sphinxes or griffins at the column's corners. There were claws and wings beating down the heads of devils.

The two men finally came to Glastonbury together on September 19th 1984, hoping firstly to find the site of the death of Phillip de Clara Vallis at the time of the anniversary of that event. They arrived in the early evening just in time to spend a few moments in the Mary Chapel crypt. Bernard saw the mosaic design again. A clairaudient voice asked him, *"Have you come to re-light the lamps?"* He then sensed the presence of a complex of underground chambers that included the room with the megalithic stone. It seemed to extend virtually the entire length of the abbey. Further guidance told him that the next site to visit was East Pennard church. An image followed of a king sitting beneath a tree who transfigured into an eagle type bird and flew away over water into the setting sun.

A swift check of a Somerset guide-book revealed that the font in East Pennard church had four carved heads of which two were sphinxes. All the figures had claws under which were horned heads. This conformed sufficiently to Bernard's last visions before departure to make it obvious they were on the right track. When Bernard checked East Pennard's location on a road map, he immediately pointed to a spot on the nearby West Bradley road as the site of his past-life death.

It was still daylight. Christian's Cross, a ploughed field shaped by three roads as a triangle, near to Kingweston, was suddenly mentioned in psychic despatches and Bernard wanted to go there immediately. On arriving, he knelt down on the earth. He saw himself in a golden sea. Many other people were all around him, striving to extricate themselves. They seemed to be priests whose strength and integrity of belief had not been sufficient to ensure them an auspicious transition. All of them had their left arms raised in a gesture of supplication that Bernard copied. The sky overhead was an orange hue and a rainbow arched over it. Suddenly a great hand appeared, reaching down from the sky. The bobbing multitudes were now convulsing in grotesque paroxyisms of disgraceful beseeching. Jewels were offered to the beckoning hand. Many tried to jump up and grab it. All to no avail.

Bernard alone was lifted up and away into a great golden whirlpool. Images came into view from outside it, rapidly replaced by others. A church. A desert area. A temple with two pillars outside. Another desert near mountains. A small town with white buildings.

A canyon near water with a square section carved out of the rock within which was a square room in which an old man, Khunata, sat amongst yellowing crumbling manuscripts on the floor. He seemed to be a Christian hermit in the Holy Land, perhaps from sometime around 800 AD. Khunata responded to Bernard's presence, telling him he revealed, *"The knowledge of Thomas. He took this back across the seas. Many have been and gone and changed it. These people were part of a wandering nomadic tribe who spread the knowledge of the people of his country. He got these ancient writings and worked them out. There is more than one centre to the Great Wheel but each centre contains a stone".*

Bernard felt that Christian's Cross was like a multi-dimensional three sided pyramid, a tetrahedron. The 'Queens Chamber' was at its centre, above ground somewhere in another vibrational level beyond the physical. He also saw a white female form somewhere within it.

Driving back to their guest-house accommodation in Butleigh, Bernard suddenly pulled the car to a halt. He had just seen a black knight carrying a shield riding on a black horse cross the road directly in front of them as if the hedges along the roadsides didn't exist. They got out of the car and Bernard heard words being shouted in their direction. *"You will never defeat me at the church."*

After breakfast the next morning, Andy and Bernard drove along the road between West Bradley and East Pennard. The location of the vision was easily located. The oaks on the hill where Robert had stood were gone but the sloping hill and nearby wood were clearly visible. In pouring rain the two took up duplicate positions to the fateful day in 1285. Bernard was only yards from the road. Andy had brought a replica medieval sword with him and held it as Robert had done on the hill. Bernard saw the whole scene exactly as before with the additional sense of some kind of connection with the black knight who was related to Scorpio.

All Saints church East Pennard proved to be as Bernard had described it. The font was indeed striking. Bernard saw a clear image of the Egyptian lioness goddess Sekhmet. He also saw a knight in red and gold surcoat holding a shield displaying a similarly coloured diamond pattern. It was later identified as belonging to the de Craon family of France, who appeared to be behind Phillip's murder. From there it was off to St. Michael and All Angels in Somerton where Andy had first made the Robert de St. Clere Somerset connection. The de Craon knight was visible again.

He stood in front of a dark cave guarded by two large dark double-headed eagle type birds. In response to requests for guidance, the knight said, "*To find the next figure is to find the green hill*". It was clear to Andy that a certain amount of replay of the saga he had already played out with Cara was occurring. The Dundon vicinity was calling once again. It had been his policy to not tell Bernard very much of what had already transpired to see what he spontaneously picked up.

In Compton Dundon church the knight and the bird-guarded cave reappeared. He turned around to face the cavernous entrance, raised his arms and walked into its darkness. Bernard felt that he and Andy were being invited to follow. He asked Andy if there was a nearby location with some sort of cave inside it. Andy confirmed that he was on the right track and Bernard proceeded to mentally 'enter' the cave with no resistance from the birds. He came to a huge underground cavern filled with light. There were two pyramids inside, their tips linked by a line of light. From each tip a figure emerged and came forth blending together in front of Bernard. The whole scene dissolved in white light. Opening his eyes again in the church, Bernard was clear that they must now go to the hill that contains the cavern. There is some kind of stone atop it.

As they climbed Dundon Beacon the rain had stopped and the sun was starting to break through the clouds. There is indeed a stone near the summit of uncertain age. Bernard could see with eyes open a column of blue light rising up from it. A laser thin line of blue was also projecting across the landscape in a south-easterly direction. Andy recalled some of Cara's material about a priestess guardian of the site and felt the need to call on her for guidance. Before he even had a chance to say anything, Bernard was telling him that he could see a medieval looking young lady in white, with blonde long flowing hair. She was holding a shield on which was a cross. She said, "*It comes of you now to enter the cones of heaven*". With this came a further glimpse of the interior of the hill with its tetrahedral pyramids and blazing light. A strong feeling immediately followed that Keinton Mandeville church, which Andy knew was situated in the Virgo figure, was a doorway to another interdimensional zone like Christian's Cross and was to be the next site on the itinerary.

Once inside the church of Mary Magdalene, both Bernard and Andy were able to see the lady again, standing in front of a cone of light. An opening could be seen in it with steps leading upwards. She was holding a small cross in one hand and a wheatsheaf in the other, and seemed to be inviting them to come inside the cone. The steps led through a dense orangey yellow light to a room in which was a huge table mirror. The lady was there, with one hand held out beckoning them to look in the mirror. In it could be seen a low tumuli-type mound with some trees upon it. She was standing upon it, holding the cross and wheatsheaf. Bernard felt the urgent necessity of going there and the certainty that she would be waiting for them.

Andy recognised the place immediately. He had visited it briefly with Chesca Potter when the Empress Matilda material had appeared. It's one of the better known Zodiac locations: Wimble Toot. It forms the breast of the Virgo effigy, the only female figure in the Glastonbury Zodiac, and is usually depicted holding out a wheatsheaf. Mrs Maltwood attributed it to the Damsel of the *High History,* along with Perceval's sister Dindrain. Mary Caine associated it more with Guenevere (who is Hydra in Maltwood's arrangement) and brought in more general goddess symbolism, including that of Ceredwen.

They arrived to fierce wind. Bernard could hear a choir of female voices. The lady was clearly visible to him, holding the cross and wheatsheaf. An approaching bank of dark cloud seemed to speak of the presence of the black knight. He was trying to block out the lady. Her voice was difficult to hear. She managed to communicate that they needed the cross she was holding and it was actually physically present at the site. Andy already had experience of such situations. He coached Bernard, asking him to get the lady to show him exactly where. The intensity of the gale increased. After a few moments of confusion Bernard was led to a large tree. The relevant episode in *Perlesvaus* depicts '*a damsel sitting under a great leafy tree*'. He began to scrape around in the soft soil near its roots. A glint of something. Frantic digging to uncover it. An ebony, brass-rimmed crucifix. Six inches long. Sunburst halo behind Christ's head. A skull and crossbones at his feet, representing Golgotha. Bernard sank to his knees, tears in his eyes. Andy leapt up in the air, letting out the yell of a man who has just scored a goal in a World Cup Final.

When a modicum of composure had been regained, Bernard stated that there was another church nearby, built by ruins of an older site. He could see the black knight there, throwing a spear into the church door which then ran with blood, dissolving into the form of a writhing serpent on blood-soaked soil. Bernard named the place. Hornblotton church in the Scorpio figure. As they departed from the Toot his last glimpse of the lady saw her holding a bow.

From Leo, to Gemini, Virgo and now into Scorpio – the fourth sign. The astonishing psychic material and the artefact discovery had built up a momentum and atmosphere that was taking the pair into another reality. On the way to St. Peter's church at Hornblotton a head-on collision with an oncoming car was narrowly avoided. This helped set the appropriate mood. The approach to the church took them along a winding track by windswept dead trees. On entering the churchyard they found two gravediggers at work on the last resting place of a man named Knight. Bernard's prior impressions were again essentially correct. The church dates from 1874 but remains of the tower of an earlier structure lie in nearby undergrowth. There was a brief scan of the place.

They knew that the black knight had to be faced. It would be a test of resolve. They had to stand their ground. Bernard felt it would happen outside. It was nearly three o'clock in the afternoon. The gravediggers had left. Finally, the rider appeared to Bernard's psychic sight. His name was Mordred. He was near the ruins. Clad completely in black, he held a lance and shield. There is an episode in *Perlesvaus* featuring a black knight carrying a spear that '*burned with a great flame*'. The shield had a distinctive heraldic design on it; deep red with a diagonal gold bar on which were displayed three frogs. Later research amazingly identified this design as being the coat of arms of Satan! A work known as the *Douce Apocalypse*, written about 1280, contained a divided illustration depicting a scene from the *Book of Revelation* showing a manacled Satan being led out of hell and also standing fully armed with a shield showing the three frogs. To the medieval imagination it seemed logical that in the great End of Days conflict, the commander-in-chief of the bad guys would require a coat of arms and battle standard around which his troops would rally. Douce was an antiquarian who had bequeathed the work to the Bodleian Library at Oxford in 1834. What on earth was the mechanics of this? The only tentative hypothesis was that Robert de St. Clere or Phillip de Clara Vallis, who were supposedly in the area at the time the work was circulating, may have been familiar with it. Bernard's mind was as primed as Bligh Bond's had been and the past-life connection probably amplified this. Whatever the case, it was an impressively weird detail.

As the black knight appeared, the whole area turned blood red. He spoke. *"Like the others who have been before, this is as far as you go."* Andy advised Bernard to be ready to visualise a pentagram of fire to project forcefully at the knight if he advanced. The apparition moved forward. Bernard flung forth the pentagram but it made no difference. The knight raised his lance. Bernard was seeing this whole scene with the vividity of physical reality. Understandably he was getting a bit worried and began to turn away as if to run. Andy had another resource at his disposal. He had brought along a magically consecrated sword which he now held aloft, threatening the black knight with the fire of the Archangel Michael and focusing with maximum intensity on the nature of that energy. Bernard saw the knight dissolving into mist and heard him say, *"You have won this time but there will be others"*. Questing site etiquette demanded that they thank the knight for letting them pass. He was the guardian of the place after all, and his demeanour was appropriate to its aspects. A request was uttered for guidance towards the next site. Bernard again saw the image of the lady with a bow and named West Pennard church in Sagittarius. They immediately departed for that location.

In the north wall of the north aisle is a commemorative window to Prince Arthur, the short-lived son of Henry VII. Bernard saw a blurred vision of a distant battle on a hill between armies of light and dark forces. Then he returned to the scene first revealed in the abbey the previous day of a king beneath a tree. This was followed by the bizarre sight of a huge bonfire with people walking in and out of it. Two rainbows arched over the fire that changed into a bird and flew into the air. It was holding in its talons a great multi-faceted crystal. It flew over a huge green lake, dropping the crystal into the water. An island slowly emerged from the ripples. The bird was the Aquarian phoenix. It was the Tor that rose from the primal waters. Bernard had seen a kind of Glastonbury foundation myth in the style of ancient Egypt.

He said that the king and the fire were on a *"high place, the place of the big serpent"*. Andy knew that this was Windmill Hill near Baltonsborough, still very much in Sagittarius. Mary Caine style etymology would link it with Bel and his fires. Andy had briefly visited the place in February 1984 after Anthony Roberts had mentioned it to him. He had seen a strange striking vision of a group of white robed women wearing head-dresses, standing around a huge bonfire. He had felt that the place had been a beacon point. The women then somehow walked through the fire. The phrase *'baptism of fire'* had repeated in Andy's head. There had been a brief glimpse of a Roman soldier but it was the fire rite that lingered. There's a waterworks on top of the hill that affords a fine view of the Tor. As their concluding act of a stunning journey Andy and Bernard climbed up to it to survey the terrain and take on the scale of what they'd just experienced. The Egyptian style Glastonbury creation myth vision repeated itself. One phase was complete. It was time to return to Essex.

1985 was supposedly the seven hundredth anniversary of Robert de St. Clere's zodiac quest. Andy was all set to complete his modern replay of it. Unfortunately, Bernard had begun to suffer from high blood pressure and had to back-off for a while. Although he was willing to continue to psychically attune to the quest, it increasingly began to look as if, just as Phillip had only accompanied Robert so far, Andy would have to physically complete the journey alone.

* * *

AEGYPT

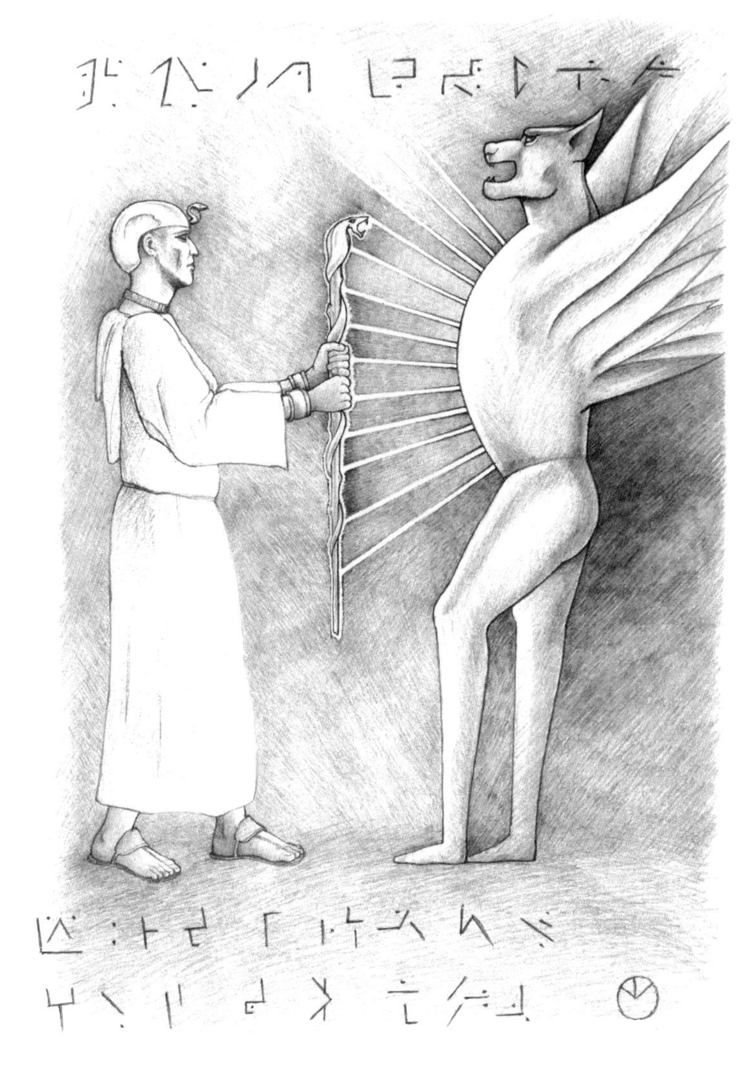

"The serpent is the guardian of the centre of the great wheel."
Americ de St. Maur.

"That which is above is like that which is below,
and that which is below is like that which is above."
Hermes Trismegistus.

THE ZODIAC QUEST HAD BEEN SPLIT IN TWO. At first it seemed that Bernard's apparently accidental high blood pressure was solely responsible. This impression soon changed. A notable omission from the sites featured in the Robert de St. Clere saga had been Park Wood, considered to be the very centre of the zodiacal wheel, the place Marion Sunderland had called the Eye of the Dragon. Before Andy's journey could recommence, the significance of the place asserted itself in a manner that ultimately placed it appropriately enough in the middle of the zodiac quest.

In February 1985, Andy returned to Glastonbury to investigate the next site in the anticipated sequence. He met Anthony Roberts in the High Street who had urgent news to convey. They retired to the *Rainbow's End* cafe. Park Wood was for sale. A number of bidders were interested. Some were from overseas and seemed to have mystical motives. With others, it was unclear. A climate of conspiracy was arising. Whatever was going on, it was clearly a vital time for the Zodiac. Roberts was sending a letter to the local MP, stating his concerns that a site of potentially huge historic significance could be damaged or lost to organisations of a dubious nature.

It is rather intriguing to discover that a couple of villages near the centre of the Zodiac have played a role in world changing events. There are two small American flags and a plaque displayed on the wall in the church at Barton St. David, located within the Libra figure. The place was the ancestral home of two American Presidents, John Adams and John Quincy Adams. Their British roots supposedly date back to the Norman Conquest. Adams ancestors could have known some of the St. Cleres. Nearby Butleigh Court had been the home of the Neville family. One of the Nevilles was responsible for bringing in the infamous Stamp Tax that put a tax on tea. John Adams and his brother Samuel were living in Boston. They were involved in the rebellion against the tax that developed into the American War of Independence.

It can be confidently stated as a matter of historical record that a number of the main movers behind the American Declaration of Independence and Constitution were Freemasons. How important a factor that may have been in the events of the time is a topic for increasing esoteric speculation. Influential early explorers and colonisers do seem to have been working to a big agenda both political and spiritual. The phrase 'New Atlantis' was in circulation from Elizabethan times. The legendary John Dee, through his royal connections and map-making skills, influenced explorers and policy makers with theories of the righteous necessity of creating a British empire that would be a logical extension of vast Arthurian domains that Geoffrey of Monmouth had claimed once existed. Some conspiracists trace the beginning of the modern phase of the notorious New World Order to this time. The word seemed to spread along the occult grapevine and a number of mystical heretical types with varying political aspirations migrated across the Atlantic from all over Western Europe.

John Adams went on from being a major game player in the great events of 1776 to become the second President of the USA. He was not a Freemason. His son John Quincy Adams even spoke out against certain aspects of the Craft during his Presidency. An aura of esotericism has attached itself to the family though. In 1823 John Adams had an engraved flat stone placed on the grave of his ancestor Henry Adams, who had emigrated from England in 1638. The inscription mentions that he *"took his flight from the Dragon persecution in Devonshire"*.

This kind of fragment is guaranteed to lead to typical occult speculation. Henry Adams, so the mythology goes, was actually the leader of the 'Dragon Society', a group variously described as initiates of the ancient earth energies known to the Druids, affiliated to the Rosicrucians, and later mixed up with the Masonic scene. Throw in hints of pre-Columbus Templar trans-Atlantic travels, and the later emergence of everybody's favourites, the Illuminati, and one has a wonderful esoteric brew. Historical documentation of this is predictably scarce but it is worth noting that some of the conspirators in the War of Independence famously met in the *Green Dragon* tavern. It was from there that the Boston Tea Party began.

In *The Temple and the Lodge,* Michael Baigent and Richard Leigh speculated on some of the more fascinating possibilities of the background to the American Revolution. It seems that players on both sides of the apparent political divide shared a Masonic connection. The wildest hypothesis is that some of the British consciously connived in events that appeared to work against them. In the light of this, the Glastonbury Zodiac roots of two families later to become so interlinked in a world-historical drama do perhaps give pause for thought.

It is fairly obvious that a place like Glastonbury will attract world-wide attention from many groups of diverse orientation. Tony Roberts was well qualified to sniff out dodgy machinations of occult forces. He had co-authored with fellow Glastonbury resident

Geoff Gilbertson a paranoid classic entitled *The Dark Gods*, published in 1980. It seems that malevolent entities have been messing with our heads since the dawn of history. Just about every single esoteric group in the western tradition reeks of diabolism and general contamination. Freemasonry is a hideous tentacled monstrosity aiming at Luciferic world domination. And so on.

After meeting Tony Roberts and hearing of the Park Wood sale, it didn't take Andy long to accept that something important was happening. The next morning, he rang Bernard from Glastonbury, wondering if any more psychic information had been forthcoming. It had. The previous day, Bernard had seen a night-time ceremony occurring at a place he knew to be Park Wood. It was led by a Templar named Americ de St. Maur, who had recently emerged as a new psychic contact. He, and five other men in dark, hoodless robes, were standing in a circle, with raised swords that were touching at their tips. To an accompanying low chant, they then moved in a circle, clockwise and anti-clockwise. They were drawing down the energy of the serpent's head and the crown. According to Katherine Maltwood the wood aligns to Draco, the dragon serpent, and its boundaries mark out the shape of a kind of Egyptian-style uraeus serpent crown.

Bernard felt considerable urgency about the conveying of the vision to him. Andy hadn't mentioned anything about the news he'd just heard about Park Wood. It was clear that the two things were connected.

The St. Maurs were descended from yet another companion of William the Conqueror. Their name evolved into Seymour during the 14th century. The family did hold land in Somerset, including Castle Cary. Americ later said that he was based in London and was the Master Templar of England in 1200. Research confirmed that an Americ de St. Maur had been Master of the Temple from 1200 to 1216. He worked on behalf of King John and was present at the signing of the Magna Carta.

His mates were also Templars, but were doing unofficial business. He named them as Roger de Auxville, Simon de Auxville, William Bradlesmire, John of Caen and Johannus de Sermet de Paignard. 'Brother John', *"had told him of the stories of the past, about the holy circle, the times of Arturio, the coming of the wanderers, the great wheel"*. Americ had no knowledge of Robert de St. Clere, whose time period was about a century later. He didn't appear to represent the kind of interests that were hostile to the St. Cleres. It's rather intriguing that these characters date from the same period of time that *Perlesvaus* is usually considered to have been written.

In the coming weeks, the details of the Park Wood ceremony expanded in detail. The sword touching practice was supposedly similar to rituals carried out in the Templar church in London. Americ said that the ritual would be done at each quarter of the year, the solstices and equinoxes. In the spring, a feast day of Joseph of Arimathea on March 17th (near enough to the equinox), was considered to be the best date. The big question was why all of this was in the psychic airwaves at the same time that Park Wood was for sale? Americ answered that, *"the energies are waning. Every practice saps the flows. Nothing is returned. Those who conduct evil on the land only destroy part of the running of the streams. It makes as a blot of ink on manuscript. It runs. It dries black. It does not disperse, it stays. Many blots on a parchment become one. The parchment becomes nothing and is fit only to be destroyed. You are acting not for yourselves but for the whole".*

Americ had also mentioned, almost in passing, a few other weighty topics. There was the little matter of a green tablet buried on the Tor. He had said that its

> *"Father is the sun, Mother the moon*
> *Wind carried it, Earth is its matron."*

There was talk of an arcane text *"from Espania, said to contain strange figures and numbers. Hearsay only. Comes from Holy Land. Very ancient".* Toledo and Cordoba were mentioned, and the name Al Kindi, a prodigious 9th century Muslim polymath. All of this served to focus attention on alchemy and Hermetica. The green tablet buried on the Tor called to mind the famous work, the 'Emerald Tablet' of Hermes Trismegistus. When Andy looked more closely he found this passage within it.

> *"The sun is its father, the moon is its mother.*
> *Wind has carried it in its belly, the Earth is its nurse."*

It was in fact directly quoted by Katherine Maltwood in *Enchantments of Britain,* a work that Bernard had now read, but he had established an entirely different context. It is considered to be a core text of alchemy. Something seemed to be trying to link Glastonbury with Hermeticism. One story tells how the fabled green tablet lay in the hands of Hermes' mummy, in a hidden chamber somewhere in the Great Pyramid. An Egyptian Glastonbury Zodiac connection had already started to appear. The mysteries of Giza were now increasingly being pointed to. It was also the first time that Bernard clearly tuned-in to alchemy. Within a few months this would lead to a moment of destiny with an inscribed spearhead in a churchyard. Whatever intelligence was guiding the psychic material, it wanted to suggest the strong likelihood that the mystical knights encountered in the zodiac quest had some knowledge of the Hermetic Gnostic alchemical transmission.

There was one detail of the Robert de St. Clere story that may reveal signs of such a lineage. Situated in modern Turkey, Harran is a city with an ancient pedigree. A cult centre of Babylonian religion, primarily dedicated to the moon god Sin, it was supposedly visited by Abraham. Its unique destiny was to survive the rise and fall of many empires, becoming a living embodiment of their cumulative traditions. It seems that a number of Alexandrian Hermeticists fled there after problems with Christians. When Islam triumphed, conquered populations had to demonstrate adherence to a sacred religious text such as the Old Testament of the Jews or Bible of the Christians to avoid persecution. The Sabians (as the Harranians became known) amazingly proclaimed the Hermetica as their scripture and got away with it. The place became a major esoteric enclave. The already syncretistic Hermetic thought further absorbed even purer elements of Mesopotamian beliefs than had been encountered in Alexandria. It all began to seep out and impact on Islamic mysticism and science. There are certainly connections with Sufism. The crusaders never took Harran but did frequent its vicinity. It seems likely, if the rest of the situation of the times is anything to go by, that they would have become aware of the strange culture nearby.

A major new work appeared out of this blend. The *Picatrix* may have been written in Spain, but shows strong signs of the influence of Harran. It became one of the most important texts in the history of western occultism and art. It's basically a mix-match of Babylonian astrological magic in a Neoplatonic context. The practical side of it showed how to bring down heavenly energies into talismans. In its most evolved form, such talismans could bring about an inner transformation, an alchemical transmutation. The practitioner of such arts was able to become a true universe in miniature, reflecting in their microcosm all of the laws and energies of the greater macrocosm, embodying the divine. The mysterious ring of Robert de St. Clere, which linked astrology and colour, can easily be seen as a prime example of the highest form of the talismanic art.

Can we find the slightest hint of such concerns in the recorded history of medieval Glastonbury? What about Chaldean solar deities and 666? Seffrid Pelochin was abbot from 1120 to 1125. He was the predecessor of Henry of Blois. Although he gave the monastery some saintly relics, he appears to have neglected the mundane, leaving the buildings in a state of collapse. Moving on to become Bishop of Chichester, he was later deposed for sodomy. Centuries later, his coffin was opened and it was discovered that he had been buried wearing a ring carved with a depiction of the Gnostic deity Abraxas.

Here indeed there seems to be a tantalising hint of heresy. What on earth was a 12th century Bishop doing wearing such an item? Quaint beliefs were circulating then about the magical properties of rings. Pope Boniface VIII, a known sexual tyrannosaurus, was accused of keeping a demon in his ring. It would come out at night and get it on with him in the papal bed! The mystery of Pelochin's ring does not arise in a vacuum. Where would he have acquired such an interest? This is one of those magnificently irritating Glastonbury maybes. One theory states that the coffin was not Pelochin's but in fact that old chestnut, another man of the same name.

Abraxas is usually depicted as having a human body with a rooster's head and legs like serpents. Sometimes he has a hawk or a lion's head. He tends to hold a whip and a shield. Abraxas rides in a chariot drawn by four white horses. The sun and moon may both be shining above him to indicate his embodiment of opposites. He is associated with one of the leading Gnostics, Basilides, who flourished in Alexandria around about 120-30 AD and made use of numbers in a way reminiscent of Pythagoras. The name Abraxas can be made to add up to 365 through the assigning of number correlations with letters. It is therefore taken to refer to the solar year in some way. From the supreme God emanated seven attributes or powers that had their correlations in the seven days of the week. There were likewise seven similar forces in every realm of the spiritual world. The complete total was 365.

One theory contends that the name comes from two words, Abir, meaning bull, and Axis, referring to the pole, and that it dates from a time when the spring equinox was in Taurus, the celestial bull. This is the same epoch that Katherine Maltwood links to the creation of the Glastonbury Zodiac. Another hypothesis derives Abraxas from the Egyptian Coptic language, taking it to mean 'holy word', perhaps in a similar way to the secret of the Qabalistic tetragrammaton which the masons claim to know.

During the peak of the Alexandrian Hermetic era, Mithras had become tremendously successful in the Roman world. In the syncretistic manner of the time, his form mutated. A complex of kindred god-forms blurred and blended. Mithras, Abraxas, Aion. A variant spelling, Meithras, adds up to 365 like Abraxas. Crowley claimed that the correct name of the idol supposedly worshipped by the Templars was *Baphometr* which meant 'Father Mithras'. This suggests the possibility of continuity between the initiatory cave chambers favoured by both groups. The underground lair of the griffons in *Perlesvaus* and the rumoured activities within the hill at Dundon may give hints in that direction.

At the time of the reception of *The Book of the Law,* Crowley stated that the old world had been destroyed by fire, at least on the inner planes. In the ancient world, some Stoic philosophers, believed to have heavily influenced Mithraism, expounded a concept called *ekpyrosis*. Vast cycles of time come to an end either through flood or fire. When it came to flame, it was a kind of alchemical process whereby all of the energy of the universe was transformed into fire. This ending was also a beginning of a new world. Mithras became the presiding deity of this process. The Mithraic Aion was the turner of the zodiacal wheel, the mover of the cycles of the heavens.

It is rather interesting that the Knights Templar made use of seals with the figure of Abraxas upon them. A surviving French example carries the inscription *Secretum Templi.* Such wording is more than enough to provoke speculation.

There are other more direct indications of Glastonbury heresy. During the same period that Americ was setting up the Park Wood ceremony, a mysterious female voice identifying itself as Melandra made a brief appearance to utter an enigmatic statement in Bernard's clairaudient ear. "*The isle holds the souls of the ancient ones. The dust of many times covers their resting. Their tombs are honoured by the chanting of the spheres for all time to come. So it must be. Fountains of the eternal light must be made as the brightness of the sun. Great troubles like the storm fast approach. Blackness edges the circling stream.*

One by one the lights will die. The time is now for the lights to rekindle."

The message contained definite echoes of one of the most obscure of all pieces of Glastonbury lore. John of Glastonbury had produced *Cronica sive Antiquitates Glastonienses Ecclesie* around 1342. He recorded words attributed to Melkin, a Dark Age Welsh bard, believed in the late Middle Ages to have been a real historical figure.

> *"The Isle of Avalon, greedy in the burial of pagans, above others in the world, decorated at the burial place of all of them with vaticinatory little spheres of prophecy, and in future it will be adorned with those who praise the Most High. Abbadare, powerful in Saphat, most noble of pagans, took his sleep there with 104,000. Amongst them Joseph de Mamore, named 'of Arimathea', took everlasting sleep. And he lies on a forked line close to the southern corner of the chapel with prepared wattle above the powerful venerable Maiden, the thirteen aforesaid sphered things occupying the place. For Joseph has with him in the tomb two white and silver vessels filled with the blood and sweat of the prophet Jesus. When his tomb is found, it will be seen whole and undefiled in the future, and will be open to all the earth. From then on, neither water nor heavenly dew will be able to be lacking for those who inhabit the most noble island. For a long time before the Day of Judgement in Josaphat will these things be open and declared to the living. Thus far Melkin."*

A tremendous amount of ingenuity has been expended in attempting to understand this bizarre material. Words and phrases get juggled around and slightly altered. The above translation/ version comes from notable Glastonbury scholar James Carley. A few things about the passage seem fairly clear. It is accepted that John had access to a version of *Perlesvaus*. The story included a scene where a sarcophagus tomb of Joseph of Arimathea was discovered and opened. The Melkin passage identifies Glastonbury as a major pagan burial site. Joseph seems to be categorised '*Amongst them*'. The reference to '*the prophet Jesus*' seems highly likely to be Muslim influenced. It simply isn't Christian parlance. Other items are more open to conjecture. The '*spheres of prophecy*' are often taken to indicate a possible zodiac design on the floor of the abbey that may be what William of Malmesbury was referring to. Others favour crystal scrying balls. The '*forked line*' has been interpreted as a geometric pointer to the location of Joseph's tomb. There may be a hint of alchemy in '*heavenly dew*'. The vessels containing blood and sweat are normally rendered in English as 'cruets'. This is not a standard Grail image and has an alchemical nuance as well.

There is also a strong indication that the abbey cemetery was one with a widespread legendary reputation for sanctity. Elsewhere in John of Glastonbury an account is given of the crusading adventures of Rainald of Marksbury who was captured by a Sultan and released only after he had obtained for his captor some earth from Glastonbury's cemetery. The sultan discusses Joseph with the crusader. This tale may well have influenced the form of the Melkin material. Assuming there is any accuracy in the story, it is intriguing to think of an Islamic Sultan believing in some special sacredness associated with Glastonbury.

John of Glastonbury represents the final coming together of the full form of the Joseph mythos. As well as the Melkin passage, a family tree linking Joseph through to Arthur is included which seems obviously influenced by *Perlesvaus*.

If Glastonbury was the famous school of forgery that its denigrators contend and the monks were not averse to manufacturing a celebrity grave then much could surely be gained from producing the Arimathean. Like Arthur they would have in their favour the fact that nobody else had already laid claim to such a relic. What actually did happen is unclear and confusing.

It may be that John's work had been stimulated by a visit from Edward III to Glastonbury in 1331. The monarch and his queen had paid lavish public respects to Arthur and Guenevere's tomb. It was another major validation of Glastonbury's status and mythology. Edward had a definite interest in such matters and this was a factor in his later foundation of the Order of the Knights of the Garter.

In 1345, royal permission was granted to a John Blome of London to search for Joseph of Arimathea's body in the grounds of Glastonbury Abbey. An anonymous East Anglian chronicler later stated that the tomb had been found in 1367. If this was the case then there would have been no need to mount a further excavation in 1419. A number of bodies were unearthed and it appears that one was tentatively identified as the saint. By 1424 an English representative at the church Council of Sienna clearly stated that Joseph had indeed been found. It might be expected that such an event would be the sensation of the Christian world and generate volumes of controversy. It all seems to fade from view until a little later the claims are being played down.

The penultimate abbot of Glastonbury, Richard Beere, developed a full-blown cult of Joseph, creating a crypt chapel for him where a statue oversaw miraculous healings. This was directly beneath the Mary Chapel and its mysterious floor design. In the years of ruination, one collapsed in to the other. The floor of today's chapel is in fact the level of the Joseph crypt. One would expect the remains of the saint, if such items were claimed to exist, to have been very much at the forefront of his crypt chapel cult scene. It all seems dimly lit now. Divergent versions remain to tantalise us.

After the dissolution a former monk named William Good stated that although Joseph was buried somewhere in Somerset, nobody knew exactly where. It may have been in the abbey grounds but a strange tradition also linked him to Montacute. Maybe Good was protecting the secret. It wasn't the best of times for relics, statues, and the tombs of saints. There are other accounts of a tomb in the crypt chapel. Modern Glastonbury folklore, as collated by the major champion of Joseph, the Rev Lionel Smithett Lewis, tells of the sarcophagus remaining in place until 1662, when it was stealthily moved by night into St. John's churchyard. It fell off the radar of awareness until 1928 when Lewis transferred it to inside the church where it remains in the present day. The tomb does seem to be late 15th century and of a size suggestive of a high status internment. Lewis claimed that it bore signs of having been moved. Known as the John Allen tomb due to the letters JA allegedly inscribed upon it, no attempt at all in the present day is made to associate it with Joseph. Indeed it is covered with a cloth. The excellent stained glass window depiction of Joseph nearby attracts far more attention. Lewis wrote a still popular work on Joseph but he is generally considered to be a virtual crank and his handling of source material has not impressed scholars.

Americ had stated that the March 17th feast of Joseph had been used for their seasonal ritual, being close enough to the Spring Equinox, and urged for it to be repeated. The saint was being subtly included in the Hermetic magical blend. There's more than a hint of magic and alchemy about the artefacts associated with his Glastonbury jaunt. The flowering staff has many possible levels of meaning, including that of a geometer's measuring rod, but is indubitably first and foremost, a wand. The chalice and cruets suggest the virtues of the philosophers' stone, the process of transmutation. The figure of Joseph that emerged during the Middle Ages has more than a hint of the Hermetic magus about him. He seems to be lying in his tomb like Christian Rosenkreutz.

Bernard did see an overwhelming vision that was perhaps a glimpse into the mystery. He was already convinced of the former existence of a whole complex of underground chambers beneath the abbey. One night he saw into the most important of all. A special feast day was being marked by a ceremony. Six monks stood around a sarcophagus. Others entered the room, carrying candles and flaming torches. Dense incense smoke filled the air. The monks chanted a low drone that the chamber's acoustics amplified into something truly extraordinary. Combined with the reverential devotion of the assembled group, the total effect was more than Bernard could handle. He felt obliged to look away, feeling he had intruded on something he was unworthy to witness. There was a definite feeling that the incumbent was Joseph of Arimathea and that what he had witnessed was a supreme sacred mystery, carefully guarded for good reasons that the world was not yet ready to know. Andy ultimately rejected any historical Joseph Glastonbury connection. I got a sense of seeing through it another glimpse of that *something*.

As well as a stone sarcophagus, there may have been other significant items that survived the dissolution destruction. One of the most enduring of Glastonbury occult legends features the Merlin-like magus, John Dee. Sir Edward Dyer, Chancellor of the Order of the Knights of the Garter, was godfather to Dee's son and lived at Sharpham Park, located only a short distance from Glastonbury and onetime home of its abbots. Dee is known to have spent a lot of time there so he would certainly have been familiar with the abbey. He and his notorious assistant Edward Kelly (who Crowley claimed as a past life) allegedly discovered some alchemical substance in the ruins around 1582. This, so the story goes, enabled Kelly to make some gold and began the duos extraordinary career as European alchemists, espionage agents, and traffickers with interdimensional entities. The tale has many variants. It is recorded in its standard form by Elias Ashmole. Some doubt the Glastonbury location. What is important is the fact that people of the time could easily believe that Glastonbury Abbey would be a place where one might expect to find such a substance. One version has Kelly finding a 'Book of Dunstan' to accompany the powder. The saint who stood at the very beginning of the abbey's medieval history was associated with alchemy and sorcery from his own lifetime and the ambiance had clearly lingered.

Dee has also become associated with the Glastonbury Zodiac. A biography of him had appeared in the sixties, written by Richard Deacon. Whilst researching his work in the Warburg Institute, he came across a Dee manuscript featuring a map of the Glastonbury area and these extraordinary words: *"the starres which agree with their reproductions on the ground do lye onlie on the celestial path of the soone, moon and planets, with the notable exception of Orion and Hercules – all the greater starres of Sagittarius fall in the hind quarters of the horse, while Altair, Tarazed and Alschain from Aquilla do fall on its cheste – thus is astrolgie carefully and exactly married and measured in a scientific reconstruction of the heavens which shews that the ancients understode all which today the learned know to be facts"*.

It would seem that this represents stupendous proof of pre-Maltwood belief in the landscape effigies. It has been subsequently quoted as such on many occasions since. It is a tad unfortunate that the incredible Dee document has never been seen from that day onwards. Not the slightest trace of it has been found. What happened here? Is Deacon a liar? He's not an esoteric author. Such deception would serve no obvious purpose. The file on this mystery is currently stamped '*Unknown*'. I feel Dee does strongly reside in the mysterious penumbral Glastonbury zone as one of the dramatis personae in the inner Avalon.

In 1989, as the time of the summer solstice approached, Andrew Collins had begun writing a book with the working title of *Godstar*. The word came from one of his favourite songs, by Psychic TV. In the context of Glastonbury, it referred to the exalted state of consciousness the Zodiac Grail quest could potentially produce. It was decided to repeat the Park Wood ritual on the weekend nearest to the solstice. It was another clear marker of transition for me. After the years rest, Pilton festival was back on again. One of my favourite bands, All About Eve, were playing. A decade on from my first visit, it never even occurred to me to attend. What I was now involved in was obviously going to bring me considerably closer to the real heart of Glastonbury.

On Saturday June 17th Andy and I travelled down to Somerset, with Alex, John, and Kerry. The weather was superb that year. My memories from spring through to autumn are of sunshine. We visited assorted Zodiac sites, doing visualisations in churches such as Kingweston and so on. I certainly felt rather strange, after having initially seen Andy on TV at Kingweston in 1986, and then hearing the whole narrative in detail, to now be stepping into that same story. The day was a definitive idyll of a British landscape of nostalgia. The abbey put us into a state of slow motion as we went over some of Bernard's 1984 material, revitalising it as we did so. It was a deliberate strategy to alert the monks of the Company of Avalon, and the mysterious guardian forces of the Zodiac in general, that we were about and what our intentions were.

As the sun began to set, the praeternatural light of the Avalonian afterglow bathed us in its beauty, shining through the trees, stirring the otherwordly aethyrs. We made our way to Park Wood. I spotted the Tor in the distance and briefly remembered the previous year's solstice. Once again I'd come a long way in my seasonal orbit around the World Mountain. We had some ceremonial accoutrements for the coming night's entertainment, primarily a collection of swords. I hasten to add that none of the Meonia model were present. The intention was to perform the ceremony as twilight came on, it being considered a time when the veil is thin. There's an uncanny atmosphere in Park Wood. Watching presences were sensed. After a period of acclimatisation, we gathered in a clearing in the middle of a striking grove of trees. It was time to begin.

We stood in a circle, holding our swords aloft, their tips touching above the centre. Energy was felt and visualised as moving through the swords to unite in the centre. Slowly we started to move clockwise and then anti-clockwise, with swords still touching, slowly chanting *Aa Shum* (which suggested something Egyptian). The two opposite circular movements focused awareness on the Ouroborus, on balance and completeness and the inward and outward spiral paths of the zodiac quest. There was also an acknowledgement of energies moving in both directions between the earth and the heavens, the unity of the serpent in the sky and in the land. A passage in *Perlesvaus* was believed by Mrs Maltwood to refer to Park Wood. "*The serpent seeth him, and cometh toward him, jaws yawning, and casteth forth fire and flame in great plenty. Perceval thrusteth his sword right through the gullet.*" Maltwood stated that, "*the equinoctial line of 2700 BC passed through the 'gullet' of this serpent*". Americ de St. Maur had spoken of how he and his companions had seen a pillar of fire descending through the rushings of air, "*as though it would melt the ground*". We put our swords into the ground in a circle together, to hold the serpent of fire in place and represent the crown of the land.

We stepped six paces back from the circle of swords, turned around and each raised our arms in a V posture. *Perlesvaus* also features a scene where a golden chain hangs down, *"loaded with precious stones, and in the midst thereof was a crown of gold"*. We visualised a golden pillar rising up through the crown of swords, blending with the fire pillar. It served as the pivot of the former pole star Draco, axis of the great wheel, and was topped by an astral crown.

The Lords of the four quarters were then called. In this case, placed as we were, they signified the royal star cross of Leo, Taurus, Aquarius, and Scorpio in its higher aspect of the eagle. They came with their respective colours, which flowed into the central pillar, blending into its gold. The pillar shimmered and pulsated, becoming solid white light, revolving, whirling forth. Streams of rainbow colours then shot out from the crown top, like a fountain. The Lords were then asked to speed to the boundaries of the great wheel, taking the outpouring of light with them. The whole Zodiac became filled with multicoloured light, slowly swirling around in a clockwise direction. This motion accelerated until the light was white, cleansing and purifying the spheres. Eventually the wheel began to come to a halt and the energies and the Lords were recalled back towards the golden pillar.

It had been noted that the ceremony was reminiscent of medieval sword dances. I was reminded of a chapter in *From Ritual to Romance* on the topic. Jessie Weston looked at various cults of swordsmen whose activities are linked to the land's fertility. The Indian Maruts are attendants of the god Indra, aiding him in his struggles against adversaries such as the great dragon Vritra. Ceremonies to them were performed at the start of the seasons. They were celebrated as bringers of food and fertility. It seems that young men of priestly caste acted out sword dance ceremonies to fulfil this function. In Greece, there were the Kouretes. Again we have mythic beings embodied by a cult clearly connected with the fertility of the land. The most interesting example from my point of view came from Roman times. The Salii were a college of Priests of Mars, who was initially primarily a god of vegetation, what we'd now think of as a Green Man/Horned God type. The point in the year when his month occurs is a good indicator of that. During March, there were extensive ceremonials to honour Mars. The Salii performed sword dances. These dances lingered on into Christian times when, dissociated from the state cult, they became strange folk practices. The Middle Ages saw many versions of this. They were widespread in England and linked with agricultural festivals.

The character of St. George often appeared in these performances, which have points of crossover with Mummer's plays and Morris dancing. George is the great dragon slayer. Some have considered that the slaying of the dragon was one of the most archaic Indo-European drama-rituals. She wondered if there was some kind of continuity *'from Salii to Templars'*. The pinning of the serpent, the revivification of the land, Templars as inheritors of the sword dances of the Salii. It felt right to me. It suggested something authentic.

On Saturday March 16th 1985, the nearest practical date to Joseph's feast, Andy had gathered a small group, including Cara, to perform the ceremony, keeping as close to the psychic details as possible. Afterwards he rang Bernard in Essex, who had been tuning in. He had seen an overview of the Zodiac with pulsating rays of light emanating from the centre. He could also hear a kind of choral chant that rose and fell with the rhythm of light. The abbey appeared, flickering back and forth from the present ruins to its past glory. Gold lights flickered in the Mary Chapel. Across the whole landscape, assorted figures from all historical periods were wandering about, as if woken by the activity. After the ceremony, Andy discovered the heraldic details of Americ de St. Maur's coat of arms. It featured a phoenix and a crown with flames emitting from the top.

The Park Wood auction eventually occurred on the summer solstice, as Andy finally set out on the concluding part of the quest, and I was pulled into the matrix. It was a favourable outcome. Access remained and no dubious groups took control. There were other ripples in the cosmic pond that were to have immense significance for Andy's future work and my own life as well.

In early October 1984 Bernard had started to talk about a feeling he had that the sphinx is far older than the pyramids. He had been reading a remarkable book by John Anthony West called *Serpent in the Sky*. West mentioned that the erosion on the sphinx looked as if it had been caused by water rather than sand. It was still a little way off from the time when he would find a professional geologist to back up his claims and his work would become a major element of the nineties Alternative Egyptology movement. In '84, Bernard felt strongly that there was truth in West's ideas. He was also stimulated by all kinds of esoteric material in the book concerning the use of sacred geometry in Egyptian temples.

Something of similar flavour had independently entered Andy's mind. He had returned to Glastonbury only a few days after the autumn equinox intensive with Chesca Potter. In *Gothic Image* he was flicking through a book on sacred geometry when a particular image seemed to switch something on in his head. It was a Fibonacci spiral.

Fibonacci was another extraordinary product of the Grail era. An Italian who travelled extensively in Muslim countries, he brought Arab and Indian mathematics, specifically decimal counting, numbers and zeros, to the west with *Liber Abaci* in 1202. This would be enough to secure him fame but he is mainly known for his discovery of a sequence of numbers that seem to represent a glimpse into the laws of creation.

The series begins with 0 and 1. After that, two numbers are added to get the next in an endless sequence where each number is the sum of the two numbers before it.

1, 2, 3, 5, 8, 13, 21, 34, 55, 89, 144, 233, 377, 610, 987, ...

When a Fibonacci number in the sequence is divided by the number before it, numbers are obtained that are very close to one another. This number is fixed after the thirteenth number in the series and known as the Golden Ratio or Phi. For example:

233 / 144 = 1.618
377 / 233 = 1.618
610 / 377 = 1.618
987 / 610 = 1.618

Although not omnipresent, the Fibonacci numbers have been found as the governing principles of form in a spectacular number of examples across the whole spectrum of creation.

In an average human body there are a number of proportional relationships that manifest the Golden Ratio and Fibonacci numerical principles. For example, if the distance between the navel and foot is taken a being one unit, the total height of the body would be the equivalent of 1.618. Leonardo da Vinci famously incorporated this knowledge into his art.

There is a particular kind of growth that develops outwards from its point of origin, increasing in size but not changing its shape. It is the form of the so-called gnomic logarithmic spiral that allows this constancy to manifest. Expressive of the Golden Ratio, it can be found throughout nature from the development of human foetuses to sea-shells. Fibonacci number ratios are also seen in such things as the arrangement of leaves on branches and the seeds of sunflowers to the breeding patterns of rabbits and the male/female ratio in honey bees.

These proportions have been considered to be the ultimate expression of aesthetic harmony, a glimpse of the mind of god at work. They have been incorporated into art and architecture. It has been suggested that the dimensions of the King's Chamber of the Great Pyramid are based upon the Golden Ratio.

In the following days, patterns started appearing in Andy's inner vision over the map of the Glastonbury Zodiac. Something was being communicated. He photocopied two different versions of the gnomic spiral and pondered upon them, feeling that a choice between them needed to be made. It would be a few months more before what was happening really unfolded but major developments were beginning. The Park Wood saga needed to play itself out first.

On April 9th 1985 Bernard was showing Andy his Mary Chapel design. He drifted into the Egyptian zone again, stating emphatically that there is a chamber beneath the Giza plateau. Andy was familiar with the famous American psychic Edgar Cayce's ideas. Perhaps primed by Theosophical and Rosicrucian input, he had talked of refugees from Atlantis travelling to Egypt and building the Sphinx and Pyramids. They also created a 'Hall of Records', an underground chamber filled with the lost knowledge of pre-deluge humanity. Cayce claimed that the place would be uncovered in 1998 and this momentous event would form part of a sequence of massive global transformations that would usher in a new epoch.

Serpent in the Sky was primarily an exposition of an immense corpus of esoteric work by the mystical polymath Rene Schwaller de Lubicz. It was he who had first suggested the possibility of water erosion on the sphinx. The man had spent fifteen years at the gigantic Luxor Karnak temple complex in Egypt. He and his team measured every inch of the place, recording each hieroglyphic and piece of artwork. Schwaller didn't have the mindset of a typical archaeologist. He was part of a potent stream of European esotericism that is sometimes overlooked in Britain and America in favour of the Golden Dawn and Theosophical legacy.

He was particularly concerned with finding evidence of phi. Conventional history credits the Greeks with this crucial mathematical geometrical discovery. Schwaller became convinced that it was known to the Egyptians. He was clear that it was a glimpse into the working of the divine, the blueprint for reality.

In his later years he told his pupil André VandenBroeck that the basic material of Fulcanelli's work on the cathedrals had been his own and the man he claimed to be behind the Fulcanelli myth, Julian Champagne, had been lent the manuscript and essentially ripped it off, adding material of his own and various associates. VandenBroeck's *Al-Kemi* tells the full story for those who may be interested. There is no doubt that Schwaller was an alchemist. He had a fully functioning laboratory in his home of which photographs exist. Anyone who looks at his Egyptian work could probably see that it is coming from a very high level of insight indeed. Schwaller stated that *"I could not have recognised the cosmology of the Pharaohs had I not known the medieval book of the cathedral"*. In his own way Bernard rapidly went through a version of the same process, from the Mary Chapel to what he began to call the Crystal Chambers beneath Giza.

* * *

As the Giza material developed, so too did the understanding of the Glastonbury Zodiac. Bernard was pulled into the Fibonnaci mystery that Andy had earlier intuited. He found himself staying up into the early hours drawing gnomic spirals over a map of Glastonbury.

(The sequence of doodled images below and on the following pages are taken directly from his notebook.)

One over Leo.

A larger one that took in most of the signs.

There seemed to be a kind of inward and outward spiral that took in two sides of the whole circuit. Some of the signs seemed to be omitted. It wasn't quite clear yet. It looked like the course already completed could be encompassed within one side of it and what remained was the flip side.

He also drew a gnomic spiral over his earlier design for the floor of the Mary Chapel.

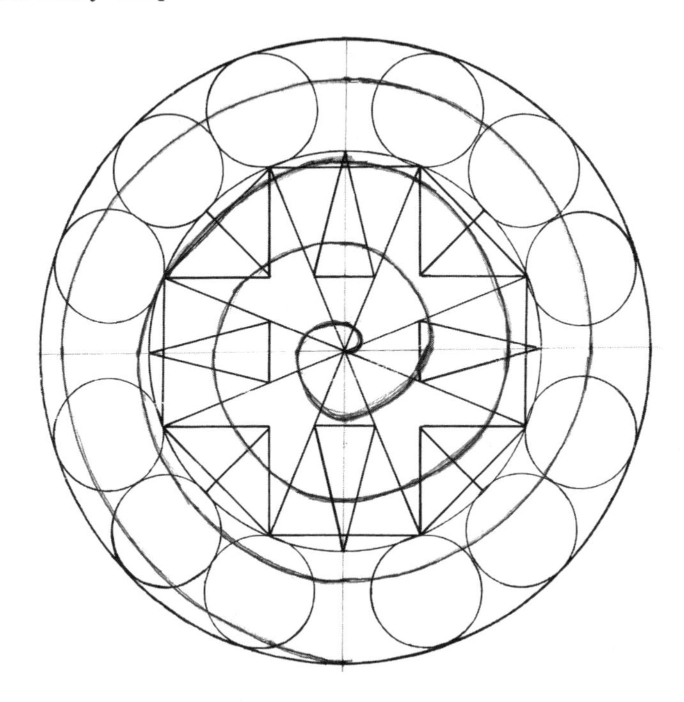

Before long, the details were clearer. The path of the first spiral took in Leo, Gemini, Virgo, Scorpio, Sagittarius and Aquarius. It missed out Capricorn and Libra. The second spiral on the other side would feature Aquarius, Pisces, Aries, Taurus, and Cancer. There was a dualistic yin yang, light dark, alchemical interplay between the two spirals. The idea of a great wheel and the spirals seemed to be more fundamental than that of a zodiac, a word that the psychic sources were scarcely using anymore. It all suggested something of the archetypal alchemical image of the ouroborus serpent, whose body is divided into light and dark, and is biting its own tail. It symbolised how, in the realm of matter, good and bad, perfection and imperfection, are inseparable.

Bernard pondered on how many triangles he had experienced in Somerset such as Christians Cross, Keinton Mandeville, and Butleigh centre. He wondered if they related to multi-dimensional pyramids. Perhaps the whole Zodiac was a massive pyramid with the twelve spheres around its edge? Are the two spirals to be seen as spiral stairways rising to the apex?

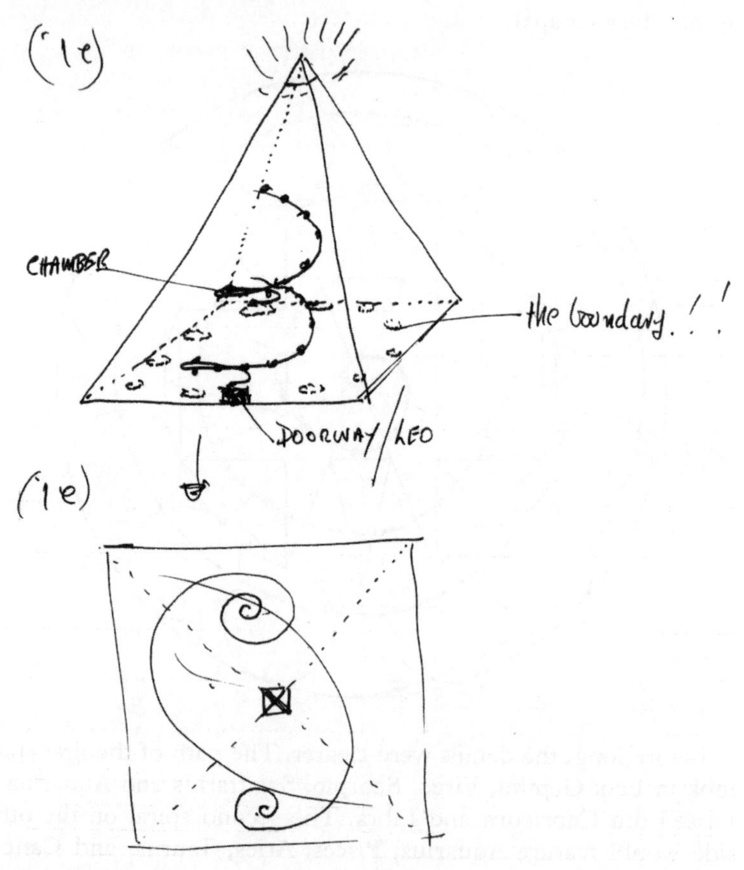

Do they relate to actual chambers inside a pyramid, with Leo as the doorway and the Queens Chamber as one of the levels? This led Bernard to ask Andy a most interesting question. *"Does any of this relate to the Tor and some kind of physical counterpart? Twisting paths going up to the top? Has anyone discovered a spiralling pathway around the Tor?"* Somehow this was all connected with the sphinx. Around it were twelve underground chambers. The great pyramid was built after obtaining knowledge about this. There was a link with the Mary Chapel design.

During the second half of April, Bernard went through an ongoing brainstorm download in which he received a detailed design and explanation for the Crystal Chambers in a similar manner to his Mary Chapel experience. Bernard came to believe that the underground complex dated from the astrological age of Leo, over 12,000 years ago. He didn't really talk about Atlantis in the usual way. It was sufficient to think in terms of a previous cycle of an advanced civilisation that had all but disappeared through planetary upheavals. He referred to the 'Elder Race'. Those dudes were a bit strange. They were etherial, extremely tall, viper-visaged, virtually albino types. They weren't standard issue Homo Sapien Sapien. They weren't ETs either. It was a now extinct line but it had bred into the current human race. Their Crystal Chambers were not a repository for books and conventional treasure but a living cosmological temple. The knowledge it held was the understanding of how the present universe came into being. It represented the form of the process of creation and the actual point of creation itself. The rites that Bernard believed to have occurred therein had a haunting otherwordly feel to them that was both archaic and futuristic. They maintained, harmonised, and adjusted the very form of the laws of nature as they functioned within the planet.

The whole complex lay beneath a mound island on a lake. At the entrance was a large rectangular panel of polished grey stone. Depicted on this in bas-relief, on the left, was a man facing right wearing an Egyptian style headdress, a skullcap with uraeus serpent. He held a red-gold staff with a curved top. Facing him was a lion with upraised griffin-esque wings, standing up on its hind legs. Ray-like spikes emanated from its stomach. There was a line of glyphs between and beneath the two figures. The leonine being seemed to be a form of the Mithraic Aion cosmocrator Lord of Time. This depicted the moment when the chambers had been sealed shut at the end of their epoch. Powerful energy remained as a guardian force.

The ground-plan was in the form of a twelve-pointed double hexagram. Domed-roofed chambers were situated on the apex points. On the floor were a series of concentric rings, slightly differently configured in each room. From their central point of emanation, there were also three straight yellow grooves cut into the floor that formed paths outward. The left and right grooves connected through doorways with adjacent chambers, forming paths that marked

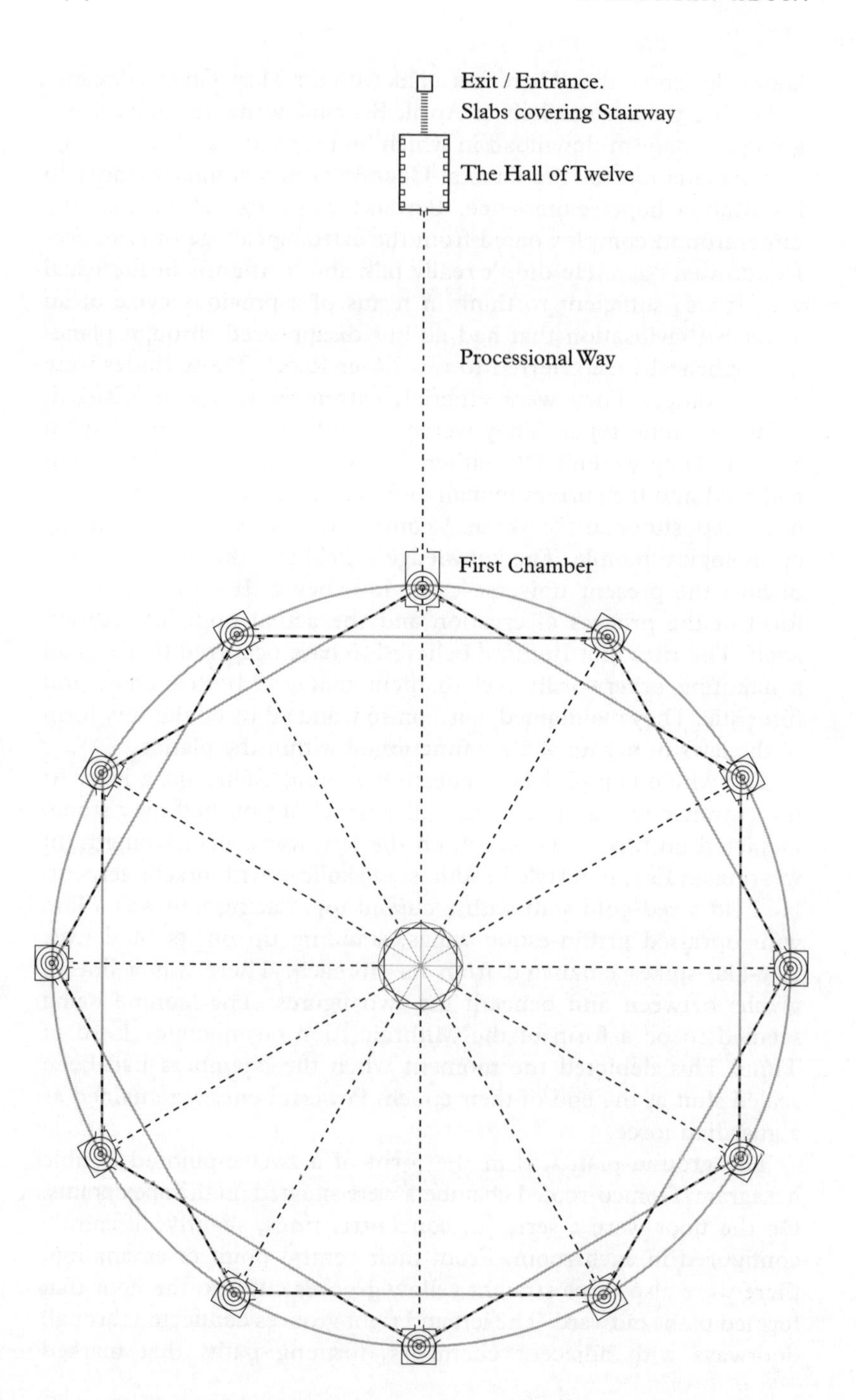
Exit / Entrance.
Slabs covering Stairway
The Hall of Twelve
Processional Way
First Chamber

the twenty four sides of the whole design. The third central groove reached down a long corridor to the central chamber producing a total effect like the spokes of a wheel.

The central chamber was twenty-four sided. In the middle was a twelve pointed, twenty-four faceted pyramidion crystal, several feet in height. It was the 'Knowledge Stone'. Its facets in combination represented all known colours, dimensions, aspects of reality etc. The last Glastonbury imagery Bernard had seen, at the climax of the first spiral of the zodiac quest, clearly recalled the Egyptian creation myth. Atum caused a hill of creation to arise out of the primordial ocean of darkness that preceded the first morning. The island became the sun temple of Heliopolis. At its centre was a black pyramidal stone with a quartz top representing the Ben-ben stone. The crystal reflected and refracted the rising sun's rays each morning. This was a living demonstration of a cosmology showing how the one became many. It seemed that the underground Giza complex with its central crystal was perhaps the original temple of this myth. The Heliopolitan form of it told of the phoenix bird that alighted upon the stone at the start of each new epoch. Bernard had seen Glastonbury Tor, the Zodiacal phoenix, arising out of the waters. It was an extraordinary mixture.

Bernard wrote that *"The Sphinx represents the `One', the omnipotent guardian of all cosmic/dualistic dimensions. Beneath sits the crystal primeval stone, the ultimate gateway, the coming into existence"*. This was literally the place where form and formlessness meet. From there, all creation emerged. This theme was Schwaller's obsession, apparent from his very first book, a short work on Pythagoras.

Time itself only began with the manifestation of form. It was considered to manifest in cycles of twelve, hence the twelve surrounding chambers. Each had an individual smaller crystal on the floor that would be held by a guardian who used it to in some way enter into the central crystal, serving as conduits for its unfolding of the process of creation. Bernard said that, *"To activate the crystal by the 'laying on of hands' is to open the door. The mind leaves the physical, enters the crystal and experiences its facets of knowledge. The entire fabric of the crystal becomes as 'one' colour and tone associated with the 'soul' pattern of the initiate that swells throughout all chambers"*.

The complex had acoustical properties designed to embody part of a cosmology that used sound to express and interact with the laws of creation. Pythagoras is said to have taught that the Earth geometrically unfolds from a point in its centre and that sound created the universe. Three notes, D, G, and E, produce the keynote C. It is that combination that Bernard believed was used by the Elder Race in their rites of morphogenesis. The rings on the floor of the twelve chambers were two-dimensional representations of the cosmic tones.

Bernard felt that the apparent crystal technology was for real. The Elders really did plug into the matrix of creation and affect the whole planet. Things had gone wrong. There had been massive climate change and catastrophe. The crystals were globally dispersed. They're still about, albeit in some hyper-dimensional zone between the worlds. One had come to Britain. Glastonbury was always the main candidate for the location. The crystal's morphogenetic power has subtly influenced much of Glastonbury's subsequent history. Eventually, a diverse group of people will rediscover them and return to Egypt. The temple remains intact and dormant. It can be switched back on.

At the very least, it was a mythic fantasy of the highest order. The Elder Race mythos was a potential minefield. Andy was well aware that the whole thing was more than a bit sci-fi. The albino Elders would not appeal to Egyptian national pride. They had an unnerving flavour of Nazi occultist Aryan master race from Atlantis fantasies. Bernard certainly felt that their value system was very different from ours. They seemed to be profoundly amoral.

Why would Bernard so thoroughly connect to such total strangeness? On the basis of his previous accuracy, Andy decided to take the gamble of tentatively accepting the scenario and seeing where it led. This was the beginning of the incredible journey that would lead to his later works *Gods of Eden* and *Beneath the Pyramids*.

It is at this point that it has to be acknowledged that some of the elements of the Glastonbury Zodiac Giza blend had, to a certain extent, been anticipated in an unlikely source. In the midst of Elizabeth Van Buren's space brother opus *Lord of the Flame* is a curious passage. Van Buren created a triangle on a map of the Glastonbury Zodiac between the eyes on the Virgo and Sagittarius figures and the eye of the Griffon. This was taken to delineate a zone coterminous with the Great Pyramid. Superimposing its inner dimensions over the triangle puts the King's Chamber in Kingweston, which Van Buren specifically names on her diagram and in the text. The church "*must certainly have been built over an ancient temple*". It is not a place which had attracted outlandish mystical speculation before. She also stated that the curling of the Leo lion tail is formed to point towards the Queen's Chamber.

Flame was published in 1981. It mentions the Hall of Records, Fibonacci, and gives considerable importance to Abraxas as a form of her interpretation of Lucifer as Christ's twin. This has been enough for me to not entirely dismiss the rather cranky work. Neither Andy or Bernard had any knowledge of Van Buren during their Glastonbury Egyptian experience. Something seemed to be broadcasting particular themes over the airwaves then and people of divergent temperaments responded according to type and destiny. These 1981 words seem somewhat prophetic of Andy's 1983 arrival: *"the quiet and secluded village of Kingweston, the focal point of great energies as its position at the heart of the pyramid suggests, has been able to keep its secret for thousands of years. Now the knowledge has been given back to us, maybe in order that we may go and silently meditate in that chamber of Initiation and ask for guidance in these fateful times".*

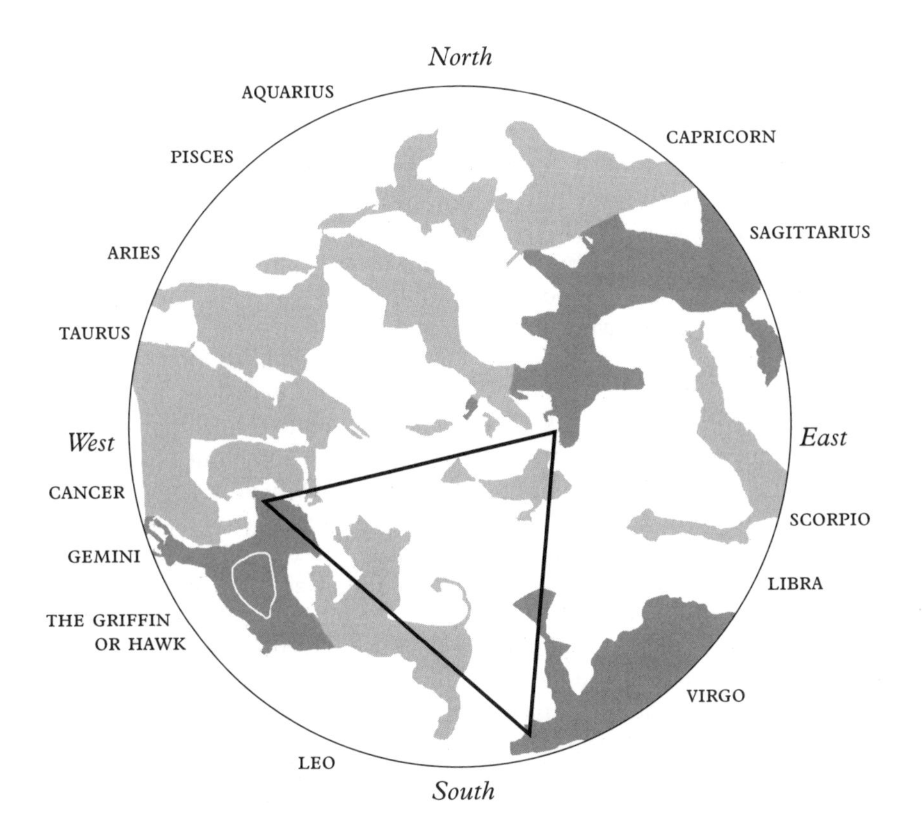

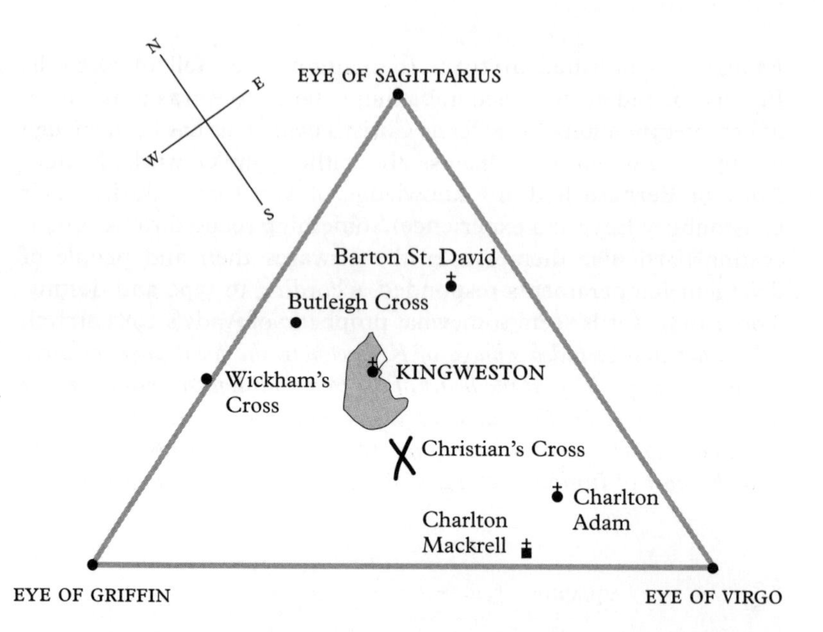

Most of the colossal corpus concerning the Crystal Chambers appeared between Andy's two adventures in the Glastonbury Zodiac spirals. This was, as always, significantly timed. It considerably affected the climax of his journey and what it ultimately led to. It seemed to sideline any ideas of wandering Sumerians but future changes of perspective would ultimately cohere the varied data.

Thelemic occultist Kenneth Grant has elucidated the crucial concept of tangential magic. There are many occasions when a magical working of some kind appears to generate results that seem to be unconnected with its original intentions, sometimes to such a degree as to throw doubt upon its success. Only after some time has passed and a wider perspective developed is it realised that the result was clearly linked with the true will behind the original impetus even if the conscious mind was not aware of it. With Andy and Bernard's Glastonbury Grail quest, the tangential developments had already extended to Egypt but there were further complications to come. Something else was gestating in darkness during that period.

Barely a week after completing his Crystal Chambers ground-plan design, on May 7th 1985, Bernard had travelled away from Essex on work related business. He realised he would be in the vicinity of Tewkesbury Abbey in Gloucestershire and made a point of finding some time to visit the place. Its founder, Robert Fitzhamon, was a member of the St. Clere family. His tomb was in the building and if recent experiences were anything to go by, getting into its proximity might generate interesting results. This was indeed the case. Fitzhamon came through. A clairaudient voice got immediately down to business by asking Bernard if he knew of something called the Stave of Nizar? It had belonged to Fitzhamon. A dying colleague had bequeathed it to him on a battlefield. He had obviously considered it to be an important legacy as he had wanted the artefact to be buried with him but it was not. Robert was clearly extremely angry about the actions of *"the bastard sons of the half-wit Robert of Montaigne"*. With this, the old knight signed off. Bernard was left to tune in to other sources to get answers. The stave had been taken but where? A loud voice exclaimed *"Wilmington"* in his ear.

When Bernard contemplated the stave and saw a powerful image of it, he realised that it was an elaborate descendant of the very same artefact depicted on the wall-carving of the entrance to the Crystal Chambers held by the priestly figure facing the guardian lion-being. As Andy later described it in *The Black Alchemist,* it was, *"a solid gold rod, some three to four feet tall, fashioned to look like the branch of a tree. Spiralling its way around the entire length was a golden snake or serpent, its head resting on the top of the rod, its mouth agape and two red rubies for eyes"*.

A sequence of staffs imbued with the same energy as the original had been passed down throughout Pharaonic times to the very end of the empire and into the Alexandrian Hermetic era. By no means everyone who had possession of them knew the original function but any psychically sensitive person would register high voltage and endorse an ongoing legend of power. Just before the first crusade it had become the property of an Egyptian Islamic caliph named Nizar. A French crusader subsequently captured it and took it to Europe where on a battlefield at home he had been mortally wounded and bequeathed it to Fitzhamon.

The stave had passed into the hands of the monks at Wilmington Priory. These were an interesting bunch, a so-called 'alien house' of French monks who enjoyed diplomatic immunity and powerful influence in the locale. There hangs around them an aura of potential heresy. Bernard believed that they knew something of the Egyptian provenance of the stave and kept its presence there a secret, using it on special ceremonial occasions.

Andy and Bernard visited the Wilmington locale in search of the

Stave of Nizar on May 30th 1985. In what appeared to be a sidetrack from the main action they found themselves at an enigmatic small mound known as Burlough Castle and a church at a place called Lullington where Bernard psychically discovered a piece of slate shaped like a spearhead inscribed with a some strange magical script.

S. F. Annett published an article in 1932 in *Sussex County Magazine* on the most notable feature of the area, the chalk figure, the Long Man of Wilmington. He made the extraordinary suggestion that the surrounding landscape was linked with a Grail romance usually considered to be thoroughly Welsh. *Peredur* features in the *Mabinogion.* The earliest written version of it could conceivably date from the same time as *Perlesvaus.* It is intriguing that Katherine Maltwood was putting the case for a tangible landscape link with a Grail romance during the same period.

Peredur visited a 'Castle of the Chessboard', involving himself with a magical board game that plays itself. He was told to go to a local wood and behead a white stag. Having done so, he was interrupted by a knight who grabbed the head and made off with it. Peredur was punished for this failure by being sent to a mound, "*beneath which is a carved man*". He recited an incantation and a giant black man emerged from the mound. Peredur had to fight him and with his victory, the adversary disappeared back into the ground. Annett believed the castle was Burlough and the wood where the stag was beheaded was the one in which Lullington church was now set. This material had later come to a wider audience through being featured in Rodney Castledon's *The Wilmington Giant.*

Bernard picked up the unusual name of Zosimos. He was the greatest of the early alchemists, living in the 4th century AD in Egypt, once known as *Khem* (referring to its black soil), from whence Alchemy derives its name, and forming part of the overall Hermetic tradition. He had a series of visions of the process of divine initiation through alchemy. The first stage involved his own beheading. This came to be a common symbol for the rebirth of the alchemist's soul.

It seemed likely that the Black Alchemist had chosen the location for his activities very deliberately. He was able to make multiple use of a mix of associations. The name of Peredur has been taken to mean 'Steel Spear'. The spearhead, symbolising his own head, was buried at a place associated with a stag beheading. Medieval alchemical symbolism featured the image of a stag's head as representing the soul of the alchemist. The most disconcerting aspect was the implication that he had wanted the spearhead to be found and removed.

Its removal by the mysterious knight would enable the black man, who was a recognised aspect of the process of the great alchemical work, the negredo, to emerge. Grail-quester Andy had been the mysterious knight, unknowingly empowering the Black Alchemist's strange work.

It soon became apparent that the Black Alchemist was strongly influenced by John Dee. A symbol known as the Monas Heiroglyphica that was Dee's glyph for the great work featured on later recovered artefacts. One idea that Zosimos was known for went unnoticed in 1985. He believed that the science of alchemy and magic was taught to humanity by a race of beings known as the Nephilim, the fallen angels of the Bible.

The stone spearhead was supposedly left at Lullington over the same weekend in March that the Templar ritual was performed in Park Wood. Pinning the head of the dragon and the beheading were occurring at the same time. Andy was right in the middle of his own alchemical death-rebirth initiation. He was about to recommence it by hurling himself into a weir on the site of Arthur's head. It was a perplexing blend.

A mini-quest in France searching for the Stave led to a dead-end in a cave but the strong belief that its energy had been encountered and assimilated into an artefact in Andy's possession sufficiently similar to carry it. Future work on Giza would benefit from this.

The Glastonbury Hermetic Aegyptian associations cohered together like a multi-faceted crystal from within which could be seen pulsating geometric light patterns, illuminating different sequences of constantly moving images on the surfaces, each facet of the crystal reflecting something of all the others.

Katherine Maltwood's tower window. Her lamplit study. She reads *Perlesvaus* with a map laid out on a table nearby. Fierce eyed Babylonians with wedge beards. Robert de St. Clere rising from a recumbent position in stone in Danbury church. Standing resplendent in solar rays in Kingweston church. Pursued on horseback. The ship of Solomon, red-cross on a white sail, moving majestically across a summerland sea, just out of reach. Al-Khem, Egypt, the black land. The face of the sphinx. An Eye of Horus in a blazing triangle. A burning phoenix. A spiral of light around Glastonbury Tor. Giant albino viper-visaged long-haired Elders, standing in strange green-walled chambers covered with unknown hieroglyphs, holding pulsating crystals. Are we looking in on them or are they looking out on us? Medieval Benedictine monks, the Company of

Avalon, standing around the Mary Chapel floor design. Cowled figures contemplating the moving colours and sounds of the Hermetic device. Joseph of Arimathea lying in his sarcophagus. An Abraxas seal. Robed figures holding swords aloft, standing in a circle in a wood. A pillar of fire descends. A glimpse of an eye of a great serpent. A crooked staff, changing form through the ages into a bejewelled stave. The constellation of Orion. A giant man-snake seemingly crucified upside-down upon it. An image of a beheading on a vivid alchemical manuscript. Storm-tossed Templar ships on the Atlantic ocean. A semi-darkened Elizabethan study. John Dee pays rapt attention to Edward Kelly as he gazes into a scrying stone. Moving nearer to it, amorphous light, shape, colour, move within. Strange angels. Unknown words. A dimly lit alchemical laboratory. A figure in shadow meticulously inscribing a script on a piece of slate. Arising between the images, sometimes seeming as if somehow present within them all, feeling as if he is near to the central matrix of the mystery, the lion headed cosmocrator, aflame with the changing aeons.

TINTAGEL

IN JUNE 1989, the day after the Park Wood ritual, the questing group relaxed in Glastonbury. John, Kerry, and Alex returned to Essex in the afternoon. A further adventure awaited Andy and I. We were off to Cornwall. Six Meonia swords had now come to light. The quest for number seven had definitely begun. A bit of backtracking was necessary. The sword discovered at Tintagel in '88 remained an unknown quantity. It became increasingly urgent to check it out. Travelling there via Glastonbury, and in the middle of magical work, felt like a fine option.

I had never visited Tintagel before. Like Glastonbury, the place infuriates sceptics due to its indissoluble links with the Arthurian mythos and the apparent nebulousness of any historical justifications. A first glimpse of the narrow, gradually winding, main road revealed cheapo tourist tackiness of exceptional grossness. Some lovely old Cornish buildings had suffered the indignity of having vulgarly grafted upon them a sequence of shop-fronts suggestive of a perverse ménage-a-trois between Blackpool seafront, English Heritage, and the New Age. Sunburnt tourist families waddled around clutching the usual Kali Yuga trash trophies, idly seeking their next dysfunctional fix.

Excalibur burgers and Merlin ball-point pens don't really help one to connect with the glories of the Grail. Things would gradually improve but in 1989, the prospect was a tad grim.

We had arrived in the perfect conditions of a superb June evening. Refreshing sea smells along with ebbing and flowing sounds of gulls carried on a warm gentle breeze soon helped to pleasantly transmute my initial impressions of the place into a more regenerative feeling.

Coming to the end of the sequence of shops, we walked down a declining path into a valley known as the Vale of Avalon leading to the cliff-top castle ruins, the famous Merlin's Cave, and the sea. Before long I realised that something about the place was affecting me as only Glastonbury had ever done before. It carried an archaic vibe of tangible magic. The larger locale contained holy wells, waterfalls, mysterious mounds, and the chapels of enigmatic Druidic Cornish saints. The septenary labyrinth design that had set Geoffrey Russell off on his spiral journeys was just a few miles away. Here was supreme 'British music'. Regardless of the strong historical arguments against the validity of their Arthurian connections, something seems to connect the legendary locations that frame his life from conception to burial. The fundamental factors are landscapes that profoundly impact on the human psyche, places that will inevitably attract a numinous mythology. I had connected with a Tintagel of the Heart.

After another perfect summer day, the all but cloudless sky had become a symphony of gradations of portentous pink focused on the sun setting into the sea. As its reflection touched the water, a rippling ray spread out from the horizon back across the foaming Mediterranean turquoise waves to the beach, like a sword of shimmering light, or a glimpse of the form of some vast devic being. From a vantage point up on the cliffs where we had gone on to climb, amongst a riot of small wild flowers, looking across at the ruined castle and down to the entrance of Merlin's Cave, I forgot all the intellectual arguments of history. I felt the Arthurian mythos alive in the very air. I *believed.*

The cliff top opposite the ruined fortress is dominated by the largest building in Tintagel, the hotel now named Camelot Castle. It seems as if the genius loci had decreed that a castle-like building of some kind needed to be strongly visible in that area. Originally built on the crest of the Tennysonian wave at the end of the 19th century, some of its rooms command views possibly as exquisite as any in the country. Over the years a cavalcade of diverse famous people had spent time there. Elgar had been inspired to write some of his second symphony. A. A. Milne, Noel Coward, and Winston Churchill make for an exquisite mix. The fifties Arthurian Hollywood epic, *Knights of the Round Table,* had been partly shot in the area and Guenevere Ava Gardner had stayed, enjoying herself so much that she allegedly still haunts the place.

The most famous work of one of my British Music discoveries was inspired by Tintagel. Arnold Bax, in the midst of an intense love affair, spent an idyllic six week holiday at the great hotel in 1917, far removed from the slaughter elsewhere. He was inspired to compose a 'tone poem'. The fifteen minute piece tried to evoke, "*the ruined castle, now so ancient and weather-worn as to seem an emanation of the rock upon which it is built*", with its Atlantic vista amidst the lingering presence of the Arthurian mythos. Wind, sea, and legend blend together. As someone who came to musical consciousness through Rock A-Z, it took a bit of effort for me to get into it but it was well worth it. I'd been listening to the piece since the spring. Now I could hear it in my head at the very location that inspired it. I felt it was another affirmation of my magical working procedures.

It was astonishing that such a small area could be such a fount of inspirational energy. At times in the summer, golden mists come off the sea and render the castle island invisible. This is suggestive of an Avalonian otherworld. Jung had come to Tintagel and later had an important dream whilst in India that seemed to reflect its influence. It featured a mysterious Grail Castle-type island citadel. It was suggestive of a mandalic representation of the structure of the Self.

Rudolf Steiner visited Tintagel in 1924, not long before his death. As he gazed upon the castle ruins, his clairvoyant vision dissolved the barrier of time. He came to believe that Tintagel had once been a Mystery Centre in the manner of Eleusis. It supposedly dated from around 1100 BC. Remember, this was the man who talked about the 'Arthurian Mysteries', an initiatory current of esoteric knowledge that served as a conduit for astrological gnosis from the days of Egypt and Babylon into the Christian era with Arthur as a sun king. Steiner's followers tended to mythologise virtually every event of the man's life. His brief visit to Tintagel seemed charged with meaning. His recognition of its former spiritual function helped to realign and reawaken it. Something profound was accomplished on the inner plane.

He and his small party, including the visionary artist Eleanor

Merry who had arranged the trip, spent some time at the big hotel as well. To the modern mind, Camelot is a fortress of the imagination, of creativity and spirituality. The new castle that exists in the same physical space as the hotel can serve that function. In an interesting continuity following through from Steiner's theories on art and the importance of light and colour, the extraordinary modern impressionist, expressionist, 'Abstract Realist', Ted Stourton would later help establish Camelot Castle Hotel as a matrix of creativity, producing a gigantic corpus of work and encouraging others to come and do likewise. Stourton and fellow hotel owners John and Irina Mappin honour the awesome genius loci in the present day.

The fact that Steiner even visited the area in the first place was probably largely down to the one man who can be credited with virtually single-handedly reviving its Arthurian charisma and creating the modern tourist industry. Tennyson's *Idylls of the King* was a massive success whose immediate influence extended through decades. Such was the extraordinary effect on the area's fortunes that one wonders whether the poet was a reincarnated hierophant of the original mystery school returned to initiate a new cycle. Something seemed to be ripe and ready in the greater scheme of things.

Geoffrey of Monmouth was the first written account we have that names Tintagel as the place of Arthur's conception. Why would he have done that? The now ruinous castle was not constructed until after Geoffrey's work. It may well be that it was intended to gain prestige through association and also to clearly show Norman control of an earlier place of power. Archaeology has established that during the post-Roman Arthurian era Tintagel was a high prestige site, probably royally connected, that was the centre of extensive trade with the Byzantine Empire. Oral tradition of some kind may have preserved the memory of Tintagel's prestige during the time of Arthur. In Geoffrey of Monmouth Arthur was conceived at Tintagel. The association has developed from conception to birth. Tennyson had him washed ashore on a wave at Merlin's Cave down on the beach beneath.

It was moving to imagine a timeless realm where a procession of illustrious people who have visited the castle and Merlin's Cave walked amongst countless shades back up the hill as golden mist and shadows ebbed and flowed around them. Steiner, Jung, Hardy, Swinburne, Tennyson, Elgar, Bax. There was no way Dion Fortune hadn't been there as well. She was amongst them.

We had experienced a perfect entry into the Tintagel zone.

After retiring to a Bed and Breakfast Guest House for the night, Andy and I began the next day focused on the reason for our visit. The Tintagel Meonia sword's story was a good one. Initial portents of its existence had come back in November 1986. At the first Psychic Questing Conference in London, Andy had been lecturing on the discovery of the Paddon swords. Whilst looking at the projected slides, Carole Young saw an image of another Meonia sword, as if hanging in the air, superimposed over the images on the screen. Within the next week the vision repeated twice. A small chapel and a cave were somehow connected. Andy's partner of the time, Gilly Street, was also separately seeing a sword hanging vertically downwards with the associated name 'Excalibur'. Only a few days later, Marion Sunderland had been contacted by a local psychic. She had seen a vision of a sword and believed that Marion would find it. From that point Marion herself received impressions of an ancient magical sword. Graham Phillips likewise tuned-in and advised Marion that it would be discovered in the area of Tintagel. Failing that, it would manifest at Dozmary Pool, a place associated with the Lady of the Lake and Excalibur. At this time Marion wasn't seeing it as a Meonia sword but she realised that the Arthurian imagery around it could be indicative of its energies as much as its appearance. In May 1987 Marion and some friends from London, including Caroline Wise, visited Tintagel. Visions of a tumbling sword continued. They checked out the main tourist attractions of the castle and Merlin's Cave. They walked past a building known as King Arthur's Hall of Chivalry but it didn't exert any pull.

In September that year, one of Andy's friends from an earlier version of Earthquest also visited Tintagel. Dave Hunt had been present at the first stirrings of the zodiac quest in 1983. In the spring of '87, he had started to write a modern day Arthurian story, not unlike one of Dion Fortune's. The central protagonist lived a directionless life in surburbia. He inherited a large sum from his mother. On that night he had a visionary dream, finding himself on a clifftop at Tintagel. In the darkness a flame materialised before him, gradually transforming into a beautiful woman, with waist length black hair, wearing a Celtic robe. She was Morgana, embodiment of the Nine Maidens of Lyonesse. She told him that he was to uncover the mysteries of Merlin. He had to begin at Tintagel, visiting the castle and cave. The church of St. Materiana had a stained-glass window vital to the quest. The woman disappeared. The dream was sufficient to inspire the hero to move to Tintagel.

By August '87 that was as far as the story had got.

Dave decided that a visit to Tintagel might stimulate inspiration. In September he drove down there with his wife. He had a certain ambivalence about the place. As he wandered about the usual locations, Dave had no sense of impending weirdness. It was all the more startling then, when he saw, at the castle ruins, a woman identical to his vision of Morgana. There was the waist length black hair. She was even wearing a plum coloured velvet cape. He stared at her in disbelief. There was a strong urge to approach her but what on earth could he say? One part of him tried to be cool and rational. It was a notable synchronicity. It didn't necessarily lead any further. Nonetheless some other part of him felt the urge to follow through the narrative of the story. This took him to St. Materiana's church. Dave wondered if a mysterious stained-glass window would provide further revelations. Unfortunately, nothing was forthcoming. He returned to Essex somewhat perplexed.

A year later he was back in Tintagel, knowing somehow that more was to come. His wife drew Dave's attention to a large neo-gothic stone building with windows full of Arthurian paraphernalia. There were heraldic shields above its entrance. This was King Arthur's Hall of Chivalry. It suggested to Dave a Tennysonian tourist trap. He had no interest in going inside. His wife wanted to visit thesupermarket and was insistent that he would be best served lingering there and meeting her later. Reluctantly, he agreed.

The building he entered was a testament to the vision of one man. Frederick Thomas Glasscock was a hugely wealthy partner in the custard firm of Monkhouse and Glasscock. TV presenter Bob was a direct descendant of the other partner. Glasscock had an abiding passion for the Arthurian mythos. After his retirement he had moved into a large house and made massive alterations to it in order to create a Hall of Chivalry. It was a major labour of love. Fifty types of stone from all over Cornwall were brought in for its reconstruction. Seventy two stained-glass windows were commissioned showing various heraldic devices and legendary scenes. The larger ones were of exceptional quality, worthy of a great cathedral. They were positioned in accordance with a precise scheme of colour that allowed rainbow light to fall upon the Hall. There were two round tables, a sword in a stone above an altar, and a throne.

Glasscock created a chivalric order, the Fellowship of the Round Table. Local men were initiated. Teenagers had a grade of Pilgrim. Younger children were Searchers, singing songs about the sagas.

When the place was officially opened on June 5th 1933, five hundred people attended. A musical programme included the Pilgrims March from Wagner's *Tannhauser*. The combination of sound, costume, and diffused coloured light must have been extremely effective.

Anyone with a taste for Arthuriana would have been aware of this Tintagel development. And that leaves uncomfortable possibilities hanging in the air. There were certainly Grail enthusiasts amongst the Nazis. At the beginning of that decade, before they even came to power, Rudolf Hess had despatched Dr. Karl Hans Fuchs to Scotland to check out Rosslyn chapel, a location little known in those days for its esoteric potency. His mission is a matter of historical record for he lectured to the Edinburgh branch of the Theosophical Society during the visit. The Hall of Chivalry opened within six months of Hitler becoming chancellor. The new regime was looking for style models to assimilate. Within a year Himmler would be equally meticulous in the creation of his Grail castle at Wewelsburg. I have a feeling that Tintagel may have been a direct influence on the Black Camelot. I do find it striking that Glasscock died in 1934, en-route to America in an attempt to spread his Order, as Wewelsburg came into being.

It seemed that his work was still-born, at least on the outer plane. Glasscock's Will bequeathed the Hall to the local Masonic Lodge of which he was a member. It was used by them and hired out for wedding receptions and so on. By the eighties the Masons only used it occasionally. It had become a gift shop and tourist oddity.

As Dave looked through leaflets on the place he started to feel more of an affinity for it. Once inside the main Hall, he realised he was alone in there. Along the top of one wall were three striking stained-glass windows depicting Arthurian scenes. The central one showed Merlin, Morgana, and the Lady of the Lake holding Excalibur. Beneath them was a large display cabinet. Dave advanced towards it. Within it were a few manuscripts, a broadsword, an axe, and something else that suddenly sharply focused his attention. On its own, almost beneath the depiction of Excalibur on the window, was a rusted Meonia sword. There was no labelling to identify it or explain its presence there. Obviously, he would inform Andy about the find the moment he returned to Essex. Somehow it felt like his strange Tintagel adventures had reached a point of closure.

In my more mystical moments I have pondered on the possibility that Glasscock's attempt to found a new Order of Chivalry was a response to Steiner's impetus. Anthroposophy considered itself to be a true Rosicrucian school. Glasscock was known to be keen on Rosicrucianism as well as Arthur.

Glasscock would probably have known of Steiner's visit. There is one work by him and one about Anthroposophy in two bookcases full of old Arthurian volumes in the main hall. The whole place seems to tremble on the edge of the etheric. I find it easy to intuit mystical nuances suggestive of vast spiritual forces at work there. It's like a chapter that got left out of *Spear of Destiny:* the Hall of Chivalry, alight with rainbow colours shining through visionary windows onto knights, pilgrims and searchers, the air thick with incense and the rising sound of choirs, the whole scene hanging between Steiner's Goetheanum and Himmler's Wewelsburg. In its midst, a Meonia sword. That's quite a mix to contemplate whilst watching a summer sunset near the castle ruins.

So what was the story of the rusting sword? It had been found in a box in the attic that had included other items like the axe also featured in the display cabinet. Nothing more was known about it. Glasscock seemed the obvious connection at first but the building's original constructor turned out to be quite an interesting character who opened up further realms of possibilities. John Douglas Cook had been a newspaper editor before retiring to Tintagel to pursue his Arthurian passion. His tomb was in St. Materiana's churchyard. It was designed by William Burges, the Victorian neo-gothic architect. This was a name we were already well familiar with. Burges was up to his neck in mystical intrigue. Psychic information had already suggested he might be involved with the Meonia swords. Space doesn't permit me to adequately sing his praises. Andy does him justice in *The Seventh Sword.* Along with Cook's tomb, there was also a commemorative window in the church. This recalled some of Dave Hunt's intuitions about the location.

Burges wasn't the only esoteric connection with Cook. He had been a good friend of Earl Stanhope. This man was closely linked to the Society Rosicruciana in Anglia, who were antecedents of the Golden Dawn. Decades later, in the twenties, there were occult groups in Tintagel. The Fellowship of the Rose Cross was founded by A. E. Waite. Another group named the Triangle of the Holy Grail were also at work in the town. It was possible that any of these people could have been in possession of the sword.

Andy had a replica Meonia sword made. On a second visit to Tintagel in early August, we were able to place the two together in order to set up a magical resonance between them so that we would effectively have a 'Tintagel' sword of our own. The return trip to Essex deliberately passed through Glastonbury. The sword was taken beneath Pomparles Bridge over the River Brue, a location linked by local mythology with Bedevere's casting away of Excalibur. It also ended up in the Tor tower.

Bernard later held the sword to see if he could pick up any information from it. He spoke of some kind of occult group in Tintagel meeting in a room with a large rose design on a wall. In Camelot Castle Hotel there is a replica of the famous Round Table at Winchester, a design that features a large rose in the centre. Although now displayed as a table that can be sat around, it had been hung on a wall for a long time. It seems quite likely that the building could have served as a meeting place for people with such interests.

Without knowing the details of our Glastonbury excursion, Bernard also saw a late 19th century scene in the abbey. Four well-dressed men were wandering amidst the ruins. One of them was William Burges. They stopped near the old High Altar. Burges took a Meonia sword from a black bag he was carrying. He pushed it into the ground near the site of Arthur's tomb. The four men then took up position at the four cardinal points, a little way back from the sword, and bowed their heads. Bernard saw a spiralling golden mist emerge from it and gradually fill the whole area. He didn't think that any of those present could actually see the radiance though. Similar visits were made to Wearyall Hill and the top of the Tor. The journeys we had made between Glastonbury and Tintagel had seemingly been following in illustrious footsteps. It still wasn't clear how the sword had come to be apparently forgotten and neglected. The period from Burges to Glasscock was obscure. What mattered was that, in some greater scheme of things, we had participated in powerful magical acts that were a statement of intent, an affirmation of lineage, and a generator of ever increasing momentum.

Andy's writing of *Godstar* had begun well in the spring. A fine account of the first part of the Zodiac adventure was soon completed. I read the early chapters just before our August Tintagel visit. A sequence of problems then arose. Andy spilled a cup of Earl Grey tea into his computer. Material was lost. He paused to regain his bearings. Other concerns demanded his attention. Work on the Glastonbury book stopped. It would never have occurred to me that, over twenty years later, it would be me who would give the first published account of the story.

* * *

THE PRIMING

AS THE SUMMER HAD PROGRESSED there was a significant addition to the Earthquest group. Twenty-one year old Deborah Benstead lived in Brentwood in Essex and had attended one of Andy's travelling lectures there. She was interested enough to come along to Leigh-on-Sea for more.

At infant school Debbie had presented problems by constantly interacting with invisible companions. Doctors and psychologists were unable to assist. An aunt suggested the possibility of psychism and a spiritualist service was recommended. Her parents reluctantly brought her along. It proved to be a rite of passage all round as her father heard for the first time a clauraudient voice that opened up a mediumistic function in him. Suddenly dad had people coming round to hear the words of some weird dude who spoke through him. This guide looked Chinese or somesuch but was happy to be known as James, a not uncommon spiritualistic device. The invisible friends remained. Amongst them were two bald oriental children who thankfully didn't want her to stay and play forever and ever. Such was Debbie's early childhood. Things stabilised as a certain level of weirdness became accepted as the norm.

Then came an afternoon on a beach, at the age of seven. It wasn't an archetypal idyllic childhood memory of buckets and spades, sandcastles, ice cream and candy-floss. It wasn't recalled against a backdrop of the sound of children's laughter and sea gulls, the comforting warmth of parental love. The tide was a long way out. Debbie and her best friend Nicky wanted to find the water's edge. Their parents let them wander off, advising them to use the group's coloured beach umbrella as a fixing marker so as to not get lost. The two friends ran towards the water, seemingly in a straight line. Debbie was moving a bit faster and stopped to let her companion catch up. Turning round, Nicky was nowhere to be seen. Nobody at all was nearby. All that was visible, some considerable distance away, was a heat-hazy coloured blurred line of people on the horizon, windbreakers, a far off dream of a happy holiday. A sudden feeling of total aloneness and panic arose. Her attention moved upwards with this inner tide of the physiology of fear. Involuntarily, her eyes followed the roaring rush, rising above the shimmering holidaymakers, to alight upon an amoebic spherical transparent pulsing something that was hovering directly above her. It was about six feet across. The sky was visible through its shimmering glittering wobbliness, its utter otherness. Time seemed to freeze as she stared, transfixed, and yet it also felt that only seconds elapsed before she began running back up the beach in terror. Although it seemed that she'd returned up the same straight path she'd followed down, when the crowds of people were reached, her parents' group were nowhere to be found. The nightmare intensified. Running along the beach, screaming and sobbing, calling for her parents. Dense crowds of tall adults in the blue sky sunshine briefly turning to look, attracted by the sounds of distress, registering perplexity and walking on. Staring children. Then hurriedly grabbed, picked up and taken. An announcement over a public address system. The first sight of her parents again.

She'd been missing for hours. The seven year old soon afterwards began to suffer recurring night terrors, strange shudders, perplexity. Special protection was called for from the spirit realms. In response a new figure appeared. Debbie came to call him the 'Jesus man'.

The oriental guide known as James also seemed to be around to help her through such episodes. She could see him. A year or so later, he announced his impending departure and spoke of a gift of some kind for Debbie, connected with her future. She experienced sitting down with him as he held her hands for some considerable time. He departed and her father never channeled him again.

When I'd first read *The Green Stone* I had wondered what effect hanging out with such characters might have on me? Would any of it rub off? It did rather seem that being in the vicinity of Andy could have a strange effect on people. I used to joke about it with him, calling it Collins' Syndrome, a previously unknown medical condition whereby people that came into contact with him started to manifest striking psychism. The most outlandish case was probably that of a teenage girl who lived in the flat downstairs from Andy with her mother and whose bedroom was directly beneath Andy's meditation room, known as the black room (because of the colour of its walls), where all the group sessions used to happen. He scarcely knew her but a random conversation revealed that she had been having dreams that were clearly about Hecate. This was a girl with no interest in the occult. For a short while afterwards she came out with a sequence of stunningly authentic material about Hecate's cult that revealed details not featured in *The Black Alchemist*.

We were about to see the definitive umbrella effect. Deb's remarkable talents were undoubtedly a natural part of her functioning but meeting Andy blew her doors of perception right off their hinges. Andy put on a sequence of weekend all-day events in Essex throughout the summer of '89. I attended them all. Debbie was increasingly present and showing definite signs of direct information psychism. There were also hints that she might be a potential focus of physical phenomenon.

THE PATH OF THE DRAGON

"Always follow the path of the dragon for at the end of that path is the source of the power you've been given."
Gwythyr (also called Uther), son of Hext.

"A beast of such power that if you were to see it whole and all complete in a single glance it would burn you to cinders."
Merlin. *Excalibur.*

"You've broken the Hills - you've broken the Hills! It hasn't happened in a thousand years."
Puck. Rudyard Kipling. *Puck of Pook's Hill.*

BY THE YEAR'S END, a dynamic core questing group had definitely assembled and gelled. Momentum was building. Little things like the fall of the Berlin Wall fuelled the psychic climate. Just what were we capable of achieving? After the Green Stone had been found, it went walkabout on the 'Lights of Knowledge' excursion, passing through Glastonbury en-route. The quest had continued down into Cornwall for the retrieval of further 'lights'. There were nine in total. *The Green Stone* told how the final one was activated at the chalk figure of the White Horse of Uffington.

I learnt from Andy that the whole Lights of Knowledge episode had been far more extensive than the published account revealed. All of the sites involved were on or near to the Michael ley line. Graham Phillips also came to feel that they somehow resonated with the energies of the Qabalistic Tree of Life in an orderly sequence.

* * *

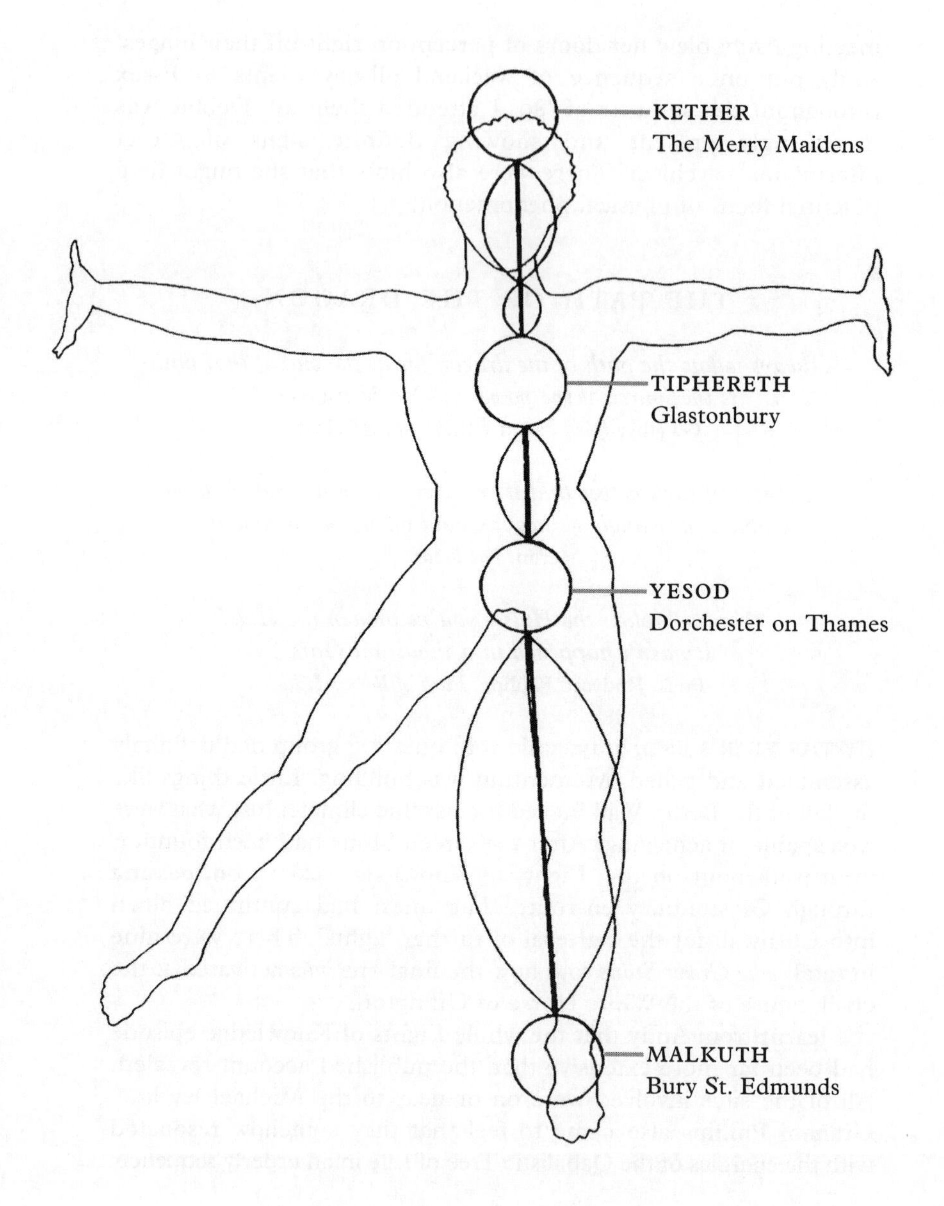

ADAM ALBION KADMON
As manifested through the St. Michael ley line

These are the basic site attributions for those who may be interested.

KETHER	*The Merry Maidens stone circle (not on the Line, but since dowsed as connected to it)*
CHOKMAH	*St. Michael's Mount.*
BINAH	*Dozmary Pool, Roche Rock, Hurlers stone circle area.*
CHESED	*Brentor.*
GEBURAH	*Crediton.*
TIPHERETH	*Glastonbury.*
NETZAH	*Avebury, Silbury Hill.*
HOD	*White Horse of Uffington, Wayland's Smithy area.*
YESOD	*Dorchester on Thames.*
MALKUTH	*A Malkuth site was never designated by Graham Phillips. I later came to feel Bury St. Edmunds was a viable option.*

The Michael line has sometimes been thought of as a possible spinal column of a Blakean Albion figure. This is not conceived of in the sense of physical earthworks in the manner that the Glastonbury Zodiac landscape supposedly models giant effigies. It somehow lives in an inner realm of the nation's consciousness. A Suffolk village named Eye has influenced views on which end of the line the head would be. After extensive ponderings on the Qabalah in 1989, I realised that Graham's material suggested another possibility. Central to Qabalistic lore is a giant cosmic being named Adam Kadmon on whom the Tree of Life can be drawn. His feet are in the earthly realms, his head at the Crown of Creation. Knowing that Blake was aware of the Qabalah, I didn't find it hard to broadly equate Albion with Adam Kadmon. Maybe the giant's head was in Cornwall?

Part of Dion Fortune's magical exploration of the Arthurian mythos involved trying to assign its characters and locations to places on the Qabalistic tree. The most extensive exposition of this work had come in Gareth Knight's *The Secret Tradition in Arthurian Legend.* I'd first read it in May 1985. Reading it again in '89, I'd found a lot of the Qabalistic material still didn't really land right with me. What did communicate itself was a flavour. Just like Mary

Caine's work, there was *something* there for me.

Graham Phillips' landscape Qabalah gave me the feeling of the doorway to that *something* opening. The Arthurian work of Fortune and Knight dealt with mythical locations, Camelot, Carbonek, the Grail Castle, and so on. Graham was talking about real physical places resonating with the energies of Qabalistic sephiroth, suggesting all kinds of magical possibilities. It seemed to me that his work was a remarkable innovation. All of these influences nicely primed me to appreciate an exquisite adventure to mark the transition into a new decade.

The Green Stone Light retrievals had been in the order of an ascent of the Tree of Life along the Michael line, until doubling back for the apparent climax at Uffington. Graham Phillips had never really thought that the process had been fully completed there. A later group outing to the Merry Maidens tried to follow it through but had been inconclusive. Although the stone had clearly been activated and all kinds of fun and games followed, the Ninth Light had the feeling of unfinished business.

Towards the end of 1989 a number of psychic hints were pulling the questing group towards Cornwall. The material was too extensive to expound in detail here. A few main themes provided the focus. In the summer, a powerful connection had been made with the Tintagel sword. A copy had been made and we were happy that we now had a sword that carried its energy. The first Meonia sword, the one found at the Knight's Pool in 1979, was in the possession of the Earl of Coventry, who owned the land on which it had been found. Another replica was made, the two brought together for a photo shoot, and a similar bit of magic worked. We had two functioning swords, one of which was 'Arthurian'. The real quest for the seventh Meonia sword needed to begin with the retrieval of the Ninth Light. We didn't have the Green Stone itself so clearly this would take the dynamic into another realm. It was also essential to interact with the most important sword bestower in British mythology, the Lady of the Lake. We would follow an Arthurian journey from the fabled site of his conception in Tintagel to his final home in Glastonbury, starting the new decade at the Avalon of the Heart. It would be a vital beginning of some kind of initiation into the land, into the energy matrix of Britain. This was primarily magical, rather than historical, questing. Nonetheless it was likely that information concerning others with similar concerns over the ages might reveal itself.

The Lady of the Lake business was most intriguing. Andy, Alex, and an occasional member of the group, a brilliant young psychic named David, all picked up on the same idea. There was a real physical woman who lived in Cornwall and was into the Lady of the Lake. Aged perhaps in her mid to late twenties, she was fairly psychic and visited sites. In some way she was able to effectively embody the energy of the archetype on a functional level. If she handed a sword to you by the side of some pool, magical force would be present. It would be no empty gesture. Strange things would follow. The psychic contact was two-way. Andy was convinced that she was aware of us to some degree. We were all being potentially pulled together. It was important to encourage this. To that end, we actively tried to send out psychic messages to her that we were coming to Cornwall and wanted to meet. This went on in varying ways throughout the Christmas period.

As well as that, Debbie had started to feel the presence of a mature woman, some kind of occultist from half a century or so ago. She had a nickname, 'Fluff'. Debbie was no reader of magical history. Along with Andy and Alex, I immediately recognised the reference. It was Dion Fortune. Plenty of people have claimed psychic contact of some kind with her since her death. She doesn't appear to be copyrighted on the inner planes. Perhaps the most useful way to assess such experiences will be to look at what they lead to.

In a group psychic session on December 23rd, Andy experienced flying over Cornwall, seeing a birds-eye panorama of the whole county. He realised that he was following the Michael line. As he began to descend, he felt that wherever he was about to land was energetically linked to Dozmary Pool, a site connected with the Lady of the Lake which we already intended to visit. He then saw his visionary destination. It was the distinctive ruined chapel at Roche Rock.

The moment that the location was identified, a flood of ideas and impressions came to him. It was important to getting back online with the Ninth Light. He should have gone there with Graham and Martin in 1981. It had been picked up on then but events had overtaken them and it had been missed out. A lot had happened there magically down through the ages, particularly during the last century or so. William Burges had visited the place. And Druidic types. Dodgy occultists with French links. Etc. We had to begin our journey there. A huge ripple effect would spread out reaching many places including Dozmary Pool.

On Friday December 29th our diverse group set out on the long car journey from Essex to Cornwall. Myself and Andy were accompanied by Debbie, Alex, John, Kerry, Lisa, Karl, and David. Shortly after entering Cornwall, Debbie saw a young deathly pale woman standing in the road directly in front of the car. Barely had she registered the impression when the car drove through the apparition confirming its otherworldly nature. Brakes were applied. The mini-convoy halted. Debbie got out. The woman was gone. All that remained was a fleeting impression that she was something to do with the Lady of the Lake. We booked in at a Guest House in Tintagel and stayed up chatting in the bar until the early hours. Something was going around in Debbie's head about nine maidens but no real details followed.

During her childhood Debbie had experienced seeing elementals; gnomes, faery folk and their kin. Like so much else, this particular talent went into abeyance. The time had come for a spectacular resurgence. Cornwall is a locale famous for Little People lore. On retiring to her room she noticed something a bit odd on the sink. Sitting on its edge was a funny little man about twenty inches high with a long moustache and straight hair sticking out from beneath a pointed helmet. He had little legs and arms and a slightly disproportionately larger body, wearing makeshift armour around which a cloak was wrapped. He was making strange noises. "Who are you little man?" *"Some call me Moray, some call me Follet."* It spoke!

A somewhat chaotic night followed. The remarkable little dude hopped around the room in typical playful Little People manner. He seemed to prefer the sink but also sat on the wardrobe and at one point on Debbie's chest. Some interesting dialogue ensued. In days gone by he and his mates had led knights into the otherworld. There they were confronted by the Old Gods. They had also invisibly moved things around to test peoples' responses to good and evil. He asked if we were coming to the Summerland, the Island of Apples? The gateway is there.

The conversation around the big breakfast table the next morning was surreally absurd but we were prepared to accept the game and play it. Debbie felt that she had picked up the follet when we had stopped after the vision of the woman in the road. Returning to her room, she found the just-made bed-clothes strewn around, along with the contents of a previously packed suitcase. As she emerged to report this we discovered from the hotel proprietors that a massive power surge had just trashed the whole building. Plumbing was leaking, the cooker broken, wiring failed and generally overloaded. They suspected, but with good humour, that we were in some unknown manner responsible. This tangible manifestation, entirely in keeping with the lore of faery, further persuaded us to accept Debbie's unlikely tales and see where it led. It set us up nicely for the coming day's agenda. We were rapidly stepping outside consensus reality.

The granite crag of Roche Rock, on the edge of Goss Moor, has an immediate visual uniqueness. It is dominated by the 15th century ruins of a tower containing a chapel and hermit's cell. On that grey wintry morning it suggested lots of possibilities for black and white photography. Local mythology links the place with a hermit who tried to act as a peacemaker in the Tristan and Iseult story. It had no obvious connection with the Arthurian material we were working with. For us, it was the Michael line/Qabalah frequency that was important that day.

It was necessary to climb a rusting metal stepladder to gain access to the upper level of the building. Once we'd settled ourselves down in the chapel, Debbie sensed a psychic contact with a woman calling herself Morgan le Fay. Somehow this was Dion Fortune but also not her. Half-sister of Arthur, Morgan le Fay is characterised in the early medieval Arthurian literature as Queen of the faery realm of Avalon in the Celtic otherworld. She is a shape-shifting sorceress and healer, learned in starlore and mathematics, a female Merlin Druidess. By the time of Malory at the end of the Middle Ages, her character had been thoroughly assassinated.

As already mentioned, Dion Fortune had worked to re-empower the archetype. The character of Vivien Le Fay Morgan in *The Sea Priestess* combined the names of the two great female sorceresses of the Arthurian sagas. There is an implication that the two are fragmented aspects of a primordial original. Fortune felt that the Celtic myths contained layers of ancient material not native to Great Britain. Arthur, Merlin, and Morgan were not solitary individuals but titles passed down through the ages from lost Atlantis. Adept refugees from the sunken continent found their way to Albion and introduced their Pendragon mysteries to the indigenous peoples. Cornish folklore of lost Lyonesse carries an echo of this. The tale of Merlin's magical overseeing of Arthur's conception refers to a genetic experiment to crossbreed the Atlantean stock of Igraine with the royal Celtic blood of Uther.

Dion Fortune helped to reactivate the Priestess function in the modern world through interaction with the Morgan archetype. This was inner-plane work done for the whole race. With the more esoteric Atlantean idea came the hint of something truly ancient in the background. Even if one doesn't believe in the standard mythology it's not too difficult to get a hint of the flavour. Just think of a cloudless night on a deserted Cornish beach, the sky full of innumerable brightly shining stars. All is silent save for gently lapping waves. Out at the sea's far horizon the slowly rising rim of a full moon reveals a shadow on the water ahead. It's a single-sailed vessel of some ancient culture. The sound of its movement through the waves begins to become audible. It is the coming of the Sea Priestess. It was this complex package that Debbie had connected with at Roche as she said that part of Dion Fortune was present that's Morgan and always will be. It was a perfect preparation to call upon the Lady of the Lake to be with us at Dozmary Pool. In many ways, she was already present.

At 11 o'clock we pressed the psychic 'on' button. The message was sent out. Those of us who knew what Dozmary Pool looked like tried to visualise it. Andy, Debbie, and David all felt that Roche Rock is a far more powerful site than most people realise. It was emanating great ripples of golden white energy across the land. The natural pattern of their flow encompassed Dozmary Pool. It was time to go there.

In Gareth Knight's Dion Fortune inspired Arthurian Qabalah,

the 'Lake' is placed on the sephiroth of Yesod. There are good reasons for this as its associations include the moon and its tides that are a potential entrance to the astral realms. In the *Sea Priestess* there are many hints of the aspects of the higher realm of Binah in the watery symbolism as well. Its 'vision' is of Marah, the dark bitter sea of sorrow, which ultimately bestows understanding. There is a sense of the matrix of the ancient origins of life, the first manifestations of form. Vivien Le Fay Morgan utters the invocation,

> *"I am that soundless, boundless bitter sea,*
> *Out of whose depths life wells eternally."*

In keeping with Graham's Michael line Qabalah, our Lake and its Lady were of Binah. The initial Morgan contact was entirely appropriate.

The Bodmin Moor landscape seemed bleakly barren on that grey December morning. The Dozmary Pool area dips down a little below the general environs. It's a mile in circumference and five hundred yards across. The waters are usually strikingly still. A few long low hills can be seen around the horizon. Other than that, only a few trees and some farm buildings lead the eye above the waters' surface. On arriving, Debbie said, *"the whole place is like the shroud of the hinterland"*. The feeling was that of the stillness after death. There was nothing inherently bad about any of this.

Local legends have come to associate the site with the Lady of the Lake and her bestowal of Excalibur upon Arthur. Andy helped to set the mood with the first of what became a series of readings from Tennyson's *Idylls of the King* on our journey.

> *"There likewise I beheld Excalibur*
> *Before him at his crowning borne, the sword*
> *That rose from out of the bosom of the lake,*
> *And Arthur rode across and took it - rich*
> *With jewels, elfin Urim, on the hilt,*
> *Bewildering heart and eye - the blade so bright*
> *That men are blinded by it."*

In honour of the movie *Excalibur* and as a rousing way to really get our adventure going, a portable cassette player was produced and *Carmina Burana* blasted out. At this cue Kerry, with the necessary protection of wellington boots, waded out into the water holding our Tintagel and Meonia swords aloft. Things had certainly been interesting and entertaining so far but we had now arrived at a crucial point in the journey. This act was intended to signify our intention to enter fully upon the quest for the seventh sword and the recognition that it would require a major interaction with the mythos of the energy matrix of Britain.

The Lady of the Lake visions needed some sort of validation. As Kerry brandished the swords, there was movement further around the edge of the Pool. A car had pulled up. A lone woman got out and began to walk in our direction. John's 20/20 hawk-eye vision could see she seemed to be in her twenties. I could tell she was paying attention to us but who wouldn't be? A group of nine people. Classical music loudly playing. A woman in the water holding swords aloft. Not a lot else was happening in the vicinity. She stopped for a while, returned to her car and departed.

Was the glass half empty or half full? Was it a result or not? We weren't exactly going to return to Essex because she hadn't come right up to us and said, "I am the embodiment of the Lady of the Lake and I have been drawn by powerful visions to come and meet you and bless your quest". What were the chances of that unknown woman coming over to such a large and potentially intimidating group and beginning a conversation even if she really was a psychic who was into the Lady of the Lake and had been drawn by inner prompting to be there at that time? It was enough for our presence and actions to have been synchronistically acknowledged. What would happen now?

We'd travelled some way across the county to get to Roche Rock from Tintagel. Now we were heading back towards it. There was only one more site on the day's itinerary; Slaughterbridge, legendary scene of Arthur's last battle. Time was comfortable. Boscastle is located just a few miles up the road from Tintagel. It is home to a unique witchcraft museum. It might be worth a quick visit. Such was our conscious reasoning. On such magical journeys it often transpires that what appear to be acts of random spontaneity can serve as portals to deeper mysteries.

Boscastle is a powerful elemental place set down in an inlet amongst the cliffs of its harbour. In the summer it presents a beautiful picture-postcard look. It's the only location along a forty-mile stretch of the north Cornish coast where a harbour is possible. At the edge of the entrance is Profile Rock, so named in recent times because it resembles, from some angles, Queen Victoria's head.

The water winds a sinuous path, difficult to navigate, through to a narrow inlet, the mouth of the Valency River, which is usually little more than a stream. During its 19th century peak, the harbour had been extremely busy. Now the main business comes from tourism. The great flood of 2004 would bring it national attention.

The summer flowers and greenery, the sunshine and Mediterranean blue waters, were absent. Very few people were about. It wasn't a total surprise to discover that the witchcraft museum was shut for the season. Further along, nearer to the mouth of the harbour, the sea foamed and crashed in surging waves upon the slate. It would be good to get closer. We crossed a small bridge over the trickling Valency River and proceeded along a walkway. The cliffs immediately to our left dripped with water. We reached the end of the path and clambered up onto a small promontory that afforded a fine view of the powerful waves some way below.

Debbie then began to see horses along the cliff-tops. Some were silver grey, others a strange purple and brown. They seemed quite solid although she was aware that they weren't. Her immediate feeling was that they were representatives of the Celtic goddess Rhiannon. The horse represented the unity of the land and the goddess and was powerfully connected to the theme of sovereignty. Somehow the vision communicated to Debbie that we had to become one with the land through the horse. The horses and the denizen of the faery realm were powerful primordial contacts. They were good omens that we were on the right track. A further meditation was in order.

There were great crashing waves full of horses coming in. The sound somehow pulled Debbie into itself. In a fleeting moment she was riding on one of the horses, back out to sea. Barely had she registered that impression when the next thing she was conscious of was standing before a group of nine women on an island. The *Spoils of Annwn* tale featured that exact number of maidens whose breath kindled the fire that heated their magical cauldron. Geoffrey of Monmouth's *Vita Merlini* tells how Morgan le Fay lived on the Isle of Avalon with her eight sisters. After the battle at Camlann Arthur was taken to them to be healed.

Why would Rhiannon and Morgan manifest together as two sides of the same experience? Some of the theories about their name derivations may supply an answer. For Morgan, *Muir gena,* meaning 'Sea Born' is one possibility that accommodates the Sea Priestess/Mistress of Avalon idea. Many also posit a likely link to the Irish Morrighan that breaks down into *Mor rigan,* 'Great Queen'. Rhiannon has been derived from *Rigantona,* also taken to mean 'Great Queen'. The way these figures seem to blur and blend, becoming confused with each other can, on one level, be seen as part of the process of later storytellers losing sight of the true nature of their female subject matter. It can also be seen as excellently evocative of the mystery of the ever-changing face and form of the Goddess. Morgan could shapeshift into animal form after all.

Debbie stood before the nine ladies grouped around the cauldron of rebirth. Her sense of who they were was completely at variance with Geoffrey of Monmouth. Grey haired black clad crone Ragnall stood with dark haired Morgana, whom was wearing celtic style trousers and cloak. There were two youngish blondes. Fee was covered in flowers. Nimue wore a lilac and blue sash and dress. The darker haired Ganied sported gold jewellery. Also present were Ninianne and two younger women, Linette and Elaine, and another whose name eluded Debbie. On coming into the company of this extraordinary group she naturally wondered what was happening and why. By way of reply she was told, *"this is the healing necromancy"*.

Three of the women named by Debbie are linked with Merlin. Ganieda is his sister in the *Vita Merlini.* Ninianne is a variant on the more famous Vivienne. Both she and Nimue are featured in stories where Merlin is seduced and entranced into an imprisonment. These stories in turn may be distorted versions of the magician and his sister retiring to an observatory of his mentioned by Geoffrey of Monmouth.

At this stage of the game it was enough that Debbie had been presented to such illustrious company as in some sense at least a candidate for admittance. It seemed that the whole nine lights business must have some resonance with these nine ladies. This was the real contact with the Lady of the Lake. Not just an individual, but a whole magical world. Celtic mythology and Arthurian literature are full of references to otherwordly zones accessed through water, whether pools, or islands such as Avalon. Archaeology has uncovered numerous Celtic votive offerings left in water, including swords. There are many maidens linked with wells and streams. An early medieval tale, *The Story of the Well-Maidens,* set in a pre-Arthurian world, portrays their tragic fate. There was once a time when the sacred wells and springs were given the necessary respect. Travellers would receive free hospitality from the ladies in attendance. A king then raped one of them and stole her golden cup. His men followed the example and likewise abused other maidens. This served to withdraw the Grail blessings and the presence of its priestesses from the world, thus ushering in the epoch of the wasteland. It's an evocative feminist fragment to put alongside the usual Fisher King stories. We had connected with their realm. The Lady of the Lake contact was already proving to be surprisingly expansive. The otherwordly waters had more in store for us over the coming months than we could ever have anticipated.

It remained a puzzle as to why this episode had unfolded as it did at Boscastle? I have wondered a bit about Profile Rock. There are some Bronze Age barrows and burial mounds and an Iron Age encampment in the vicinity. What would those people have made of the formation? A crone goddess perhaps? It looks out over the small island of Meachard in the harbour entrance. Might there have been some group of nine witchy priestess-type women in the area? Such groups weren't just fiction. An island in the Seine was famously home to one. If Boscastle did have such a history, the site memory would act as a perfect trigger to activate the early medieval mythology into a potent magical matrix. The witchcraft museum was probably some factor in the equation. A mystery remains. Watch a full moon rising over Boscastle harbour and ponder upon it.

We doubled back on ourselves, heading for an area just beyond Tintagel. Slaughterbridge crosses the River Camel when it's little more than a stream. Through the usual etymological gymnastics the place has become linked with the legendary Battle of Camlann where Arthur and Mordred finally met in combat and the King received his fatal wounds. It's no great surprise to discover that history and mythology are slightly at variance there. A stone slab known as 'Arthur's Grave' supposedly dates from a battle during the Saxon conquest of Cornwall in 825 AD, a few centuries too late.

These were the days before the current visitor centre was built with its elevated wooden tracks marking a path above the stream. Access to the stone itself was easier then. There had been a few hints of what was coming. Kerry seemed to carry the Morgan energy very well. It had already been activated at Dozmary Pool when she took on a powerful archetypal magical role. As we arrived at the Slaughterbridge site she wasn't feeling too good anymore. There were stomach pains and overwhelming emotions that brought tears. She was emphatic that there was no way she was going down to the river. She waited in John's car as we walked away down a slope into the self-contained bowl of the site. Her state didn't improve when she saw a ghostly woman in white over in the direction we were heading who she felt was trying to compel her to join us.

Things were very different for Debbie. As we got nearer to the bridge by the river, she told us that she could hear our Tintagel sword singing. In fact she could sing us the whole song.

> *"When the knights won their spurs in the stories of old,*
> *they were gentle and brave, they were gallant and bold.*
> *With a shield on their arms and a lance in their hands,*
> *for good and for valour they rode through the land.*
>
> *No charger have I and no sword by my side,*
> *yet still to adventure and battle I ride.*
> *Though back into storyland giants have fled,*
> *and the knights are no more and the dragons are dead,*
> *let faith be my shield and let truth be my steed,*
> *gainst the dragons of anger, the ogres of greed.*
> *And true to our quest may the light be our path*
> *gainst the castle of darkness, the fire kings of wrath."*

It repeated a number of times. Debbie could have a wide-eyed childish innocence about her at times and her singing of this song very much brought out those qualities. Most of the group recognised the song. I could remember singing it at Junior School. Hearing it again brought a cold-tingling poignant nostalgia of the feelings that my mother's bedtime reading to me from Enid Blyton's *Tales of Brave Adventure* had stirred. It was possible that Glassock's young Searchers and Pilgrims may have sung it in the Hall of Chivalry. That would partly explain why our Tintagel sword somehow carried it as part of its program.

Some of the words seemed a bit different from my memories though. The seventh sword was singing to us as well, although at that moment it was almost inaudible to even the most psychically attuned ears. It was no wholesome feeling of childhood and chivalry and gentle patriotism that was beginning to sound a rising tone in our direction either. It was a wail of Sumer, the sun shadowed by the moon. A little hint of its flavour would very soon be upon us, suggesting that the dragons weren't dead, the giants were returning, and the fire kings of wrath were a force to be reckoned with.

Tennyson had set the battle at the time, *"when the great light of heaven burn'd at his lowest in the rolling year"*, so we were nicely synchronised with that. Once again, Andy used the poet, coupled with his own directions, to good effect to conjure up the appropriate scene.

> *"– The splintering spear, the hard mail hewn*
> *Shield breakings, and the clash of brands, the crash*
> *Of battleaxes on shatter'd helms, and shrieks*
> *After the Christ, of those who falling down*
> *Look'd up for heaven, and only saw the mist;*
> *And shouts of heathen and the traitor knights,*
> *Oaths, insult, filth, and monstrous blasphemies,*
> *Sweat, writhings, anguish, labouring of the lungs."*

The vivid words, in combination with countless viewings of *Excalibur,* made it easy enough to enter into a reverie on the theme. What followed seemed a bit more intense than the average visualisation. Initially John saw the battle with exceptional vividness. He started to glimpse the events before Andy had mentioned them and with more detail. When Arthur killed Mordred with a single sword blow, John actually felt the sword enter his own body with such extreme accompanying pain that the former soldier was forced to sit down. David received a sword blow on his head. He felt his eyes filling with blood.

It all led to the final moments of Arthur. With his fatal swoon, the magic sword had to be returned to the Lady of the Lake. There was blood upon it that needed to be cleansed. Andy walked down by the bridge and immersed our swords in the running water, asking the Lady of the Lake to cleanse them so that they could only be used for light, never hatred or evil.

The female form that manifested bore little resemblance to the usual Pre-Raphaelite depiction. She was more akin to the Irish Morrigan who was connected to battlefield funerary functions. Alex saw what he described as a hideous demoness come out of the ground. She was ten feet tall with great curved oxen type horns on her head. She had black sunken eyes in a deathly white face. Uprooting herself, she charged at Alex and pinned him against a rock with her horns. Fortunately, he experienced no pain beyond the shock of the unexpected vision. David saw his own version of the female form. He simply described her as 'Black Isis'. Her blackness began to turn to gold. As it did so he could see what he described as the *"energy vortex of the site turning in on itself"*.

Debbie had no real sense of the battle at all but did see her own version of the mysterious woman on the other side of the river-bank. She had a young face, long black hair streaked with red and blonde. Wearing a dark blue robe with red and purple sashes, she held up a serpent staff with wings on the top like a caduceus. Her name was Morgausanne. This was a strange mix. Geoffrey of Monmouth has Anna as Arthur's sister. She later marries Lot of Lothian and gives birth to Mordred and Gawain. In Malory, Morgause is one of Arthur's half sisters. She also marries the Scottish king and mothers Mordred. Some versions have her conceiving the usurper with Arthur. The Cornish background of 'Morgausanne' and her status as Mordred's mother made her presence at his death appropriate.

John was at that time becoming increasingly connected with Gawain, a process that would generate a superb quest in 1990 that's outside the scope of this narrative. If Gawain was Mordred's brother, at least in some versions, this might explain why the sight of his death affected John so strongly. None of these details were known by John or Debbie. The results were not particularly significant but are noted as examples of a type of a bizarre psychism of obscure details that manifested regularly on our subsequent adventures.

When Andy put the swords in the water, Debbie saw Morgausanne somehow absorbing energy from the blood-stain cleansing and push it back out in the form of a multitude of small red wriggling serpents which dispersed down river, spreading their colour through the water as they went. Then, like the turning of a tide, they began to come back. This didn't quite seem like the ideal outcome. Debbie communicated what she was seeing.

Andy had been involved in a not dissimilar space. He'd seen a fiery female form that seemed to be a distorted version of the Lake Lady funerary Morrigan one could expect and accept in such a situation. He had called upon the Archangel Michael to send his protective fire into our swords and the whole locale. He had seen the woman dissolve into tiny red dragons before Debbie had spoken. Now the creatures were returning.

The archangel Gabriel was called on for additional assistance. Debbie saw him appear. A tall, pale, black-eyed being with straight wet hair, he wore a dark-blue hooded cloak over a royal blue robe. He was holding one hand against his chest. The other was held out palm outstretched, a stream of bright blue liquid flowing from it. We visualised blue energy radiating from our swords and spreading out throughout the adjoining woods and water. Gold light was then pushed out over the top of that. The water no longer flowed with blood. The trees were suffused with gold. The colours blended into an emerald green. A sense of harmony had been restored to the place of slaughter.

I felt at the time that the site and others like it might carry battle and death associations from way back before the Bronze Age. Perhaps people deliberately chose to fight at places already sacred to death goddesses and their ancestors. We had no intention of behaving like New Age Lightworkers and trying to cleanse the place permanently of some imagined deep dark evil. It seemed unbalanced, but in its own terms. It's not always wrong for places to carry memories of history and death. We had played out our drama and emerged on the other side. Others coming to the site in future might have to navigate their own versions of the same process. That's okay. It's what the place is supposed to do. Sacred site doesn't necessarily mean cotton wool and candy-floss.

After the final battle Arthur was taken to a chapel. It suited our purposes to use the clifftop church of St. Materiana in Tintagel as the focus for this episode. By the time we arrived it was dark. This amplified the elemental qualities of the place. A crashing sea sounded loudly from down below us. Debbie spoke of feeling Rhiannon present as the Night Mare.

We settled down in the churchyard for the next stage of the Arthurian journey, the beginning of the grand finale that would help set us off on the road to Glastonbury the following day. The idea was to visualise being in the boat with the wounded Arthur and the three Queens.

> *"I am going a long way...*
> *To the island-valley of Avilion;*
> *Where falls not hail, or rain, or any snow,*
> *Nor ever wind blows loudly; but it lies*
> *Deep-meadow'd, happy, fair with orchard lawns*
> *And bowery hollows crowned with summer sea."*

It should have been very beautiful. Debbie felt that someone else was also present behind her. She mentally questioned who it was and received the instant answer, 'The Vortigern'.

He asked her, *"Do you wish to know of the dragon's egg?"* Sounds interesting. Yes, of course. Debbie half expected an explanation or a vision of a site. No. She barely had time to register the sense of something amiss when the imposing figure somehow forced some strange object inside her. She later described Vortigern's communication as being along the lines of, "give birth to that, bitch". Everything turned black and red. She opened her eyes and it was still the same. Her legs buckled and she slumped to the floor. Coming back to consciousness she tried to get back up but couldn't. She had a feeling of something very bad inside her. It was like a sharp egg-shaped object was rapidly turning around, exerting an intense pressure on her whole system. The movement slowed down and the central core of the 'egg' seemed to disperse into numerous smaller objects that dissolved throughout Debbie's body.

This was the first time that she had got into such difficulties. The group visualised white light pouring into her and expanding into an aura around her body. After a little while she seemed to be physically recovered but had obviously found the whole thing to be a bit disturbing. Later that evening, in the Guest-House we took stock of the situation.

Modern occult and New Age mythology speculates that in the lost golden age humanity was at one with natural forces. The shamans and magicians had profound knowledge of the inner workings of the world and possessed extraordinary paranormal powers. This was the epoch when the ley system was fully activated. Then came a fall of some kind. Climate changed. Harvests failed. Nothing was ever quite the same again.

There may have been a sequence of rise and falls. It's common now to talk of pole shifts and geological upheavals destroying previous civilisations. In the evolving questing lore there was the tale of the shutting down of the Crystal Chambers. Thousands of years later, at a time of hope, Akhenaten's experiment was wrecked by the Santorini event, remembered in distorted form in the Moses *Exodus* story. The ripples of this major biggie messed-up the British energy matrix. Similar forces of climatic disruption were at work on a global scale during the Arthurian era.

If there can be said to be some kind of life force that flows through a planetary grid then such humungous turmoil will assuredly change the nature of the flow. The relation to cosmic forces, such as the constellation of dragon Draco would certainly be different after a polc-shift. The serpent power, the Pendragon, might just have turned a bit nasty. David was talking of the 'Black Dragon'. Some religious elites who perhaps really were tuned in to the land and wielded its power might have got warped-out by the shift and their cults turned 'black'. Whatever its 6th century focus, the Arthurian mythos quite probably did contain material immeasurably older, dating back at least to the Bronze Age. When David stated that it was the Black Dragon that turned Vortigern into a bad guy it might be pointing to a recurring cycle of events that have left a powerful imprint in the etheric timeline.

Something of the energies of that intense and deep mystery was stirred by the Green Stone story. A distorted magical force lingering since the end of the megalithic era and periodically resurfacing as a dangerous adversarial limitation on collective reawakening was confronted. In 1989, 'The Vortigern' served as our Dweller on the Threshold to that realm. We were getting an increasing taste of what it was going to mean to enter it.

It had been understood by the psychics for some time that the seventh sword was the 'black' sword. In *Excalibur,* as Arthur learnt from Merlin about the dragon, he had realised that his sword was, *"part of the dragon too"*. The seventh sword was part of the black dragon and intense alchemical magical work would be necessary to safely manifest it.

Some of the group got significantly drunk that night in the guest-house bar. A conga-chain up the road to the Hall of Chivalry had been one of the consequences. By 2.30am, back indoors, Andy and David were attempting to talk to the follet through Debbie. He told them his name was Trebor, which is Robert backwards and indubitably very silly. They asked him for advice on the trip to Glastonbury the next day. He stated that we would connect with Melchizedec, Lord of Fire, who had come from far away to become part of the old gods of England.

Melchizedec is one of the most enigmatic characters in the Bible and therefore an esoteric favourite. He has a walk-on part in chapter 14 of *Genesis* when he meets Abraham after the latter has achieved victory in a battle. "*Melchizidec king of Salem brought forth bread and wine: and he was priest of God Most High. And he blessed him, and said, Blessed be Abraham of God Most high, possessor of heaven and earth.*" So, he is a priest and a king and he has the authority to dispense blessings to the father of the Jewish race before the time of Moses. In Christian times he came to be regarded as some kind of mysterious pre-figuration of Christ for his proto-eucharistic feast, getting another brief mention in the *Epistle to the Hebrews* on that basis.

Rene Guenon stated that 'Melki-Tsedeq' was acting on behalf of the spiritual hierarchy of the planet and embodies the Lord of the

World spoken of in connection with Agharttha and Shambhala. The meeting with Abraham was, "*a spiritual investiture, wherein is found the exact point of union between the Hebraic and the great primordial tradition*". Melchizedek appears in some Byzantine artwork and is later depicted by statues in some of the Gothic cathedrals such as Chartres, Notre Dame and Reims. As the bearer of a chalice it's not surprising that he has been linked with the Grail and the possibility of some hidden cultus.

St. Paul mentions the little matter that Melchizedek, "*is without father, without mother, without origin – has neither beginning nor end to his life*" and, "*dwells as Priest in perpetuity*". This seems to suggest immortality. It's on that basis that he now functions as what the New Agers call an Ascended Master.

The most immediate relevance of his name-check by Trebor was that it was another Dion Fortune connection. Melchizedek was the head honcho of her magical order, which featured three 'rays' of emanation. Each ray also had a subsidiary Master in charge of it. The Green Ray was an Earth Mysteries path. It involved connection to the faery realm. These ideas had crystallised for Dion Fortune during time spent at Glastonbury. She had contacted Melchizedec on the Tor and he had shown her the three rays and their Lords. Debbie knew nothing of any of this. For the follet to talk of Melchizedec, calling him a Lord of Flame and mention that he had come from far away to join the old gods of England was a clear indicator that we were making a strong connection with the Dion Fortune current and that the spiritual forces behind her were on our case.

Andy asked Trebor if he could name any other humans that he had communicated with. He claimed that he only ever spoke to women. The name Christine Hartley was mentioned. He had conveyed messages to her from Melchizedec. The plot was continuing to thicken. Hartley had been an associate of Dion Fortune who branched out away from her and later wrote a well-received book, *The Western Mystery Tradition*. I'd read it at the start of the year. It was known that she likewise worked with Melchizedec and was concerned with faery lore but I wasn't aware of any known biographical details that would confirm what Trebor was saying. She might not have seen him with the visual vividness of Debbie. It may have been an inner inspiration. For the moment I took it to mean that it would be a mistake to think that we were connecting exclusively to Dion Fortune. Her work and legacy spread out some considerable way.

What could Trebor tell us about Debbie's intense experience with Vortigern and the mystery of the dragon's egg? Some enigmatic utterances followed. The connection between the black dragon and the seventh sword was confirmed. The egg is something that's been placed at various points at different times. It embodies aspects of the black dragon like lots of babies. There are three of them. The fire will hatch them. Debbie had been vaccinated now.

What about Avalon? He referred to it as the *"isle of the sun king"*, where, "*Morgan from the city of the sea, the place you call Atlantis"*, would be waiting. *"She was mother of the king and the sister and daughter of the king"*. The female follets are her attendants. Merlin was an Atlantean priest. Trebor asked Andy if he was, *"a sun man, a sun pilgrim?"* He answered in the affirmative and invited the follet to accompany us to Glastonbury. The artefact-conscious Andy also asked Trebor if he could bring us some item that related to his world. He promised something personal to Debbie from the sea daughter Morgan. His good-night message was, *"I'll see you in the cave of the heart"*. It had been a long day. We'd first heard news of Trebor the follet over the breakfast table. He now seemed like an old mate, an eye and guide to millennia of Albion's landscape.

The Land's End peninsula is dense with megalithic remains. These include four intriguingly similar stone circles within ten miles of each other; Boskednan, Tregeseal, Boscawen-Un and the Merry Maidens. At 21-24m in diameter, they're all about the same size, having nineteen stones each. Despite the stone count, they all became known as 'Nine Maidens' with associated tales that the stones were women petrified in punishment for dancing on the Sabbath. The nine women designation seemed all the more intriguing after the Boscastle experience. Arguments continue over whether the four circles are part of an enormous system of alignments on the ground and against the heavens. At the very least, there seems to be a strong likelihood that they link with lunar cycles.

On the morning of the last day of the decade, in honour of *Monty Python and the Holy Grail*, Andy led us in a line towards the Merry Maidens stone circle, knocking two coconut shell halves together to make the sound of horses' hooves. All that remains of the original site now is a circle of stones ranging from 0.4 to 1.4m in height. There had once been another circle and various outlying stones. Fifteen assorted standing stones remain within a mile, two of which would be important to us.

In comparison to somewhere like Avebury it seems a tiny place, a parish church compared to a cathedral. Was this really supposed to be the Qabalistic Kether of the great Michael ley line? Did the limitless ocean of divine light break through here? The site has to be considered in the bigger context of the whole antiquity packed peninsula. All kinds of subtle stuff passes between these places and then out and beyond across the country. There were accumulations and discharges of energy. The Merry Maidens could serve as a conduit through to the Michael line system. How? What? We chose to simply accept that something of that nature was the case and to see where we got with it.

The site has had a few name changes over the years. In 1201 it was recorded as *Rosmoderet,* meaning 'Mordred's rough land'. There are more than three hundred place names in the Land's End area and this is the only one with Arthurian associations. Slaughterbridge is actually the nearest location with any such connection and it's fifty miles away. A further resonance with that site was the folk belief that the circle was raised as a memorial to a battle in 936 AD when the last of the Cornish Celts were finally defeated by the Saxons.

A number of British stone circles have associated folklore tales of maidens coaxed into dancing by the devil on a sabbath being turned to stone by the vengeful Christian god. In this case, the two tallest stones in Cornwall, known as the Pipers, four and five metres high in an adjacent field about a quarter of a mile away, are the frozen remains of the tempters. Two evil spirits took on the form of pipers to lead the maidens into sin. A flash of lightning in a clear sky froze the whole group into stone.

Andy had picked up in advance of the trip that the Pipers were important. Shortly afterwards, he was driving in his car when Led Zeppelin's *Stairway to Heaven* had come on the radio. Something about the words, *"the piper's calling you to join him"* did funny things to his head. He started to feel that the two stones would lead us away to yet another site that was important. There was a stream nearby and a path. David had also sensed the pull of a secondary site. He picked-up on a path, and something about a merman. A quick map check showed that the pipers do align to a strange man-made cave known by the Cornish name of fogou. A stream did indeed run nearby down to Lamorna cove, a place known for mermaid lore.

Having reached the Merry Maidens, the magical procedure was intuited. We would work simultaneously at the two different sites. Debbie would supervise a reawakening of the petrified maidens.

Her introduction to Morgan and her sisterhood the previous day felt like a preparation for this task amongst other things. David and John would take one Meonia sword to the Pipers. It would be struck like a tuning fork and its tones would set up a ripple of energy that would activate the dancing maidens who would have been suitably primed by the rest of us under Debbie's supervision working with the Tintagel sword.

We took up our respective positions and began. Over at the Pipers, David saw a group of about twenty megalithic wanderers. It was the Egyptian magicians who had left the Lights of the Green Stone along the line. They were led by a known character from the saga named Yuya Neb, who was holding a staff wand of some kind. Strange unpronounceable words started to fill David's head. At this point, the sword was struck, its tone vibrating outwards on many levels. An awesome vision unfolded to David's psychic eyes. A giant flaming arrow spear flew up into the air and across the sky like a fireball comet. On the ground beneath, following its path, a huge wall of flame leapt up as if from deep within the earth. This was the Michael line and the spear of Lugh. It moved right across the country, beginning to fan out into an arrowhead awen shape beyond Oxfordshire.

It wasn't possible to physically hear the sound of the sword back at the Merry Maidens but Debbie's psychic sensibilities felt the resonations. She saw Archangel Michael appear. He had long curly red hair and yellow eyes. An orangey red cloak was worn over a ruby red robe. He wielded a flaming sword. Its fire entered the Tintagel sword that to her touch seemed to tangibly heat up. This energy was fed into the stones.

The occultists of Dion Fortune's epoch thought of Melchizedek and the Archangel Michael as two separate beings. Today's New Agers have taken that on. Debbie felt that they were one and the same. There is historical validation for this. Some of the Dead Sea Scrolls literature discovered in 1947 makes it clear that there were apocalypse obsessed Jews who felt likewise a few thousand years ago. Rudolf Steiner believed that Michael was a later form of the Babylonian god, Bel Marduk. Here were hints of things to come. A lot further down the path, Debbie would journey back through layers of historical angelology to come to some profoundly unsettling realisations. Cornwall would be involved again, a site not that far from the Merry Maidens and another group of travellers from overseas.

Enlivened by the fiery sword, the stones shimmered with a kind of heat haze. Female forms tentatively emerged from them, soon rejoicing in their freedom by dancing in a great circle. As they did so, the very land itself seemed to share the feeling of celebration. And so did the great Piper Pan, the satyr of the sea, the albino king, the dolphin leader from Lyonesse, come forth to join them. This figure seemed to carry a hint of the Irish sea god, Manannan. Christine Hartley had written that our "*shores were guarded by the Merriemaids or Fairy Girls, daughters of the great Manannan, whom today we call Mermaids*". David could see Rhiannon's horses. For Kerry, it was flying sea-horses. Debbie heard three tones as three men came to stand behind Pan. They were sons of Neptune. The tones became the calling of Sirens. From Lamorna. We needed to get to the stream that led down there immediately.

It seemed like two of the archetypes from Dion Fortune's novels were coming together. The day before had been *The Sea Priestess.* Now it was *The Goatfoot God.* In Qabalistic terms, it was a meeting of Chokmah and Binah.

Another look at a map pinpointed the fogou. Debbie and David both agreed with a feeling Andy was getting that this was Daath, where Chokmah and Binah met. The car convoy set out to try and locate this strange place barely a mile up the road. More detailed scanning of guide-books revealed that it's in the grounds of a house called Rosemerryn. Debbie had noticed the name on a sign as we had driven past earlier on. She'd pointed it out, feeling there was something significant about it. A halfway decent parking place was found. The stream we were looking for seemed to be in nearby woods. That seemed to be the first order of business so we wandered in to search for it. Once again Kerry was overwhelmed by strong emotion and decided to stay behind. The stream was located. As we stood around planning our next move, a woman with a dog appeared. Andy began chatting with her. It turned out that we had unwittingly made our way into the grounds of Rosemerryn. Yes, she would take us to the fogou and it would be okay for us to spend a short time inside it. This was an excellent development.

Boleigh fogou is situated within the remains of a small fortified Iron Age camp that appears to date from the period just before the coming of the Romans. It seems a safe bet that the place served no practical secular purpose. Etymologists argue over the site's name. 'Boleigh' has been taken to mean, 'the dwelling by the flat slab'. More interesting from our point of view was the version that says it means 'place of slaughter', referring to the battle that the Merry

Maidens supposedly commemorate. Local lore tells how the stream that leads down to Lamorna cove ran red with blood. This was yet another connection with our experiences the previous day. It was odd that Kerry was getting her own emotional replay of Slaughterbridge. Perhaps we had got something out of the way there that otherwise would have problematically intruded into our current magical agenda? More recent legends associate the site with witches dancing with the devil and that further followed through from the Merry Maidens.

Psychic questing mythology speaks of site perpetuation, guardians, and how ancient places are responsive to interaction. We had no idea at the time but we'd been drawn to one of the best examples in the whole country. The house and grounds were rumoured to be cursed. A succession of owners had died before their time. Assorted ghostly poltergeist style phenomenon came and went. Stories about the place seemed to date back a millennium.

Jo May came from an early seventies human-potential-movement psychotherapy background. He became owner of the estate through the usual synchronicities. Having arrived, he and his family and friends soon started having weird experiences. One of them vividly saw with their inner eye an Iron Age character in period costume who conveyed to her the importance of the locale as a place of power. This was the beginning of an opening up to the feeling of the lingering presence of those ancient ones and their radically different world. Psychotherapist May began to feel that he was being given clues to understand what the modern alienated mind needs to recover its lost balance. The house became a centre for personal growth workshop type events and the fogou was incorporated into the process. Over the years, shamans from around the world had visited it and conducted ceremonies there, venturing their opinions on the place. Some reasonable conjectures could be made as to what the place was all about. It seemed to be a womb and tomb, a place of death and rebirth in the body of mother earth. May allowed himself to be open to guidance from the site itself as to what was appropriate. It was fortunate that we had arrived at a time when the space was clear for us to just walk right in.

We walked past the house, noticing a panel with a carving of a Neptune figure on it leaning up against a wall. The fogou cave is set at a slight angle into the ground. Roofed and walled with granite slabs, it has a main passage about thirty five feet long and a smaller adjacent side chamber. A carving had been uncovered on a boulder near the entrance that is unique in Britain. It seems to depict a male figure holding a spear with his right hand and what appears to be a coiled serpent with his left. Plenty of scope for speculation there.

The lady and her dog left us to it. We cautiously entered down into the darkened gloom with only a weak torchlight to guide us. This was a moment I'll always remember. However incredible and engrossing the psychic material had been, I'd kept on an even keel. I hadn't experienced any crippling sword blows or been pinned to a rock by a giant horned demoness, never mind having a dragon egg inserted inside me. I couldn't actually see any of it at first hand. I was visualising it as the psychics relayed the details. It was vivid but not visceral. Something snapped in my head as we entered that fogou. How the fuck had we ended up in there? It was somebody's back garden for god's sake. Half an hour ago we scarcely knew the place existed and yet it was clearly the *'cave of the heart'* that the preposterous Trebor the follet had spoken of in the early hours of the morning in the aftermath of the drunken conga chain. It finally dawned on me. Something pretty weird's going on here.

The place was so damp that the walls dripped with water that formed some considerable puddles on the floor. Trying to avoid stepping in them as we entered deeper inside, we realised that there were some small candles alight in the chamber. As our eyes became accustomed to the gloom we began to notice a few quartz crystals strategically placed along it. Of more immediate concern to some were a number of spectacular cocoon-like spider web formations, suggesting the possibility of large arachnids concealed in the darkness.

Debbie began speaking of the place as Daath, the abyss, as Trebor appeared. He told her that we were in the heart of the land, the centre of all things. To arrive at our journey's end we had to pass through that centre, into the underworld, down dark tunnels to the mother spider who would weave us into her realm. We must pass through this to the light we seek, the Ninth Light at the fortunate isle. We were about to go back down the line to its heart, guarded by the watcher of the line. The cave of the heart experience suggested that the underworld is not inevitably a place of fear and danger. In the land, the body of the mother, there can be love and inspiration. This was a preparation for Glastonbury. We were going to enter on a particular frequency, and now, because of our entry into the earth, it was known we were coming. Debbie told us that the Little People of Avalon were already stocking up on food and booze for the big beano that night. They were apparently well excited that we were on our way. We'd entered the woods seeking the stream that led down to the cove. Somehow the fogou adventure rendered the Lamorna connection irrelevant. Our task in Cornwall was complete. The time had come to journey to the Summerland.

After a brief visit to Burrow Mump, our Glastonbury workings began in earnest on Wearyall Hill. Night had now fallen. Assembling by the Holy Thorn, we looked out across to the dim shape of the Tor, looming in the distance above the twinkling town lights. We stood around a stone slab by the side of the tree. Its original inscription has faded to illegibility. It was believed to commemorate the site of the original far larger two-trunk thorn that had been felled in puritan days. The modern descendant had only been planted there in 1950.

The very last words of Tennyson's *Idylls* set the scene. "*The new sun rose bringing the new year.*" We visualised a growing dawn light revealing ever more fully the mythic Glastonbury landscape, the summerland apple isles. Its holy hills rose from a glass-like sea. Water lapped around the base of Wearyall. A boat was coming towards us. It contained the wounded Arthur and the three Queens. It docked at the foot of the hill. The ailing King was carefully stretchered from it by waiting attendants. The women led a slow procession along a gradual path up to the hilltop where Arthur was laid down. A great feeling of sorrow and pain pervaded the place. It had to be healed. The three women raised their arms to salute and invoke Avalon as the sun rose above the horizon. Arthur was then carried back down the hill as the scene faded.

We called on Morgan as Queen of the fairies to come and heal his wounds. Debbie saw her with the other maidens gathered around the cauldron of rebirth. Arthur was laid before it. Morgan gave him liquid from it so that he could rest in eternal peace until the time of his reawakening. With this accomplished, we then asked Morgan to be with us.

At this point, a giant red-capped man, nearly nine feet tall, dressed mainly in khaki green, appeared behind us. Avallach. He entered our circle and welcomed us to Yns Witrin. Reaching down, he lifted open the stone slab by our feet like a door. Silver light poured out from within. On either side of the open gateway, purple glass pillars appeared. Morgan's subjects poured out to greet us. First came her attendants, knee high dark haired dusky maiden elves, clad in purest linen. Trebor the follet followed, picking up the two

Meonia swords and leading Andy and Debbie along the way down. Silver light engulfed them as they entered into another plane, to Goloc, the faery realm. The rest of the group followed. A great throng of the little folk approached, singing, dancing, pulling at us all. As we entered ever deeper the light became golden. At its heart, a feast was laid out before us on a round table.

Each species greeted Andy in turn and then the rest of us. Firstly, the wizened morays. The women were thin, each carrying a stick and wearing their long hair up in a bun. The gnomic men carried a pipe and bow. They were bald on top, their hair starting at the side and hanging down. Then the extremely strange shire fey. The bottom half of the males was like a walking tree trunk, whereas the females were like mini-centaurs, half shetland horse. The gilliups came. Winged dancing fat female cherubs in white linen dresses, flowers on their heads and clothes, some with wings. Brownies as well, like fluffy-furred monkeys with round heads and bodies, thin arms, and hairless faces hands and feet. And a whole throng of follets.

Trebor then led Joseph of Arimathea towards us. Tall with short white hair, he wore a brown cloak over a white tunic. His feet were bare. He brought a crown of thorns. Taking on the role of the sun man, Andy knelt down to receive it. With this coronation, the crown burst forth with the radiance of the limitless light. Avallach then approached to bestow the golden Ninth Light, which blended the crown, the circle, the line, the orb, and the sceptre. Their combined energies flowed into the Meonia swords. With its crown in place, we would be able to reconstruct the tree of life. It stood shining in the underworld. Its trunk was a downward pointing Meonia sword. Its surrounding hovering coloured sephirotic spheres contained different gem stones. Morgan watched the whole scene. She approached Andy, acknowledging his initiation. It seemed that Andy was now considered fit to take on some specialised task that was subtly different from his previous Glastonbury work. It was much connected with sovereignty and the land.

Trebor led us through silver light back to the doorway. Avallach then opened it. We stepped back out into the circle. He then closed the gateway, sealing it with a line and lock of fire from the Tintagel sword. He had bestowed upon Andy the duty of watchman. Avallach departed in the direction from whence he came. His final words were, *"the dragon will greet you tomorrow at the druids' oak tree shrine"*.

Debbie had talked us through the entire process, describing what she was seeing as it happened and imparting whatever was being communicated to her. The assorted species on display were a mighty weird blend. Some conformed to Victorian specifications. Others were post-Tolkien. Commentators from Jacques Vallée to R. J. Stewart have noted how faery folk clothe themselves from the human psyche. Whatever Debbie's mind gave to the stimuli, they were configured around classic archaic material. It was becoming increasingly obvious that she was a magical visionary of the highest order and was rapidly developing her full capacities.

People tend to focus on the Tor for a hollow faery hill. Joseph of Arimathea is not normally thought of as a ruler in such a realm or pictured with short white hair. What none of us knew at the time was that in 1921, early on in her magical career, Dion Fortune had worked as a medium for Frederick Bligh Bond. In an anticipation of her later opinions concerning Arthur, Merlin, and Morgan, she stated that Joseph of Arimathea was not a solitary individual but a title. Likewise, the Holy Thorn tradition predated Christianity. There had once been a major mystery cult centre in Glastonbury on Wearyall Hill. People came from the Middle East in ships of the tin trade to receive initiations there. There was a strong Druidical elemental flavour to the work. I really am inclined to believe that Debbie had genuinely tuned-in to a particular transmission. The invisible watchers of the Glastonbury aquarium had noted our arrival and were giving us every encouragement.

After that, the evening's work was done. The group retired to the *Rifleman's Arms.* The place was packed solid as one would expect on such a night. Amongst the heaving host, Andy caught sight of the giant form of Tony Roberts. It was certainly rather synchronous to hear that he was very much concerned with the faery realm at the time. He talked to Andy about its most famous 'abduction' case, the Reverend Kirk, light-heartedly proposing a rescue mission. It was also interesting for Andy to meet the man who had served as the guardian of the Glastonbury Light as we took up that quest again. In the midst of the merry multitude I was oblivious of the meeting. I never got a chance to talk to Tony Roberts. I wish I had. Eventually the group climbed the Tor amongst many raucous revellers. So did my eighties end. Andy and Debbie ascended the Tor separately. They started the new decade by walking down hand in hand. A lot was happening at a rapid rate.

It wasn't difficult to figure out where the *"Druids' oak tree shrine"* was located. Two famous old trees known as Gog and Magog are fabled in Glastonbury mythology as the last remains of a grove and ceremonial oak avenue. As we approached them, on the first morning of the new decade, Debbie saw a phantom flight of unknown birds and could smell elderflower, mandrake and helsbane. She began talking about a *"lost shrine of the acorn"*.

The two trees stand in a small fenced-off enclosure by the side of a country lane. As Debbie opened her mind up to the locale she soon repeated the general idea that they're the last remnants of a once extensive processional way that she believed had some dragon connection. There were many other trees around as well. Some stood in a circle. The 'lost shrine' was a small building made of wood that had stood nearby.

Three men, all wearing skullcaps, were seen coming from the direction of the shrine. Vortigern was dressed all in black. Merlin was in dark mauve and white. Mertridus, clothed in light green, held a staff. He used it to summon two spiralling serpent dragons, black and green. The formidable group stood opposite Andy. He was told he must choose between the dragon's breath, sight, or claw. He chose sight. Mertridus presented it to him in the form of a red stone that he was told to hold. Looking more closely into it, Debbie saw it as a glowing golden ball with a dark swirling centre. It could be used in the future to see answers. The three powerful figures left in different directions. The spiralling dragons rose upwards into the air to dissolve in the clouds.

We decided to visit the abbey. Nothing was particularly planned. The journey's magical itinerary was complete. Or so we thought. Down in the Mary Chapel crypt, Debbie was startled by the appearance of a dwarf-sized monk who seemed to be beckoning her to follow him. He was moving surprisingly quickly so she ran out after him. The rest of the group followed her. The strange little friar called out that he was heading for the fishpond. Debbie had never visited the abbey before and didn't know where it was. Nonetheless she was successfully led to it from the ruins through the apple-less winter orchard. As if things weren't ridiculous enough anyway, Debbie could now see our mate Trebor in the water. He swam over to a pipe that feeds water into the pond from the distant Chalice Well. Trebor then climbed up upon the stone rim to squat in a similar posture to the one of his first appearance. Debbie moved nearer. Trebor seemed to be encouraging her to investigate the pipe. Something was happening inside it.

Andy tried to put his hand in the pipe but it wouldn't fit. He encouraged Debbie to have a go. She held her hands in the flowing water at the very end of the pipe. There was an atmosphere of expectation. David heard a sound like a kind of subtle snapping in the air. At that moment Debbie snatched at something she had felt in motion in the water, catching hold of it. She raised and opened her hand, revealing a small black horse figurine. Here was the promised present, personal to her, from the sea-daughter, here was Rhiannon, sovereignty, the land, the Goddess. Debbie came to feel that the siddhi of manifestation was the parting gift that the oriental spiritualistic contact of her childhood, James, had promised her.

Was I satisfied that no trickery was involved? Yes. Entirely. Cheers and applause broke out. John threw his hat in the air. This was all too much for me. A hole had been ripped in the fabric of reality. We'd done it! Our qualifications for future adventures had been established. What a way to start a new decade. I burst into tears muttering something about this being my own version of the sound of one hand clapping. The illusion of the 3D world was rent asunder by the intrusion of another level of functioning altogether. Mind was helpless before it.

Recovering from the initial shock, we noticed that a definite vesica piscis shape had become visible on the surface of the water. It was marked out by water lilies and general pond slime. It was a peculiar and striking manifestation. The shape strongly featured in works on the sacred geometry of the abbey and fitted the theme of form emerging from formlessness.

Later on in the afternoon we also made a point of checking out Park Wood. As we revisited the site of the June Templar ritual, Andy announced that during the midsummer period he intended to take us all around the whole Glastonbury Zodiac. What he had taken years to complete, we would navigate in a few days. It would be an attempt to stretch reality to the limits. We'd have minimal sleep and maximum sites. Most ominously for me was the news that it would involve a jump into the weir at Baltonsborough Flights. I can barely swim and it was a worrying prospect. Whatever the case, it set the year up a treat. I couldn't ask for anything better to propel me towards the solstice. Riding on the tide of exhilaration that had accompanied the artefact, it was in fact a perfect start to a whole decade.

Not long into the New Year, still full of Glastonbury and the promise of June's epic journey, we heard some news that confirmed that powerful processes were at work there. On the night of February 8th Anthony Roberts had met John Michell in the *Beckets* pub in

Glastonbury. In the course of a good-natured evening he had said that he would like to die on the Tor and be buried there. On the afternoon of the following day there was an eclipse of the full moon. Tony and his son Michael ascended the Tor to mark the occasion. It proved to be a journey to a truly legendary Glastonbury transition as he collapsed with a heart attack, dying on the slopes. He had just completed an article on the Zodiac entitled *Glimpses of Eternity,* which he considered to be the best thing he'd ever written. Of all the great enthusiasts on the subject, he had been the one who had actually lived the longest amidst the mystery. He had served the function of guardian for Andy and Graham during the Lights of Knowledge quest in 1981, acting as a major catalyst to Andy's Zodiac experiences. His alerting of Andy to the Park Wood situation in 1985, an event which set off the strange ceremony then performed there, showed his profound connection to the work we were all involved in. As John Michell said at his funeral, *"His life was dedicated to the Vision of Albion, the quest in Avalon and the fulfilment of the paradisal prophecies of Glastonbury"*. Now he was gone, and at the point when things were clearly going ballistic for us, as we had pledged ourselves in Park Wood to undertake the zodiac quest. Tony Roberts is buried in the same cemetery as Dion Fortune, with the legend *'From Atlantis to Avalon and Beyond'* carved upon his megalithic-style tombstone.

PERSPECTIVES: ON THE SPEAR OF DESTINY AND TERMA TREASURES

AS THE SEVENTH SWORD QUEST began in earnest, I tried to place our activities in as wide a context as I could. We were clearly part of the wider history of magic. There was an illustrious lineage pedigree back to Egypt redolent of Hermeticism. This took in all the usual suspects through the ages such as Akhenaten and the Knights Templar until our check-in with the flavour of Dion Fortune's work. Crowley was somewhere in the background. I really felt that for all the identifiable diverse influences around us, we were genuinely moving into fresh unknown territory. Our blend was unique. I knew enough occult history to be quite clear about that. The quality of the repeated psychism from the Green Stone story through to Bernard's Glastonbury Zodiac, Elder race and Black Alchemist material and the current adventure was out there on its own. It was a truly epic magical mythology and it seemed to be based, in a manner no other previous work had been, on real events. Or at least something very mysterious indeed was trying to convey that impression and making a good job of it. The artefacts were the icing on the cake.

There was only one example of comparable psychism I was aware of. It was detailed in Trevor Ravenscroft's cult classic, *The Spear of Destiny.* The contents of this work, which deals at length with the alleged occultism of Hitler, are contentious to say the least. Large chunks of it have been rubbished over the years for various reasons so the following material has an air of uncertainty about it but serves to make interesting comparisons nonetheless.

The legend of the Spear of Destiny suggests that it is the very weapon that pierced the side of Christ on the cross. The Roman soldier responsible for this act supposedly held the fate of the world in his hand as his act prevented the legs of Christ from being broken to accelerate his death. If he had been thus injured it would have messed with a Jewish messianic prophecy telling about no bones being broken on the body of the chosen one. I wasn't interested in whether or not that was really true. In order to believe that side of the story it would be necessary to fully endorse Christianity, to accept the Jesus drama as a unique world-redeeming event. I wasn't ready to go that far.

What did seem plausible was that a spearhead *believed* to be that very artefact had indeed been in the possession of an impressive sequence of major historical game-players, at least from Charlemagne onwards, right through to Hitler. Somehow it had become magically spiritually powerful. That was the concept that really fascinated me. It seemed to serve as a potential portal to a kind of Time Spirit that could see history in its totality, the rise and fall of empires, monarchs, and messiahs. Extraordinary episodes in the inner life of the founder of Anthroposophy, Rudolf Steiner, and his follower Walter Johannes Stein had allegedly occurred in its physical proximity in a Vienna museum. This access to the Time Spirit or the Akashic records seemed to provoke the telling of previously hidden or neglected historical tales from a new perspective.

Stein is the main protagonist of *Spear.* His psychic awakening, as Ravenscroft recounts it, began in earnest when he was studying the famous Grail romance *Parzival* by Wolfram von Eschenbach. In a strange space between sleeping and waking, he found himself reciting words in the original old German dialect of its composition.

Writing them down on waking, he was perplexed to discover their verbatim accuracy with the original text further on from where he had already read. This led him into a lifelong study of the Grail mysteries. A faculty of 'Higher Memory' developed, whereby detailed visions of historical events unknown to him led to research that seemed to confirm their truth and unfold a coherent narrative. Being in the presence of the spear significantly moved the process along. Stein's greatest achievement was his book *The Ninth Century,* which connected events of that time with the later composition and contents of the Grail Romances.

A major aspect of this uncovering of the hidden spiritual dimension of the historical process was the tracing of strands of reincarnational identities across the millennia. The most dramatic example concerns Stein's belief that Hitler had been one Llandulf of Capua, a notorious necromancer based in 9th century Sicily who had allegedly provided the model for the wicked sorcerer Klingsor in Wolfram von Eschenbach's *Parzival.* According to Ravenscroft, Steiner and Stein also psychically picked up on hideous magical rites practised by Nazi occultists and tried to counteract them.

I cross-referenced what I'd read in *Spear* with the data I was now gathering concerning the Meonia saga. A huge historical narrative was being unfolded. It involved a mixture of famous and obscure figures in a spiritual drama that was working towards some kind of contemporary culmination. It had a sense of contending forces and high stakes. The modern Meonia players were conspicuously different from Steiners' Anthroposophical circle though. I didn't quite imagine Walter Johannes Stein getting fifteen cans of Guinness down his neck before a session of writing *The Ninth Century*. I rather think a jukebox might have disturbed Rudolf Steiner's contemplations as well. What really blew my mind was realising that, in many ways, the Direct Information Psychism of the likes of Graham Phillips and Bernard was of a higher quality in terms of its minute historical details than what was recounted in *Spear.* It also wasn't as flavoured by religious and metaphysical beliefs. The strong reincarnational theme was largely absent. Details of the occult workings of the opposition were more informed with credible knowledge and not as lurid. I pondered the two powerful 'transmissions' in *Spear* and *The Green Stone* and wondered what guiding intelligence determined why and when such details were ready to release? What factors were involved in the selection of the human vehicles for this process?

There was an even bigger perspective that helped make sense of our peculiar mode of functioning. After the Green Stone saga Andy became interested in seeing if he could find similar phenomenon in other historical periods and cultures. The Tibetan Terma tradition provided the most fruitful material. Buddhism was brought to Tibet in the 8th century AD by the great adept Padmasambhava. To say this being was a bit of a paranormal force would be an understatement. He was toting quite a package of empowered teachings and energies. In fact he didn't think the Tibetans were ready for the whole deal so he withdrew some of it from circulation in a variety of increasingly strange ways. In the most simple examples he might take a scroll of teachings, a statue or a ritual artefact, and hide them in a cave behind some rocks or bury them in the ground or somesuch. This was consigning them to the element of earth. A fire concealment would literally mean incinerating the material. Water would require casting it into a river, waterfall or sacred lake. For the element of air, a true shamanic sorcerer's performance was required whereby Padmasambhava threw something up from his hands and it dematerialised. These elemental treasures, known as Termas, went into a kind of suspended animation, awaiting the time of their return.

In the centuries ahead, unusual visionaries would be inspired to find them. These characters (called Tertons) would often seem a bit crazy. They would be mystics who didn't conform to normal monastic-type patterns. Strange dreams, omens and visions of saints and deities, would lead them to particular places. The earth element retrievals are comparatively straightforward. The Terton would rummage around some rocks in a cave and uncover a scroll or statue. One of the most famous scriptures in the world, the so-called *Tibetan Book of the Dead*, is considered to be a Terma treasure found in such a manner. It is believed to have been written by Padmasambhava. Modern textual analysis suggests it dates from the time of its alleged recovery but the belief remains. The other elemental retrievals are weirder by far. A Terton may build a fire and then reach into it and pull out an artefact. Likewise a waterfall or lake. And thin air. Most rarefied of all are the 'mind treasures' that disappeared into the element of ether. These were whole teachings on consciousness, reality, and mystical processes of attainment. They weren't just verbal formula and ideas. They were charged with blessing power, alive with energy for transformation. Anyone receiving such a teaching in a ceremonial empowerment would find it coming to life within them if they upheld the necessary practice. Tertons might suddenly get a complete download from a wisdom deity and something forgotten had returned to the world. The increasingly popular energy transmission of Reiki seems to be an example of a mind treasure.

The strange 'Siddhi' or paranormal power of manifestation appeared to accompany the Green Stone Meonia sword transmission. Along with this, the unparalleled density of direct information psychism could likewise be seen as a siddhi unique to the particular frequency. Other western occult schools didn't really seem to have anything like this combination in terms of intensity. We would come to meet a number of people who had diligently practiced various disciplines and had psychic experiences for decades but never experienced anything like what became normal for us and therefore distrusted or actively disbelieved what they heard of our activities. The fact that we were in many ways a right larey bunch made it even worse. And it seemed like we were only just getting going on some great work that could fulfil a titanic remit. That was quite a feeling to take from Glastonbury at the start of a new decade when I was perfectly willing to believe we had received a Terma treasure.

Most importantly of all for Questing mythology, the mysterious morphogenesis crystals of the Elder Race that had been globally dispersed from their original home in the Giza Crystal Chambers were considered to be held between the worlds, waiting for the right time and person to facilitate their reappearance.

INITIATION OF THE ORACLE

IN FEBRUARY AN OPPORTUNITY AROSE for Debbie to come into contact with the two Meonia swords that had been discovered in the Milton Keynes wood by Colin and Angela Paddon. It was an interesting test of her psychometry abilities. This wild talent involves being able to tell an object's history, sometimes by seeing vivid scenes, simply by touching it. It was also a test of what level of voltage was running through these unusual items. We would not be disappointed. Another startling unnerving adventure immediately developed.

Debbie's first impression on handling the swords was that they represented a male and female pair, embodying power and knowledge respectively. Others had been cast at the same time, which was round about 1880, from European models. There was a lineage link through assorted Masonic neo-Templar orders in France and Germany. Vivid visual impressions soon followed. Dense woods. A clearing containing the ruins of a chapel. A broken arch. Dilapidated walls. A plinth and altar of some kind. Nearby graves. Where was this? Near the place of the swans in Dorset. Abbotsbury? The chapel had been used for mystical gatherings of some kind in the thirties.

A character called Robert Firth was of central importance in the sword mystery. He was a Rosicrucian of some kind with close contacts amongst Golden Dawn associated people. Debbie picked him up as strongly linked with Christine Hartley and Charles 'the Colonel' Seymour. Robert Firth did magical workings at the chapel and other locations in Dorset. There were more hints of material that had been present in Cornwall. Colonel Seymour had used the Tintagel and male Paddon Meonia swords on Michael Line sites. Christine Hartley had magically programmed the female sword. They were aware to some extent of previous models but not necessarily the Meonia story in full.

Debbie was clear that Robert was related to Dion Fortune. On a piece of kitchen towel, a family tree was hurriedly written down by Andy as Debbie seemed to tune in to the enigmatic Firth family. Thomas Firth senior was a steelworker who had three sons, Mark, John, and Thomas junior. Although all were involved with Firth steel, Mark was the most important. John married Katherine Harding. They had five sons. Edward was born in Wales and later connected with Winchester Cathedral, possibly ordained. Lewis or Louis John had a French wife. They were the parents of Robert. Arthur married Sarah Smith, who he met in a Welsh town, daughter of John Smith, a Yorkshire man. They were the parents of Violet, who became Dion Fortune. The other two sons of John and Katherine were Henry and Thomas.

On February 22nd Debbie dreamed of a circle of people gathered in the ruined chapel that included Christine Hartley and Robert Firth. There was a woman called Paula, and also a Margaret and Mary. Dion Fortune was not present. Some kind of initiation was occurring. A very specific date, June 28th 1938. Something to do with the goddess Ishtar, who Debbie mentioned as identical to Astarte and Ashterah. These were Canaanite goddesses of love and fertility very similar to the famous Babylonian. The writers of the Old Testament weren't great fans of them as they became popular with the Jews, corrupting their monotheistic male purity. *Astarte Syriaca* was beautifully depicted by Dante Gabriel Rossetti in one of his most iconic paintings, the title of which indicates the general geographical zone of her veneration. Although these goddesses may have originated in different areas, their cults eventually began to blend and they tend to cohere together on the inner plane.

Seymour was aware of the Forgotten Chapel gathering but was not present. The male sword was involved. It had helped to take them to the Qabalistic plane of Yesod, which served as an entrance to the 'Fields of Ishtar'. The group psychism seemed to experience a message from the Babylonian goddess. *"I am not the Virgin Mary. This is not the fullness of my worship."* Ishtar gave Christine Hartley a bunch of violets and Paula a silver star. She was then seen taking hold of the Meonia sword and summoning things with it. People on horseback came out of the woods. *"Now you may ride with the hosts of the Shee."* Hartley couldn't let go and join them. Firth told her not to worry about it.

The 'Shee' is a phonetic rendering of Sidhe. This host have a little in common with the Wild Hunt. They are the Irish faery folk, no prissy bunch of Victorian Tinkerbells but a human size glorious regal horny bunch, vibrating with the soul of poetry and magic. It is often stated that they are a folk memory of the Tuatha De Danaan, an ancient race conquered by invaders, who vanished into the hollow hills of the old burial mounds where they now exist in a strange interdimensional state. They are considered to be a living presence in much of Ireland to this day and accounts of interaction with them are innumerable.

On another occasion, Firth had done a magical working in the woods by the chapel with the two swords. Something strange happened that was difficult to determine. He may have physically buried them. In effect, they disappeared from that moment for nearly fifty years and resurfaced in superbly strange circumstances in Milton Keynes in 1985. Robert Firth also had a purple Yesodic stone to go with his male sword. He considered himself to be a priest of the horned moon god and this item was somehow given to him by the deity. It seemed clear that apports were involved in these events. Alongside mysterious destiny factors, Colin Paddon's strong interest in the Qabalah had helped to attract the swords towards him.

Was it possible to get a reality-check on any of this? Regarding the Firth family, Debbie had got the names of Dion Fortune's parents and grandfather correct. The remaining details were not to be found in the usual books and the time and resources to research them fully were not available. The very existence of Robert remained unproven.

It was known that Hartley and Seymour conducted a series of magical workings together in the thirties. A recent book by Dion Fortune's biographer Alan Richardson called *Dancers to the Gods* gave a good account of them. In general they involved varying amounts of Golden Dawn style preparations. Robes were usually worn, banishing pentagrams might be drawn, angels invoked, the Qabalistic tree built up within the inner body and so on. The main business usually consisted of something not dissimilar to one of our psychic sessions. The participants would often end up sitting in chairs with their eyes closed and trying to pick up material that they would become interactive with. Sometimes hefty dudes like Melchizedek would appear and convey power, blessings, and instructions. There were many glimpses of past lives. Egypt was strongly featured, alongside Norse, Celtic, Greek and alleged Atlantean material. There are a few telling Babylonian snippets. Dion Fortune and a few others were occasionally present but the book shows that Seymour and Hartley were a dynamic pair of great competence in their own right. There is no indication in *Dancers* that any of the featured workings happened outdoors or anywhere other than London.

A passing reference confirms that Seymour did visit Tintagel at least once. He had a rock from Merlin's Cave that he gave Hartley to psychometrise. It is stated quite clearly that she herself had never been there and had no knowledge of the place. This followed on from a working in February 1938 where Hartley had seen herself as a Sea Priestess Morgan type arriving at Tintagel in a vastly ancient past not long after the Atlantean dispersion.

Hartley and Seymour were certainly very into Celtic, and in particular, Irish mythology. The Sidhe were well known to them. An anthology of the Colonel's writings, *The Forgotten Mage,* contained most interesting material on this subject. I actually started reading it on the same day that Debbie's material started appearing, independently of any knowledge of what she and Andy were getting into. There was no copy of *Dancers* or *Mage* in Andy's library but a few of the rest of the group were familiar with them. In the light of what followed I tend to feel it was a kind of Bligh Bond situation where it was necessary that certain foundational material existed in our group mind for the magical psychism to latch on to and then develop further. Once the material began to flow, Andy consulted the relevant volumes for confirmation.

Dion Fortune herself was clearly involved, through her magical novels and Priestess work, with the larger process in the collective mind of the return of women's mysteries. The post-war rebirth of witchcraft was another manifestation of this. Although the redoubtable Gerald Gardner was the prime mover in the material plane, stirrings from the inner plane were being registered for some time beforehand. Of all the material in *Dancers,* one working has attracted the most attention, being increasingly seen as part of that larger dynamic. It is the entry for June 28th 1938.

Anyone who has read it could be forgiven for refusing to believe that Debbie had no prior knowledge. Christine Hartley reported feeling *"extremely desirous of being a witch"*. She soon began seeing *"little pictures of Ishtar worship through the ages, the most common being one of silhouetted witches in pointed hats and ragged skirts dancing round a fire. Then it seemed to focus a little more steadily and I was aware of the goddess standing before us mistily veiled"*. Ishtar spoke to her of the need for love and celebration and lamented how she had been turned into the Virgin Mary which was not, *"the fullness of her worship"*. Another of the Inner Light magical group named Paula Trevanion was also present and it is mentioned that Ishtar gave her a silver star. It was Seymour who was given the flowers. Ishtar enfolded Hartley with her veils and began to ascend with her to the threshold of the *'Fields of Ishtar'* but an inner resistance curtailed the process.

The details are very similar but there are also considerable additions in Debbie's version. A stronger connection was being made between the Shining Ones of Irish mythology and the Middle East, in particular, Babylon. In years to come this apparently tenuous tangent would yield extraordinary fruit.

She was making a controversial assertion in claiming that there was a lot more going on than the written records depicted, with magical action at outdoor sites and a far larger cast of characters involved. The Cornish adventure had carried a strong flavour of Dion Fortune's magical current and affirmed the virtue of going along with the various promptings with excellent results. It was obvious that we would visit the Forgotten Chapel as soon as possible. Debbie had seen the general location clearly enough to create a very detailed navigable map that checked out superbly. This in itself was spectacularly accurate psychism. Andy was doing an Occult all-day event in Brighton on Saturday March 3rd. We decided to travel on to Dorset afterwards.

In the week leading up to it, a surreal episode occurred when Debbie was travelling with Andy in his car on the M25. She suddenly seemed to be outside on the bonnet looking back in through the window at herself. Somebody was talking through her mouth. Andy's tape recorded Ashterah saying, *"It is vitally important that you come to me. Visit the site of the Forgotten Chapel. Ascend with me to the Fields of Ishtar. It is a matter to do with the lost stone"*. On February 27th a further psychic snippet about the chapel mentioned being fed information on a silver spoon.

On the Saturday night journey to Dorset, Debbie began to describe herself as blindfolded and feeling increasingly out of control and unwell. There were odd sensations in her stomach and head. Country roads took us into an archetypal middle of nowhere. We parked up in a place with a wide view of dark rolling landscape, wooded hills, a profound unknown. Thanks to the combination of earlier psychic material and mapwork, we had a good idea of the general direction we were heading but there would come a point when we would be navigating through woods with only a torch and Debbie's intuitive radar to guide us.

Every little detail of her psychic map proved to be accurate. We emerged tentatively out of primal dense dark woods as torch-lights picked out the ruined walls of the Forgotten Chapel. What a place! The atmosphere of it was haunting beyond our strange collective mind-set. It felt like nature was re-claiming the site and the balance of energy between the chapel and the forest was continually ebbing and flowing. Debbie was stunned by her psychic navigation. Her mind became increasingly blown as we discovered a small number of graves that included some exact names she had picked up on. Looking further around it was clear that the site was being used in some way. There were a few flower offerings and crescent moon images both drawn and carved in small subtle places. Thoroughly tuned in, she led us virtually straight to the altar and immediately proclaimed that an artefact lay concealed there. Beneath a stone, a silver spoon was discovered. Precisely such an item had been mentioned a few days before in an apparently nonsensical fragment.

We proceeded to enter into our most elaborate ceremonial working since Park Wood the previous summer. Andy had consulted *Dancers to the Gods* for some of the visuals, in particular an earlier Ishtar entry for October 8th 1937. A magic circle was traced around us on the ground with representations of the elements laid out at the four quarters. Banishing pentagrams were drawn in the air. A cross of light was visualised inside us. The four archangels were invoked. We began our journey by particularly focusing on Gabriel, seeing him in blue light, which cleared to find us located on a mountain covered in snow and ice, the ridge at the edge of the world, Malkuth. The sky was dark blue, lit by a bright silver star cupped by a crescent moon. At our feet was an edelweiss flower, the colour and shape of a star. It was picked, enlarging until it filled the scene, becoming the swirling entrance into a silvery grey tunnel tinged with blue. We moved along it into the sphere of Yesod, domain of the moon.

The sky there was purple, the realm varying shades of it, violet, and mauve. We found ourselves at the base of a huge hill fort in front of a gateway to a wall that surrounded its base. The path beyond the gateway ascended up to a plateau on which stood a tall four-sided tower displaying the horns of the crescent moon on its roof. Standing beyond the gate was a figure in a bright mauve robe with face of a white haired stag, silver starry eyes, long albino blonde hair, and horns of the crescent moon upon his head. He was the moon god of Yesod. On the ground at the foot of the gateway lay a violet flower. This we picked and, with it in our hands, we asked the moon god to install us with the virtues of the sphere of Yesod. He allowed us to climb towards the tower, which had four doors, one on each side. They represented the attainment of the sphere, mentally, emotionally, spiritually, physically. We entered the first door and passed through to the back door that was then opened.

In front of us now lay a lilac-coloured swirling tunnel of mist that we entered into and journeyed along. In the distance the tunnel mist was turning to emerald green. The door of the tunnel likewise changed to green. The mist cleared to reveal a strange landscape all about us. A sky of light pastel violet lit a rolling landscape of bright green fields. We had entered the Fields of Ishtar in the realms between Yesod and the emerald green of Netzah and Venus. We were in the domain of Ashterah who we called to be with us.

We tried to see and hear her approaching, riding on a huge white stallion across the glowing green fields of Ishtar. Appearing to be perhaps around thirty years old, she was tall and slender, with long fawn coloured hair flowing around a soft, serene, intelligent face. Spiralling goats horns protruded from the side of her head, seemingly woven into her hair. Upon her head was a golden sun-disk and around her neck on a chain was a silver seven-pointed star. These indicated her dual solar/lunar aspects. She wore a long golden robe with a purple latticework down to the waist. A green cloak covered her back.

We greeted her and were invited to ride with her to her temple. The structure consisted of three huge pillars in a circle holding up a decayed roof. It was surrounded by bushes, around which grew freesia flowers in gold, green, and purple. As we moved closer we could see in the centre of the circular floor a bowl on a stand and an altar of stone. At this point Debbie took over.

She experienced riding off with Ashterah into an ever-brightening sunset. From out of the light gathered twelve figures, six male and six female. There were four Lords of Flame, four of Mind, and four of Love. They were presided over by Melchizedek and Ashterah (who were Lords of Flame and Love respectively). The group was told that we are all creatures of the Summerland and was asked to mentally build the temple, kindle a fire at the altar, and dance around the fire. We pledged ourselves to help Ashterah rebuild the temple and began our imaginings.

At this point Debbie began to cough. The sound rapidly developed into a disturbing choking that transfixed everyone's attention. Something intense was going down. Debbie was clearly having a very unpleasant experience. She could feel a strange inner pressure pushing out from within her neck. The more she tried to breathe in, the stronger a feeling of some horrible resistant outer flow of force became. She felt a small hard object bang against her teeth from inside her mouth, which she opened to cough again. *"Something's come out, something's there"*, she feebly said, followed by an even quieter, *"I don't feel well"*. Andy switched on a small torch and scanned the ground in front of her. A mass chorus of *"Oh my god"* and *"fucking hell"* immediately arose as the beam picked out a small purple crystal. *"There's a bit of Yesod for you"*, I remarked. Debbie was totally shell-shocked, confused, unable to understand.

We all believed that this stone had somehow apported from out of her body. It was a paranormal phenomenon and she wasn't employing conjuring tricks to produce it. Surely no such nonsense ever happens anywhere at all ever. It is indubitably a lot to take on. There has been at least one notable case of someone allegedly demonstrating a similar strange talent. Indian holy man Sai Baba put on a yearly performance of manifesting a stone from his mouth to a huge audience but he has been reviled as a charlatan as well as being revered as a miracle-working avatar. As usual I decided to accept it all in the spirit of the game and see where it led.

As we left the Forgotten Chapel, Debbie was convinced that the place would play a major role in the future for her. The flowering of her talents during the New Year adventure had been in many respects on behalf of Andy to help him and the group enter into a landscape initiation and properly commence the seventh sword quest. This was also part of the expanding group magical dynamic but was more personal to Debbie. In mythical magical terms, she was now the Delphic oracle to Andy's Apollo. It was confirmation of a process that had begun with her presentation to the nine women of the cauldron. In the following weeks, the group took turns to sleep with the dream stone under their pillows. It all served the creation of a collective magical mind.

MOON MAGIC

ALONGSIDE THE INCREDIBLE QUESTING ADVENTURES, an apparently random minor turn of events towards the end of 1989 had also developed considerable momentum by the spring of 1990. It had started in October on the day of the Questing Conference in London. The event was supposed to conclude with an outdoor meditation at a venue to be announced. It was the full moon that night and many of us looked forward to being out beneath it. Unforeseen circumstances led to Andy being detained elsewhere, so the projected scenario had to be cancelled, almost at the last minute. A few carloads of Earthquest regulars drove back to Essex. The moon beamed out magnificently. There was a really strong feeling that something wanted to happen. We decided to do our own full moon meditation. There was a suitable location in a wooded area in Brentwood that wasn't too much of a diversion from our common route home.

Before long, we were all standing in a circle in a clearing lit by an outrageously vibing moon. Just doing something that simple felt quite extraordinary. It seemed familiar, supremely natural, and intensely beautiful. I was nominated to focus whatever ensued. None of us really knew what it was we were going to do. I scarcely gave it any forethought, trusting I would be suitably inspired to pretty much make it up as I went along. Guided visualisations we'd done with Andy certainly helped set it off. Something of the Park

Wood working was present but this had the sense of being subtly different. It was a drawing down of the moon. We tried to see, with our eyes closed, a point of sparkling, transparent lunar light, circling around the group at ground level. It increased in speed until it seemed like a solid ring. This now rose up like a curtain of light all around us. The top tapered off above, into a funnel that reached all the way to the moon. A conduit for lunar energy was thus formed. The moon shone even more brightly and its energy came down to fully bathe us in bliss. As it finally fully filled the funnel, we then imagined that beams of light shot out from our circle across the landscape. They began to move like spokes of a slowly turning wheel. There was the hope that the blessings of the Moon Goddess were permeating the very earth and the consciousness of all living things upon it, bringing peace, inspiration, and connection to all of the qualities of the divine feminine. It was really very simple, but many felt powerfully moved.

With no real sense of what we were doing or where it might lead, we were soon preparing for the next full moon and then the one after that. Much of the accoutrements of Wicca and ceremonial magic seemed to naturally become involved. A small hardcore group consisting of myself, Alex, John, Kerry and Lisa became full moon regulars. Assorted others came and went. In a circle of candles, including big outdoor barbecue ones on sticks at the four quarters, we created sacred space, with swords and daggers, broom and banishment. Mighty Watchtowers were summoned and stirred. In the early days we invoked Diana. Eventually we came to Isis.

The Egyptian Goddess Aset, whose name meant 'throne', was connected with sovereignty, Sirius, and the great gifts of the Nile on which her nation depended. She later became hugely popular throughout the Roman world, rendered by Greek translators as Isis. Her aspects and influences were multiple, covering the whole spectrum of life and death, extending through fertility, love, inspiration, creativity, nature, and resurrection. She was mistress of magic.

One of the most famous tales of a divine family concerns Isis and her husband Osiris. He is murdered and dismembered by his deceitful brother Set. Isis seeks out the scattered body parts and installs him as Lord of the Underworld, in the process conceiving their son and avenger, Horus. The iconography of Isis and the infant Horus was undoubtedly a major influence on the Madonna and child of the Christian era. Crowley used the family group to explain his aeons of history.

When I was studying comparative religion at university, one of the set texts was an anthology by Mircea Eliade entitled *From Primitives to Zen.* In there I had first seen a numinous vision of Isis that powerfully affected me. It came from a 2nd century AD work by Lucius Apuleius called *The Golden Ass*, an almost unclassifiable mix of magic, mysticism, sex, mythology, humour and psychodrama. I believe it to be a genuine document of initiation. It dates from the same period when Isis was featuring in the Hermetic texts that had such a huge effect on the western mystery tradition. At that time, shortly before the triumph of Christianity, she had become 'Isis of ten thousand names', taking on the visual attributes and aspects of many of the other goddesses of the Empire until she was seen in a form that embodied them all. The climax of *The Golden Ass* comes when the main protagonist, who is lying on a beach on a full moon night, sees Isis emerging from out of the sea. A detailed description is given of her that evokes the feeling of all of the goddesses of the ancient world in one. It burned a hole in my brain into which moonlight had been shining ever since. I introduced the others to the Apuleius material and they were likewise impressed.

We began to use that form of Isis for our workings. The description would be read out and we would all try and visualise her as vividly as possible, including a moment when she laid her hands on each person's head. The rest of the ceremonial details we made up ourselves, from a mix of Gerald Gardner, Starhawk and our own inspiration. Eventually we gave ourselves a name, the *Grove of the Sky Dancers.* A Grove because we were an open group rather than a Coven. I took this designation from Margot Adler's *Drawing down the Moon.* We found a regular site that became our physical grove. It wasn't that far away from where the Hadleigh Downs tepee had been constructed in the summer of '79. It felt like a good development for me on a landscape full of personal associations that went back to my childhood. None of us were in the slightest bit interested in any Wiccan controversies over who was truly initiated to set such things in motion. All we cared about was that it felt totally incredible. So began a parallel dynamic to the questing momentum, one that didn't involve Andy. I could never have imagined the nature of the Glastonbury climax it would one day lead me towards.

I'd been talking on the phone with my old university friend Jane Satchwell, who I'd re-met in the 1985 Pilton mud. She was involved with the Sufi Peace Dance group that had been present on the Tor in June '88. On that occasion she had been unable to attend because she was in the process of moving into a new home. Shortly afterwards, I spoke to her at length about my enthusiasm for everything that I'd seen that night. She knew a large number of the chants and songs I'd heard on the Tor but couldn't properly remember. She sang them down the phone, enabling me to then introduce such material to the full moon group. Post-ritual chanting became a regular feature.

At this time, things began to significantly change for the better at work. I was joined by a new colleague. As he sat down next to me for the first time, I noticed that Oliver Gillespie was wearing a badge with an image of Glastonbury Tor on it. He was a musician with an impressive array of electronic keyboards in his Basildon home. Tangerine Dream were his main influence but he was also heavily into David Sylvian and with his dyed hair and fashion sense looked like he could have played in an early eighties electro pop combo. Before long I was mutating his tastes with Steve Hillage. He was already aware of *The Black Alchemist* and we soon talked extensively about the weird things I was involved in. The full moon gatherings particularly interested him as his first wife had been a witch and he began to periodically attend them.

The moon workings inevitably brought us into the orbit of the Fellowship of Isis. This extraordinary grouping was founded on the spring equinox of 1976 by the Baron of Strathloch, Lawrence Durdin-Robertson, generally known as Derry, his wife Pamela and sister Olivia. It was based at Clonegal Castle in rural Ireland, one of the last such edifices, dating from 1625. Built on the site of an abbey, that in turn superseded a Druid community, a sacred well remains within the castle grounds. In the basement are rooms dedicated to the signs of the zodiac and their associated goddesses. Priestesses and priests are ordained within them.

Derry had theological training and had worked as a rector. Studies in comparative religion and occult theosophical realms gradually mutated his consciousness. In 1966 he experienced the revelation that essentially *'God was female'*. Archaeology seemed to confirm that the earliest religious icons represented mother goddesses. Veneration of the divine feminine had survived medieval intolerance through being focused in the Virgin Mary cult. The modern visions and manifestations of her are essentially the Goddess in a form acceptable to the psyches of the recipients.

Olivia was a natural mediumistic visionary, helping spirits pass on from childhood and becoming adept at trance journeys. She was a cousin of another great advocate of the goddess, Robert Graves, and could remember being told childhood stories sat on the knee of W. B. Yeats. Although a pre-war leftie pacifist, she supported the war against Hitler, experiencing something of the inner realms of that conflict. Concerned with social issues and a prolific writer, Olivia allowed the pull of the visionary realms to transform her until she became a kind of early hippie. With the death of Derry, she became the leading force in the Fellowship, attaining legendary status amongst lovers of the divine feminine as Lady Olivia.

The FOI believed that after the closing down of the mystery cults of the classical world, the Isis initiation school remained alive on the inner planes and was now ready to expand again into manifestation beyond the small numbers who had been responsive during the intervening epoch.

All religions are welcome in the Fellowship. There is worldwide free membership, strong in Africa, particularly Nigeria. Pets can be registered in the Animal Family of Isis. It was the first goddess organisation to be recognised by the World Parliament of Religions. Rituals and meditations feature deities from different traditions all together. Olivia produced a large number of visualisation trance journeys to connect with them. There are no vows or commitments to secrecy. Love, beauty, and abundance are affirmed against asceticism.

Members may work alone or come together in Iseums of varying sizes dedicated to particular goddesses. Lyceums promulgate more detailed teachings. There are assorted initiations but these are not obligatory. The whole configuration is given over not to the set forms of the patriarchal cults but to the expression of the free-flowing creativity that characterises nature and the goddesses that personify her.

As we began our moon magic, the FOI dynamic was becoming ever stronger. London Conventions with multi-national audiences would shortly follow. Membership would expand at an exponential rate. There were a number of people who were involved in both questing and the FOI such as Caroline Wise, Steve Wilson and John Merron. A mysterious common ground would occasionally reveal itself.

A musical theme was definitely stirring with the Grove. Strange inspirations visited the Sky Dancer group that seemed nicely in keeping with the creative associations of the divine feminine. Lisa heard a complete unknown song in a dream and could remember it all on waking. When she sang it to us (and she has a great singing voice) we dissolved in cold shivers. On another occasion a second complete song came to her spontaneously, unsought. The day after one of the rituals, I suddenly found myself writing a poem/invocation inspired by Apuleius. I had stopped reading a completely unrelated book in mid-sentence and weirdly watched myself picking up a pen and paper and starting to write. The words simply flowed automatically with no conscious thought involved. There were no pauses. The whole thing was just written straight down in one go. I later only needed to make the most minor adjustments for its final form. I was a bit more used to these kinds of manifestations than the others but the result was richly satisfying to me.

ISIS

Deep down in the darkness of the sea
(in depths arising far inside of me),
stir strange feelings I have grown to know,
secret tremblings of truth that come and go.
I know these feelings as a lady, summon her to sight.
Mistress of the darkness, lead me to the light.

She is older than the ocean,
she is pulling like the moon.
I've been waiting so long for her,
I feel she is coming soon, coming soon.

Many times I've sought her, longing in my heart,
yet somehow she eludes me, she is set apart.
I feel now things are changing, she's drawing very near.
Ocean roaring, heart pounding, I start to fear:
for when I meet her, she'll play a deadly game,
destroy everything I once was, won't let me stay the same.

She is deeper than the ocean,
she is madness like the moon.
I am going to be with her,
consummation's coming soon, coming soon.

Out of the waves she rises to my sight,
black cloak of stars reflecting lunar light.
I kneel before her, she raises up her hands,
her power fills me and now, I understand.

I was washed up on the seashore, shattered, all alone.
I'm back now with my beginnings, feel at last I'm home.
She's coming back. Why did we send her far away?
Should have known she'd have to come back again some day.
And now at last, as I kiss her perfumed feet,
the division inside me's ended, I'm complete.

She's our mother like the ocean,
she's our lover like the moon.
She is what we've all been missing:
night's dark wisdom returning soon, returning soon,
the Goddess,
the fullness,
of the moon.

What was great about the full moon gatherings was that they fulfilled a deep need for something that stimulated an ongoing feeling of passion and creativity. All this felt important for my preparation for the Zodiac journey. I knew I needed to cultivate such sensibilities to the max in order for me to get the most out of the coming epic. It seemed very close to the zone occupied by John Cowper Powys and his relationship to the Grail. In his late novel, *The Brazen Head,* a character utters a prayer to the moon that seemed to sum it all up.

"O great Goddess – grant us, we beseech thee, an influence, a virtue, a secret, a touch, a mystery, from the heart of that which continueth forever! – Heal us, therefore, O Goddess, of the hurts and wounds in our souls that ache and bleed today because of the false doctrines about gods and men that have been inflicted upon us, false doctrines about all things in heaven and earth! Have they not taken on themselves, these priests of pain, these ministers of blood, to invent signs and tokens and symbols and sacraments out of privation and deprivation, out of suppression and frustration, out of denial and negation? Have they not thus defied the revelations made by thy blessed mystery, and turned to nothing the secret of thy holy rapture, of thy sacred madness, of thy entranced, thy transporting ecstasy? Make them give us back the pulse of our life, great Goddess, give us back the beat of our heart, give us back the dance of our blood!'

⋆ ⋆ ⋆

THE WHITE LADY, THE BLACK KING, AND THE DRAGON'S EGGS

IN EARLY JANUARY, Andy and David had met up with Graham Phillips to discuss the apparent fulfilment of the old Lights of Knowledge quest. He felt that Vortigern was the key to the seventh sword, the black sword, 'the sword that corrupts'. Shortly after that, Debbie had begun speaking of a 'basilisk stone' connected with Vortigern that stood alone in a field somewhere in Wales. Andy realised that he and Bernard had picked up on it as far back as 1984. Bernard referred to 'ways of the wyvern'. They felt that the stone was in North Wales and was permeated with a dodgy energy that needed sorting out. Before going there Debbie believed we had to approach the black king as his sword was aligned to the energy of the seventh sword. He was a kind of guardian of it. This would have to be done at the hillfort associated with him named Dinas Emrys. After the basilisk stone we would then proceed to a waterfall. Kerry and Lisa had also both been dreaming of a waterfall that they believed to be in Wales and connected with the seventh sword quest.

By the end of January the important locations had been clearly identified. The basilisk stone was a twelve-foot tall pillar known locally as Post Coch, the red pillar, or Post-y-Wiber, the pillar of the serpent or viper, in Powys near the Berwyn mountains. The local folklore told of a winged serpent known as a Gwiberod that fed on animals and abducted humans. It was eventually killed by a cunning ruse. A large pillar was erected and covered in spikes. A red cloth was draped over it to attract the beastie in matador style. It rushed at the stone and stupidly repeatedly rammed against it until dying of blood loss. It was believed that the stone had been quarried from a nearby location adjacent to a waterfall at Pistyll Rhaeadr, at 240ft the highest in England and Wales. A major excursion was planned for late April. A lot of anticipation built up around it.

A good indicator of the extent to which things were warping-out occurred in early April. Andy was contacted by someone familiar with *The Black Alchemist* who had some strange experiences under hypnosis that he felt may have a magical meaning that Andy could help unravel. The two men spoke at length on the phone, with Andy increasingly realising that he was talking to someone who was extremely interesting and clued-in. Andy mentioned his love of the *Robin of Sherwood* TV show for its strong magical mystical content and themes not dissimilar to questing. His caller responded that he knew it very well as he was in it! Actor Mark Ryan played the Saracen swordsman Nasir, who happened to be the general favourite character of the group.

The two men soon met up and were joined by David for a psychic session. Since he was a teenager, Ryan had been aware of the abiding presence of a female guardian spirit of some kind, a woman in white. On one occasion, after he had slept near a waterfall, he awoke with the memory that she had somehow emerged from it to be with him. This would prove to be a fundamental element in the mystery of what followed. The Californian hypnosis session was intended to investigate possible past lives. In going back through random layers of childhood memories to generally set the process in motion, something unforeseen intervened. Ryan vividly saw a 19th century stone folly called Lund's Tower on a ridge of hills named Earl Crag, near Skipton in the West Riding of Yorkshire. He had visited the place once twenty years previously and had fond memories of the day. It wasn't that past event that came to mind though. He seemed to be seeing the place in the present day. There was an immediate feeling that something was badly wrong there. A distorted occult force of wild anger and rage filled the place. It seemed like a beast was chained there. A voice told Mark Ryan that he would have to deal with the situation and would know who to contact. Somewhere in the whole weird scene, the woman in white was also present.

Andy and David were rapidly able to tune in to the Yorkshire landscape, providing precise details of the vicinity that Mark Ryan was able to confirm. David spoke of a local tradition concerning a dragon in a cave, believing that the tower had been deliberately placed to connect with it. This prompted Ryan to remember something for the first time. On his visit twenty years ago, he had talked with his companion of a dragon coming across the land to the tower. David also felt that the white lady was more than just a personal guide and would prove to be important. Andy was feeling the same and was seeing her with an expanse of water he felt was nearby. The sense of some kind of Lady of the Lake scenario with this white goddess rapidly grew. David, in a strange echo of the Christmas Dozmary Pool episode, proclaimed that a woman who was in tune with the site and the lady would be important as well. He stated that she was an artist or photographer.

What was remarkable about this session was how much of the

material proved to be accurate. Both Andy and David saw a wealth of topographical detail on a landscape of which they had no prior knowledge. The lake proved to exist in the exact region Andy had seen. It was called Eshton Tarn. Going on to check a detailed map of the area he started to notice the frequency of place names with El, Elle, Elen or Helen in them. There was a St. Helen's well near to the lake. It was clear that the white lady was the goddess Elen.

The main source for our ideas concerning Elen is the *Mabinogion* story, *The Dream of Macsen Wledig*. She is responsible for building a series of roads. This has led to her being considered as a presiding deity force of the ley system. She embodies the energies of the 'shining paths'. Her name supposedly derives from the ancient seed root 'El', found in many contexts and cultures, primarily meaning 'light'. Her *Mabinogion* tale was written down by medieval monks who probably had very little idea of the archaic motifs it contained. Thanks to their recording of the basic narrative we can recover meanings unknown to them. Helen was the mother of the Emperor Constantine. As she assumed saintly status, it seems she took on attributes of a pagan predecessor in a manner similar to the Irish Brigit. A well dedicated to St. Helen suggested prior veneration of Elen.

In a considerable upgrade from Cornwall, the identity of the woman who knew the landscape and the white goddess was discovered. Amazingly enough, it was Chesca Potter! She and Caroline Wise had produced a booklet, *The Green Lady,* on the subject. It turned out that the Yorkshire sites were known to her. It was increasingly clear that what was unfolding was not some peripheral side-show but an integral part of the main questing dynamic.

Things moved rapidly. A swift visit to the tower was proposed. David was unable to attend. Andy introduced Debbie to the scenario at short notice and she accompanied him. She soon came to feel that Elen had been seen as the body, blood, and spirit of the land. Her arrival on the scene had obvious continuity with our landscape goddess sovereignty adventure over the New-Year. She was possibly an extremely archaic figure who the aspects of the landscape goddess we had already encountered had all originated from.

Whilst listening to a tape recording of the psychic session with Mark Ryan, Debbie started doodling on a notepad. Two designs repeated themselves into increasing detail. One was a Celtic cross whose four arms were waves like water. The circle behind them had the scales of a snake. Alongside that was a caduceus, two serpents wound around a central staff with wings at its tip. It had been late at night and no explanation was forthcoming before she fell asleep. The next day would see a long drive from Essex to Yorkshire.

On Saturday April 14th, Andy, Debbie, and Mark Ryan visited Lund's Tower. Almost immediately a magical artefact of the kind frequently encountered in the Black Alchemist saga was discovered. This served to confirm that the site was being used for potentially dubious purposes.

Lund is a variant of the legendary Lud, onetime ruler of London according to Geoffrey of Monmouth. A *Mabinogion* tale of Lludd tells of a scream heard across Britain on May Eve caused by two dragons fighting. They are discovered at the exact centre of the realm, which in this tale is at Oxford. Once captured, they are imprisoned at the fortress of Dinas Emrys in North Wales, known for being the stronghold of Vortigern. Another earlier version of the fighting dragons tale recounted by Nennius tells how Vortigern's tower repeatedly collapsed during its construction. His Druids advised a sacrifice and a young boy named Emrys was selected. In Geoffrey of Monmouth he is Merlin. The superior magical vision of the boy detects the real problem in the form of the two fighting dragons. Some strange archaic theme was being retold in distorted forms in these slightly different stories. A major quest involving the whole group was set for the following weekend. We were already going to visit Dinas Emrys. Lund's Tower and the dragon strongly echoed an already established theme.

After spending some time in the tower, Debbie felt the place was built on a Celtic site and was linked to two dragons, one black and the other white, which were in some kind of continual conflict. Recent magical activity had messed with the balance, turning the white dragon to a very angry red. This then blended with the darker dragon to produce one mean beast that was trapped in the tower, deliberately held in place to spread distorted energy around the local energy matrix.

Having got a sense of the place it was decided to check out Eshton Tarn lake and return later. On arriving, Debbie stood at the very edge of the water and peered out. Before long she could see a stunning female figure floating across the surface towards her. As Andy later described her in *The Seventh Sword,* Elen "*had long strawberry-blonde hair, and a pale, finely featured face. Her white robe was of a thick flannel-like material, diagonally wrapped across her chest and gathered around her waist*". She stopped barely ten feet away from Debbie and seemed to communicate a message for Mark Ryan, asking him to help her by "*releasing the bonds of the dragon*". Elen then pointed downwards, seemingly towards the water, maintaining the gesture in apparent emphasis. Debbie began to feel there might be something there and began feeling around in the mud and the reeds. She started to walk out into the water. Only a few paces in she paused and put her hand down. There was something there. It was solid and strangely shaped. Her fingers grasped it securely and retrieved it from the water, holding it triumphantly aloft. She turned with a smile to display a three-inch long turquoise glazed white plaster caduceus. It was the classic design of two serpents wound around a central staff topped by a winged sphere. Along with wing feathers and snake scales, inscribed detail also included two tiny Celtic crosses inscribed on the serpent's necks. An eyehole suggested the artefact had been used as a pendant.

How did it get there? The plaster it was made from could not survive for long in water. Sceptics would obviously maintain that Debbie had somehow managed to obtain an item entirely appropriate to someone else's psychic material that she had only been exposed to for the first time the previous night and then produced it with a deceptive dramatic flourish. The questing group, being the bunch of space-cases we were and not giving a shit about Occam and his razor, quite happily accepted that the laws of physics had been trashed again and anticipated an excellent adventure the following weekend in Wales.

The Yorkshire saga hadn't ended there though. The next stop was St. Helen's well. Carved Celtic stone heads discovered below the water line had been sufficient proof of pre-Christian veneration. The whole area had yielded many remains indicative of the presence of a Bronze and Iron Age population. Elen appeared once again to Debbie. She told her that, *"the caduceus is the sign of balance"*. It represented deep mysteries within the land. Its purpose went far beyond the activities of the weekend. As for the business at the tower, two Meonia swords that Andy had brought along should be used to sever the dragon's bonds.

Using visualisation and concentration as they walked around the base of the tower, the three questers made the necessary magical use of the swords to free the dragon. Debbie saw Elen coming towards the tower at the same time as a strange small black four-legged dragon likewise advanced. They met in the middle of the tower and the beast rose up on two legs like a heraldic image as Elen became a white unicorn that similarly reared up. The image froze and then slowly dissolved into the stone tower. The thoroughly bizarre mission had been accomplished.

In an appropriate development, Mark Ryan would later meet Chesca Potter and work with her on the creation of the *Greenwood Tarot*, a project that beautifully fulfilled his *Robin of Sherwood* and Elen inspirations and experiences.

One week after the dramatic appearance of Elen, the Welsh adventure began, seeing us very much on the trail of the man who had so impolitely introduced himself and the mystery of the dragon eggs to Debbie in Cornwall. After Lund's tower it seemed obvious that a journey to the lair of Vortigern himself would produce results.

The Seventh Sword gives a detailed account of what followed. Elementals were again in evidence. This time it was the Cymric contingent, the Tylwyth Tegs. A few powerful sites were visited before the ascent of Dinas Emrys. John and Karl went for the full mountaineering approach on one rock face. The rest of the group chose a more gradual climb. We all came together in a hollow between four ruined walls on the summit. The view was suitably spectacular, taking in a lake called Llyn Dinas. It was easy enough to get into a powerful reverie on ancient mythology. We began by visualising the fighting dragons beneath the ground. They were seen biting each other's tails and in a state of continual motion.

Debbie soon saw Vortigern as he had appeared on New Year's Day, bearded, with powerful eyes, wearing a black robe and metal skullcap. He was holding out two egg shaped black crystals that she knew were part of the dragon. There are three such eggs. Trebor had told us this after Vortigern's first brutal appearance. The fire would hatch them. Vortigern stated that we had already received one and he was now forced to give us the second. With this, he turned around to face the direction of Llyn Dinas and cast one of the dragon eggs towards it. The egg entered the lake with a mighty splash and the sound of hissing. Water churned and boiled as a mighty dragon rose from it. It looked quite similar to the red dragon of the Welsh flag, although more serpentine. It flew in a circle of diminishing size until it was biting its tail. Water was pouring from it into four quartered streams forming a cross of light. The image gradually faded, leaving Vortigern to enigmatically proclaim that he awaited his release at the time of change. He made a dramatic emphasis by moving the third and final egg behind his back and disappearing in a dark haze.

Shortly before the trip, Debbie had seen a brief vision of blossom falling from thorn trees in what she felt was a Druidic site. Andy quickly identified it as Cell-y-Dewiniaid, the Grove of the Magicians. It was located below Dinas Emrys and had once supposedly been the place where Vortigern's Druids had met. When one of them died, so the local folklore went, a white thorn tree and a stone marked their grave that would then be covered by blossom each year. After meeting Vortigern on the summit, Debbie felt that we should find the Grove next. This involved some blind navigating driving around and asking assorted walkers along the roads. Typical questing luck eventually brought us towards a woman driving a farm vehicle on her way out to feed lambs. Andy talked to her about the place and she realised it was actually on her own land. We had assuredly met the site guardian. She was able to tell us that recent archaeology had uncovered burials that supported the local traditions.

There were only a few thorn trees now. On settling down by one, Debbie saw a small ball of golden light appear from within it. It rapidly expanded into a classic archetypal form of a purple-robed, skullcap wearing, white-bearded old man. He identified himself as Myrddin, a Welsh variant of Merlin. He asked if we wanted to finish the quest to find the seventh sword of destiny so that we could open the gates of power? Not exactly a hard question to answer! He bade us understand, *"the four symbols of the universe"*, the spiral, line, cross, and circle. Myrrdin now held in one hand a flaming gold caduceus staff and in the other a shining Celtic cross. *"These are the four keys of the universe. The nature of the cosmos. There is one other. It is a messenger, the third dragon's egg held by Vortigern. If you possess each one, then you shall be ready to hold the sword."* It was beginning to seem that the previous week's caduceus apport was an embodiment of one of the mysterious dragon's eggs of which there appeared to be three in total. There was little time to ponder too deeply. We had a hectic itinerary to meet.

Sunday April 22nd involved a meeting with a dragon. Although we would be entering into a story that involved a dragon killing, that was not our ultimate intention. It was more of a case of perhaps helping to heal a wound in the local matrix of the pendragon force that in turn would free up the flow throughout the land.

To link into the story we would drape a large red tablecloth over the stone and use a Meonia sword to impale the beast. Its blood-red energy would move through the sword, down through the stone and into the ground, turning white as it did so. When it was discovered that basilisks are considered to be tiny creatures only a few inches long we developed a false sense of the ease of the magical task at hand. This feeling soon dissipated.

Debbie had been dreaming of a winged dragon that she referred to as Saraph. The name was possibly derived from the biblical Seraph that means 'fiery serpent'. Near to the stone was a place named Sarffle, taken to mean the Serpent's Hole. Perhaps the various factors involved were larger and more complex than we had initially anticipated.

At sunset, having sought the permission of the landowner to enter the field, we gathered by the stone. John did his mountaineering man thing by climbing up to put the tablecloth over it. Debbie stood with her back to the stone holding the sword. The rest of us were arranged either side of her in a horseshoe formation open to the north from whence we would call forth the dragon. We visualised white shining crosses of light within ourselves as a kind of psychic protection against the rigours of what was to come.

To start with we imagined a blood-red glow like a rising sun and then left things to develop of their own accord. It wasn't long before Debbie's otherworldly perceptions became aware of a stirring ahead and the news wasn't good! Some kind of gaseous red cloud that stretched along the entire horizon was beginning to move towards us in a slow rippling motion. It blotted out the sky behind it as it progressed. She was filled with terror. As the vast energy drew nearer it began to take on a recognisable form.

Its body seemed to stretch from the far horizon to the very edge of the field we were standing in. There were wings that were closed against its generally serpentine bulk. Eyes of merciless fire stared down into Debbie. Others in the group began to see glimpses with the inner eye as well. The growing fear was tangible. Debbie brandished the sword aloft and the great wyvern head moved as if to strike. She let loose a series of screams sufficient in volume and emotional intensity to have alerted anyone within earshot to phone the emergency services immediately. Fortunately for us, the area was only sparsely populated and we attracted no attention. It's one thing to become habituated to such manifestations as a cliché of horror movies but something else altogether to hear such sounds for real coming from someone you know clearly on the edge of terrifying oblivion. Debbie's legs gave way. Andy rushed forward to support her and keep the sword raised. Under his directions we tried to fulfil the plan by seeing the dragon repeatedly bashing its head onto the sword and blood pouring along it, through Debbie and into the stone. It would change to pink and then white as it descended into the ground and then spiralled outwards. The distorted form of the dragon would eventually fade. It took a bit of doing. Massive mental effort was concentrated for what seemed a long time before it was felt that the drama was completed.

Debbie was barely conscious by the end of the process. She slumped onto the ground, later unsteadily rising to silently slowly stagger around. After a while she purposefully started to walk away towards the field gate. She finally spoke to Andy, expressing the urgent need to get to the nearby Pistyll Rhaeadr waterfall. It was as if she was covered in blood in a totally red world. It needed to be thoroughly cleansed. And there was urgency about it. The sun had set and twilight was rapidly drawing in. There were scavengers abroad now, alerted by the smell of blood, who would come for her and us. She called them the 'Gruach'. The brief journey through darkening country lanes was intense. I was in Alex's car with Andy and Debbie in the back. It was like we were rushing her to hospital. In the other vehicle, driver John was somewhat perplexed by the sight of a huge bat flying alongside. Kerry, Lisa, and Karl could all see it. Was it real? Can bats fly that fast? John then clearly saw a wolf running ahead of the car. This time he was alone in the vision but it seemed totally real.

We had previously checked out the awesome waterfall in daylight. This night-time conclusion had always been intended but the flavour of the circumstance had not been adequately anticipated. It was fortunate that we had some sense of the location and were thus able to make our way to the water's edge for a ritual cleansing. I had realised that the primal elemental location would have an immensely powerful atmosphere after dark but the immediate raw effect was still stunning. Whilst Andy helped Debbie to slowly stumble along, amongst others there was almost a sense of running for our lives. Hairs were rising with the fears of the primordial forest. Karl heard a definite growling in the darkness and Lisa saw two glowing eyes. It was worse for John. The open mouth of a pouncing wolf loomed suddenly, sending him into a frantic dash for the water. Our shouts of alarm were as nothing against the backdrop of the thundering waterfall. We needed to watch our feet. The path became precarious.

At the foot of the waterfall was a large pool. A stone platform afforded access to it. Parts of the water were not that deep. Debbie waded straight into it fully clothed and crouched on all fours as the spray from the waterfall drenched her. The rest of the group were a little more reserved in their ablutions. Andy cleansed the Meonia sword.

When Debbie eventually began to stand up she saw three ghostly white women standing together in front of the waterfall. Barely had she registered their presence when they blended into one form instantly recognisable as Elen. In what rapidly followed nobody actually spoke to anyone else about what they were experiencing until after it was over. It all unfolded simultaneously. Kerry could see a white lady in the middle of the waterfall as well. Debbie saw Elen raise her hands upwards with her palms facing the direction of the flowing water. John began to look up at this point and saw a point of white light strangely moving down through the first level of the waterfall. It then reappeared a little further down. Debbie saw a horizontal band of light coming down towards Elen's hands. John saw his point of light coming down the final cascade and with it came the feeling that a physical artefact had landed in the water in front of us. Kerry came to a similar feeling and bent down to put her hands in the water. Alex was now quite close to Debbie. He could see a ripple of light underneath the water in front of her. It instantly changed into some sort of object that hadn't been there a micro-second earlier. It rose and fell in the water. Karl and Lisa caught a glimpse of it. For the second weekend in succession, Debbie put her hand down into water. Moments later she had thrown something aloft in the manner of a cricketer celebrating a spectacular catch. We watched something spinning upwards and turning back down to be caught again and displayed to the spray-drenched group. Another turquoise blue-glazed artefact, a Celtic cross with a serpent circle. The four arms had a wave-like pattern on them. It was about four inches long and two wide. A collective howl arose of an intensity appropriate to signify the nuking of our brains. Alex stared into space, repeatedly muttering his new mantra, "I saw it materialise".

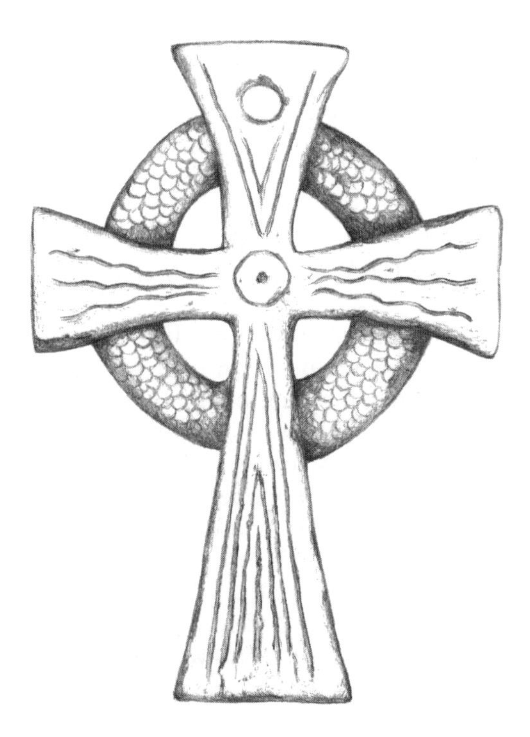

It had been a bit of a week really. From Debbie's idle doodles whilst listening to the tape of the Mark Ryan psychic session through the appearance of Elen to the retrieval from water of two dragon egg Keys of Balance, the impetus that had begun in Cornwall and Glastonbury at the New Year was now unfolding spectacularly.

After the first Key of Balance episode, Mark Ryan had expressed an interest in coming out on one of the larger group excursions. The Welsh trip was too soon. Another opportunity arose on John's Gawain quest. One Saturday in early May, we were all set up to spend the night in a cave at a place called Dovedale in Derbyshire, a location well off the beaten track. Mark Ryan came along. At that time there was serious talk of getting a Robin of Sherwood movie together. Resources were being assembled. It never happened and the project gradually developed into the Kevin Costner vehicle. In May '90 Mark Ryan had grown his hair and beard again so that he once again looked the part of Nasir. Not only that, Andy had mentioned to him how we were all fans of his distinctive two-sword fighting style. He had said that he still had the swords and would bring then along. This resulted in him appearing looking essentially identical to his Nasir character, even to the extent of having the swords scabbarded over his shoulders behind his back. He seemed to fit into the Nasir role amongst us as well, following along behind, as if keeping look-out and so on. I felt that something had completely snapped. I was now convinced that we had fucked up reality completely.

GLASTONBURY ZODIAC VISION QUEST

FROM THE FIRST DAY OF JUNE I tried to up the intensity of my preparation for the zodiac quest. On that day I read *Avalon of the Heart.* I proceeded into the month feeding on a relentless diet of Glastonbury material. On Tuesday June 19th I watched *Excalibur* for the umpteenth time. As scenes of Pre-Raphaelite beauty and Maloryian vitality were played out before my eyes, accompanied by the disturbingly stirring Wagner soundtrack, I brooded still further over the imminent leap into the weir. The weather forecast was not auspicious. Rain seemed likely. What if we were subjected to conditions like '85? Doing the Zodiac in pouring rain would surely be a major bummer but what if the weir was swollen like it had been then? I really did not want it to be like that. I had got the Fear.

Common sense told me that the immersion would be fine. John was lending me an inflatable life jacket and some goggles. I would rise back up to the surface in a matter of seconds. He and Karl would be standing right by me as I jumped. That still wasn't enough. I forced myself to rise above it. This was to be my last indulgence in such concerns.

Along with Alex Langstone, I had decided to start the process a day ahead of the rest of the group. We couldn't resist the whole Tor solstice sunrise scenario with its attendant knees-up. It seemed like an ideal way to enter into the mythos and generally relax and limber up in readiness for the intense times ahead. That Wednesday began with a definite indication that we were involved in something that rippled out further than our strange head-spaces. I went out early to buy the *New Musical Express*. I already knew what to expect but it was mighty weird to see it nonetheless. That edition was a Glastonbury festival special. On the cover were bill toppers the Happy Mondays, who were then on the crest of their chemical wave of success. Inside was a large feature on the Ecstasy New Age spirit of the time, including material on Andy with large pictures of him and Debbie, separately on adjoining pages. My personal background of multiple festival experiences and the mysterious road that had led me to what I was about to do made me feel that this mixture was a strong affirmation to me personally that I was very much on the right track.

A large crowd carpeted the Tor top by sunset. The tower was full of drummers. Singing, chanting, whooping, cheering and sounds of wild euphoria gradually blended into an ever-greater tide of familiar intensity. A number of nutters had come out of the woodwork as always. I particularly noticed, in the midst of the melee in the tower, a solitary guy who was just standing still repeating the words, "I come from hell, you know me well". He wasn't looking at me or anyone else in particular, just staring ahead. As I glanced at the people packed solid around him, it seemed like I was the only one aware of him and his strange mantra. Time dissolved. At the crucial moment of sunrise, the weather was mercifully kind. A clear sky heralded yet another glorious solstice golden dawn. Alex and I, standing in the tower, noted that people seemed to want to acknowledge the sunrise somehow but didn't quite know what to do. There were no large groups to focus it like the witches and Sufis in '88. We began to sing the Hopi sun chant in alternate Hopi and English. Before long a number of others had joined in.

This felt as if it met the requirements of the energy of the moment.

Eventually it began to cloud over. We'd had no sleep all night. Time to find a place on the slopes and make use of our trusty German Army sleeping bags. John Horrigan had turned the questing group on to these choice items and we all got a lot of mileage out of them in 1990. It rained lightly for some hours. Even though I'd been awake for a long time I didn't really fall asleep. I seldom did in the normal manner when I stayed out at some ancient site. It was more a case of passing into a trance condition between sleeping and waking.

The rest of the solstice was a bit of a blur. The sun came out again later. We spent hours at a time sitting on benches, either on the Tor or its adjacent field, just watching the humans walk by. I affirmed a feeling that welled up inside me and was to be a crucial preset for my coming experience. "It's all true. Everything that all of the mystics and magicians have ever said about Glastonbury, it really is all true. Even the most spaced-out of all of them got something right. All the bits that might seem to contradict each other or have no historical validation. All true. I know this like I know I've got two arms, two legs, and a head." That night the whole group gathered in a guest-house. Something I had been building up to for nearly six months was finally about to begin.

The great adventure started at midday on Friday June 22nd at Kingweston. Inside the church, Andy proclaimed our wish to embark upon the Grail quest, asking the guardian forces of the Zodiac for acceptance. We immediately established the basic working procedure for the whole journey. Andy had brought a gold coloured chalice with him. At each site we visited it would be placed on the ground and we would stand or sit around it. This was the cue to begin visualising transparent electric blue light expanding from within the chalice to encompass us in a sparkling sphere. Andy would then take us through a guided meditation based on his own achievement of being the first known person in modern times to complete the Glastonbury Zodiac, initially working with Bernard, and then for the final half working entirely alone. He would now bring that powerful knowledge to use here again, yet also provide every opportunity to leave us time to explore it alone and see what transpired. Debbie would be a vital part of the group alchemy. One of the most interesting aspects of the coming excursion was to see to what extent her psychic material would duplicate or develop from the experiences in the mid-eighties, of which she knew only the vaguest of details. After the Welsh adventure, we were open to limitless possibilities. Who was to say that some groovy Grail chalice or general Arthurian artefact might not somehow manifest?

With our eyes closed we firstly tried to see the church as it was in physical reality. Outside, a huge solar wheel with pulsating sunray spokes was descending from the sky above it. The building seemed to be attracting solar energies from all directions. The sun shone mightily through all the windows. Golden light totally filled the church like a thickening mist. By the early Norman font and doorway, beneath a stained glass window, we saw the king of the western lands seated on a throne. He was a figure in his prime, resplendent in deep red royal regalia. His throne was also red, its arms ending in carved lion's heads. The king held a shining gold orb. Below the throne was a stone of destiny, likewise emanating golden light. It was a vision not unlike the depiction of the Emperor by Lady Frieda Harris in Crowley's Tarot deck.

The church was now a powerhouse beacon of solar energies. The light within it began a clockwise swirling, radiating back out through the windows and transparently vibrant walls, across the land in spoke-like shafts. The quality of that light rapidly shifted, denoting the change from midday to evening setting sun. The rays streaming through the church windows were now redder. The whole countryside was bathed in an orangey-red afterglow. The wall of the church behind the king vanished. A portal entrance to a dark tunnel had appeared. It was guarded by two figures holding lances across it, clearly barring our way. We needed their permission to pass. The tunnel would be entered at the next site. We would have to meet them again there.

Who was it that stood in our path? Debbie had suggested that we would encounter some kind of guardian figure at each site we visited. In the church, she saw the two warriors before Andy had even mentioned them. She identified them as Cath Palug and Lancelot. Cath Palug had a dark orange complexion, bright red eyes and long blonde hair. He was wearing black and gold armour and holding a lance. Lancelot was pale faced with blue eyes. Wearing shining bronze armour, with a red and white plumed helmet, he held a lance in one hand and a shield with the other. It was down by his side and turned away so as not to display any heraldic device. Debbie saw Cath Palug dip his lance down into our chalice and three drops of blood were seen to drip from its tip.

Our next destination was another church, St. Michael and

All Angels, in nearby Somerton. It was there that Andy had first connected Robert de St. Clere with Somerset. Now we were in a location within the usual Zodiac. I rather like the parish church. Visitors would probably most notice the amazing wooden carved roof. It's full of angels and men and weird wyvern dragons. Always nice to see a devil with a pig's snout as well. We settled down in the supremely peaceful chapel of the Holy Spirit where the St. Clere coat of arms and Robert's name are unobtrusively displayed.

Once again we saw the two knights holding their lances across the beckoning tunnel entrance. Cath Palug communicated to Debbie the need for us to utter an oath of intention in order to enter the tunnel. At his dictation we recited, *"I renounce all dominance over my destiny, discard my pride and am willing to be led by the divine child of Gemini"*. He then gave the obscure advice, *"do not be afraid to reach for the star, you will not be pecked"*. John then mentioned that he had been seeing a bird in flight.

Debbie experienced being handed a spear by Lancelot and a stone by Cath Palug who said, *"This makes you kings. The lance will guard your way"*. *"Now you have become the beast king do not be afraid to be led, otherwise when you turn to Merlin he will not be by your side."* The objects obviously signified two of the Grail Hallows, a set of four elemental objects featured in the tales. The reference to the *'beast king'* was an example of enigmatic utterances that Debbie would hear from various figures throughout the journey. Sometimes they revealed their meaning at another location in the context of the unfolding quest. Occasionally they seemed to contain obscure and not obviously relevant references to assorted Arthuriana and Glastonbury lore. And some of it simply remained indecipherable.

St. Andrew's church in Compton Dundon was the first of the Gemini sites on our itinerary. A magnificent giant yew tree in the graveyard is the most notable feature of the place. The church seemed quite sparse in comparison with where we'd just been in Somerton. Once inside, we reconnected to the imagery as we'd left it.

This time the building filled with blue light. The swirling tunnel portal appeared, unguarded, opening into darkness. We needed to dare to enter over its threshold into the inner realms of the next site, the nearby Dundon Beacon. Once inside the tunnel, Debbie saw a small bright star far ahead in the distance. Two shadowy male figures appeared in front of her, silhouetted strongly by the light behind them. One stood with his hands raised above his head, palms touching forming the shape of the upper half of a diamond.

The other figure's hands were likewise palms together but facing downwards. Like Lancelot and Cath Palug, they clearly represented guardian figures, posing a challenge, blocking the way with their strange gestures. They communicated that they were Tammuz and Adonai Dionysis. With this, they began to change, metamorphosing through a sudden dark mist into glowing yellow figures that then identified themselves as Perceval and Galahad. Debbie moved through them towards the shining star, in which she then saw a small child, wearing a crown, who proclaimed, *"I am Bel, Adonai, Tammuz, Dionysis, Pollux, Atlas, I am Orion"*.

Debbie also now partly explained her earlier reference to the 'beast king'. It was the lion of Leo and it was to be 'led' by the child of Gemini. We had to identify with the figures and characters along the journey, to internalise the process. The tunnels and their guardians that we were encountering had the flavour of visionary pathworkings between the Qabalistic spheres in the Golden Dawn tradition. In this case we were using real physical locations as a grand Hermetic memory theatre.

John had found himself in Solomon's Temple. He saw two angelic figures guarding its inner sanctum. As a mason it was not surprising that such imagery arose. It clearly fitted in with the material that Andy and Cara had worked with concerning the Holy Sepulchre, which was supposedly built above the ruins of Solomon's edifice.

From the church, we now prepared to ascend the 'dark hill'. Debbie saw a large number of human skulls on poles all around its base. As we were walking through woods up to the summit, she stopped, staring into space as we'd often seen her do before. Nobody noticed as we left her behind and she disappeared from sight. When she regained her focus, she realised she'd lost us and was unsure of the path. At this point, a dark featureless human shadow shape figure appeared before her, beckoning. She felt no sense of danger and began to follow it, thinking it would lead her back to the group. The mysterious shadow figure seemed to disappear. Looking around, she located it again in a nearby meadow clearing, full of sapling trees. Moving towards it she now saw that it was holding a shining gold grail out towards her. Understandably, she advanced towards it. Suddenly something flew out of the chalice and expanded, rapidly followed by a whole dark host. They were small human skeleton creatures with enlarged skulls and black-feathered wings. Here was a veritable Ray Harryhausen special effect, worthy of the Jason or Sinbad movies. Unfortunately for

Debbie, the whole thing was being experienced as physical reality. She turned and tried to run but everything seemed to have gone into slow motion. Something pushed her from behind right off her feet to land face down amidst the saplings. She could feel the creatures swarming all over her. There was tremendous pressure on her back. It felt like it would have to break. Suddenly the whole tumult ceased. The feeling of the presence of the creatures had abruptly ended. Slowly and cautiously she picked herself up, looking around. Everything looked grey. She started calling out hoping to find us, whilst trying to walk upwards to the top of the hill. Three divergent paths presented themselves. They all seemed like grey tunnels. Two were investigated and proved to be incorrect.

By now we had realised that Debbie was definitely missing and were actively searching for her. Sounds of distant distress alerted us. When we found her, she was upset and confused. She told us of her encounter with the bizarre creatures. Lifting the back of her top she revealed scratches and red marks on her skin. It was an archetypal episode with the threshold guardians of Chapel Perilous. They communicated an attempt to discourage her from the quest. It didn't work. She regained her equilibrium and we continued.

We took up positions on top of the beacon point. In the opening Grail chalice visualisation, we spread light out across the land. Then, it was briefly back into the tunnel, to see ourselves rapidly emerging out of it onto the hilltop bathed in shining light. Debbie saw a gigantic goddess figure, shining with a blue white light, who lifted her up on the palm of her hand. As Debbie rose into the air, a shaft of gold light shot across the sky towards the figure, changing its colour to gold as well. Two further shafts become visible on either side of her, marking out paths to the left and right of the hill. *"These are the three bars."* Above them could be glimpsed white fluttering wings. As she saw this pre-figuration of imagery that would later become important on the journey, Debbie was being taken up into the heavens towards Orion.

The titan goddess indeed identified herself as Orion. She told Debbie that she had experienced the two sides of Gemini, moving through its deceptiveness. And there were the now familiarly flavoured cryptic utterances. *"The head is unburied and the griffin is split. The raven is free, it no longer circles. The lion is flightless"*. A griffin could now be seen flying around in the sky above. The Orion goddess confirmed that we had passed the Dundon test. Debbie saw a church building and then a field with a small mound topped with clumps of trees. Our way forward had been indicated in a manner that clearly recalled Bernard's 1984 experience there.

Andy was curious about what might happen at the locations that had produced particular highlights in the mid-eighties. The Virgo area was the first of these to be entered. Keinton Mandeville church had opened the 'cones of heaven' and led to the nun's gift on Wimble Toot. Experiences at each of the sites so far contained prefigurations of what was to come. This was deliberate but still produced surprises. The Orion goddess was a form of the Virgo figure.

The church of St. Mary Magdalene was, in my opinion, the least interesting of all those we visited on the journey. It seemed a well-scrubbed characterless example of uninspired Victorian restoration and therefore unworthy of its controversial patron saint. It nonetheless proved to be an effective doorway once again. Debbie was inspired to make an addition to our operational procedure. The horse figurine apport was placed in the chalice. Perhaps themes of the land and sovereignty were about to manifest. The Virgo figure is the only depiction of a female in the Glastonbury Zodiac. It inevitably resonates with the complete Goddess frequency.

Debbie saw a woman near the font, in the form of Ceres the corn mother, dressed in white and gold, holding an orangey-red shaft of corn. In a sense, the wheat sheaf was a condensed physical form of the three shafts of light, the celestial Awen experienced at Dundon and certain to be encountered again later on in the journey. It's also the corn baby, the divine child itself. Debbie told us that the shaft which Ceres had reaped strangles the Gemini child, so that brought the ideas together.

We asked Ceres for permission to let us pass through her territory. *"You must accept the hag and destructress as your mother, not as your enemy. This will dispel the concept of fear. You fear the part of you that will grow old"*. She then took seeds from the corn and placed one into each of the group. *"This is the seed of your mother. If you accept the seed in its true form you will have no fear. Accept the root that is your fear."* The seeds inside us became bright red. Now, Debbie told us, we were within her power and the sheaf of corn that she has would also strangle us. It was all part of the natural process of things. The connection of mother and child will never break. The strangulation of the child continues throughout its growth. We must accept it as Gemini accepted Virgo's strangulation. If we were to accept it, we could accept the milk of life and of knowledge that would guide our way.

The sheaf of Ceres turned golden again. She held it upside down, moving nearer to the font, which was full of milk. The sheaf transformed into an inverted grail. Gold light poured from it into the font, turning the milk red. *"The cup and the sword will be gathered in the mist of battle. Pick them up as they lay on the ground."* As the blood in the font seemed to swirl around, so the rest of the church turned blue. Debbie could now see beyond the walls to a field of flowers outside. Lancelot was there, in chains. He wanted to be with us but couldn't as he didn't have the hallows. Following this glimpse, the Ceres figure split into five parts that dispersed in different directions, leaving the message, *"Go to the flowers where you'll be fed the knowledge of the mother"*.

It was time to go to Wimble Toot, where in 1984 a spectral nun had led Andy and Bernard to a special gift. Debbie's immediate feeling was that something was wrong there. In Mary Caine's work the Virgo figure, and particularly the Toot, are associated with Guenevere. In the Arthurian cycle, after the disgrace of her affair with Lancelot, she retires to a nunnery. In the true form of the mythos she was a representative of sovereignty and the land. Debbie felt that the nun needed to be restored to the form of the flower maiden.

On the low tree-covered tumulus, all visualised the approach of the tall veiled figure of the nun queen, inviting her towards our circle and requesting her to manifest her aspect as ruler of fruitfulness, flowers, crops and vegetation. She removed her veil, revealing a serene wise countenance. With a subtle Leonardo-esque smile, her face regained a radiant youthfulness. In a rippling of the air and a sudden strong fragrance of flowers, her nun's habit was gone, replaced by a velvet-textured dress of gorgeous green. She raised her arms, flinging back her long red hair as she did so. Sparkling rainbow light radiated out from her hands, falling as droplets of light across the Toot and the surrounding fields. This milk of the land caused flowers rapidly to grow and sprout.

The lady spoke to Debbie. "*What will flow will be the earth, the moon and the sea. You must learn to be still, then that power can be taken with you wherever you go and in the battles to come you must yield. What is stronger? The oak or a blade or grass? What will snap in a hurricane? Yield. Be small. Be soft. Beware of the monster that walks the land and the sea. Beware of the false king, the green king of water and of land. The monster will be his protector.*"

The young psychic then saw herself being given a small gold

bowl. *"Take this bowl and all darkness that flies overhead will be contained within it and you will be the controller."* This was possibly the Krater constellation cup that Mary Caine considered to be situated by the Virgo figure's lips.

Before departing from Virgo, we asked Guenevere to bless our own physical cup with her green golden light. In return, we walked all around the Toot, visualising it covered in flowers and the surrounding fields full of golden corn.

Debbie then saw an image of green grass, a graveyard, a stone gate. There's darkness within it. Something is waiting to come out of it. The ecliptic line must be used as a pulling point out of there to the next site or we'll never escape the sign that stings. Avoid the pincer that can cut off the ecliptic line. No prizes for guessing the next sign on the journey.

At 5.15 we arrived at St. Peter's church in Hornblottom, the doorway to our Scorpio experience and a place all too familiar to Andy. Wandering about inside, an interesting grave plaque on a wall was soon spotted. It showed a cup and sword, calling to mind Guenevere's earlier words and alerting us to the fact they that would supposedly be found, *"in the mist of battle"*. These representations completed the set of Hallows after what we'd been given in Leo. Such were the preliminaries. The real fun and games were set for outside.

We sat down in the graveyard to await death, decay, war, blood and despair, the black knight, the false king Mordred, in whatever form he manifested. Andy's 1984 visit with Bernard had been intense. We needed to protect ourselves. This was an episode that required a certain *Devil Rides Out* style to cultivate its essential flavour. A tangible circle of protection was created. Ash saved from a ritual fire earlier in the year was scattered around it. The chalice was specially filled with holy water, some of which was also sprinkled outside the circle. There were two crucifixes at opposite quarters. A church candle was burning. Clouds of incense were smoking. We were aware of the necessity of standing our ground no matter what happened. It was broad daylight in June, but in keeping with the dreamtime momentum we were generating, nobody else intruded upon the strange scene.

Andy called forth Mordred from the ruins of the old church. The first hints came when John saw the bird he'd been seeing since Somerton land in front of him and stand looking at us. It was a large raven type creature. Debbie saw it still in flight with silver rings round its ankles, circling anti-clockwise around us, trying to draw off our power. She then started hearing hissing and squelching sounds. Suddenly, from the nearby old chapel ruin, a line of fire moved across the ground towards us, burning the grass, scorching a black path. It heralded the spectacular appearance of a shining silver armoured knight on horseback. He was holding a silver shield and appeared to be weapon-less. Mordred's armour was like a mirror, reflecting everything back at us so we didn't see his true form. Debbie felt it was unwise to look at him. Andy called on Mordred, telling him we wished to pass through and asking his permission.

The rider revealed his true form. His black armour was pointed at the shoulders, coming down to a breast-plate like two circles joined. Ribbed ridges completed the upper section. Beneath the armour, red undergarments could be glimpsed. His coat of arms depicted a gold pentagram shape, but not with lines inside it. Three diagonally slanted green serpents lay across the design, one in the middle of the star. He slowly rode towards us, brandishing a raised sword, seemingly poised to strike. As he approached, Debbie experienced a host of small green snakes covering her. We affirmed that he couldn't defeat us, telling him to stand down. We called on the archangel Michael, firing a flaming pentagram into and through Mordred. This didn't do Debbie much good. The snakes turned into sharp teethed eels inside her body. *"I'm going to puke my insides up"* was her immediate assessment of the situation. Andy helped her to visualise them turning into green light and fading away. Mordred was still riding around us brandishing his raised sword. His next trick was to encircle us with a ring of fire. Our response was to create a ring of green ice between us and him. He seemed to retreat back along the scorched line into the chapel. Our green ice melted into vapour and liquid in the sun, extinguishing the ring and line of fire and then surrounding the chapel and church. We tried to pump up the energy until Mordred and his horse were forced to swim through the vibrant green liquid. It soon filled the ruin and a hole within it from whence Mordred had come. It looked like we were winning until Debbie cried an urgent halt. In an echo of Bernard's experience, a giant demon frog was emerging from the hole. *"I feel all slimy"* was Debbie's sad lament. At least it wasn't a killer rabbit. Send for Gabriel, archangel of water. Blue light cocooned the frog and despatched it back down the hole. Mordred galloped back out again. An ice blue pentagram was directed against horse and rider. They shrank within the star.

The chapel turned white. Mordred spoke for the first time, saying, *"the seat of the king is empty for your taking"*.

A tall archer now appeared in the churchyard. He was dressed in a kind of suede green outfit, trousers and a top. A flaming arrow was fired into the air. It went through the chapel ruin and beyond. This was the ecliptic line mentioned at Wimble Toot. With this came the feeling of Sagittarius as the 'seat of the king'. Debbie saw a bend in a river. A spiralling cone going downward into the earth. A setting sun. We had to catch the flaming arrow where it lands. This would be at a hill that was connected with fire. Some sort of mound on top of it. A further ordeal awaited us there. Andy knew the site but didn't mention the name to see if Debbie could pick it up. She did. Go to *"Pennard Hill"* and *"meet your initiator"*.

The hill is near enough to the site of the Pilton festival to give a clear view of the multitudes. As we had approached, the roads were full of typical characters. It was a strange and poignant moment for me. Memories rapidly arose. My 1979 solstice journey. The sequence of transitional moments culminating in the mystery of 1985. And now this. It was a very obvious point of ever-greater transition. What I'd dimly intuited as driving me on in 1979, what I'd tried to connect with through the eighties, was now no longer in the future as some far off ideal. It was in the present moment. However much still lay ahead unknown, I had arrived.

On the hilltop we began by visualising the flaming arrow flying through the sky towards us, gradually coming down until it landed almost at our feet. With my eyes closed I could still hear the constant sound of festival traffic back on the road, laughing, beeping car horns and so on. Debbie's first impression was that the site was linked with the Druids. She saw a tiny red glow beginning to form on the horizon by a small hill. It rapidly expanded, moving through the sky towards us. It was a wingless red dragon serpent, long-bodied with small front and hind legs. There was a glimpse of Druidic figures riding on its back. It spiralled directly above us and then seemed to engulf us in its body as mouth and tail connected in ouroboros fashion. The daunting message received reminded us of one of the constant background questing themes, *"we are perpetually part of it, there is no turning back"*. The dragon would be our initiator, guiding us through the next barrier before we could reach the seat of the king. Flames had been lit inside us. The dragon left us, returning back to the point on the horizon from whence it had come, spiralling down into the earth there.

Debbie then saw a ring of fire on top of a hill. The place was a focal point of some kind. It was time for a baptism of fire to purge us before we could leap, emptied, into the long-anticipated waters. Here began the second spiral. In 1984, Bernard had described the same place from West Pennard church just down the road as, *"the place of fire, on a high place, the place of the big serpent"*. It was on to Windmill Hill near Baltonborough, place of Bel.

At first we stood in a line. The sun was seen spectacularly setting behind the Tor. It became an awesome blood red sphere reminiscent of the climactic *Morte de Arthur* moment in *Excalibur.* It invited a Wagnerian soundtrack. We called on the pendragon force of the serpent initiator of the baptism of fire to come from the sunset to us. The creature came forth from the great fireball, moving across the sky in a line towards us. It brought the fire of Bel down, igniting the ground. The conflagration was about eight feet tall and wide. It did not seem to feed on any fuel, blazing out of the earth itself. This was the purificatory fire of the death of the sun king. We physically walked round the psychic fire with half open eyes, forming a circle after one circuit. The shamanic inferno was cold but burnt skin and bones away, leaving only our souls within the flame.

Debbie could now see the dragon again. This time it was on the ground. There were five Druids on its back. It was they who had been glimpsed in flight over Pennard Hill. They climbed off and began to walk around our circle, carrying flaming metal bowls, coming to a halt in a pentagram star formation with us in the middle. The fire in the bowls was then thrown upon us, turning to blood on impact. It moved down through us like oil. When it reached the ground, it re-ascended, emerging out of the top of our heads as red serpents. At this point, the flaming arrow initially loosed by the archer at Hornblotton re-appeared, multiplied and landed, piercing each serpent, leaving them burnt upon the ground. We remained glowing red, the ring of fire within us now. Fallen leaves lay all around us. Bel's dragon was now visible only as a ball of light. Debbie saw a triangle. *"Before you achieve the triple sight can you seat yourself upon the watery throne, the king's last act of majesty?"* Something about his last time on the throne, his last breath. His soul would be released upon the rising of the sun. From Aquarius.

It was at this site in 1984 that Bernard had seen the dying sun king figure sitting beneath a tree, followed by the flight of the phoenix with the crystal over the primordial waters. Andy had restarted the quest alone there in June 1985 by taking up the imagery again. He had identified himself with the king, visualising a fire springing up from the earth to engulf him. His soul was purified and released in the form of a bird. The soul bird then flew over the primeval waters of Glastonbury/Aquarius, a landscape void of form. He saw again the bird holding a crystal in its talons that was then dropped into the waters. The mound of creation emerged. Andy then returned to the consciousness of being on the ground again whilst his soul was in flight, understanding that he would reconnect with it if the quest was successfully completed.

The sun had set. A slight chill set in with the onset of twilight. It was nearing the time to physically enact a ritual death. Time to face our own reflections in the waters. Death and rebirth. Survival was the entrance ticket for the rest of the quest. And the waters connected to the realm of the feminine as a balance to the solar energy of the sun king. Baltonsborough Flights is located on the forehead of the Arthur figure. For those willing to entertain the possibility that the figures may even contain some kind of chakra system, it is considered to be the third-eye point and therefore an auspicious location for visionary undertakings.

The Libran dove is positioned as if it has flown from Arthur's head. Something of this was reflected in the 1985 imagery of the soul spirit bird leaving the dying sun king. The great immersion was scheduled for around midnight, the exact opposite time of the sun's maximum energy. We had some time to spare. It was spent in a pub in Baltonsborough. It didn't feel much like any previous Friday nights in pubs I had known. After closing time it wasn't going to be a case of finding a party or going back to someone's home and getting stoned with some good sounds. No. This was the prelude to an experience that might prove to be one of unhinging terror for me. Some of the others did consume some alcohol but in my case it didn't feel appropriate.

After what seemed an interminable wait, we finally drove out into the real country dark night. The narrow roads pulled us onwards like the tunnels of our pathworkings. A mile or so later, the cars stopped by the side of the road. There was a walk of a few hundred yards across fields. John and Karl, who were acting as life-guards, went to check out the site for possible company. John also did an investigative dive to make sure there were no underwater hazards to snare us. He discovered that there was a sheer drop of about fifteen feet where we were jumping. Fresh water coming off a weir at midnight would be a tad cold and carry a bit of momentum. An inevitable rising tide of hysteria began to grip us. Thus prepared, the process began.

Back in 1985, Andy did it at midnight in the pouring rain, with the weir swollen with flood water. Crazily, he deliberately expelled all air and sank to the bottom in order to fully immerse himself in the shadow of death, before going on to experience a moment of ecstatic rebirth. It almost seemed too easy. Incredibly enough, to ensure he really had experienced sufficient intensity and danger, he threw himself in a second time.

Kerry and Lisa jumped in together holding hands. Despite being good swimmers, they had both felt fear before the leap. Once submerged, their experiences were strangely similar. Somehow in the underwater darkness, they saw myriad points of dancing blue lights. And those lights brought bliss. Fear dissolved. They surfaced laughing, ecstatic. Andy didn't experience anything like the intensity of 1985 but he also saw the lights and commented on how striking and unusual they were.

Debbie had mixed feelings on the leap. There was real fear on arrival at the Flights even though she too was a good swimmer. There was also a sense that she didn't need to do it. The whole death-rebirth thing was already happening in her. On jumping, as she hit the water she felt part of herself was still standing back on the bank. At the very moment of this realisation, she was resurfacing. Swimming back to shore it seemed like something bit her ankle, causing her to flounder as she tried to get back on the bank. John helped pull her out. Beneath the water, Debbie had seen nothing but darkness. Walking away, she could now see huge fiery bonfires filling the heavens. Great bursts of white light were exploding all around at ground level as well. The very ethers were aflame as the rest of us leapt into the water. As the doors of perception were opening, we were setting the night on fire.

I was one of the last to take the big plunge. I had heard the sounds of the laughing ladies in the distance. It threw me back on the inevitable difference between our experiences due to that tiny little factor of my lack of swimming prowess. I put on the inflatable jacket whilst watching Alex jump in. On went the goggles. A moment I had been psyching up for months had finally arrived. I stood at the muddy edge of the dank, dark water, listening to the rushing weir and all of the voices in my head that had had ever said "no". Carlos Castaneda's *The Teachings of Don Juan* had stated that the first enemy of a man of knowledge is fear. I also recalled the scene at the end of his fourth book, *Tales of Power.* The whole thing is set up to climax so that Castaneda and a group of sorcerer's apprentices are required literally to leap off a cliff and fly on fibres of light they have been magically cultivating inside themselves. Did it really happen? To me, it was what it represented that mattered. I felt that in some way this was my own version of such a test and I was making a magical policy statement of intent to the unseen powers of Glastonbury. "This is how far I'm prepared to go, I'm prepared to do something that scares the shit out of me, that may even be physically harmful to me, this is how important this place is to me, this is a measure of what I believe about it."

I seemed to hesitate for an eternity but the outcome was never really in question. The whole experience was rapid, intense, and all encompassing. Sinking downwards through dark freezing water. No mind. Nothing for it to connect to. Nothing from the rational world of consensus symbols to make a map of understanding with. Raw, primal awareness. The return. Ascending upwards. Emerging from the waters and letting loose a mighty primal screaming. All of this synaesthetically simultaneous. One total experience.

There are some photos somewhere showing me curled up in a foetal ball by the edge of the water. John and Karl left me to recover and I came to conscious awareness of my state. I felt incredible. Totally cleared out, *"Agitated by an exceptional stir of heightened consciousness"*, as Powys put it. Vibrant. Throbbing with life. I gazed up at the night sky and thought of Nuit's words from *The Book of the Law, "I am above you and in you"*, *"bring the glory of the stars into the hearts of men"*. The *'lithe body'* of Nuit heaved and breathed with rippling stars as I had seen it do on acid. All of that and more, in non-linear synchronisation, as I walked back alone from the weir across darkened buzzing fields to the others by the parked cars.

It had been an evening of some small energy expenditure. After the intensity of the weir, a brief interlude was scheduled prior to resumption of an all-night itinerary. We drove into the centre of Glastonbury. Some were hoping the Indian restaurant might still be open and some food available. It was. The streets were deserted. It felt as if we were the only people on Earth and that the restaurant had materialised out of some other-worldly zone to meet our needs. John Horrigan and I weren't up for the curry challenge. We sat on the pavement over the road where John set up a primer stove to boil up some water for some pot-noodles we were going to share. A few of the others began to drift out after their meal. Our attention was suddenly focused by the sound of screeching brakes from the bottom of the High Street a few hundred metres away. We watched in amazement as a jeep mounted the pavement and crashed into a front door pillar of the *George and Pilgrim* hotel. Two figures leapt from the vehicle and legged-it up the road, soon passing us.

Our sense of reality was somewhat mutable at this point and it was difficult to assess the situation. Myself and John, with Kerry, Lisa, and Karl, decided to wander down and check it out. The obviously stolen jeep had taken a fair sized chunk of masonry out of the wall. A large drunken crowd of loud rowdy youths and middle-aged men had now assembled. They seemed to me to be a group of Powys and Hardyesque rustics rendered in nightlight by Bosch, Brueghel and Hogarth. Somehow they were collectively cohering through the magnetic attraction of the rapidly manifesting matrix of bizarre chaos.

A lone elderly rotund policeman, looking not unlike *Dixon of Dock Green*, was struggling to keep a semblance of order. It appeared as if he was about to be heaved through a shop window. At this point a man calmly walked up and asked us if we wanted a fight. We said "no thanks", and he turned away. The etiquette of such scenarios was somewhat different on Southend sea-front. It was clearly time to extricate ourselves from the volatile situation. The smallest of things could potentially take us badly off course. In the afterglow of my baptismal gnosis everything was still acid sparkly clear. It seemed only to be expected that, in the midst of such realities, the normal world could not be expected to be functioning normally.

Departing from the raucous scene, we retired to a place called Stone Down Hill in the vicinity of the Capricorn figure, anticipating a vigil likely to last until dawn. In early 1985 Bernard had picked up on a cave of some kind that was the entrance to a tunnel near sacred waters that led under the Tor and was guarded by Templars. There was a small pool near the cave. It was situated in a gully amidst boulders and trees. A woman named Eve sat under a tree by the pool. She pointed to the water. Below the rippling surface could be seen a round dark-red jewel stone set in a golden clasp that showed two serpents. Their necks intertwined with the heads facing in different directions, unlike the famous caduceus. At the bottom their tails spiralled together to form a point. A man wearing a grey cloak was then seen standing by the pool. This had been the first appearance of Americ de St. Maur. Soon he was joined by companions in rough plain clothes. The site was further identified as *'the place of the rising'*. The jewel somehow 'fixed' the site. The woman seemed to date from an earlier period to the Templars but there were tantalising hints of some sort of connection that were never expanded upon. Americ had said to Bernard that, "*It is told that the pool is the home of the priestess. That is all*".

This fitted in very nicely with a fragment in Katherine Maltwood's *Temple of the Stars* where she had mentioned that, "*It is thought the Knights Templars guarded the spring that flows forth at Paradise above Wick*". It has never been entirely clear where she got that idea. She went on to say that, "*its lovely valley might have been looked upon as the 'cave of the rising' (which according to ancient Akkadai, belonged to Capricornus)*". This is an even more obscure statement, but in 1985 Bernard had picked up on a *'place of the rising'* and this indicated a closer look was necessary, so Andy had put it into his itinerary then.

There were deeper and stranger resonances with and elaborations from Maltwood's work in Bernard's psychic material as well. In the Capricorn chapter of *Temple of the Stars* there is an odd section on *'King Arthur's Queen'*. She is identified with the stars of Hydra, the water snake. Maltwood refers to her as "*Queen of the Serpents*". A famous statuette of a Cretan snake priestess also gets a mention, leading into some etymological conjuring where the name Guen-ever links with Eve. Arthur's Queen supposedly, "*belonged to that earlier Water worshipping stock, which element was symbolized all over the world by snakes and women, in conjunction with the Pole Star Tree of Life*". I get a flavour of Dion Fortune's Atlantean Morgan here. It's all far too loose a sequence of associations surely? Hydra is nowhere near Capricorn. Its significant areas are closer to Leo and Virgo. Maltwood does dwell on Lancelot for that very reason. She only seems to place the reference at that point in the text to briefly refer to Hercules holding three heads of the hydra in later mythology and he is linked with the Sagittarius Arthur figure. One wonders whether Maltwood intuitively felt the need to mention a certain grouping of ideas in Capricorn but didn't really understand why. Bernard's snake priestess Eve by the pool by the tree also recalled the ongoing theme of the damsels of the wells, the ladies of sovereignty. Seeing Americ de St. Maur and his Templar group in that context was redolent with mystery. The whole package together was yet another potent magical glyph.

Maltwood's Glastonbury mythology also mentions the rising dawn sun shining through the entrance of the 'cave of the rising' and along a waterway tunnel to be visible out of the base of the Tor by Chalice Well. Its route is one of many Glastonbury collapsed tunnel tales. On the zodiac quest this tunnel serves as the path into Aquarius. We would enter it and emerge to greet an Aquarian phoenix resurrection dawn on the Tor.

We followed a public footpath through an area known as Paradise. Climbing over a stile in a path-side hedgerow dimly revealed through the darkness a great dip down into a field bounded by terraced slopes. We kept parallel with the higher path, edging our way down and round towards a lone tree near a muddy shallow pool by a mound in which the remains of some kind of wall could vaguely be discerned.

In 1985, after his death-like weir leap, Andy had spent a long cold wet vigil by the pool until dawn's twilight, waiting for the Templars to complete their own obscure business and leave. Americ de St. Maur as guardian of the doorway into Aquarius. We tried to visualise him and his Templar associates. Through the gently rippling waters of the pool could be seen the double caduceus jewel. It somehow represented the serpent of Eden. This place was the scene of the original temptation. The Templars began to fade from view. It was as if the scene at the spring was moving even further back in time. A snake priestess guardian could be seen at the water. She had long dark hair and was wearing a vertically divided red and blue dress. We stated our desire to seek entrance along the underground waterways from the cave of the rising to the Tor. The lady moved away to sit cross-legged at the base of the tree of knowledge.

New details supplied by Debbie completed the scene. She had anticipated the arrival of a unicorn, later to be followed by Merlin. The mythical beast approached. It was greeted by the lady. Capricorn is usually linked with a goat. Mary Caine, inspired by certain landscape features, favoured a Glastonbury unicorn, evoking royal heraldry and alchemy. Debbie felt that the animal had been somehow bound at the site and was unable to leave. We needed to sit-out a vigil of unknown length, probably until dawn. There was a sense that the snake priestess would leave when she felt we were ready. Time passed. It was the darkest hour before the first hints of dawn. Many of us were very near to sleep.

Suddenly Debbie saw the lady rise and walk away. As she did so,

Merlin walked into view by the tree. With his connections to the horned god, he was a more obvious Capricorn figure. The unicorn was to be set free. It galloped away across the hills, its white form and graceful motion vividly highlighted against the dark shades of the night landscape. The path it followed would lead to transformation and transmutation. Merlin then shape-shifted into a dragon-like being. Purple mist rapidly arose all around him. This called to mind the similar manifestation on New Year's Day. Gog and Magog were not that far away. The being spoke to Debbie. *"Go to the heights of Aquarius and release the soul of the dead king. Draw all four questing beasts to you; lion, unicorn, phoenix, griffin. Marry them. They wish to join for they are part of each other."* In conclusion, we visualised ourselves entering into a cave by the spring and tree which led into underground tunnels of water which we swam through in primal darkness until reaching the inside of the Tor, slowly rising upwards. We left Paradise in the hazy twilight of dawn's first stirrings.

The Tor was climbed by the shorter steeper path from Stone Down Lane. As we were ascending, the dawn chorus was beginning. It could be heard from all across the landscape out around beneath us. The way the beautiful sounds were subtly spread by differing distances and heights across a vast space by birds at rest and in motion was most striking. In my altered state there didn't seem anything random about it. It was a harmonious symphony of the very song of the Earth. The Tor summit was oddly deserted for the time of year. A few people drifted around, as if in slow motion. It was strange to recall that 48 hours previously myself and Alex had been at the same location in somewhat larger company.

Initially we returned to the dark waterways ascent. We broke through turf to climb out on the Tor top as the sun appeared on the horizon. As its rays reached the Tor, the hill was engulfed in a vast fire from which a giant golden phoenix arose into the sky. A griffin could now be seen flying through the air. It came down to land at one end of the summit. The phoenix descended to take up position opposite it. They rose up in the air facing each other, fading away. A red lion could then be seen making its way across the land, likewise the white unicorn we'd just set free. They were both of normal stature. Each climbed one of the two pathways up the Tor to meet on the summit, then rose up like heraldic devices, before stopping in frozen motion and dissolving. Debbie felt that some alchemical process had occurred, whereby the joining of the beasts had combined with the fire that we had ignited inside ourselves and then extinguished in the water. The ashes had together formed a rose that was somehow present in our Tor space at that moment but we had yet to fully come out of the winter.

That seemed to complete the group meditation. John, Kerry, Lisa and Karl started to walk back down the Tor to the parked cars. The rest of us lingered on the summit as a Powys sun began to appear above the horizon. "*Roaring, cresting, heaving, gathering, mounting, advancing, the enormous fire thoughts of the huge luminary surged resistlessly, evoking a turbulent aura of psychic activity.*" Debbie began to hear singing and music. Suddenly an old friend appeared. Trebor the follet! I suppose if there was anywhere in the country one could expect to encounter such a being it was here. This place was a supposed entrance to the underworld and its old lord Gwyn was the leader of the faery folk. Trebor was smaller than before. Sitting crouching as he had done in Cornwall, he had longer hair and wasn't wearing a helmet. It was great to know he was about but why had he appeared now? Our last encounter with him had led to the massive threshold crossing of the abbey pond apport. We asked him if he knew what we were up to and whether or not we were doing okay? A bunch of his mates appeared and the whole group laughed heartily at us. Trebor confirmed that we had to visit Chalice Well next. He also referred to the, "*song of the Fisher King*". When asked to explain, he would only say that, "*you cannot learn it yet*".

He beckoned Debbie to the edge of the summit and indicated that she should descend a little way down the side. Andy, Alex, and I followed her. Trebor halted at a piece of ground, about twenty feet down, where the soil was eroded by many rabbit holes. Debbie felt that he wanted her to dig into one of them. The angle of the slope was such that we were unable to stand and were therefore half sitting, half lying down. The whole of the side of the Tor we clung to was now bathed in golden sunlight. As she rolled her sleeve up to start digging out some earth, I moved my face as near to the action as possible and was looking at the whole scene with total focus from barely a few feet away, smelling the earth and slightly moist grass in the cool dawn air. After a few moments, something gold suddenly glinted in the rising sun's rays. Something that had been buried in the earth in the rabbit hole had been partly uncovered. Careful excavation revealed its full form. It was a tiny crucifix, barely an inch long. A gift from the faery folk on Glastonbury Tor! Trebor communicated that it was nothing specific to our zodiac quest but was a talisman of personal protection for Debbie. It was interesting that the denizens of Gwyn's underworld would make a present of a Christian artefact. I preferred to believe that the earliest saints of the so-called Celtic Church had been more in harmony with the elemental powers than the later miserable old gits personified by St. Collen. The event had a certain resonance with the crucifix that Bernard had found on Wimble Toot in 1984. It had been a most unusual day. Reality was not even a concept any more. I had jumped into a weir about six hours before. My brief glimpse of consensus was a blurred memory of a jeep crashing into a wall. It was dawn and I'd witnessed the uncovering of a prezzie from the little people.

A brief rest was now scheduled. There were a few hours before the immense second sequence began. Whilst the rest of the group adjourned to cars, Alex and I returned to the slopes of the Tor with our sleeping bags. If I did actually fall asleep, it barely registered. The immense non-ordinary impetus was too powerful to be tranquillised.

According to the Zodiac mythos, the Chalice Well is situated in the beak of the Aquarian phoenix. The great firebird is partaking of its alchemical waters. That morning we were amongst the first people in the gardens. The place usually induces some sort of reverie in me. After the night's entertainment I didn't exactly offer much resistance. An all-encompassing warm glow of sunlight through leaves, multi-coloured strongly fragrant flowers and the sounds of flowing waters and birdsong thoroughly permeated me. Our visualisation was short and simple. A bird took divine nectar from a grail chalice and flew off.

As we prepared to enter Pisces I realised that a truly profound delirium had set in. I was sitting in the back of John's car. I began to experience the well-known phenomenon of 'nodding'. I kept slipping into sleep. My head would suddenly nod forward and its movement send a shudder through my body that would jerk me back into wakefulness. This was happening repeatedly and with absurd rapidity. It seemed barely a second after twitching out from a slumping nod that I was nodding back again. It was probably as near to being simultaneously awake and asleep as I'd ever been in my life.

We departed slightly from the cosmic spiral course. There was a detail that Bernard had picked up on that was featured in *Perlesvaus* and seemed important to conform to. The Castle of King Fisherman had to be approached by crossing three bridges. There is a stretch of road that passes along the space between Glastonbury and the neighbouring town of Street. Within a few hundred yards or so there are three bridges that cross the River Brue and some rhyne dykes. If you're driving along that road, two of them are barely noticeable. Cars were parked up and we walked out to the edge of Street and turned back towards Wearyall Hill and Glastonbury. The Pisces effigies consist of two fishes. Wearyall Hill itself is one of them.

Once out of the car and walking, my nodding and twitching abated. I was aware of certain consensus co-ordinates. It was Saturday morning. Hectic busy traffic was rapidly rushing by. My sleep-deprived, reality-warped, heightened sensibilities were starting to distort its constant aural backdrop into some sort of semi synthesiser sound in the manner of the helicopters in *Apocalypse Now*. Three times we stepped off the side of the road, precariously picking our way down to the confined spaces beneath the bridges, to stand unsteadily on uncertain muddy, slippery, sloping footholds by the slowly running, somewhat stagnant waters, the rising smell of which blended with that of sodden earth into something faintly nauseous. The bridges shielded me from the traffic synth noise that slightly receded into the background as I tried to focus on the sound of the rhynes and river.

We did a visualisation under all of the bridges. Gradually everything was becoming a visualisation. On each occasion we tried to see a mighty river in full flow with no bridge across it. We had to create our own and clearly imagine ourselves to be walking over it in order to proceed. Any faltering meant a return to the bank to begin the task again. The first bridge was to be made of iron and represented the element of fire.

The second of the bridges is the most obvious of the three. It crosses the Brue, which we had thrown ourselves into further upstream on some distant occasion centuries beforehand. Glastonbury mythology links it with the very bridge from which Excalibur was cast away at the climax of the Arthurian story. Since late medieval times at least, it has been known as Pomparles or some variant thereof. For that reason, Andy and I had brought the duplicate Tintagel Meonia sword there the previous summer. It did require quite an effort of psychogeographical imagination to conjure up the magical aspects of the location from beyond its physical characteristics. Powys, from the vantage point of the bridge, had noted the, "*old cans, old pieces of rusty iron, drowned cats and dogs, human abortions, vegetable garbage, tramps' discarded boots, heads and entrails of fishes, brick-shards, empty tobacco tins, broken bottles, and so forth, which are to be seen sticking in the Brue-mud".* Things had improved a bit since the nineteen-twenties but it was easy to believe that he'd been an accurate observer. From Pomparles we crossed an airy bridge of ice.

The third bridge, of earth/stone, stands on the threshold of a site that came to represent for decades Glastonbury's tangible waste-land, the abandoned and ever more ruinous and melancholy Morlands industrial estate. Its immediate proximity to a site identified with the Fisher King's castle is perhaps a post-Powys example of the mythical personality of the landscape asserting itself. Emerging from under the bridge after our completed visionary crossing, we then turned to our right, proceeding on foot past the last of the row of houses known as Northover, and up a raised path in Roman Way onto the end of Wearyall Hill itself.

From there, we saw ourselves back at Pomparles, having just crossed the bridge. We wandered across fields to the former site of a small chapel of St. Brigit on top of a low mound. 'Celtic nuns' became visible as we approached. *If* there was ever a community of druidic women resident there as modern Glastonbury mythology asserts, they *may* have presided over the occasional Celtic sword offering unto the waters. A dim memory of that *might* have lingered as an influence on the Pomparles Bridge tales. We visualised St. Brigit, dressed in vibrant white, standing inside the chapel, by the altar. We sought her permission, as guardian of a sacred well at the doorway to Avalon, to enter the land of the Fisher King. With her blessing we returned to the bridge and looked towards the base of the hill, which had now transformed into a giant fish. As we moved forward, its gaping mouth closed around us. We began a journey down its darkened gullet to the palace of the Fisher King. Opening our eyes, we briefly looked out from the top of the hill across the landscape, noticing both Bride's Mound and the desolate Morlands site, before preparing to drive along to the other, more famous end of Wearyall Hill, to meet the Fisher King.

We reconvened by the Holy Thorn. Sitting comfortably on that gradually warming and brightening morning, refreshed by the gentlest of breezes, we took in perhaps the definitive Glastonbury view. From just a little way further up the hill behind the thorn, it's possible to see the thorn itself, the Tor, Chalice Hill, and the abbey ruins. I feel it may be the most condensed mythic panorama able to be fitted in a single visual field available anywhere in Britain. Thus fortified and inspired, we entered into the internal landscape of the hill. It was significantly different to the realm of the little people seen on the previous New Year's Eve.

At first, we were moving again down through the dimly lit ribbed wet passage ever deeper inside the devouring fish. Our path was suddenly halted by the appearance of an entrance to an old dark castle with an open door. Along empty cold stony corridors, echoing with our footsteps, we continued. A thick wooden door was pushed open to reveal a chamber lit by a shaft of light from above, although no obvious window indicated its source.

The place was like the belly of a huge fish in which was situated a medieval throne room. Rounded connecting corridors had green/red ribbed ridged walls. The beam shone directly down over the sad old wise weary figure of the Fisher King, seated on a stone throne. The guardian of springtime had long white hair and wore a plain white robe, which starkly highlighted blood that was slowly trickling from a wound in his thigh down onto the ground. In this form he was destined to die and we had to let him but we needed his permission to continue the quest. He asked us to wait with him for a while. The air rippled as he transformed into the green man. Behind the king a veil hung across the chamber. The light revealed hints of human shapes behind it. A sublime angelic chanting began to sound from its direction. Debbie saw five women enter the throne room from the left. A larger procession of males appeared from the right. There were old men at the front and younger behind, carrying the Grail hallows. One held a bell which he slowly struck, its tone echoing around the huge ribbed room. It was the cue for strange haunting music to fill the chamber. It sounded like it was being played on some kind of medieval harpsichord. Debbie intuitively knew that this was the 'Fisher King's Song' she had been told of on the Tor. It was somehow the sound of the transition from one era to another. In this case, not the current entry into Aquarius, but the previous one into the Piscean Christian age. There was also an accompanying chant from the procession. The words were not immediately clear. They kept trying to return and be understood. Years later, in a Scottish Grail chapel, Debbie finally fully heard them.

"The head of the King is the seat of all knowledge.
The knowledge is the Grail. The Grail is the word.
The word is the vine.
The vine is the land, the land is the King.
The head of the King is the seat of all knowledge."

The male procession halted before the green king, presenting the Grail to him. Without drinking from it, he dematerialised, leaving the Grail on the throne. It was a small simple vessel with no jewelled decoration but it was continually changing colour; gold, red, blue, and green. Then from within it, came a kind of waterspout out of which the shape-shifting monarch returned in the form of a kingfisher, flying around the room and then out into the sky, as the voice of the Fisher King could be heard saying, *"follow me and your spirits will be regained for I am their pathway"*. The bird flew off across a blooded desolate wasteland as the music and chanting faded.

The Celtic head theme had been a recurring presence in the journey. There had been Golgotha Dundon, the radiant brow on the place of the skull. We'd been through a death-rebirth immersion at the head of the king. A bird flew forth from his forehead. Now the Rich Fisher Brons, who called to mind archaic Bran, most famous of British severed heads, had likewise taken flight. The infamous Baphomet of the Templars was probably somewhere in there as well.

In Street churchyard we made the move from Pisces to Aries. This involved imagining re-crossing the three bridges in reverse sequence. From there we followed Maltwood's *Perlesvaus* topography but with an alteration of the chief protagonist. We substituted Gawain for Lancelot. John had strongly taken on the aspect of Gawain all year and we had only recently returned from a memorable episode where he led a quest through Gawain's most famous adventure, the saga of the Green Knight and the beheading test. An interestingly similar test featured in the upcoming section of *Perlesvaus.*

It began with us imagining entering into a forested area where we saw the armoured form of Messire Gawain riding on horseback ahead of us. We followed behind him. He led us deep inside the woods to a mighty citadel protected by huge walls with '*one entrance thereinto'*. A large gate became visible. Maltwood locates it at Portway on the neck of the effigy. It opened to allow us inside the city. Gawain was greeted by rapturous cheers, accompanied by bagpipe and flute music, as he neared the central court. Again Maltwood is very specific. The *Piper's Inn* on the road to Ashcott marks the location for that. The crowd hailed him as their new king. He refused the crown, feeling that some greater spiritual destiny was his true path. In pursuit of that aim, he turns towards a small church. John clearly saw a doorway in a church beckoning at that point.

This Wall-Town of *Perlesvaus* is Walton, near Street on the back of the Aries lamb. The church there was our next location. Gawain was seen approaching the building, dismounting and entering. He strode up to the altar and unhesitatingly prostrated himself before it. He was laying on the sacrificial Lamb of God and in so doing becoming part of it. It was time for a confession of sins, an unburdening of the past. We all took on the process but John physically knelt before the altar, taking communion as Gawain. The cup and wafer gave union with the blood of land, lamb and Christ.

The archer who earlier fired the blazing arrow reappeared. He became the green knight. To him, Gawain again renounces kingship. This sets in motion the beheading test. The green knight brought his axe down upon Gawain's neck, misses the target and throws the weapon down. The whole group had mentally offered themselves as sacrifices at this point. This was not needed but a purging of some kind still awaited in Taurus. We departed seeing fields of corn surrounded by a wasteland and mist. Such was the state of the land after the death of the king. April rain started falling, beginning the process of the healing of the land.

A crossroads at a place named Marshall's Farm leads from Aries into Taurus. The ridge of Compton Dundon woods forms most of its bull effigy that consists of just the head, neck and front paws. A tall pillar monument has been nicely placed where the horn would begin. It's a memorial to Sir Samuel Hood, describing him as, "*Baronet knight of the most honourable order of the bar and nominated grand cross bearer of knight of Saint Ferdinand and of merit, knight grand cross of the sword, Vice Admiral of the white and Commander in Chief of his Majesty's fleet in the East Indies*" and more besides. He died in 1814. It's fairly clear that he moved in strange Masonic type circles. One can only wonder what his family may have believed about the local landscape and its history.

In 1985 Andy, on his own Grail journey, noticed that the site of the bull's eye was a place called Tray's Farm. The word is very near to the widespread 'Troy' which often occurs in the vicinity of turf mazes and labyrinths. The most famous labyrinth tale is that of the Minotaur, a creature most appropriate to the area of Taurus. It suggested to Andy the need to confront one's personal Minotaur in the labyrinth. The force symbolised by the Minotaur needed to be externalised and triumphed over. This would involve identifying to some extent with the hero Theseus and seeking the guidance of Ariadne who laid a thread for him to follow back out. In a clearing Andy found great lengths of bunched up vine that called to mind Ariadne's thread. He collected some to mark his path in and out of the woods.

In 1990, we tried to repeat the process of the transmutation through externalisation of our shadow selves. This meant acknowledging one's deepest strangest aspects and visualising them as somehow embodied, perhaps as a beast or picture of Dorian Gray. Things would emerge that were better left behind. They would probably try and get straight back in. Other oddities maybe just need to be looked at a bit differently. In this bizarre psychodrama the relationship to the shadow side of the psyche would hopefully change for the better, freeing up energy and enabling us to finally move beyond the underworld part of the journey that had been a fairly constant theme. So the pathways through the woods became our labyrinth. We all went off alone to find a place that felt comfortable to do it.

The encounter with the Minotaur finally completed the sequence of underworld shadow side experiences. The climax of the quest now beckoned. From there we needed to listen for the sound of the bell of Solomon's ship. Where on a bull's head would one listen for a bell? On its ear, which lies on the wooded slopes around the Hood monument, looking out across to the area of Argo Navis. Debbie began to hear pipe music and the slow tolling of a heavy bell. A number of the group could hear the wind starting to sound like waves on the sea.

Bernard had said that Robert de St. Clere failed the 1285 quest in this vicinity. He had made a mistake concerning the bell of the ship. The obvious thing to do having first heard it would be to then head for the site of the bell itself, a place now occupied by Hurst's Farm near Dundon Beacon. Robert was ambushed for the second time as a result of this wrong turn. In 1985 Andy realised that Theseus retraced his path back out of the labyrinth. The Taurus effigy is out of place within the perimeter circle of the rest of the effigies. It was necessary to return back out of Taurus and into Aries, thus rejoining the circle and then connect to the Argo Navis at Walton Drove below Walton Hill where Maltwood seems to refer to the coming of the ship from across King Sedgemoor.

It was appropriate that it was by a monument to an Admiral, topped by a carved ship, that we turned our attention to the majestic Ship of Solomon. We saw the sky as if the sun had just set, full of afterglow hues across dramatic clouds. A pinpoint of darkness, coming out of the horizon, silhouetted against it, was moving very slowly towards us. A slow tolling bell reverberated from it across the waters through the sound of their lapping. A number of the group heard the bell very clearly, along with the waves and the smell of sea air.

In 1985 Andy Collins had moved from the Hood monument to sit at the foot of Walton Hill in the pouring rain, looking out across the drove and rhynes that make up the figure of the Argo Navis Cancer ship, waiting to hear its bell again. He eventually heard it three times, coming from the direction of Kings Sedgemoor. With this came a vision of a great sea shrouded in mist. Above the distant horizon was a faint golden glow. From it slowly emerged an intense white light, the first indication that the ship was on its way. This was similar to Perceval's first glimpse of it in *Perlesvaus.*

The boat eventually pulled up and docked. Andy felt beckoned towards it and jumped over a gate to enter a field where he could see it waiting. Again he paused to try and psychically connect to the scene more strongly. A gang-plank was lowered. He boarded the vessel. We were taken through the same sequence of events, leaving the shoreline of Walton Hill with our parked cars behind to sail into the last signs of the coloured sunset the boat had appeared from. Debbie saw the whole sky on fire and in motion.

In 1985, Andy was in unknown territory. He had the *High History*, Katherine Maltwood, and Bernard to guide him up to a certain point. Beyond that he was on his own. A lot of the quest had already covered new ground. The climax was impossible to predict. I already knew, up to a point, what was coming. It had been two years since I'd first heard the story. Would the preparation and extreme vision quest conditions be sufficient to produce the unexpected?

From that moment, in 1985 and 1990, a number of sites were visited as the ship progressed towards its ultimate destination. In 1985, the appearance of the ship had begun a complete mutation of reality for Andy. He started to see it serenely sailing across the sea-like fields whilst he was driving along from site to site in his car. Lisa saw it in the same way in 1990, with her eyes open. It took quite a bit of effort to get to some of the next sequence of locations. We wandered through farmyards and up on hills. Things blurred more and more. It was the gaps between the visualisations that were beginning to seem dreamlike.

We kept up the pace until the early evening and then retired for some sleep with the intention of trying to somehow stay on the ship through the night. If we awoke at any time, the idea was to try and immediately recall the ship imagery and that the journey was still in motion. We were back up at 3am, heading out to an orchard near

Butleigh, for a recapitulation of the whole journey on the boat, up along the three bars of its mast to our final destination, the enclosure of the sun, the Zodiac's inner temple. By the time of the final session, Andy combined the details of the ship as he had seen it in 1985 with the glimpses Debbie had just seen as it approached. Solomon's vessel was blending with Arthur's death barge and his ship Prydwen in the kind of Celtic/medieval mix typical of *Perlesvaus.* It was on this extraordinary vessel that we undertook the climactic visionary journey, each of us taking the role of the Grail hero(ine) Gemini babe on the boat. I was mindful of a Gnostic design reproduced in one of Israel Regardie's books showing the infant Horus Harpocrates child on a boat displaying the forefinger to the lips gesture seen in Crowley's Aeon tarot card.

The ship was made of wood, coloured red, white and green, taken from Eve's Tree of Knowledge. Its tall mast had a large sail depicting the upward pointing Druidic awen arrowhead. A carved griffin's head adorned the prow. The bow was tall and pointed, the galley wide and flat. On a raised cubic edifice at the rear stood a male figure holding a staff who flickered between two forms; Merlin, cowled, robed in black, holding a staff, and Solomon in golden finery. Down on the deck, laid out on plinths, were two dead bodies, Arthur and Dindraine. Nearby, the nine Queens of Narguelles, in cowled brown and blue robes, sat cross-legged in a circle around a copper cauldron of Annwn. Some of them seemed to flicker in and out of view, between realities. *"The shape of cancer is the cauldron of Annwn. It cradles the babe of Gemini. It is maternal. It is the moon, the womb and the tomb. It is the end and the beginning."* The most important of the women was the Lady Vivienne, the ultimate healer. Her cowl fell back, revealing her pale skin and long straight strawberry hair. She held out a hand, a small flickering flame dancing on the palm. It communicated something of that Annwn underworld, to which the cauldron gave entrance, *"the fire of that hell is healing"*.

Out of the sea ahead, a gigantic waterspout appeared, more than a thousand feet tall, rapidly taking the form of a three-sided aquamarine coloured tetrahedron pyramid of ice-like light. As we approached, it seemed as if it was made of crystal. The ship passed through into it. As the new realm was entered, the ship imagery vanished, although the feeling of being on it remained. All was aquamarine, with the exception of a vertical pillar of light around me. Three shafts of horizontal pulsing orange lightning fire suddenly shot towards a common source in a faint red glow in the distance ahead. One moved through me, marking my path. Two moved to my right. As I went more deeply into the zone, all that remained of the boat and the column was the sense of moving in a small vehicle of light. Apart from that and the three shafts, everything else had now become a dark void. The destination was the land of the Grail. The darkness began to recede as the source of the three converging shafts came nearer.

The white light I was travelling in came to be perceived as the soul bird, the dove of spirit, carrying me forward into the centre of the shining golden orange void of the land of the Grail. The three rays of orange lightning became white light rays flowing from behind the wings and tail of the bird, each emanating one of three divine tones. The bird seemed to somehow land, vanishing as it did so. Now, from its centre, the golden orange space could be seen as configured in the form of a large triangle. There were pillars of light at each corner. Red, emerald-green, white. Each pillar contained a Grail maiden who governed four signs of the zodiac. The one in the red pillar carried a copper chalice. Green had a silver one. White had gold. The pillars disappeared. The women floated towards the centre, drifting through golden orange light. They blended together as one white lady with a singular Grail. She was asked who it serves? The answer came back in a strong voice, "LIFE", as shimmering, she dissolved into a column of light. Powerful, pulsating, it moved forwards, engulfing me. All other imagery had gone. Below my feet, a brief vision of a huge crystal rose opened a vortex that I fell spiralling down into, aware that the soul bird of earlier on had reappeared above and was rapidly descending with me. As I landed, it passed right down through me. Suddenly I was in a vast crystal lattice with thousands of triangular shaped facets. Looking at them, I saw myself reflected in each. The visions then changed into multitudinous glimpses of the past of the Zodiac and potential futures. The crystal visions faded with the feeling of being thrust into a great void of interstellar darkness. I could hear a low tonal humming drone, soon joined by two other notes, medium and higher. Blobs of light began to appear around me. Everything stopped. There was a deep red humming light directly in front of me. I entered into and joined it. Back to primal creation. The point where all minds are one, where all is one in this and all other universes and dimensions.

At the climax of the journey we were left to our own experience. I allowed myself to accept whatever reverie arose. I did not want to bring my normal mind into the situation. I wasn't disappointed. A supremely satisfying Glastonbury vision overwhelmed me. I sobbed with joy. The exact form of it will be revealed further on in the narrative. Gradually I came back to something resembling normal consciousness in the growing dawn light. My feet and the bottom of my trousers were soaked through standing in tall grass in the dew. Looking blearily around, the first thing I noticed was that Debbie was lying flat on her back in the wet with her eyes open and entirely vacant. She remained that way for quite a while. It would be a number of years before we both realised the extent of the differing downloads we'd both received.

She was able to share one portentous detail with us at the time. At the point in the final sequence when the bird had appeared amidst the converging three light rays, Debbie had started to hear a strange chanting accompanied by high pipe music. The repeating words had sounded something like "wool mo sarra". The bird was the Libran dove. Zodiac critics have had a problem with it. Firstly it's not the usual depiction associated with the sign. In the planispheric overlay, the stars of Libra don't even fall on the bird. They're in the Scorpio figure. Mary Caine mentions that it is actually the seven stars of Ursa Major that are contained in the bird. According to her, the Chaldeans called the constellation, *"Wul mo sarra"*, meaning "The Lord, Voice of the Universe", Wul being a form of Bel. Typically enough, she gives no reference for this information. I knew Debbie enough to be certain that she had never read this odd obscure detail. Why then would she pick up a supposed chant to this particular Babylonian deity as we reached the climax of our journey?

We had supposedly travelled along an equinoctial line from Taurus tuned to Babylonian New Year 2700 BC. Our final destination had seen us at the centre of the royal star cross. As Maltwood had said in *Enchantments*, quoting clay tablets, Marduk, *'instituted the year and divided it into twelve months in order that all the gods should have their image visible in the sky'*. The bell of the ship had invoked Bel. That seemed fairly straightforward. It would later turn out to be a lot more complicated.

We all returned to the guest-house for a few hours sleep. On awaking, I immediately wrote down as much of my dawn reverie as possible. It was vital to get it whilst it was still fresh and I remained in an altered state. As we shall see, I would later be extremely grateful that I had made that effort. In '85 Andy had likewise spent the morning after the completion of the quest writing down his immediate thoughts that undoubtedly showed something of the morphogenesis flavour of the Egyptian Crystal Chambers material. "*The Grail is but a superficial image created in a modern age. The true Grail is a multi-dimensional crystalline complex that forms the blueprint to cosmic order and form, from the centre of the universe, the moment of the big bang. It includes all life in this universe, its influence setting the standards of life for a cycle of time. It is the co-ordinator of the cosmic pulse of life and exists on many levels, the heartbeat of the world, it's a cosmic computer, controller of the destinies of Time.*"

At crucial times in the unfolding of the time spiral, some of the world's sacred sites open to allow new influences to re-encode the planetary matrix for the new dispensation. Now is such a time, hence the revealing of the Glastonbury Zodiac, the call of the Giza plateau. In '85, Andy had written, "*These heart/brain/minds of the Earth are not natural. They are representative of the central creative source of the universe and were placed here by beings who attained the stage of light millions of years ago. Cultures are co-ordinated to perpetuate the influence of their particular spheres, continually updating the existing imagery and archetypes, thus ensuring the quest can still be taken. This also serves the secondary purpose of a symbolic representation in imagery, stories and traditions of the cycles of the seasons, the cosmos and man himself, thus providing a place of learning.*" The "beings who attained the stage of light" were named by Andy as *Morphians*. Over the coming decades he would periodically ponder over what they might be. The medieval layer of site memory was the last major update, hence its powerful lingering presence.

After a late breakfast we drove into Glastonbury and visited the church of St. John the Baptist in the High Street. It was actually his main feast day, June 24th, so it was yet another severed head acknowledgement. The place is best known for a cutting of the Holy Thorn in the churchyard and its stain glass window depiction of Joseph of Arimathea. I'd got some good mileage out of the postcard reproduction I'd bought back in 1985. After a Grail quest it seemed only proper to pay our respects to the figure who had first associated Glastonbury with the Grail, whatever the historical reality behind it could be said to be. As we moved to stand in front of the window, Debbie noticed a piano. She mentioned that she could still remember the 'Fisher King's song' that she'd heard on Wearyall Hill and could probably play it. The church seemed empty so we encouraged her to go for it. Fortunately there were two tape recorders on hand to record the moment for posterity.

Piano sounds filled the building. Cold shivers tingled all over me. This was something very special. It affected me like the piano music of Gurdjieff. I had no doubt that it had come from a very high level of inspiration. None of us suspected it would one day be heard in an American cathedral.

That afternoon I returned to the Tor top with Alex, Andy, and Debbie, for what proved to be a moving finale. Debbie felt something was imminent so we sat down to tune in. Anthony Roberts appeared to her. He was dressed in green and embodying something of site guardian, primordial Gwyn. On New Year's Day Andy had received the gift of the dragon sight. This had helped the whole group somehow in our odyssey into the mythic matrix of Britain. It was apparently now needed by someone else. An offer was made to exchange it for what was termed the 'Heart of Avalon'. Andy accepted. Debbie could see Tony Roberts now standing directly in front of Andy offering him a bright orange rose. At this point all of us could detect a unique aroma in the air that was a mix of orange and rose! Andy took it with thanks, being told it could take us directly to Glastonbury whenever it was necessary. One day it would also need to be passed on.

We asked the author of *The Dark Gods* about the state of Glastonbury. Was anything happening that was out of balance with how it should be? Had the passionate idealist found further causes to uphold on the other side? He simply said, "let it be". It was appropriate we were told no more at that point. It was necessary to assimilate the initial impact of the Zodiac journey. We would soon have our own answers to the first question. In conclusion Andy asked for a sign of confirmation and we departed.

The 'sign' came a few days later when Andy and Debbie walked into their living room first thing in the morning to find an orange rose, fresh with dew, inexplicably positioned on the floor. None of the neighbouring gardens as viewed from the perspective of Andy's first-floor windows seemed to contain such a specimen. One would later be located at the Chalice Well. It was a mysterious process but something of the qualities it seemed to represent would soon be needed to help us through a definite *Dark Gods* Glastonbury episode.

On the tiring journey home from the zodiac quest I enjoyed speculating about how far out the ripples in the cosmic pond extended if part of us really had stepped beyond spacetime. What effect did it have on the past and future? Might some lake village coracler have caught a perplexing glimpse of Solomon's ship and the tetrahedron? Might our activities have given strange twinges, nights of not quite remembered dreams for Dion Fortune and Frederick Bligh Bond? If some archaic mighty magicians of the landscape really had created the Glastonbury star temple might they have intuited our presence? Did we even potentially affect its creation?

The feature in the *New Musical Express* on Andy had been part of the backdrop to our Glastonbury journey. I was sure it would get some kind of significant response, especially following on from our reality-smashing endeavours. It came in July. A publisher contacted Andy after seeing the piece. He was commissioned to produce a book that would tell the Green Stone story in greater detail than ever before and follow through into our own work on Meonia. It was a task that would increasingly occupy him in the coming months. *The Seventh Sword* would be published just over a year later. The book would only mention Glastonbury in passing but its existence seemed to have subtly emerged from the ripples following the zodiac quest.

This highlighted a bigger issue of timing and sequence as well. After the climax of his 1985 experiences Andy had written of '*The true Grail*', *"its influence setting the standards of life for a cycle of time". "Cultures are co-ordinated to perpetuate the influence of their particular spheres, continually updating the existing imagery and archetypes, thus ensuring the quest can still be taken."* He had come to feel that his completion of the Glastonbury Zodiac quest had prepared him to enter the matrix and potentially help update the program. Once he was ready, the full seven sword quest was activated when the Paddon swords were found in August 1985. To emphasise the connectedness, it was the TV screening of a feature on Andy talking about the Zodiac that had helped set everything in motion.

* * *

FROM HELL

"Through the darkness of futures past,
The magician longs to see.
One chants out between two worlds,
Fire walk with me."
Twin Peaks. Bob.

"It can generate madness and death as easily as it can produce tranquillity and revelation."
Glastonbury: Ancient Avalon New Jerusalem.
Anthony Roberts.

"'What none of you people in Glastonbury seem to understand,' Mr Evans went on now, 'is that the place is charged and soaked with a desperate invisible struggle.'"
A Glastonbury Romance. John Cowper Powys.

"Was this any more than a local conspiracy? Or is the cycle even now turning on us? As the century dies will another pattern of sacrifice be demanded? Do we slowly begin to understand only because we are about to become performers in the same blind ritual?"
White Chappell Scarlet Tracings. Iain Sinclair.

THE QUEST FOR THE SEVENTH 'BLACK' SWORD remained a major concern of ours. Since early 1990 Debbie had been picking up snippets about its history. Masonic lodges and neo-Templar groupings whose personnel and influences travelled back and forth between Britain and France were a consistent feature. Some of this material and the research it stimulated would be included in the *Prophets of Hell* chapter in *The Seventh Sword.*

In July there was more and it led to one of our more perplexing adventures. Dion Fortune had suggested a profound mysterious relationship exists between Glastonbury and London. In some ways it was like the heart and head of the British body-politic. Forms brewed and built up in Glastonbury manifested through London. The pilgrimage route of the Great West Road, eloquently discussed in *Avalon of the Heart,* served as an external indicator of some psychic arterial connection. This idea would remain somewhere in the back of my mind during what followed.

The mixture of material seemed fragmentary on one level.

Attempts to establish linear causality between its apparently disparate elements were not possible. Something else was happening though. There was a unity there, in another realm that could be intuited by the nightside of the mind. It was part of the arising of a magical realm that was prophetic of things that were to come a year further on.

During the 19th century, so Debbie said, a number of occult mystical groups turned their attention towards Glastonbury. At the centre of activities were enthusiasts of the British Israelite movement, a loose affiliation that shared in common a belief that the British are the descendants of the Lost Tribes of Israel. This was an idea that had been present somewhere in the background of British esotericism for a long time but came strongly to the surface in the 19th century.

Some of the British Israelites were well-connected and considered themselves to be spiritual visionaries of Britain's global mission. Certain groups monitored and infiltrated their circles to manipulate the mythology to their own ends and work other influences into the current. Just as in the present day, ideas and people moved between groups that shared at least a little common ground. British Israelites and Druid revivalists could find things to talk about with the kind of Qabalistic enthusiasts who would make up Golden Dawn lodges. Freemasonry often served as the meeting place. Gnosticism and Neo-Templarism were in the air. In this, the French took a leading role.

Debbie believed that Dundon Beacon was considered to be extremely important. It was another strand in the Golgotha mystery that Andy had first encountered back in 1983 at the start of his Zodiac adventures. In July, she repeated and expanded on material from a few weeks before. Dundon had been a Druid site. Many have died there. There were rites involving drinking a potion based on apples out of skulls. A ring of skulls on poles had circled the base of the hill. The medieval imagery repeated most evocatively. There was the knight in the sepulchre cave again. He hadn't got the power to hold the sword much longer. The programme was exhausted. Soon the sword would slip from his hands. We had to be there to catch it because Andy had already approached him once so he would not refuse.

There were British Israelites who saw Glastonbury as the New Jerusalem and heart of Britain. Dundon was Golgotha and contained the Holy Sepulchre. Some of the medieval knowledge had lingered amongst esoteric coteries. French influence from a group called the Ordre du Temple was involved. Dundon would play a crucial role in the preparation for the Second Coming of Christ.

Property was secured in the vicinity. An extraordinary clandestine project was begun to equip the cave that existed in the heart of the hill as a new Temple of Solomon. A chequerboard floor was laid down. French Gnostic occultists brought some items they believed had come from Britain in the Middle Ages and needed to be returned. Amongst them was a sword that had belonged to a leading Templar who had some connection with the Rennes Le Chateau area. The persistent image of the recumbent knight was due to the presence of a real pickled one as per the Danbury St. Clere. He was a Templar. There was a 'Pillar of Jacob' and a representation of the Crown of Thorns. The seven twigs of the crown were in some way linked with the seven swords. And with this came the feeling that the black sword had been physically present. It was connected with the Gnostic Ordre de Temple. Debbie was convinced that the hill was full of tunnels. She even expanded existing Glastonbury mythology by talking of other extensive tunnels linking Zodiac sites. Somehow all of this activity was able to happen without the general populace having any knowledge of it. These were wild ideas that no research was able to back up but something about the scenario was magically compelling.

Debbie thickened the plot by speaking of a Masonic-inspired magical order known as the Knights of David formed in nearby Bath. They believed that the Jewish monarch was the first true divine king. Their conception of his beliefs was a tad unusual. He worshipped a primal deity named Saloman who created the earth from volcanic fire and was the first god of magic. His rites involved fire and blood. A variant of his name was given to the man who founded the famous temple that was being reconfigured. Melchizedek was in the blend as well. Some members of the Knights of David were part of the Dundon operation. Others were active in London.

A legendary figure in Meonia mythology was John Newton Langley. He had appeared in psychic material from the Green Stone days right through into the Seventh Sword quest. Research identified him as a real person from the 19th century although any occult links could not be established. His image will be familiar to readers of the Phillips and Keatman *Eye of Fire*. A photograph was taken at Brinklow Hill in Staffordshire that when developed showed an image of a dark silhouetted form of an archetypal male Victorian figure wearing a long cape and top hat. Langley was the bad guy, a representative of an ancient grouping of international occultists known for convenience in Green Stone mythology as the Wheel. He had been responsible for destroying the Victorian Meonia group through malevolent magic and machinations, gaining possession of the black sword. As well as living in Wolverhampton, the major scene of his battles with Meonia, it was discovered that he later lived in Bristol, easily within travelling distance of Glastonbury.

Debbie believed that Langley had associations with the 19th century's most notable prophet of hell, Eugene Vintras. After a bizarre encounter in 1839 with an old man who Vintras believed was the Archangel Michael, he decided that he was the prophet Elijah reborn and began proclaiming that medieval favourite, the imminent dawning of the age of the Holy Spirit which would involve the 'reign of love'. What this meant became a tad controversial. Accusations of mass nudity in church services soon arose. There was talk of a strange masturbatory prayer and homosexuality. It was, as Eliphas Levi said in *The History of Magic*, *"like the orgies of the old Gnostics"* or something from the medieval golden age of wacko heresies portrayed in *The Pursuit of the Millennium*.

Things were a bit intense in the prophet's head. On one occasion he had seen all around him, *"an abyss full of hideous monsters who called me brother"*. He called on the Virgin Mary for help and she duly appeared. *"Her eyes of heavenly blue were filled with fire, her red lips were violet, her mild and divine voice had become terrible and like a thunderbolt she hurled these words at me: 'writhe, proud one, in the burning regions inhabited by devils'."*

Although the great French magus Levi was far from impressed, Vintras was widely considered to be quite a preacher, attracting a large following that included members of the upper echelons of society. Wild paranormal phenomenon allegedly accompanied his liturgical performances. Blood appeared on consecrated hosts and out of previously empty chalices. The fact that Vintras wore an inverted cross during services was the icing on the cake. Of course he was excommunicated. The resulting independent church had both male and female priests. To make matters even worse he had strange political beliefs, supporting a figure claiming to be the true king of France. Vintras ended up in prison. On his release the heretic decamped to London for a decade before finally returning to France.

Debbie believed that Vintras had been in possession of the black sword. It was stolen from him by a woman who brought it to the British Meonia group. He met Langley in London, possibly informing him of the black sword business, and was active in the Midlands at places that featured in Meonia material such as Ranton and Combe Abbey, meeting up with representatives of other groupings such as German Rosicrucians.

So was Vintras on the dark side of the force? In some circles he is revered as an important figure in the Gnostic revival. A peculiar little episode demonstrated our conscious ambiguity around black sword issues. I can only mention the briefest of details. Andy and Debbie came into contact with a most unusual vicar somewhere in Essex. This guy was vibing way beyond the standard C of E dullard. He was packing some Holy Spirit power for certain. Debbie came to feel he was the reincarnation of Vintras! Andy, in typical manner, told him this. Amazingly enough he kind of took it on board. The questing group actually attended one of his services and took communion from him. I'm entirely happy to think of a possible Vintras reincarnation making the sign of the cross on my forehead with holy water.

Langley managed to somehow involve himself with the Knights of David. He visited Dundon on a few occasions. Power struggles ensued. Langley gained possession of the black sword and removed it. Whether this was through outright theft was unclear.

Onto the scene came Meonia hero William Burges. He had associations through a wealthy patron with another Masonic Templar order, the Knights of the Holy Sepulchre. These guys were extremely rich, and serious in their intent. A candidate had to travel to Jerusalem to be initiated. With their interests it's no surprise that word of the Dundon project reached them along with dodgy dealings around it.

A bit of an occult tussle ensued. It was possible that Bernard's 1989 psychic vision of William Burges and his companions working magic with the Tintagel sword at Glastonbury locations may have been linked. It could have been some kind of counter-balance to Langley's use of the black sword. It was believed that the two swords were both relics of an 18th century casting and were older than the others in the current set. They were the fundamental power holders, functioning at different extremes of the spectrum. The Knights of the Sepulchre briefly retrieved the sword from Langley again. Quite what this involved on a human level remained obscure. The sword seemed to do a bit of a yo-yo back and forth between the two sides until crossing the channel back to France towards the end of the 19th century.

At the same time, the great Dundon Beacon project was abandoned. The temple was closed down. The cave remains along with some of the artefacts that had been gathered there. Something of the knowledge and associations had lingered amongst the people who had allegedly been involved in Templar style activities in Glastonbury in the eighties. Tim Henry wasn't specifically mentioned this time but the feeling was that a few of the people he knew may have been aware of events a century earlier. Debbie was sure that the black sword had been back in the Glastonbury area during the eighties, perhaps even during the time of Andy's Zodiac adventures. Whether those in possession of it knew its provenance was unclear.

During July 1990, as the Dundon Langley material was appearing, there had also been further attention given to his time in London. Other 19th century strands from the capital began to intrude. The Jack the Ripper murders began surfacing in psychic material that had a Meonia slant on it. I had been aware of ideas suggesting royal and Masonic connections to the crimes for a long time. The most famous portrayal of the themes was in Stephen Knight's *Jack the Ripper: the Final Solution,* which had in turn inspired Alan Moore's legendary graphic novel *From Hell.*

Most conducive to my own temperament though was the material produced by poet novelist Iain Sinclair in *Lud Heat* on the architect of some notable London churches, Nicholas Hawksmoor. Five of these buildings, dating from the reconstruction after the great fire of 1666, and expressing all manner of Masonic and Aegyptian influences, lie in an allegedly deliberate pentagramic configuration anchoring an arcane matrix of powerful influences that have called forth murder and mayhem over the years. The last and most hideous of the Ripper's murders was committed in the immediate proximity of a Hawksmoor church. When Debbie began picking up on some of this flavour I pointed Andy in the direction of Sinclair's material. Before long, Langley was stalking the streets near the Hawksmoor churches. The ghostly Brinklow photograph was a classic archetype of the Ripper after all. There are no definite sightings of the Victorian killer, only a few possible glimpses. None of them conform to the now standard mythic image.

The spooky thing about this was that it wasn't just Debbie who was picking up on this stuff. The London psychic Helen, who Andy had played out his notable 1979 Crowley episode with, had reappeared on the scene in 1989. A strong sequence of black questing had occurred after she had read *The Black Alchemist.* Quite a lot of these adventures are featured in *The Second Coming.* It had all been a bit much and she had departed again but during 1990 she occasionally surfaced. A considerably unpleasant Ripper scenario followed which is beyond the scope of this narrative. Suffice it to say that she identified Langley as definitely involved. She also went into exceptional detail about William Gull, surgeon to Queen Victoria who has received consistent attention for decades as a major suspect. Alongside his name stand the masons and the royals in a classic conspiracy. A number of compelling and creative books and movies have come out of the zone. Hardcore Ripperologists reject Gull for many reasons. In 1990 the material around him seemed to be broadcasting on the psychic airwaves in our direction.

I came to mull over what I came to call the London 1888 matrix. I had already figured out a lot of the details before coming to Alan Moore's comprehensive catalogue. On 8/8/88, the Lyceum theatre premiered a stage version of Robert Louis Stephenson's *Dr. Jekyll and Mister Hyde.* It was an immediate sensation, evoking strong responses in its audience. The leading actor's transformations from the figure of a pillar of the community to a monster right in front of their eyes was horrific stuff for a pre-psychoanalytical culture with no real sense of any lurking inner demons. It proved to be a powerful experience for the young Irish manager of the theatre, Abraham 'Bram' Stoker. Within a decade he would be inspired to conjure a figure of equal power from the collective unconscious to stand alongside Mr. Hyde on the streets of London. Something strange was stirring. Just a few weeks after the play's opening the first of the Whitechapel murders occurred. The 'autumn of terror' had begun.

This was the London where Madame Blavatsky was living out her last years, publishing the epochal *Secret Doctrine* in 1888. A few miles away from the Ripper's Whitechapel, in 1887, coroner Wynn Westcott claimed to have discovered cipher manuscripts in some books bought on the Farringdon Road. With the aid of an associate knowledgeable in the occult, Samuel Liddell Macgregor Mathers, he set about translating the information that led to the foundation of the Hermetic Order of the Golden Dawn the following year. Or so the mythology goes.

And lots of other evocative little fragments contributed to a particular flavour. The Elephant Man was coming to public attention. One of the greatest fictional characters in British consciousness,

Sherlock Holmes, had just set out on his first published case, *A Study in Scarlet.* And Hitler was in the womb during the time of the Ripper murders.

In the midst of the strange brew featuring Langley around Glastonbury and London with its backdrop of murder, 19th century French occultism, Gnosticism, and Old Testament heresies, Debbie began to pick up details of magical goings on in the Glastonbury area that would not have been out of place in ancient Canaan and would indubitably have earned the major wroth of any passing prophet and the bringing down of a bolt of lightning at the very least from Yahweh.

An unpleasant little episode was being set up to link to the energy of the 'dog days' that follow from the heliacal rising of Sirius in Egypt. The evocative phrase 'the blood of the bitch' opened the door to psychically spy on a ritual occurring outdoors in a large garden. Its presiding priestess was a woman with the magical name of Stella who was already familiar from previous psychic despatches. She was an older woman, perhaps in her late fifties but having a glamour of youth around her, wearing a ground length low-cut blue dress. Her long straight blonde hair was possibly a wig. She was gaudily made-up with red lipstick and long golden finger-nails.

There were three altars, based on black, red, and white. Three older men in black suits holding swords stood in front of them. Two young men and two young women were also in attendance. In front of the black altar Stella called upon Isis and Black Annis. Two large silver grey dogs, a male and female were brought out. In a true gross-out scenario Stella had sex with the male dog whilst one of the young men sprinkled sparkling stuff from a bowl over her. The female dog had a small black statuette inserted inside it and was then pulled up on it legs and slit down the middle, the blood being collected in bowls that were put on the red altar. Something was added to them and they were set on fire. The group began a chant of "the burning blood of the bitch".

Stella stood in front of the black altar. The two young men and young women knelt before her, putting one of the fire-bowls and the strange bowl of sparkly stars at her feet along with the black statue that had been inside the female dog. The older men assembled in front of Stella. The whole group now prostrated themselves before her, paying homage to her as a goddess.

This ceremony was yet to occur. It was believed to be set to happen on the night of Saturday July 21st. The location was somewhere in the Glastonbury environs which we were able to discover. A plan was made to stake the place out and later go and camp on Dundon Beacon. The nature of this kind of material was such that one couldn't say whether it was symbolic or that such nasties were really going to happen. Debbie's track record was good enough for us to know that it was likely that *something* was in the air and set to go down. It led to us all returning, one month after the zodiac quest.

A few days before setting off we were stopped in our tracks by powerful disturbing news from Glastonbury. On Friday June 15th an almost decapitated decomposed body was found in an irrigation ditch near Drove Road in Butleigh. A suspect had appeared in court by Monday 18th. Local papers published on the solstice Thursday revealed the barest of details. Further information followed. A self-professed 'magician' called Phillip Bennett, supposedly engaged in a process of 'collecting souls', had taken *"a face from the ancient gallery"* and murdered a Frenchman known as Jean Luc with a hatchet in the immediate proximity of the centre of the Zodiac, matrix of the alchemy of light and dark. I remembered the persistent weirdo in the Tor tower that solstice-eve who had repeatedly affirmed, "I come from hell, you know me well". It was enough to elicit an involuntary shudder.

That was plenty to be going with but there was more. At the start of the week that would conclude with us back in Glastonbury, Bennett had escaped from a police van and was on the loose. Against the psychic backdrop of ghastly imagery there stalked potentially a real life black magic murderer!

No, we didn't stumble across some weird sacrificial bestiality rite. Our night on the beacon was not uneventful though. John used his army training to try and give us a sense of security. It gave him an excuse to get his camouflage gear on and crawl around in the bushes on patrol. He also rigged up a system of trip-wires connected to large stones that he spent considerable time positioning up in trees. Once we were in place for the night he set this up so that anyone walking through the wires would get a big stone on their head. Unfortunately we hadn't anticipated the arrival of a hippie couple out for an evening stroll. They were somewhat surprised when a rock fell out of the air and landed at their feet. It was a close call and it seemed best to dismantle the armed camp and simply rely on a collection of machetes, hammers, and clubs to defend ourselves in a worst-case scenario. This all might seem a bit extreme. Probably not that many people have spent a night out at an isolated location, in the middle of an occult episode, with a black magic murderer on the loose. There isn't really a manual for such eventualities so we made it up as we went along. Sleep eventually came upon us. We were awoken from our slumbers by the nearby sound of a shotgun. Logic eventually pacified us with the probability that it was a poacher but the initial waking moments were not ones to cherish. We survived the night.

I was later led to ponder on the gruesome Glastonbury murder again. The stimulus was the cult TV series *Twin Peaks,* set Stateside and not seen in Britain in the summer of 1990. Central to the plot was an otherworldly location that served as either the 'Black Lodge' or the 'White Lodge' depending on what state of mind you entered with. It was accessible through a kind of dimensional doorway physically located at a place only identified in the closing episodes as 'Glastonberry Grove', a circle of twelve sycamore trees with a small ring of stones and a strange pool of oil in its centre. One line of dialogue concerning the British site's link with King Arthur is enough to make the intended link clear. A local Native American legend stated that every soul must pass through the Black Lodge on it way to perfection. In there one meets the shadow-self, the Dweller on the Threshold. The possibility of failure and annihilation exists. It was easy for me to link Glastonberry Grove with Park Wood and the grove of trees within which we had performed the Templar ritual.

In *Twin Peaks* a malevolent being named Bob came forth from the Black Lodge through the dimensional portal in the grove. He was a kind of evil spirit who took people over and motivated them to murder. He claimed to be hunting souls.

The programme is most strongly associated with David Lynch. There were also major contributions from Mark Frost. Frost had worked on *Hill Street Blues* and helped to anchor the complex plotting of *Peaks.* He also had a serious interest in the occult. This later manifested in the form of a novel, *The List of Seven.* Its cover featured a scene in Whitby Abbey just as Andy's *Second Coming* did. In fact there are many ideas and motifs that connect the work to magic we'd been involved with including the Ripper murders. Something mysterious seems to be going down in cases like this. Where do artists get their inspiration? Certain ideas appear to be hanging in the air waiting to interface with human consciousness.

So what was really happening to us in July 1990? Do I believe that a physical cave exists in the Dundon Beacon hill that was set up as a magical temple in the 19th century? Maybe. Do I believe that the Stella ritual actually happened? Perhaps. Do I believe in the standard William Gull Masonic royal Ripper myth? For a long time I did. Despite the compelling and creative works that have come from that hypothesis and the wealth of psychic material and hard-core weirdness in 1990 I have some doubts now. Do I believe that these ideas somehow stimulated us to enter into an experience that put us in the waiting room of the Black Lodge facing the Dweller on the Threshold in the form of the image of Langley? Yes. The 1985 and '89 Park Wood Templar ritual was not separate from all this.

The timing that led to us, with our particular mindset and magical capabilities, being in Glastonbury during the same period as the murder and its repercussions were all part of some bigger process that nobody ever gets to see more than a comparative glimpse of. Something sought expression in a diverse manner at that time and we participated in it. We were agents of the programme and I of course wondered just what kind of programme it was that contained such horror and darkness? The invisible watchers of the Glastonbury aquarium know but they're not telling anybody yet.

The 1888 matrix will provide further revelations, inspirations, and horror for a long time to come. The flavour of 19th century French occultism lingers around Glastonbury. Eliphas Levi himself, who did spend time in Britain, has made some enigmatic psychic guest appearances over the years. Andy would later be drawn into an artefact retrieval episode in the Dundon environs in darkness in 2003 during the writing of *Twenty-First Century Grail*. The story will never be over.

The brooding underworld quality of Glastonbury is as much a part of its essential make-up as the gnosis of light. The more it's ignored or denied the more it will demand to assert itself. The greater the fear and repression, the more distorted and horrific the balancing compensation.

BABYLON RISING

IN EARLY AUGUST, the ambassadors of America, Britain and the USSR left Kuwait. Two days later, in a completely surprise attack, the army of Iraq invaded. It was immediately clear that it was not good news. Dictator Saddam Hussein was a classic evil bastard nutter. He was larging it in Kuwait, seeing just how much he could get away with. Armageddon watchers twitched. It showed a lot of promise for a potential Middle Eastern mega-death scenario into which all of the major powers could get pulled. Thelemites had an angle on it as well. In the ferocious third chapter of *The Book of the Law* there was a cryptic statement from Ra-Hoor-Khuit, "*I am the warrior Lord of the Forties: the Eighties cower before me and are abased*". Some took 1904 to be year one. That meant that the forties had begun in 1944 of the Christian calendar, with the climax of Hitler's genocidal atrocities, followed the next year by Hiroshima and Nagasaki. 1990 was still in the eighties. I did get a bit worried. Saddam was not your bog-standard dictator. He did exhibit a number of the usual symptoms but the West continually failed to understand him. He was more like something out of the Old Testament, a fierce Assyrian warlord. That was pretty obvious to me for little reasons like the fact that he was rebuilding Babylon in its original form and putting up huge public images of himself dressed in a leopard-skin, riding in a chariot.

As we were leaving for the zodiac quest, the England World Cup squad's official anthem by New Order had been proclaiming, "*love's got the world in motion*". It now seemed that we'd entered into another reality. A new phase was beginning in the greater life of the world. For the rest of the year, as Andy got down to writing *The Seventh Sword,* the war vibe intensified. I never doubted it would come to that. The issue was just how bad might it get?

On November 22nd the Thatcher era ended, not with a bang but a whimper. Opinions on her will probably polarise as sharply as those on Oliver Cromwell. I was at work when I heard the news. The temptation to howl with joy and utter biblical denunciatory curses was a strong one but I had to resist. I wasn't at university anymore. The people around me had never seen a live miner. The blue-rinse set and night-club boys would have kicked me to death. Wilhelm Reich once said that the fact that Hitler was a political genius says more about the true nature of politics than any other single fact can. The fact that Thatcher was an icon of eighties Essex perhaps says more about the true nature of the estuary culture of the time than any other single fact can.

It had been centuries since she'd come to power. My first visit to Glastonbury had been barely a month later. Now, as a personal epoch had culminated with the zodiac quest, so a cycle in the body-politic likewise concluded. There's no doubting that the monstrous grocer's daughter was some kind of uber-fraulein. Whether you loved or hated her, her titan status was obvious. Perhaps, as Trevor Ravenscroft claimed about Heinrich Himmler, she was an empty vessel completely controlled by a demonic entity.

Suddenly John Major was Prime Minister. How did such a ludicrous scenario ever occur? He was like something out of a Samuel Beckett play where some hollow nowhere man buried up to their neck in sand delivers a three-hour monologue about bus tickets. He was thrown in at the deep end as well. An End Times extravaganza was brewing.

It was an appropriate time to look at Gurdjieff literature. Ouspensky's *In Search of the Miraculous* had never felt more potent. Sleepwalking humanity was at it again. The 1990 equivalent of those trucks full of artificial limbs that had awakened Ouspensky to the horror of the situation were on their way to the front once more. This time it was helicopters loaded with body-bags. Casualty calculations were being made. All sorts of jargon masked the terrifying reality. I believed the war was going to happen. I fully accepted that Saddam, to use Essex terminology, needed a slap, and that the cause was generally just. I was grateful that Reagan and Thatcher had departed. Bush and Major were far from inspiring but I felt marginally more confident in their judgements.

In December I bought the current issue of the New Age magazine, *Kindred Spirit*. I liked to keep up on New Age thinking and it usually helped me to identify the major trends without having to wade through volumes of dross to do so. I found something in it that entered my head with a sense of urgency and wouldn't let go. In an interview with an American trance channel named Kevin Ryerson I read about something called the 'Harmonic Convergence'. He described it as a *"metaphysical social revolution"*. What was it? I'd never heard of it. Apparently it had been inspired by a book called *The Mayan Factor* that had been about that ancient culture's incredibly complex calendar. A period of a few days in the mid-eighties were considered auspicious for a potential immense global event. The idea was that if enough people went out to sacred sites across the planet like the Tor and Mt. Shasta, some kind of change in global consciousness would ensue. Word had spread on the New Age grapevine. The media had got hold of it. The event happened bigtime. *Essence* magazine called it a *"New Age Woodstock"*. *Discover* however, referred to it as the *"pseudo-scientific event of the decade"*. The event's adherents pointed to the amazing pace of subsequent events such as the fall of the Berlin Wall and the reunification of

Germany as proof of its effects. *Kindred Spirit* itself came into being as a result of this humungous episode. How the hell could such a biggie come and go without me having any knowledge of it? I couldn't recall Andy or any of his friends ever mentioning it. Those words 'Harmonic Convergence' had a real ring to them. And the Mayan calendar. I loved that Mesoamerican stuff. I was absolutely determined to find out all about it. *The Mayan Factor* became top of my shopping list. I discovered that it was written by someone named José Argüelles and he'd done a couple more on similar themes, *Earth Ascending* and *Surfers of the Zuvuya*. I ordered them all, eagerly anticipating gorging my brain in one huge download.

New Year's Eve saw the whole questing crew back in Glastonbury. It was a full moon that night. The Sky Dancer contingent decided to get up to the top of the Tor before the multitudes arrived and at least commune with the force. This was a time of great significance for us. The combination of musical elements in the group equation had finally taken on a life of their own. Oliver was a brilliant keyboard player already functioning in a band called the Prayer with a superb guitarist named Nigel Roberts on board. This guy was a truly stunning talent. He could play like Jimmy Page or Steve Hillage. Songs and invocations and generally strange inspired stuff had been coming strongly through. It all felt incredible. A few nights earlier we resolved to make a recording of our efforts. Oliver was sure he could get Nigel to play guitar with us.

Being on the Tor on a full moon was a ritual in itself. We didn't feel the need for overt ceremonial. A major hoedown was sure to develop later. We left Andy and Debbie in the *Rifleman's Arms* and let the spectacularly rising moon guide us up the Tor. It was a powerful contemplative vibe up there. People settled into their own spaces. As I gazed up at the moon and tried to take stock of the immensity of 1990 it all got too much. I started crying my eyes out. It didn't subside for quite some time. People began to assemble. The standard drum-out sing-song kicked off. We were right there in the middle of it. Nearer to midnight I noticed a group forming a circle. They wanted us all to be quiet for a few moments at the turning of the year. It was a meditation for world peace, an attempt to stop the war. I respected the dignity of their intention but felt that at that stage of the game things were way too far-gone for such action to make any difference.

In the lead up to Christmas, knowing that another Glastonbury New Year visit was looming, Debbie inevitably found herself looking back on the events of 1990, in particular the ongoing dragon theme that had led to the two Key of Balance eggs amongst much else. She became agitated with the feeling that the dragon was even more important than we had realised. There was something that we had so far not understood. She wondered what was coming next?

It had been perplexing that we had received two Keys on subsequent weekends and then had to wait so long for the third. There had been a number of occasions when things appeared to be set up for number three and then not quite happened. The actual form it would take seemed mutable. The destiny matrix kept reconfiguring. Debbie believed that a set of the artefacts had been constructed during the 20th century by a man who was now dead. The one that would manifest as the third Key would determine massive future karma. The mechanism of all this was impossible to understand. How the set had been put into hyperspace as Terma type treasures could barely be speculated upon. It was clear that whatever the hell it was we were up to it was not separate from the bigger world drama. The Gulf crisis might well be a significant factor.

From December 23rd, Debbie began to repeatedly see an image of an arched stone bridge and an eastern, maybe Sumerian, looking priest leaning over it towards the river beneath in which lurked a huge, monstrous, open-mouthed dragon. The priest was tossing a red stone into its gaping jaws. It was an offering made in order to be able to cross over the bridge. The feeling was that this character had physically come to Glastonbury from Mesopotamia bringing dragon power of some kind with him. Every time the scene appeared it would conclude by turning into turquoise stone. This seemed to be a clear Key of Balance indicator. It was all connected with very powerful Glastonbury dragon energies.

In a dream she found herself present in the scene which she now knew was somewhere in the Glastonbury vicinity. The bridge had been located. She could hear chanting. The last words of the sequence were "Ehieh Metatron" and each time they repeated, a blinding flash of light was seen on the water. Debbie ran across the bridge saying urgently, "it's there, we must get it". She put her hand down into muddy water by the riverbank only to find her arm then being eaten by something beneath the surface. The excruciating pain caused her to leave her body and watch herself screaming. A procession of ten Sumerian-looking men appeared, crossing the bridge, repeating the chant for the third and final time. An unknown person, connected in some way with our group, threw something into the water. This sacrificial offering was sufficient for the beast to release Debbie. Some of the Sumerians helped pull her from the water. Her arm had mutated. There was a blue disc stuck to her stump on which was a picture of a dragon being fed the stone. The perplexing thought arose that just because we got it didn't mean we'd succeeded. In fact we failed because they got across the bridge. The same dream repeated twice.

The chanting words heard were clearly Jewish Qabalistic and both associated with the sephiroth of Kether. Why would they be recited by alleged Sumerians? There were all kinds of nuances in the air. Abraham, the founder of Judaism, originated in the famous Sumerian city of Ur. The Jews took much from the Babylonians (heirs to Sumeria). Metatron, so the story goes, had once been a human being named Enoch who had attained unique archangelic status. A book concerning him was present in some versions of the Bible and he was of some significance in underground esoteric lore. As was so often the case with Debbie's psychic material, there were seeds of future developments in what seemed to be peripheral details.

A further vision then followed on the 29th where Debbie was standing on a windswept hilltop. A strange young man named Eserkyll was with her. He had dark skin and hair and sported a bizarre inverted cone-shaped brown and gold hat. He also wore a thick necklace and a long white robe, enlivened by zigzag and square designs with a kind of squashed eye in the middle. He told her that an oath should to be taken on the hill on which they stood and then, from the starting point of a tree, the path of the beast needed to be walked to the crossway. *"On oath the bridge is in sight."* There was talk of the River Pharet.

There was enough information for Andy to understand where we were being directed. Oath Hill is a well-known site in the region of the girt dog and also lies in an area that Somerset folklore says was once terrorised by a dragon that used to fly between Curry Rivel and Aller. It was slain by a man named Hext. In Loham Church, the spear allegedly used to kill it is displayed on the wall. Janet Roberts, wife of Tony, had looked closely at the landscape of the legend and believed it to hide a dragon effigy to add to the girt dog as a Zodiac guardian figure. There is an article by her discussing it in *Glastonbury: Ancient Avalon, New Jerusalem.* About nine miles long, the serpentine creature has a head at each end, one of which was at the foot of Oath Hill. Churches in the general vicinity do seem to contain an abnormal amount of carvings of dragons and associated saints.

The area is full of evocative history and legend that strongly hints at ancient mysteries. It was in this area that Alfred the Great was based during the darkest days of the war between Wessex and the Vikings. After his victory, the mighty Dane Guthrum and his warriors were baptised at Aller, which is situated on the back of the girt doggie. As for offerings to the beast, it was also in the vicinity that the famous tale of the burnt cakes comes. Some have speculated that they were a ritual burnt offering put into the mouth of the Zodiac dog in a manner similar to Greek offerings to Cerberus the guardian hound of the underworld.

In a semi-dream state Debbie saw a place she named the Temple of the Blue Flame. It was in Mesopotamia and constructed around natural flame from the earth. The disc was seen tumbling through blue flame. Something untoward had occurred there. A presiding priestess had been murdered. Some group of travellers had carried the flame away. They had the Key.

As the Glastonbury visit got nearer, Debbie's feelings on what was involved became more strongly focused. She believed that during the Christmas/New Year period a kind of astral video of an event that really happened replays. A Sumerian boat sailed up the River Parrett. It left the Key and loads more temporarily available there. The vessel sailed on to Glastonbury. It was red, white and green, colours associated with the travellers' home city. They came at a time of unusual flooding that was primarily natural but also amplified in some occult manner by the powerful magical contingent. They stayed on board for a while before making landfall. Subsequent imagery such as the Ship of Solomon derives from these people. The great hero Gilgamesh was the son of one of them, who in turn was connected to the original form of Noah.

It was clear that a Sumero-Babylonian Key of Balance hung in the air. If we wanted it we had to bring the boat back to us. The third Key would take us to the root of our myths, in particular the dragon. The retrieval of the first Key had involved releasing a dragon. The second involved facing one. For the third, we needed to make an offering to it. They all represented very archaic magical acts.

On New Year's Day the group diverged somewhat. Some had other business to attend to. I accompanied Andy and Debbie out towards Burrow Mump. An interesting dream of hers from the previous night was the first point of discussion. She was standing on Oath Hill in the company of a warrior king named Gwythyr who was directly descended from the wandering Mesopotamians. His name meant Head Dragon. He was also known as Uther and was the son of Hext who was also Hercules. He was the father of someone called either Amhearty or Amahita, which were versions of Arthur.

This was a bewildering blend worthy of Mary Caine. We were being invited to contemplate a series of potential associations. Gwythyr is primarily known for his role in the *Mabinogion* story of *Culch and Olwen*. He was betrothed to a beautiful maiden who is abducted by Gwyn ap Nudd. Arthur intervenes and rules that the two shall fight each other for her hand every Mayday until doomsday. The two protagonists appear to represent summer and winter. Their potential prize Creiddylyd, in some variants Cordelia, is the landscape goddess, sovereignty. Things start to get a bit complex when it is realised that she is daughter of Lludd who likewise features in a tale of Mayday conflict involving the two dragons that get buried at Dinas Emrys. Gwythyr was appearing for us in the middle of a two-headed dragon. If he was a Head Dragon, a pendragon, then it seems that he and Gwyn and their contention represent another pair of fighting dragons. There was a sense of thematic continuity in this from the first two Keys and all the way back to Cornwall. To suggest that these Celtic warrior types were descended from Sumero-Babylonian wanderers was a weird variant on the recurring eccentric British Israelite theme.

Debbie was only just getting warmed up for the day though. Having mentioned the previous night's dream, she turned her attention to the present moment, picking up on the girt doggie. It's not the guardian of the Zodiac, it's the creator. This is where the mysterious boat travellers first let loose the power they had. It was in the form of the dragon because of 'Mardek'. She began to use this alternative to the usual Marduk. Bel Mardek is god of light like the Celtic Lugh. More than that, he's the oldest god of light, the first source of power for all sun kings and sun men, all god of light imagery. He was light, and a serpent, born of a fish. The ancient middle-eastern travellers believed life came from the sea. The old ones came and lived in the sea before any gods were formed in man's mind. Baal, son of Dagon, came from the sea as knowledge and light. When priests acknowledged Bel the first knowledge began. Bel was the serpent of knowledge, symbolised by a flame above the head. He turned the wheel of man's advancement. Something went wrong. They believed they'd got the wrong apple, temptation, and banished him, cutting off his arms and legs, making him into a serpent. Some priests stuck by him. They left in a boat and travelled to Britain, bringing Bel's serpent power. At Burrow Mump they first let it loose. It's not a dog, it's a dragon. The dog is a later layer like Uffington's horse over a dragon. The Gilgamesh legend reflects this. The Merdek name carried through to the Druids as Myrrdin. The Merlin archetype is a wielder of dragon power. 'Bel Merdek' was an initiatory title passed down that had mutated into Merlin. In Wales in April, at the foot of Dinas Emrys in the Grove of the Magicians, Myrrdin had spoken of the distinctive difference of the third Key. Our journey to the dog was becoming a journey to the origins of the source of the Matter of Britain and our work.

There were definite echoes of Dion Fortune in this material. The idea that Arthur, Merlin, and Morgan were titles passed down from an Atlantean lineage was one we had already made some kind of connection with in Cornwall. I noted that the location she used for her novel *The Sea Priestess* was at a powerful primal promontory called Brean Down by the Bristol Channel just before Weston-super-Mare. It would have been a location that foreign seafarers in the Somerset vicinity would surely have been aware of. Debbie believed that the lineage connected by Dion Fortune to Atlantis was proper to Sumeria. It came to this country from the Middle East and not the mid-Atlantic. Its more ancient antecedents were not immediately relevant.

On a muddy, rainy, and windy New Year's Day afternoon, we climbed to the top of Oath Hill and did our best to visualise the boat coming up river. Gwythawr appeared. He spoke of the two-headed dragon that flew between the nearby Crimson Hill and Red Hill. The nose of the Mump is the flame of fire from the dragon's mouth. He asked, *"do we come to strangle Cerberus or do we come to offer her?"* We replied, *"offer"*. Having earlier been linked to Hercules, this was a clear link to his myth cycle. We were instructed to cross the bridge where the two rivers Tone and Parret meet, the area of the mouth of the dog or dragon. Gwythawr's final advice was to, *"always follow the path of the dragon for at the end of that path is the source of the power you've been given"*.

On the bridge we offered up an artefact that had once been found in the usual bizarre circumstances by Bernard. It was a serpent bracelet with an orange stone set into it. We went to stand where the rivers meet. At first nothing seemed to be happening. Debbie then began to hear a tone coming from the ruined church atop Burrow Mump, which was clearly visible from where we were. It was the same sound that a Meonia sword made if struck. This was an obvious encouragement for Andy to use a sword he had with him for a similar purpose. To Debbie's psychic hearing, the sounds met. Orange flames were seen ascending from the church tower and coming down to the water. Along each of the two rivers, a dark green shadow moved along, underneath the water. They converged at the meeting of the rivers, where the fire had touched the water. Debbie then started to hear the chanting from her dream of the procession.

We rushed back to the bridge, anticipating the appearance of the Sumerians. There was no sign of them. Debbie rapidly became confused and then upset. No instructions were forthcoming. We began to randomly search on the riverbank for the elusive Key but to no avail. Time passed. The mood was becoming increasingly despondent.

Suddenly, a typically strange Sumero-Babylonian type appeared on the opposite end of the bridge, identifying himself as Utnapishtim. The procession stood behind him but not very vividly. This was indeed an A List magical celebrity. He features in one of the most ancient extant myth sagas of the human race, the Epic of Gilgamesh, recorded on cuneiform tablets in the Assyrian capital of Nineveh but much older and found in varying forms across the Middle East. Gilgamesh is a proto-hero whose long journey in search of immortality finds later echoes in stories of the labours of Hercules, Jason and the Argonauts and the Grail sagas. He may have originally been a real historical king who ruled from the city of Uruk around 2700 BC, an interesting date for Glastonbury Zodiac enthusiasts. Within the cycle is a flood tale that is clearly a major influence on the Bible story, including an Ark full of animals. Utnapishtim (known as Ziusudra in earlier Sumerian) is the main protagonist, a Babylonian Noah. He was once a king and seeds a new wave of the human race. Utnapishtim and his wife were made immortal after the flood. He was taken by the gods to live forever at 'the mouth of the rivers'. This makes him a kind of Ascended Master although I'm not aware of any New Agers channelling him. I felt it was interesting to put him alongside Melchizedek who had made his presence felt over the previous New Year.

This was an obvious further development of some of the fragments of material which had come out over the previous week where Gilgamesh and Noah had been mentioned along with a flood. The hero was indeed descended from Utnapishtim but wasn't his son in the known versions. It suggested Ark connotations for the Sumerian boat.

Utnapishtim swept his arms through the riverbank rushes a few times. *"Where did you find Moses?"* he said. Aha! This set us off into frantic investigation amongst the rushes. It was Andy who found it.

Debbie's initial response was not jubilation but tears. She shook her head saying, *"No, this isn't supposed to be this way, this is wrong,"* shuddering with an intimation of the path that had now been laid out ahead. There was no escaping Saddam's rebuilding of Babylon and what was returning with it.

So what was this strange artefact? What did it depict? It was obviously part of the same batch as the first two Keys. The plaster and turquoise finish were identical. It was circular, about an inch and a half across. The design carved upon it was faded and difficult to discern at first but it was undoubtedly Debbie's repeating vision.

Despite her earlier successes with the first two Keys, she was profoundly shocked to see her imagery physically displayed in front of her, especially as on this occasion it was so distinctly unusual. There was a mountain in the background. A bridge stretched over an expanse of water. A robed figure standing on it, lent over the handrail to put a small spherical object into the gaping jaws of some dragon/crocodile type creature in the water. There was a tree by the right end of the bridge. What did it mean? They came down from the mountain and crossed the bridge over four rivers. The figure was feeding the dream stone, the word the oracle speaks, back to the land, the dragon serpent, the beast, the father. Everything we do he will take from us. Our fruits will be offered to him. If we want to cross the bridge to where they've come from that's the price we pay. Some kind of sacrifice might be involved. The hand that gives the offering could be torn off by the beast. It would be a long time before the immensity of what that really meant became clear. In the short term, Debbie was convinced that the final Key would act as a homing beacon for the seventh 'black' sword. We wouldn't have to go and dig it up somewhere. It would find *us*. All we had to do was ensure that certain things were set in motion and to keep calling to it.

Back in Essex, after yet another extraordinary New Year's Day, Andy and Debbie retired for the night. The three Keys had been brought together for the first time in the bedroom by a mirror. Before long, a small very bright ball of powerful dark blue energy appeared out of the darkness, seeming to arise from the combined presence of the three artefacts. It was pulsating like a snake's tongue, sensing, waiting. Debbie realised that she was paralysed and could barely speak to alert Andy about what was occurring. It moved towards her. One side of her face became ice cold. She had trouble breathing. This was seriously scary. The small ball of light entered her head, slowly moving down through her body. She began to hear a deep, slow, voice that sounded as if it was echoing through immense caverns. It wasn't speaking directly to her. She was overhearing something but could only hear some of the words. The energy finally left through her feet and she was released.

A feeling of powerful lingering presences in the flat remained for days. After a week, one night around 5am, Debbie became aware of not being asleep anymore. It felt like the bed was floating but this was not unpleasant. A sudden sense of urgency made her feel it was important to sit up. She then realised that she was incapable of moving. Looking in the direction of the window, it seemed to disappear in glowing darkness. It was as if the night came through the window. It had a very long face with glowing eyes, long pale hands with long fingers that came ever nearer, making snaking movements across her body. The night then tapped its hands together, uttering a strange incantation that sounded like *"ulab anhadre"*. Debbie tried to force her face away feeling that if she looked for too long she would become the darkness.

ROCK ME ASMODEUS

WAR IN THE GULF LOOMED EVER NEARER. The Babylonian Key had manifested. More from that distinctive frequency seemed inevitable. On Saturday January 12th, there was a social gathering at John and Kerry's. I remember that night for a few reasons. Oliver had bought the recently released Ozric Tentacles album *Erpland* that afternoon. He had a knowing smile on his face. It went on the sound system. Within ten seconds of the guitar coming in on the very first track, I was grinning from ear to ear. At last! At long bloody last. The legacy of Gong and Steve Hillage had been brought up to date. This was supreme head-mashing instrumental glissando guitar psychedelic rock for the nineties. It was often played against a backdrop of ethnic percussion samples and so forth that conjured up Mesoamerican, Arabian and African vistas. The final track on *Erpland* was so intense it made me think of Crowley and Neuberg's visionary journey across the desert. It was almost enough to make me want to take acid again. I was glad there was an appropriately intense soundtrack available for such possible End Times. Enigma had appeared on the scene as well. Their hit chart album was the best I'd heard in aeons. It was an actual Album like they used to make in the seventies, not just a collection of possible singles. With its Gregorian chant synthesiser sounds and samplings from the likes of Aphrodite's Child's 666, it had a haunting, decadent, end of an era feel to it.

Perhaps best of all, a work colleague, Kirk Butcher, had

introduced me to the astoundingly brilliant music of Dead Can Dance. The most immediately noticeable thing about their sound was Lisa Gerard. Her wordless vocals could call to mind a Sophianic shekhinah expressing the light within the Grail in a manner Hildegard of Bingen would have approved of, or a priestess of Ishtar in some middle-eastern mystery cult. Male vocalist and lyricist Brendan Perry created works that conjured up Frank Sinatra singing Nietzsche or Jim Morrison singing Baudelaire. Their musical styles evoked every period of history from Babylon to a Goth Fin de Siecle. It was transcendental and melancholic, a call to the soul, absolutely out there on its own. I had noticed for some time that Kirk had their name painted on the back of his leather jacket. Why had I never checked them out? Because such a major event had to wait for the perfect time.

I had once been amused by a tale Andy told from Green Stone days when the intrepid Parasearch team of himself, Graham Phillips, and Martin Keatman had been based in a flat in Wolverhampton. As things had first started to get very strange they had tried to relieve the tension by having a party and inviting random people from the local pub. It all seemed to be going smoothly enough until a young woman who they barely knew collapsed on the floor in a disturbing trance-like state and began repeating the word "Akhenaten". On later recovering, she had no knowledge of what had happened to her. We had reached the point ourselves where a 'normal' evening was becoming increasingly unlikely.

The Horrigan home had already seen some outlandish phenomenon. Almost a year before, in early February 1990, John had become engrossed in reading *The Eye of Fire,* the Phillips and Keatman follow up to *The Green Stone*. It was another juggernaut of excessive paranormal adventures. The climax saw the retrieval of a red stone that complemented the green. Some of the locations featured had started to spontaneously arise in the questing material of early 1990. Some of it would lead into the Welsh trip. There were also links with John's Gawain quest, hence the intensity of his interest.

The power of the original stone had been psychically handed back to its source by Gaynor Sunderland. *"It is not for us,"* she had said. These words had lingered with John as he tried to get to sleep after a marathon stint one Sunday night when he had completed reading the book. A loud cracking sound suddenly disturbed him and Kerry in the darkness. It seemed to originate in the hall. This was followed by bangs and the sound of footsteps. They convinced themselves it was coming from the flat upstairs and managed to fall asleep. The next morning, as the couple were getting ready for work, the light bulb in the hall started to rapidly flicker in a strobe effect before extinguishing altogether simultaneous to a sudden sound from its vicinity like a thin piece of wood snapping. One brief further flicker drew attention to something now present on the carpet in front of them.

The mystery object was an orange red carnelian stone, about three-quarters of an inch long and half an inch wide. It was another Eye of Fire, proof positive that reading weird books can be injurious to your reality. There was shouting, screaming, tears, cigarettes, and cups of tea. The respective days at work were somewhat dreamlike. *The Seventh Sword* tells something of how the stone became part of the story. In late December 1990, as the Babylonian Key material had emerged, Debbie had started linking the original Eye of Fire with the Middle East.

None of this was in the forefront of our minds as we convened for what was intended to be a convivial light-hearted gathering of merriment and perhaps some intoxication. John had placed a red ornamental foliate face on a wall in the hall. It had been there for some time and we were all familiar with it. Sitting in the living room, Debbie started to stare upwards at the ceiling. The red face had come out of the carving and was floating there. She registered the weirdness but tried not to give it too much attention. When she later walked past it in the hall, it appeared in a full body of fire, standing right in front of her and saying, *"I am the true guardian of the treasure at this place and when the master of this place wore a costume of night and godman of green it was I. He must realise it was I, for I am the red man and can only serve an honourable brother"*. Debbie puked up on the spot. The bottle of wine she had drunk was certainly a contributory factor but this was a full-on manifestation for sure.

Who or what was this fierce being? He was called Asmodeus. Once his name was mentioned a few of us knew enough about him to make some preliminary speculations about what was happening. He was a kind of lord of the storm, generally considered to be a demon, who had helped Solomon in the construction of his temple. He is associated with treasure and its locating and was therefore perhaps the most appropriate demon to manifest to psychic questers. John's Masonic connections were a possible reason why it had visited him rather than any of the rest of us, hence the reference to an *"honourable brother"*. The treasure mentioned was surely the Eye of Fire stone. Further tuning in to the situation suggested that the demon had been around for a while. He had probably helped the Eye of Fire to manifest. Now the build up of fiery energy might just be too much. Andy advised John to take care it didn't blow a psychic fuse-box in his head. He recommended putting the stone in the mouth of the red man face and sealing the two in a box of some kind. John was happy to go along with this and the items were soon taped inside a cardboard package.

From that night onwards, it was obvious that immense power was building up. When John first entered the living room on Monday morning he noticed that a large armchair had moved across the floor to sit adjacent to the box. His immediate assumption was that he or Kerry had moved it the night before but forgotten they'd done it. On the morning of Wednesday 16th, John heard a sound suggestive of paper rustling coming from the living room that was empty at the time. A little later the phone rang from there. He and Kerry both entered, John vaguely noticing that the box had moved as he took the call. Kerry paid closer attention. There was a noticeable bulge now within the package. Some of the tape was starting to come undone but the box remained sealed. She undid the tape. John was soon forced to rapidly conclude his phone conversation as an astonishing nine-inch brass dagger letter-opener revealed itself as an addition to the face and stone. There was a design that seemed to represent Joan of Arc carved upon it.

To say this manifestation blew John and Kerry's minds would be an understatement. The Eye of Fire had been more than enough to deal with but as John said in a classic dazed message left on Andy's phone, *"this makes the stone look like getting a Smartie out of a tube. Oh dear"*. The next day, the 17th, Operation Desert Storm began. It was an intense night as the group gathered to see the latest questing artefact. A few things were immediately striking. It seemed clear that Asmodeus had pulled it through. A prezzie from a storm demon as Desert Storm got underway. The Joan of Arc design and general 19th century look of the thing strongly suggested a French origin. January 17th is also a date familiar to devotees of *The Holy Blood and the Holy Grail.* An above average number of events connected with alleged machinations of the notorious Priory of Sion seem to occur on that date. The whole mystery was focused on a priest who obtained a strange fortune and, amongst other things, set up a striking statue of none other than Asmodeus in a French church. On handling the dagger for the first time, Debbie felt it to be burning hot and that the whole of the Horrigan home was pulsating. She was sure that this same entity was definitely connected to the French mystery.

The group retired for the night to their respective abodes to settle into the new late-night routine of watching the computer game special effects entertainment that was Gulf War 1. Not surprisingly, Debbie soon began to pick up on snippets of occult background to the Saddam scenario. There were supposedly dudes out in the desert raising tempests with the aid of djinn and so on. It never reached a level of intensity that invited involvement. For a while the option of a classic *Key of Solomon* goetic ceremony to raise Asmodeus was considered. It didn't happen and probably a good job too. It could well have been a distraction on what would soon unfold as the final part of the journey along the path of the dragon and there would be more than enough of the flavour of the demonic to accompany us.

THE MAYAN FACTOR

SO THE GULF WAR KICKED-OFF to searing glissando guitar, monks backed by synthesisers, Sophianic exaltations, and a demon dagger apport. On the next day my Argüelles package arrived. I dived straight into *The Mayan Factor*. As always, the timing was perfect. When did I develop an interest in Mesoamerican civilisations? It's an intriguing issue for me to contemplate. When I was quite young, barely of school age, I had a habitual strategy for falling asleep. Once I'd closed my eyes, I kind of looked at the back of my eyelids, seeing nothing but darkness. After a while, images would emerge out of this darkness, framed against it. They were usually colourfully dressed strange long-headed people, floating in space. Sometimes there were peculiar patterns. They would loom into the foreground and rapidly float up and away out of sight, tropical fish in my internal aquarium. I used to wait for them every night. They were the inevitable precursors of sleep and this process seemed perfectly normal to me. Psychologists call this kind of thing 'hypnagogic imagery'. One night they didn't appear. I was disappointed. The next night I was waiting for them, hoping they'd be back. They never returned. I realised I had to formulate another falling asleep manoeuvre. A few years later, when I was ten, I was looking through some school history books. I came upon pictures of Aztec stuff. Their artwork and clothing reminded me very much of the old hypnagogics. I never really thought much about it then. It didn't freak me out or start a huge interest in the Aztecs either. In later years it all seemed increasingly mysterious. I'd fantasised about visiting Mexico in 1979 but the history was a vague backdrop to mescaline and tequila. Now it looked like it might be time for another hidden program to be released.

Who, where and when were the Maya? Why has so much interest arisen around them? Their culture primarily existed through some distinct phases between 200 and 900 AD in a Central American zone currently occupied by bits of Mexico, Honduras, Guatamala and Belize. The Maya had a shamanic worldview similar to that found in many traditional cultures. There were the three realms of Heaven, Earth, and Underworld. Heaven was a thirteen tiered pyramid, with a God for each level. The Underworld was an inverted pyramid of nine layers. The Gods of Death hung out down there, skeletal dudes, smoking big cigars. Between the two pyramids was the Earth and Sky. The Earth was seen as a flat surface resting on the back of a crocodile or caiman floating in the middle of a cosmic pond full of water lilies. A world tree grew from out of the crocodile. It was usually depicted in the form of a cross that later confused and upset the pious Spaniards. Both of the classic images of the sacred centre; the world tree and world-mountain, are present. The world tree stretched to the heavens. The Milky Way was its visible symbol. From that central point, the world was quartered by the four directions in a manner found throughout the Americas. The centre is considered to be a direction in itself.

This cosmology was carefully reflected and actualised in the layout of their cities in a way recognisable from Babylon. The temple of the Feathered Serpent at Chichen Itza is perhaps the best example of their style of functioning. It is famously constructed so that the spring equinox sunrise sends a shadow down its steps in the manner of a snake. This snake seems analogous to the Hindu Kundalini. The Maya may have had esoteric teachings concerning internal subtle anatomy similar to the yogic chakra system. This has been affirmed in modern times by Hunbatz Men in *Secrets of Mayan Science/Religion.*

To contemporary western sensibilities there is much that seems distant and alien about the Maya. New Agers probably need to get real about the fact that these people were not tree hugging hippies.

Their aristocratic priestly caste would offer their own blood up to the sun as a magical rite of life force invocation. The ladies would rasp their tongues with thorns. The men would behave likewise with their penises. Not exactly my idea of a good start to the day. And the archaeological data is in now. Along with most Mesoamerican cultures there were human sacrifices and some of them were children.

On the other hand, we wouldn't ignore the Hubble telescope and the human genome project because of the faults of the western capitalistic democracies. Here was a culture that didn't even have the wheel but the Mayan elite had a prodigious talent for astronomy and mathematics that was intimately connected with their cosmology and way of life. This is the legacy that has now surfaced so spectacularly in the current age.

Tony Shearer was an American of Lakota blood who, during the Vietnam era, experienced growing feelings of rage against the mistreatment of all Native Americans, north and south, from the time of Columbus to the present day. He went on a kind of beat-poet flute playing odyssey to Mexico. In the Valley of Oaxaca he encountered a Zapotec woman who essentially functioned as some kind of priestess as she introduced him to tribal elders and shamans who shared secrets with him, including details of the remarkable Mesoamerican calendar system, most famously refined by the Maya. This transformed his destiny, sending him back out into the world as a man with a mission.

His 1971 poetic work *Lord of the Dawn* carried a prophecy of the return of the great deity Quetzalcoatl. He wrote of cycles of thirteen heavens and nine hells, each lasting 52 years. The first heaven began in 843 AD. It was on the day that Cortes landed in 1519, a time already considered likely to see the return of Quetzalcoatl, that the nine hells began. Shearer believed that the last hell cycle ended on August 16th 1987. It was then that the Lord of the Dawn (thus named through his link with Venus) would again return. A 1975 follow-up, *Beneath the Moon and under the Sun,* expanded the calendrical details. Shearer passionately spread the word of the prophecy, often accompanying it with his flute playing.

He had already met the person who would most strongly respond to it before *Lord of the Dawn* was in print. As a young teenager José Argüelles had climbed the pyramid of Teotihuacan in the early fifties and was filled with an intense desire to understand the Mesoamerican cultures. Growing to become a visionary artist with a further background in Tibetan Buddhism, he met Tony Shearer in 1969. In 1972 Argüelles was teaching in a college and was able to invite Shearer to come along and expound his ideas in detail. This proved to be a strong foundation for the extraordinary edifice that Argüelles would construct.

Earth Ascending, published in 1984, was Argüelles' first major work. It's full of detailed charts and artwork with terminology that could easily deter the casual reader. How about *"Psi Matrix Flow-Pattern as Template of Psychocultural Transformation Showing the Eight Stages of Holonomic Recollection"*? Argüelles was influenced by Oliver Reiser. There was talk of the Noosphere Psi Bank emerging global consciousness and the natural laws governing its development. These could be demonstrated, for example, in the striking resonance between the binary form of the 64 trigrams of the I Ching and the structure of DNA. Argüelles stated that perhaps the most important of the hidden laws governing the holistic planet Earth system are demonstrated through the Mayan calendar with its detailed examination of the varied influences at play on the planet during gigantic periods.

The number 260 plays an important role in different layers of Mayan interlocking calendars. It is considered to represent initially the number of days in human gestation and also the period between planting and harvesting maize. There is a 260 day cycle known as the Tzolkin that works with the numbers 1 to 13 repeated in order 20 times. Imagine it laid out as a 13 by 20 number square. Begin at the top of the left hand column and work down. Go to the top of the next column and continue. It begins with day 1 of the 260 day cycle and ends with 260 in the bottom right. It was Argüelles insight, strongly stated in *The Mayan Factor,* that this cycle had a clear relationship to another far larger one extending 5125 years between 3114 BC and 2012 known as the 13 Baktun cycle. A Baktun is about four hundred years long. The big cycle can be mapped out on the Tzolkin grid. The top left square starts in 3114 BC. Each unit is a further sub-division of a Baktun called a Katun that lasts nearly twenty years. The last one shows the period from 1992 to 2012. If each day has a potential relationship to one of the Katuns we get a hint of our connectedness to the bigger beam, to vertical 4D time. Argüelles called this symmetry *"an inter-dimensional galactic constant"*. In *Earth Ascending* Argüelles matched the world's history against these Baktuns to see if the influences supposedly functioning in them corresponded to actual events.

Argüelles believed that the Earth entered some kind of cosmic beam at the start of the greater cycle in 3114 BC and will emerge out of the end in 2012. Within the smaller cycles are moments when things get a kick-start or fall apart or whatever. In 2012 there are awesome possibilities for humanity if we've got ourselves sorted. In the lead in to the final hoedown, a 5 year wobble of the Earth's etheric gyroscope seemed scheduled between 1987 to 1992. There was a period of 3 days in August 1987 when this potentially iffy phase began. This was the time specified by Shearer. Argüelles felt it would be a good idea to stake out every sacred site in the world and engage in appropriate activity to help the coming phase of massive acceleration to be safely navigated. He promoted this idea in *The Mayan Factor* and it spread very quickly through the New Age grapevine coming to pass in a big way as the Harmonic Convergence.

There was no doubt that things had been rather extraordinary during the years following the event. As well as the Berlin Wall spectacularly coming down and Germany being reunited, the USSR was falling to bits and Eastern Europe was rapidly transforming. Nelson Mandela was out of prison and South Africa was never going to be the same. In Britain, the emergence of Ecstasy and Rave culture had been a profound process of social change. Now we had the interesting challenge of the Gulf War.

Argüelles material proved to be a spectacularly mind-expanding overview in the middle of the Armageddon matrix. For all the comparative data there were no obvious Aeon of Horus pointers but I considered the timing of this material entering my consciousness to be one. This was not a passive experience where I pondered some interesting ideas from my armchair. It felt like everything was massively switched on and great issues were at stake. Would the mysterious cosmic Mayan factor offset the ferocity of the Aeon of Horus? Argüelles had said that, "*when the light hits, the dark gets tough*".

When the war ended it was not possible to realise that the defining event of the decade had occurred at its very start. The immediate mood was one of relief. Things could have been so much worse. It was over in no time at all. A general Middle East conflagration had been avoided. Despite scud provocation Israel had not got involved. Chemical weapons were not deployed. As in 1918 and 1945 though, the Allied powers once again demonstrated that although they could win a war they could also disastrously fail to properly manage its conclusion and the subsequent 'peace'.

It was clear that it had been a mighty strange affair. Consensus reality appeared to have been detrimentally warped-out by the conflict. French Post-Modern cultural theorist and all-round wind-up artist, Jean Baudrillard, suggested that the war had never happened. In this he was perhaps inviting a redefinition of the word 'war' to accommodate the situation. The allied powers had assuredly 'won'. Absurdly disproportionate casualty figures affirmed that. Saddam remained in power however, and immediately set about brutally crushing internal opponents who the west had given encouragement to revolt and were then left to be slaughtered. No war had ever had such a level of media attention but the 'truth' was difficult to determine. Journalists near to the front were effectively managed by the military so that they had no better idea of what was occurring than TV audiences a continent away. In this, they and their viewers and readers were in certain respects hostages alongside Saddam's famous human shields. People had died horribly amidst the clean calculated victory and this raw human fact seemed continually elusive, receding into an indeterminate background behind computer game smart bomb collateral damage jargon data. What the hell had really happened and what was it all about? Did anyone, including the intelligence agencies of both sets of protagonists, actually know? The confusion was guaranteed to generate conspiracy theories.

It seemed to some observers that a web of electronic media cyber-information now stood as a simulated reality masquerading as the genuine article somewhere between any observer and what they might be trying to observe. In functional terms it could be argued that it had in effect become reality. It dramatised the eastern concept of maya, the veil of illusion. To some it would seem to be the controlling chains of a shadowy new world order. Others intuited its mutability and potential to be the battleground for a new epoch of reality wars between the techno-sorcerers of divergent philosophies.

I had one overriding feeling as my meta-perspective on the situation. It was my favourite theme of eternal return. Western civilisation began in Sumeria. A whole package of innovations started there. Now, as we seemed to be nearing the end of a huge cycle, something massive was happening in the same geographical region again as jets flew over Abraham's Ur. After the episode of the Babylonian Key I could easily believe that powerful forces were stirring. The timing of our Glastonbury Zodiac quest took on increasingly strange connotations. It looked like the deities of Babylon were on the move and were set to play a role in our destiny.

DANCERS OF THE DREAMTIME

BY EARLY JUNE, Andy was involved in the final editing of his book. The Sky Dancer crew had virtually completed recording what would be called *Moon Magic*. Lisa's beautiful songs had been done justice. Oliver put some spacey keyboards behind me reciting my *Isis*. John contributed a poetic invocation of the three faces of the goddess. Most satisfying of all was a twenty minute epic entitled *Nuit Isis* where guitarist Nigel put in a blistering performance worthy of Jimmy Page.

A measure of the creativity of the Moon Magic project was the nature of a seemingly random contribution from Debbie. One afternoon she heard Kerry and Lisa singing the famous chant *We are all Part of the Goddess*. "Why are you only singing some of the words?" she innocently asked. What other words are there? She immediately sang back an eerie invocational chant that closely resembled some of the fragments of ritual in Dion Fortune's *Sea Priestess*. There were differences. It was extraordinary. The sisters learned the words from Debbie immediately and it became incorporated into our album. We were invited to perform some of it at the Fellowship of Isis convention in London in September. This all felt rather splendid.

As the solstice approached, there was a brief pause in the multifaceted proceedings. Glastonbury was calling. I was relieved that no leaps into weirs at midnight would be required this year. Enjoyment of the season in the spirit of classic past Junes was totally acceptable. Early in the evening of June 20th I was picked up by John and Kerry and we left Southend for Glastonbury. The weather was perfect. *Victorialand* by the Cocteau Twins provided a suitably etherial soundtrack. We were meeting up with Alex and Kirk Butcher, who were already in Glastonbury. John had grabbed one part of a drum kit and was all set to carry the fairly large item up the Tor. There were already a lot of drummers and didg players up there.

It was not long since *The Doors* movie had been on general release. I had a feeling most of those present had seen it. Opinion was divided as to its merits. Some of it was inaccurate at Jim Morrison's expense. Nonetheless I had been trashed by it in a manner no movie had managed since *Apocalypse Now.* When I'd heard the film was being made I'd felt it was inevitably doomed because nobody could be expected to realistically portray Jim Morrison. Val Kilmer was paranormally good in the role. Not so much acting as possession. I was amazed that he actually contributed credible vocals as well. Some of Oliver Stone's imaginative interpolations were very effective. One scene seemed to linger in everyone's minds. The band are giving a typically transcendent performance at an outdoor gig. There's a bonfire out in the audience that naked people are dancing round. Jim is in an altered state on stage, moving like a shaman. Keyboard player Ray Manzarek is staring at him and is forced into a double-take as a group of ghostly Native Americans join in with Morrison's dance. Something of that was present on the Tor that night, an invitation to the dancers of the dreamtime, of all cultures and periods, to join us.

Our drum was the biggest and loudest up there. Inevitably it attracted attention and participation. We soon settled into a stomp between the worlds. At one point, a young hippie guy joined us and sang the Morrison classic *My Wild Love,* inevitably amplifying the feeling that was already there. To some cynical bastard, looking on from the outside and determined to resist the vibe, it would have been easy to dismiss the whole thing as a bunch of kiddies playing pretend Red Indians. When we played Indians though, weird shit happened. At the Earthquest 1990 Christmas party, a similar hoedown had spontaneously developed. John Horrigan had collapsed on the floor as psychics saw Native Americans walking through the walls into the room. All his vital signs disappeared as he lay there, white and motionless. The ambulance option was seriously considered before he twitched back into consciousness. He had found himself out in a desert with some shaman-type who had offered him a sequence of initiatory items. It was the beginning of a mini-saga for John. We knew that us playing silly-buggers always carried the possibility of stirring something up.

That night on the Tor, time dissolved. I really don't know where the energy came from as none of us were on drugs. Somehow a continual dancing and chanting and drumming was maintained from just after sunset until dawn. I remember vaguely coming back to some sort of sense of separate identity, as a guy with bagpipes serenaded the sunrise. Bagpipes may sound crap at the Edinburgh Military Tattoo but they're a hauntingly evocative instrument when played by someone in the right headspace. Our piper at the gates of dawn sounded forth an atavistic invocation of the ancestors that tingled deep down inside our DNA.

The solstice became the usual blissful blur. In the afternoon we lingered by the abbey fishpond. Off came shoes and socks as feet were dangled in. It was discovered that fish eat bananas. By evening, we were back on the Tor, our appetite for drum-outs unabated. This time John set up his great device in the Tor tower. As the usual sunset watchers milled around outside, we made a lot of noise. It rose and fell on unseen tides. Before it was dark we finally ceased, entirely exhausted. A couple of ladies came into the tower and told us an extraordinary tale. During our shamanic stomp a number of people outside had clearly seen the image of a distinctly Native American face appearing in the clouds. It had a headdress. The more noise we made, the clearer it got. When we quietened down, it started to fade. This rhythm persisted for a while, until it finally faded entirely at the very moment we stopped. Result! It's a bit of a shame nobody came in to tell us about what was happening. I would rather have liked to have seen such an outlandish manifestation. It would have been a good game to see just how interactive we could have got with it. Never mind. Obviously it was supposed to have been that way.

PACT WITH THE DEVIL

"If you gaze into the abyss, then the abyss also gazes into you."
Friedrich Nietzsche.

"If the thing did happen, then man must be prepared to accept notions of the cosmos, and of his own place in the seething vortex of time, whose merest mention is paralysing. He must, too, be placed on guard against a specific lurking peril which, though it will never engulf the whole race, may impose monstrous and unguessable horrors upon certain venturesome members of it."
H. P. Lovecraft. *The Shadow Out of Time.*

ONE NIGHT IN EARLY MARCH 1991, shortly after the Gulf War had ended, an unsettling atmosphere had once again arisen in Andy's flat. There was a series of unexplained bangs and crashes. Debbie passed into the usual visionary zone, finding herself in a cave. The place was intensely hot. She knew that it was filled with spirits that had been there for untold ages. Some kind of illumination enabled her to see carvings of spiral patterns and men and animals on the walls. She touched one depiction of a man with spirals for eyes. Something came out of the spirals to form an

Egyptian-style eye made of bright light. A voice said, *"look into the black eye of Horus"*. Inside it, a flame was discernable which she was told was *"the fire of essence"*. Black smoke could then be seen around it that began curling around, forming into a cobra. *"I am the Apep, I am the line that runs deep, the only essence in each one of you. Build the fires of essence. Now is the time. I can take you down the line knowing something you wouldn't know in an incarnation of light."*

Debbie backed away but the eye seemed to follow her, getting progressively bigger. Her attention was briefly diverted back to the area of the original carving of the figure from which the eye had appeared. It had been replaced by a sword. She reached out to touch it, taking hold of it to throw into the eye. As it entered it began tumbling over and over in space. Suddenly the snake had reappeared and struck out at her. There was a sharp pain and the experience was over. She was back in the Black Room but still feeling like she had been bitten. A glance at her hand revealed an odd little mark and some blood. The feeling was that the cave location was real and in Britain. We would have to go there.

Others in the group were having cave dreams during the same period. Kerry remembered a fragment that involved crawling along into a large chamber. It was John who soon identified where it was. He knew the locale well and had been having periodic dreams about it since January 1990. It was Symonds Yat on the river Wye. Yat means gateway. Canoeist John knew that the Wye in that area was the most hazardous course in England. People had drowned there. It could easily be seen as a place of sacrifice. In the general vicinity there are a number of caves that have yielded archaeological finds dating back to the Stone Age. Our trip there was projected forward to sometime in the summer.

With the Middle Eastern situation changed there was also talk of a group project that was set to be our greatest adventure yet, a trip to Egypt. For various reasons it never happened but by psychically tuning into what such a journey would involve remarkable things were set in motion. It wasn't clear at first but it was all leading to a moment of destiny in the cave at Symonds Yat.

In a series of group meditation sessions and dreams, Debbie kept returning to a situation in modern day Egypt that gradually developed. Initially she was led to the back room of a shop. Sitting there was a man named Hareesh. He was about fifty years old, with a high forehead, moustache, and small intense eyes. He was wearing a head-scarf from which protruded wild tufts of grey hair.

In front of him was placed a clay model of a two-headed crocodile. It was painted with a pattern of wavy and zigzag lines with dots. Debbie became aware that she was wearing a dress decorated with similar designs.

Hareesh led her out into a valley that Debbie believed had once been a former tributary of the Nile, one of seven. It had become a sacred path when it dried up thousands of years earlier. The journey culminated at an old ruined mosque. There was a tomb beneath connected to a very important figure, a kind of forerunner of Akhenaten in terms of monotheism. One corner of the crypt featured ancient imagery, a large dragon, a fish, and skulls. The rest was decorated in Arab style. In further subterranean levels was a chamber that connected to a deep source of water that contained strange creatures.

On one occasion, Hareesh cleared an area of dirt and rubbish on the floor of the ruined mosque to mark out an equal armed cross, which he then sat down in the middle of, placing his strange crocodile totem in front of him. He was descended from an archaic shamanic lineage of rainmakers who had once been figures of great importance as far back as pre-dynastic times. He somehow invoked, through visualisation, the waters beneath and brought them up from primordial darkness, along with the strange creatures that lived in them, to become sparkling purple, running down the arms of the cross on the ground and out into the valley recreating the original waterway in a manner linked with the great inundation of the Nile at the time of the rising of Sirius.

At the completion of the process Debbie noticed that the painted patterns had been cleaned away from the crocodile totem and that her dress was now plain white. Hareesh had a white and purple light shining from his mouth. He raised his hand to it, displaying a small circular transparent purple-tinged stone. It was given to Debbie with the strange instruction to drop it down a flight of stone stairs she had suddenly become aware of. They seemed to descend forever. There was a small piece, a chip, missing from the stone. For some unknown reason Debbie felt a compulsion to put it in her mouth and eat it. She was now aware that Hareesh was singing and it was raining outside.

A powerful atmosphere lingered the following day in the flat. Events in the evening were enough to convince Andy and Debbie that important things were happening. Lights started flickering. Looking out of the window and then walking out into the street confirmed something inexplicable. Along half of the road on both sides there was a complete electrical failure with the sole exception of Andy's first-floor flat. There was actually a policeman in attendance. Andy was an infamously known local figure by this time and the copper suggested that the phenomenon was probably something to do with the demons he had been raising. In the midst of this strangeness a small circular transparent purple-tinged stone with a small chip on one edge was found under an old wooden ottoman that doubled up as an altar in the Black Room. Every one of our mysterious artefact appearances offered up plenty of ammunition for the sceptics. What we noticed was how increasingly they coincided with bizarre external events.

The rainmaking stone episode with Hareesh proved to be a catalyst for a Middle Eastern heretical magical history lesson lasting throughout the spring of 1991 that sat very evocatively alongside various Old Testament themes. It began from the subterranean realms beneath the ruined mosque. Holding a flaming torch, Debbie descended down the stone steps into the nethermost caverns.

Along a tall corridor, square tiered chambers were set into the walls. Each contained a sarcophagus. Further labyrinthine tunnels contained hundreds more. Other smaller square holes were used to climb up and down for access. There were Sumerian bodies down there. This was Egypt. How had they got there? One chamber had a blue mauve flame burning inside. This detail took Debbie back to something she had briefly picked up on after the finding of the third Key of Balance.

In a Sumerian city there had once been a temple built over and around a deep cavern that emitted gas that burned blue. The flame was considered to be a gateway to the source of knowledge and creation from whence was born the mother of all. It was a supremely magically potent place governed by powerful taboos. Profane outsiders who glimpsed it could be punished by death. Debbie felt that it was somehow possible for specially prepared adepts to physically stand inside the flame and not be burnt. It could only be carried by a sacred priestess from one place to another. Not only were they able to physically light fires from the original, they also had inner techniques, perhaps analogous to Kundalini Tantra for somehow carrying the flame within them.

There is one blue flame reference that has found its way into popular culture and could be seen as a possible stimulus for Debbie's ideas. It features in the movie of H. Rider Haggard's novel

She, made by Hammer with Ursula Andress in the title role in 1965. Queen Ayesha remains eternally young through having stepped into a mysterious blue flame. It wasn't blue in the original novel however and is never actually referred to as such in the movie. It's simply an imaginative special effect to suggest the periodic coolness of the flame at times of special heavenly alignments that allow someone to stand within it.

Although the group were unaware of it at the time, there are known examples of natural gas fissure flames becoming the focus for temples in more than one tradition. Jyalamukhi in the foothills of the Himalayas is a major Hindu goddess shrine. In some versions, its blue flame is considered to be the tongue of Kali. More significant in retrospect for Andy's future work was the number of such places in Azerbaijan that had a link to the ancient Iranian religion of Zoroastrianism.

Some great political and religious upheaval in Sumeria changed everything. It seemed like the end of the world and that Tiamat would destroy the Temple of the Blue Flame in anger. There was something dangerous about the knowledge held there, which included elements of what would later become the Qabalah, something about their origins, which put them in peril. A priest prince of Mardek and Dagon kidnapped the highest priestess who carried the flame within. It was believed that the flame was about to be corrupted and turned red and this was the only way to save it. He left with a large group, travelling in the direction of Egypt with the intention of recreating the temple there. Fragments of this saga had been glimpsed around the turning of the year. The third Key had been seen in blue flame. The departing group had it with them in some sense. An epic journey began.

Debbie's telling of the story ebbed and flowed over a period of months. A few details changed. Basic themes remained. At first she said that it was Melchizedek who brought the blue flame out of Sumeria. Soon the details started to coalesce with the tale of the most famous traveller between Sumeria and Egypt. She began speaking of someone named I Ra Han. It became clear that he was the Biblical Abraham although the tale being told was apocryphal in the extreme. His wife Sarah sometimes seemed to be the blue flame priestess. He is remembered for the powerful themes of pact and sacrifice, having formed the covenant with Yahweh that began the nation of Israel and then showed his willingness to kill his own son for that deity if the need arose.

There was consistent mention of Mount Nebo, a location usually associated with Moses. It was on its summit that he saw the promised land he had led his people out of slavery to claim but he was never to enter it for he died shortly afterwards. Things seemed to mixmatch with the usual Sinai story.

Something big happened on Nebo when the wanderers stopped there. A temple of some kind, perhaps a stone circle, had been constructed. I Ra Han was crowned and God spoke to him, imparting sacred words and names to be used in the newly evolving forms of knowledge. There may have also been a further ritual joining with the priestess of the blue flame lineage, the woman the Bible calls Sarah. It was also a place of sacrifice. Perhaps the wildest claim that Debbie made was that amongst the multi-cultural party were a small number of Megalithic people who took some Sumerians back to Britain where they let loose the power of the dragon.

Debbie also consistently referred to it as the High Place. She stated more than once during the spring months that we too were travelling to that High Place in terms suggestive of it being a return rather than discovery. The significance of the terminology was then unknown but it would later prove to be a clue as to the source and psychic airwave frequency of the narrative.

The ultimate Egyptian destination was named as Zoan. This ancient city was better known by its later Greek name of Tanis and has achieved a certain fame in the modern age through featuring heavily in *Raiders of the Lost Ark*. The *Book of Numbers* mentions Zoan saying it was built seven years after Hebron was founded. This was the area most famously associated with Abraham. Tanis was situated on the north-east part of the Nile delta. It had been the capital of Egypt during a period when it was under the control of a people known as the Hyksos. Although chronology is often disputed this may well have been the time when Abraham arrived in Egypt. It does seem that the traveller and his wife were important people who soon came into contact with the pharaoh of the time. Debbie mentioned on various occasions such incidental details as that a Sumerian who had ruled Egypt had been erased from history. I Ra Han was once referred to by her as *'King of Two Lands'*.

A lot of other material came up as well, covering themes that were already familiar and would continue through the years in the works of Andy and Graham Phillips. There was talk of multi-coloured dreamcoat Joseph and links between Moses and Akhenaten with the general sense that they were one and the same person.

The group carried on across the desert. Years passed. Eventually they came to the Nile delta at a point where seven rivers had once joined. There they constructed a huge underground tomb complex. It was initially to house bodies of priests that they had laboriously taken with them from Sumeria. The travellers provided a high-level cultural infusion into Egypt through general knowledge and architectural influences. Things seemed okay for a short period. Disputes arose amongst the Sumerian group. They were waiting for the arrival of others from home but things didn't work out. The drying up of the Nile tributary seemed to demonstrate a sense of being cursed, that something had gone wrong.

The accession of a strong Egyptian pharaoh forced many of them to depart in an earlier version of the Exodus. I Ra Han returned to Nebo, the memory of his monotheism remaining as an undercurrent that would stimulate Akhenaten. His wife influenced a lineage of priestesses with arcane star cult knowledge that later resurfaced in the reign of the female queen Sobek Nofru Re. Big plans to return in triumph came to nothing.

On June 7th, Debbie was in a very deep trance, speaking almost inaudibly. Andy's constant practice of holding a portable tape recorder near her mouth during such episodes preserved the peculiar words for later inspection. *"Black as the sun. Garden. Dark king. She cometh. Tiamareth: the gate. Aden adoreth the bounteous gate. And she offereth fruit of the gate. The seven stave holded the oriflame. Aden put down his stave for the gate. The seventh stave go with Aden. Gilgatr leave with the second stave. Hunra with the third. The path of the dragon Dagon. He is the cord which bindeth your land with mine. By air, by land, by sea, the dragon will fly, maketh the path. The seventh stave must behold the flame. You will find it in the hands of him who adoreth the gate and her bounty of chaos."*

She saw a woman standing in the blue flame, naked save for a large eye design on her stomach. This was the gateway. There were people around pointing staves of some kind at her. Power was flowing between them all. She stepped out of the flame, which seemed to turn black. Behind her was a chasm, a complete black hole. It seemed very real. She approached one of the shadowy figures and touched his stave, transforming it to black. Others turned around in different directions and walked away. It was understood that this was something to do with the dispersal of a lineage of knowledge and the genesis of the black seventh sword.

On Sunday June 9th the group travelled to Gloucestershire. It was a big day for me because the site we were visiting had come to light through my own experiences, yet another thread of our multi-faceted sagas that can't be included here. Situated between Cheltenham and Cirencester, Seven Springs was considered by some to be the source of the River Thames and this excursion was the climax to a three-month journey along the river that had coincided with the gradual appearance of the Old Testament style material. The whole journey had always had a strong Egyptian flavour for me but events were to take an unexpected turn. As with the Middle Eastern saga, there was to be a blending with Sumerian themes.

The name Seven Springs and its significance as source of the River Isis (as some of the Thames is still called), with the hint of some archaic goddess strata behind the myth of Old Father Thames had evoked all kinds of poetic fantasies in me. The site itself however is far from spectacular, being immediately to the side of a road over the other side of which is a large pub restaurant. From a small car park area, steps lead down to a corner where two walls join, one of which is beneath the levels of the road. A faded Latin inscription, dating from the 19th century, was the only acknowledgement of the importance of the place. At the base of both walls can be seen small niches where the springs arise into a stony pool where the water is barely inches deep. After nightfall though, the atmosphere changed. Surrounding trees helped create the feeling of an enclosed zone. It was most conducive to strange magical business. Being beneath road level helped as well. A few small candles were lit and incense burnt.

Debbie soon found that the place served as a gateway into what she called on this occasion, the Scorpion Temple of the Blue Flame. We were invited to each step into it. An option was offered of staying there or stepping back out. Only Debbie and I decided to stay.

Her experience was a bit more intense than mine. She stood at the centre of the blue flame, naked apart from a large eye design on her stomach, becoming one with the original priestesses and their goddess. In that identification a function of manifestation already working through her was amplified still further. Through the flame, outside, could be seen the shadowy presence of seven figures with staffs pointing towards her. She was the pole star around which they revolved. The eye was not just a painted design but a real doorway to the void, to Daath, the womb of the divine feminine where all life comes from nothing. This was a stellar experience in a timeless realm where the usual opposites that help define our consensus reality had dissolved. No up and down or hot and cold. No motion. The distinctions of form and formlessness, being and becoming, had annihilated each other. It was in this realm, in this existential maelstrom, that the seventh sword resided.

A group meditation in Andy's Black Room on the night of July 6th was a memorable one. Something that had first come into view shortly after the arrival of the third Key of Balance recurred with terrifying amplification. Debbie had been in the usual visionary space seeing something or another from the desert realms of the Middle East but it vanished from view leaving no memory behind. Everything had gone dark. There was a feeling of apprehension, of imminence. A lurking fear. She could hear a guttural humming sound. Something was coming. It was difficult to tell if she was in the room or some visionary space. Breathing became difficult. She opened her eyes. The group were still visible but everything was very dimly lit as if the candles had been extinguished. The velvet curtains were not drawn. The night sky was visible through the window. This comforting glimpse of consensus reality was all too brief. The window frame unbelievably began to dissolve. To her horror, the night seemed to creep and pour itself into the room, pulsating as a tentacled blackness, coagulating to take the form of a nearly ten feet tall humanoid entity. It had three pairs of wings protruding behind it, from above its head, and behind its shoulders and back. Some kind of robe was apparent. Long probing fingers. And a strange elongated face, not unlike the famous visage of Akhenaten. There was a short Babylonian style beard on its chin. The haunter of the dark was entirely black, created from the night, apart from slanted eyes of brilliant burning azure blue. No pupils, no whites, just laser blue. It leaned over her, its face horrifyingly close, a face that seemed to burn itself into the back of Debbie's retina where it's stayed ever since. The being spoke in an incomprehensible language whilst making hand passes over her. Debbie felt as if her insides had gathered up into one ball and been pulled out.

In the midst of such transfixing horror, she seemed to suddenly slip away and reconfigure standing on stairs that were carved out of a mountain. A remarkable winged woman stood before here. She had a dark-skinned Egyptian kind of face with the neck and forehead painted red and head adorned in gold. Debbie followed her up the stairs to see an opening where a river could be seen flowing down beneath. There was a cave above it on the opposite side in the mouth of which was a statue of a muscular two-headed man. One head had eyes open, the other closed. It had the now familiar three pairs of wings and was holding a long staff. The woman pointed towards the cave and water. Debbie looked into the water and could see half men/half fish creatures swimming about. There was a feeling that if she tried to cross the river they would eat her. Suddenly there was a glimpse of something white in the cave. The woman transformed into a big bird and flew across. Debbie did likewise. At the moment of touchdown a veritable monsoon began. From out of the cave emerged a figure in white somewhat obscured by a curtain of water. It told Debbie she could not enter unless she had offered a sacrifice and made an oath at Hebron. The woman still had bird claws on the end of her arms. She walked into the water and pulled out one of the manfish creatures. In a thoroughly bizarre scenario, she shook it up till it was limp and then squeezed it until eggs fell out of its tail area. Debbie inwardly asked where she was and received the words *"Gulah Mamre"*. She tried to approach the statue but a powerful force blocked her like a punch in the chest. She could feel a pulling sensation again and found herself back in the Black Room with the nightmare being still leaning over her, virtually face to face.

It seemed as if it was some form of Bel Marduk that stood before her but Debbie also knew that it was really something even more ancient, something terrible to behold but great nonetheless. A dark god, but God the father of civilisation as we know it. From his spindly fingers silver threads connected to everyone else still lying silently on the floor with their eyes closed. Like a puppet master he began to pull on the threads and as he did so people began to writhe and twitch with physical symptoms; Alex with asthma stirrings, Lisa with cramps, and so on. Debbie herself felt like her own thread was connected to lots of other fine ones inside her. If the pull had been any stronger they would have all ripped apart. In the two years since meeting Andy rather a lot had happened. This, finally, was too much. She began to scream. The group were instantly transported back from diverse locations into the room. We all put our hands upon her and visualised light pouring through us into her. This helped her regain some sort of equilibrium. Debbie later came to believe that her willingness to stare directly into the eyes of oblivion, the face of the dragon, and survive, won her the right to bear the black sword. Containing its power would be nothing compared to that encounter.

On July 14th a meditation contained hints at a coming full-circle. Debbie saw a barrow from which emerged a tall man with long brown hair, wearing purple and dark green robes. Somehow she knew that despite a changed appearance this was our old mate the follet. There was also a woman who seemed to have come from a tree. She was dressed in dark blue with blonde hair. Suddenly she was standing by Dozmary Pool. She identified herself as Eve and offered some magical advice. "*Tune into the pool to go through the gate because now you have the keys to use it as a gate. Then you must go to the cave of the silver eel. Your knowledge of the dragon, will you grab it by the tail? Or will you let go?*"

Andy was seeing similarly themed things at the same time. He saw Dave Hunt at Tintagel-head looking at his Morgana woman. This rapidly switched to the Hall of Chivalry and the display cabinet containing the Meonia sword. It broke out and hung glowing in the air, transformed into an archetypal jewel-encrusted Excalibur-type weapon. It then shrank back down in to the case. The Tintagel sword had hardly come to mind all year. There was never any thought of going back down to Cornwall but something was brewing around our connections there.

On the afternoon of Tuesday July 23rd, the group drove down to Dorset to return to the Forgotten Chapel, where Debbie had first been accepted as the oracle. During one of her recent encounters with Hareesh in the ruined mosque he had shown her an image of the place, indicating we should return. We were going to spend the night there. The soundtrack in Andy's car included *Floodland* by the Sisters of Mercy. It helped set the mood for what followed. This time we didn't have to locate the site in darkness. There was time to comfortably wander through the woods, arrive and settle down. Night came slowly as a powerful vibe seemed to close in around us.

Our intention was to achieve a transition from one magical state to another. It would involve a ritual in rainmaking linked with the Nile inundation and the heliacal rising of Sirius. The process began with the cleansing of the site. Alex drew banishing pentagrams of light at the four quarters. The night featured a strong theme of purification by water so the pentagrams were specifically not of fire. A temple bell was struck. Lots of Egyptian khyphi incense was burnt. We visualised a veil of white mist drawn around the place. A circle was created within the ruined chapel. Andy and I sat back to back by the altar. Debbie sat opposite. The rest of the group sat in a circle around us.

Qabalistically speaking, our first visit to the Forgotten Chapel in March 1990 had been a Yesodic experience. It was from there that Debbie's oracular function had been bestowed. Now she would dare to go into the void from Yesod up the middle pillar of the Tree of Life, beyond the comfort of solar Tiphareth to Daath and sacrifice her role on one level to become a dark priestess. Why? Because the seventh 'black' sword was in Daath. For some time a recurring image of the weapon tumbling in the void had featured in her dreams and meditations. She knew that she had to retrieve it from the fathomless depths of Daath. The tarot trump of the High Priestess lies along the middle pillar between Tiphareth and Kether, crossing the abyss of Daath. If Debbie wasn't set up by now to take on such a task she never would be.

A portable tape machine had been brought along. Jean Michel Jarre's uncharacteristic ambient underwater track *Waiting for Cousteau* had a proven track record of putting Debbie instantly into the zone all through the unfolding Sumerian Biblical saga.

With Jarre playing gently in the background, we imagined ourselves to be in the lost temple in the woods familiar to us from our previous visit. This morphed into the Temple of the Blue Flame. The intention was to carry the flame out with us on a journey. It led us forward, showing a blue fiery path on the ground. We became like fire walking into a desert wilderness. Vultures flew above us. In the distance ahead was a Silbury-sized black mound. It loomed ever nearer until we began to climb it. By now, the sky was purple and water was suddenly all around us. Sirius shone brightly above. Having reached the top of the mound, we proceeded to draw down the female power of the star to manifest as mist coming up from the mound as if she was part of the black earth, forming a woman with the large eye design on her stomach.

Tiamat would help us make rain. She would perform the dance. We would do the calling. Part of this would involve actually making a totem out of modelling clay that would be our version of the crocodile figurine that Hareesh had used. The group had been asked in advance to meditate upon a suitable form for each individual. It would be offered up with the request for Tiamat to release it from us. Then we would make the rain come down by offering the totem and a chant that Debbie had heard in her head and would recite with us repeating her words.

The chant was very strange. Barbarous words. Unrecognisable. Just about possible to repeat at the time. Unfortunately impossible to phonetically render as writing. With Jarre in the background they at least served the purpose of heightening the already spooky atmosphere. Under Debbie's direction, we imagined clouds forming over the purple night sky, the sound of thunder, and then the water of the moon falling as a deluge. Beneath us, simultaneously, the inundation began to rise. What was once asleep had now been awakened. The water had soon risen above our heads, covering the mound, and we could see nothing except a murky violet haze. From within the water could be heard the sounds of creatures coming towards us. Out of the murkiness came the first demon of the delta, a crocodile with burning eyes, gaping jaws, and gleaming teeth. Barely had it appeared when it slipped back away into the dark void. A new form was revealed. The large round bulk of a hippo, sacred horse of water, again with wide-open mouth. It was, in turn, replaced by a fiery-eyed serpent. The fourth delta demon was introduced as a creature not of the water but spawned there whose destiny was to become a god. It was a large black beetle with eyes of burning gold. It scuttled past. Next came a scorpion. Then a bizarre half dog half monkey thing barked its entrance and disappeared into the void. The last demon was in the form of a man burning with golden light and eyes of fire. He too was destined to become a god.

The water that was above our heads began to subside back into the earth. A light above was drying out the water. It was welcoming us, pulling us towards the surface. It was the light of the sun, the first light of first morning of the first day. It was now possible to look around from the mound. The land was renewed. A river, trees, greenery, flowers.

Looking down upon the mound at our feet, a silver disc had appeared. Picking it up and turning it over revealed an ancient script spelling the names of power, of creation, the names of the soul in every man and woman, the names that return us to the one of creation. They are known now as the spheres of the Qabalah and its limitless light. We climbed down from the mound with the disc in our hands and the names within our hearts, for our quest had only just begun. After briefly exploring the new land that the water had revealed we journeyed back to float in a dark timeless spaceless void, coming to land as the darkness cleared to reveal the temple from which we started, the forgotten temple in the woods. We sat back down inside ourselves, becoming aware of our physical bodies again.

For a moment, everything seemed fine. It wasn't. Debbie was not happy. Our previous visit was enough to establish a feeling of caution on her behalf. The fear was well-founded. She had pains that felt like *"burning ice"*. *"Get it out. Please."* Distressing moments ensued. Soon we were gazing with shock and horror on what immediately became known as the Eye of Tiamat, a piece of sodalite, about an inch by an inch and a half in size. I recommended to Debbie that she never return to the place again. Sceptics are welcome to feast on this if they wish. Reality had shifted and now something was coming that would leave us with no doubts.

When all of the lights had been extinguished and we tried to settle down in our German army sleeping bags, the atmosphere in the woods around us was as uncanny as any place we had yet known. Of course, the night's events had served to heighten our sensitivity but this was extreme. Strange sounds came from what seemed like not that far away. Growling. Sighing. Forget black questing on Chanctonbury Ring in the fog on the anniversary of the hurricane. Never mind Dundon Beacon with a black magic murderer on the loose. This was a night that none of those present will ever forget.

The form of the wood emerged from darkness with the gentle summer dawn. Sombre and subdued we departed, seeking out a weary bleary-eyed breakfast at a *Little Chef* restaurant. Debbie was convinced that, more than ever before, the mysterious forces that drove us on were observing us and that the next phase would now begin. It was a statement that she had never made before. Back at home in Southend, I slept for a while and then finished off John Symonds' *The Great Beast,* which I'd been reading for the last week.

In the early evening, John rang. Andy had contacted him and mysteriously requested that we gather at his home as he had urgent news to convey that required our physical presence. He wouldn't let slip a single detail. Only with the group gathered would he reveal what was happening. Of course we were curious. Travelling from Southend to Leigh with John, Kerry, Karl and Lisa, there was plenty of speculation but none of us guessed the truth.

That day he had heard from a local arms and armoury expert who he had left a photo of a Meonia sword with some years before, asking the man to keep an eye out for such an item. This gentleman now had one. Was Andy still interested?

The preposterous denouement was that the sword came into the dealer's possession from a source in Leigh-on-Sea, barely a quarter of a mile from Andy's home. It had been part of a job-lot of indeterminate origin that had included unspecified Nazi artefacts. The dealer had obtained it on the previous Saturday. Now it finally came into Andy's possession barely twelve hours after the manifestation of the Eye of Tiamat. Andy produced the tangibly blackened darker-coloured seventh sword for our inspection. He had the look of a man in a state of ecstatic gnosis about him. Kerry began crying. John spoke on behalf of the males with a cup-final-goal-shout and air-punch-salute. After aeons, it had finally arrived. It was impossible to take it all in. It had been an outrageous couple of days. One gigantic phase was complete. Another was assuredly beginning.

In the first instance, a major episode scheduled for the coming Saturday was now significantly reconfigured. We already knew when we arrived at the Forgotten Chapel that the next stage of the magical journey was to Hebron to make the pact. Months after its first appearance in psychic material, it was finally time to visit Symonds Yat.

During the horrific appearance of the Marduk figure a few weeks before, in the visionary sequence with the winged woman and the two-headed statue, there were references to Hebron and Gulah Mamre. Mamre is a place of Biblical significance in the region of Hebron in what is now Israel. It's an oak grove where Abraham built a huge tent prior to his strange meeting with three 'angels' whom he sat down and shared a meal with. One of them was the *Lord.* The other two wandered on down with him on a cheerful trip to Sodom where the local lads took a lascivious liking to them and got quite vocal in their demands for some angel ass. Things were already looking bad for Sodom in the eyes of the Lord and this kind of thing helped lead to its nuking.

There is a very obvious indication that the angels were flesh and blood beings although clearly different from the surrounding cultural norm. The meal with Abraham may have been ritualistic in nature and calls to mind his earlier meeting with Melchizedek. And Bel means Lord. The mystery of Abraham's meeting with the angels and our magical connection to this was part of the beginning of an opening up of mysteries that would lead Andy to the creation of his masterpiece *From the Ashes of Angels.*

Saturday July 27th was a year and a week since we had been led by the call of the black sword sent forth by the Dweller on the Threshold to our strange night on Dundon Beacon with a killer on the loose. Strange symmetry was at work, inviting consideration of potential unity within two disparate episodes. 1991 saw the group climbing up a rock face into the mouth of a cave that archaeology had shown was used by humans during the earliest stages of habitation in Britain. This made it perhaps the most archaic and primal site we had yet visited. On arriving our immediate intention was simply making ourselves feel at home. We were going to be spending a long time there. After a few hours in a far from consensus environment reality did begin to blur. For a while we sat with faces painted with shamanic designs by Debbie. After the sun had set, a fire 'of essence' was lit in the mouth of the cave. This was a bit naughty and went against a code of practice for the area so we limited the size of it.

A fairly strange scene had been set up for us. An eel had been caught in the river. It had been put in a big container of water and brought up with us. We might be required to kill and eat it in a strange communion pact meal that would accompany an oath we would be making to the One, a path represented by the path of the dragon. The next morning we would cast away our clay totems as a sacrifice into the river from a point high above it. This all felt a bit uncomfortable. There were vegetarians in the group including Andy. We had almost immediately named the eel Eddie and got rather fond of it. Hacking him up seemed a bit hardcore but it seemed we needed to show willingness. Maybe the dragon lord would let him live.

Behind the cave mouth was another chamber. To reach it we had to crawl on our stomachs through a passage barely a few feet high. Torchlight was necessary to then orientate ourselves. Once it was extinguished it soon became apparent that we were in the darkest place in the universe. Not a photon of light was able to reach us from outside. This was a primal blackness the like of which none of us had ever experienced before. Daath had given us the seventh sword and it was in Daath that we must take the oath in return. This was no cave of the heart and Trebor the follet was not in evidence.

On the sunny side of the Tree of Life Adam Kadmon can be seen. Qabalistic lore talks of a kind of anti-matter shadow zone beneath the tree. In a controversial elaboration, Kenneth Grant places it directly behind it. The connecting zone between the two is Daath. The denizens of its paths and spheres have been mapped out. Grant has given particular attention to what he calls the Tunnels of Set in *Nightside of Eden*. There must be a kind of dark Adam Kadmon. The two sides are not in opposition. In theory, they are a complementary balance. Indeed, in the magical system of

Abra-Melin, once the holy guardian angel has been invoked successfully, one then has to summon every demon in hell to demonstrate ones power over them. There's a profound psychology here but there's also no doubt that the road is strewn with casualties.

In the Golden Dawn system of magic there are some important diagrams and teachings concerning the Garden of Eden before and after the Fall. They conform more to general Qabalistic teachings. Originally, the sleeping seven-headed red dragon Leviathan who symbolised the Seven Infernal Palaces which contain the Ten Averse Sephiroth, lay at the foot of the Tree of Life. Configured around the top three sephiroth was Aima Elohim, the Supernal Mother. Where Daath lay, four rivers flowed out forming a cross upon which was Adam. After the Fall, Leviathan was awoken and rose from Malkuth up to Daath and the feet of the Supernal Mother. A flaming sword was placed between the fallen garden and supernal Eden. All too familiar imagery for us.

We were somewhere in the zone. All kinds of motifs from this material were present in our adventure. Hareesh sitting in the cross raising the four rivers. The Thames as a great serpent dragon Leviathan or Tiamat, Seven Infernal Palaces, Ten Averse Sephiroth. All around the feet of the High Priestess of the Supernal Mother in the Blue Flame. We had lived, dreamt, felt, and experienced this imagery as all too real over the past year. It had begun with Vortigern and then Langley. Dwellers on the Threshold of Daath for us. The motif of the black sword and the black dragon had finally fully come together in the vision of Marduk.

It was time to make an oath of allegiance to the force that we now believed was behind the entire epic journey we had set out on at the turning of the decade in Cornwall. The source of the great dragon energy behind the seven swords was a ten-feet tall being of infinite blackness, a being known as a Babylonian deity but older by far. The name on the contract was Bel Marduk but who he really was remained to be seen. Steiner believed that Marduk was an earlier form of Archangel Michael. Bel was normally a solar figure. A few have realised there's a bit more to it. Some have seen a mile high Daath Vader-type form framed against the night sky of Glastonbury and called it Dark Angel Michael. Names like Shemyaza and Melek Taus would only come into view through Debbie later as the *Ashes of Angels* saga began to unfold. Perhaps Ishtar and Tiamat were female aspects of the same light and dark configuration.

Debbie felt that the arrival of the third Key of Balance was like the contract coming through. Now was the time to sign it. Did nobody smell the stench of the pit here? Were we completely insane? During the journey down Debbie had become intensely aware of an unknown large insect asserting its presence in Andy's car with a persistent loud buzzing. Opening the window didn't shift it. Something about it didn't feel right. It called to mind the ambiance of desert demons.

There's no doubt that this was a moment of tumultuous destiny. In a zone we tried to imagine as infinite stellar darkness Debbie spoke the words of the agreement we were entering into and it made clear that any deviance from the pact we were committing ourselves to would have uncomfortable consequences. We would be cast into the Tunnels of Set for all eternity. This thing was binding and it was for keeps. A hard bargain. The option to decline was offered to each individual. Nobody turned away. We said yes to the Babylonian night. We were from Essex. We thought we were *that hard.*

Within a few years the relationships of Andy and Debbie, John and Kerry, and Lisa and Karl would all be over. Andy would find himself addressing a rally of thousands of Kurds in Trafalgar Square telling them they were descended from angels. It's a funny old life.

When I had first been strangely captivated by Eliade's accounts of the Babylonian New Year festivities involving Tiamat and Marduk I could never in my wildest drug-fuelled dreaming have imagined quite where that would lead me. Both figures embodied something of the greater mystery of the dragon serpent. It was an earlier form of the enigma of Michael and the dragon. The combat and slaying are not the full story.

For the time being we were happy campers. Bel Marduk considered it a decent night's work to have our souls so Eddie the eel had been spared. We would rejoice over his return to the river tomorrow. I tried to get to sleep. Despite the buffer of my padded sleeping bag, it was difficult to get comfortable on the floor of the stony cave-mouth. Eventually I nodded out, passing into a most unusual state. I dreamt I was lying at the back of the cave looking outwards in dawn twilight. In the mouth was the still smoking remains of the previous night's fire. A figure was huddled by it. It was not a member of the group because they were all around me in their sleeping bags. Debbie was muttering something about Bel Marduk in her sleep. I heard the phrase 'break the dream' repeated twice from an unknown source as an urgent injunction and awoke.

I found I was staring at *exactly* the same scene. The mouth of the cave and the fire occupied the same position with my eyes open. It was more like blinking than awaking from a dream but the figure was gone. Somehow I knew that the timeline of my destiny had subtly diverged from the others who had dreamed with me in the same cave. I had made an oath and on one level it was binding. I still shared a unique magical destiny with my companions in that dream but other possibilities lay ahead for me as well.

Once everyone had awoken we walked to the edge of a precipice that looked out over the river below. On the way up there I had a brief startlingly vivid minds-eye glimpse of a long wriggly centipede-type creature with a human head sporting a Babylonian beard and hat. This was a tad disconcerting. It was time to complete the process by casting away as bizarre sacrifices the clay totem beasts we had created to represent ourselves at the Forgotten Chapel. In the void where the oath was made we were seen by Marduk as we really were and not as we appeared to be. The totem beasts were an expression of our true forms. Away they went into the river far below us.

We knew, from psychic material initially picked up by Graham Phillips and Bernard, that the seven swords were to be brought together in a series of ceremonies at a place in the English landscape known as the Heart of the Rose. These actions would assist an enormous process whereby the multi-layered mythos of Britain would increasingly connect with the rest of the world, particularly Egypt, as the millennium approached.

In *City of Revelation* John Michell mentioned literature known as the Welsh Triads, supposedly of Dark Age provenance, which contain references to 'three Perpetual Choirs of Britain'. They are named as being Glastonbury, Llantwit Major and Amesbury. Supposedly, at each of these places, teams of monks were chanting continually. Michell drew lines on maps, and extrapolated a huge landscape decagon incorporating the choir sites. At the centre was White Leaved Oak in the Malverns. This was the Heart of the Rose. The main action was some way ahead though. A massive further personal preparation was required before I would bring everything I knew into the climax of that scenario in 1998.

The journey home provided a welcome respite from recent intensity in the form of a superb reconnection with British Music. The ruins of Tintern Abbey were not that far away. A brief stop-over seemed a good idea. Vaughan Williams *Fantasia on a Theme by Thomas Tallis* played in Andy's car as we came in sight of the sunlit place, set in a huge natural amphitheatre with extensive wooded hills all around. I bought a copy of Wordsworth's immortal poem in the abbey shop and wandered through into the grounds to refresh my soul and rid my mind of Babylonian centipedes. I found an inspiring vantage point amongst the ruins and made myself as fully present as possible in the fatiguing circumstances of little sleep and a pact with the devil. The lines of poetry caressed me with cold shivers. "*A sense of something far more deeply interfused.*" I was still alive and valued such spiritual sustenance more than ever. Now what?

PART THREE

CONVERGENCE: COSMIC TRIGGER

"My mind is immersed in Infinite Intelligence which can deliver information to me about my past, present and future."

Leonard Orr. *Rebirthing affirmation.*

SURFING THE ZUVUYA: SYNCHRONICITY GAMES

"The world will only change once we accept and PLAY with the next dimension - the fourth dimension!"
José Argüelles. *Surfers of the Zuvuya.*

JULY '91 HAD SHAPED UP AS A MIGHTY STRANGE TIME. The huge seven swords quest had obviously reached a conclusion. The actual sword had been found and the book was written and soon to appear. The full moon adventures were set to climax with the appearance of a music tape and a live performance at the Fellowship of Isis Convention.

After the weird breaking of the dream, I felt that I needed to ensure I was properly connected to my own unique path. My obsessions with time and anniversaries had been encouraged and amplified by psychic questing so I decided to undertake a series of experiments to try and provoke synchronicity.

I was greatly inspired by José Argüelles' *Surfers of the Zuvuya.* Zuvuya was defined by him as a Mayan term for "*interdimensional thread*", or "*big memory circuit*". *"It connects equally to the future as well as the past."* Wherever you are in the present moment can be modelled as the centre point of an infinity loop, a figure eight on its side. One side of that loop represents the past, the other, the future. The loop is not static but continually in motion. "*The past and future are continuously circulating their memories to you.*" 4D time is *"past and future all at once"*.

Wherever you're at is being constantly defined and determined by the memories meeting in the present moment. Zuvuya "*works individually and collectively*" and can be entered any time and place. "*It is what fuels synchronicity, and consequently, it is the pipeline for magic.*" Once consciously connected to, it becomes obvious you've always been part of it. If out of touch with it, life feels meaningless.

So where is it inside us that we connect to the Zuvuya? How does it actually work through us? Argüelles' book deals with inter-dimensional reality. Its central theme considers the idea that we all exist simultaneously in other realms and we have, in some way, other bodies that function in them. Those 'bodies' are not separate from our physical selves that live in the consensus 3D world. They are in a constant state of communication. Our cultural conditioning has messed up our natural modes of being so that we may not hear these messages at all or we may lack the means to make best use of them.

Argüelles began to have experiences of contact with his 'dimensional double'. This was undoubtedly facilitated by a great personal tragedy. Barely a month after the Harmonic Convergence, in September 1987, his eighteen year old son Josh was killed in a car crash. This major event shaped the form of the book. Argüelles felt that the two could not be separated. The death of his son forced the issue of connections between different realms into Argüelles' consciousness so forcefully that he was opened up to a profound accelerated process. He had already started writing *Surfers* with the intention of helping to explain the Harmonic Convergence to the younger generation. This theme was inevitably amplified. The book is pretty hip and humorous for all its cosmic Californianisms.

"Harmonic Convergence was and is the interdimensional zap of the Zuvuya riding the consciousness of the human race, giving it the signal that something else is going on." Argüelles felt he had heard the signal and wanted to track it to its source. This set him up to surf the Zuvuya. "*The Zuvuya is the wave, and to surf this wave is to be at the dynamic crest that interfaces our third-dimensional physical reality with the reality of the fourth-dimension - the dimension of our dream bodies, energy bodies, or light bodies."* Argüelles stated that the fundamental personal meaning of the Harmonic Convergence for him was the conscious union with his dimensional double. He felt that many other people had connected to their 'converged' selves as well. It seemed fairly clear that something radical had happened to me since August 1987 so I was willing to hear him out.

He named his 4D self Uncle Joe Zuvuya. It manifested as a kind of playful trickster shaman type, telling him *"I'm your memory circuit, hotline keeper, your Zuvuya keeper. I'm the one who keeps the score on what you're up to. I'm also the one who sees to it that whatever information I can get from upstairs gets to you."* Uncle Joe advised Argüelles that, *"we're in this together. You're my third dimensional property. But I'm only as good as you are clear. The more clear you can get about your intentions on this planet, the more light I can pour into you; the more light I can pour into you, the easier you make my job"*.

Beyond 4D is 5D.The fifth dimension is where beings in charge of the planetary programs hang out. Broadcasts come from the sun. The sun in turn gets its stuff from other stars and galactic central, Hunab Ku. Hunab Ku sends out light waves, radio waves, gravity waves and other stuff of greater subtlety, genetic coding transmissions etc. Get sorted with your 4D light body and it in turn can make better connections with the 5D realm. Each one of us is a planetary program from the sun. Uncle Joe suggests that *"maybe you're a broadcast, a special service announcement meant to be played just for this time period?" "You're the result of a particular set of DNA programs. This set of programs is your wave form. – DNA has its own vibratory structure. It's a wave form because you're also electromagnetic."* We can't be separate from the Earth and Sun. Our wave forms are linked to theirs. We can potentially process the full spectrum of wave transmissions from galactic central.

There are many people who, inspired by Argüelles' work, have taken to using the Mayan calendar to make their connection to the Zuvuya. In the summer of 1991 I didn't feel I needed to do that yet. It was already happening to me. I believed that my head was so full of such material that if I played games with time it would be enough to warp-out reality and help my 4D body do its stuff. I would use my own biography as the experimental raw material. My diaries contained the necessary magical formula. I'd been keeping daily one-line entries, written on A4 paper, since 1976. In the eighties I increased the information that basic one line would carry to include things like books I was reading and films I'd seen. Later still, I began recording exercise sessions or drug and booze binges. This basic data has proved priceless to me again and again. I would never have been able to write this book without it. I've also kept long-standing dream diaries and more detailed general diaries. I cannot recommend highly enough the necessity of keeping such records. Crowley emphatically insisted on the practice in his students. It requires very little effort and as this book will hopefully make clear, can potentially generate immense rewards.

Here is an example of one of my one-line entries.

Sun19. y, m.r., pizza, Raj Zen video, Total Recall.

That tells me that on a particular Sunday the 19th, I did some yoga (y), went for a run first thing in the morning (m.r.), dined out on a pizza, watched a video of Rajneesh talking about Zen and then saw Arnie in *Total Recall* at the cinema that night. If I'd started or finished a book that day, I'd have mentioned that. A spliff would have registered as 'spl' with a number afterwards indicating how many were smoked. Separate sheets for each year also kept lists of books read and movies seen in sequence. On an everyday sort of level, it was useful to see if I was smoking too many spliffs or missing too many days exercise. A balanced together month can serve as a great stimulus to later endeavours by proving it can be done. It's an easy way to keep track of one's functioning. It also helped me to set in motion some bizarre processes that soon took on a life of their own and swept me off to an unimaginable convergence.

It was the very last day of July that kicked off the next phase of my mutation. A mate of mine had borrowed some books four years previously and still hadn't returned them. I had vivid memories of the time I'd last visited his home and lent them to him. It was at the time when my relationship with Jane had crossed a crisis threshold into meltdown. I felt that reclaiming those books was very necessary as a kind of little physical sign of bringing that period to closure. They seemed to symbolise something left undone and incomplete. A few associations lingered in my mind. I'd visited him on July 31st 1987. When I got back home, I watched the movie *Big Trouble in Little China.* I smoked three spliffs that night. The next day I began reading a book about Rajneesh, *Death Comes Dancing* by Ma Satya Bharti. I recalled that it seemed that was precisely what then started to happen. How typical of the incomparable Osho. A strange idea came upon me in '91. I would try and retrieve my books on the exact same day, July 31st. Once it was confirmed that my friend was available for a visit, I expanded the whole thing. I got *Big Trouble in Little China* out on video. When I got back with my books, I watched it, also smoking a spliff to further enhance the associations. The following day I started reading *Death Comes Dancing* again. I had no expectations as to what all this was likely to stir up. The day after that was a Friday. High summer. Gloriously hot. During my lunch break, I spoke with Kirk Butcher about a growing Glastonbury hunger. It would be magnificent to be there. I rang Alex. He didn't take much persuading. By early evening, the three of us were driving westward, ready to take our sleeping bags up on to the Tor.

Next morning, at the first hint of sunrise, I registered footsteps nearby. I poked my head out of the sleeping bag cocoon to see an elderly woman walking towards the direction finding plinth at the summit's edge. She stopped and sang *Amazing Grace* to the sunrise. After completing it, she simply turned around to depart down the hill. As she passed me, we exchanged smiles. What was her story? I didn't need to know. I was back in the realm of the Avalon of the Heart and that was all that mattered.

In the morning we aimlessly wandered from shop to shop. I walked out of *Gothic Image* and there was Jane! She was carrying a baby and with her new partner. I had known about this development. She was living in Somerset but a little way from Glastonbury. I'd never seen her there in all my numerous visits during the questing days. On the same dates that things had gone wonky in '87, and immediately following my anniversary games, the matrix repeated on a new twist of the spiral. Later that day we met up again atop the Tor to groove with the ripe sunset. The last time I'd been on the Tor with Jane was the June '86 full moon during Pilton. One week before, I'd been in primordial darkness with Bel Marduk. What a life! I'd known that the completion of the seven swords quest was the culmination of a cycle that probably started on one level in 1985. My return to Essex and the ending of my relationship were all part of it. It was mighty fine to feel something in motion that connected me with a profound continuity, stretching back to my university days, and affirming a mysterious symmetry and destiny at work. Another Glastonbury classic.

I felt that my experiment with synchronicity had got off to a superb start. My methodology was vindicated. From that point onwards I continued the same strategies for a couple of years. If I felt like rereading a particular book and vaguely recalled having previously read it round about that time of year, I'd check my diaries and then arrange to read it again on the exact same date. Likewise with movies. If I felt that the vibe of some year from the past was in the air and something unresolved needed clearing, I'd find out what I was reading and watching and doing on that month in that year and strategically repeat some of it. Sometimes I just replayed things for entertainment. August '91 was full of good examples of how I worked it and the kind of total strangeness that came back on me.

On the 15th I took a day off work. I'd done likewise in 1989. I firstly read Thomas and Olga De Hartmann's *Our Life with Mr Gurdjieff* which I'd read on that day in '87. I then polished off Colin Wilson's *The War Against Sleep* repeating 15/8/82. I moved from that into the *Bhagavad Gita*. I'd taken it with me on my journey to appear in court in Salisbury in 1981. When I got up the next morning I was conscious that the pivotal event was ten years ago that day. Whatever else was in motion I was pleased to think that the whole episode was long gone. Or so I thought. An official looking letter was waiting for me on the doormat. It was a summons to appear in court for non-payment of Poll Tax. The amount owed, £250.00, was exactly the same amount of money I'd been fined in 1981.

This was indubitably a major drag but I was actually quite exhilarated. I was even more convinced that my peculiar experiments with Time to provoke synchronicity were working. I had no control whatever on the results but somehow they were always going to be appropriate because it was the very fabric of my life that I was playing with so I could only get back more of my life in response. As Argüelles said, Zuvuya "*circulates the memories you need for whatever situation comes up*".

However much I'd read on synchronicity, I felt I was to some extent in uncharted territory. I came to feel that it was delivering a teaching that reminded me of the so-called 'Crazy Wisdom' of wild Zen and Tibetan masters. I was being continually slapped about in an uproarious manner and taken beyond my limited sense of everyday identity with the encouragement to abide in something greater. It was magnificent fun.

On the first weekend in September, I had the remarkable experience of performing my *Isis* poem against a backdrop of Oliver's keyboards at the Fellowship of Isis Convention in London. Most of the *Moon Magic* album was performed. Everyone had a chance to take stage centre. It was a hugely satisfying moment for me to have played a part in helping to stimulate and manifest such creativity. It was also immediately apparent that the project was a self-contained one-off episode. The impetus to continue full moon workings was no longer there. We were all moving in different directions. There would be no part two. My connections to the questing group, and in particular to Andy's work, were profound but at that time it was clear that I was being thrown back on my own resources and the next phase was upon me.

DARSHAN

"Come just one step forward, I shall take a hundred towards you."
Satya Sai Baba.

THE GENERAL AFTERMATH of the Glastonbury Zodiac experience in 1990 had been so multi-faceted and immense that I have been forced to omit innumerable strange tales. There had been a truly epic autumnal quest in Cumbria involving St. Bega. Another remarkable episode in November had seen the Sky Dancer group perform to a gathering of Hindus celebrating the birthday of the guru Sai Baba. As 1991 neared its end, the event came back round again with significantly amplified results.

Standing just over five feet tall, sporting fuzzy black afro hair and usually wearing a full length orange robe, Satya Sai Baba's distinctive appearance immediately sets him apart. He is perhaps the most famous of all 20th century Indian holy men and his influence throughout New Age circles has been immense and increasingly controversial.

Baba has claimed to be the world's only living avatar, a full incarnation of divinity. In dark epochs such beings allegedly appear on earth to help the transition from one world age to another. Christians believe there is only one such case. Hindus accept a multiplicity.

More paranormal phenomenon are claimed for Sai Baba than any other person in recorded history. All this has occurred in the modern age in full view of countless people over a period of seventy years. He has said, *"My power is divine and has no limit. I have the power to change the earth into the sky and the sky into the earth. – I am beyond any obstacle, and there is no force, natural or supernatural, that can stop me or my mission"*. That's some boast really. It makes him a kind of Muhammad Ali of gurudom.

Many believe he really is an avatar. There are powerful politicians, industrialists, and media people supporting him. Vast numbers of Indians accept him. He appears to authenticate their traditions. Others consider that he is a miracle working Anti-Christ, one of the false prophets foretold by the *Book of Revelation*. There are stories denouncing him as a prodigious paedophile extraordinaire, a manipulator of the Indian government and judicial system. Some merely grind their teeth at the mention of his name, considering him to be a charlatan conjurer street magician and explain how someone like David Blaine could duplicate all of his tricks.

I'd been aware of Baba for ten years and had read the best-known study of him by a westerner, Howard Murphet's devotional *Sai Baba: Man of Miracles*. I was more enthralled by *Riders of the Cosmic Circuit* by Tal Brooke though. This book was a classic of its kind. Brooke had been with Baba in the early seventies when there weren't that many westerners around him. He had risen to a high position of responsibility and spoken to crowds of twenty thousand people on Baba's behalf. Then he decided that Satya Sai was in fact an Anti-Christ and resolved to expose him to the world. He also made it part of his mission to similarly educate us on the demonic background of Rajneesh and Kundalini Yoga superstar, Swami Muktananda. I've now read his ripping yarn nine times and, with me at least, Brooke has entirely failed in his purpose, as I simply found myself ever more fascinated by these astonishing characters and the mystery they represent.

I found the discourses of Rajneesh far more inspirational but I had met a number of people who were into Sai Baba, all with wild tales to tell. That was what was most immediately compelling about him. It seemed that anyone who got into him soon had remarkable strange experiences to confirm they were on the right track.

An Indian woman who worked in the VAT HQ knew my keyboard-playing friend Oliver. She ran a local Sai Baba group. Every year, on the nearest Sunday to his birthday in November, they hosted a celebration at a school, converting the Assembly Hall into a Hindu temple for the day. She asked Oliver if he would like to perform some music for the occasion. This was a daunting proposition as he knew little of Baba and Hinduism in general. Playing to an audience of five hundred or so Indians who were venerating their guru, who many believed to be God incarnate, would undoubtedly be an honour. The innumerable tales of Baba's paranormal powers also suggested it wouldn't be an average gig. Being aware that I had a long-standing affinity for all things Indian and was usually up for anything, he asked me if I fancied getting involved. I accepted the challenge and soon persuaded the rest of the moon magic Sky Dancer crew to join in. Such had been the roots of our 1990 gig.

In my usual spirit of experimentation I resolved to hang on in there with the mystery. I reserved the right to periodic reality checks. I recognised that I was not going to find out where, if anywhere, I stood with Sai Baba, if I held back or walked away. For the time being I took a huge gamble and was willing to give him the benefit of the doubt. It turned out to be an excellent day and we were warmly received, mainly due to the singing of Kerry and Lisa.

When the invitation for a repeat performance came in 1991, things had considerably changed. All that remained of the Sky Dancer group was myself, Oliver and Alex Langstone. I was keen to go for it but Alex and I were not necessarily the world's greatest vocalists. Oliver assured us that, with all his keyboards and effects, he could make us sound acceptable. We agreed to the challenge. I had a tape and booklet I'd bought in Glastonbury produced by the 1988 solstice shindig Universal Peace Dancers. It featured a selection of chants from the world's religions. Amongst them was a version of *Om Nama Shivaya* that I particularly liked.

I was very interested in Sai Baba's affirmation of his Shiva aspect, which he had regularly demonstrated over a period of years at the festival of Mahashivaratri. There is a symbol of Shiva, widespread in Indian culture, known as the *lingam*. This is usually a stone, ellipsoid in shape. It is often considered to be simply a phallic symbol. There is a deeper philosophy behind the appearance though. It is understood to represent the emergence of form from formlessness, the breaking through into the material realm of the powers of divine creation. On a number of occasions Sai Baba supposedly miraculously produced lingams from within his own body, from out of his mouth. These amazing performances certainly have a touch of show-business about them and invite scepticism

During the sixties the Mahshivaratri routine took on an almost standardised form. Thousands of people would gather at Baba's ashram home at Prasanthi Nilayam. An atmosphere of intense expectancy would build up for days beforehand. Baba claimed to be a reincarnation of a famous miracle working saint named Shirdi Sai Baba who had died in 1918. On stage would be a large silver statue of Shirdi Sai. Satya Sai would come and stand beside it. An assistant brought on a foot high wooden urn filled with sacred ash called vibhuti. This would be held over the head of the statue, letting the ash fall over it until it was empty. Satya Sai then thrust his own arm into the urn making a churning motion. With that the ash began flowing again and would continue until he removed his arm. After repeating the process for a while, the statue would end up completely buried in an amount of ash that was obviously more than the urn could possibly hold. I had seen a film of one of these episodes and it was a bizarre sight.

Lots of devotional songs would be sung, often led by Baba himself. At some point in the evening he would start to appear unwell. He might run a high temperature beforehand. In the midst of the public performance his voice would waver and he would have to be helped to sit down. It reminded me of how James Brown would famously perform, theatrically pushing himself to a state of apparent exhaustion where a helper would cover him with a blanket before resuming. Everyone in Baba's audience would know what it meant and the fervour of devotional singing would increase. Shortly after this he would cough up one, or even more (one year there were *nine*), lingams. They would then be displayed to the audience and later taken away to form the centre-piece of ceremonials. It may appear to be a case of sleight of hand and misdirecting of attention. Some of the lingams have been so large they have appeared to split the sides of his mouth open and produce blood. Why am I willing to believe that these episodes just might be genuine? My experiences in psychic questing had shown me similar phenomenon, albeit scaled down. I had been present when Debbie Benstead had produced the dream stone and the Eye of Tiamat. I was entirely satisfied that they were genuine phenomenon.

With all of that background in my head, I felt it would be a good undertaking to attempt a version of the Peace Dancers *Om Nama Shivaya*. We wouldn't be leading a dance though. This was going to be a thudding electronic drumbeat, floor vibrating, cosmic floaty synth number. Children might start crying. Elderly Indian ladies, who barely spoke a word of English, could become distressed. There was always a possibility that we might empty the place. It was a gamble, but one that we were prepared to take.

We convened for rehearsals the night before the gig in Oliver's living room at his flat in Basildon. It was a dodgy area and his upstairs neighbour occasionally gave cause for concern. This was most clearly demonstrated in an incident that occurred some time after our musical adventures. It was about five o'clock on a Friday afternoon. Oliver's partner of the time, Joanne, was in the living room when she was suddenly startled by the sound of glass shattering from upstairs. This was immediately followed by the sight of a human form falling from above, past the window. Having hit the ground amidst a flurry of broken glass, it picked itself up and ran off down the road shouting "help, they're trying to kill me!" Soon after this came the sound of mass brake-screeching as a number of police cars (who had been keeping the place under surveillance) arrived outside. Apparently a drug gang were in the process of torturing someone upstairs and were about to start sticking swords through him when he decided that jumping through a first storey window was a better option. It was in the midst of this veritable matrix of the Kali-Yuga that we attuned ourselves to the sacred. The whole *Moon Magic* album had already been recorded there.

The next afternoon we arrived at the school hall in good time for our performance, to find the event in full swing. The stage was dense with different-sized flower-decorated images of saints and deities. Long garlands hung everywhere. Devotional songs, known as bhajans, were being sung. I stood at the back of the hall, soaking up the atmosphere. With the completion of the preliminary mood setting, the main program of events commenced. A well known episode in the life of Shirdi Sai Baba was portrayed in a dramatic mime to the accompaniment of a musical narrative on tape.

I had come to have a real affinity for the supposed previous incarnation of Satya Sai, whose form he allegedly still took for certain manifestations. Shirdi Sai Baba was one of India's most famous and popular miracle-working saints. Pictures of his face, white bearded and wearing a bandana headband, can be seen all over India and increasingly often in Britain.

Making his home in the village of Shirdi in a ruined mosque, he had kept a permanent fire burning and lit the inside with oil lamps at night. Most of the villagers initially considered him to be a mad fakir. He depended on charity for food and material needs. Oil was required for the lamps. One evening a shop keeper who usually supplied it claimed he didn't have any as a joke to amuse some local youths. He and they secretly followed Shirdi Sai back to the mosque to see what he would do and have a laugh at his expense. Water jars are kept in mosques for people to wash their feet before entering. At dusk Shirdi Sai was seen to take water from the jars and pour it into the lamps. He then lit the lamps and they burned and continued to do so. The watchers now fell at his feet, totally freaked out.

As he began to demonstrate the full range of siddhis it became clear that one reason for the constant fire in the mosque was to provide ash which he then used for healing. The production of vibhuti ash by Satya Sai Baba is considered to be a demonstration of continuity with the Shirdi form. Some of the stories associated with him are quite outlandish, including the apparent taking of other forms such as a beggar, a hermit, a workman, or even a dog or a cat. Many around him firmly believed that he constantly demonstrated knowledge of what his devotees were doing hundreds of miles away. Blindness was cured and evil spirits cast out. On one occasion he allowed a man with advanced leprosy to come and wash his legs. Instead of Shirdi Sai catching the disease himself, the leper was cured.

Learned pundits who thought him illiterate found he could discourse on the scriptures with more profundity than anyone they had ever met. His prime teaching was Love, Devotion and Surrender. By 1910 he was so feted that he might be seated in a silver chariot and, surrounded by horses and elephants, be taken in procession through the streets. His personality remained essentially the same and he still begged for food. When he died he had just enough money to pay for his burial. His tomb attracts pilgrims of all persuasions to this day.

I paid close attention to the dramatic scene being played out on stage. It showed an occasion when he had asked a devotee to guard his body as he was 'going to Allah'. The instruction was left that if he was not back in three days his body should be buried. As he settled into a trance state it appeared very much that he had indeed died. Officials ordered the corpse buried. The devotee who had been left on guard, with the help of others, successfully resisted this move. They prayed that he would return. Finally, after an absence of three days, his inert body stirred, to much rejoicing. During the performance a man dressed as Shirdi Sai, with an absurd false beard, white bandana and robe, lay on a bed, centre stage. A group of men and women were gathered around him, gesticulating grief, concern, and exhortations to the audience. As I watched this somewhat kitsch scene of amateur dramatics I was aware of powerful cold tingles running up and down my arms and legs. I got the feeling that something strange was definitely happening. There was no time to ponder the mystery as our performance was imminent.

The curtains parted and we faced our audience. A deep space synth sound now emanated from the stage. Bells reverberated. A slow drum machine rhythm vibrated the floor. Cue Alex and I:

Om Nama Shivaya.
Om Nama Shivo.

Shivaya Namaho Shivaya Namaho
Shivaya Namaho Shivaya Namahoo

Shiva, Shiva, Shiva, Shiva, Nama Shivaya
Shiva, Shiva, Shiva, Shiva, Nama Shivaya.

With the completion of the chant, Oliver played a quick flourish of the riff of George Harrison's *It's All Too Much* (covered so superbly by Steve Hillage), which we deemed an appropriate sentiment to express before the mystery of Baba. From there it segued into a sung recitation of the mantra *Om Sai Ram*. Up to this point I felt the vocals had been just about acceptable. Subsequent listening to a recording of the performance leaves me in no doubt that we lost it from then on in. Nonetheless, we were enthusiastically received and the feeling afterwards was very splendid indeed. It had been an honour and a great pleasure.

Only later did the most unprecedented reverberations hit us. The whole event was being videoed from the back of the hall. The man holding the camera was somewhat stunned to notice, early on in the proceedings, the spirit form of Shirdi Sai Baba walk through the door, down the aisle and up onto the stage. This disturbed his equilibrium enough to make his camera work a bit erratic. He hoped to actually get something of this apparition on tape. No wonder I'd gone down with a case of the tingles whilst watching the play.

What came out on the video was a bit unusual. Part of the Hindu tradition of guru worship involves setting aside a chair onto which the divine presence is invited. It may be decorated by flowers. No-one would even consider sitting on it. Sometimes some subtle sign may be seen to reveal the guru's manifestation. If, for example, at a climactic point in the ceremonial, a flower fell from atop the chair it would be considered an auspicious sign. Now that might not seem much to a cynic. On this occasion we had a bit more to be dealing with.

The chair was positioned behind where I'd stood with Alex, so on the video, it appeared exactly between us. It was straight-backed, uniformly dark red in colour, with no design but decorated with some flowers. Some strange trick of the lighting and the video recording helped create an image of Shidi Sai Baba's head, as if floating above the seat. The characteristic bandana headband and beard seem to be discernable. It's not exactly a CGI quality special effect. The entire recording goes continually in and out of focus and generally wobbles around. Shirdi Sai remains for the duration though. I've since shown the footage to a number of people whose responses have varied. Some have simply acknowledged an oddity of some kind in the lighting effect that is vaguely suggestive of an image of Shirdi Sai. Others have seen his face very clearly and felt a definite force emanating.

I am aware that from a paranormal researcher's point of view there are many problems with this story. I never actually spoke to the person who had recorded the film. I don't know how many retellings of the tale had happened before it reached me. The quality of the film is poor. Nonetheless, at the time, the effect was overwhelming for me. There, on video, were Alex and I chanting to Shiva, with the apparition of the head of a miracle-working Indian guru floating in space between us. I pondered my choice of the Shiva chant, the involvement of the statue of Shirdi Sai in the Mahashivaratri Festival, and the mysterious play suggesting he had the ability to function beyond the confines of his body and go walkabout. All of these elements had coalesced. It seemed to have been specially laid on for me personally. Of course it was possible that other viewers of the footage could have their special personal associations to render it similarly meaningful for them.

One of the most important teachings of Hinduism concerns what is known as d*arshan*. This means basically, the sighting of a holy being. It is considered that the most fortunate of all circumstances is to spend time in the company of such a one. Even if it is only a brief glance in the midst of some huge ceremonial, a blessing is transmitted for those sufficiently open to receive it. Indian culture is full of tales of people who have undergone extraordinary difficulties simply in order to have sighting of a saint. I hadn't realised it while it was actually occurring but this was perhaps, in its own peculiar way, my first darshan. And it was strangely typical of my unfolding process. Once again something mysterious and life changing had happened to me. I'd made a profound connection and hadn't actually realised it whilst it was happening. It was only later that the bigger picture was revealed, like the whole 1985 Glastonbury Zodiac and Qabalah episodes. The amount of time that elapsed before I was catching up on myself now was no longer measured in years.

What was I really connecting to with Sai Baba though? Everything felt supremely fine about it all. Nonetheless, in a year of hardcore occultism, a pact with the devil even, I needed to remain open to all possibilities. Perhaps Baba's emergence in my life synchronous to the Babylonian Gulf War Bel Marduk scenario wasn't an indication of his redeeming avatar status but his kinship with the returning spawn of the abyss. Tal Brooke certainly would have thought so. A major moment in *Riders of the Cosmic Circuit* changed his life forever. In India in spring 1971, he experienced an occult vision not unlike a scene from Spielberg's *Young Sherlock Holmes* (and to be fair to him, his account was published before the movie appeared). The location was Cairo. Down at the docks, a huge stone temple was disguised by the facade of a warehouse. Brooke entered through a dark doorway in a high windowless wall and ascended up stairs and through further doors until joining a hypnotically chanting procession in the dim flickering light provided by two black candles on an altar. A burning censer perfumed the room. Two hooded priest figures appeared to be officiating. Brooke recognised one of them as principal of the Vedic school at Baba's ashram. At this point, fear set in. Dominating the eerie chamber were two fifteen-foot tall statues of Set and Anubis. Curtains parted to reveal another beckoning priest, holding a candle before a giant stairway, covered in hieroglyphs, that led upwards towards another chamber that seemed to have no other entrance or exit. The two giant statues suddenly jerked into motion, detaching themselves from the wall, eyes opening to reveal furnace like lights. Brooke heard their footsteps '*sound like hydraulic hammers*' as a wind entered the chamber. The priests moved up the giant staircase, leading the statues. The procession shuffled as if preparing to follow. One of the statues stopped, scanning the group with magnetic intensity, as if to demand their obedience. Brooke wondered why the great initiatory thresholds have to stink of the pit of hell, intuited something was badly wrong, and ran for his life, calling the name of Jesus, which served to return him to normal consciousness.

This undoubtedly remarkable visionary episode focused all of Brooke's concerns about Baba. It was a turning point. From then on, he became convinced that a genuine Anti-Christ is amongst us. The big question seems to be "did he bottle it?" Should he have followed the priests and the living statues into the chamber of no return? Would he have been asked to kiss the devil's goatish backside and then discover on acquiescing (as is said to have occurred at Mendes) that he was in fact presented with the beautiful face of a maiden priestess?

Brooke also wrote a book on Baba alone, entitled *Avatar of Night*, which is available in shortened form as *Lord of the Air*. Here it becomes clear that he had a strong Christian background before immersing himself in all things Indian and that he never really freed himself from certain attitudes that would inevitably generate conflict later. Having led us to the lair of the devil incarnate what horrifying charges is he ultimately able to bring against him? What is it that most clearly reveals Baba as Anti-Christ? Apparently the fact that he is not Jesus but works genuine miracles and that Brooke believes him to be homosexual or hermaphroditic in some weird way, puts Satya Sai up there with Hitler and Stalin as one of history's great villains.

Brooke tells weird tales, variants of which persist to this day, that

Satya Sai has a huge appetite for young boys and has also made homosexual advances towards older westerners, including Brooke himself. According to this corpus of material, if you are male, a private audience with Baba may well involve him unzipping your trousers and having a good fiddle around. As for all of the free hospitals he has set up around India, they are simply the front for traffic in human organs and other repulsive crimes. I must admit that when I first heard these tales they halted me in my tracks somewhat. Since those far off innocent days, effusions by the likes of David Icke have recounted the personal testimonies of people who have, for example, been raped in a black magic ritual by former British Prime Minister Edward Heath. A woman told of taking her young son to see President George Bush senior and the lad emerged with a bleeding rectum. The British Royal family are revealed as extra-terrestrial lizards with a taste for human blood. Icke's contacts talk of witnessing human sacrifice rituals conducted by the dreaded Illuminati and involving prominent world leaders. I neither believe nor disbelieve these tales. I merely note a realm of extreme mutability where personal consciousness is a vital factor.

Nonetheless, in 1993 something real and entirely ghastly would occur at Baba'a ashram. Versions of what happened are wildly divergent. At its conclusion five people lay dead through bullet wounds. In one reality tunnel, a young boy suffered serious anal injury as a result of a major shafting from the avatar. This enraged some students at a nearby Baba college who had become increasingly sickened by endless repetition of such shenanigans. A small group of them marched into Prasanthi Nilayam determined to confront the culprit. Baba's security guards killed them all to definitively enforce silence. Another version has fanatical Hindu nationalists who objected to Baba's multi-faith tolerance mounting an armed assassination attempt that is only foiled through bloodshed. The official version has internal ashram politics generating jealousies and power struggles that ended in death.

In November '91, I again marvelled at the impenetrable mystery of Baba and decided to continue giving him the benefit of the doubt. My deepest feelings were that he was not exactly in league with Bel Marduk in the way Tal Brooke might believe but he was more of a lord of the underworld than many of his devotees realised. The Indians and Tibetans have a more profound psychology concerning their apparently dark deities. It was whilst singing the praises of Shiva, who is simultaneously creator and destroyer that the Baba manifestation had occurred. It seemed pretty obvious to me that Baba had appeared as a benevolent force during a truly extraordinary period in my life. It was also worth pondering that the devotees of Shirdi Sai Baba do not all accept Satya Sai as reincarnation. My powerful experience was not with the form of Satya Sai. I couldn't deny that I personally had nonetheless experienced the exact opposite of the negative stories around him. The karma attendant on the Glastonbury Zodiac quest and the Symonds Yat oath was complex and fraught with peril. Where others might come to grief, I was being helped.

SIRIUS MYSTERY AND EXPONENTIAL ACCELERATION

COSMIC TRIGGER by Robert Anton Wilson was probably the book that I had most enjoyed in my whole life. During the period of decade transition I had taken to reading it with the kind of regularity I had once given to *In Search of the Miraculous.* I was being gradually primed to become interactive with its contents.

Wilson had co-authored with Robert Shea the cult classic *Illuminatus* trilogy. *Trigger* told the story of the background of their researches into the mystery of the Order of the Illuminati, a secret group many believe have far-reaching occult connections and exert a powerful and nefarious influence on world events.

Although the authors initially used the cultural legend as a means of satirising politics and cultism, as the writing progressed, things began to get increasingly weird. A process was set in motion whereby Wilson was led to question to what extent there was a reality behind the mythos of the Illuminati. Information revealed itself in an impressively synchronistic manner, suggesting to him that he may have connected psychically to a magickal current that really did extend back down the ages to an astonishing source. Things he thought he'd made up proved to be the apparent calling cards of the mysterious ones. The way in which the whole thing unfolded was way beyond the sifting of data and ideas by an armchair academic to arrive at some kind of theory.

These ideas seemed to be alive. Connecting to them inevitably generated weirdness. "*In researching occult conspiracies, one eventually faces a crossroad of mythic proportions (called Chapel Perilous in the trade).*" "*Everything you fear is waiting with slavering jaws – but if you are armed with the wand of intuition, the cup of sympathy, the sword of reason and the pentacle of valor, you will find there (the legends say) the Medicine of Metals, the Elixir of Life, the Philosopher's Stone, True Wisdom and Perfect Happiness." "You come out the other side either a stone paranoid or an agnostic; there is no third way. I came out an agnostic."* It didn't necessarily follow that the Illuminati were the bad guys. This was crucial stuff to me. Symonds Yat and Sai Baba were in that zone. What Wilson underwent was a kind of initiation. It forced him to look at the very nature of reality and personal identity. It put him through intense personal dramas and all of it was strangely synchronised with the bigger picture of the madness of the sixties. I was thrilled to find that the enigma of Aleister Crowley was central to the narrative.

Wilson stated that his entry to Chapel Perilous began when he was reading Crowley's *The Book of Lies* in 1971. It is a book full of codes and riddles, Zen-type epigrams, poetry, jokes and magick. Crowley had stated that somewhere within it was concealed the inner secret of Freemasonry and Illuminism. Wilson experienced a flash of insight whereby he felt he'd cracked the code. It dealt with sex magick. This led him to suspect that the Illuminati had possibly been the lineage holders of methods of altering consciousness through sex and perhaps drugs as well. This stuff had to be kept secret as it carried a potential death sentence. Outsiders looking in experienced the immediate horrors of the threshold of Chapel Perilous, suffering as they probably were from Christian conditioning.

Already an experienced psychedelic voyager, Wilson decided to test his theory by combining acid with serious experimentation in Crowley's magickal techniques. As a result of this he found that synchronicities and strange experiences rapidly increased. It was through this doorway that information suggestive of an Illuminati signature fortuitously clustered around him. During the writing of *Illuminatus,* Wilson was inspired to make major use of the symbol of the eye in the triangle, treating it as a motif of the secret brotherhood. He knew that its portrayal on the dollar bill had been linked to Freemasonry. Gradually he came to know that it connects with the Egyptian Eye of Horus design and was used on ceremonial headgear by Crowley. The Beast referred to his work as *'scientific illuminism'*, and occasionally to himself as *'Epopt of the Illuminati'*. Wilson began to notice that the number 23 seemed to appear in his synchronicities a disproportionate amount of times. William Burroughs had introduced him to the idea that some kind of strangeness surrounds the number. At first he wondered if it was a case of selective attention.

The process built up to a peak in 1973. On July 22nd Wilson performed a customised Crowleyan ceremony with his wife involving '*Tantric sex-trance*'. The next morning he "*awoke with an urgent message from Dreamland*". It stated that "*Sirius is very important*". Looking for relevant information in his occult books, he struck gold in Kenneth Grant's *The Magical Revival.* Grant knew Crowley and, along with John Symonds, was one of his literary executors. He had become one of his leading advocates, heading a version of one of Crowley's magickal orders, the OTO (Order of the Templars of the Orient). Wilson was impressed to read that "*Phoenix was Crowley's secret name in the Ordo Templi Orientis... The Phoenix was also an ancient constellation in which Sothis, or Sirius, was the chief star*". "*Crowley identified the heart of his magical current with one particular Star. In Occult Tradition, this is 'the sun behind the sun', the Hidden God, the vast star Sirius*". Indeed, the Order that Crowley created himself, the AA, has been generally taken to mean 'Argenteum Astrum' or Silver Star. The part of Wilson that was a careful researcher hesitated to weird-out too much as he had looked through some of Grant's book before and may have subconsciously absorbed some of the data.

Later on, at a public library, his doubts were dissolved. He read that July 23rd, that very day, was the date when the so-called 'dog days' began. Sirius has come to be known as the dog star. This dates from Graeco-Roman times. It's located in the constellation of Canis Major, the Great Dog. It follows Orion the hunter as the dog at his heels. The ancient Egyptian calendar began when it was seen to rise above the horizon, behind the sun, at dawn, after a long period of absence from the sky. This return was noted across the classical world as the beginning of the season of scorching summer sun, the dog days. In Egypt, it was once broadly synchronised with the inundation of the Nile. The river dominated the agricultural cycle of Egyptian life so it was inevitable that the star heralding the season of its blessings would be regarded as important. To the Egyptians, Sirius was the star of the Goddess Isis. The river's fertile gifts could easily be associated with a divine mother. Nuit is not separate from Isis, rather a more expansive cosmic form of her. In *The Book of the Law* Nuit says, "*I am Infinite Space and the Infinite Stars thereof,*" showing how Isis is within her. Despite the preponderance of Egyptian motifs in Thelemic magick, Grant also traced its lineage to Sumero-Babylonian times.

Wilson was obviously stunned by this. He couldn't resist speculating as to whether, via Crowley's work, he may have tuned in to a magickal frequency that really did link Earth to Sirius through hyperspace. Somehow he had been led to the most auspicious date in the calendar to make that connection. The eye in the triangle represented Sirius. Perhaps the 23 enigma had been leading him towards the July 23rd event. Things he had been pondering on for years seemed to have been inexorably leading him to that moment of revelation. I paused for thought as well, when I remembered something that Wilson didn't mention. The birthday of Rose Crowley, who had been so instrumental in the reception of *The Book of the Law*, was also on July 23rd.

From that moment on, Wilson was willing to entertain the possibility that he might be in contact with an intelligence connected with Sirius. This episode lasted for over a year. *Trigger* contains an extensive consideration of the 'contact' phenomenon.

It wasn't just Crowley who seemed to be linked with Sirius. Idries Shah stated that the Illuminati had arisen from a Sufi impetus. He focused on a particular verse in the *Koran* considered central to the secret doctrines of this lineage. *"Allah is the Light of the heavens and earth. His light is resembled by a lamp within a niche. The lamp is within a crystal, like a shining star."* Wilson felt that the star in question could well be Sirius. OTO documents, approved by Crowley, trace their origin to a famous martyred Sufi saint, Mansur el Hallaj. I later learnt that Crowley was actually studying under a Sufi Sheikh at the very time that the events leading to the reception of *The Book of the Law* began. The teacher was of the school of the Sidi Isawiyya. Founded by Sidi Ibn Isa (1425-1526), they incorporated pre-Islamic shamanic magical rites into their practices, and were considered heretical in some Arab countries. Crowley made extensive use of one of the most notable Sufi techniques, the Zikhr. This is similar to Mantra Yoga, involving repetition of holy verses whilst cultivating exalted emotional states. In 1909, whilst walking across the Algerian desert, he recited a verse from the *Koran* 1001 times, prostrating himself in the sand with each repetition.

Gurdjieff, has also been strongly linked to Sufism, and Wilson was led to connect him to the mystery as well. One of his most important followers, J. G. Bennett, had been willing to accept *Meetings with Remarkable Men* as primarily based on real events.

He tried to discover the locations it mentions with a view to finding the Sarmoun Brotherhood. Links with the Khwajagan and Naqshibindi Sufis seemed very likely. The idea of a Babylonian beginning was deemed acceptable. I had read his book on this quest, *Gurdjieff: Making a New World,* and considered it to be outstanding. Wilson focused on a passage that mentioned Gurdjieff discussing why he rewrote some of his book *Beelzebub's Tales.* Passages were made deliberately obscure in order to *'bury the dog deeper'*. Some thought that he meant to say "bone". He explained that the dog he was speaking of was Sirius, "*which stands for the spirit of wisdom in the Zoroastrian tradition*". *Beelzebub's Tales* can be taken on one level as a kind of science fiction tale. It is set on board a space ship named Karnak. Wilson wondered whether this plot device was more than just a vehicle for allegorical teaching? There may be an implication that the source of Gurdjieff's teaching was extraterrestrial. Sirius was originally present in a way that revealed too much so it needed to be hidden.

I found confirmation of this in the revised updated version of Thomas and Olga DeHartmann's *Our Life with Mister Gurdjieff.* The original had been the memoirs of Thomas. To this was added material from his wife. Olga had been Gurdjieff's secretary when he had begun *Beelzebub's Tales.* She had taken dictation of the initial draft. Included in the memoir was the original version of the very first page. The spaceship Karnak was specifically stated to be journeying from Sirius.

That there was a profound connection between Crowley and Gurdjieff has been demonstrated satisfactorily to me by something that others seem to have missed. I cover it in more detail in *Aleister Crowley and the Aeon of Horus*. In *Beelzebub's Tales,* Gurdjieff mentions a group of Tibetans who understood the energy of warfare as a global phenomenon, and were able to exercise occult influence to keep it from overwhelming the world. When the British Younghusband expedition entered Tibet the group leader was killed during a confrontation with the invader that had intended to negotiate peace but gone disastrously wrong. Gurdjieff stated that this resulted in the dogs of war being unleashed into the world in a way previously unknown.

There is one obvious candidate for this episode in the historical narrative and it happened on March 31st 1904. Gurdjieff was supposedly in Tibet himself at the time. Himalayan mountaineer Crowley was already in Cairo. A few days before, he had been informed that the old world was about to disappear in flames. Barely a week later, he took dictation of *The Book of the Law.* The two most significant magus figures of the 20th century both stated that a cataclysmic new epoch had been unleashed upon the world that would be characterised by ferocious warfare. Not only that, they both dated its beginning to exactly the same period of time.

On July 23rd 1976 Wilson was inspired to perform, "*using all the paraphernalia of ceremonial magick*", an invocation of Hadit, having linked this aspect of Crowley's cosmology with the eye of Horus, which is Sirius. There was a sense that the explosive energies at the very heart of matter and consciousness, characteristic of the Aeon of Horus, were an expression of a greater cosmic process linked with Sirius. Nothing as immediately obvious as the events of 1973 immediately manifested as potential validation. Within a week however, Robert Temple's *The Sirius Mystery* appeared, to great publicity and amazement. It was difficult not to feel that the two events were connected, but no normal laws of causality could explain how.

Temple's book rapidly attained cult classic status. It takes the reader on a memorable journey. I'd first read it in 1980 and it had blown my mind. The West African Dogon tribe know that Sirius has an invisible companion, although our modern astronomy didn't prove this until the 20th century. They know its orbital period of 50 years and that it's one of the 'heaviest' stars. They say that they know this because a visitor from Sirius told them, thousands of years ago. These beliefs are central to their whole culture and the rituals of its religious calendrical mythology. Temple believed that this information was carried, over a long period of time, across Africa from Egypt. He lingers there on the subject of Nuit/Isis, Anubis, and the Nile. He eventually postulates a starting point in Mesopotamia, involving an actual physical 'contact'. There are also glimpses of a kind of esoteric cultural package, partially inspired by those events, surviving down through the ages. Fragments of it can be spotted within the western mystery tradition.

Temple seemed generally unaware of the fact that the tradition remains alive and that Egyptian and Babylonian deities are invoked to this day. His historical search nicely complemented Wilson's. Robert Temple postulates 'contact' at a similar time and place to where J. G. Bennett eventually came to believe that the lineage behind the Sarmoun Brotherhood originated, and Kenneth Grant traced back the Thelemic current. It all leads back to the origins of our civilisation in Sumero-Babylonian times, with links also to Egypt. If the Glastonbury mythology was correct, this was when the creators of its terrestrial zodiac had travelled to Britain. Questing lore had also expanded my sense of those enigmatic dudes.

Temple concluded by wondering if the human race has been left with a kind of initiative test. The beings from Sirius may have been monitoring our progress, waiting for us to finally realise the implications of the cultural package they have left us. They may be waiting to resume the contact. Perhaps *The Sirius Mystery* could represent a crucial moment? "*If what I propose in this book really is true, then am I pulling a cosmic trigger?*" Wilson was happy to affirm the possibilities and took the phrase for his own book's title.

It could be argued that Wilson's Sirius experiences originated solely in his own brain. Evolutionary games like magick and psychedelia activate normally latent faculties that produce major weirdness. Different bits of our heads start having dialogues together and the result brings dreaming and waking together. We can affect the external world. Increased synchronicity can be a symptom of such stirrings. Shamans and yogis know the landscape. Our rational culture doesn't, hence confusion. The contact experience may be with parts of our own higher selves, dressed by our dream weavers in the cultural fabric of fears and expectations.

The immense amount of information and ideas in *Cosmic Trigger* (of which I have omitted much) climaxed with Wilson's summary of the most outlandish psychedelic prophecy imaginable. He set the scene by discussing the topic of acceleration. Henry Adams (a descendant by the way of the presidential family who had fled the 'Dragon persecution') suggested that the development of technology follows an exponential sequence. In other words, rather than following a 1-2-3-4 sequence, information doubles itself: 2-4-8-16 etc. This doubling process is occurring at an increasingly rapid rate. There are more scientists alive now than in all of previous history added together, so it's a safe bet that this modern age will see more breakthroughs than any other time.

The Invisible Landscape by Terence and Dennis McKenna suggests that the intensity has barely begun. The brothers' background included anthropology, biology, chemistry and botany. In March 1971 they travelled to the upper Amazon basin and sampled the local hallucinogens. A major mutation of consciousness occurred. In trying to figure out what had happened to them they came to regard the universe as a hologram created by the action of two hyper-universes, just as an ordinary hologram is created by the interaction of two lasers. If this is true it means that every part contains the information of the whole. Every atom contains the brain of the whole universe. 'As above, so below.'

This memorable fancy is only the starting point for the McKennas. There are supposedly 64 timescales in the hologram of our universe that relate to the 64 *I Ching* hexagrams. What we call 'mind' or 'consciousness' could be modelled as a standing wave form in these 64 time systems. As the two hyper-universes making up the hologram of our universe interact in time, 'mind' manifests further in our continuum. This means that we are riding 64 evolutionary waves all mounting towards a point of cosmic awakening. Some drugs may enable one to be in a number of the zones at once.

All 64 timescales peak in 2012 and they include some very interesting sequences. Wilson details:

> *"A 4,300 year cycle from urbanisation to the dawn of modern science.*
> *A 384 year cycle of science.*
> *A 67 year cycle from the technological breakthroughs of the 1940s, including nuclear energy and DNA in which there will be more acceleration than between Galileo and Hiroshima.*
> *A 384 day cycle in 2011-12 where there will be more transformations than in all of the previous cycles.*
> *A 6 day cycle at the end of increasing acceleration that peaks in the last 135 minutes when 18 barriers comparable to the appearance of life, the invention of language or the achievement of immortality will be crossed, 13 of them in the last 75 x 10-4 seconds."*

I didn't have any idea about how the McKennas had worked out the various cycles in that list. It wouldn't have surprised me if they were open to criticism. Exponential increase is not inevitably involved in all processes. For example, by 2012, if their current rate of expansion continues, one quarter of the entire global population will be official Elvis impersonators. I have my doubts about that scenario. Nonetheless, from my first reading of *Cosmic Trigger* I accepted the basic principle of acceleration. Wilson was an optimist, foreseeing a profound mutation of humanity for the better as imminent. I was mindful of the vast power and resources of the forces of reaction and conservatism. What I did take away with me from reading *Trigger* was the belief that the kind of changes Wilson was advocating *were* possible and the rate of acceleration was always going to be increasing. One day something like the McKenna scenario might happen. Assuming we didn't nuke or pollute ourselves into extinction it probably would do. If the Sirius hypothesis had any validity help might be available. I didn't feel it would come in the way that many New Agers expected. Fleets of flying saucers full of smiling benevolent Space Brothers seemed like a fifties Disney fantasy. That's why Wilson set my head on fire. He brought in the most credible sources I knew, Crowley and Gurdjieff and the whole massive lineages they connected to, as witnesses for his speculations.

As time passed, for me and many others, it became increasingly interesting that the end of 2012 had been flagged by both the McKennas, starting from the I Ching, and Argüelles, from the Mayan perspective. The Sirius mystery, 2012, and the idea of many cycles of varying lengths culminating together germinated somewhere in the back of my mind, awaiting a time when they would emerge in my personal life.

REAMALGAMERGENCE

"How can we find my original quantum state and return me to it?"
Commander Worf.

As the Christmas season approached I felt the need to do something to help me assimilate the passing year and connect to the mysteries of what lay ahead. Jane Satchwell was the former girlfriend of mine from university days who I'd met up with again at the Pilton '85 mudbath. We'd kept in touch from then on. By 1991 she was living in Frome, which is about forty minutes drive from Glastonbury. We'd talked of the possibilities of me staying with her for a weekend on a number of occasions. It would be a great opportunity to step apart from my normal life by going on a journey alone, instead of with my usual companions. As it was Glastonbury I was heading for, it was more than likely that something would happen that was in continuity with the essential dynamic of my destiny. A weekend in early December presented itself when we were both available. It was only after the date was set that I realised that it fell on the exact tenth anniversary of my first meeting with her. That was typical of the recent flavour of synchronicities and primed me to anticipate something interesting.

That first week of December turned out to be fairly lively. A mate of mine sorted me out with a new sound system. I procured a large bag of weed, put up the crimbo decorations and settled into the zone. Having not smoked for nearly five months, it was guaranteed to strongly affect me. The night before my journey to Somerset I had an after-dinner spliff, relaxing to Christmas tree lights and the music of Andreas Vollenweider's *White Winds* album. I soon drifted into a general pondering on the state of my life.

I realised that my imminent journey was the first time I'd been to Glastonbury alone since the classic '88 solstice. That led me to recall that night again. I'd arrived as a major drum-out was in motion. It had really stirred me up and I'd felt how good it would be to try and get something like it happening in Essex. I did. The most fulfilling manifestation of it had been barely six months previously, when the Sky Dancers had drummed and chanted a visionary shaman into appearance in the clouds above the Tor. A satisfying full circle. In '88, the Sufis had then appeared. I'd loved their Universal Service with chants from the worlds' religions and wanted to do something like it myself. Just two weeks previously, I'd been on stage in front of hundreds of Hindus, performing a version of a chant I'd got from a tape made by those very same Sufis. Shirdi Sai Baba had seemingly manifested in the process. I think it was safe to say that little part of my '88 desires had been fulfilled as well. The Sufis had been followed by the witches and their brilliant Sabbat. Once again I'd felt a huge yearning to do something like it myself. Since then, the whole Sky Dancer episode had occurred. I'd been a major catalyst in getting a group of people together who went on to manage a superb sequence of Wiccan lunar and seasonal rituals. Great inspiration had come from it. Three months previously, the performance of *Moon Magic* at the Fellowship of Isis Convention had completed that dynamic. I'd have to say, 'result'. On leaving Glastonbury in '88, I'd read *The Green Stone* on the way back to Southend. I really wanted something of that story to start again and for me to be part of it. Three and a half years later, the seventh sword quest had arisen and was now complete. A book had been written, was on sale in the shops and I was in it! Another result.

Hang on a minute.

Whoa! Cold tingles covered me as an awesome realisation made itself felt. I'd got my moneys worth from June '88 really, hadn't I? The sheer comprehensiveness of it all overwhelmed me. I had made a totally full-on connection to every single thing that was happening on the Tor that night and then some. Any one of those aspects would have been enough for most people. What the fuck was happening? Somehow I had clearly played out a hidden plan to perfection. That night on the Tor had assuredly been a gigantic initiatory process. I felt like I had received some kind of microdot programming in hyperspace. I remembered the movie *Close Encounters of the Third Kind.* The main protagonist Roy Neary, played by Richard Dreyfuss, is out driving a truck when he encounters an alien vessel that hovers above him. He looks out of his window up at it and sees a brief flashing light and hears barely audible tones. He had received a destiny download that his conscious mind was unaware of. After that, he is pulled ever more strongly towards an unknown culmination. Images of a strange mountain increasingly fill his head. He has to repeatedly paint and model it, striving to understand it as his marriage and job disintegrates. Finally it leads him to the mother-ship. I'd always loved that movie. Now it provided the best model I could find for understanding the kind of thing that seemed to have happened to me. Global heart chakra and mobile third eye indeed!

Ever since 1979 I'd dreamed of some kind of ultimate event I would experience in relation to Glastonbury Tor. It had pulled me back into its vicinity again and again. Solstice '88 delivered the goods. I knew it at the time but of course it needed all of its elements to fully unfold in time for the whole picture to become clear. The 1985 convergence with Andy had been a similar kind of thing. The Glastonbury Qabalah was another. This seemed to be of a greater level of magnitude again. And it had all happened when I'd barely met Andy.

At a time when I was wondering where my life was leading, this realisation of 4D planning helped me transcend petty egoic doubts and relax into the awesome mystery that was clearly present. Still reeling from the contemplation of the1988 microdot, I then realised something else. I'd caught up on myself again in another of those Streiber type moments. I was thinking about the last time I'd been to Glastonbury alone. I was going back there the very next day. A huge cycle had completed itself. The implication was surely there that the next biggie was about to kick off. It was not unreasonable to wonder if another download might happen over the next few days. Something told me it wouldn't take three and a half years to complete this time. Acceleration was increasing. With this further mutation of my consciousness, I wondered if I was being invited to look out for the process and maybe be aware of it whilst it was actually happening. Whatever the case, I was as well primed for the coming Glastonbury visit as any I'd ever made.

On Friday December 6th I travelled to Frome. During the train journey I read *Avalon of the Heart*. It felt like the right thing to do. It was great to see Jane again. She lived with her two cats in a house dating from the 18th century. Coming to her home seemed another example of the culminating of big cycles that the previous night's perspective had revealed to me. As well as the ten-year thing there were some definite 4D mysteries in our connection and the timing of my visit. It had been Jane who had introduced me to *Cosmic Trigger* in 1982. At Pilton '85, I'd bumped into her in the middle of the infinitely mysterious matrix that had connected me to Andy Collins and the Glastonbury Zodiac. We'd lost touch but were set up to re-establish contact again. She had been the agency whereby the 1988 solstice Sufi and pagan chants had found their way into the Sky Dancer situation. If I hadn't met her at that point, it's quite possible that the *Moon Magic* episode would have been significantly different. Hearing her tales of the Sufis also primed me to buy the tape featuring *Om Namah Shivaya* and that led to the particular form of the Shirdi Sai Baba event of only a few weeks before. There was a very strong feeling of continuity. When was it that I really first experienced the big download? Jane was somehow connected to a number of the major threshold crossings of my life. That was great and it was also puzzling. Our temperaments were massively different. Back in the university days she had never been a drug-crazed dementoid like me. There was no way we could sustain a relationship. She had ascetic tendencies and a definite distaste for Crowley. Over the years she'd become a bit of a New Ager. After ten years of knowing each other there was a sense of 4D mystery. In the midst of a brain-nuke I was grateful for assistance.

On the first night, we caught up on general gossip and I raved and drooled over the perfection of June '88. I told her of my belief that a major new phase was primed to begin for me and I was on the lookout for it. Somehow the conversation turned to Tarot. Jane had a deck and we gave each other readings. No great revelations emerged. It had been a long day and enough was enough. I retired for the night to charge myself up for the imminent visit to Glastonbury. Saturday was overcast in the manner one would expect of December. The town was decorated for the Christmas season. Of course, we ascended the Tor. As in '88, I internally spoke to the unknown forces presiding there. I confessed my total awe at the comprehensiveness of the solstice microdot and expressed my desire to be worthy of it and to be able to connect with the next part of the process. No mother-ships appeared. No Ascended Masters materialised before me. That was fine. I knew with total certainty *something* was going down, right there and then. It would reveal itself to me. In the meantime I would search the shops for goodies. In *The Crystal Star* I found a book that instantly struck me as an essential purchase. It was *The Way of the Secret Lover: Tantra, Tarot and the Holy Guardian Angel* by Christopher Hyatt and Lon Milo DuQuette. The title was more than enough to be going on with. I knew Hyatt's work anyway. There was no way it was going to be anything less than excellent. I bought it.

Saturday night was chilled. Jane gave me a foot massage by candlelight to the accompaniment of floaty music. It had been a regenerative weekend. Nothing overtly spectacular had happened. The culmination of the cycle begun in '88 and my realisation of it was quite sufficient unto itself. Things were obviously moving into another realm of functioning. It was part of my adventures in synchronicity and games with time, my surfing of the Zuvuya. I was back in Southend by Sunday night. Monday had been secured as a holiday. I would devour Hyatt and DuQuette's book then.

Within twenty pages I was convinced that I had found the next part of the program. *Way of the Secret Lover* had only been published that year. The central theme of the book was something haunting and immediately familiar to me. We all have a Secret Lover, a profound inner aspect of our most fundamental identity, "*an ideal lover who has adored us since the beginning of our individual existence and who will never abandon us until the instant we merge our being in absolute Godhead*". Our awareness of this may take the form of a response to certain types we might repeatedly fall in love with. Sexual ecstasy can be a doorway to communion with it, likewise the effects of the Arts. Our relationship with the Secret Lover, however unconscious it may be, nonetheless forms a kind of standard against which everything else may be compared. This can lead to melancholy, aching nostalgia, and general pangs for that which seems so near yet unattainable. Surrendering to the Secret Lover can be considered to be a fundamental process at the real heart of all religions. Unfortunately, the assorted orthodoxies have always acted in ways that have prevented their adherents from experiencing the blessings of such a communion. Accounts that exist leave no doubt that the most obvious ways of expressing it always use the symbols of enraptured love and sexual ecstasy. This mode of being was never a favourite of the Inquisition. In the western mysteries the Secret Lover has been called the Higher Genius, Adonai, and the Daemon. The Golden Dawn/Crowley Tradition used the term 'Holy Guardian Angel'. 'Knowledge and Conversation of the Holy Guardian Angel' was the fundamental task of any would-be magus. Only thus equipped could the higher levels of initiation be navigated.

When I'd got busted in 1981 I began to recognise some sort of process of magickal destiny at work in me. It was amplified in 1988 when I met Andy and recognised what had been set up in June '85. In December '91, having caught up on the '88 microdot, I had an even stronger sense of some astounding fundamental part of my identity that was masterfully living my life. It was as close as my breathing. I slept with it every night. Truly it was my Higher Genius, my Daemon, my 4D light body or whatever terminology best revealed it at any given moment. I was enraptured by it. I could readily accept it as my 'Secret Lover'. It had steered me through eastern mysticism, western magick and psychology, the whole Glastonbury mythos and the immense Questing adventures. A remarkable diversity. With the same kind of perfect timing that had brought me to *King Arthur's Avalon* a decade before in 1981, Hyatt and DuQuette brought everything together for me.

It was all summed up in the aphoristic statement that "*the will toward self mastery and the will to surrender are the head and tail of the same snake*". The exposition of that idea dealt with very powerful issues indeed. Surrender has been known to cause many a twitch amongst westerners, especially narcissistic magicians. "*It is unfortunate but true that most of life's misery is caused by our inability to surrender to love. In a desperate attempt to fill this void people become addicted to alcohol, food, sex, endless affairs, fame, fortune and of course drugs.*" Surrender appears to be a negation of the will. The impression can be given that something of vital importance can be lost, integrity, or even the very soul itself. Hyatt and DuQuette assert that "*though the boundaries of the individual must necessarily fade away there is no way in the world that you can lose your Self. Your true Self is hard wired in and even if it were possible to lose one's self or be possessed it would have to be the result of one's true will".*

Accounts of experiences of mystical surrender tend to agree that they are centred in the heart region, whether it be the Qabalistic Tiphereth with its Holy Gurdian Angel contact, or the yogic Anahata heart chakra. It marks a major stage in the activation of the True Will. My own version of this process was inextricably linked with Glastonbury, the alleged global Anahata.

The Way of the Secret Lover centres on a Tarot ritual the authors call the 'Ultimate Divination'. They consider it to be a possible means to contact and communion with the Holy Guardian Angel. The images depicted by the cards seem to cover all possible human situations. They are "*the visual spiritual equivalent to an encyclopaedia of man's collected knowledge*". Occult mythology tells of the origins of the Tarot in Egypt. It has been seen as a product of Thoth, the God of Wisdom. There are endless disputes over its true history. By the late 19th century, the cards had been linked to the Hebrew alphabet and Qabalah. Whether this idea was of recent invention need not concern us here. The connection has been a fruitful one. They do seem to fit together rather well. Golden Dawn teachings included the Qabalistic Tarot. Crowley got a tremendous amount of mileage from the associations, eventually producing his *Book of Thoth* masterpiece.

Hyatt and DuQuette believe that the Tarot has the potential to connect one to the deepest realms of the psyche and the most fundamental issues of our lives. For that to occur one must function from a level beyond that normally required for a standard divination. In fact one must connect with the Secret Lover in order to ask it the big question for the 'Ultimate Divination', "What is the true purpose of my life?" It simply isn't possible to get into that space without sustained preparation on all levels.

The authors consider one's birthday to be the most auspicious time for the performance of the ritual. My birthday was in four months time. It wasn't just any old birthday either. It was the mystically vibing 33. It had been a big year for Jesus and I was already determined I was going to get a result out of it as well. The basic idea of the Tarot/Holy Guardian Angel ceremony was perfect. It had a strong sexual aspect as well that, in the absence of a partner, could not be fulfilled but I was sure I could still make something awesome of it.

There was one obvious prerequisite. I didn't have a Tarot deck. I'd owned Crowley's but sold it during a period of poverty, after my hypnotherapy business failed in 1985. I wasted no time. The day after completing the book, I went out and bought the cards again. Inevitably, I spent many hours looking at them. Much of the time I was stoned. That helped me get into the imagery all the more easily. An idea came to me that seemed extravagant. It kept nagging away at me through the Christmas period. Finally, on the morning of New Year's Eve, I gave in to it. I took the twenty two major arcana cards to the library and got them all laser colour-copied up to A4 size. It cost me £25.00. In those days, that was not a sum of money I could sensibly afford, but the idea was so powerful, it was impossible to resist. I'd worked out that there was enough space in my hallway to put them up as a gallery. As I saw them coming off the machine, I was in awe. They looked incredible. I was wildly excited and wondering what this would set in motion. Back home, I affixed them to the wall with blu-tack. There was about a hand's width between each image. I could only think of one good way to press the 'on' button. A monster spliff was in order. Having smoked it, I walked very slowly along the hall, looking at each card. I found that, after a few moments, they went three-dimensional. After that, there came a point when I seemed to feel a sense of presence, that the scenes depicted were in some way alive. This was the necessary sign I was intuitively awaiting. It took a long time to walk along the hall. From that moment onwards, for a few months, all journeys between rooms in my home, even if I was intending to visit the toilet, involved long distractions in the Tarot gallery.

It was perfectly calculated as the best way to totally internalise the imagery and the various magickal associations of the cards. For example, each one of them was assigned to a path on the Qabalistic Tree of Life. There were planetary and/or astrological attributions. Hebrew letters were likewise designated and they all carry their own visual associations. For example *The Magus* gets placed on the path between Kether and Binah. Its symbolism includes the planet Mercury and the Hebrew letter Beth, which means 'house'. I already had some of this material in my mental filing cabinet but didn't have the whole thing memorised. If I was going to respect the hidden dynamic that had connected me to Hyatt and DuQuette's book, if I really meant to make the most of it on my birthday, I needed to complete that mental work. With the astounding gallery right there in my face, it was not going to be a hard slog. In fact, it was going to be magnificent fun. I was sure that once the inner machine was switched on, and the full range of magickal symbolic connections made, it would all start to work on its own, regardless of whatever I was consciously doing. It was a great way to end the year and to set myself up for the rest of that very day, which involved a trip down to Glastonbury for the midnight transition. The events of the night weren't particularly spectacular. I travelled with Alex and Kirk. Andy was about but very much involved in his work of the time, producing a book on the crop circle phenomenon. I was happy to conclude another astounding year on the Tor and open myself up for more adventures.

My first task of 1992 was to become fully engaged in Qabalistic Tarot studies. The basic attributions were memorised in a few weeks. I read the whole of Crowley's *Book of Thoth* to go into greater depth. I was performing the Lesser Banishing Ritual of the Pentagram (of which, more later) everyday. I'd worked out a schedule for the gradual intensification of my magickal practices as my birthday drew nearer. I pondered on the strange relationship of Glastonbury and the Qabalah in my inner life. The revealing of the Tree of Life in my living room in December '88 had been a major threshold crossing. On another turn of the spiral, another visit to Glastonbury was now pulling me even deeper into such studies.

REBIRTHING

> *"For mind and body alike there is no purgative like Pranayama,no purgative like Pranayama."*
>
> Aleister Crowley. The Book of Lies.

I'D PLUGGED IN A MAGICKAL SELF-MASTERY EPISODE for my birthday. What about the surrender? There was a New Age shop in the Southend Victoria Centre called *Dimensions.* I'd been gradually getting to know the owners, Joan and Dana Lee. Joan was a former Rajneesh sannyasin who was now into Sai Baba. Dana Lee was into radical politics, Rajneesh, shamanic dancing and the rock 'n' roll lifestyle with attitude. I enjoyed talking to her. There was a backroom behind the shop that was large enough for gatherings. One day I popped in after work and saw a poster on the wall. A group Rebirthing day was happening there on Sunday April 5th. My

33rd birthday. And I'd been born on a Sunday. This was barely five minutes walk from my home. It really seemed it had been laid on for my benefit. I immediately affirmed I was up for it.

On Monday March 16th, I was walking along Southend High Street after work. I suddenly diverged from my path and entered into the huge *Keddies* department store. It was a split consciousness episode. Mr 3D was curious. "Oh, I'm going in here. Why am I doing that? Am I heading for the *HMV* section? Is there some music or videos in there I need to find? Looks like I'm going up the escalator, so it's not *HMV*. Must be the *Dillon's* bookstore. Yes. I've got off on that floor and I'm walking in there. I wonder what section I'm going to look at? I seem to be heading straight for the New Age stuff. What's that there? Of course!" I'd been guided straight to *Rebirthing in the New Age* by Leonard Orr and Sondra Ray. It was the first copy of it I'd ever seen. In just under three weeks I was going for the biggie. It seemed I was being given the chance to thoroughly prepare.

Leonard Orr was the founder of Rebirthing. I believe him to be one of the most extraordinary New Age figures, an eccentric in the best sense of the term, a true innovator. For those interested in the subtle chain of the transmission of ideas, in the sixties, Orr was briefly associated with Werner Erhard, the founder of EST (Erhard Seminars Training), who in turn had a Scientology background. Orr's written works cover a giddying spectrum of subject matter ranging from community politics, millionaire prosperity consciousness and fire purification ceremonies to physical immortality. Rebirthing, at first glance, has seemed to some to be a typical Californian New Age Me-Generation cult. Others have seen it as a modern manifestation of ancient yogic teachings. It has been known to provoke strong responses of affinity and aversion. So what's it all about?

Orr's uniquely individual contribution began in earnest when he noticed a sign in a sauna stating that fifteen minutes was considered to be the maximum safe duration for a session. This made him curious enough to find out what might happen if the limit was exceeded. He later crawled out, barely conscious, believing that he had accessed some kind of womb memory stored in his body. This led to him spending long experimental sessions in his bathtub, developing a technique that he called Conscious Connected Breathing as part of a process that came to be known as Rebirthing. Most simply put by Orr himself, "*Rebirthing is primarily a relaxed continuous breathing rhythm in which the inhale is connected to the exhale in a continuous circle"*. The inhale gets consciously pulled in whilst the exhale should be simply let go. There should be no gap between the two.

So what's the womb/birth/breath connection? A good case can be made for criticising the modern way of birth as conducive to the creation of numerous possible dysfunctions. At regular intervals over the years I've read of some 'new' breakthrough suggesting that babies are far more self-aware than previously understood and that perhaps more care should be taken around the birthing environment. L. Ron Hubbard was saying this as far back as 1948. Scientologists advocate silence around a birth to minimise the possibility of the vulnerable child inputting weird scripts that will later warp it out. For example, if someone says "there's a problem here", this somehow registers with the preverbal child simultaneous to the physical freak-out of birth and can later come back as a subtle unconscious loser script whereby "there's a problem here" refers to its entire life. This can readily be considered contentious psychology but I believe that somewhere in these theories lie profound bioenergetic truths about our emotional lives and Rebirthing seems to access and clear them very rapidly and efficaciously.

The standard western birth does seem a tad brutal. Bright lights may well be shone on the mother's pelvis. Babies are light sensitive even inside the womb. The first experience of emergence can become linked with blinding light and burning liquid in the eyes. In the womb, the sounds of heartbeat and inner squelchings and pulsings are quiet and peaceful. The noise of the hospital delivery room may be a painful assault on sensitive eardrums. After the womb's warmth, a sudden temperature drop of about twenty degrees can further shock the naked wet creature. Rebirthers believe that 'temperature trauma' can be the cause of many psychosomatic disorders. Most fundamentally of all, the first breath outside the womb may be a hideous experience of inexplicable pain. The umbilical cord may be cut quite quickly and the child held upside down and spanked. In such a circumstance, the first intake of air will be one of the most powerful events that ever befall most people in their whole lives. So the first breath may be experienced as part of a simultaneous total package combining blinding light, deafening sound, massive temperature decrease and violent assault. If that wasn't enough, the child may well be taken away from its mother who it has experienced as the one and only total reality for the whole of its existence. Breathing can become linked with pain and fear, setting up ongoing anxiety that will be suppressed by patterns of shallow breathing that may leave an individual contracted upon themselves for the rest of their lives, never able to fully experience the free flow of emotional sexual and spiritual energies through their bodies. Looking at the whole thing from such a perspective one can only marvel that any of us even manage to get out of bed in the morning. So, "*rebirthing primarily means the rehabilitation of breathing*", "*the transformation of the subconscious impression of birth from one of primal pain to one of pleasure*".

The conscious connected breathing technique can induce immensely powerful physiological processes which Rebirthers believe stir up primal imprinted patterns, potentially releasing blockages and contractions. Vibrating and tingling may be felt throughout the body. "*This energy reconnects your body to the universal energy by vibrating out tension which is the manifestation of negative mental mass.*" "*All discomfort in conjunction with rebirthing comes from holding on to negativity, misery or pain.*" A resistance to this flow, which Wilhelm Reich would have recognised, may arise in the form of symptoms known as tetany. This cramping and paralysis is a sign of what is usually called hyperventilation, a syndrome full of negative connotations for the medical profession. On the basis of his own personal experimentation, Leonard Orr came to believe that the onset of such symptoms should not be resisted despite the discomfort and fear that tends to accompany them. If one persists with the breathing technique, "*Negative energy patterns held in the mind and body start to dissolve.*" A spectacular 'breathing release' can lie on the other side of the pain. Laughing, crying, and screaming may be the obvious external signs of this, "*critical release of all your resistance to life*".

Various stuff may arise in the midst of the physiological fireworks. There are accounts of vivid memory restimulation involving full-sense recall. During sessions and their aftermath a variety of illnesses have been supposedly alleviated or cured: bad eyesight, sinus problems, backache, dermatitis, to name just a few of many. Orr was nonetheless careful to state that "*We recommend those who have a condition they are concerned about stay in constant communication with their physician. Rebirthing is not a treatment and no claim is made as to its ability to cure symptoms or reverse illness.*" Contrariwise, assorted bizarre symptoms of previous illnesses may temporarily manifest. Psychological emotional patterns may be transformed: distrust, sexual stuff, relationship issues, claustrophobia, anxiety.

There may be mood swing hangovers; highs and lows in exaggerated form. Rebirthing has always been more concerned with the letting go of trauma rather than the meticulous re-experiencing of it. Many old forms of psychotherapy may endlessly mull over the nature of a dysfunction and its possible causes rather than simply removing it. And why is it called Rebirthing? At the heart of the vibrating layers of primal crud lies the energetic core memory of the birth event. In a session this can be totally relived, re-energised, re-programmed. People can end up crying and gurgling like babies on the floor! Such are the claims of the Rebirthers.

There have certainly been criticisms of the technique and the philosophy. In *New Age and Armageddon*, Monica Sjöö detailed some extremely unfortunate events involving some Rebirthers when her son became seriously ill. These people do seem to have exploited him into neglecting conventional treatment to instead feed them with lots of money and terminally decline despite a diet of affirmations and endless hours of conscious connected breathing. They had clearly ignored Orr's advice about remaining in communication with a doctor and that although all kinds of conditions can be transformed, "*Rebirthing is not a treatment*". That seemed clear enough. There does appear to be a recognisable syndrome that when some people connect to a powerful transformative technique the incredible highs it generates fool them into over-generalising about its appropriate applicability. And some do perhaps keep too much of an eye on their bank balances. Sjöö recounted a tragic tale but I was already forewarned against such things.

Once the full breathing release has been experienced, subsequent sessions are unlikely to induce the same intensity of response. Something else begins to happen. Just as Dianetics evolved into the realms of Scientology, Rebirthing expanded its scope. "*Ultimately we may learn that rebirthing is a physical experience of Infinite Being which is not exclusively to do with the birth trauma.*" It becomes, "*a biological experience of religion*". For the breathing technique to work most effectively one must allow the great surging flow of bioenergy that arises to be felt as divine prana. This is accomplished simply through surrendering into the feeling that such a thing can really happen. The more one can luxuriate in the exquisite subtlety of the force at work, the more miraculous it feels. Orr came to feel that Rebirthing was not simply a self-help cult but an authentic American yoga.

* * *

TRUE WILL

"If the Biblical symbol for breath is fire, then hyperventilation may be the baptism of fire which Jesus talked about."
Leonard Orr.

THE SOUTHEND REBIRTHING SCENARIO had presented itself with unmistakeable appropriateness. It was right there on a plate for me on my actual birthday. I hadn't the slightest doubt that I was meant to do it. I had also been rather strongly pointed in the direction of the Tarot ritual. My birthday was ideal for that as well. The Rebirthing started in the morning. It would probably be concluded by early evening. This gave me the superb opportunity to pursue both options, Hyatt and DuQuette's two ends of the same snake. The ritual would conclude the day. As it drew ever nearer, I was increasingly in awe of it. I couldn't recall a day in my life that had been so comprehensively set up.

By the start of April I had correlated all possible data to assist the birthday meltdown. My Qabalistic Tarot studies had been comprehensive. I had also looked at my astrological birth chart and sought advice on all of its complex ramifications. The total effect was a complete focus on the fundamental question, "who am I and what will be my destiny?" I'd been performing the Lesser Banishing Ritual of the Pentagram regularly throughout the year. Midway through March I'd added the Hexagram Ritual (explained below). I reread the whole of *Secret Lover.* I spent the last day of my 32nd year alone in introspective preparation. I deliberately tried to recall details from as many previous birthdays as possible. They all represented snapshots of my life. Remembering them in sequence connected me to a greater continuity.

I had been noticing that in recent mini-divinations with the Crowley deck, the Aeon card had seemed to manifest with increasing regularity. This led to me studying it all the more closely and adopting it as the general signifier of the bigger picture surrounding my extraordinary 33rd birthday.

The twentieth tarot trump has been generally named as Judgement in the majority of decks. Its usual imagery tends to be like something from *Revelations,* a trumpet-blowing angel hovering in the sky above resurrecting dead stepping from their graves, and so on. To Crowley, the formula of dying and reborn deities like Christ has been superseded so, more than any other trumps, this particular card requires a new representation in accordance with the new law.

Crowley's Aeon card strongly recalls the Stele of Revealing. Once again Nuit arches over the scene. Beneath her sits Ra Hoor Khuit on his throne. This time he is not depicted in profile but facing outwards. Transparently in front of him stands a naked Hoor Paar Kraat, Harpocrates, the infant Horus, right forefinger raised to his mouth in an enigmatic gesture of silence. It was from the Stele that the formula of the Aeon of Horus was revealed, so the use of its imagery on the tarot trump basically proclaims, "Do what thou wilt shall be the whole of the Law" instead of the Christian Judgement formula.

Leonard Orr spoke of the Rebirthing alchemy where there comes a place in the process where one begins to breathe divine energy. I was mindful of this idea as I noted some interesting associations in the Golden Dawn tradition from the original Judgement card and in particular, the meaning of its Hebrew letter, 'Shin'. It has a double elemental attribution of Fire and Spirit with associations of the energy that enlivens matter. The great holy Hebrew God formula YHVH, which permeated the Qabalah, represented the basic forces at work in the universe. There was a missing ingredient though. In *Genesis,* God breathed life into the whole thing. This breath of the Holy Spirit was called *Ruach Elohim.* Its gematria was 300. Shin has the same number. This supposedly shows that it represents some aspect of that force. Christian Qabalistic Occultists like Pico della Mirandola claimed that one could prove the divinity of Jesus through this. If you put Shin in the middle of the Tetragrammaton it spelled YHShVH, a Hebrew version of the name of Jesus. When tongues of fire came down into the disciples at Pentecost, it was the spirit/fire of Shin in operation. I felt it was not unlike the Kundalini/Shaktipat spirit baptism of Hinduism. Crowley had kept the Shin attribution for Aeon.

I awoke on my 33rd birthday with a feeling of excited anticipation. There was quite simply no way that what was coming could be anything other than extraordinary. By 11 o'clock I was in the back room at *Dimensions* sitting in a circle of chairs with a group of about fifteen people. I only knew two of them. Dana Lee was present on behalf of the shop. I got the feeling she was looking forward to seeing my brain explode. The day was presented in a sort of general New Age format common to many group gatherings. We all introduced ourselves and said a few words about why we were there and what our intentions were. One bearded middle-aged man looked around the group with a painfully sincere smile telling us it was his fifty fourth session and he was there to sort out some of his issues with women. Etc. I simply said, "Hi, I'm Paul. It's my 33rd birthday today. It was a big year for Jesus and I'm looking for a major result myself. I'm hoping for a napalm strike on my karma right now. Let's do it."

The group divided into pairs. There would be two mass breathing sessions where each participant would watch over their partner, supervised by the facilitating team. I was eager to go first. Early Rebirthing had been done in water. This still happened in the more advanced trainings but this was to be a 'dry' event. I lay on the floor, covered in a few blankets in anticipation of likely massive temperature change experience. The conscious connected breathing began. I was breathing through my mouth. I later discovered that this is more likely to stir up strong emotions. On the whole, Orr advocates nose breathing as a deeper more subtle pranayama. I wasn't up for subtlety that day.

Before long the full gamut of symptoms I'd read about in *Rebirthing in the New Age* were starting to manifest. A kind of pins and needles feeling began to fill my whole body but I could feel multiple streamings pulsing through it. I recognised signs of the dreaded tetany as my hands seemed to raise themselves automatically in front of me, contracting into claws. Bizarre growling sounds accompanied this process. Once a certain threshold of intensity was crossed a seemingly deranged outpouring of roller coaster emotional extremes erupted from me in rapid succession. One moment I was grinding my teeth and howling and screaming like a wild beast. Shortly afterwards I was laughing like the man who has finally discovered that god is a frog in a pit of slime but that's really okay. Dana Lee, who was sitting right next to me, later used one word to sum up her response to what was happening. 'Fear'. And she was a qualified Rebirther. Her psychic senses could perceive "eighteen different voices coming out of you simultaneously". She reckoned that if she had somehow been able to record what she could hear it would have made a brilliant soundtrack to a future *Exorcist* movie. I had no fear at all of what was happening. This enabled me to flow screaming through the tetany barrier into an even more primal space. A demonic craziness was now alternating with the increasing emergence of an all-pervading dynamic ecstatic bliss. The screaming rage and deranged laughter gave way to sobbing and then huge convulsive crying like a baby. Yes, like a baby.

Anything resembling normal thought processes had disappeared fairly early on in the proceedings. For a man rather used to having a head full of words it was a measure of the unique nature of the experience that there were no words in my head at all. It seems clear that some connection exists between the Rebirthing event and my 1990 zodiac quest weir jump and its attendant primal scream. I can readily intuit a 4D continuity in terms of the unfolding form of my initiatory drama. In 1990 though, I was full of cross-referencing memories, the words and sensibilities of assorted poets and mystics, and so on. It had assuredly been a moment of alchemical transmutation, a baptism and some kind of rebirth, but this was an event of an altogether different level of magnitude. It wasn't just that there were no words. There were no memories with any visual associations anywhere in my conscious mind. That's quite a big thing really. Everyday life generates zillions of them and when one ponders the great emotional rites of passage they usually conjure up the weather, the time of day, season of the year, music that was playing etc. And ever afterwards the repetition of one of those stimuli may well stir up the strong emotions of the time they became inextricably associated with. There I was, overwhelmed by the strongest emotions of my entire life, but they weren't accompanied by any normal memory associations at all.

So where was it all coming from? There was one distinct feeling that I was aware of as the increasing centre of gravity of the situation. Without ever formulating it in words, I knew that, "something is missing". One of the female Rebirthing team who had been keeping a close eye on me understood exactly. She sat down by me and cradled my head to her breast. Cue floods of tears. When I say I was crying like a baby I want to differentiate between what the most skilled adult mimic could manage as an impersonation of how a baby might cry and someone who was *crying like a baby*, as I was doing then. In the days following the event I believed that I had, pretty much as far as such a thing can remotely be considered to be possible, relived my birth. I had been reborn. And I still believe that now.

The incredible bliss and buckets of tears went on and on. Eventually I opened my eyes. A group of strangely huge heads were circled around looking down at me and smiling. I might just as well have been in a pram. The first words I eventually spoke were, "At last! Reality!" Not many more words followed for some considerable time afterwards. A later diary entry unhesitatingly referred to, "the most primal and awesome experience of my life since my birth".

My skin was softly tingling all over me. Looking in a mirror, I saw my eyes were wide as saucers and an imbecilic grin occupied most of my face. A few thoughts eventually started to arise, drifting like white clouds across my sky of mind. I watched them float by, having no involvement with them at all. I was in the Rajneesh zone for sure. This was what he had always said meditation was all about. I was completely emptied out but in that nothingness was a tremendous fullness that was entirely sufficient unto itself. I'd been reading him for over a decade and finally I had really experienced what he was talking about and understood it.

There was a lunchbreak of some kind. I don't really know what happened during it although I assume that I probably eat something. The afternoon session convened. I sat beside my breathing partner. Did anyone else experience anything remotely comparable to me? No. One person started gently sobbing at one point. Another mentioned that she had fallen asleep a few times. I had hoped that my enthusiastic participation might have encouraged some to let go of any reluctance to completely go for it. It obviously wasn't appropriate for anyone else that day. My awesome altered state had in no way dissipated when the event concluded. I could easily have wall-stared for hours but this was only part one of my day's entertainment.

It was dark when I finally left *Dimensions.* I could see enormous rainbow haloes around streetlights. Everything was stunningly vibrant. It reminded me of what the world looked like coming up on acid, just before the hallucinations and real weirdness kicked-in. Once I got home it was obvious there was someone I had to speak to. I rang my mother. I had told my parents about the Rebirthing event. I'd even attempted to summarise *Rebirthing in the New Age* for them. I had tried to quiz them on any potentially formative external influences playing upon me whilst I was in the womb. My mother told me that she was particularly conscious of repeatedly hearing Sylvester and Tweetie Pie's *I Tawt I Taw a Puddy Cat* on the radio during the time she was carrying me. It could be that some extensive Dianetics auditing might be needed to unravel that particular strand. My father was somewhat uncomprehending about the latest load of total weirdness I was babbling on about but my mother made supportive noises, her main concern being that I might somehow strain or injure myself if I was rolling about on the floor screaming my brains out. She had advised caution. Now I could report back. No problem mum. Sorted. Born on the floor. Nice one. I did discover that I had been separated from her immediately after birth. This was what the whole "something's missing" episode had been about. Incredible.

Leonard Orr had said that, *"The breathing release puts the power of your life-force into your thoughts"*. Bearing that in mind, it was time to further alter my state. The womb. The void. The ocean of possibilities. Nuit. Me. Newly born and silent. The child. The birth of the true self. Harpocrates.

I robed-up in my candlelit living room and then also lit a large circle of small nightlights on the floor around me. Standing at its centre, facing east with eyes closed, I began some deep conscious connected breathing. I imagined that the external form of the room was rapidly dissolving and I was growing to giant stature, my height reaching to the vault of heaven as a vast limitless light above me came increasingly into view. I raised my arms up until my hands were cupped together stretched above me in the ocean of white. They became infused with an essence of that supernal energy which I proceeded to pull down as a column of light, firstly into the top of my head, where I intoned the appropriate Hebrew, "Ateh"(Unto Thee). My still cupped hands moved down the front of my body, stopping at the point of the maximum length of their extension as I visualised the column reaching down to my feet, "El Malkuth" (the Kingdom). I touched my right shoulder, "Ve Geburah" (the Power), beginning a horizontal line of light to balance the vertical. It crossed to my left shoulder, "Ve Gedulah" (the Glory). With the cross of light thus formulated, I brought my hands together at my heart to complete the invocatory prayer, "Le-Olam. Amen". The light of the cross became ever brighter, expanding outwards to fill my whole body and move out in the form of a great auric egg.

Beginning in the east where I was already facing, I stretched out my right hand to draw, starting at the lower left tip, a large banishing pentagram of blue fire. Once it was completed, I forcefully intoned "Ye-ho-vah", thrusting my finger into the pentagram centre and seeing it blaze all the more brightly as I did so. Moving round on the balls of my feet from the same centre point to my right, the south, I repeated the pentagram drawing, this time intoning "Ah-do-nai". Continuing to move clockwise, the western Hebrew name was "Eh-He-Yeh", the north, "Ah-ge-lah".

Returning to face east, I now imagined myself to be standing in the midst of four flaming pentagrams. It was like they formed the centre of four sides of a great cube of light in which I was hovering in the middle with a cross of light within.

I now extended my arms at my side to form a cross. "Before me stands Ra-phay-el." The archangel was visualised beyond the eastern pentagram with an attempt to imagine his associated qualities. He was adorned in a flowing robe of yellowy gold, flecked with orange, holding aloft a large caduceus wand. A gentle breeze accompanied him along with a feeling of healing.

Without moving, I changed focus. "On my right, Me-kay-el." In reds, orange, and gold, Michael was brandishing a large flaming sword. He was obviously a spiritual warrior, emanating the feeling of the powers of protection, purification and transformation that are the spiritual qualities of fire.

"Behind me, Ga-bray-el." Clothed in robes of blue and silver, he stood in an audible waterfall, holding a chalice between his hands communicating receptivity and creativity.

"On my left, Ur-ray-el." He came walking out of a forest, dressed in dark greens and browns, holding a sheaf of corn, resonating the qualities of groundedness and stability.

"Around me shine the pentagrams of fire. In my heart and in the column blazes the six-rayed star." I visualised an upright six-pointed Seal of Solomon star around my heart region and repeated the Qabalstic cross prayer. It was the same as before but with one extra detail. The cube had now been formulated. The face above and below had a blazing six-pointed star on it. When bringing the Kether light down it was as if it was coming down through a Seal of Solomon. As it went through the heart region, the star previously visualised became horizontal like a lotus chakra so the light went down through the middle of it and further down through the one on the cube face beneath.

The process of the Middle Pillar followed. This involved a visualisation focus on the spheres in the central column of the tree of life. A point of light came down as a column through my head to each one in turn. As it did I intoned the associated Hebrew mantra and thought of the relevant colours. Once I had worked my way down, a further technique known as the circulation of the light completed the exercise. With each exhalation, light was imagined moving down the left side of my body. When it reached the foot it moved to the right to ascend the right side of my body with the subsequent inhalation. This was repeated ten times. Then the flow was moved to descend directly down the front and then up the back, seeming to exit the crown like a fountain that bathed the whole aura in its emanations. This sequence was likewise repeated ten times.

The final preliminary was the Lesser Banishing Ritual of the Hexagram. The hexagram is a six-pointed star whose points represent planets surrounding the sun of Tiphareth as the pentagram does the elements. It connects to the greater world of the macrocosm rather than the personal elemental world of the individual practitioner. The union of the five and six, the elemental microcosmic realm and the six, the planetary macrocosmic world is the area where union with the angel is facilitated.

It began with the recitation of a resurrection formula.

> *"INRI*
> *Yod. Nun. Resh. Yod.*
> *Virgo, Isis, Mighty mother.*
> *Scorpio, Apophis, Destroyer.*
> *Sol, Osiris, Slain and Risen.*
> *Isis, Apophis, Osiris, IAO"*

I extended my arms outwards at my sides making the shape of a cross, intoning, "the sign of Osiris slain". I then raised my right arm directly upwards and my left arm out to form an L. "The sign of Isis mourning." A V shape above my head was "the sign of Apophis-Typhon". Crossing my arms across my chest and bowing my head made "the sign of Osiris risen". They were stretched out and crossed once again. "LVX, Lux, the Light of the Cross." A series of different types of six-pointed stars were then drawn at the four quarters before the INRI formula was repeated.

I added a mixture of some of Crowley's poetry to the ritual, invocations to the Higher Self I'd found over the years in *The Eye in the Triangle* and *The Great Beast.* I recited them aloud, robed in that candlelit room at the climax of an epic day,

> *"O Self Divine O Living Lord of Me!*
> *Self-shining flame, begotten of Beyond!*
> *Godhead immaculate! Swift tongue of fire,*
> *Kindled from thy immeasurable light*
> *The boundless, the immutable. Come forth,*

My God, my lover, spirit of my heart,
Heart of my soul, white virgin of the Dawn,
My Queen of all perfection, come thou forth
From thine abode beyond the Silences
To me the prisoner, me the mortal man,
Shrined in this clay, come forth to me I say, to me,
Initiate my quickened soul; draw near
And let the glory of thy Godhead shine.

Come forth
My actual Self! Come forth, O dazzling one,
Wrapped in the glory of the Holy Place
Whence I have called thee: Come thou forth to me,
And permeate my being, till my face
Shine with the light reflected, till my brows
Gleam with thy starry symbol, till my voice
Reach the ineffable: Come forth, I say
And make me one with thee; that all my ways
May glitter with thy holy influence,
That I may be found worthy at the end.

I shuffled the cards for about ten minutes whilst contemplating the issue of my higher self. The whole deck was then spread out face down on the floor in front of me in a fan shape. I imagined a kind of wide focus beam shining out of my forehead, scanning the cards. I used its subtle promptings to select ten. I then laid them out in the tree of life format. Having done so, I turned them over one at a time. When the whole spread was revealed I simply stared at them for a few minutes allowing the first level of assimilation. I wrote down the details. For the sake of this narrative it doesn't matter what the actual cards were. The whole procedure was then concluded with a second performance of the lesser banishing ritual of the pentagram. I wrote in my diary, just before midnight, that I'd experienced *'the greatest affirmation of my true self I'd ever made in a single day'*. Like Harpocrates, I had vibrated some kind of magickal formula. It was now time to let it go, abandoning any lust of result but knowing that ripples would later return at an appropriate moment.

* * *

RIPPLES

THERE WERE MANY TANGIBLE SIGNS that something enormous had happened and a new phase of my life begun. I'd written an article in an Earth Mysteries journal *ASH* (Albion's Sacred Heritage) that Alex Langstone was involved with. It was about a journey along the Michael ley line (yet another one of the multi-faceted sagas excluded here for space reasons). At the start of 1992 I received a letter from a woman in response. An exchange of correspondence followed resulting in a meeting in May. I could not remotely have anticipated the level of affinity and attraction that would be present between us. It was overwhelming. It had been nearly five years since the break-up of my previous relationship. I had been completely physically alone during all that time. That was not at all pleasant for a healthy guy aged between 28 and 33. It had taken some extra-ordinary adventures to stop me getting dangerously distressed. Now, suddenly, it was like an angel had come down out of heaven. There was one little problem though. She was already in a long-established serious relationship that she had no intention of ending. During May and June there were some blissful assignations but the intensity of the realisation of the inevitable short-term nature of the scenario put me into an unbearably heightened emotional state.

During the same spring period, Alex, who had always been an above-average psychic, went into overdrive and his abilities massively increased. He was seeing and communicating with various discarnate dudes and picking up all sorts of stuff about sites and magic. Such was the weird blend as Glastonbury and the solstice once again beckoned

On Saturday June 20th, Daevid Allen was playing in the Assembly Rooms. Alex took a car full to Glastonbury. Kirk joined us, along with Oliver's partner Joanne and her sister. The weekend became an experience of extreme opposites. When we first arrived in the afternoon, a lot of traveller/crustie types had been in evidence in the centre of town. There was a big contingent in St. John's churchyard. These people were not emanating a Summer of Love vibe. Many of them were clearly hostile and disdainful to everybody. Period. They were engaged in ongoing serious intoxication. I was far from enamoured at the prospect of their company. For the first time since '79, I'd started growing my hair long again. It was about shoulder length. At heart I was still a Woodstock case. The sight of the massed ranks of Altamont characters made me decide to have it all cut off again.

In the psychically dense atmosphere of Glastonbury my perspective on these people was not one that dwelt on socio-economic political factors. I wondered if groups of some defeated dark-age war band had reincarnated en-masse to play out its confusion and resentment. Perhaps some of them had been sacrificed like the famous bog-people to placate the primal deities of archaic Avalon's dark waters. Maybe some remnants of the Duke of Monmouth's rebel army, traumatised and semi-psychotic, were still reeling from their 1685 reverses. Some of them had been hanged in the area where the entrance to the Assembly Rooms now lies. A wall plaque anchors that psychogeographical factor in the multitudinous aethyrs. Who knows how many layers of history are being played out on any summer Saturday afternoon in Glastonbury High Street?

No hanged men intruded onto my entrance into the Assembly Rooms that night. The first part of the evening was incredible. An amazing cast of characters assembled for the gig. I was stunned to realise that I was in the company of people who represented my experience of every single solstice year since my first 1979 visit. There were a few who had been with me at Stonehenge and Pilton then. I was sitting with people I'd known at sixth-form college and a few years later at university. There were two former partners. Alex was my continuity with all the questing years. Fourteen years. I wrote in my diary that the *"whole thing stinks of burnt karma on toast"*. Daevid Allen was brilliant. He performed all of my favourite songs, taking me back to the formative period that had led me to Pilton in the first place. It was a stunningly satisfying continuity. Something was being summed up, recapitulated, prior to a new step forward. I couldn't resist that feeling of imminence. I'd never felt more connected to Glastonbury. It was clearly my true home. I had to live there one day.

After the gig, it was off to the Tor. Up on the summit something had changed. There was drumming in the tower and didgs. Lots of spliffs were in evidence. The usual elements at first glance. It soon became apparent that the desire to become totally intoxicated had become the prevalent concern. There were some seriously out of it people up there. Drug dealers were wandering around shouting out the nature of their merchandise. Others desperately howled their requirements. Alcohol was now widely in evidence. A lot of empty cans already littered the place. I had a feeling that few of these people had any sense of the place or occasion other than it being a rebellious rave of some kind. The Geordie piss-heads had been in evidence in '88 but there had been Sufis and Witches to keep the right balance. Nothing like them was anywhere to be seen this time. Joanne and her sister had never been on the Tor for a solstice eve shindig so they had nothing to compare it with. Alex, Kirk, and I, left them there. To us, it was ghastly. The top of Chalice Hill seemed an infinitely better prospect to greet the dawn. A few people were about there but it was a haven of tranquillity compared to the Tor. Noise wafted over from the summit. Some dork was periodically screaming "I want some acid" at the top of his voice. The general vibe of a bad-trip piss-up in a Brueghel painting seemed to float across the psychic airwaves. Daylight came. We headed back to the car to meet the ladies.

Some old loyalty compelled me to re-ascend the Tor. Alex and Kirk didn't want to know. The sight that greeted me was far from inspiring. A group of Morris dancers lay slumped-out by the tower, their arcane paraphernalia scattered on the ground, inert and meaningless. Strange creatures stumbled amongst the carpet of beer cans. One naked long-hair, clutching an almost empty vodka bottle, burbled obscurely to an unspecified audience as he surveyed the stirrings of an erection. I wished there had been a huge tanker full of holy water parked down by the road. It would have had a mile long high-pressure pipe attached. I would take it up to the summit and hose the scumbags off. I would then petition the Archangel Michael for a psychic napalm strike of his holy fire to further purge the place of their rancid presence. Omigawd! Had I become a total fascist bastard? Did I now believe that a spot of National Service was necessary to build their character? Was I going to vote Tory at the next Election? Hopefully not. Something had shifted. It wasn't just me getting older and leaving the days of intoxication behind. There were considerable differences to the classic 1988 gathering. They were microcosmic symptoms of bigger processes in the body-politic. The glorious outpouring of the Ecstasy inspired Rave culture had hit levels of turbulence. Heroin and gangsters, Bad quality E. In some crucial quarters, the idealism had dissipated. People were just getting wasted for the sake of it. It was a sense of party unto death, with someone else paying the bill and clearing up the mess. Partying with no sense of responsibility. Similar things had happened at the end of the sixties.

As the solstice morning progressed, an instructive episode was played out in front of *Gothic Image*. We were walking down the

High Street towards it when a long-haired bearded man loomed into view, moving unsteadily in our direction. Staring into my eyes, he lurched to about two feet away from me and said "Do you read that crap in there?" Cheerily, I pushed him away with the friendly reply, "get out of my face you fucking scumbag". He grabbed me by the left wrist and began a pseudo magical psychotic tirade about ravens. Two different states of consciousness were functioning simultaneously in me. The ultra-violence option was considered. I noted my position in relation to the creature that was holding on to me. Distances were calculated. I had enough space to kick him in the head. I could pull him towards me and either punch him in the throat or stick two fingers into his eyeballs. In the initial shock after that, he would let go of me and I could heave him through the window of *Gothic Image* or maybe grab his head and smash it repeatedly against the wall. Alex psychically saw me starting to transfigure into Pan. Horns were appearing on my head and fire was in my eyes. Another part of me was issuing urgent instructions. "Paul, defuse this situation immediately. This represents an initiatory test. Look at last night. The whole of your life affirmed. It's the morning of the solstice, your favourite day of the year. You're in Glastonbury, the most important place in the whole world to your destiny. Look, you're outside *Gothic Image*. Remember 1985 dude. You bought *Earthquest News* and the pictures that became the Glastonbury Qabalah in there. If you lob this dirtbag through the window you've lost it man." All of this was happening at lightning speed. I chilled him out. Just. He continued his progress up the High Street, still shouting stuff about ravens at me. I was fairly freaked-out by the whole business. There were high stakes involved. I hoped that I'd passed the test.

We sought sanctuary at the Chalice Well gardens. Alex soon announced that he was involved in some kind of dialogue with Dion Fortune. I did not immediately enter into unconditional belief of what Alex was saying and neither did he. My previous experiences suggested to me that I should go along with the whole business and see what followed. That solstice morning at the Well, she dictated a visualisation through Alex concerning the magical protection of Glastonbury. It wasn't something I was familiar with from any of her books.

When we got back I was obviously fired up with the possibilities of the Dion Fortune contact and started to reread *Priestess*. I noted that she was born on December 6th. The year was actually 1890 but she herself, for reasons unknown, used to say it was 1891. When I had travelled to Glastonbury at the start of the previous December, in search of the new programme, it had actually been her birthday. By her own reckoning it had been the centenary. And I had read *Avalon of the Heart* during a journey that would take me further into the Qabalah than ever before. Hmm. For some reason I was only intended to consciously become aware of that date synchronisation at that time. I could perhaps have realised it once the date for that journey was set. I probably would have decided to read *Avalon of the Heart* anyway. That subtle nuance was only revealed the day after an alleged psychic contact with Dion Fortune was made. This was exactly the kind of detail that I would have looked for to help me assess its genuineness.

ISIS OF AVALON

"In the Temple of Love, shine like thunder – cry like rain."
Andrew Eldritch. *Temple of Love*. The Sisters of Mercy.

"There are times when my mind is an explosion of feelings.
I'm trying to hold on to the soul inside."
Marc Almond. *Soul Inside*. Soft Cell.

THE LAST DAY OF JUNE was both a new moon and a solar eclipse (although not visible from Britain). It was also the halfway point of what had already proved to be an immense year. I decided to take stock by reading my diaries since January, whilst listening to some of the music that conjured up the year's experiences. I smoked a few spliffs. They were the first since I'd switched on the Tarot gallery the previous New Year's Eve. Before going into the diaries, I did a one card Tarot reading, seeking a key for the evening ahead. I got the *High Priestess.* I began to recapitulate the amazing birthday process and my romantic emotional extremis.

At twilight, during a track on the Gabrielle Roth *Wave* album called *Spirit,* a strange feeling came over me. I was staring out of the window but suddenly felt compelled to look at a statue of Isis on the fireplace. It was unquestionably vibing. Some kind of force was emanating from it. I could feel it tingling throughout my body, above and beyond the cannabis. This was an interesting development. I hadn't really thought much about Isis since the '91 Convention when the *Moon Magic* saga had concluded. I'd always associated her with the full moon. Whatever the case, I'd learned to go along with these things. I lit some candles and arranged them in front of her. On went my tape of Anne Williams' *Song of Isis,* stunning harp music recorded in the Great Pyramid during the Harmonic Convergence. I then lit some *Starchild* Isis incense. I knelt down before the statue, holding up the smoking bowl in supplication. I saw this image of myself reflected in a mirror behind her and it seemed to trigger some ancient memory. Dion Fortune was surely somehow involved in this. I rang Alex to let him know my feelings that something big was in the air and to recommend the virtues of some Isis devotion. He had actually just been sitting in front of his own statue of Isis and the infant Horus, with candles and incense on the go. This led to him pondering on Dion Fortune and she'd appeared to him, as if physically present, in his temple room. The *High Priestess* Tarot key to the night had proved to be spectacularly accurate. Dion Fortune was assuredly a High Priestess and the card represented Isis in many ways as well. After an astounding six months it didn't seem out of the question that more was to come.

As July began, I felt I was being torn apart by the glimpse of romantic possibilities and their lack of fulfilment. On the 6th, I again pulled the *High Priestess* as my Tarot key to the evening ahead. Mindful of the powerful results a few nights before, I smoked a spliff to enhance my potential sensitivity to what might be in the airwaves awaiting me. My emotional horrors were amplified. Why the fuck did I have to be put through this shit? I protested to Dion Fortune, to Isis, and anyone else who might be listening. After a while, I took the *High Priestess* card and held it in my hand in front of me, staring into it. I then looked out of my window to a point in the sky where the full moon tended to rise at that time of year. I found it very easy to imagine that moon out there with a vast figure of Isis behind it. I called on Isis, and Dion Fortune and mentally put them all together in the expanding vision. I then saw the scene framed by the two pillars of the Temple. Without any sense of what I was doing, I took some Chalice Well water and anointed the headband of the figure on the Tarot card and my own forehead. I was sitting in the lotus posture in the centre of the room. I stretched my arms out in a cross, palms upraised. I was imagining a cross of light within me. At this point, the visionary reverie shifted its location and increased in detail until it had included the entire contents of my mental filing cabinet pertinent to the *High Priestess* card, revealing far more than I had ever realised was in there.

Closing my eyes, I imagined myself to be in the Tor tower at night, with my back to the town, gazing out upon the enchanted landscape, which soon came alive with the sounds of owls hooting and a distant barking of dogs. In the great deep soundless, boundless sea, of infinite space and infinite stars, the silver moon was rising, riding through scudding clouds that cleared, leaving the naked brilliance of the voluptuous night sky. As the hour of the high full moon drew near, beyond the deepest pools of emptiness, infinitesimal ripples in the creative silence of the first cause stirred forth a wave, an emanation. A silvery cloud of pale moon mist formed a shimmering pillar that spanned the space from moon to earth. Beneath the heaven tree of stars hung with humid night blue fruit, it vibrated with energies of flux and reflux. Within an aura of a lambent flame of blue it began to coalesce into a human form, becoming ever clearer, until revealing itself as Isis of Avalon, Queen of Heaven, Spirit of the Moon, whose cosmic love and inspiration radiates eternally. Here was the mistress of the tides, the secret silent tides of death and birth, tides of men's souls and dreams and destiny, tides that rise in our hearts and minds.

The tresses of her hair were long and thick and streamed down softly, flowing and curling about her divine neck. On her head she wore as a crown twelve stars entwined with many garlands of flowers. On her forehead shone white and glowing, a round mirror-like full moon disc. On its right and left it was supported by the furrowed coils of rising vipers with ears of corn bristling beside them. Her tunic was of many colours, woven of the finest linen, gleaming multi-coloured, at first glance with snowy whiteness, then yellow like a crocus, rosy-red like a flame. Her cloak was deep black, glistening with sable sheen. It was cast about her, passing under her right arm and brought together on her left shoulder. Part of it hung down like a shield and drooped in many a fold, the whole reaching to the lower edge of her garment with tasselled fringe. Here and there, along its embroidered border, and also on its surface, were scattered sequins of sparkling stars. In their midst the full moon shone forth like a flame of fire. All along the border of that gorgeous robe there was an unbroken garland of all kinds of flowers and fruits. In her right hand she carried a bronze sistrum rattle. In her left was held a golden cup, an alchemical Grail, from which rose a snake. Her soft feet, not hurting the little flowers, were shod with sandals woven of the palm of victory. Perfumes of resinous woods and gums wafted through the air. Out of the timeless she had come down into time. Out of the un-named she had come down into human symbols. In the land that had called her, amidst the people whose hearts she alone can fill, she was calling forth the flame of the hearts of all. Thus she abided. A thing of beauty and a joy forever.

Extending her right arm, she shook her sistrum, sounding soft celestial bells. From it, like falling stars floating to earth, a sparkling shower of crystalline moon blessings descended, touching the whole of the sacred landscape, resonating through its multitudinous aethyrs, all touching, all penetrant. The Tor maze began to glow a gentle gold that pulsated as if emerging from just beneath the ground. The moonlit sparkling abbey hummed as the face of Isis of Avalon was also seen in the Mary Chapel. All across the land fell the glory of the stars into the hearts of men. The Chalice Well, its cover open, reflected in its water the holy face as the ground seemed to exhale in a great relaxation. Spreading out and touching the Wearyall Hill thorn, to Bride's Mound and beyond, out in all directions the gratuitous grace extended, until finally, the outlines of the signs of the Glastonbury Zodiac were seen to light up and energise.

It was one of the most intense, magnificent reveries of the whole of my life and a notable contrast to the *Birdie Song* scenario just over a decade before. The appearance of Isis was essentially that contained within the *Golden Ass* of Apulieus. The full moon rituals had involved the Sky Dancer group building up the image over a long period of time. Now it had suddenly expanded into another realm altogether. I had no doubt that the hidden part of me, which I had been systematically invoking by all possible means, was functioning more fully than ever before. That perspective kept me from dissolving in grief. Two days later, I found a letter lying on my doormat. Before I'd even got close enough to recognise the handwriting, I could feel a weird dead quality emanating from it. My brief romance was definitively over. The strain was too much for her, as she was committed to her existing partner. There was no way she could ever see me again. Great start to the day. I got into a pathetic state. I asked the Tarot and I Ching an unhealthy amount of questions about the situation and the general state of my life. I managed a day at work and then had to take two off.

The ongoing mystery of the increasingly strong presence of Dion Fortune was not forgotten. I made the decision that, over the next few days, I would reread both of her major novels, *The Sea Priestess* and *Moon Magic*. They were both concerned with the mysteries of Isis. It was those very books that had initially attracted me to that sublime goddess. Harp music, candles, incense, and general devotion would accompany this. That new moon had been enough to be going on with. The Glastonbury full moon vision invited me to give over to it completely. I started *The Sea Priestess* on Friday July 10th, one of my days off work. Good progress was made amidst a few spliffs, despite a constant backdrop of emotional blah and repeated Tarot and I Ching questions.

On Saturday morning, I awoke earlier than normal, feeling hideous and hollow, the prospect of a long empty day ahead. I went out shopping to Sainsburys with a frustrating feeling that there was somewhere I had to go, somewhere else I was supposed to be. I put aside the obvious immediate thought. Glastonbury was not an option. Nobody was potentially available who might be interested in driving down there that weekend. The morning was already almost gone. It would take ages to get there and cost a stupid amount of money I simply couldn't spare.

Back home, divination frenzy began. I Ching hexagram 2, *The Receptive* told me it was "*favourable to seek friends in the west*". Tarot cards were also chucked about. I passed into a bizarre altered state. Under remote control, I slung some bits and pieces into a bag and walked out of the door to the train station. I finished *The Sea Priestess* en-route to Bristol. An hour was then spent in dull drizzle at a bus stop. Eventually I strode grimly up the Tor, as the rain gently continued. I was feeling a tad demented. In my head I was shaking my fist at the sky screaming, "what do you fucking want from me?" It wasn't a standard moment of Glastonbury ecstasy. Nonetheless, it still seemed like I'd acted on my best option. The prospect of a long day alone in Southend felt like an atrocity. If I was going to connect with the hidden dynamic behind my turmoil then Glastonbury Tor was the place for me to be. I came down and rang Jane Satchwell. Thankfully she was about and it was okay for me to stay. On Sunday we were back in Glastonbury again. It was sunny this time and the Tor and Chalice Well recharged my batteries. I began reading *Moon Magic* on the way home.

Tuesday July 14th was the full moon in Capricorn. The new moon had been a powerful one so I was curious to see what its fullness might bring. Whilst eating breakfast, I had the feeling that I needed to pull a Tarot card and meditate on it during the day at work. I'd recently bought the Haindl deck to complement Crowley's. Dana Lee had introduced me to it in *Dimensions*. It was an extraordinary work. Hermann Haindl was a concentration camp survivor. His deck was broadly based on Crowley. There was an *Aeon* trump instead of *Judgement*. Celtic, Norse, Egyptian and Native American imagery was skilfully used within that framework. Some of the cards had Glastonbury references. He had visited the place and had a visionary experience of light atop the Tor. I'd been getting increasingly impressive results through use of the deck. That full moon morning, I decided I would seek the key to the day there, instead of in the *Book of Thoth*.

I pulled *Aeon*. To me, it had always been the most interesting Haindl card. The imagery combined aspects of Crowley's ideas with the traditional *Judgement*. Two rivers wind across a wasteland. One contains blue water, the other, red liquid fire. They lead the eye towards a landmark at a central far horizon. Glastonbury Tor. Above it looms a stormy sky, full of clouds and strange suggestive shapes. It carries a *Book of Revelation* vibe. A clearly visible eye, stated by Haindl to be of a Goddess, looks out through the miasma. Droplets of blue rain descend. Individual tongues of red fire ascend. At the middle of the image, as the obvious focus, can be seen a large transparent egg of blue. Within it, lies an upside-down foetus, finger to its mouth in the gesture of Harpocrates. The stirring archetypal motif was consciously taken from the final moments of Kubrick's *2001: a Space Odyssey*. In that seminal movie, the image of a foetus floating in outer space above the Earth, had deeply stirred many in a way that defied rational analysis. It spoke of a mythological truth. In Haindl's Tarot card, the babe of the New Aeon descends from the Goddess to be born at Glastonbury. In the amazing mix of old and new Aeon imagery are suggestions of both the disease and its cure. We are locked into a destructive myth cycle of the end days. *Revelation* and Nostradamus dominate the western collective unconscious. Ways must be found to dissolve such self-fulfilling prophetic scripts. The Goddess and the Tor, the Aeon babe, and the birth of a new humanity represent possible paths across the abyss.

I was well primed to enter into the depths of this Tarot masterpiece. The morning at work was really just an extended reverie upon it. Kirk then suddenly remembered a vision he had experienced on the previous day. He saw me standing, robed, in the Tor tower. His communication of this seemed to instantaneously set off a rapid train of thought. We should try and bring down Sirius energy into the Tor, through the maze within the Aquarius sign that serves as potential matrix for the New Age/Aeon. It would be an act inspired by Reiser's embryogenesis ideas. I glanced at my desk calendar. The weekend of July 25th/26th stood out at me. It was the nearest practical time to the July 23rd *Cosmic Trigger* synchro-mesh date that a group of us could be mustered to get down to Glastonbury.

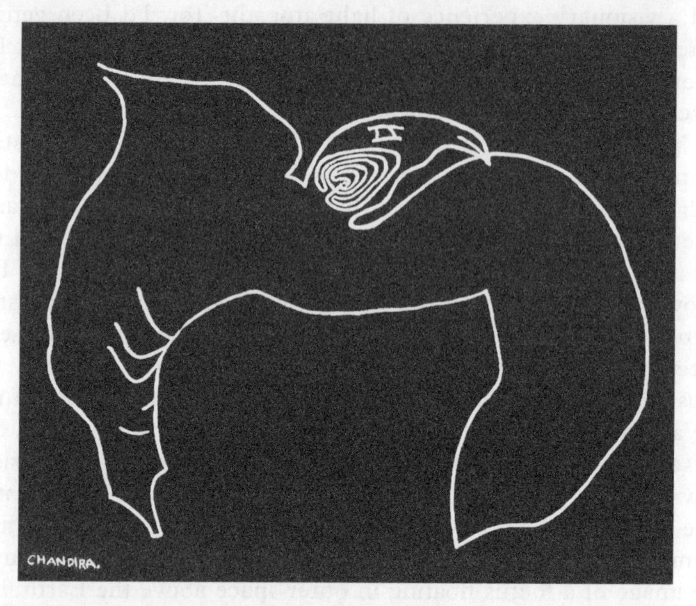

My two Tarot visions of the *High Priestess* and *Aeon* seemed to be strongly connected and to carry a reverberation from my visit to Glastonbury on Dion Fortune's birthday in December '91, when I had keyed in an unparalleled period of Tarot study. The new blueprint I had gone in search of was surely approaching its apogee. That full moon evening, back at home, I reconnected with the Isis of Avalon vision and found it readily expanded to accommodate the day's musings. It began with a void of stars from which shone the outline shape of a great phoenix. Within it was the golden form of a maze, a brain, the morphogenetic field pattern for the embryogenesis of the world sensorium. It was resonating and communicating with the sun behind the sun. Ursa Major's seven stars transparently appeared through the maze for a brief moment. The image of the Tor and the surrounding landscape and night sky then emerged. The maze remained, glowing and pulsating around the slopes. The larger shape of the phoenix was also still visible, lit up across the ground. In the sky above the Tor, a blue point of light appeared and grew bigger, beginning to descend. It floated down slowly towards the Tor, as Isis of Avalon beamed her grace upon it. A babe in an egg of blue. The New Aeon, the New Age. Coming to birth as its devotees in Glastonbury send healing and magick out unto the entire world and beyond; yea out unto the entire world and beyond.

TIME SHIFT: CASTING THE DREAMSPELL

"Self-divination is the Art form of the Dreamspell.
Through self-divination, you become your own authority
in charge of your own destiny."
"Who owns your time, owns your mind.
Own your own time and you will know your own mind."
José Argüelles.

ON THE FOLLOWING DAY, Wednesday July 15th, I was told that the next big New Age extravaganza was happening over the week-end of July 25th/26th and Glastonbury was involved! No further details were available. This brought me to some kind of fever pitch. I desperately wanted to know more. A fragment of material could, perhaps, resonate very strongly with me and expand my understand-ing of what we were up to. Remember, this was the age before mass internet access. In later years such details would be easy to find.

For a few days I carried the visionary *High Priestess/Aeon* package around in my head, nurturing it. If we were really going to work magick with those themes in Glastonbury, there was only a week to prepare. I accepted that if we were supposed to discover any information in advance about the upcoming New Age event then it would somehow come to us. That still didn't stop me from remaining wired-out with the desire for details.

Saturday July 18th was Oliver's birthday. He was hosting a bit of a gathering. It was a chance for me to discuss the situation with Alex. I had no expectations for the evening, beyond good company and perhaps a little bit of a respite from the mounting intensity. I started talking to a musician mate of Oliver's named Nick Ashron. He just happened to have some printed material on the coming biggie with him. It had already been assimilated. I was welcome to take it away with me. So much for a quiet night. There were eleven pages to digest. One thing was immediately clear: the prime source of the material was José Argüelles and his wife, Lloydine. I had known that, according to the Harmonic Convergence enthusiasts, at some point in 1992, we were going to emerge from the five year wobble point and into the final sequence leading to 2012 but the exact date wasn't in the books. Now I discovered that it was a week away from Part Two of the Harmonic Convergence! Was I finally about to catch up on myself?

Argüelles offered a prophetic critique of the established calendar and the way it dictates our relationship with Time. He referred to the current *'third-dimensional timing frequency,'*of '12:60'. We have a 12 month year and a 60 minute hour. This has been determined by the 360 degree circle rather than the natural orbits of the Moon and Earth. The western Gregorian calendar mechanised Time. *"By the beginning of the 17th century,* the *12:60 timing frequency was in place, creating a purely third-dimensional mental bubble around the planet. Thus was made possible the revolution of scientific materialism, followed by the Industrial Revolution, and, in quick succession, the various democratic and socialist revolutions of the past two centuries. All of these 12:60 clockwise revolutions have been accompanied by a staggering increase of human population, a rapid spread of materialism, and the environmental pollution and degradation of the current world crisis."*

He believed that our calendar has played a major role in the current global crisis. *"The entire purpose of education and socialization in the modern world is to fit children into a 12:60 slot so that they can carry on the burdensome business of materialism"*, which Argüelles called a *'Time Drug'. "Time is money" is based on the 12:60 ratio. Everything is valued according to how much you can get out of 60 minutes."* Reforming the calendar would literally change Reality. Argüelles announced *"the Time Shift, July 26, 1992 – the moment when the 12:60 frequency attains maximum entropy".*

The Dreamspell Peace Plan was inaugurated in which people, *"agree to follow the 13-moon calendar, effective July 26, 1992, the Time Shift. The 13-moon calendar measures the solar year according to thirteen perfect months of 28 days each. The 12-month Gregorian calendar (the current global standard) distributes the thirteenth month as 28 extra days randomly added to eleven of the twelve months. (One extra day, the 365th, is accounted for in the Dreamspell as Green Day, July 25.)"* This would enable the human race to make *"the transition from*

12:60 third-dimensional time to 13:20 fourth dimensional time," best represented by the Mayan 13 x 20 Tzolkin. For someone as obsessed with Time as me, these were astounding ideas.

One thing struck me very strongly. I had no knowledge of the Harmonic Convergence in 1987 but looking back in my diaries I discovered that during the exact three days of its occurrence I had been reading *Cosmic Trigger,* a work with a spectacular 2012 conclusion. I started reading it on the 16th and finished on the 18th. It was also the time of the intense end of my five-year relationship, one of the most significant transitional moments in my life. This was enough to give me pause for thought. Like the 1985 mystery, I rather felt that some part of me *was* responding to this event and that there was something of importance I needed to pay attention to.

The upcoming 1992 pivotal moment was being linked in many New Age circles with the increasing vogue for Earth Change prophecies. Californians are understandably more conscious of the possibilities of epic earthquakes that might sink the state. Some began to feel it was inevitable. Various visionaries focused the fear.

Gordon Michael Scallion was an interesting and disturbing case. He had made a series of very specific predictions about earthquakes and they'd initially been fulfilled with a worryingly high percentage of accuracy. A number of noticeable quakes had disturbed the sunshine state around the turn of the decade. Scallion believed it was all a prequel to a three-stage break up of California that would get underway in June '92. He stated there was a 50 % likelihood of a major quake in the Los Angeles vicinity between April 17th -22nd. On the 22nd a biggie occurred within a hundred miles. In June he claimed a 65% probability of a 7.6 scale event before the end of July. A 7.5 quake occurred on June 28th. He expected further action within a few months that would complete the beginning of the fracturing of California. I guess we can understand that American Earth Change freaks were beginning to feel a bit twitchy.

So, California was about to slide into the sea, 3D was about to give over to 4D. Argüelles himself was expecting a pole shift but not until May 2000. Not only that, some New Agers believed that all electricity on the planet was set to fail. My printed material advised stocking up on candles as it could get a bit dismal before the space brothers sorted it out. Regardless of such flakiness, Scallion's earthquake predictions did seem to have real-world consensus co-ordinates.

I needed to put the whole thing in perspective. Someone else had seen it all before. Dion Fortune wrote in *Avalon of the Heart*, *"The last thing of interest to happen here was the end of the world, which has now occurred three times. Glastonbury is very conveniently situated for this event, for it has been prophesied that the top of the Tor will stick out of the waters when the end comes, and all who gather thereon shall be saved. People have come to live in Glastonbury for this reason, and whenever the date for the end of the world is announced they rush home from their holidays, and pack picnic baskets, and put them handy in the hall. Two ladies once gave away all their winter woollies because the end of the world had been prophesied for a date early in September, and when November came, and no end of the world, had to ask for them back again, to the great disgust of the recipient, who had now missed the July sales."*

It was interesting for me to contemplate how the nature of the messenger can determine how and where their message may be heard. If some of Argüelles ideas on the 12:60 Time is Money matrix had been espoused by some French Neo-Marxist post-modern types like Derida or Baudrillard they would probably be taught on university courses by now, having become part of political debate. It hasn't quite worked out that way but a zone of interface between different ends of the philosophical spectrum can sometimes be discerned.

Beyond the strange mindset of New Agers, with the approach of the millennium, a general theme of 'Endism' was emerging amongst post-modern cultural theorists. One major work saw the theme break the surface of the mainstream that very year and generate ferocious debate. In 1992 American political theorist Francis Fukuyama published *The End of History and the Last Man*, a completed form of arguments that had initially appeared in journals a few years previously. It's quite interesting and instructive to compare and contrast him with Argüelles. It was mighty strange to see their two apparently divergent perspectives appearing about the same time. Fukuyama likewise pondered the extraordinary rate of change best represented by the fall of the Berlin Wall and Soviet communism. He also felt that a huge epoch had culminated. In this case though, Fukuyama came to strikingly different conclusions. He believed that, rather than indicating the demise of the 12:60 reality-tunnel, such events were in fact a sign of its ultimate and most worthy triumph. American capitalistic liberal democracy cannot be improved upon. It represents the ultimate perfection of human culture and all other systems will inevitably fail before it.

The only worry for Fukuyama was that the Last Men of his title might find such perfection a tad boring and maybe be dumb enough to restart the general nonsense of history for want of something better to do. Little episodes like Stalin's Russia and Nazi Germany were minor aberrations on the obvious road to perfection. Howls of protest and derision greeted Fukuyama but he remained unphased. He continues to affirm his theories in the present day, 9/11 notwithstanding.

Some post-modernists rejected anything that could be called a 'meta-narrative', a bigger picture that explained why history and cultures worked the way they did, whether it was the Bible or Karl Marx. Crowley's Aeon of Horus was a meta-narrative. Argüelles' Mayan calendar likewise. What the PoMo contingent didn't seem to grasp was that any concept of an era that was 'post' something previous was also a meta-narrative. I found both Argüelles and Fukuyama to be part of a bigger picture that Eliade had outlined for me a decade before. It was that old theme of the ending and regeneration of history/time.

In the midst of the party, I tried to assimilate the extraordinary ideas. It might not be the end of the world in the way most people thought of it but something was surely going down and the part of my consciousness I'd been cultivating for more than a decade was responding to it, somehow intimately involved in it. I staggered away from Oliver's to Alex's Temple room to further ponder the situation. We asked Dion Fortune what was happening? The contact confirmed that my Sirius musings were correct and that she had assisted me in their reception. She promised more help later.

It now felt as if the whole package was coming back round together for me. After the massive input of Argüelles' ideas, I needed to refocus on what it was that had initially made me consider the coming period of July to be so significant. I felt that July 23rd was the most important date in my magickal calendar. *Cosmic Trigger* was fundamental to that realisation. It had linked together the heliacal rising of Sirius, Isis, Crowley's Thelema, and Gurdjieff.

The date also had very strong Psychic Questing links. The most outrageous of all the stories from the Green Stone era concerned Graham Phillips' ceremonial raising of an Egyptian Queen. In 1981, after the Lights of Knowledge adventure, Graham experienced dreams and visions of an obscure female Pharaoh named Sobek-Nofru-Re or Sa-Re. She gave him details of how to bring her back to life using the Green Stone. He complied with instructions that included the drawing of large Egyptian figures on the walls of his home. The end result saw the visible appearance of the lady, spectacularly floating in mid-air, to three witnesses. Andy's *The Seventh Sword* gives a full account. It was possibly my favourite paranormal tale. The whole extravaganza had occurred on July 22nd and been linked with Isis and Sirius. A decade later, the actual seventh sword itself had manifested immediately after events on July 23rd.

All kinds of data in the magickal filing cabinet part of my brain began arising unsought throughout the coming days in strangely suggestive manner. The full title of the tarot trump that had inspired my Isis of Avalon vision was 'Priestess of the Silver Star'. It was accepted that the star in question was Sirius. The inundation of the Nile is also the birth of Horus so the dog days are a good Aeon of Horus time. And there was a Sirius phoenix link. Egyptian mythology tells how the phoenix returns to Heliopolis once every five hundred years. Due to imperfections in Egyptian calendars, the rising of Sirius and the inundation gradually wandered away from the month dedicated to it. Approximately once every five hundred years it was readjusted to return to harmony with the Great Sothic year. It seemed to represent the hawk-headed sun god returning. Kenneth Grant stated in *The Magical Revival* that Sirius had once been in an ancient constellation called the phoenix. This little mix was enough to affirm for me my magickal Isis Aeon babe Aquarian phoenix Tor configuration. Perhaps most inexplicably, the Sirius calendar seemed to be at the root of the western 12:60 system. It had been sacred once. Now it was distorted and in need of major reform.

Crowley had visited Mexico in 1900. He climbed mountains and imbibed the culture. The country retained a special place in his heart. It was there that he had begun the systematic invocation of the Enochian universe of John Dee. His first act was to assume the god-form of Harpocrates, standing with finger to mouth in a visualised giant crystal. The skrying mirror that Dee had used for the original operations had supposedly been of Aztec origin. There was some not-quite-graspable nuance there. It had the flavour of trying to intuit the meaning of some atmospheric dream that contained an odd mixture of elements that seemed important but couldn't quite be consciously understood. I could only really come away from it with the feeling that Crowley and the Mesoamerican calendar system were linked in my own destiny and in the bigger picture somehow.

Argüelles had talked of the July 25th/26th period as being New Year in the Mayan calendar. If Sirius was the significant stellar factor in the Egyptian calendar, the Pleiades are probably the Mesoamerican equivalent but the important dates associated with them fall in May and November. With July, a solar alignment is of primary importance. In Europe and America during the course of a year the sun rises in the south east and sets in the south west marking a modest arc across the sky that reaches it maximum length and height at the summer solstice. It never crosses the very centre of the sky. The Mesoamerican area is situated in the tropics. The sun does attain a true central zenith and the dates are of considerable importance to understanding the ancient cultures. On the exact Tropic of Cancer, the sun reaches the zenith on the summer solstice. As one moves south, the zenith will manifest twice on either side of the sun's path towards and away from the June solstice. In the Mesoamerican zones this will be in May and July. At the famous Chichen Itza site, it's July 23rd. A bit further south the Yucatec Maya celebrate July 26th.

There have been differently oriented cosmologies used by Mesoamerican cultures along with periodic attempts to reconcile them. One interesting example can be found with the Chorti Maya of Honduras who perform a ritual known as 'raising the sky' to re-enact the creation of the world. July 25th marks the intersection of the Milky Way and the Gemini ecliptic directly overhead at the zenith at that latitude. It makes a cross in the sky that they consider to be their world tree. It defines the fourfold division of their sacred space. And Sirius did actually have significance for some Mayan groups in the Yucatan who began their New Year cycles around July 26th as Sirius returned to visibility in their vicinity. If the mix of data was bewildering, the most important thing for me in July 1992 was that a Sirius Mesoamerican synchromesh was unfolding in my life and I was aware of it whilst it was happening rather than waiting years to discover it.

THE TURNING POINT

ON THE SUNDAY NIGHT FOLLOWING THE PARTY I decided to seek guidance from the *I Ching* as to what the coming week might bring. The response was Hexagram 24, *The Turning Point*. As a fan of early Pink Floyd it was familiar to me. Syd Barrett had used it in the lyrics of *Chapter 24* on *The Piper at the Gates of Dawn* album. It had also been the inspiration for the title of a book by Fritjof Capra on new paradigms that I had particularly liked.

So what did it tell me? "*After the decay comes the turning point. The light that was banished returns. – Change return success. – Action brings good fortune.*" That sounded promising. What would it take to confirm its accuracy? I didn't give the matter much thought. The most immediate return I had to think about was the one to 12:60 the next day at work even if I was going to dissolve into 13:20 by the weekend.

Watching Monday's early evening local TV news, I discovered that rain and thunder were forecast for later on. This was great to hear. I hoped it would be fairly early so I could go out for a run in it. Running in electric storms happens to be one of my favourite activities. Not many opportunities arise in Britain to enjoy such a hobby so I'm always keen to make the most of them. Round about eight o'clock, the sky suddenly darkened. Perfect! Time to quickly limber up. Out came the Cult album *Love*. On went the classic track, *Rain*. At literally the very second it began, lightning lit the sky. A further flash exactly coincided with the concluding drum-beat. Excellent. Heavy rain had started to fall. I ran out into the street feeling like a deranged maniac. People were dashing for cover. I was heading joyfully into the heart of the maelstrom. I ran up along Victoria Avenue, past my place of work, part of a row of office skyscrapers. I came to a garden area by the roadside and got off the pavement. The earth was wet and fragrant. Church bells were ringing. I passed through a smell of bonfires. I could imagine it was the odour of the sky on fire. A blinding forked lightning flash snaked across the heavens with a searing rip of a sound suggesting the sky was about to explode. No thunderous retort followed though, just even heavier rain. It was one of the best runs of my life. Out in that elemental fury, soaking wet and breathing hard, exhilaratingly alive and vibrant, I suddenly remembered that *I Ching* hexagram. It was based on the trigram, *The Arousing/Thunder.* I'd had a few prime Tarot moments in '92. Now it seemed that I was having a unique *I Ching* experience. What did that tell me? It was surely another enormous indicator that a major 'turning point' really had arrived.

The next day, I was completely knackered at work. Time dragged. That night a passive Osho meditation was scheduled in *Dimensions.* I felt it could provide a necessary contrast to the intensity of the previous night and went along, happy with the idea of sitting silently and thinking of nothing. Things had reached the point of input overload and once again, I hoped for a brief respite. In the back room, where I'd screamed my lungs out a few months before, I found that my mind refused to empty itself. I kept on coming back to a vision of me sitting cross-legged on the Tor, near to the tower. I accepted the scene and stayed with it. Nothing developed. There was no further *High Priestess/Aeon* type episode. At the end though, I was a bit startled when Dana Lee asked what I was doing sitting on the Tor when it was supposed to be a meditation void of form? I was aware that she was an above-average psychic but this compelled my attention. She knew all about what was going on and I was very happy to hear that she was willing to accompany us to Glastonbury for the biggie. Her vision of me suggested that my presence on the Tor was more than just normal imagination. It was part of the build up to the coming weekend. I remembered the *Turning Point* again. Alongside *The Arousing/Thunder*, the other trigram that made up the hexagram was *The Receptive/Earth.* My Tor-top passive meditation seemed to exactly embody those qualities. When I got home I wrote in my diary, "*even shagged out, I can have a virtual satori on the I Ching*". It had got to the point where there was hardly any difference between my inner and outer world.

On Wednesday July 22nd, I was looking back in my diaries to previous July 23rds. When scanning 1985, I casually looked up the page to the Saturday when I'd first put up my Glastonbury Qabalah pictures. I consciously clocked something I'd never fully realised before. I could have done on many occasions. With typical timing it saved itself for then to show me what I already knew in my guts, that I was about to conclude and somehow fulfil a huge cycle of my life started in 1985. The book I was reading over that weekend, for the first time, was *Avalon of the Heart.* In February 1988 I had read *Priestess* at a great transitional moment in my life. It now seemed as if Dion Fortune had been standing, as my guardian of the threshold, beckoning me over, before I made the connection to Andy Collins and his work. I also recalled how later in '88, the impetus to go to my great solstice rendezvous with destiny was reading *Avalon of the Heart* for the second time, on the first day of my sacred month of June. Adding that to the mysteries of the 1991 birthday pilgrimage was enough to give me the cold shivers. I couldn't help but feel that this was an unmistakeable sign suggesting Dion Fortune's nurturing and protective influence in my life. This amazed me all the more because if I'd made a list of people I considered to be my great teachers at that point, Gurdjieff, Crowley, Rajneesh etc., she probably wouldn't have made the top ten and there she was, involved in the most awesome experiences of my life.

Thursday July 23rd saw the launch of Andy's *The Circlemakers* at *Atlantis Books* in London. It was a strange night. The events of exactly a year ago seemed extremely distant. The seventh sword was history. As for crop circles, I'd received a copy of Andy's book a few days before and rapidly read it. It seemed to be obviously the best yet written on the subject. He would soon be inspired to carry out, over two summers in 1993 and '94, an extensive extraordinary series of experiments in the heart of crop circle country to test the full spectrum of a hypothesis linking Wilhelm Reich's orgone energy with the phenomenon. The resulting limited edition account of that work, *Alien Energy,* I consider to be an unjustly neglected masterpiece. It would amaze and exasperate me in years to come to see new books bring up orgone as possibly related to crop circles and not even mention Andy's work in the bibliography, especially when I knew that there was no way that the authors in question couldn't be aware of it. Perhaps Andy's basic belief that the majority of the recent elaborate pictograms were man-made didn't help. Most interestingly he discovered that humans creating a crop formation could stimulate orgonic manifestations, seemingly through the disruption of the crops.

I talked to Andy a bit about having another big Glastonbury adventure lined up. It barely registered. The new book was obviously the main thing on his mind. He was actually going to be in Glastonbury himself over the coming weekend, lecturing at the Crop Circle Symposium in the Assembly Rooms. For the time being, we were on divergent paths.

On Friday night there was a final preparatory psychic session at Alex's. He was sure that I would be able to receive Dion Fortune's instructions for what we were supposed to be doing the next day. I spontaneously envisaged a meditational ritual and the details seemed to be acceptable to those present, both alive and dead. Through Alex, I mentioned my Glastonbury Qabalah to her and she said, *"yes, I was around you then, but you put it in your own head"*.

Monica Sjöö's made major criticisms in *New Age and Armageddon* of the Harmonic Convergence and the New Age in general claiming that it appeared to be a very gender imbalanced phenomenon.

Sjöö called the major male New Age figures, *'White Light Patriarchs'*. She suggested that beneath the external veneer of the new lay the same old apocalyptic Christianity that had suppressed the feminine and abused the planet for so long. The return of Quetzalcoatl and the Harmonic Convergence were just another form of the Second Coming of Christ Rapture of the evangelicals. For all the fine-sounding talk of Gaia the living planet it was the fertilising seed of the white light deity that always seemed to be ultimately the most important necessary ingredient. The Goddess was noticeably absent. Some New Agers came up with strange sounding stuff about her as well. A lot of fluffy bunnies aren't at all comfortable in physical bodies. The flesh is evil. We must ascend up and away in our light bodies asap.

A final set of motifs came to mind to complete my preparation. Something was out of balance and the cosmic Goddess force was needed to sort it. I recalled Gerald Massey's idea of the world mountain and its septenary spiral path as throne of the Goddess. The name of Isis was taken to mean throne and the hieroglyph representing her was a picture of one. The Hopi labyrinth, which is the same design as the one on the Tor, symbolises the emergence of a new world from the old. Their world age concept is part of the same Mesoamerican group of ideas as the ones that influenced Shearer and Argüelles. Is that one of the reasons why the maze has made itself visible again in the current epoch? Is it part of an energetic template involved in the transition from one epoch to the next? And that old Eliade favourite theme, the abolition and regeneration of time. It all settled into my head together as I went to sleep on the night before the big event.

Early on Saturday evening a car full of people left Southend for Glastonbury. Work commitments had prevented an earlier departure. Alex was driving. We were to be accompanied by Kirk and Dana Lee. It was nearly dark when we arrived at about nine-thirty. I still had no idea what Harmonic Convergence stuff was happening. We went straight to the Tor. There were further echoes from 1985 and the whole process since, as Jane Satchwell was able to participate. We met her on the summit. She'd just seen Andy Collins in town. As in '85, he was a mile down the road. Like themes in a novel, like a sort of symphony, motifs from the start were being restated at the end. I'd been through a lot. It seemed I was about to come out on the other side.

After taking a little bit of time to acclimatise and go over the business in hand, it was time for the meditational ritual. We wandered over to the area near the direction finding plinth and stood in a circle. As we did so, it started to rain with a light drizzle. This worked in our favour as hardly anyone else was around to distract us. We began by visualising the whole of the Tor hill as flat. At each corner of the tower stood one of the Watchers of Avalon, the indigenous site Guardians, seen as tall dark hooded figures.

For our purposes the guardians of the four quarters were to be the four sons of Horus. Dion Fortune had explained the previous night that although Sumerian/Babylonian stuff was at the heart of the Zodiac, we were using Egyptian forms as they resonate more strongly in the collective unconscious, were easier to use and most of the group present had a strong Egyptian background. It also helped affirm the link to the Elder culture and the Green Stone wanderers.

In the east was Duamutef. He had a jackal head like Anubis. In the west was the hawk-headed Quebsenuf. Ape-headed Hapi guarded the north. Imsety, with human head, false Egyptian beard and painted eyes took the south. We started to walk slowly, anti-clockwise, around our circle, seeing the maze pattern lighting up from beneath the ground in a gentle golden glow, activating the vortex to bring the energy down. Mists of Avalon were visualised as rising all around us until the whole world had disappeared, apart from the flattened shining maze and Tor tower.

The four sons of Horus hovered just above the edge of the glowing maze, against the background of mist Thus prepared, the space was ready to receive the celestial energy. A small ball of light was seen in the body of Nuit, directly above us. The Isis/Sirius force came down in the form of a golden beam. Like lightning Hadit kundalini it downloaded into the Grail receptacle maze brain of the phoenix, sending ripples of light out through the spiral pattern.

Later on, in a tent at the Avalon camp-site, Alex and Dana Lee got into stuff that can best be described as 'beam me up Scotty' material that I won't inflict on you. It was a measure of how cosmic the whole thing had got. I retired to my tent alone. Sleep easily came. I stirred in the early light of dawn, feeling immediately that something was happening. I could feel a kind of force vibrating through the ground. My initial response was to want to get up and gallop off to the Tor, but it was a few miles away and I was still very tired. I dozed off again. When everyone had emerged, a few hours later, I told them what I'd experienced. Dana Lee had heard at dawn an Om so loud it had made the earth move. In Glastonbury town centre we finally saw the flyers for the Harmonic Convergence event. There was to be a gathering at dawn on the Tor that Sunday morning, to sound a great Om! I was amazed. I was convinced that I had actually felt it, vibrating through the ground.

I went home well happy. My brain was annihilated, which was just as well because the meeting place of all this is not the brain. I'd used my mind but gone beyond it. My heart was primed. On Monday night I was looking through a folder of assorted notes when I saw, sticking out a little way from the rest of the material, what I recognised as the piece of paper on which I'd written my 1990 Zodiac vision a few hours after it had occurred. I thought it was odd that, with all the retrospective process I'd been engaged in, I hadn't reread it. I'd taken it for granted that it had opened my heart and helped me to accept that all that was said about Glastonbury by the most spaced out mystics was true. It had been the greatest experience of my life. But the actual precise details. What were they? Of course, it was a timing special. To have reread it at any point in the last few months would have changed everything. It was only now that I was supposed to make the necessary connections. This was what I read ...

"I saw a Glastonbury solstice dawn, symbolic dawn, dawn of the Aquarian age, New Aeon, New Age. Mists of Avalon are rising from the ground, vaporising into the air as they roll across the land. The Tor. The Abbey. Chalice Well. A hum, like organ music, gently but powerfully rising. A sense of the Abbey's perpetual choir. Celestial voices are emerging from the hum. On this new turn of the time spiral, other voices join the monks of the Celtic Church. There are native American and Indian intonations. Bells, at first sounding Christian, but then reverberating Tibetan style, sound a background. This dawn will bring a greater awakening and what we've done, our vision quest, purging and purifying ourselves, traversing the Zodiac in set sequence, we're in the same dawn, adding a tone to the great choir, an old tone that was known before, added again, but different in the way it relates to the greater whole, as this is a new era. What we've done, whatever individuals may or may not have got from it has contributed to the rising choir. Glastonbury is waking. Now the Tor, a glass isle, a hollow hill, filled with elementals, ancestors, faery folk. Vast angelic forms, Watchers of Avalon, are on guard. The Monks of the Company of Avalon are

smiling, as the Abbey/Chalice Well current is absorbed into the beak of the Aquarian phoenix, the fire heart rising with the sun. In underground tunnels beneath the town, through the whole ground, the great humming sounds. All around, in enchanted sleep, are the dreamers, seventy-five thousand at the festival, the mystics in Glastonbury itself. Because of all these people and us and what we've done, the choir sings louder and the inner bodies of those with right intentions are responding/resonating. Messages are being left deep inside. They are all singers of the song, though they carry different notes, different lines of the song. The more and the further they spread the notes and different lines of the song, the more people may start to hear the whole song. As they gather at places like Glastonbury the whole song will be heard more and more, louder and louder. We must resonate together and a part of our task is to revitalise the tuning forks of stone and wind chimes of water that are the energy matrix of Britain. A hundredth monkey point will come in this process: the more it happens the less anyone can do to stop it and at the quantum leap point - bang! - we're there, we're everywhere. It's all true. All that the visionaries have ever said of Glastonbury. It really is all true."

I immediately realised the piece could very aptly be titled 'Harmonic Convergence'. In June 1990 I'd never heard of it. The rising tone was some kind of global Om that the Sunday dawn was part of. It was a call to 2012. My Vision Quest had generated a genuine vision and I had actually participated in the beginning of the living out of its manifestation. All of the divergent stuff I'd been into had been a personal harmonic convergence omega point, fulfilling and transcending my entire inner life until that moment, enabling me to be properly prepared for July '92. Twenty minutes later, I picked myself off the floor and stopped crying as the waves of cold shivers began to abate.

A massive high stayed with me for a few days after the Glastonbury biggie. Lots of little affirmative things clustered together to enhance it. Looking back in Hyatt and DuQuette's tarot book I was interested to see it stated that the opening of the heart chakra enables one to hear Om with the inner ear. It was nice to discover that one of Mary Caine's seminal Glastonbury experiences had come when she accompanied the Druid order to which she belonged to Glastonbury some time in the sixties. The eclectic bunch had sounded a mass Om in memorable manner from the

Tor top one night. It was the logic of poetry and dreams but that was fine because that is also the logic of magick.

The *Cosmic Trigger* Sirius mystery had initially drawn me towards the period in July when my inner life had so spectacularly converged. From Robert Anton Wilson's book, which I had now read an absurd number of times, I had taken the information that in Egypt, after its absence from the sky for a long period, Sirius rises on July 23rd. That may have been true once but it wasn't anymore. The date had shifted. It was now early August. What I have come to respect is that the July 22/23 time remains a most potent magical time to connect with certain energies.

When it came to the Argüelles material a veritable nightmare confronted me. The starting point had been Tony Shearer's time specific prophecy that produced the Harmonic Convergence, dates calculated forwards from the Spanish arrival in Mexico. A detailed critique is outside the scope of this work but it does seem that he got it considerably wrong and Argüelles followed him in that. As for the big July '92 Dreamspell transition into the final phase leading to 2012, some authorities on the Mayan calendar would actually point to April 1993 as being the real start of that process. Whilst Argüelles Dreamspell became increasingly popular in New Age circles and many, including Mayan elders themselves, came to regard him as an authority on the subject, it seemed best to regard his work as a new version of the Mayan calendar. His day counts did not match those that had remained in continuous use by some Mayans ever since the conquest.

Despite these details, I never had any doubts about the importance of what had happened to me. It was obvious from the previous decade of my life that the seemingly endless process of the revealing of a bigger picture was part of an exquisite ongoing mystery. Sealed orders from the future were revealed at pre-determined places on the path. I trusted it. Both *Cosmic Trigger* and the Argüelles material shared a common point of culmination in 2012. This was always considered to be the ultimate omega point convergence. All manner of things would come into alignment by then. It was where I was being led. All of my adventures would surely repeat on another twist of the spiral.

[illegible] for one night. It was the realm of poetry and dreams but that was fine because that is also the [illegible] of magic.

The Cosmic Trigger [illegible] quest had finally drawn me towards the period in July when my inner life had so spectacularly converged [illegible] Robert Anton Wilson's book, which I had now read an [illegible] number of times. I had taken on the information that in Egypt, after its absence from the sky for a long period, Sirius rises on July 23rd. That may have been true once but it wasn't anymore. The date had shifted. It was now early August. What I have come to suspect is that the July 23rd [illegible] remains a most potent magical [illegible] connected with certain energies.

When it came to the Aeonics [illegible] at a veritable nightmare [illegible]. The starting point had been Tony Shearer's [illegible] [illegible] [illegible] [illegible] [illegible] the [illegible] [illegible] [illegible] [illegible] the [illegible] [illegible] [illegible] [illegible] [illegible] [illegible] [illegible] [illegible] the [illegible] [illegible] [illegible] [illegible] 2012, [illegible] [illegible] [illegible] the Mayan calendar [illegible] [illegible] [illegible] [illegible] as being the real end of that process. Whilst [illegible] [illegible] [illegible] [illegible] in New Age circles and many [illegible] [illegible] [illegible] themselves came to regard him as an authority on the subject, it seemed best to regard his work as a new version of the Mayan calendar. [illegible] [illegible] did not match those that had [illegible] in [illegible] [illegible] [illegible] Mayan [illegible] since the conquest.

Despite these details I never had any doubts about the importance of what had happened to me. It was obvious from the previous decade of my life that my seemingly endless process of the revealing of a bigger picture was part of an [illegible] ongoing mystery. [illegible] orders from the future were revealed at pre-determined places on the [illegible] [illegible] [illegible] [illegible] and the Aeonics [illegible] [illegible] a common point of culmination in 2012. That was always considered to be the ultimate omega point. [illegible] [illegible] manner of things would come into alignment by then. It was where I was being led. All of my adventures would [illegible] [illegible] [illegible] [illegible] of the [illegible].

PART FOUR

FLASH FORWARD: AQUARIAN PHOENIX

The following material serves as a conclusion to *Avalonian Aeon* and a bridge into the follow-up, *Aquarian Phoenix*, in which it will feature in an expanded context.

STRANGE ATTRACTOR

IN JUNE 1995, after numerous intense adventures that will be detailed elsewhere, I finally fulfilled my greatest dream and moved to Glastonbury. I wasted no time in going into action. Within two weeks of arriving, I had arranged for my first public lecture there. Over the next four years I would put on one hundred events of some kind. I had been immensely encouraged by things soon after my arrival that affirmed to me that the vast process that had led me through Questing, the Glastonbury Zodiac, Sirius, and into the mysteries of the Mayan calendar, was still ongoing and was something that needed to be shared.

On the morning of July 25th 1995 I wandered into the courtyard of the *Glastonbury Experience* at the bottom of the High St. Scanning the notice-board I saw that a video was to be shown upstairs in the Georges Room that afternoon, featuring José and Lloydine Argüelles discussing the 13 Moon Mayan calendar. It was exactly three years since my personal 'convergence'. I'd never seen film footage of José before. It seemed like a fine way to spend the afternoon and to affirm continuity with one of the great turning points of my life. When I returned after lunch, I unexpectedly bumped into Chandira Hensey. She was one of the first people I'd met after moving to Glastonbury. I'd already had a few unusual experiences in her company and recognised a great psychic and spiritual potential emerging in her life. I mentioned the video showing and said a few words about José and she decided to accompany me upstairs.

It was great to finally see a man who had such a mysterious influence on my life. I still felt that his critique of the 12:60 Reality Grid was profound. The World Peace Plan Mayan Calendar ideal was wisely sane. I never entertained the slightest hope of a real tangible world calendar reform but the whole campaign was powerful shamanic magic subtly mutating consciousness and reality and I knew it was still worth persevering with.

The video was presented by a couple who were representatives of Argüelles' work in Britain. They were promoting his version of the Mayan calendar for the forthcoming year that began the next day. An invitation was put out to join them on the Tor that evening, at sunset, for a meditational ceremony to commemorate the special time. I asked Chandira if she was interested and if she wanted to see if she could access some of the Mayan mysteries psychically. She affirmed that she was happy to go for it. We returned to my flat and I showed her a magical image I had once been given by one of the July '92 crew, Dana Lee. It was supposed to be a doorway into the Mesoamerican realms. In a matter of moments Chandira was transported into visionary spaces that meant nothing to her but were richly suggestive to me. Some of it seemed to represent prophecies for the coming transition to 2012 via the millennium. The Glastonbury airwaves were full of that sort of stuff then. There was a white horse archer. Beyond that, a striking image of a bird entity holding a black obsidian pyramid full of golden liquid fire energy, crystal caverns beneath the Tor, bird star shapes, Nazca lines, stars, meteorites, DNA sections being replaced, collapsing buildings, skyscrapers, cathedrals, mosques, birds going up in a spiral, multiple many sized triangles. There was Metatron, light shining from his face, bringing a flaming torch down on the world, a solar eclipse, a line of pyramids on fire, Jesus and weird bird figures spiralling down.

After a break for our respective evening meals we met again to ascend the Tor. It was a muggy night, typical of the hot summer of that year. A 'tongues of fire' wind blew. When we reached the summit there was no sign of the awaited group. To temporarily escape the uncomfortably choking wind we descended to the egg stone maze centre, a place of embryogenesis, and a suitable spot to contemplate a new cycle. Chandira went back into the visionary realm. She found herself atop a ruined step pyramid in a desolate landscape. A group of the bird beings she'd seen earlier flew in and landed with her. They then took her flying into a place that became the Tor. A sort of etheric Mayan pyramid appeared and transposed itself over the Tor so that both were visible. The bird beings remained in attendance.

All of this could conceivably have been an evening's entertainment in its own right but it proved to be a prelude and preparation. When we returned to the Tor top, the group we had been intending to meet were assembling. The uncomfortable wind was commented on. Someone said they knew a great place, just off the top of the Tor, where it would be possible to retire for an undisturbed meditation. Chandira and I soon intuited that something strange was afoot as we were led back to the egg stone within a quarter of an hour of our earlier episode. Nothing too complex unfolded as far as external events were concerned but it was sufficient to blow my brain yet again. Basically, ten people joined hands and intoned a triple Om. Looking around, Chandira could see the bird shamans and a few other characters who looked as if they were indigenous site guardians, megalithic hippies. For me this was an obvious further development of the astounding process that I had connected to in June 1990 and experienced as coming to life in 1992. Now I was actually on the Tor and part of the Om whilst it was happening. In a perfect affirmation of the whole business of the dissolving of 12:60 into 13:20, the barriers between my 3D and 4D continued to disappear. The great vision was becoming ever more real. I was being welcomed into Glastonbury and assured that more was to come. We couldn't help feeling that we had somehow prepared the inner plane space for the simple ceremonial. The Tor had been connected to Mayan realms and mysterious presences were in attendance. I had been given a glimpse of potential functions I could fulfil in my new life.

Knowledge of the astronomy around the 2012 event and how a number of the world's sacred traditions seemed to carry some aspects of it was increasingly emerging, My perplexity over the multiple elements of the 1992 experience would soon be resolved as I was being pulled towards the peak of a process that was already in motion.

THE STELE REVEALED

IN CROWLEY'S *Book of the Law* the number ninety-three has great significance. The word *Thelema* itself has that enumeration by gematria of the Greek Qabalah. So does *agape*, a form of love. The Love under Will formula is thus encapsulated. A variant spelling on the mysterious messenger of the aeon, Aiwaz, has the same result. 1997 was year ninety-three of the Thelemic epoch. It seemed a safe bet that some Thelemic vibes would be in the air.

In late March I met Robert Coon in Glastonbury. He was back in the country for a short period. I was interested to know what he had been up to in recent times and was sure a number of other people would be as well. I mentioned to him that it was very easy then to arrange public presentations in the Library of Avalon at short notice. It was something I did regularly. I encouraged him to contemplate the option. Shortly afterwards he told me he was going to go for it. When he outlined the subject matter my head went into meltdown. I had known, from brief references in his writings that, in 1979, he had been in Egypt and located the Stele of Revealing. Although in recent years many Thelemites have seen it, back then it seemed to have fallen off the radar. This had been a vital moment in Coon's Crowleyan odyssey. For various reasons he had never made public the details of that adventure. He decided that the upcoming perihelion (meaning the moment when it passed closest to the sun) of the comet Hale Bopp was the time, and Glastonbury the place, to update and complete the saga. *Avalon and the AA* would be presented in the Library on April 1st. I noted the Cosmic Joker's date signature and anticipated a magnificent evening.

The contents of the lecture were summarised in a small booklet *The Cairo Working* published on the day in an edition of eleven copies. This, along with my existing knowledge of his work, enabled me to see it in a large timescale as never before and to set it against the backdrop of other significant events during the same period. This proved to be a process of immense importance for me.

What was it about this specific time in Thelemic year '93 that had convinced Coon to make such a significant magickal gesture? Comets were an important theme in his work. To begin with, when Crowley died in 1947 it was twenty four hours before the perihelion of a comet.

The 1967 full-physical manifestation of the Elijah being was the major moment of Coon's personal activation. Robert affirmed that he had been initiated into the Melchizedek Priesthood. He was allegedly empowered to reactivate Crowley's magickal order the AA (Argenteum Astrum) which he also referred to as the Omega Point Foundation. A massive download was received for a twenty-six year global work. Elijah instructed him to release the information in astrologically timed stages through until 1993.

Some of the details that appeared during the same summer of '67 concerned the Aztec calendar. In common with Tony Shearer at round about the same time, he focused on August 17th 1987 as a time of major transformation involving the primary Meso-american deity Quetzalcoatl. He envisaged a male dragon force that circles the planet being activated then from two main sites in Mexico, El Tule and Palenque. This was twenty years in advance of the date and considerably pre-empted Argüelles. Both men's visions were centred on the tree of life concept. Whilst Shearer was being inspired with his thirteen heavens vision, Robert was working on what became the thirteen sphere Enochian Cabala presented in *Voyage to Avalon*.

In January 1971 Robert publicly proclaimed that Glastonbury is planetary heart chakra (although not in any published form like Kenneth Grant the following year) and that the global omega point would be activated at Easter sunrise 1984 atop the Tor along with a female dragon energy, complementary to the male, that likewise circles the world.

On Christmas Day 1973, as Comet Kohoutek passed behind the sun, Robert said he had his only meeting with Melchizedek. The instructions he received began his great global chakra work with the *'Shasta-Great Pyramid-Glastonbury formula'*. This was *"opening the Heart of Gaia so that the feminine Rainbow Serpent current could flow without restriction around the world"*. In 1976, during the time of the appearance of Comet West, Robert was in El Tule burying a ruby and an emerald magickally set to activate eleven years later at the moment of sunrise on August 17th 1987.

Working with a profound belief in the possibility of physical immortality and that a planetary throat chakra is focused in Cairo, Robert Coon's mission was to ensure that, *"the archetypal thought of Physical Immortality, the Key Word of the Aquarian Aeon, was energized within the collective consciousness of humanity"*. Timing was of vital importance in this grand plan and two major magickal acts would be involved.

Coon believed that it was vital for him to be in Cairo at the time of the 1979 Autumn Equinox. This was partly inspired by studying strange prophecies derived from the dimensions of the Great Pyramid, in particular by Adam Rutherford, who although meticulous in his adherence to genuine measurements could readily be described as a Bible nut and fellow traveller of the likes of Jehovah's Witness founder Charles Taze Russell who had earlier used the pyramid to support an extreme evangelical prophesying. Basically, the epoch of the Second Coming of Christ would begin in 1979 ushering in a millennium lasting until 2979. This material has very specific locations within the pyramid linked to it. The entrance to the Queen's Chamber marked the 1979 moment.

Robert accepted that a new era was set to unfold and it would involve a shift in consciousness which he linked with his major concern, Immortalism. He informed Rutherford's group that he intended to actually be inside the pyramid in the Queen's Chamber at the exact moment of the prophecies' fulfilment. They had a bit of a fire and brimstone attitude to what was upcoming. The response was one of fear with a definite warning to stay away.

Following on from the prophetic moment in the pyramid Robert Coon would then immediately set out to rediscover and *'realign'* the Stele of Revealing and recite an appropriate invocation in its vicinity. It's an oddity of Thelemic history that after the great events of 1904 the actual physical artefact disappears from view. Considering its importance it seems strange that world-traveller Crowley never returned to look at it again. None of his followers are on record as having checked it out either.

On September 24th 1979, Coon invoked various deities and angels in front of the Stele. The culmination was a spontaneous outpouring which included the words:

"May the total frequencies,
May the full force,
May the unique True Will
Of the Stele of Revealing
Be directed upon this first day of the Millennium
Unto the Total Purification
Of every Heart – individual and planetary –
And unto the Complete Manifestation
Of the Revelation of Everlasting Life!"

Coon considered that the single most important element of the 1997 presentation was the magickal affirmation of the new museum exhibit number of the Stele. He believed it had not been publicly discussed before. The original 666 designation was a major part of the story of how Crowley was drawn towards the reception of *The Book of the Law.* 9422 doesn't seem anywhere near as promising. Coon believed that in fact Gematria higher intelligence was definitely on the case. '*Immediately after the consecration of the Stele*' he was inspired to write down a sequence of twelve numbers incorporating two of Crowley's favourites, 666 and 777. Thus:

777666666777

This was followed by a sequence of multiplication and addition symbols.

.+.+.+.

This led to

7.7 + 7.666 + 666.7 + 7.7 = 9422

I can understand why this blew Robert Coon's mind in 1979 and left him feeling like he was definitely on a winner. I am not making any big claims about it but it is rather interesting and deserves to be better known. More 9422 numerical material was presented in *The Cairo Working* but that is Coon's story to tell. The pamphlet does periodically surface online and is worth keeping an eye out for.

A deliberate magickal link between Egypt and Glastonbury, the throat and heart chakras, was made when Robert came to Chalice Hill a few weeks later on October 7th 1979. This was all part of the bigger picture of preparation for the Global Omega Point in 1984.

The rainbow serpents mated at Wesak, the Scorpio full moon, in May 1987 in the Andes, primarily focused on Lake Titicaca. This was the last major preparatory process before the event that thanks to José Argüelles has become known as the Harmonic Convergence.

The *'psychic Woodstock'* attracted a lot of attention in Glastonbury. Robert was strongly involved, serving as the focus for some large groups of people. In his estimation, *"At Sunrise of 17th August, 1987, the Living Quetzalcoatl arose from El Tule to activate a new 52 year Heaven cycle on earth."* Robert was not particularly into Argüelles. He emphasised the Aztec as opposed to Mayan calendar and made no mention of 2012 in his general prophetic blueprint.

Monica Sjöö in *New Age and Armageddon* took Robert Coon to task for ignoring the feminine in his Glastonbury Harmonic Convergence work. In his defence it needs to be remembered that as part of the 1984 Tor Omega Point event, he believed that a great female dragon current that encircled the planet had been activated. Harmony of male-female polarity was implicit in his concept of the two dragons.

The *'Planetary Christ Body'* had returned at the Easter 1984 Omega Point event and been in the womb until Harmonic Convergence. A further process lasting decades to bring it to birth was now activated. This involved a huge grid of sites that constituted the 'Planetary New Jerusalem'. Six additional sites to the fixed continental chakras constitute the *"12 Planetary Gates of the New Jerusalem"*. They are located on Bali, Palenque, Mount Fuji, Haleakala Crater Hawaii, Lake Taupo-Tongariro in New Zealand, and Table Mountain near Capetown South Africa. Of these 12, 8 are 'Driver Wheels', 4 are 'Spinner Wheels'; the Great Pyramid, Table Mountain, Lake Taupo and Haleakala. A 13th gate was set to open in Russia during the nineties. Further unfolding of this data ultimately leads to a total of 156 sites finally fully activated as a complete New Jerusalem global grid by 2065. The grid is the body of Christ. The process of its creation shows the expansion of the Omega Point into an Omega Sphere. These details were published in a 1990 booklet, *Glastonbury and the Planetary New Jerusalem.*

Fundamental to all this work was the meta-concept of Aeon shift. With the start of each new astrological age, the focus of the energies of the time moves thirty degrees of longitude, or a twelfth of the circumference of the Earth, to the west. The age of Taurus was initiated around the Altai Mountains region. It was the beginning of the Shambhalic initiative that Geoffrey Ashe investigated in *The Ancient Wisdom.* The Zoroastrians presided over the start of the fire age of Aries from modern day Iran. At the start of each period there are deliberate connections made between the preceding and upcoming locations. The Piscean epoch was birthed in a longitudinal corridor that contains Jerusalem, Mt. Sinai and the Great Pyramid. The Persian Magi are stated to have been present at the nativity of Christ. Joseph of Arimathea came to Glastonbury and not only brought the dispensation for the dawning Christian era but also staked out the location of the inception of the Aquarian Age. At this moment in time people will be going back and forth between Glastonbury, the Great Pyramid and Jerusalem. The next epoch of Capricorn will be anchored on the north-east tip of Brazil. The mobile Shambhalic focus shifts with the aeons across the globe and is currently conjunct with the Glastonbury heart chakra for the activation of the 'Aquarian Aeon of the Immortal Child'.

Not long before my Zodiac adventures, between April 10th - 22nd 1990, the 'Aquarian Cross Ritual' occurred. This was a physical representation of the Aeon shift timed immediately after the perihelion of Comet Austin on April 9th (right in the middle of the three-day feast of the writing of *The Book of the Law*) A cross was brought from the Mount of Olives to the Tor. This accomplished on another twist of the spiral what the three magi did at the birth of Christ. At noon on April 21st, the peak of the ritual process, Anthony Roberts *"materialized atop the Tor and sang Blake's Jerusalem"*. Coon considered that, after much discussion on the global New Jerusalem, Tony Roberts had now become a powerful inner plane co-worker in the process. It was intriguing that Roberts also appeared at the climax of the Questing group's Zodiac journey.

The mix of Crowley, Glastonbury and the bigger global picture including Egypt and Mesoamerican calendar systems nicely blended with my previous decade. One apparently minor detail though blazed forth to me like an inner comet in my consciousness. More than anything else, I would remember the evening for some data correlation that I was able to do myself. My neurotic faculty for storing names, dates, and places, catapulted me into an astonishing situation. I suddenly realised something that nobody else did. It was part of a bigger picture that had always been present but no individual had been consciously aware of. At that moment, I had come to see it. And it made stunning sense to me, affirming my intuitive sense that some of my diverse interests were not so separate after all.

Robert had, to use his own terminology, obtained and realigned the Stele of Revealing on September 24th 1979. As far as he was concerned, he had effectively reformulated Crowley's magickal order at that point. During that same period in '79, Andrew Collins was also engaged in a Crowleyan journey. He was being called to the Abbey of Thelema in Sicily to likewise revive Crowley's work. There was a moment in that story when he had conclusively pulled out, thus enabling the Green Stone and Seven Swords epics to unfold. It had happened when he was visiting the Sunderland family and a tooth had apparently apported and split in two. It had been around midnight on the transition between September 23rd and 24th 1979. The start of the very same day that Robert in Egypt connected to the Stele. The two men had been involved in a synchronous saga, both seeking similar aims. As one succeeded, so the other was switched onto another timeline. They had actually met years later whilst both working on the Glastonbury Zodiac but neither of them realised the 1979 connection. It had waited to now to be made visible and it had become clear in Glastonbury in the midst of a profoundly Thelemic event. And it was me that had seen it.

There was a possible touch of Gematria at work as well. Hebrew letters are ideograms. Shin, which features on the *Aeon* card, represents a tooth. I was willing to entertain the possibility that the apported tooth which split in half was a strange signifier of the diverging Thelemic destinies that were decided in that moment. Remember, the *Aeon* card was designed as a depiction of the forces on the Stele. It features Nuit, the winged disc Hadit, and Ra-Hoor-Khuit, as well as Harpocrates. Maybe you need to have a completely magickally conditioned mind to think that reality might ever work that way. Recognising that it was April Fools day, I nonetheless felt that the synchronicity machine had virtually exploded with this one.

I assimilated the basic data for a few days. I knew I would have to communicate it to Andy but I needed to ponder it for a while.

I felt that it was massively important and that something had changed forever but what that would actually mean in real terms, I had no idea. A few days later, on my birthday, Andy rang me. He was putting together the details for the years' Questing Conference and wondered if I would be interested in talking on Crowley's connection with Questing! He was thinking of the Helen and the Beast material and the spectacular 1988 Cairo manifestation. Following the Robert Coon lecture I was able to add to it.

A further idea quickly came to me. I knew that Andy was soon to visit Egypt. I suggested he could set himself up for a massive full circle by checking out the Stele. He could take some slides and I could then show them in my lecture. Crowley commissioned a copy of both sides of the Stele of Revealing. Images of this reproduction are what feature in any books displaying it right up into the nineties. I wasn't sure if an actual photo of the Stele had ever been seen in public before.

It was inevitable that I came to ponder the strange destiny that had led from my meeting Andy on my birthday in 1988 to this. It was another one of those destiny microdots and contained both Glastonbury and Crowley. My other classic birthday in 1992 stood interestingly between them.

Andy managed to take some photos. Since those days it has become impossible to do that in the Cairo Museum on pain of expulsion and possible arrest. I did indeed feature a slide of the Stele in my Questing Conference presentation. It was certainly done as a very deliberate year '93 magickal act further sending out the Glastonbury ripples from Robert Coon's perihelion event, an affirmation of my Avalonian Aeon process, the indivisibility of my Glastonbury, Questing, Crowley, Egyptian and Mesoamerican experiences.

* * *

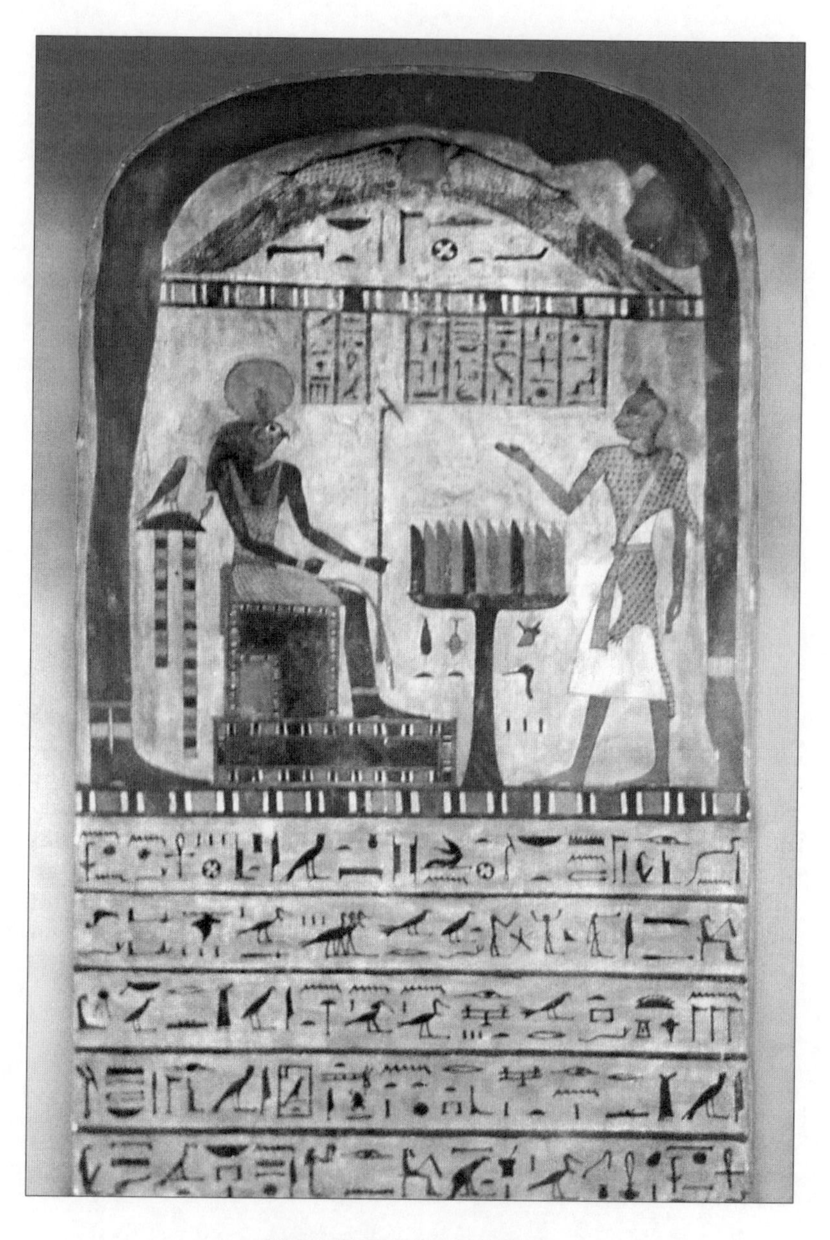

THE STELE OF REVEALING.
PHOTO TAKEN BY ANDREW COLLINS IN 1997.
ENHANCED BY SUE COLLINS.

In April 2009, as part of the climax to my *Aleister Crowley and the Aeon of Horus* project (which had grown out of the writing of *Avalonian Aeon*) I would be in Egypt with my partner Rachel and Andy and his wife Sue on the occasion of my fiftieth birthday. Sue and I share the same birthday. My collapse in front of the Sphinx and the subsequent change of plans leading to Andy and Sue being given, in the usual bizarre circumstances, a serpent stone linked to the guardian of the Giza underworld is a story that will have to be told elsewhere. A few days later the Cairo Museum was visited three times during *The Book of the Law* dates. On the 9th, twenty four years to the day since Bernard mentioned to Andy his belief that there are chambers beneath Giza, he had his first meeting with Zahi Hawass to discuss his extraordinary underground discoveries detailed in *Beneath the Pyramids* that would be published with the dating of September 23rd later in the year. As Andy spoke with Hawass, I was reciting the second chapter of *The Book of the Law* in front of the Stele. The 1997 Stele photo seen opposite would eventually appear in colour in a new edition of Kenneth Grant's *The Magical Revival* in 2010. The convergence never ends.

AFTERWORD

I WOULD CONSCIOUSLY TRY AND MANIFEST my 1990 vision still further through the concept of the Circle of Perpetual Choirs, initiating a musical project that would lead to the Fisher King's song being heard in a cathedral, a Shambhalic manifestation of the Medicine Buddha in the English landscape, and ultimately a bringing together of my Glastonbury Zodiac experience, the Egyptian Crystal Chambers, and 2012, as part of the climax of the seven swords ceremonies at the Heart of the Rose with a spectacular Quetzalcoatl conclusion.

That millennial story, flavoured by the Nephilim, crop circles, 11:11, the 1999 eclipse, Giza, Druidism, and the harmonisation of multiple celestial alignments through the galactic centre matrix, will feature in

AQUARIAN PHOENIX

There were giants on the Tor in those days. Mighty men of renown.

BIBLIOGRAPHY

Ackroyd, Peter, *Albion*, Chatto & Windus, London, 2002.

Adams, Henry, *The Education of Henry Adams,* Massachusetts Historical Society, 1918.

Apuleius, Lucius, *The Golden Ass.* Robert Graves trans., Cardinal, NY, 1952.

Allen, Daevid, *Gong Dreaming 1*, SAF Publishing Ltd, UK, 2006.

Argüelles, José, *Earth Ascending,* Shambhala Publications, USA, 1984.

Argüelles, José, *The Mayan Factor,* Bear & Co, Santa Fe, NM, 1987.

Argüelles, José, *Surfers of the Zuvuya*, Bear & Co, Santa Fe, NM, 1989.

Argüelles, José, & Argüelles, Lloydine, *Dreamspell,* Chelsea Pacific, HI, USA, 1990.

Ashe, Geoffrey, *King Arthur's Avalon,* London, 1957.

Ashe, Geoffrey, *Camelot and the Vision of Albion,* William Heinemann, UK, 1971.

Ashe, Geoffrey, *The Ancient Wisdom,* Macmillan, London, 1977.

Ashe, Geoffrey, *Avalonian Quest,* Methuen, London, 1982.

Ashe, Geoffrey, *The Finger and the Moon,* William Heinemann Ltd., 1973.

Aston, Michael, & Burrow, Ian, Eds., *The Archaeology of Somerset,* Somerset County Council, 1982.

Baigent, Michael, & Leigh, Richard, & Lincoln, Henry, *The Holy Blood and the Holy Grail,* Corgi, 1983.

Baigent, Michael & Leigh, Richard, *The Temple and the Lodge,* Corgi Books, UK, 1990.

Baigent, Michael & Leigh, Richard, *The Elixir and the Stone*, Viking, England, 1997.

Barber, Richard, *The Devil's Crown,* BBC, London, 1978.

Barber, Richard, *The Holy Grail,* Allen Lane, London, 2004.

Bauval, Robert, *Secret Chamber,* Century, London, 1999.

Benham, Patrick, *The Avalonians,* Gothic Image, Glastonbury, 1993.

Bennett, J. G., *Gurdjieff: Making a New World,* Harper & Row, UK, 1973.

Bharti, Ma Satya, *Death Comes Dancing,* Routeledge & Kegan Paul, 1981.

Biddle, Martin, *King Arthur's Round Table,* Boydell Press, UK, 2000.

Blyton, Enid, *Tales of Brave Adventure,* Deans International Publishing, London, 1963.

Boorman John, *Adventures of a Suburban Boy,* Faber and Faber, London, 2003.

Booth, Martin, *A Magick Life,* Hodder & Stoughton, London, 2000.

Bradley, Marion Zimmer, *The Mists of Avalon,* Del Rey books, USA, 1987.

Broadhurst, Paul, *Tintagel and the Arthurian Mythos,* Pendragon Press, Cornwall, 1992.

Brooke, Tal, *Avatar of Night*, End Run Publishing, 1999.

Brooke, Tal, *Riders of the Cosmic Circuit,* Lion, England, 1986.

Brown, Rosemary Alicia, *Katherine Emma Maltwood Artist 1878-1961,* Sono Nis Press, Victoria BC, Canada, 1981.

Bryant, Nigel, Translator, *The High Book of the Grail,* D. S. Brewer, Cambridge, 1996.

Burl, Aubrey, *Great Stone Circles,* Yale University, USA, 1999.

Caine, Mary, *The Glastonbury Zodiac,* Surrey, 1978.

Caine, Mary, *Celtic Saints and the Glastonbury Zodiac,* Capall Bann, Berks, 1998.

Carley, James P., *Melkin the Bard and Esoteric Tradition at Glastonbury Abbey*, Downside Review, Vol. 99, Bath, 1981.

Carley, James P., *Glastonbury Abbey,* Gothic Image Publications, Somerset, 1996.

Castaneda, Carlos, The Teachings of Don Juan, Penguin Books, UK, 1970.

Castaneda, Carlos, Tales of Power, Penguin Books, UK, 1976.

Cavendish, Richard, *The Black Arts*, Macmillan, UK, 1969.

Cavendish, Richard, *King Arthur and the Grail,* Granada Publishing, St. Albans, 1980.

Chapman, Janine, *Quest For Dion Fortune,* Weiser, Maine, USA, 1993.

Cohn, Norman, *The Pursuit of the Millennium,* Oxford University Press, 1970.

Cohn, Norman, *Europe's Inner Demons*, Pimlico, UK, 1998.

Collins, Andrew, *The Knights of Danbury,* Earthquest Books, Essex, 1985.

Collins, Andrew, *The Black Alchemist,* ABC Books, 1988.

Collins, Andrew, *Helen and the Beast,* ABC pamphlet, 1988.

Collins, Andrew, *The Seventh Sword,* Random Century Ltd., London, 1991.

Collins, Andrew, *The Circlemakers,* ABC Books, 1992.

Collins, Andrew, *The Second Coming,* Century, London, 1993.

Collins, Andrew, *Alien Energy,* ABC Books, 1994.

Collins, Andrew, *From the Ashes of Angels,* Michael Joseph, London, 1996.

Collins, Andrew, *Gods of Eden,* Headline, London, 1998.

Collins, Andrew, *Twenty-First Century Grail,* Virgin, London, 2004.

Collins, Andrew, *Beneath the Pyramids,* 4th Dimension Press, ARE, USA, 2009.

Coon, Robert, *Elliptical Navigations through the Multitudinous Aethyrs of Avalon,* Excalibur Press, Somerset, 1984.

Coon, Robert, *Voyage to Avalon,* Griffon Gold Publications, Somerset, 1986.

Coon, Robert, *Glastonbury and the Planetary New Jerusalem,* Excalibur Press, Glastonbury, 1990.

Coon, Robert, *The Glastonbury Zodiac,* Avalon, 1993.

Coon, Robert, *The Cairo Working,* Glastonbury, 1997.

Crowley, Aleister, *The Book of the Law,* Red Wheel/Weiser centennial edition, USA 2004.

Crowley, Aleister, *Aha!,* New Falcon, USA, 1983.

Crowley, Aleister, & Neuberg, Victor, & Desti, Mary, *The Vision and the Voice,* Red Wheel/Weiser, USA, 1998.

Crowley, Aleister, *The Book of Lies,* Red Wheel/Weiser, USA, 1981.

Crowley, Aleister, *Magick: Liber ABA Book Four,* Red Wheel/Weiser, USA, 1998.

Crowley, Aleister, *The Book of Thoth,* Red Wheel/Weiser, USA, 1981.

Darrah, John, *The Real Camelot,* Thames and Hudson, London, 1981.

de Hartmann, Thomas, & de Hartmann, Olga, *Our Life with Mr Gurdjieff,* Arkana, 1992.

de Ropp, Robert S., *The Master Game,* Picador, London, 1974.

Drury, Neville, *Don Juan, Mescalito, and Modern Magic*, Routledge & Kegan Paul, London, 1978.

DuQuette, Lon Milo, *The Magick of Thelema,* Red Wheel/Weiser, New York, 2003.

Eliade, Mircea, *The Myth of the Eternal Return,* Bollingen Foundation, 1954.

Eliade, Mircea, *From Primitives to Zen,* Fount, 1978.

Elstob, Lynne and Howes, Anne, *The Glastonbury Festivals,* Gothic Image, Glastonbury, 1987.

Evans, Sebastian, Translator, *The High History of the Holy Grail,* James Clarke & Co. Ltd., Cambridge.

Evola, Julius, *The Mystery of the Grail,* Inner Traditions International, 1997.

Fortune, Dion, *Avalon of the Heart*, London, 1934.

Fortune Dion, *The Mystical Qabalah,* London, 1935.

Fortune, Dion, *The Sea Priestess,* Red Wheel Weiser, NY, USA, 1979.

Fortune, Dion, *Moon Magic*, Red Wheel Weiser, NY, USA, 1979.

Frazer, J. G., *The Golden Bough* (abridged single volume), Macmillan, 1975.

Frost, Mark, *The List of Seven*, Avon Books, 1995.

Fukuyama, Francis, *The End of History and the Last Man,* The Free Press, 1992.

Fulcanelli, *Le Mystere Des Cathedrals,* Neville Spearman Ltd., London, 1971.

Gale, Jack, *The Circle and the Square,* Capall Bann, Berkshire, 1997.

Geoffrey of Monmouth, *The History of the Kings of Britain,* Penguin Books, London, 1966.

Godwin, Joscelyn, *Arktos,* Thames and Hudson, London, 1993.

Goodrich, Norma Lorre, *The Holy Grail,* Harper Collins Publishers, New York, 1992.

Grant, Kenneth, *The Magical Revival,* Frederick Muller Ltd., London, 1972.

Grant, Kenneth, *Aleister Crowley and the Hidden God,* Frederick Muller, London, 1973.

Grant, Kenneth, *Nightside of Eden*, Frederick Muller, London, 1977.

Grant, Kenneth, *Outer Gateways,* Skoob Books Publishing, London, 1994.

Grigsby, John, *Warriors of the Wasteland,* Watkins , London, 2003.

Guenon, Rene, *The Lord of the World,* Coombe Springs Press, North Yorkshire, 1983.

Guenon, Rene, *Symbols of Sacred Science,* Sophian Perennis, Hillsdale, NY, USA, 2004.

Gurdjieff, G. I., *Beelzebub's Tales to his Grandson*, Penguin Books, 2000.

Gurdjieff, G. I., *Meetings with Remarkable Men*, E. P. Dutton, UK, 1979.

Hancock, Graham, *The Sign and the Seal,* Arrow, London, 1993.

Harrison, Hank, *The Cauldron and the Grail,* The Archives Press, California, 1992.

Hartley, Christine, *The Western Mystery Tradition,* London, 1967.

Hay, George, Ed., *The Necronomicon,* Skoob, London, 1992.

Hershon, Cyril, P., *The Castles of Cary,* Pavalas Press, Bristol, 1990.

Hoeller, Stephan A., *The Gnostic Jung and the Seven Sermons to the Dead,* Quest, Illinois, 1982.

Hurd, Michael, *Rutland Boughton and the Glastonbury Festivals,* Oxford University Press, 1993.

Hyatt, Christopher, & DuQuette, Lon Milo, *The Way of the Secret Lover,* New Falcon, USA, 1991.

Jenkins, John Major, *Maya Cosmogenesis 2012,* Bear & Company, Santa Fe, NM, 1998.

Jenkins, Stephen, *The Undiscovered Country*, Neville Spearman, Suffolk, UK, 1976.

Johnson, Kenneth, *Jaguar Wisdom,* Llewellyn Publications, St. Paul, MN, USA, 1997.

Kahanne, Henry, & Kahanne Renee, *The Krater and the Grail: Hermetic Sources of the Parzival,* University of Illinois Press, USA, 1965.

Keys, David, *Catastrophe,* Arrow Books, London, 2000.

Kipling, Rudyard, *Pucks of Pook's Hill,* Macmillan & Co., London, 1926.

Knight, Christopher and Lomas, Robert, *The Second Messiah,* Century Books Ltd., UK, 1997.

Knight, Gareth, *The Secret Tradition in Arthurian Legend,* Aquarian Press, Wellingborough, 1983.

Knight, Gareth, *The Magical Battle of Britain,* SIL, England, 1993.

Knight, Gareth, *Dion Fortune & the Inner Light,* Thoth Publications, Loughborough, 2000.

Knight, Stephen, *Jack the Ripper: the Final Solution*, Harper Collins, 1979.

Leary, Timothy, *The Politics of Ecstasy,* G. P. Putnam, USA, 1968.

Leitch, Yuri, *Gwyn: Ancient god of Glastonbury and key to the Glastonbury Zodiac,* The Temple Publications, Somerset, 2007.

Le Page,Victoria, **Shambhala**, Quest Books, US, 1996.

Leviton, Richard, *Looking for Arthur,* Station Hill Openings, New York, 1997.

Loomis, Roger Sherman, *The Grail. From Celtic Myth to Christian Symbol,* Columbia University Press, USA, 1963.

Maltwood, Katherine, E., *A Guide to Glastonbury's Temple of the Stars,* James Clarke & Co., Cambridge, 1934.

Maltwood, Katherine, E., *The Enchantments of Britain,* James Clarke & Co., Cambridge, 1944.

Mann, Nicholas, R., *The Isle of Avalon,* Llewellyn, USA, 1996.

Marlow Louis, *Welsh Ambassadors,* Chapman and Hall Ltd., London, 1936.

Matthews, Caitlín & John, *Ladies of the Lake,* Aquarian Press, London, 1992.

Matthews, John, Ed., *A Glastonbury Reader*, Aquarian Press, London, 1991.

May, Jo, *Fogou*, Gothic Image, Somerset, 1996.

McKenna, Terence, & McKenna, Dennis, *The Invisible Landscape*, Harper Collins, Australia, 1994.

Mellers, Wilfrid, *Vaughan Williams and the Vision of Albion*, Barrie and Jenkins Ltd., London, 1989.

Men, Hunbatz, *Secrets of Mayan Science/Religion*, Bear & Company, Santa Fe, NM, 1990.

Merry, Eleanor, *The Flaming Door*, Rider & Co., London, 1936.

Michell, John, *The Flying Saucer Vision*, Sidgwick and Jackson Ltd., UK, 1967.

Michell, John, *The View Over Atlantis*, Sago Press, Great Britain, 1969.

Michell, John, *City of Revelation*, Abacus, UK, 1972.

Michell, John, *Eccentric Lives and Peculiar Notions*, Thames & Hudson, London, 1984.

Michell, John, *New Light on the Ancient Mystery of Glastonbury*, Gothic Image, Glastonbury, 1990.

Miller, Hamish, & Broadhurst, Paul, *The Sun and the Serpent*, Pendragon Press, Cornwall, 1989.

Minnit, Stephen, & Coles, John, *The Lake Villages of Somerset*, Glastonbury Antiquarian Society, Somerset Levels Project & Somerset County Council Museums Service, 1996.

Moore, Alan, & Campbell, Eddie, *From Hell*, Knockabout Comics, 2008.

Morton, H. V., *In Search of England*, Methuen, London, 1927.

Murphet, Howard, *Sai Baba, Man of Miracles*, Frederick Muller Ltd., London, 1971.

Newton, Toyne, *The Demonic Connection*, Blandford Press, Dorset, 1987.

Newton, Toyne, *The Dark Worship*, Vega, London, 2002.

Nicoll, Maurice, *Living Time*, Watkins, London, 1976.

Nitze, William A. & collaborators, *Perlesvaus, Volume 2*, Phaeton Press, New York, 1972.

Noll, Richard, *The Aryan Christ*, Macmillan, London, 1997.

Olschki, Leonardo, *The Grail Castle and its Mysteries*, Manchester University Press, UK, 1966.

Orr, Leonard & Ray, Sondra, *Rebirthing in the New Age*, Celestial Arts, California, 1983.

Ouspensky, P. D., *A New Model of the Universe*, Routledge & Kegan Paul Ltd., London, 1931.

Ouspensky, P. D., *In Search of the Miraculous*, Harcourt Inc., USA, 1949.

Phillips, Graham, & Keatman, Martin, *The Green Stone,* Granada, London, 1984.

Phillips, Graham & Keatman, Martin, *The Eye of Fire,* Grafton, London, 1988.

Picknett Lynn & Prince, Clive, *The Stargate Conspiracy,* Little Brown & Co., UK, 1999.

Pollack, Rachel, *The Haindl Tarot Volume 1 Major Arcana,* Newcastle Publishing Co., US, 1990.

Powys, John Cowper, *A Glastonbury Romance,* Picador, London, 1975.

Powys, John Cowper, *Autobiography,* Bodley Head, London, 1934.

Powys, John Cowper, *Petrushka & the Dancer, The Diaries of John Cowper Powys 1929-1939.* Edited by Morine Krissdottir. Carcanet Press Ltd., Manchester, 1995.

Rahtz, Philip, & Watts, Lorna, *Glastonbury. Myth and Archaeology.* Tempus Publishing Ltd., Gloucestershire, 2003.

Randles, Jenny, & Whetnall, Paul, *Alien Contact*, Neville Spearman, Suffolk, UK, 1981.

Ravenscroft, Trevor, *The Spear of Destiny,* Corgi, London, 1974.

Regardie, Israel, *The Eye in the Triangle,* (Edition with introduction by Robert Anton Wilson and Preface by Christopher S. Hyatt, PhD.) Falcon Press, Phoenix, Arizona, USA, 1982.

Reiser, Oliver L., *This Holyest Erthe,* Perennial Books, London, 1974.

Richardson, Alan, *Dancers to the Gods,* Aquarian Press, Wellingborough, UK, 1985.

Richardson, Alan, *Priestess,* Thoth Publications, Loughborough, 2007.

Roberts, Anthony, *Atlantean Traditions in Ancient Britain*, Rider, UK, 1977.

Roberts, Anthony, Ed, *Glastonbury. Ancient Avalon, New Jerusalem.* Rider & Co., London, 1978.

Roberts, Anthony, *Geomancy*, Zodiac House Publications, Glastonbury, UK, 1980.

Roberts, Anthony & Gilbertson, Geoff, *The Dark Gods,* Rider/Hutchinson & Co. (Publishers) Ltd., 1980.

Robertson, Olivia, *The Call of Isis,* Neptune Press, London, 1993.

Robinson, Stephen, *Somerset Place Names,* The Dovecote Press, Dorset, 1992.

Rothovius, Andrew, *The Dragon Tradition in the New World*, East West Magazine article, August 1977.

Sahukar, Mani, *Sai Baba, The Saint of Shirdi,* Somaiya publications, PVT Ltd., Bombay, 1971.

Scott, Ernest, *The People of the Secret,* Octagon Press Ltd., London, 1983.

Seddon, Richard, *The Mystery of Arthur at Tintagel,* Rudolf Steiner Press, London, 1990.

Shearer, Tony, *Lord of the Dawn,* Naturegraph Publishers, CA, USA, 1995.

Sinclair, Andrew, *The Discovery of the Grail,* Century, London, 1998.

Sinclair, Iain, *Lud Heat and Suicide Bridge,* Vintage, London, 1995.

Sinclair, Iain, *White Chappell Scarlet Tracings,* Vintage, London, 1995.

Sjöö, Monica, *New Age & Armageddon,* The Women's Press Ltd., London, 1992.

Smithett Lewis, Lionel, *Glastonbury "The Mother of Saints" Her Saints,* A. R. Mowbray & Co. Ltd., London, 1925.

Smithett Lewis, Lionel, St Joseph of Arimathea at Glastonbury, A. R. Mowbray & Co., 1937.

Spence, Lewis, *The Mysteries of Britain,* Senate, Middlesex, 1994.

Stein, Walter Johannes, *The Ninth Century,* Temple Lodge Press, London, 1991.

Stein, Walter Johannes, *The Death of Merlin,* Floris Books, Edinburgh, 1989.

Steiner, Rudolf, *The Holy Grail,* Sophia Books, East Sussex, 2001.

Stewart, R. J., *The Underworld Initiation,* Aquarian Press, Wellingborough, 1985.

Stewart, R. J., *Merlin: The Prophetic Vision and the Mystic Life,* Arkana, UK, 1994.

Stone, C. J., *Fierce Dancing,* Faber & Faber, UK, 1996.

Strachan, Gordon, *Chartres,* Floris Books, Edinburgh, 2003.

Streiber, Whitley, *Communion,* Morrow, New York, 1987.

Suster, Gerald, *Hitler and the Age of Horus,* Sphere Books, London, 1981.

Symonds, John, *The Great Beast,* Mayflower, UK, 1974.

Teilhard de Chardin, Pierre, *The Phenomenon of Man,* Fontana Books, 1965.

Temple, Robert, *The Sirius Mystery,* Century, UK, 1998.

Tennyson, Alfred, The Works of Alfred Lord Tennyson, Macmillan & Co., London, 1889.

Thompson, Damian, *The End of Time,* Minerva, London, 1997.

Thompson, Hunter S., *Fear and Loathing in Las Vegas,* Flamingo, 1993.

Thondup Rinpoche, Tulku, *Hidden Teachings of Tibet,* Wisdom Publications, London, 1986.

Trevelyan, George, *Operation Redemption,* Turnstone Press, UK, 1981.

Ulansey, David, *The Origins of the Mithraic Mysteries,* Oxford University Press, New York, 1989.

Vallée, Jacques, *Passport to Magonia,* Neville Spearman Ltd, UK, 1970.

Van Buren, Elizabeth, *Lord of the Flame,* Neville Spearman, Suffolk, 1981.

Various, *From Atlantis to Avalon and Beyond,* Zodiac House Publications, Glastonbury, UK, 1990.

Various, *Glastonbury & Britain - A Study in Patterns,* RILKO, Lodon, 1990.

Wasserman, James (Ed.), *Aleister Crowley and the Practice of the Magical Diary,* New Falcon, USA, 1993.

West, John Anthony, *Serpent in the Sky*, Quest Books, Wheaton, IL, USA, 1993.

Weston, Jessie, *From Ritual to Romance,* Princeton University Press, West Sussex, 1993.

Weston, Paul, *Mysterium Artorius,* Avalonian Aeon Publications, Glastonbury, UK, 2007.

Weston, Paul, *Aleister Crowley and the Aeon of Horus,* Avalonian Aeon Publications, Glastonbury, UK, 2009.

Wilson, Colin, *The Outsider,* Victor Gollancz, London, 1956.

Wilson, Colin, *Introduction to the New Existentialism,* Hutchinson & Co., London, 1966.

Wilson, Colin, *The Occult,* Hodder & Stoughton Ltd., Great Britain, 1971.

Wilson, Colin, *New Pathways in Psychology,* Victor Gollancz, London, 1972.

Wilson, Colin, *Mysteries,* Grafton, London, 1979.

Wilson Knight, G., *The Saturnian Quest,* Methuen & Co. Ltd., London, 1964.

Wilson, Robert Anton, *Cosmic Trigger: Final Secret of the Illuminati,* And/Or Press, USA, 1977.

Wilson, Robert Anton, *Prometheus Rising,* New Falcon, USA, 1983.

Wilson, Robert Anton, *The New Inquisition,* New Falcon, USA, 1986.

Wilson, Robert Anton, *Cosmic Trigger II,* New Falcon, USA, 1988.

Wilson, Robert Anton, *Quantum Psychology,* New Falcon, USA, 1990.

Wood, Michael, *In Search of England,* Penguin Books, London, 2000.

Woodcock, Peter, *This Enchanted Isle,* Gothic Image, Glastonbury, 2000.

A note on Hank Harrison

I have read a number of online articles by Harrison, primarily on *Perlesvaus*. They included *Signs of Divinity, Eleanore's Ghost, The Mystery, Gawain's Quest, Who Wrote Y Saent Graal?, Who Was Ina?* and *The Grail in the Stones*. They periodically disappear from view. At the time of this publication **www.arkives.com** is the current place to find Harrison's material. *Crown of Stars* gathers much of the above together. It would be great to see his stuff in print one day. The man deserves recognition.

THEMATIC GUIDE

MOST OF ALL, this work is an affirmation of the great blend that is the Glastonbury experience, so many themes are continually coalescing and only the full narrative serves as reference there.

Nonetheless with such a wide range of material covered, knowing where to find some of it may prove useful.

A further spread of references typical of the *Avalonian Aeon* mix includes